Kaplan Publishing are consta
ways to make a difference to
exciting online resources rea g
different to students looking for exam success.

This book comes with free MyKaplan online resources so that you can study anytime, anywhere. This free online resource is not sold separately and is included in the price of the book.

Having purchased this book, you have access to the following online study materials:

CONTENT	ACCA (including FFA,FAB,FMA)		FIA (excluding FFA,FAB,FMA)	
	Text	Kit	Text	Kit
Eletronic version of the book	✓	✓	✓	✓
Check Your Understanding Test with instant answers	✓			
Material updates	✓	✓	✓	✓
Latest official ACCA exam questions*		✓		
Extra question assistance using the signpost icon**		✓		
Timed questions with an online tutor debrief using clock icon***		✓		
Interim assessment including questions and answers	✓		✓	
Technical answers	✓	✓	✓	✓

* Excludes F1, F2, F3, F4, FAB, FMA and FFA; for all other papers includes a selection of questions, as released by ACCA

** For ACCA P1-P7 only

*** Excludes F1, F2, F3, F4, FAB, FMA and FFA

How to access your online resources

Kaplan Financial students will already have a MyKaplan account and these extra resources will be available to you online. You do not need to register again, as this process was completed when you enrolled. If you are having problems accessing online materials, please ask your course administrator.

If you are not studying with Kaplan and did not purchase your book via a Kaplan website, to unlock your extra online resources please go to www.mykaplan.co.uk/addabook (even if you have set up an account and registered books previously). You will then need to enter the ISBN number (on the title page and back cover) and the unique pass key number contained in the scratch panel below to gain access.

You will also be required to enter additional information during this process to set up or confirm your account details.

If you purchased through Kaplan Flexible Learning or via the Kaplan Publishing website you will automatically receive an e-mail invitation to MyKaplan. Please register your details using this email to gain access to your content. If you do not receive the e-mail or book content, please contact Kaplan Publishing.

Your Code and Information

This code can only be used once for the registration of one book online. This registration and your online content will expire when the final sittings for the examinations covered by this book have taken place. Please allow one hour from the time you submit your book details for us to process your request.

Please scratch the film to access your MyKaplan code.

Please be aware that this code is case-sensitive and you will need to include the dashes within the passcode, but not when entering the ISBN. For further technical support, please visit www.MyKaplan.co.uk

KAPLAN PUBLISHING

Professional Examinations

Paper P7 (INT & UK)

ADVANCED AUDIT AND ASSURANCE

EXAM KIT

KAPLAN
PUBLISHING

British Library Cataloguing-in-Publication Data

A catalogue record for this book is available from the British Library.

Published by:

Kaplan Publishing UK
Unit 2 The Business Centre
Molly Millar's Lane
Wokingham
Berkshire
RG41 2QZ

ISBN: 978-1-78415-840-8

Acknowledgements

This Product includes propriety content of the International Accounting Standards Board which is overseen by the IFRS Foundation, and is used with the express permission of the IFRS Foundation under licence. All rights reserved. No part of this publication may be reproduced, stored in a retrieval system, or transmitted in any form or by any means, electronic, mechanical, photocopying, recording, or otherwise, without prior written permission of Kaplan Publishing and the IFRS Foundation.

IFRS

IFRS

Trade Marks

CONTENTS

Section

This document references IFRS® Standards and IAS® Standards, which are authored by the International Accounting Standards Board (the Board), and published in the 2016 IFRS Standards Red Book.

Key features in this edition

In addition to providing a wide ranging bank of real past exam questions, we have also included in this edition:

- An analysis of the recent new syllabus examination papers.
- Paper specific information and advice on exam technique.
- Our recommended approach to make your revision for this particular subject as effective as possible.

  This includes step by step guidance on how best to use our Kaplan material (Study Text, pocket notes and exam kit) at this stage in your studies.
- Enhanced tutorial answers packed with specific key answer tips, technical tutorial notes and exam technique tips from our experienced tutors.
- Complementary online resources including full tutor debriefs and question assistance to point you in the right direction when you get stuck.

You will find a wealth of other resources to help you with your studies on the following sites:

www.MyKaplan.co.uk

http://www.accaglobal.com/gb/en/student.html

Quality and accuracy are of the utmost importance to us so if you spot an error in any of our products, please send an email to mykaplanreporting@kaplan.com with full details.

Our Quality Co-ordinator will work with our technical team to verify the error and take action to ensure it is corrected in future editions.

INDEX TO QUESTIONS AND ANSWERS

INTRODUCTION

The style of current Paper P7 exam questions is different to older versions of the syllabus and changes have been made to questions in order to reflect changes in question style and syllabus updates.

Accordingly any older ACCA questions within this kit have been adapted to reflect the new style of paper and the new guidance. If changed in any way from the original version, this is indicated in the end column of the index below with the mark *(A)*.

Note that all of the questions within the kit are past ACCA exam questions.

The pilot paper is included at the end of the kit.

KEY TO THE INDEX

PAPER ENHANCEMENTS

We have added the following enhancements to the answers in this exam kit:

Key answer tips

All answers include key answer tips to help your understanding of each question.

Tutorial note

All answers include more tutorial notes to explain some of the technical points in more detail.

Top tutor tips

For selected questions, we 'walk through the answer' giving guidance on how to approach the questions with helpful 'tips from a top tutor', together with technical tutor notes.

These answers are indicated with the 'footsteps' icon in the index.

ONLINE ENHANCEMENTS

Timed question with online tutor debrief

For selected questions, we recommend that they are to be completed in full exam conditions (i.e. properly timed in a closed book environment).

In addition to the examiner's technical answer, enhanced with key answer tips and tutorial notes in this exam kit, you can find an answer debrief online by a top tutor that:

- works through the question in full
- points out how to approach the question
- discusses how to ensure that the easy marks are obtained as quickly as possible, and
- emphasises how to tackle exam questions and exam technique.

These questions are indicated with the 'clock' icon in the index.

INT Syllabus only

ANALYSIS OF PAST PAPERS

The table below summarises the key topics that have been tested in the new syllabus examinations to date.

	Jun 14	Dec 14	Jun 15	Sept/ Dec 15	March/ June 16	Sept/ Dec 16
Regulatory Environment						
Regulatory framework						✓
Money laundering	✓				✓	
Laws and regulations			✓			
Professional & ethical considerations						
Code of ethics	✓	✓	✓	✓	✓	✓
Fraud and error					✓	
Professional liability						
Practice Management						
Quality control	✓	✓	✓	✓	✓	✓
Advertising				✓		
Tendering		✓				
Professional appointments	✓					
Audit of historical information						
Risk assessment:						
Audit risk	✓		✓	✓	✓	✓
Business risk		✓				
Material misstatement		✓				
Planning and materiality			✓			
Professional scepticism			✓			
Audit evidence:						
Sufficient/appropriate						
Specific procedures		✓	✓	✓		✓
Analytical procedures					✓	
Related parties						
Written representations						
Work of experts		✓				
Work of internal audit						
Group audits	✓	✓	✓	✓	✓	✓

	Jun 14	Dec 14	Jun 15	Sept/ Dec 15	March/ June 16	Sept/ Dec 16
Joint audits						
Evaluation/review						
Review procedures		✓				✓
Matters and evidence	✓	✓	✓		✓	
Initial engagements						
Comparatives						
Subsequent events						
Going concern	✓			✓		
Other assignments						
Levels of assurance					✓	
Advantages and disadvantages of audit					✓	
Interim review						
Due diligence				✓		
Prospective financial information	✓					✓
Social/environmental audit		✓				
Forensic audit			✓			
Internal audit						
Outsourcing	✓					
Insolvency (UK only)	✓			✓		
Performance information (INT only)				✓		
Reporting						
Reporting implications		✓	✓	✓	✓	✓
Critical appraisal of a draft report	✓			✓		
Reporting in relation to other information published with FS						
Reports to those charged with governance						✓
Current Issues						
Professional and ethical developments						
Transnational audits						
Other current issues	✓					

EXAM TECHNIQUE

- **Skim through the whole paper**, assessing the level of difficulty of each question and identifying which **two** of the section B questions you wish to attempt.
- **Divide the time** you spend on questions in proportion to the marks on offer:
  - There are 1.95 minutes available per mark in the examination.
  - Within that, try to allow time at the end of each question to review your answer and address any obvious issues.

  Whatever happens, always keep your eye on the clock and **do not over run on any part of any question!**
- **Decide the order** in which you think you will attempt each question:
  - A common approach is to tackle the question you think is the easiest and you are most comfortable with first.
  - Others may prefer to tackle the longest questions first as this has the most marks attributable and you cannot afford to leave this question to last and find that you have run out of time to complete it fully. The examiner has commented that students who do not attempt Q1 first tend to do badly in the exam.
  - It is usual, however, that students tackle their least favourite topic and/or the most difficult question last.
  - Whatever your approach, you must make sure that you leave enough time to attempt all questions fully and be very strict with yourself in timing each question.
- At the beginning of the exam take time to:
  - **read the questions and examination requirements carefully** so that you understand them, and
  - **plan** your answers.
- Spend the last **five minutes** of the examination:
  - reading through your answers, and
  - **making any additions or corrections.**
- If you **get completely stuck** with a question:
  - leave space in your answer book, and
  - **return to it later.**
- Stick to the question and **tailor your answer** to what you are asked.
  - pay particular attention to the verbs in the question.
- If you do not understand what a question is asking, **state your assumptions**.

  Even if you do not answer in precisely the way the examiner hoped, you may be given some credit, if your assumptions are reasonable.
- You should do everything you can to make things easy for the marker.

  The marker will find it easier to identify the points you have made if your **answers are legible**.

- **Written questions**:

  P7 marks are normally awarded for depth of explanation and discussion. For this reason lists and bullet points should be avoided unless specifically requested. Your answer should:

  – Have a clear structure using subheadings to improve the quality and clarity of your response.

  – Be concise, get to the point!

  – Address a broad range of points: it is usually better to write a little about a lot of different points than a great deal about one or two points.

- **Reports, memos and other documents**:

  Some questions ask you to present your answer in the form of briefing notes or a report. Professional marks are awarded for these questions so do not ignore their format.

  Make sure that you use the correct format – there could be easy marks to gain here.

PAPER SPECIFIC INFORMATION

THE EXAM

FORMAT OF THE P7 EXAM

		Number of marks
Section A:	2 compulsory questions	
	Question 1:	35
	Question 2:	25
Section B:	2 questions from 3 (20 marks each)	40
		100
Total time allowed:	3 hours and 15 minutes.	

Note that:

- Section A questions normally focus on reasonably large scenarios. The first question usually requires some form of risk assessment. The second question normally considers another form of engagement or a specialised area of audit, such as group auditing.
- Most of the marks available for question 1 are for applying your knowledge of audit procedures to the scenario, rather than simple 'knowledge dumping.'
- Section B questions normally include:
  - a discussion of the ethical and professional issues relevant to a few short scenarios.
  - reporting, typically audit reports, although reports to those charged with governance are also possible. You normally have to discuss the impact of certain issues on the wording of the report and the assurance opinion offered.
- Questions are no longer restricted to particular topics. Any topic could appear in any question, including within the compulsory questions (1 and 2).
- All requirements will be broken into numerous sub-requirements that test a range of topics.
- The majority of marks available on P7 are for applying your knowledge to specific case studies. There is little scope for 'knowledge dumping,' so only do this if the question specifically asks for it, e.g. when a definition is requested.
- Current issues and developments within the profession are examinable. For these types of questions it is likely that a technical article on the relevant topic will be issued in the months preceding the exam. Students are advised to check for any recent technical articles published by the ACCA Examining Team. Examiner's reports emphasise the need for students to read up on current issues and recommend that students do not solely depend on the text books for this exam.
- Discussion questions are generally disliked by students, possibly because there is no right or wrong answer. The way to approach these questions is to provide a balanced argument. Where a statement is given that you are required to discuss, give reasons why you agree with the statement and reasons why you disagree with the statement.

UK VARIANT SPECIFIC INFORMATION

The following are the key differences between the UK and INT variant exams:

- The requirement for question one in the UK exam will not be broken down in the same way as the INT variant. This may appear to make the question more difficult however this means that the marking scheme will be more flexible. It is recommended that you use the INT variant papers as a guide for how many marks are typically awarded for the different requirements and apply this in your exam. The questions included in this exam kit are from the INT papers so take notice of the breakdown of the marks to help you.
- Questions on ethics and audit reports will require knowledge of UK guidance e.g. the FRC Ethical Standard and UK versions of the ISAs. The basic knowledge is the same for UK and INT but there are some variations in ethical safeguards and the elements of a UK audit report.
- Insolvency is a syllabus area which is only relevant for UK variant exams. This will not necessarily be examined every sitting. If it is examined it is likely to be one requirement that is changed from the INT variant paper.
- Practise the UK specific questions in the Study Text and this exam kit to help prepare you for any UK specific questions.

PASS MARK

The pass mark for all ACCA Qualification examination papers is 50%.

DETAILED SYLLABUS

The detailed syllabus and study guide written by the ACCA can be found at:

www.accaglobal.com/students/

KAPLAN'S RECOMMENDED REVISION APPROACH

QUESTION PRACTICE IS THE KEY TO SUCCESS

Success in professional examinations relies upon you acquiring a firm grasp of the required knowledge at the tuition phase. In order to be able to do the questions, knowledge is essential.

However, the difference between success and failure often hinges on your exam technique on the day and making the most of the revision phase of your studies.

The **Kaplan Study Text** is the starting point, designed to provide the underpinning knowledge to tackle all questions. However, in the revision phase, pouring over text books is not the answer.

Kaplan online progress tests help you consolidate your knowledge and understanding and are a useful tool to check whether you can remember key topic areas.

Kaplan pocket notes are designed to help you quickly revise a topic area, however you then need to practice questions. There is a need to progress to full exam standard questions as soon as possible, and to tie your exam technique and technical knowledge together.

The importance of question practice cannot be over-emphasised.

The recommended approach below is designed by expert tutors in the field, in conjunction with their knowledge of the examiner and their recent real exams.

The approach taken for the fundamental papers is to revise by topic area. However, with the professional stage papers, a multi topic approach is required to answer the scenario based questions.

You need to practice as many questions as possible in the time you have left.

OUR AIM

Our aim is to get you to the stage where you can attempt exam standard questions confidently, to time, in a closed book environment, with no supplementary help (i.e. to simulate the real examination experience).

Practising your exam technique on real past examination questions, in timed conditions, is also vitally important for you to assess your progress and identify areas of weakness that may need more attention in the final run up to the examination.

In order to achieve this we recognise that initially you may feel the need to practice some questions with open book help and exceed the required time.

The approach below shows you which questions you should use to build up to coping with exam standard question practice, and references to the sources of information available should you need to revisit a topic area in more detail.

Remember that in the real examination, all you have to do is:

- attempt all questions required by the exam
- only spend the allotted time on each question, and
- get at least 50% of the marks allocated!

Try and practice this approach on every question you attempt from now to the real exam.

EXAMINER COMMENTS

We have included the examiners comments to the specific new syllabus examination questions in this kit for you to see the main pitfalls that students fall into with regard to technical content.

However, too many times in the general section of the report, the examiner comments that students had failed due to:

- 'misallocation of time'
- 'running out of time' and
- showing signs of 'spending too much time on an earlier question and clearly rushing the answer to a subsequent question'.

Good exam technique is vital.

THE KAPLAN PAPER P7 REVISION PLAN

Stage 1: Assess areas of strengths and weaknesses

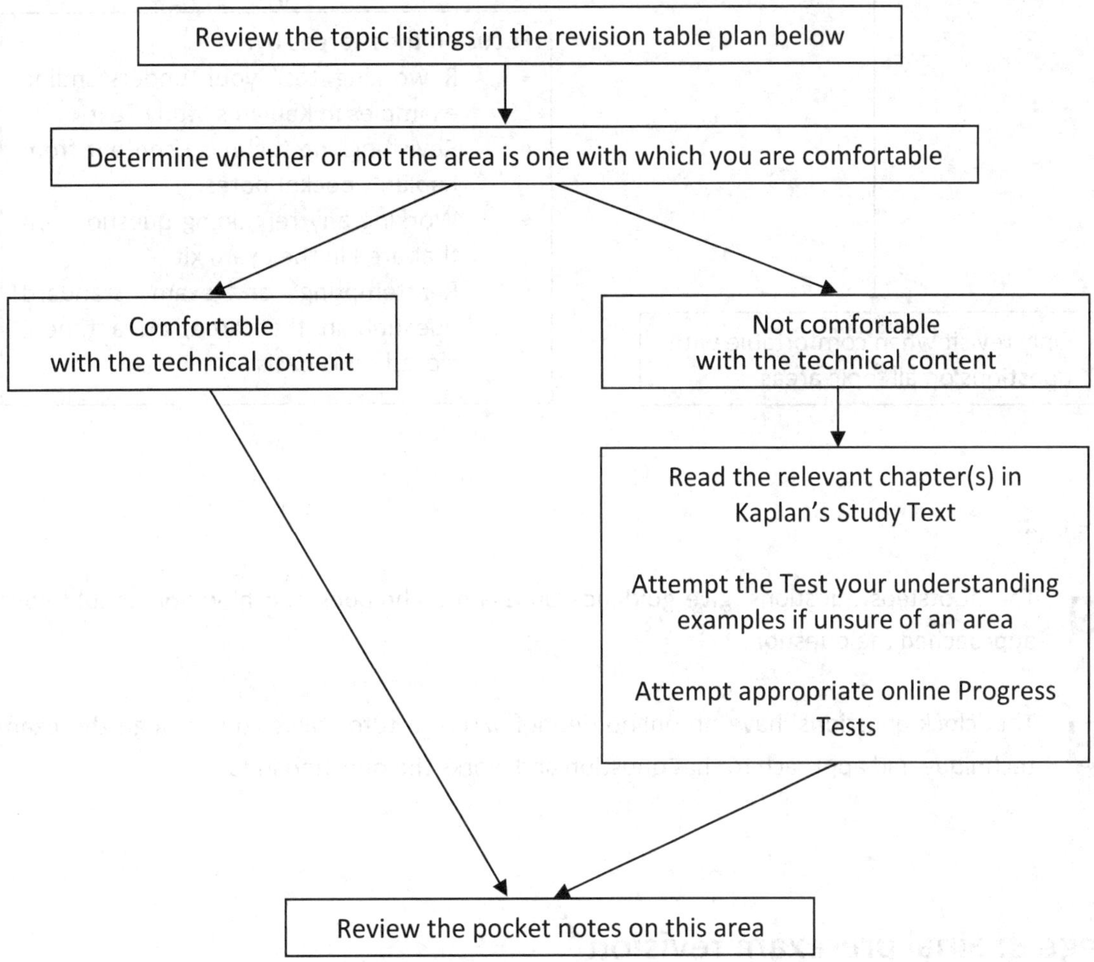

Stage 2: Practice questions

Follow the order of revision of topics as recommended in the revision table plan below and attempt the questions in the order suggested.

Try to avoid referring to text books and notes and the model answer until you have completed your attempt.

Try to answer the question in the allotted time.

Review your attempt with the model answer and assess how much of the answer you achieved in the allocated exam time.

Fill in the self-assessment box below and decide on your best course of action.

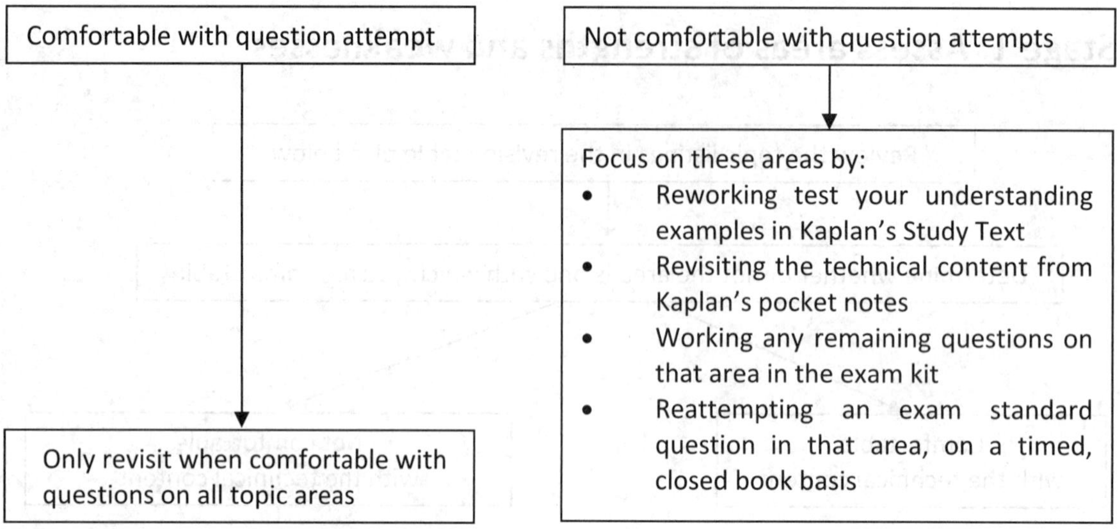

Note that:

The 'footsteps questions' give guidance on exam techniques and how you should have approached the question.

The 'clock questions' have an online debrief where a tutor talks you through the exam technique and approach to that question and works the question in full.

Stage 3: Final pre-exam revision

We recommend that you **attempt at least one three hour mock examination** containing a set of previously unseen exam standard questions.

It is important that you get a feel for the breadth of coverage of a real exam without advanced knowledge of the topic areas covered – just as you will expect to see on the real exam day.

Ideally this mock should be sat in timed, closed book, real exam conditions and could be:

- a mock examination offered by your tuition provider, and/or
- the pilot paper in the back of this exam kit, and/or
- the last real examination paper (available shortly afterwards on MyKaplan with 'enhanced walk through answers' and a full 'tutor debrief').

KAPLAN'S DETAILED REVISION PLAN

Topics	*Study Text (and Pocket Note) Chapter*	*Questions to attempt*	*Tutor guidance*	*Date attempted*	*Self assessment*
1 Audit planning, risk assessment and materiality including group audits.	9, 10, 11	1 2 3 5 7	Audit risk, business and risk of material misstatement is fundamental to P7. However, rather than discussing definitions you need to be able to perform a risk assessment for specific information given in a scenario. It is imperative to understand the difference between the three types of risk in order to answer the question correctly.		
2 Other assignments	15 - 21	11 15 18 20	There are many non-audit engagements that you could be asked to discuss. Therefore ensure that you know: the typical sorts of engagement; how they are planned, performed and reviewed. You also need to consider the ethical/professional impact of an auditor accepting these engagements.		
3 Evaluation and review	12	21 23 26	At the review stage of an audit you need to consider a number of issues: whether there is sufficient appropriate evidence on file; if the audit plan has been followed; whether there are any material errors in the information under review; and the impact of these issues on the reports you will have to issue.		

4	Professional and ethical considerations	1 – 8	28 30 32 36 38	You need to be able to discuss and apply the code of ethics to given scenarios. In addition you also need to consider a wide range of practice management issues, such as: internal quality control; legal requirements; commercial strategy; and professional liability.		
5	Reporting	13 & 14	43 44 45 49	One of the fundamental weaknesses identified by the examiner is a lack of understanding regarding the nature of audit report modifications. It is therefore important that you are able to assess a scenario and identify how it might impact upon your audit opinion. You also need to be able to discuss the content and purpose of reports to those charged with governance.		
6	UK Syllabus: Insolvency	20	52 53 54 55	Students studying for the UK variant of P7 need to understand the procedures for placing a company into liquidation or administration.		
7	INT syllabus: Performance information in the public sector	21	57 58	Students studying for the INT variant of the paper need to be able to comment on the relevance and measurability of performance information as well as describe procedures that can be used to audit such information.		

Note that not all of the questions are referred to in the programme above. We have recommended an approach to build up from the basic to exam standard questions. The remaining questions are available in the kit for extra practice for those who require more question practise on some areas.

Section 1

PRACTICE QUESTIONS – SECTION A

RISK ASSESSMENT

1 ZED COMMUNICATIONS GROUP *Walk in the footsteps of a top tutor*

The Zed Communications Group (ZCG) is an audit client of your firm, Tarantino & Co, with a financial year ending 31 December 2016. You are the manager assigned to the forthcoming audit. ZCG is a listed entity, one of the largest telecommunications providers in the country and is seeking to expand internationally. ZCG also provides broadband and fixed telephone line services.

You have just received the following email from the audit engagement partner:

To: Audit engagement manager

From: Vincent Vega, audit engagement partner

Subject: ZCG audit planning

Hello

We need to begin planning the final audit of ZCG, which as you know is one of our largest audit clients. I met with the Group's finance director yesterday and I have provided you with notes from this meeting along with extracts from the latest management accounts. We also discussed the possibility of using the Group's internal audit team to improve audit efficiency. I have provided you with an extract from the latest report of the internal audit department.

Using all of the information provided, you are required to prepare briefing notes for my use in which you:

(a) Evaluate the audit risks relevant to planning the final audit of ZCG **(14 marks)**

(b) Discuss the matters to be considered in determining the assistance which could be provided by, and the amount of reliance, if any, which can be placed on the work of ZCG's internal audit department **(7 marks)**

(c) Recommend the principal audit procedures to be performed on:

(i) The classification of the 50% equity shareholding in WTC as a joint venture, and **(4 marks)**

(ii) The measurement of the intangible asset recognised in respect of the licence to operate in Farland. **(6 marks)**

Thank you.

Notes from meeting with finance director

One of ZCG's strategic aims is to expand internationally, either by acquiring existing telecommunications providers in other countries, or by purchasing licences to operate in foreign countries.

In March 2016, ZCG purchased a 50% equity shareholding in Wallace Telecoms Co (WTC), a company operating in several countries where ZCG previously had no interests. The other 50% is held by Wolf Communications Co. The cost of the 50% equity shareholding was $45 million. ZCG is planning to account for its investment in WTC as a joint venture in the Group financial statements.

On 1 January 2015, ZCG purchased a licence to operate in Farland, a rapidly expanding economy, at a cost of $65 million. The licence lasts for 10 years from the date that it was purchased. Since purchasing the licence, ZCG has established its network coverage in Farland and the network became operational on 1 July 2016. The licence was recognised as an intangible asset at cost in the Group statement of financial position at 31 December 2015. Since the network became operational, customer demand has been less than anticipated due to a competitor offering a special deal to its existing customers to encourage them not to change providers.

Most of ZCG's mobile phone customers sign a contract under which they pay a fixed amount each month to use ZCG's mobile network, paying extra if they exceed the agreed data usage and airtime limits. The contract also allows connection to a fixed landline and internet access using broadband connection and most contracts run for two or three years. For the first time this year, the Group is adopting IFRS® 15 *Revenue from Contracts with Customers*.

In order to extend its broadband services, ZCG has started to purchase network capacity from third party companies. ZCG enters a fixed-term contract to use a specified amount of the seller's network capacity, with the seller determining which of its network assets are used by ZCG in supplying network services to its customers. In the first six months of 2016, ZCG purchased $17.8 million of network capacity from a range of suppliers, with the contract periods varying from twelve months to three years. The cost has been capitalised as an intangible asset.

Internal audit

ZCG has a well-established internal audit department which is tasked with a range of activities including providing assurance to management over internal controls and assisting the Group's risk management team. The internal audit department is managed by Jules Winfield, a qualified accountant with many years' experience. An extract from the executive summary of the latest internal audit report to the Group finance director is shown below:

'We are pleased to report that ZCG's internal controls are working well and there have been no significant changes to systems and controls during the year. As a result of our testing of controls we uncovered only two financial irregularities which related to:

- Failure to obtain appropriate authorisation and approval of senior management expense claims, such as travel and other reimbursements. The unsubstantiated expense claims amounted to $575,000.
- Inadequate access controls over the Group's IT systems which resulted in a payroll fraud amounting to $750,000.'

Financial information – extracts from latest management accounts

	8 months to 31 August 2016 $ million	Audited financial statements to 31 December 2015 $ million
Revenue:		
Europe	106	102
Americas	30	68
South East Asia	33	30
India	29	20
Total	198	220

	At 31 August 2016 $ million	At 31 December 2015 $ million
Total assets	598	565

Required:

Respond to the instructions in the audit engagement partner's email. **(31 marks)**

Note: The split of the mark allocation is shown in the partner's email.

Professional marks will be awarded for the presentation of the briefing notes and the clarity of the explanations provided. **(4 marks)**

(Total: 35 marks)

2 VANCOUVER GROUP *Walk in the footsteps of a top tutor*

You are an audit manager in Montreal & Co, a firm of Chartered Certified Accountants, and you are responsible for the audit of the Vancouver Group (the Group). The Group operates in the supply chain management sector, offering distribution, warehousing and container handling services.

The Group comprises a parent company, Vancouver Co, and two subsidiaries, Toronto Co and Calgary Co. Both of the subsidiaries were acquired as wholly owned subsidiaries many years ago. Montreal & Co audits all of the individual company financial statements as well as the Group consolidated financial statements.

You are beginning to plan the Group audit for the financial year ending 31 July 2016, and the audit engagement partner has sent you the following email:

To: Audit manager

From: Albert Franks, audit engagement partner

Subject: The Vancouver Group – audit planning

Hello

I held a meeting yesterday with Hannah Peters, the Group finance director. A representative of the Group audit committee was also at the meeting to discuss two issues raised for our attention by the committee. Hannah gave me some projected financial information for the Group's forthcoming year end, along with comparatives and explanatory notes, and we discussed some matters relevant to the Group this year. I am preparing for the audit team briefing next week at which there will be a number of recent recruits into the audit department whose first assignment will be the Vancouver Group.

I have attached some notes from my meeting as well as the financial information provided by Hannah. Using this information you are required to prepare briefing notes for use in the audit team briefing in which you:

(a) Explain why analytical procedures are performed as a fundamental part of our risk assessment at the planning stage of the audit. **(5 marks)**

(b) Identify and explain the audit risks which should be considered in planning the Group audit. You should ensure that you consider all of the information provided as well as utilising analytical procedures, where relevant, to identify the audit risks. **(18 marks)**

(c) Discuss the ethical issues relevant to Montreal & Co, and recommend any actions which should be taken by our firm. **(8 marks)**

Thank you.

Notes from meeting with the Group finance director and audit committee representative

The Group has not changed its operations significantly this year. However, it has completed a modernisation programme of its warehousing facilities at a cost of $25 million. The programme was financed with cash raised from two sources: $5 million was raised from a debenture issue, and $20 million from the sale of 5% of the share capital of Calgary Co, with the shares being purchased by an institutional investor.

An investigation into the Group's tax affairs started in January 2016. The tax authorities are investigating the possible underpayment of taxes by each of the companies in the Group, claiming that tax laws have been breached. The Group's tax planning was performed by another firm of accountants, Victoria & Co, but the Group's audit committee has asked if our firm will support the Group by looking into its tax position and liaising with the tax authorities in respect of the tax investigation on its behalf. Victoria & Co has resigned from their engagement to provide tax advice to the Group. The matter is to be resolved by a tribunal which is scheduled to take place in September 2016.

The Group audit committee has also asked whether one of Montreal & Co's audit partners can be appointed as a non-executive director and serve on the audit committee. The audit committee lacks a financial reporting expert, and the appointment of an audit partner would bring much needed knowledge and experience.

Financial information provided by the Group finance director

Consolidated statement of financial position

	Note	*Projected 31 July 2016* $m	*Actual 31 July 2015* $m
Assets			
Non-current assets			
Property, plant and equipment	1	230	187
Intangible assets – goodwill		30	30
Deferred tax asset	2	10	15
Total non-current assets		270	232
Current assets			
Inventories		35	28
Trade and other receivables		62	45
Cash and cash equivalents		–	10
Total current assets		97	83
Total assets		367	315
Equity and liabilities			
Equity			
Equity share capital		50	50
Retained earnings		126	103
Non-controlling interest	3	5	–
Total equity		181	153
Non-current liabilities			
Debenture		60	55
Provisions	4	6	12
Total non-current liabilities		66	67
Current liabilities			
Trade and other payables		105	95
Overdraft		15	–
Total current liabilities		120	95
Total liabilities		186	162
Total equity and liabilities		367	315

Consolidated statement of profit or loss for the year to 31 July

	Projected	*Actual*
	2016	*2015*
	$m	$m
Revenue	375	315
Operating expenses	(348)	(277)
Operating profit	27	38
Profit on disposal of shares in Calgary Co	10	–
Finance costs	(4)	(3)
Profit before tax	33	35
Tax expense	(10)	(15)
Profit for the year	23	20

Notes:

1 Several old warehouses were modernised during the year. The modernisation involved the redesign of the layout of each warehouse, the installation of new computer systems, and the replacement of electrical systems.

2 The deferred tax asset is in respect of unused tax losses (tax credits) which accumulated when Toronto Co was loss making for a period of three years from 2009 to 2012.

3 The non-controlling interest has arisen on the disposal of shares in Calgary Co. On 1 January 2016, a 5% equity shareholding in Calgary Co was sold, raising cash of $20 million. The profit made on the disposal is separately recognised in the Group statement of profit or loss.

4 The provisions relate to onerous leases in respect of vacant properties which are surplus to the Group's requirements.

Required:

Respond to the instructions in the partner's email. **(31 marks)**

Note: The split of the mark allocation is shown within the email.

Professional marks will be awarded for presentation, logical flow, and clarity of explanations provided. **(4 marks)**

(Total: 35 marks)

3 DALI *Walk in the footsteps of a top tutor*

You are a manager in the audit department of Mondrian & Co, a firm of Chartered Certified Accountants. You are responsible for the audit of Dali Co, a listed company specialising in the design and manufacture of equipment and machinery used in the quarrying industry. You are planning the audit of the financial statements for the year ending 31 December 2015. The projected financial statements for the 2015 year end recognise revenue of $138 million (2014 – $135 million), profit before tax of $9·8 million (2014 – $9.2 million) and total assets of $90 million (2014 – $85 million). Dali Co became listed in its home jurisdiction on 1 March 2015, and is hoping to achieve a listing on a foreign stock exchange in June 2016.

You have just received the following email from the audit engagement partner.

To: **Audit manager**

From: **Audit engagement partner, Sam Hockney**

Regarding: **Audit planning – Dali Co**

Hello

I need you to start planning the audit of Dali Co. I know you are new to this audit client, so I have provided you with some background information, the results of some preliminary analytical review performed by one of the audit team members, and notes from a discussion I had with the company's audit committee yesterday. I require you to prepare briefing notes for use in the audit planning meeting which will be held next week. In these notes you are required to:

(a) (i) **Evaluate the audit risks to be considered in planning the audit of Dali Co.** **(18 marks)**

(ii) **Recommend the additional information which would be relevant in the evaluation of audit risk.** **(5 marks)**

(b) **Explain the principal audit procedures to be performed in respect of:**

(i) **The valuation of work in progress.** **(4 marks)**

(ii) **The recognition and measurement of the government grant.** **(4 marks)**

Thank you.

Company background

Dali Co was established 20 years ago and has become known as a leading supplier of machinery used in the quarrying industry, with its customers operating quarries which extract stone used mainly for construction. Its customer base is located solely in its country of incorporation but most of the components used in Dali Co's manufacturing process are imported from foreign suppliers.

The machines and equipment made by Dali Co are mostly made to order in the company's three manufacturing sites. Customers approach Dali Co to design and develop a machine or piece of equipment specific to their needs. Where management considers that the design work will be significant, the customer is required to pay a 30% payment in advance, which is used to fund the design work. The remaining 70% is paid on delivery of the machine to the customer.

Typically, a machine takes three months to build, and a smaller piece of equipment takes on average six weeks. The design and manufacture of bespoke machinery involving payments in advance has increased during the year. Dali Co also manufactures a range of generic products which are offered for sale to all customers, including drills, conveyors and crushing equipment.

Notes from meeting with Dali Co audit committee

This year has been successful from a strategic point of view in that Dali Co achieved its stock exchange listing in March 2015, and in doing so raised a significant amount of equity finance. The company's corporate governance was reviewed as part of the flotation process, resulting in the recruitment of three new non-executive directors and a new finance director.

In March 2015, a cash-settled share-based payment plan was introduced for senior executives, who will receive a bonus on 31 December 2017. The amount of the bonus will be based on the increase in Dali Co's share price from that at the date of the flotation, when it was \$2·90, to the share price at 31 December 2017. On the advice of the newly appointed finance director, no accounting entries have been made in respect of the plan, but the details relating to the cash-settled share-based payment plan will be disclosed in the notes to the financial statements.

The finance director recommended that the company's manufacturing sites should be revalued. An external valuation was performed in June 2015, resulting in a revaluation surplus of \$3·5 million being recognised in equity. The finance director has informed the audit committee that no deferred tax needs to be provided in respect of the valuation because the property is part of continuing operations and there is no plan for disposal.

In July 2015, a government grant of \$10 million was received as part of a government scheme to subsidise companies which operate in deprived areas. Specifically \$2 million of the grant compensates the company for wages and salaries incurred in the year to 31 December 2015. The remaining grant relates to the continued operations in the deprived area, with a condition of the grant being that the manufacturing site in that area will remain operational until July 2020.

All of the company's manufacturing sites will be closed at the year end to allow the inventory counts to take place. According to the most recent management accounts which are available, at 30 November 2015 work in progress is valued at \$12 million (2014 – \$9.5 million) and the majority of these orders will not be complete until after the year end. In recent weeks several customers have returned equipment due to faults, and Dali Co offers a warranty to guarantee that defective items will be replaced free of charge.

Preliminary analytical review (extract) and other financial information

	Based on projected figures to 31 December 2015	*Based on audited figures to 31 December 2014*
Operating margin	15%	13%
Inventory days	175 days	150 days
Receivables collection period	90 days	70 days
Trade payables payment period	60 days	55 days
Earnings per share	75 cents per share	–
Share price	\$3·50	–

Required:

Respond to the instructions.in the audit partner's email. **(31 marks)**

Note: The split of the mark allocation is shown in the email.

Professional marks will be awarded for the presentation of the briefing notes and for the clarity of explanations provided. **(4 marks)**

(Total: 35 marks)

4 TED *Walk in the footsteps of a top tutor*

You are a manager in the audit department of Craggy & Co, a firm of Chartered Certified Accountants, and you have just been assigned to the audit of Ted Co, a new audit client of your firm, with a financial year ended 31 May 2015. Ted Co, a newly listed company, is a computer games designer and developer, and has grown rapidly in the last few years. The audit engagement partner, Jack Hackett, has sent you the following email:

To: **Audit manager**

From: **Jack Hackett**

Regarding: **Ted Co audit planning**

Hello

There are several tasks I require you to perform in respect of planning the audit of Ted Co. I held a meeting with the company's finance director, Len Brennan, yesterday, and I have provided you with some information from that meeting. In addition, I have asked one of the audit seniors to begin to carry out preliminary analytical review procedures on Ted Co's draft financial statements, and the results of the review performed so far are also provided to you.

Using this information and your audit planning knowledge, you are required to prepare briefing notes for me to use when briefing the audit team. In the briefing notes you should:

(a) Discuss the matters specific to the planning of an initial audit engagement which should be considered in developing the audit strategy. **(6 marks)**

(b) Evaluate the audit risks to be considered in planning the audit of Ted Co. **(17 marks)**

(c) Recommend the principal audit procedures to be performed in the audit of:

(i) The portfolio of short-term investments, and

(ii) The earnings per share figure. **(8 marks)**

Thank you.

Notes from meeting with Len Brennan

Ted Co was formed ten years ago by Dougal Doyle, a graduate in multimedia computing. The company designs, develops and publishes computer games including many highly successful games which have won industry awards. In the last two years the company invested $100m in creating games designed to appeal to a broad, global audience and sales are now made in over 60 countries. The software used in the computer games is developed in this country, but the manufacture of the physical product takes place overseas.

Computer games are largely sold through retail outlets, but approximately 25% of Ted Co's revenue is generated through sales made on the company's website. In some countries Ted Co's products are distributed under licences which give the licence holder the exclusive right to sell the products in that country. The cost of each licence to the distributor depends on the estimated sales in the country to which it relates, and licences last for an average of five years. The income which Ted Co receives from the sale of a licence is deferred over the period of the licence. At 31 May 2015 the total amount of deferred income recognised in Ted Co's statement of financial position is $18 million.

As part of a five-year strategic plan, Ted Co obtained a stock market listing in December 2014. The listing and related share issue raised a significant amount of finance, and many shares are held by institutional investors. Dougal Doyle retains a 20% equity shareholding, and a further 10% of the company's shares are held by his family members.

Despite being listed, the company does not have an internal audit department, and there is only one non-executive director on the board. These issues are explained in the company's annual report, as required by the applicable corporate governance code.

Recently, a small treasury management function was established to manage the company's foreign currency transactions, which include forward exchange currency contracts. The treasury management function also deals with short-term investments. In January 2015, cash of $8 million was invested in a portfolio of equity shares held in listed companies, which is to be held in the short term as a speculative investment. The shares are recognised as a financial asset at cost of $8 million in the draft statement of financial position. The fair value of the shares at 31 May 2015 is $6 million.

As a listed company, Ted Co is required to disclose its earnings per share figure. Dougal Doyle would like this to be based on an adjusted earnings figure which does not include depreciation or amortisation expenses.

The previous auditors of Ted Co, a small firm called Crilly & Co, resigned in September 2014. The audit opinion on the financial statements for the year ended 31 May 2014 was unmodified.

Extract of draft financial statements and results of preliminary analytical review

Statement of profit or loss (extract)

	Year to 31 May 2015	*Year to 31 May 2014*	*% change*
	Draft	*Actual*	
	$000	$000	
Revenue	98,000	67,000	46.3% increase
Gross profit	65,000	40,000	62.5% increase
Operating profit	12,000	9,200	30.4% increase
Finance charge	4,000	3,800	5.3% increase
Profit before tax	8,000	5,400	48.1% increase
Earnings per share	89.6 cents per share	–	

Note: Earnings per share has been calculated as follows:

	$000
Profit before tax	8,000
Add: Depreciation	1,100
Amortisation	6,000
Adjusted profit before tax	15,100
Adjusted profit before tax	15,100,000
Number of equity shares at 31 May 2015	16,850,000 = 89.6 cents per share

Statement of financial position (extract)

	31 May 2015 *Draft* $000	*31 May 2014* *Actual* $000	% change
Non-current assets:			
Intangible assets – development costs	58,000	35,000	65.7% increase
Total assets	134,000	105,000	27.6% increase

Required:

Respond to the email from the audit partner. (31 marks)

Professional marks will be awarded for the presentation, clarity of explanations and logical flow of the briefing notes. (4 marks)

(Total: 35 marks)

5 CONNOLLY *Walk in the footsteps of a top tutor*

Timed question with online tutor debrief

You are an audit manager in Davies & Co, responsible for the audit of Connolly Co, a listed company operating in the pharmaceutical industry. You are planning the audit of the financial statements for the year ending 31 December 2014, and the audit partner, Ali Stone, has sent you this email:

To: **Audit manager**
From: **Ali Stone, Audit partner**
Subject: **Audit planning – Connolly Co**

Hello

I would like you to start planning the audit of Connolly Co. The company's finance director, Maggie Ram, has sent to me this morning some key financial information discussed at the latest board meeting. I have also provided you with minutes of a meeting I had with Maggie last week and some background information about the company. Using this information I would like you to prepare briefing notes for my use in which you:

(a) Evaluate the business risks faced by Connolly Co. (11 marks)

(b) Identify and explain FOUR risks of material misstatement to be considered in planning the audit. (8 marks)

(c) Recommend the principal audit procedures to be performed in respect of the acquired 'Cold Comforts' brand name. (5 marks)

(d) Discuss the ethical issues relevant to the audit firm, and recommend appropriate actions to be taken. (7 marks)

Thank you.

Background information

Connolly Co is a pharmaceutical company, developing drugs to be licensed for use around the world. Products include medicines such as tablets and medical gels and creams. Some drugs are sold over the counter at pharmacy stores, while others can only be prescribed for use by a doctor. Products are heavily advertised to support the company's brand names. In some countries television advertising is not allowed for prescription drugs.

The market is very competitive, encouraging rapid product innovation. New products are continually in development and improvements are made to existing formulations. Four new drugs are in the research and development phase. Drugs have to meet very stringent regulatory requirements prior to being licensed for production and sale. Research and development involves human clinical trials, the results of which are scrutinised by the licensing authorities.

It is common in the industry for patents to be acquired for new drugs and patent rights are rigorously defended, sometimes resulting in legal action against potential infringement.

Minutes from Ali Stone's meeting with Maggie Ram

Connolly Co has approached its bank to extend its borrowing facilities. An extension of $10 million is being sought to its existing loan to support the on-going development of new drugs. Our firm has been asked by the bank to provide a guarantee in respect of this loan extension.

In addition, the company has asked the bank to make cash of $3 million available in the event that an existing court case against the company is successful. The court case is being brought by an individual who suffered severe and debilitating side effects when participating in a clinical trial in 2013.

In January 2014, Connolly Co began to sell into a new market – that of animal health. This has been very successful, and the sales of veterinary pharmaceuticals and grooming products for livestock and pets amount to approximately 15% of total revenue for 2014.

Another success in 2014 was the acquisition of the 'Cold Comforts' brand from a rival company. Products to alleviate the symptoms of coughs and colds are sold under this brand. The brand cost $5 million and is being amortised over an estimated useful life of 15 years.

Connolly Co's accounting and management information systems are out of date. This is not considered to create any significant control deficiencies, but the company would like to develop and implement new systems next year. Management has asked our firm to give advice on the new systems as they have little specialist in-house knowledge in this area.

Key financial information

	2014 – Projected unaudited	2013 – Actual audited
	$000	$000
Revenue	40,000	38,000
Operating profit	8,100	9,085
Operating margin	20%	24%
Earnings per share	25c	29c
Net cash flow	(1,200)	6,000
Research and development cash outflow in the year	(3,000)	(2,800)
Total development intangible asset recognised at the year end	50,000	48,000
Total assets	200,000	195,000
Gearing ratio (debt/equity)	0.8	0.9

Required:

Respond to the email from the audit partner. **(31 marks)**

Professional marks will be awarded in question 1 for the presentation, clarity of explanations and logical flow of the answer. **(4 marks)**

(Total: 35 marks)

Calculate your allowed time, allocate the time to the separate parts..............

6 STOW GROUP *Walk in the footsteps of a top tutor*

You are an audit manager in Compton & Co, responsible for the audit of the Stow Group (the Group). You are planning the audit of the Group financial statements for the year ending 31 December 2013. The Group's projected profit before tax for the year is $200 million and projected total assets at 31 December are $2,500 million.

The Group is a car manufacturer. Its operations are divided between a number of subsidiaries, some of which focus on manufacturing and distributing the cars, while others deal mainly with marketing and retail. All components of the Group have the same year end. The Group audit engagement partner, Chad Woodstock, has just sent you the following email.

To:	**Audit manager**
From:	**Chad Woodstock, audit partner**
Subject:	**The Stow Group – audit planning**

Hello

We need to start planning the audit of The Stow Group. Yesterday I met with the Group finance director, Marta Bidford, and we discussed some restructuring of the Group which has taken place this year. A new wholly-owned subsidiary has been acquired – Zennor Co, which is located overseas in Farland. Another subsidiary, Broadway Co, was disposed of.

I have provided you with a summary of issues which I discussed with Marta, and using this information I would like you to prepare briefing notes for my use in which you:

(a) (i) Explain the risks of material misstatement to be considered in planning the Group audit, commenting on their materiality to the Group financial statements. (12 marks)

(ii) Identify any further information that may be needed. (4 marks)

(b) Recommend the principal audit procedures to be performed in respect of the disposal of Broadway Co. (8 marks)

Marta has told me that Zennor Co has a well established internal audit team. She has suggested that we use the internal audit team as much as possible when performing our audit of Zennor Co as this will reduce the audit fee. The Group audit committee appreciates that with the audit of the new subsidiary there will be some increase in our costs, but has requested that the audit fee for the Group as a whole is not increased from last year's fee. I have provided you with some information about the internal audit team and in your briefing notes I would like you to:

(c) Discuss how Marta's suggestion impacts on the planning of the audit of Zennor Co's and of the Group's financial statements, and comment on any ethical issue raised. (7 marks)

Thank you.

Acquisition of Zennor Co

In order to expand overseas, the Group acquired 100% of the share capital of Zennor Co on 1 February 2013. Zennor Co is located in Farland, where it owns a chain of car dealerships. Zennor Co's financial statements are prepared using International Financial Reporting Standards and are measured and presented using the local currency of Farland, the Dingu. At the present time, the exchange rate is 4 Dingu = $1. Zennor Co has the same year end as the Group, and its projected profit for the year ending 31 December 2013 is 90 million Dingu, with projected assets at the same date of 800 million Dingu.

Zennor Co is supplied with cars from the Group's manufacturing plant. The cars are sent on cargo ships and take approximately six weeks to reach the main port in Farland, where they are stored until delivered to the dealerships. At today's date there are cars in transit to Zennor Co with a selling price of $58 million.

A local firm of auditors was engaged by the Group to perform a due diligence review on Zennor Co prior to its acquisition. The Group's statement of financial position recognises goodwill at acquisition of $60 million.

Compton & Co was appointed as auditor of Zennor Co on 1 March 2013.

Disposal of Broadway Co

On 1 September 2013, the Group disposed of its wholly-owned subsidiary, Broadway Co, for proceeds of $180 million. Broadway Co operated a distribution centre in this country. The Group's statement of profit or loss includes a profit of $25 million in respect of the disposal.

Broadway Co was acquired by a retail organisation, the Cornwall Group, which wished to bring its distribution operations in house in order to save costs. Compton & Co resigned as auditor to Broadway Co on 15 September 2013 to be replaced by the group auditor of the Cornwall Group.

Zennor Co – Internal audit team

The internal audit team was established several years ago and is headed up by a qualified accountant, Jo Evesham, who has a lot of experience in designing systems and controls. Jo and her team monitor the effectiveness of operating and financial reporting controls, and report to the board of directors. Zennor Co does not have an audit committee as corporate governance rules in Farland do not require an internal audit function or an audit committee to be established.

During the year, the internal audit team performed several value for money exercises such as reviewing the terms negotiated with suppliers.

Required:

Respond to the instructions in the partner's email. (31 marks)

Note: The mark allocation is shown against each of the instructions in the partner's email above.

Professional marks will be awarded for the structure and presentation of the briefing notes and for the clarity of explanations. (4 marks)

(Total: 35 marks)

7 GROHL *Walk in the footsteps of a top tutor*

(a) You are a manager in Foo & Co, responsible for the audit of Grohl Co, a company which produces circuit boards which are sold to manufacturers of electrical equipment such as computers and mobile phones. It is the first time that you have managed this audit client, taking over from the previous audit manager, Bob Halen, last month. The audit planning for the year ended 30 November 2012 is about to commence, and you have just received an email from Mia Vai, the audit engagement partner.

To: **Audit manager**

From: Mia Vai, Audit partner, Foo & Co

Subject: **Grohl Co – audit planning**

Hello

I am meeting with the other audit partners tomorrow to discuss forthcoming audits and related issues. I understand that you recently had a meeting with Mo Satriani, the finance director of Grohl Co.

Using the information from your meeting, I would like you to prepare briefing notes for my use in which you:

(i) Evaluate the business risks faced by Grohl Co. (12 marks)

(ii) Identify and explain FOUR risks of material misstatement to be considered in planning the audit. (8 marks)

(iii) Discuss any ethical issues raised, and recommend the relevant actions to be taken by our firm. (6 marks)

Thank you.

Comments made by Mo Satriani in your meeting

Business overview

Grohl Co's principal business activity remains the production of circuit boards. One of the key materials used in production is copper wiring, all of which is imported. As a cost cutting measure, in April 2012 a contract with a new overseas supplier was signed, and all of the company's copper wiring is now supplied under this contract. Purchases are denominated in a foreign currency, but the company does not use forward exchange contracts in relation to its imports of copper wiring.

Grohl Co has two production facilities, one of which produces goods for the export market, and the other produces goods for the domestic market. About half of its goods are exported, but the export market is suffering due to competition from cheaper producers overseas. Most domestic sales are made under contract with approximately 20 customers.

Recent developments

In early November 2012, production was halted for a week at the production facility which supplies the domestic market. A number of customers had returned goods, claiming faults in the circuit boards supplied. On inspection, it was found that the copper used in the circuit boards was corroded and therefore unsuitable for use. The corrosion is difficult to spot as it cannot be identified by eye, and relies on electrical testing.

All customers were contacted immediately and, where necessary, products recalled and replaced. The corroded copper remaining in inventory has been identified and separated from the rest of the copper.

Work has recently started on a new production line which will ensure that Grohl Co meets new regulatory requirements prohibiting the use of certain chemicals, which come into force in March 2013. In July 2012, a loan of $30 million with an interest rate of 4% was negotiated with Grohl Co's bank, the main purpose of the loan being to fund the capital expenditure necessary for the new production line. $2.5 million of the loan represents an overdraft which was converted into long-term finance.

Other matters

Several of Grohl Co's executive directors and the financial controller left in October 2012, to set up a company specialising in the recycling of old electronic equipment. This new company is not considered to be in competition with Grohl Co's operations. The directors left on good terms, and replacements for the directors have been recruited.

One of Foo & Co's audit managers, Bob Halen, is being interviewed for the role of financial controller at Grohl Co. Bob is a good candidate for the position, as he developed good knowledge of Grohl Co's business when he was managing the audit.

At Grohl Co's most recent board meeting, the audit fee was discussed. The board members expressed concern over the size of the audit fee, given the company's loss for the year. The board members would like to know whether the audit can be performed on a contingent fee basis.

Financial Information provided by Mo Satriani

Extract from draft statement of profit or loss for the year ended 30 November 2012

	2012 Draft	*2011 Actual*
	$000	$000
Revenue	12,500	13,800
Operating costs	(12,000)	(12,800)
Operating profit	500	1,000
Finance costs	(800)	(800)
Profit/(loss) before tax	(300)	200

The draft statement of financial position has not yet been prepared, but Mo states that the total assets of Grohl Co at 30 November 2012 are $180 million, and cash at bank is $130,000. Based on draft figures, the company's current ratio is 1.1, and the quick ratio is 0.8.

Required:

Respond to the email from the audit partner. **(26 marks)**

Professional marks will be awarded for the presentation, structure, logical flow and clarity of your answer. **(4 marks)**

(b) You have just received a phone call from Mo Satriani, Grohl Co's finance director, in which he made the following comments:

'There is something I forgot to mention in our meeting. Our business insurance covers us for specific occasions when business is interrupted. I put in a claim on 28 November 2012 for $5 million which I have estimated to cover the period when our production was halted due to the problem with the corroded copper. This is not yet recognised in the financial statements, but I want to make an adjustment to recognise the $5 million as a receivable as at 30 November.'

Required:

Comment on the matters that should be considered, and recommend the audit procedures to be performed, in respect of the insurance claim. (5 marks)

(Total: 35 marks)

8 JOVI GROUP *Walk in the footsteps of a top tutor*

(a) You are a manager in Sambora & Co, responsible for the audit of the Jovi Group (the Group), which is listed. The Group's main activity is steel manufacturing and it comprises a parent company and five subsidiaries. Sambora & Co currently audits all components of the Group.

You are working on the audit of the Group's financial statements for the year ended 30 June 2012. This morning the audit engagement partner left a note for you:

> **Hello**
>
> The audit senior has provided you with the draft consolidated financial statements and accompanying notes which summarise the key audit findings and some background information.
>
> At the planning stage, materiality was initially determined to be $900,000, and was c materiality is now determined to be $700,000. One of the audit juniors was unsure as to why the materiality level had been revised. There are two matters you need to deal with:
>
> (i) Explain why auditors may need to reassess materiality as the audit progresses. **(4 marks)**
>
> (ii) Assess the implications of the key audit findings for the completion of the audit. Your assessment must consider whether the key audit findings indicate a risk of material misstatement. Where the key audit findings refer to audit evidence, you must also consider the adequacy of the audit evidence obtained, but you do not need to recommend further specific procedures. **(15 marks)**
>
> Thank you

The Group's draft consolidated financial statements, with notes referenced to key audit findings, are shown below:

Draft consolidated statement of profit or loss

	Note	*30 June 2012 Draft*	*30 June 2011 Actual*
		$000	$000
Revenue	1	98,795	103,100
Cost of sales		(75,250)	(74,560)
Gross profit		23,545	28,540
Operating expenses	2	(14,900)	(17,500)
Operating profit		8,645	11,040
Share of profit of associate		1,010	900
Finance costs		(380)	(340)
Profit before tax		9,275	11,600
Taxation		(3,200)	(3,500)
Profit for the year		6,075	8,100
Other comprehensive income/expense for the year, net of tax:			
Gains on property revaluation	3	800	–
Actuarial losses on defined benefit plan	4	(1,100)	(200)
Other comprehensive income/expense		(300)	(200)
Total comprehensive income for the year		5,775	7,900

Notes: Key audit findings – statement of profit or loss

(1) Revenue has been stable for all components of the Group with the exception of one subsidiary, Copeland Co, which has recognised a 25% decrease in revenue.

(2) Operating expenses for the year to June 2012 is shown net of a profit on a property disposal of $2 million. Our evidence includes agreeing the cash receipts to bank statement and sale documentation, and we have confirmed that the property has been removed from the non-current asset register. The audit junior noted when reviewing the sale document, that there is an option to repurchase the property in five years time, but did not discuss the matter with management.

(3) The property revaluation relates to the Group's head office. The audit team have not obtained evidence on the revaluation, as the gain was immaterial based on the initial calculation of materiality.

(4) The actuarial loss is attributed to an unexpected stock market crash. The Group's pension plan is managed by Axle Co – a firm of independent fund managers who maintain the necessary accounting records relating to the plan. Axle Co has supplied written representation as to the value of the defined benefit plan's assets and liabilities at 30 June 2012. No other audit work has been performed other than to agree the figure from the financial statements to supporting documentation supplied by Axle Co.

Draft consolidated statement of financial position

	Note	*30 June 2012* *Draft* $000	*30 June 2011* *Actual* $000
ASSETS			
Non-current assets			
Property, plant and equipment		81,800	76,300
Goodwill	5	5,350	5,350
Investment in associate	6	4,230	4,230
Assets classified as held for sale	7	7,800	–
		99,180	85,880
Current assets			
Inventory		8,600	8,000
Receivables		8,540	7,800
Cash and cash equivalents		2,100	2,420
		19,240	18,220
Total assets		118,420	104,100
EQUITY AND LIABILITIES			
Equity			
Share capital		12,500	12,500
Revaluation reserve		3,300	2,500
Retained earnings		33,600	29,400
Non-controlling interest	8	4,350	4,000
Total equity		53,750	48,400
Non-current liabilities			
Defined benefit pension plan		10,820	9,250
Long-term borrowings	9	43,000	35,000
Deferred tax		1,950	1,350
Total non-current liabilities		55,770	45,600

Current liabilities		
Trade and other payables	6,200	7,300
Provisions	2,700	2,800
Total current liabilities	8,900	10,100
Total liabilities	64,670	55,700
Total equity and liabilities	118,420	104,100

Notes: Key audit findings – statement of financial position

(5) The goodwill relates to each of the subsidiaries in the Group. Management has confirmed in writing that goodwill is stated correctly, and our other audit procedure was to arithmetically check the impairment review conducted by management.

(6) The associate is a 30% holding in James Co, purchased to provide investment income. The audit team have not obtained evidence regarding the associate as there is no movement in the amount recognised in the statement of financial position.

(7) The assets held for sale relate to a trading division of one of the subsidiaries, which represents one third of that subsidiary's net assets. The sale of the division was announced in May 2012, and is expected to be complete by 31 December 2012. Audit evidence obtained includes a review of the sales agreement and confirmation from the buyer, obtained in July 2012, that the sale will take place.

(8) Two of the Group's subsidiaries are partly owned by shareholders external to the Group.

(9) A loan of $8 million was taken out in October 2011, carrying an interest rate of 2%, payable annually in arrears. The terms of the loan have been confirmed to documentation provided by the bank.

Required:

Respond to the note from the audit engagement partner. **(19 marks)**

(b) The audit engagement partner now sends a further note regarding the Jovi Group:

'The Group finance director has just informed me that last week the Group purchased 100% of the share capital of May Co, a company located overseas in Farland. The Group audit committee has suggested that due to the distant location of May Co, a joint audit could be performed, starting with the next financial statements for the year ending 30 June 2013. May Co's current auditors are a small local firm called Moore & Co who operate only in Farland.'

Required:

Discuss the advantages and disadvantages of a joint audit being performed on the financial statements of May Co. **(6 marks)**

(Total: 25 marks)

9 CS GROUP *Walk in the footsteps of a top tutor*

You are a manager in Magpie & Co, responsible for the audit of the CS Group. An extract from the permanent audit file describing the CS Group's history and operations is shown below:

Permanent file (extract)

Crow Co was incorporated 100 years ago. It was founded by Joseph Crow, who established a small pottery making tableware such as dishes, plates and cups. The products quickly grew popular, with one range of products becoming highly sought after when it was used at a royal wedding. The company's products have retained their popularity over the decades, and the Crow brand enjoys a strong identity and good market share.

Ten years ago, Crow Co made its first acquisition by purchasing 100% of the share capital of Starling Co. Both companies benefited from the newly formed CS Group, as Starling Co itself had a strong brand name in the pottery market. The CS Group has a history of steady profitability and stable management.

Crow Co and Starling Co have a financial year ending 31 July 2012, and your firm has audited both companies for several years.

(a) You have received an email from Jo Daw, the audit engagement partner:

To: **Audit manager**

From: **Jo Daw**

Regarding: **CS Group audit planning**

Hello

I have just been to a meeting with Steve Eagle, the finance director of the CS Group. We were discussing recent events which will have a bearing on our forthcoming audit, and my notes from the meeting are attached to this email. One of the issues discussed is the change in group structure due to the acquisition of Canary Co earlier this year. Our firm has been appointed as auditor of Canary Co, which has a year ending 30 June 2012, and the terms of the engagement have been agreed with the client. We need to start planning the audits of the three components of the Group, and of the consolidated financial statements.

Using the attached information, you are required to:

(i) Identify and explain the implications of the acquisition of Canary Co for the audit planning of the individual and consolidated financial statements of the CS Group. **(8 marks)**

(ii) Evaluate the risks of material misstatement to be considered in the audit planning of the individual and consolidated financial statements of the CS Group. **(18 marks)**

(iii) Recommend the principal audit procedures to be performed in respect of the goodwill initially recognised on the acquisition of Canary Co. **(5 marks)**

Thank you.

Attachment: Notes from meeting with Steve Eagle, finance director of the CS Group

Acquisition of Canary Co

The most significant event for the CS Group this year was the acquisition of Canary Co, which took place on 1 February 2012. Crow Co purchased all of Canary Co's equity shares for cash consideration of $125 million, and further contingent consideration of $30 million will be paid on the third anniversary of the acquisition, if the Group's revenue grows by at least 8% per annum. Crow Co engaged an external provider to perform due diligence on Canary Co, whose report indicated that the fair value of Canary Co's net assets was estimated to be $110 million at the date of acquisition. Goodwill arising on the acquisition has been calculated as follows:

	$ million
Fair value of consideration:	
Cash consideration	125
Contingent consideration	30
	155
Less: fair value of identifiable net assets acquired	(110)
Goodwill	45

To help finance the acquisition, Crow Co issued loan stock at par on 31 January 2012, raising cash of $100 million. The loan has a five-year term, and will be repaid at a premium of $20 million. 5% interest is payable annually in arrears. It is Group accounting policy to recognise financial liabilities at amortised cost.

Canary Co manufactures pottery figurines and ornaments. The company is considered a good strategic fit to the Group, as its products are luxury items like those of Crow Co and Starling Co, and its acquisition will enable the Group to diversify into a different market. Approximately 30% of its sales are made online, and it is hoped that online sales can soon be introduced for the rest of the Group's products. Canary Co has only ever operated as a single company, so this is the first year that it is part of a group of companies.

Financial performance and position

The Group has performed well this year, with forecast consolidated revenue for the year to 31 July 2012 of $135 million (2011 – $125 million), and profit before tax of $8.5 million (2011 – $8.4 million). A breakdown of the Group's forecast revenue and profit is shown below:

	Crow Co	*Starling Co*	*Canary Co*	*CS Group*
	$ million	$ million	$ million	$ million
Revenue	69	50	16	135
Profit before tax	3.5	3	2	8.5

Note: Canary Co's results have been included from 1 February 2012 (date of acquisition), and forecast up to 31 July 2012, the CS Group's financial year end.

The forecast consolidated statement of financial position at 31 July 2012 recognises total assets of $550 million.

Other matters

Starling Co received a grant of $35 million on 1 March 2012 in relation to redevelopment of its main manufacturing site. The government is providing grants to companies for capital expenditure on environmentally friendly assets. Starling Co has spent $25 million of the amount received on solar panels which generate electricity, and intends to spend the remaining $10 million on upgrading its production and packaging lines.

On 1 January 2012, a new IT system was introduced to Crow Co and Starling Co, with the aim of improving financial reporting controls and to standardise processes across the two companies. Unfortunately, Starling Co's finance director left the company last week.

Required:

Respond to the email from the partner. (31 marks)

Professional marks will be awarded in question 1 for the presentation, clarity of explanations and logical flow of the answer. (4 marks)

(Total: 35 marks)

10 JOLIE *Walk in the footsteps of a top tutor*

Jolie Co is a large company, operating in the retail industry, with a year ended 30 November 2010. You are a manager in Jen & Co, responsible for the audit of Jolie Co, and you have recently attended a planning meeting with Mo Pitt, the finance director of the company. As this is the first year that your firm will be acting as auditor for Jolie Co, you need to gain an understanding of the business risks facing the new client.

Notes from planning meeting

Jolie Co sells clothing, with a strategy of selling high fashion items under the JLC brand name. New ranges of clothes are introduced to stores every eight weeks. The company relies on a team of highly skilled designers to develop new fashion ranges. The designers must be able to anticipate and quickly respond to changes in consumer preferences.

There is a high staff turnover in the design team.

Most sales are made in-store, but there is also a very popular catalogue, from which customers can place an order on-line, or over the phone. The company has recently upgraded the computer system and improved the website, at significant cost, in order to integrate the website sales directly into the general ledger, and to provide an easier interface for customers to use when ordering and entering their credit card details. The new on-line sales system has allowed overseas sales for the first time.

The system for phone ordering has recently been outsourced. The contract for outsourcing went out to tender and Jolie Co awarded the contract to the company offering the least cost. The company providing the service uses an overseas phone call centre where staff costs are very low.

Jolie Co has recently joined the Ethical Trading Initiative. This is a 'fair-trade' initiative, which means that any products bearing the JLC brand name must have been produced in a manner which is clean and safe for employees, and minimises the environmental impact of the manufacturing process. A significant advertising campaign promoting Jolie Co's involvement with this initiative has recently taken place. The JLC brand name was purchased a number of years ago and is recognised at cost as an intangible asset, which is not amortised. The brand represents 12% of the total assets recognised on the statement of financial position.

The company owns numerous distribution centres, some of which operate close to residential areas. A licence to operate the distribution centres is issued by each local government authority in which a centre is located. One of the conditions of the licence is that deliveries must only take place between 8 am and 6 pm. The authority also monitors the noise level of each centre, and can revoke the operating licence if a certain noise limit is breached. Two licences were revoked for a period of three months during the year.

You have just received the following e-mail from the audit engagement partner, Toni Pacino:

To: **Audit manager**

From: **Toni Pacino**

Regarding: **Audit planning for Jolie Co**

I would like you to begin the audit planning for our new audit client, Jolie Co. Mo Pitt has just sent to me extracts from Jolie Co's draft accounts and comparative figures, which should help you to prepare some briefing notes which will be used at the audit planning meeting. I understand you met recently with Mo, and I am sure you discussed a variety of issues relevant to the audit planning. In your briefing notes, you should evaluate the business risks facing Jolie Co. The notes will be used to brief the audit team members about the issues facing the client, and to help them gain some business understanding of Jolie Co.

Thanks, Toni

Extract from draft statement of profit or loss:

Year ending 30 November	*2010 Draft* $ million	*2009 Actual* $ million
Revenue:		
Retail outlets	1,030	1,140
Phone and on-line sales	425	395
Total revenue	**1,455**	**1,535**
Operating profit	245	275
Finance costs	(25)	(22)
Profit before tax	**220**	**253**
Additional information:		
Number of stores	210	208
Average revenue per store	$4.905 million	$5.77 million
Number of phone orders	680,000	790,000
Number of on-line orders	1,020,000	526,667
Average spend per order	$250	$300

Required:

(a) Respond to the e-mail from the partner. (15 marks)

Professional marks will be awarded in part (a) for the format of the answer and the clarity of the evaluation. (4 marks)

(b) Using the information provided, identify and explain FIVE risks of material misstatement in the financial statements of Jolie Co. (10 marks)

(c) Recommend the principal audit procedures to be performed in respect of the valuation of the JLC brand name. (6 marks)

(Total: 35 marks)

OTHER ASSIGNMENTS

11 ROPE *Walk in the footsteps of a top tutor*

You are the manager responsible for the audit of Rope Co for the year ended 30 September 2016. During a visit to the team performing the fieldwork, the audit senior shows you a cash flow forecast covering six-month periods to 30 September 2018 as prepared by management as part of their assessment of the going concern status of the company. The audit senior asks whether any of the forecast cash flows disclosed require any further investigation during the audit fieldwork.

The actual and forecast six-monthly cash flows for Rope Co for the periods ended:

	Actual		Forecast			
	31 March 2016	30 Sept 2016	31 March 2017	30 Sept 2017	31 March 2018	30 Sept 2018
	$000	$000	$000	$000	$000	$000
Operating cash flows						
Receipts from customers	13,935	14,050	14,300	14,700	14,950	15,400
Payments to suppliers	(10,725)	(10,850)	(11,050)	(11,400)	(11,600)	(12,000)
Salaries	(1,250)	(1,300)	(1,275)	(1,326)	(1,301)	(1,353)
Other operating cash payments	(1,875)	(1,850)	(1,913)	(1,887)	(1,951)	(1,925)
Other cash flows						
Sale of investments	–	–	–	–	–	500
Repayment of J Stewart loan	–	–	–	–	–	(500)
Repayment of bank loan	–	–	–	–	(1,500)	–
Receipt of bank loan	–	–	–	–	1,500	–
Cash flow for the period	85	50	62	87	98	122
Opening cash	(275)	(190)	(140)	(78)	9	107
Closing cash	(190)	(140)	(78)	9	107	229

The following additional information has been provided in support of the forecasts:

- Receipts from customers and payments to suppliers have been estimated based on detailed sales forecasts prepared by the sales director.
- Salaries and overheads have been estimated as the prior year cost plus general inflation of 2%.
- The bank loan expires on 5 January 2018. The finance director expects to take out a matching facility with the current lender to pay off the existing debt.
- On 1 October 2015, the chief executive, Mr J Stewart, gave the company a three-year, interest free loan secured by a fixed charge over the operational assets of Rope Co. The audit team was unaware of this loan prior to obtaining the cash flow forecast. Related parties ?
- The directors plan to sell some investments in listed shares to fund the repayment of the chief executive's loan. At 30 September 2016, the investments were carried in the statement of financial position at their fair value of $350,000.

Required:

(a) Evaluate the appropriateness of the cash flow forecast prepared by Rope Co and recommend the further audit procedures which should be performed. (14 marks)

(b) Comment on the matters to be considered in respect of the loan from Mr J Stewart and recommend the further audit procedures to be performed. (6 marks)

(Total: 20 marks)

12 WATERS *Walk in the footsteps of a top tutor*

> ***Timed question with online tutor debrief***

You are a manager in Hunt & Co, a firm which offers a range of services to audit and non-audit clients. You have been asked to consider a potential engagement to review and provide a report on the prospective financial information of Waters Co, a company which has been an audit client of Hunt & Co for six years. The audit of the financial statements for the year ended 30 April 2014 has just commenced.

Waters Co operates a chain of cinemas across the country. Currently its cinemas are out of date and use projectors which cannot show films made using new technology, which are becoming more popular. Management is planning to invest in all of its cinemas in order to attract more customers. The company has sufficient cash to fund half of the necessary capital expenditure, but has approached its bank with a loan application of $8 million for the remainder of the funds required. Most of the cash will be used to invest in equipment and fittings, such as new projectors and larger screens, enabling new technology films to be shown in all cinemas. The remaining cash will be used for refurbishment of the cinemas.

The draft forecast statements of profit or loss for the years ending 30 April 2015 and 2016 are shown below, along with the key assumptions which have been used in their preparation. The unaudited statement of profit or loss for the year ended 30 April 2014 is also shown below. The forecast has been prepared for use by the bank in making its lending decision, and will be accompanied by other prospective financial information including a forecast statement of cash flows.

Forecast statement of profit or loss

	Year ended 30 April 2014 Unaudited $000	*Note relevant to forecast information*	*Year ending 30 April 2015 Forecast* $000	*Year ending 30 April 2016 Forecast* $000
Revenue	35,000	1	43,000	46,000
Operating expenses	(28,250)	2	(31,500)	(32,100)
Operating profit	6,750		11,500	13,900
Finance costs	(1,700)		(2,000)	(1,900)
Profit before tax	5,050		9,500	12,000

Note 1: The forecast increase in revenue is based on the following assumptions:

(i) All cinemas will be fitted with new projectors and larger screens to show new technology films by September 2014.

(ii) Ticket prices will increase from $7.50 to $10 from 1 September 2014.

Note 2: Operating expenses include mainly staff costs, depreciation of property and equipment, and repairs and maintenance to the cinemas.

Required:

(a) (i) Explain the matters to be considered by Hunt & Co before accepting the engagement to review and report on Waters Co's prospective financial information. (6 marks)

(ii) Assuming the engagement is accepted, describe the examination procedures to be used in respect of the forecast statement of profit or loss. (8 marks)

(b) The audit strategy relevant to the audit of Waters Co concludes that the company has a relatively high risk associated with money laundering, largely due to the cash-based nature of its activities. The majority of customers purchase their cinema tickets and refreshments in cash, and the company transfers its cash to overseas bank accounts on a regular basis.

Required:

(i) Explain the stages used in laundering money, commenting on why Waters Co has been identified as high risk. (5 marks)

(ii) Recommend FOUR elements of an anti-money laundering programme which audit firms such as Hunt & Co should have in place. (6 marks)

(Total: 25 marks)

Calculate your allowed time, allocate the time to the separate parts..............

13 HAWK *Walk in the footsteps of a top tutor*

(a) You are a manager in Lapwing & Co. One of your audit clients is Hawk Co which operates commercial real estate properties typically comprising several floors of retail units and leisure facilities such as cinemas and health clubs, which are rented out to provide rental income.

Your firm has just been approached to provide an additional engagement for Hawk Co, to review and provide a report on the company's business plan, including forecast financial statements for the 12-month period to 31 May 2013. Hawk Co is in the process of negotiating a new bank loan of $30 million and the report on the business plan is at the request of the bank. It is anticipated that the loan would be advanced in August 2012 and would carry an interest rate of 4%. The report would be provided by your firm's business advisory department and a second partner review will be conducted which will reduce any threat to objectivity to an acceptable level.

Extracts from the forecast financial statements included in the business plan are given below:

Statement of Profit or Loss (extract)

	Note	*FORECAST 12 months to 31 May 2013*	*UNAUDITED 12 months to 31 May 2012*
		$000	$000
Revenue		25,000	20,600
Operating expenses		(16,550)	(14,420)
Operating profit		8,450	6,180
Profit on disposal of Beak Retail	1	4,720	–
Finance costs		(2,650)	(1,690)
Profit before tax		10,520	4,490

Statement of financial position

	Note	*FORECAST 12 months to 31 May 2013*	*UNAUDITED 12 months to 31 May 2012*
Assets		$000	$000
Non-current assets			
Property, plant and equipment	2	330,150	293,000
Current assets			
Inventory		500	450
Receivables		3,600	3,300
Cash and cash equivalents		2,250	3,750
		6,350	7,500
Total assets		336,500	300,500

Equity and liabilities			
Equity			
Share capital		105,000	100,000
Retained earnings		93,400	92,600
Total equity		198,400	192,600
Non-current liabilities			
Long-term borrowings	2	82,500	52,500
Deferred tax		50,000	50,000
Current liabilities			
Trade payables		5,600	5,400
Total liabilities		138,100	107,900
Total equity and liabilities		336,500	300,500

Notes:

(1) Beak Retail is a retail park which is underperforming. Its sale is currently being negotiated, and is expected to take place in September 2012.

(2) Hawk Co is planning to invest the cash raised from the bank loan in a new retail and leisure park which is being developed jointly with another company, Kestrel Co.

Required:

In respect of the engagement to provide a report on Hawk Co's business plan:

(i) Identify and explain the matters that should be considered in agreeing the terms of the engagement, and

Note: You are NOT required to consider ethical threats to objectivity.

(6 marks)

(ii) Recommend the procedures that should be performed in order to examine and report on the forecast financial statements of Hawk Co for the year to 31 May 2013. (15 marks)

(b) You are also responsible for the audit of Osprey Co, which has a financial year ended 31 May 2012. The audit engagement partner, Bill Kingfisher, sent you the following email this morning:

To: **Audit manager**

From: **Bill Kingfisher, audit engagement partner, Osprey Co**

Regarding: **Environmental incident**

Hello

Osprey Co's finance director called me yesterday to explain that unfortunately over the last few weeks, one of its four factories leaked a small amount of toxic chemicals into the atmosphere. The factory's operations were halted immediately and a decision has been taken to permanently close the site. Though this is a significant event for the company and will result in relocation and some restructuring of operations, it is not considered to be a threat to its going concern status. Costs of closure of the factory have been estimated to be $1.25 million, which is expected to be material to the financial statements, and a provision has been set up in respect of these costs.

Osprey Co is keen to highlight its previous excellent record on socio-environmental matters. Management is preparing a report to be published with the financial statements which will describe the commitment of the company to socio-environmental matters, and state its target of reducing environmental damage caused by its operations. The report will contain a selection of targets and key performance indicators to show performance in areas such as energy use, water consumption and employee satisfaction. Our firm may be asked to provide an assurance report on the key performance indicators.

I am asking you to prepare briefing notes for my use in which you:

(i) Recommend the principal audit procedures to be performed in respect of the costs of closure of the factory. **(6 marks)**

(ii) Discuss the difficulties in measuring and reporting on environmental and social performance. **(4 marks)**

Thank you.

Required:

Respond to the partner's email. **(10 marks)**

Professional marks will be awarded in part (b) for the presentation and clarity of your answer. **(4 marks)**

(Total: 35 marks)

14 APRICOT *Walk in the footsteps of a top tutor*

Your audit client, Apricot Co, is intending to purchase a new warehouse at a cost of $500,000. One of the directors of the company, Pik Choi, has agreed to make the necessary finance available through a director's loan to the company. This arrangement has been approved by the other directors, and the cash will be provided on 30 March 2010, one day before the purchase is due to be completed. Pik's financial advisor has asked to see a cash flow projection of Apricot Co for the next three months. Your firm has been asked to provide an assurance report to Pik's financial advisor on this prospective financial information.

The cash flow forecast is shown below:

	January 2010	*February 2010*	*March 2010*
	$000	$000	$000
Operating cash receipts:			
Cash sales	125	135	140
Receipts from credit sales	580	600	625
Operating cash payments:			
Purchases of inventory	(410)	(425)	(425)
Salaries	(100)	(100)	(100)
Overheads	(175)	(175)	(175)
Other cash flows:			
Dividend payment		(80)	
Purchase of new licence	(35)		
Fixtures for new warehouse			(60)
Loan receipt			500
Payment for warehouse			(500)
Cash flow for the month	(15)	(45)	5
Opening cash	100	85	40
Closing cash	85	40	45

The following information is relevant:

(1) Apricot Co is a wholesaler of catering equipment and frozen food. Its customers are mostly restaurant chains and fast food outlets.

(2) Customers who pay in cash receive a 10% discount. Analysis has been provided showing that for sales made on credit, 20% of customers pay in the month of the sale, 60% pay after 45 days, 10% after 65 days, 5% after 90 days, and the remainder are bad debts.

(3) Apricot Co pays for all purchases within 30 days in order to take advantage of a 12% discount from suppliers.

(4) Overheads are mainly property rentals, utility bills, insurance premiums and general office expenses.

(5) Apricot Co needs to have a health and safety licence as it sells food. Each licence is valid for one year and is issued once an inspection has taken place.

(6) A profit forecast has also been prepared for the year ending 31 December 2010 to help with internal planning and budgeting.

This is the first time that Apricot Co has requested an assurance report, and the directors are unsure about the contents of the report that your firm will issue. They understand that it is similar in format to an auditor's report, but that the specific contents are not the same.

Required:

(a) Recommend the procedures that should be performed on the cash flow forecast for the three months ending 31 March 2010 in order to provide an assurance report as requested by Apricot Co. (15 marks)

(b) Explain the main contents of the report that will be issued on the prospective financial information. (5 marks)

(Total: 20 marks)

15 SANZIO *Walk in the footsteps of a top tutor*

You are a manager in the assurance department at Raphael & Co, a firm of Chartered Certified Accountants. Your firm has been appointed by Sanzio Co to perform a due diligence review of a potential acquisition target, Titian Tyres Co. As part of the due diligence review and to allow for consideration of an appropriate offer price, Sanzio Co has requested that you identify and value all the assets and liabilities of Titian Tyres Co, including items which may not currently be reported in the statement of financial position.

Sanzio Co is a large, privately owned company operating only in this country, which sells spare parts and accessories for cars, vans and bicycles. Titian Tyres Co is a national chain of vehicle service centres, specialising in the repair and replacement of tyres, although the company also offers a complete range of engine and bodywork services as well. If the acquisition is successful, the management of Sanzio Co intends to open a Titian Tyres service centre in each of its stores.

One of the reasons for Titian Tyres Co's success is their internally generated customer database, which records all customer service details. Using the information contained on the database software, the company's operating system automatically informs previous customers when their vehicle is due for its next service via email, mobile phone text or automated letter. It also informs a customer service team to telephone the customer if they fail to book a service within two weeks of receiving the notification. According to the management of Titian Tyres Co, repeat business makes up over 60% of annual sales and management believes that this is a distinct competitive advantage over other service centres.

Titian Tyres Co also recently purchased a licence to distribute a new, innovative tyre which was designed and patented in the United States. The tyre is made of 100% recycled materials and, due to a new manufacturing process, is more hardwearing and therefore needs replacing less often. Titian Tyres Co paid $5 million for the licence in January 2015 and the company is currently the sole, licenced distributor in this country.

During a brief review of Titian Tyres Co's financial statements for the year ended 30 June 2015, you notice a contingent liability disclosure in the notes relating to compensation claims made after the fitting of faulty engine parts during 2014. The management of Titian Tyres Co has stated that the fault lies with the manufacturer of the part and that they have made a claim against the manufacturer for the total amount sought by the affected customers.

Required:

(a) Describe the purpose of a due diligence assignment and compare the scope of a due diligence assignment with that of an audit of historical financial statements.
(6 marks)

(b) (i) Recommend, with reasons, the principal additional information which should be made available to assist with your valuation of Titian Tyres Co's intangible assets.

(ii) Explain the specific enquiries you should make of Titian Tyres Co's management relevant to the contingent liability disclosed in the financial statements.

Note: The total marks will be split equally between each part. (14 marks)

(Total: 20 marks)

16 BALTIMORE *Walk in the footsteps of a top tutor*

Timed question with online tutor debrief

You are a manager in the business advisory department of Goleen & Co. Your firm has been approached to provide assurance to Baltimore Co, a company which is not an audit client of your firm, on a potential acquisition. You have just had a conversation with Mark Clear, Baltimore Co's managing director, who made the following comments:

'Baltimore Co is a book publisher specialising in publishing textbooks and academic journals. In the last few years the market has changed significantly, with the majority of customers purchasing books from online sellers. This has led to a reduction in profits, and we recognise that we need to diversify our product range in order to survive. As a result of this, we decided to offer a subscription-based website to customers, which would provide the customer with access to our full range of textbooks and journals online.

'On investigating how to set up this website, we found that we lack sufficient knowledge and resources to develop it ourselves and began to look for another company which has the necessary skills, with a view to acquiring the company. We have identified Mizzen Co as a potential acquisition, and we have approached the bank for a loan which will be used to finance the acquisition if it goes ahead.

'Baltimore Co has not previously acquired another company. We would like to engage your firm to provide guidance regarding the acquisition. I understand that a due diligence review would be advisable prior to deciding on whether to go ahead with the acquisition, but the other directors are not sure that this is required, and they don't understand what the review would involve. They are also unsure about the type of conclusion that would be issued and whether it would be similar to the opinion in an auditor's report.

'To help me brief the other directors and using the information I have provided, I would like you to:

Required:

(a) Discuss THREE benefits to Baltimore Co of a due diligence review being performed on Mizzen Co. (6 marks)

(b) Identify and explain the matters which you would focus on in your due diligence review and recommend the additional information which you will need to perform your work. (16 marks)

(c) Describe the type of conclusion which would be issued for a due diligence report and compare this to an auditor's report.' (3 marks)

Mark Clear has sent you the following information about Mizzen Co:

Company background

Mizzen Co was established four years ago by two university graduates, Vic Sandhu and Lou Lien, who secured funds from a venture capitalist company, BizGrow, to set up the company. Vic and Lou created a new type of website interface which has proven extremely popular, and which led to the company growing rapidly and building a good reputation. They continue to innovate and have won awards for website design. Vic and Lou have a minority shareholding in Mizzen Co.

Mizzen Co employs 50 people and operates from premises owned by BizGrow, for which a nominal rent of $1,000 is paid annually. The company uses few assets other than computer equipment and fixtures and fittings. The biggest expense is wages and salaries and due to increased demand for website development, freelance specialists have been used in the last six months. According to the most recent audited financial statements, Mizzen Co has a bank balance of $500,000.

The company has three revenue streams:

(1) Developing and maintaining websites for corporate customers. Mizzen Co charges a one-off fee to its customers for the initial development of a website and for maintaining the website for two years. The amount of this fee depends on the size and complexity of the website and averages at $10,000 per website. The customer can then choose to pay another one-off fee, averaging $2,000, for Mizzen Co to provide maintenance for a further five years.

(2) Mizzen Co has also developed a subscription-based website on which it provides access to technical material for computer specialists. Customers pay an annual fee of $250 which gives them unlimited access to the website. This accounts for approximately 30% of Mizzen Co's total revenue.

(3) The company has built up several customer databases which are made available, for a fee, to other companies for marketing purposes. This is the smallest revenue stream, accounting for approximately 20% of Mizzen Co's total revenue.

Extracts from audited financial statements

Statement of profit or loss

	Year ended 30 September 2013	*Year ended 30 September 2012*	*Year ended 30 September 2011*	*Year ended 30 September 2010*
	$000	$000	$000	$000
Revenue	4,268	3,450	2,150	500
Operating expenses	(2,118)	(2,010)	(1,290)	(1,000)
Operating profit/(loss)	2,150	1,440	860	(500)
Finance costs	(250)	(250)	(250)	–
Profit/(loss) before tax	1,900	1,190	610	(500)
Tax expense	(475)	(300)	(140)	–
Profit/(loss) for the year	1,425	890	470	(500)

There were no items of other comprehensive income recognised in any year.

Required:

Respond to the request from Mark Clear.

(Total: 25 marks)

Calculate your allowed time, allocate the time to the separate parts..............

17 JACOB *Walk in the footsteps of a top tutor*

Jacob Co, an audit client of your firm, is a large privately owned company whose operations involve a repair and maintenance service for domestic customers. The company offers a range of services, such as plumbing and electrical repairs and maintenance, and the repair of domestic appliances such as washing machines and cookers, as well as dealing with emergencies such as damage caused by flooding. All work is covered by a two-year warranty.

The directors of Jacob Co have been seeking to acquire expertise in the repair and maintenance of swimming pools and hot-tubs as this is a service increasingly requested, but not offered by the company. They have recently identified Locke Co as a potential acquisition. Preliminary discussions have been held between the directors of the two companies with a view to the acquisition of Locke Co by Jacob Co. This will be the first acquisition performed by the current management team of Jacob Co. Your firm has been asked to perform a due diligence review on Locke Co prior to further discussions taking place. You have been provided with the following information regarding Locke Co:

Locke Co is owner-managed, with three of the five board members being the original founders of the company, which was incorporated thirty years ago. The head office is located in a prestigious building, which is owned by the founders' family estate. The company recently acquired a separate piece of land on which a new head office is to be built.

The company has grown rapidly in the last three years as more affluent customers can afford the cost of installing and maintaining swimming pools and hot-tubs. The expansion was funded by a significant bank loan. The company relies on an overdraft facility in the winter months when less operating cash inflows arise from maintenance work.

Locke Co enjoys a good reputation, though this was tarnished last year by a complaint by a famous actor who claimed that, following maintenance of his swimming pool by Locke Co's employees, the water contained a chemical which damaged his skin. A court case is on-going and is attracting media attention.

The company's financial year end is 31 August. Its accounting function is outsourced to Austin Co, a local provider of accounting and tax services.

Required:

(a) Explain THREE potential benefits of an externally provided due diligence review to Jacob Co. (6 marks)

(b) Recommend additional information which should be made available for your firm's due diligence review, and explain the need for the information. (14 marks)

(Total: 20 marks)

18 FASTER JETS *Walk in the footsteps of a top tutor*

Timed question with online tutor debrief

Faster Jets Co is an airline company and is a new audit client of Brown & Co. You are responsible for the audit of the financial statements for the year ended 30 November 2014. The draft financial statements recognise revenue of $150 million and total assets of $250 million.

(a) During the year, Faster Jets Co purchased several large plots of land located near major airports at a cost of $12.5 million. The land is currently rented out and is classified as investment property, which is recognised in the draft financial statements at a fair value of $14.5 million. The audit partner has suggested the use of an auditor's expert to obtain evidence in respect of the fair value of the land.

Required:

In respect of the land recognised as investment property:

(i) Explain the additional information which you require to plan the audit of the land; and

(ii) Explain the matters to be considered in assessing the reliance which can be placed on the work of an auditor's expert.

Note: The total marks will be split equally between each part. (10 marks)

(b) Your firm has also been engaged to perform a separate assurance engagement on Faster Jets Co's corporate social responsibility (CSR) report. This engagement will be performed by Brown & Co's specialist social and environmental assurance department and there are no ethical threats created by the provision of this service in addition to the audit. An extract from the draft CSR report is shown below:

CSR objective	**CSR target**	**Performance in 2014**
Continue to invest in local communities and contribute to charitable causes	Make direct charitable cash donations to local charities	Donations of $550,000 were made to local charities
	Build relationships with global charities and offer free flights to charitable organisations	800 free flights with a value of $560,000 were provided to charities
	Develop our Local Learning Initiative and offer free one day education programmes to schools	$750,000 was spent on the Local Learning Initiative and 2,250 children attended education days
Reduce environmental impact of operations	Reduce the amount of vehicle fuel used on business travel by our employees	The number of miles travelled in vehicles reduced by 5%, and the amount spent on vehicle fuel reduced by 7%

Required:

(i) **Discuss the difficulties in measuring and reporting on social and environmental performance; and** **(4 marks)**

(ii) **Recommend the procedures to be used to gain assurance on the validity of the performance information in Faster Jets Co's CSR report.** **(6 marks)**

(Total: 20 marks)

Calculate your allowed time, allocate the time to the separate parts..............

19 NEWMAN & CO *Walk in the footsteps of a top tutor*

You are a manager in Newman & Co, a global firm of Chartered Certified Accountants. You are responsible for evaluating proposed engagements and for recommending to a team of partners whether or not an engagement should be accepted by your firm.

Eastwood Co, a listed company, is an existing audit client and is an international mail services operator, with a global network including 220 countries and 300,000 employees. The company offers mail and freight services to individual and corporate customers, as well as storage and logistical services.

Eastwood Co takes its corporate social responsibility seriously, and publishes social and environmental key performance indicators (KPIs) in a Sustainability Report, which is published with the financial statements in the annual report. Partly in response to requests from shareholders and pressure groups, Eastwood Co's management has decided that in the forthcoming annual report, the KPIs should be accompanied by an independent assurance report. An approach has been made to your firm to provide this report in addition to the audit.

To help in your evaluation of this potential engagement, you have been given an extract from the draft Sustainability Report, containing some of the KPIs published by Eastwood Co. In total, 25 environmental KPIs, and 50 social KPIs are disclosed.

Extract from Sustainability Report:

Year ended 31 October	*2010 Draft*	*2009 Actual*
CO_2 emissions (million tonnes)	26.8	28.3
Energy use (million kilowatt hours)	4,895	5,250
Charitable donations ($ million)	10.5	8.2
Number of serious accidents in the workplace	60	68
Average annual spend on training per employee	$180	$175

You have also had a meeting with Ali Monroe, the manager responsible for the audit of Eastwood Co, and notes of the meeting are given below:

Notes from meeting with audit manager, Ali Monroe

Newman & Co has audited Eastwood Co for three years, and it is a major audit client of our firm, due to its global presence and recent listing on two major stock exchanges. The audit is managed from our office in Oldtown, which is also the location of the global headquarters of Eastwood Co.

We have not done any work on the KPIs, other than review them for consistency, as we would with any 'other information' issued with the financial statements. The KPIs are produced by Eastwood Co's Sustainability Department, located in Fartown.

We have performed audit procedures on the charitable donations, as this is disclosed in a note to the financial statements, and our evidence indicates that there have been donations of $9 million this year, which is the amount disclosed in the note. However, the draft KPI is a different figure – $10.5 million, and this is the figure highlighted in the draft Chairman's Statement as well as the draft Sustainability Report. $9 million is material to the financial statements.

The audit work is nearly complete, and the annual report is to be published in about four weeks, in time for the company meeting, scheduled for 31 January 2011.

Your firm has recently established a sustainability reporting assurance team based in Oldtown, and if the engagement to report on the Sustainability Report is accepted, it would be performed by members of that team, who would not be involved with the audit.

Required:

(a) Identify and explain the matters that should be considered in evaluating the invitation to perform an assurance engagement on the Sustainability Report of Eastwood Co. (12 marks)

(b) Recommend procedures that could be used to verify the following draft KPIs:

(i) The number of serious accidents in the workplace; and

(ii) The average annual spend on training per employee. (5 marks)

You have a trainee accountant assigned to you, who has read the notes taken at your meeting with Ali Monroe.

She is unsure of the implications of the charitable donations being disclosed as a different figure in the financial statements compared with the other information published in the annual report.

Required:

(c) (i) Explain the responsibility of the auditor in relation to other information published with the financial statements; and

(ii) Recommend the action to be taken by Newman & Co if the figure relating to charitable donations in the other information is not amended. (8 marks)

(Total: 25 marks)

20 CHESTNUT *Walk in the footsteps of a top tutor*

You are an audit manager in Cedar & Co, responsible for the audit of Chestnut Co, a large company which provides information technology services to business customers. The finance director of Chestnut Co, Jack Privet, contacted you this morning, saying:

'I was alerted yesterday to a fraud being conducted by members of our sales team. It appears that several sales representatives have been claiming reimbursement for fictitious travel and client entertaining expenses and inflating actual expenses incurred. Specifically, it has been alleged that the sales representatives have claimed on expenses for items such as gifts for clients and office supplies which were never actually purchased, claimed for business-class airline tickets but in reality had purchased economy tickets, claimed for non-existent business mileage and used the company credit card to purchase items for personal use.

I am very worried about the scale of this fraud, as travel and client entertainment is one of our biggest expenses. All of the alleged fraudsters have been suspended pending an investigation, which I would like your firm to conduct. We will prosecute these employees to attempt to recoup our losses if evidence shows that a fraud has indeed occurred, so your firm would need to provide an expert witness in the event of a court case. Can we meet tomorrow to discuss this potential assignment?'

Chestnut Co has a small internal audit department and in previous years the evidence obtained by Cedar & Co as part of the external audit has indicated that the control environment of the company is generally good. The audit opinion on the financial statements for the year ended 31 March 2011 was unmodified.

Required:

(a) Assess the ethical and professional issues raised by the request for your firm to investigate the alleged fraudulent activity. (7 marks)

(b) Explain the matters that should be discussed in the meeting with Jack Privet in respect of planning the investigation into the alleged fraudulent activity. (7 marks)

(c) Evaluate the arguments for and against the prohibition of auditors providing non-audit services to audit clients. (6 marks)

(Total: 20 marks)

EVALUATION AND REVIEW

21 THURMAN *Walk in the footsteps of a top tutor*

You are the manager responsible for the audit of Thurman Co, a manufacturing company which supplies stainless steel components to a wide range of industries. The company's financial year ended on 31 July 2016 and you are reviewing the audit work which has been completed on a number of material balances and transactions: assets held for sale, capital expenditure and payroll expenses. A summary of the work which has been performed is given below and in each case the description of the audit work indicates the full extent of the audit procedures carried out by the audit team.

(a) Assets held for sale

Due to the planned disposal of one of Thurman Co's factory sites, the property and associated assets have been classified as held for sale in the financial statements. A manual journal has been posted by the finance director to reclassify the assets as current assets and to adjust the value of the assets for impairment and reversal of depreciation charged from the date at which the assets met the criteria to be classified as held for sale. The finance director asked the audit senior to check the journal before it was posted on the basis of there being no one with the relevant knowledge to do this at Thurman Co.

The planned disposal was discussed with management. A brief note has been put into the audit working papers stating that in management's opinion the accounting treatment to classify the factory as held for sale is correct. The manual journal has been arithmetically checked by a different member of the audit team, and the amounts agreed back to the non-current asset register. **(9 marks)**

(b) Capital expenditure

When auditing the company's capital expenditure, the audit team selected a material transaction to test and found that key internal controls over capital expenditure were not operating effectively. Authorisation had not been obtained for an order placed for several vehicles, and appropriate segregation of duties over initiating and processing the transaction was not maintained.

The audit team noted details of the internal control deficiencies and updated the systems notes on the permanent audit file to reflect the deficiencies. The audit work completed on this order was to agree the purchase of the vehicles to purchase invoices and to the cash book and bank statement. The rest of the audit work on capital expenditure was completed in accordance with the audit programme.

(7 marks)

(c) Payroll expenses

The payroll function is outsourced to Jackson Co, a service organisation which processes all of Thurman Co's salary expenses. The payroll expenses recognised in the financial statements have been traced back to year-end reports issued by Jackson Co. The audit team has had no direct contact with Jackson Co as the year-end reports were sent to Thurman Co's finance director who then passed them to the audit team.

Thurman Co employs a few casual workers who are paid in cash at the end of each month and are not entered into the payroll system. The audit team has agreed the cash payment made back to the petty cash records and the amounts involved are considered immaterial. **(9 marks)**

Required:

In respect of each of the three matters described above:

(i) Comment on the sufficiency and appropriateness of the audit evidence obtained

(ii) Recommend further audit procedures to be performed by the audit team, and

(iii) Explain the matters which should be included in a report in accordance with ISA 265 *Communicating Deficiencies in Internal Controls to Those Charged with Governance and Management.*

Note: The split of the mark allocation is shown against each of the matters above.

(Total: 25 marks)

22 ADDER GROUP *Walk in the footsteps of a top tutor*

The Adder Group (the Group) has been an audit client of your firm for several years. You have recently been assigned to act as audit manager, replacing a manager who has fallen ill, and the audit of the Group financial statements for the year ended 31 March 2015 is underway. The Group's activities include property management and the provision of large storage facilities in warehouses owned by the Group. The draft consolidated financial statements recognise total assets of $150 million, and profit before tax of $20 million.

(a) The audit engagement partner, Edmund Black, has asked you to review the audit working papers in relation to two audit issues which have been highlighted by the audit senior. Information on each of these issues is given below:

(i) In December 2014, a leisure centre complex was sold for proceeds equivalent to its fair value of $35 million, the related assets have been derecognised from the Group statement of financial position, and a profit on disposal of $8 million is included in the Group statement of profit or loss for the year. The remaining useful life of the leisure centre complex was 21 years at the date of disposal.

The Group is leasing back the leisure centre complex to use in its ongoing operations, paying rentals annually in arrears. At the end of the 20-year lease arrangement, the Group has the option to repurchase the leisure centre complex for its market value at that time.

(ii) In January 2015, the Group acquired 52% of the equity shares of Baldrick Co. This company has not been consolidated into the Group as a subsidiary, and is instead accounted for as an associate. The Group finance director's reason for this accounting treatment is that Baldrick Co's operations have not yet been integrated with those of the rest of the Group. Baldrick Co's financial statements recognise total assets of $18 million and a loss for the year to 31 March 2015 of $5 million.

Required:

In respect of the issues described above:

Comment on the matters to be considered, and explain the audit evidence you should expect to find in your review of the audit working papers.

Note: The marks will be split equally between each part. **(16 marks)**

(b) The audit senior also left the following note for your attention:

'I have been working on the audit of properties, including the Group's storage facility warehouses. Customers rent individual self-contained storage areas of a warehouse, for which they are given keys allowing access by the customer at any time. The Group's employees rarely enter the customers' storage areas.

It seems the Group's policy for storage contracts which generate revenue of less than $10,000, is that very little documentation is required, and the nature of the items being stored is not always known. While visiting one of the Group's warehouses, the door to one of the customers' storage areas was open, so I looked in and saw what appeared to be potentially hazardous chemicals, stored in large metal drums marked with warning signs. I asked the warehouse manager about the items being stored, and he became very aggressive, refusing to allow me to ask other employees about the matter, and threatening me if I alerted management to the storage of these items. I did not mention the matter to anyone else at the client.'

Required:

Discuss the implications of the audit senior's note for the completion of the audit, commenting on the auditor's responsibilities in relation to laws and regulations, and on any ethical matters arising. **(9 marks)**

(Total: 25 marks)

23 FRANCIS GROUP *Walk in the footsteps of a top tutor*

Timed question with online tutor debrief

You are a manager in the audit department of Williams & Co and you are reviewing the audit working papers in relation to the Francis Group (the Group), whose financial year ended on 31 July 2014. Your firm audits all components of the Group, which consists of a parent company and three subsidiaries – Marks Co, Roberts Co and Teapot Co.

The Group manufactures engines which are then supplied to the car industry. The draft consolidated financial statements recognise profit for the year to 31 July 2014 of $23 million (2013 – $33 million) and total assets of $450 million (2013 – $455 million).

Information in respect of three issues has been highlighted for your attention during the file review.

(a) An 80% equity shareholding in Teapot Co was acquired on 1 August 2013. Goodwill on the acquisition of $27 million was calculated at that date and remains recognised as an intangible asset at that value at the year end. The goodwill calculation performed by the Group's management is shown below:

	$000
Purchase consideration	75,000
Fair value of 20% non-controlling interest	13,000
	88,000
Less: Fair value of Teapot Co's identifiable net assets at acquisition	(61,000)
Goodwill	27,000

In determining the fair value of identifiable net assets at acquisition, an upwards fair value adjustment of $300,000 was made to the book value of a property recognised in Teapot Co's financial statements at a carrying value of $600,000.

A loan of $60 million was taken out on 1 August 2013 to help finance the acquisition. The loan carries an annual interest rate of 6%, with interest payments made annually in arrears. The loan will be repaid in 20 years at a premium of $5 million. **(12 marks)**

(b) In September 2014, a natural disaster caused severe damage to the property complex housing the Group's head office and main manufacturing site. For health and safety reasons, a decision was made to demolish the property complex. The demolition took place three weeks after the damage was caused. The property had a carrying value of $16 million at 31 July 2014.

A contingent asset of $18 million has been recognised as a current asset and as deferred income in the Group statement of financial position at 31 July 2014, representing the amount claimed under the Group's insurance policy in respect of the disaster. **(7 marks)**

(c) Marks Co supplies some of the components used by Roberts Co in its manufacturing process. At the year end, an intercompany receivable of $20 million is recognised in Marks Co's financial statements. Roberts Co's financial statements include a corresponding intercompany payables balance of $20 million and inventory supplied from Marks Co valued at $50 million. **(6 marks)**

Required:

Comment on the matters to be considered, and explain the audit evidence you should expect to find during your review of the audit working papers in respect of each of the issues described above.

(Total: 25 marks)

Calculate your allowed time, allocate the time to the separate parts..............

24 COOPER *Walk in the footsteps of a top tutor*

(a) You are an audit manager in Rose & Co, responsible for the audit of Cooper Co. You are reviewing the audit working papers relating to the financial year ended 31 January 2014. Cooper Co is a manufacturer of chemicals used in the agricultural industry. The draft financial statements recognise profit for the year to 31 January 2014 of $15 million (2013 – $20 million) and total assets of $240 million (2013 – $230 million).

The audit senior, Max Turner, has brought several matters to your attention:

(i) Cooper Co's factories are recognised within property, plant and equipment at a carrying value of $60 million. Half of the factories produce a chemical which is used in farm animal feed. Recently the government has introduced a regulation stipulating that the chemical is phased out over the next three years. Sales of the chemical are still buoyant, however, and are projected to account for 45% of Cooper Co's revenue for the year ending 31 January 2015. Cooper Co has started to research a replacement chemical which is allowed under the new regulation, and has spent $1 million on a feasibility study into the development of this chemical. **(8 marks)**

(ii) In October 2013, Cooper Co's finance director, Hannah Osbourne, purchased a car from the company. The carrying value of the car at the date of its disposal to Hannah was $50,000, and its market value was $75,000. Cooper Co raised an invoice for $50,000 in respect of the disposal, which is still outstanding for payment. **(7 marks)**

Required:

Comment on the matters to be considered and explain the audit evidence you should expect to find during your review of the audit working papers in respect of each of the issues described above.

(b) Max noticed that a section of the audit file had not been completed on the previous year's audit. The incomplete section relates to expenditure incurred in the year to 31 January 2013, which appears not to have been audited at all in the prior year. The expenditure of $1.2 million was incurred in the development of an internally generated brand name. The amount was capitalised as an intangible asset at 31 January 2013, and that amount is still recognised at 31 January 2014.

Required:

Explain the implications of this matter for the completion of the audit, and any other professional issues raised, recommending any actions to be taken by the auditor. **(5 marks)**

(Total: 20 marks)

25 DASSET *Walk in the footsteps of a top tutor*

Dasset Co operates in the coal mining industry. The company owns ten mines across the country from which coal is extracted before being sold onto customers who are energy providers. Coal mining companies operate under licence from the National Coal Mining Authority, an organisation which monitors the environmental impact of coal mining operations, and requires coal mines to be operated in compliance with strict health and safety regulations.

You are an audit manager in Burton & Co, responsible for the audit of Dasset Co and you are reviewing the audit working papers for the year ended 31 August 2013. The draft financial statements recognise profit before tax of $18 million and total assets of $175 million. The audit senior has left a note for your attention:

Accident at the Ledge Hill Mine

On 15 August 2013, there was an accident at the Ledge Hill Mine, where several of the tunnels in the mine collapsed, causing other tunnels to become flooded. This has resulted in one-third of the mine becoming inaccessible and for safety reasons, the tunnels will be permanently closed. However, Dasset Co's management thinks that the rest of the mine can remain operational, as long as improvements are made to ensure that the mine meets health and safety regulations.

Luckily no one was injured in the accident. However, the collapse caused subsidence which has damaged several residential properties in a village located above the mine. A surveyor has been commissioned to report on whether the properties need to be demolished or whether they can be safely repaired. A group of 20 residents has been relocated to rental properties in the local area and Dasset Co is meeting all expenses in relation to this.

The Ledge Hill Mine was acquired several years ago and is recognised in the draft statement of financial position at $10 million. As no employees were injured in the accident, Dasset Co's management has decided not to report the accident to the National Coal Mining Authority.

Required:

In respect of the accident at the Ledge Hill Mine:

(a) (i) Comment on the matters which you should consider, and

(ii) Describe the audit evidence which you should expect to find,

in undertaking your review of the audit working papers and financial statements of Dasset Co.

Note: The total marks will be split equally between each part. (14 marks)

(b) In relation to management's decision not to report the accident to the National Coal Mining Authority, discuss Burton & Co's responsibilities and recommend the actions which should be taken by the firm. (6 marks)

(Total: 20 marks)

26 SETTER STORES *Walk in the footsteps of a top tutor*

You are the manager responsible for the audit of Setter Stores Co, a company which operates supermarkets across the country. The final audit for the year ended 31 January 2013 is nearing completion and you are reviewing the audit working papers. The draft financial statements recognise total assets of $300 million, revenue of $620 million and profit before tax of $47.5 million.

Three issues from the audit working papers are summarised below:

(a) Assets held for sale

Setter Stores Co owns a number of properties which have been classified as assets held for sale in the statement of financial position. The notes to the financial statements state that the properties are all due to be sold within one year. On classification as held for sale, in October 2012, the properties were re-measured from carrying value of $26 million to fair value less cost to sell of $24 million, which is the amount recognised in the statement of financial position at the year end. **(8 marks)**

(b) Sale and leaseback arrangement

A sale and leaseback arrangement involving a large property complex was entered into on 31 January 2013. The property complex is a large warehousing facility, which was sold for $37 million, its fair value at the date of the disposal. The facility had a carrying value at that date of $27 million. The only accounting entry recognised in respect of the proceeds raised was to record the cash received and recognise a non-current liability classified as 'Lease obligations'. The lease term is for 8 years, while the remaining useful life of the property complex was 20 years. The present value of the annual lease payments is $16 million. **(7 marks)**

(c) Distribution licence

The statement of financial position includes an intangible asset of $15 million, which is the cost of a distribution licence acquired on 1 September 2012. The licence gives Setter Stores Co the exclusive right to distribute a popular branded soft drink in its stores for a period of five years. **(5 marks)**

Required:

Comment on the matters to be considered, and explain the audit evidence you should expect to find during your file review in respect of each of the issues described above.

(Total: 20 marks)

27 ROBSTER CO *Walk in the footsteps of a top tutor*

Robster Co is a company which manufactures tractors and other machinery to be used in the agricultural industry. You are the manager responsible for the audit of Robster Co, and you are reviewing the audit working papers for the year ended 28 February 2009. The draft financial statements show revenue of $10.5 million, profit before tax of $3.2 million, and total assets of $45 million.

Two matters have been brought to your attention by the audit senior, both of which relate to assets recognised in the statement of financial position for the first time this year:

Leases

In July 2008, Robster Co entered into five new leases of land and buildings. The leases have been capitalised and the statement of financial position includes leased assets presented as non-current assets at a value of $3.6 million, and a total lease liability of $3.2 million presented as a non-current liability.

Financial assets

Non-current assets include financial assets recognised at $1.26 million. A note to the financial statements describes these financial assets as investments classified as 'fair value through profit or loss', and the investments are described in the note as 'held for trading'. The investments are all shares in listed companies. A gain of $350,000 has been recognised in net profit in respect of the revaluation of these investments.

Required:

(a) In your review of the audit working papers, comment on the matters you should consider, and state the audit evidence you should expect to find in respect of:

(i) the leases **(9 marks)**

(ii) the financial assets. **(5 marks)**

You are aware that Robster Co is seeking a listing in September 2009. The listing rules in this jurisdiction require that interim financial information is published half-way through the accounting period, and that the information should be accompanied by a review report issued by the company's independent auditor.

Required:

(b) Explain the principal analytical procedures that should be used to gather evidence in a review of interim financial information. **(6 marks)**

(Total: 20 marks)

Section 2

PRACTICE QUESTIONS – SECTION B

PROFESSIONAL AND ETHICAL CONSIDERATIONS

28 THORNHILL & CO *Walk in the footsteps of a top tutor*

You are an audit manager at Thornhill & Co responsible for the audit of Northwest Co, a subsidiary of Valerian Co. A different audit firm is responsible for the audit of Valerian Co and the Valerian Group financial statements.

The audit of the financial statements of Northwest Co for the year ended 31 July 2016 is nearing completion, but the following issues require your attention before the auditor's report is signed and your final communication is made to the group auditor in response to their request for information. The draft financial statements of Northwest Co recognise a loss before tax of $50,000.

Northwest Co has been loss making for several years and it generates insufficient cash to meet its significant debt obligations. The company relies on support from Valerian Co in order to continue trading. The management of Valerian Co has confirmed verbally that it will continue to support Northwest Co, but has not provided a formal letter of support despite a number of requests.

You are aware that Valerian Co is the subject of a major lawsuit following an industrial accident which resulted in significant pollution of local agricultural land and, most seriously, loss of life. You attempted to discuss the matter with the directors of Valerian Co but they refused, saying that it had already been investigated by the group auditor. The group auditor informed you that the case is ongoing and that they have obtained satisfactory representations from both management and legal advisers stating that they were confident of successfully defending the claim. When you asked for copies of the representations, the group auditor refused saying it was a matter relevant to the parent company and that it was not relevant to the audit of Northwest Co.

Shortly after making your enquiries, you received a phone call from the group engagement partner who said that the board of Valerian Co was concerned that you might modify the auditor's report of Northwest Co. He also said that, as the only person with full oversight of audit matters relating to the Valerian Group, he did not think that it would be necessary to modify the auditor's report of Northwest Co and that he would oppose any attempt to do so. He suggested that if the debt in the financial statements of Northwest Co was the reason for seeking parental support that he would transfer it to the Group and the letter of support would no longer be necessary.

Required:

(a) Discuss how professional scepticism should be applied to the statements made by the management and auditors of Valerian Co regarding the outstanding legal case. **(6 marks)**

(b) Comment on the ethical and professional issues raised, considering any implications for completion of the audit, in respect of:

(i) The evidence obtained in relation to the support offered by Valerian Co.

(ii) The request not to modify the auditor's report of Northwest Co.

Note: The total marks will be split equally between each part. **(14 marks)**

(Total: 20 marks)

29 CHENNAI & CO *Walk in the footsteps of a top tutor*

You are a manager at Chennai & Co, a firm of Chartered Certified Accountants. One of the partners has asked you to investigate and respond to a number of issues which have arisen with two different companies.

(a) Delhi Co, a potential new client, is a privately owned and rapidly expanding company which currently operates below the audit threshold in the country in which it is based. The company's management is currently considering having either a full audit or a limited assurance review of their financial statements. The partner would like you to assist the management of Delhi Co by writing a response to them in which you:

(i) Explain the difference between an audit of historical financial statements and a limited assurance review. **(4 marks)**

(ii) Discuss the relative advantages and disadvantages to Delhi Co of having an audit of their historical financial statements as opposed to a limited assurance review. **(8 marks)**

Delhi Co was incorporated in 2005, with founder and chief executive Mr Nimesh Dattani as the sole shareholder. After a period of rapid growth, Delhi Co took out a ten-year bank loan facility in June 2007 to finance Mr Dattani's ambitious expansion plans. This was supported by a further injection of financial capital in 2014 through a new issue of shares in the company. The shares were sold to Mr Robert Hyland, an ex-business partner of Mr Dattani. The sale gave Mr Hyland a 40% shareholding in Delhi Co. He has no involvement in the management of the company.

Until recently Delhi Co operated with a small accounting department, comprising one full-time member of staff and one part-time employee. Due to the expansion of the company and Mr Dattani's plans to expand the customer base internationally, it has been necessary to increase the size of the accounting function to include two new full-time members of staff. Both of the new recruits are part-qualified accountants and Mr Dattani has committed to sponsoring them through their remaining training and ACCA examinations.

Required:

Prepare the response to the management of Delhi Co as requested by the partner.

Note: The split of the mark allocation is shown against each of the issues above.

(b) The audit committee of another client, Mumbai Co, has asked the partner to consider whether it would be possible for the audit team to perform a review of the company's internal control system. A number of recent incidents have raised concerns amongst the management team that controls have deteriorated and that this has increased the risk of fraud, as well as inefficient commercial practices. The auditor's report for the audit of the financial statements of Mumbai Co for the year ended 31 March 2016 was signed a few weeks ago. Mumbai Co is a listed company.

Required:

In respect of the request for Chennai & Co to review Mumbai Co's internal control systems:

Identify and discuss the relevant ethical and professional issues raised, and recommend any actions necessary. **(8 marks)**

(Total: 20 marks)

30 MONET & CO *Walk in the footsteps of a top tutor*

You are a manager in Monet & Co, a firm of accountants which has 12 offices and 30 partners, 10 of whom are members of ACCA. As an expert in ethics and professional conduct, you have been asked to advise the partners on the following issues, which were raised at a recent meeting.

(a) An advertisement has been drafted as part of the firm's drive to increase the number of clients. It is suggested that it should be placed in a number of quality national as well as local newspapers:

> Have you had enough of your accountant charging you too much for poor quality services?
>
> Does your business need a kick-start?
>
> Look no further; Monet & Co provides the most comprehensive range of finance and accountancy services in the country as well as having the leading tax team in the country who are just waiting to save you money.
>
> Still not sure? We guarantee to be cheaper than your existing service provider and for the month of January we are offering free business advice to all new audit clients.
>
> Drop in and see us at your local office for a free consultation.
>
> Monet & Co, Chartered Certified Accountants.

(7 marks)

(b) The planning for the audit of Renoir Co's financial statements for the year ending 31 March 2016 will commence shortly. In preparation the audit partner telephoned Renoir Co's finance director, Jim Cassatt, to set up a planning meeting and to remind him that fees relating to a tax engagement from the previous year were still outstanding. Mr Cassatt raised concerns about the conduct of the previous audit, stating numerous examples of when he and his staff had been interrupted when they were busy. He stated that he wanted guarantees that this year's audit will be more efficient, less intrusive and cheaper, otherwise he will seek an alternative auditor. **(7 marks)**

(c) Your firm audits the publisher Homer Winslow Co. During its recent audit, the company's finance director commented on growing competition in the digital publishing sector. One rapidly expanding competitor, Pissarro Co, was specifically referred to. You are aware that your firm recently acquired another accountancy firm, Maar Associates, and that Pissarro Co is one of their clients. It is hoped that the audit of Pissarro Co will be transferred to your department to take advantage of your specialism in media and publishing. **(6 marks)**

Required:

Evaluate each of the issues described above, commenting on the ethical and professional issues raised and recommend any actions necessary in response to the issues identified.

(Total: 20 marks)

31 BUNK & CO *Walk in the footsteps of a top tutor*

You are a senior manager in Bunk & Co, a global audit firm with offices in more than 30 countries. You are responsible for monitoring audit quality and ethical situations which arise in relation to audit clients. Wire Co is an audit client whose operations involve haulage and distribution. The auditor's report for the financial statements of Wire Co for the year ended 31 December 2014 was issued last week. You are conducting a review of the quality of that audit, and of any ethical issues which arose in relation to it. Relevant information obtained from a discussion with Lester Freeman, the audit engagement partner, is given below.

(a) Wire Co's audit committee refused to agree to an increase in audit fees despite the company's operations expanding into new locations. In response to this, the materiality level was increased during the audit, and some review procedures were not carried out. To reduce sample sizes used in tests of detail, the samples were selected based on judgement rather than statistical methods. In addition, only parts of the population being tested were sampled, for example, certain locations were not included in the sample of non-current assets selected for physical verification. **(6 marks)**

(b) Some of the audit work was performed by an overseas office of Bunk & Co in an 'off-shoring' arrangement. This practice is encouraged by Bunk & Co, whose managing partners see it as a way of improving audit efficiency. The overseas office performs the work at a lower cost, and it was largely low-risk, non-judgemental work included in this arrangement for the audit of Wire Co, for example, numerical checks on documentation. In addition, the overseas office read the minutes of board meetings to identify issues relevant to the audit. **(5 marks)**

(c) In July 2014, Russell Bell, Wire Co's former finance director, joined Bunk & Co as an audit partner, working in the same office as Lester Freeman. Although Russell was not a member of the audit team, he did update Lester on some business developments which had taken place at the company during the period before he left. Russell held a number of equity shares in Wire Co, which he sold in January 2015. Since joining Bunk & Co, Russell has been developing initiatives to increase the firm's income. One initiative is that audit team members should be encouraged to cross-sell non-audit services and references to targets for the cross-selling of non-audit services to audit clients is now included in partner and employee appraisal documentation. **(9 marks)**

Required:

Comment on the quality control, ethical and professional issues raised in respect of the audit of Wire Co and the firm-wide policies of Bunk & Co, and recommend any actions to be taken by the audit firm.

(Total: 20 marks)

32 RYDER & CO *Walk in the footsteps of a top tutor*

Timed question with online tutor debrief

You are a manager in Ryder & Co, a firm of Chartered Certified Accountants, and you have taken on the responsibility for providing support and guidance to new members of the firm. Ryder & Co has recently recruited a new audit junior, Sam Tyler, who has come across several issues in his first few months at the firm which he would like your guidance on. Sam's comments and questions are shown below:

(a) I know that auditors are required to assess risks of material misstatement by developing an understanding of the business risks of an audit client, but I am not clear on the relationship between business risk and risk of material misstatement. Can you explain the two types of risk, and how identifying business risk relates to risk of material misstatement? **(4 marks)**

(b) I worked on the interim audit of Crow Co, a manufacturing company which outsources its payroll function. I know that for Crow Co payroll is material. How does the outsourcing of payroll affect our audit planning? **(4 marks)**

(c) Crow Co is tendering for an important contract to supply Hatfield Co. I know that Hatfield Co is also an audit client of our firm, and I have heard that Crow Co's management has requested our firm to provide advice on the tender it is preparing. What matters should our firm consider in deciding whether to provide advice to Crow Co on the tender? **(5 marks)**

(d) I also worked on the audit of Campbell Co, where I heard the managing director, Ting Campbell, discussing a potential new business opportunity with the audit engagement partner. Campbell Co is an events organiser, and is planning to run a programme of nationwide events for accountants, at which speakers will discuss technical updates to financial reporting, tax and audit regulations. Ting proposed that our firm could invest some cash in the business opportunity, supply the speakers, market the events to our audit clients, and that any profit made would be shared between Ryder & Co and Campbell Co. What would be the implications of our firm considering this business opportunity? **(7 marks)**

Required:

For each of the issues raised, respond to the audit junior, explaining the ethical and professional matters arising from the audit junior's comments.

(Total: 20 marks)

Calculate your allowed time, allocate the time to the separate parts..............

33 CHESTER & CO *Walk in the footsteps of a top tutor*

You are an audit manager in Chester & Co, and you are reviewing three situations which have recently arisen with respect to potential and existing audit clients of your firm.

Tetbury Co's managing director, Juan Stanton, has approached Chester & Co to invite the firm to tender for its audit. Tetbury Co is a small, owner-managed company providing financial services such as arranging mortgages and advising on pension plans. The company's previous auditors recently resigned. Juan Stanton states that this was due to 'a disagreement on the accounting treatment of commission earned, and because they thought our controls were not very good.' You are aware that Tetbury Co has been investigated by the financial services authority for alleged noncompliance with its regulations. As well as performing the audit, Juan would like Chester & Co to give business development advice.

The audit of Stratford Co's financial statements for the year ended 30 November 2013 will commence shortly. You are aware that the company is in financial difficulties. Stratford Co's managing director, Colin Charlecote, has requested that the audit engagement partner accompanies him to a meeting with the bank where a new loan will be discussed, and the draft financial statements reviewed. Colin has hinted that if the partner does not accompany him to the meeting, he will put the audit out to tender. In addition, an invoice relating to interim audit work performed in August 2013 has not yet been paid.

Banbury Co is a listed entity, and its audit committee has asked Chester & Co to perform an actuarial valuation on the company's defined benefit pension plan. One of the audit partners is a qualified actuary and has the necessary skills and expertise to perform the service. Banbury Co has a year ending 28 February 2014, and the audit planning is due to commence next week. Its financial statements for the year ended 28 February 2013, in respect of which the auditor's report was unmodified, included total assets of $35 million and a pension liability of $105,000.

Required:

Identify and discuss the ethical and other professional issues raised, and recommend any actions that should be taken in respect of:

(a)	**Tetbury Co**	**(8 marks)**
(b)	**Stratford Co**	**(6 marks)**
(c)	**Banbury Co.**	**(6 marks)**
		(Total: 20 marks)

34 WESTON & CO *Walk in the footsteps of a top tutor*

(a) You are an audit manager in Weston & Co which is an international firm of Chartered Certified Accountants with branches in many countries and which offers a range of audit and assurance services to its clients. Your responsibilities include reviewing ethical matters which arise with audit clients, and dealing with approaches from prospective audit clients.

The management of Jones Co has invited Weston & Co to submit an audit proposal (tender document) for their consideration. Jones Co was established only two years ago, but has grown rapidly, and this will be the first year that an audit is required. In previous years a limited assurance review was performed on its financial statements by an unrelated audit firm. The company specialises in the recruitment of medical personnel and some of its start-up funding was raised from a venture capital company. There are plans for the company to open branches overseas to help recruit personnel from foreign countries.

Jones Co has one full-time accountant who uses an off-the-shelf accounting package to record transactions and to prepare financial information. The company has a financial year ending 31 March 2015.

The following comment was made by Bentley Jones, the company's founder and owner-manager, in relation to the audit proposal and potential audit fee:

'I am looking for a firm of auditors who will give me a competitive audit fee. I am hoping that the fee will be quite low, as I am willing to pay more for services that I consider more beneficial to the business, such as strategic advice. I would like the audit fee to be linked to Jones Co's success in expanding overseas as a result of the audit firm's advice. Hopefully the audit will not be too disruptive and I would like it completed within four months of the year end.'

Required:

(i) Explain the specific matters to be included in the audit proposal (tender document), other than those relating to the audit fee; and (8 marks)

(ii) Assuming that Weston & Co is appointed to provide the audit service to Jones Co, discuss the issues to be considered by the audit firm in determining a fee for the audit including any ethical matters raised. (6 marks)

(b) Ordway Co is a long-standing audit client of your firm and is a listed company. Bobby Wellington has acted as audit engagement partner for seven years and understands that a new audit partner needs to be appointed to take his place. Bobby is hoping to stay in contact with the client and act as the engagement quality control reviewer in forthcoming audits of Ordway Co.

Required:

Explain the ethical threats raised by the long association of senior audit personnel with an audit client and the relevant safeguards to be applied, and discuss whether Bobby Wellington can act as engagement quality control reviewer in the future audits of Ordway Co. (6 marks)

(Total: 20 marks)

35 WELLER & CO *Walk in the footsteps of a top tutor*

(a) You are an audit manager in Weller & Co, an audit firm which operates as part of an international network of firms. This morning you received a note from a partner regarding a potential new audit client:

'I have been approached by the audit committee of the Plant Group, which operates in the mobile telecommunications sector. Our firm has been invited to tender for the audit of the individual and group financial statements for the year ending 31 March 2013, and I would like your help in preparing the tender document. This would be a major new client for our firm's telecoms audit department.

The Plant Group comprises a parent company and six subsidiaries, one of which is located overseas. The audit committee is looking for a cost effective audit, and hopes that the strength of the Plant Group's governance and internal control mean that the audit can be conducted quickly, with a proposed deadline of 31 May 2013. The Plant Group has expanded rapidly in the last few years and significant finance was raised in July 2012 through a stock exchange listing.'

Required:

Identify and explain the specific matters to be included in the tender document for the audit of the Plant Group. (7 marks)

(b) Weller & Co is facing competition from other audit firms, and the partners have been considering how the firm's revenue could be increased. Two suggestions have been made:

(1) Audit partners and managers can be encouraged to sell non-audit services to audit clients by including in their remuneration package a bonus for successful sales.

(2) All audit managers should suggest to their audit clients that as well as providing the external audit service, Weller & Co can provide the internal audit service as part of an 'extended audit' service.

Required:

Comment on the ethical and professional issues raised by the suggestions to increase the firm's revenue. (8 marks)

(Total: 15 marks)

36 DRAGON GROUP *Walk in the footsteps of a top tutor*

Timed question with online tutor debrief

(a) Explain FOUR reasons why a firm of auditors may decide NOT to seek re-election as auditor. (4 marks)

The Dragon Group is a large group of companies operating in the furniture retail trade. The group has expanded rapidly in the last three years, by acquiring several subsidiaries each year. The management of the parent company, Dragon Co, a listed company, has decided to put the audit of the group and all subsidiaries out to tender, as the current audit firm is not seeking re-election. The financial year end of the Dragon Group is 30 September 2009.

You are a senior manager in Unicorn & Co, a global firm of Chartered Certified Accountants, with offices in over 150 countries across the world. Unicorn & Co has been invited to tender for the Dragon Group audit (including the audit of all subsidiaries). You manage a department within the firm which specialises in the audit of retail companies, and you have been assigned the task of drafting the tender document. You recently held a meeting with Edmund Jalousie, the group finance director, in which you discussed the current group structure, recent acquisitions, and the group's plans for future expansion.

Meeting notes – Dragon Group

Group structure

The parent company owns 20 subsidiaries, all of which are wholly owned. Half of the subsidiaries are located in the same country as the parent, and half overseas. Most of the foreign subsidiaries report under the same financial reporting framework as Dragon Co, but several prepare financial statements using local accounting rules.

Acquisitions during the year

Two companies were purchased in March 2009, both located in this country:

(i) Mermaid Co, a company which operates 20 furniture retail outlets. The audit opinion expressed by the incumbent auditors on the financial statements for the year ended 30 September 2008 was modified by a disagreement over the non-disclosure of a contingent liability. The contingent liability relates to a court case which is still on-going.

(ii) Minotaur Co, a large company, whose operations are distribution and warehousing. This represents a diversification away from retail, and it is hoped that the Dragon Group will benefit from significant economies of scale as a result of the acquisition.

Other matters

The acquisitive strategy of the group over the last few years has led to significant growth. Group revenue has increased by 25% in the last three years, and is predicted to increase by a further 35% in the next four years as the acquisition of more subsidiaries is planned. The Dragon Group has raised finance for the acquisitions in the past by becoming listed on the stock exchanges of three different countries. A new listing on a foreign stock exchange is planned for January 2010. For this reason, management would like the group audit completed by 31 December 2009.

Required:

(b) **Recommend and describe the principal matters to be included in your firm's tender document to provide the audit service to the Dragon Group.** **(8 marks)**

(c) **Using the specific information provided, evaluate the matters that should be considered before accepting the audit engagement, in the event of your firm being successful in the tender.** **(6 marks)**

(d) **(i)** **Define 'transnational audit', and explain the relevance of the term to the audit of the Dragon Group.** **(3 marks)**

(ii) **Discuss TWO features of a transnational audit that may contribute to a high level of audit risk in such an engagement.** **(4 marks)**

(Total: 25 marks)

Calculate your allowed time, allocate the time to the separate parts..............

37 MACAU & CO *Walk in the footsteps of a top tutor*

You are a senior manager in Macau & Co, a firm of Chartered Certified Accountants. In your capacity as engagement quality control reviewer, you have been asked to review the audit files of Stanley Co and Kowloon Co, both of which have a financial year ended 31 December 2015, and the audits of both companies are nearing completion.

(a) Stanley Co is a frozen food processor, selling its products to wholesalers and supermarkets. From your review of the audit working papers, you have noted that the level of materiality was determined to be $1.5 million at the planning stage, and this materiality threshold has been used throughout the audit. There is no evidence on the audit file that this threshold has been reviewed during the course of the audit.

From your review of the audit planning, you know that a new packing machine with a cost of $1.6 million was acquired by Stanley Co in March 2015, and is recognised in the draft statement of financial position at a carrying amount of $1.4 million at 31 December 2015. The packing machine is located at the premises of Aberdeen Co, a distribution company which is used to pack and distribute a significant proportion of Stanley Co's products. The machine has not been physically verified by a member of the audit team. The audit working papers conclude that 'we have obtained the purchase invoice and order in relation to the machine, and therefore can conclude that the asset is appropriately valued and that it exists. In addition, the managing director of Aberdeen Co has confirmed in writing that the machine is located at their premises and is in working order. No further work is needed in respect of this item.'

Inventory is recognised at $2 million in the draft statement of financial position. You have reviewed the results of audit procedures performed at the inventory count, where the test counts performed by the audit team indicated that the count of some items performed by the company's staff was not correct. The working papers state that 'the inventory count was not well organised' and conclude that 'however, the discrepancies were immaterial, so no further action is required'.

The audit senior spoke to you yesterday, voicing some concerns about the performance of the audit. A summary of his comments is shown below:

'The audit manager and audit engagement partner came to review the audit working papers on the same day towards the completion of the audit fieldwork. The audit partner asked me if there had been any issues on the sections of the audit which I had worked on, and when I said there had been no problems, he signed off the working papers after a quick look through them.

When reading the company's board minutes, I found several references to the audit engagement partner, Joe Lantau. It appears that Joe recommended that the company use the services of his brother, Mick Lantau, for advice on business development, as Mick is a management consultant. Based on that recommendation, Mick has provided a consultancy service to Stanley Co since September 2015. I mentioned this to Joe, and he told me not to record it in the audit working papers or to discuss it with anyone.'

Required:

Comment on the quality of the audit performed discussing the quality control, ethical and other professional issues raised. (13 marks)

(b) Kowloon Co works on contracts to design and manufacture large items of medical equipment such as radiotherapy and X-ray machines. The company specialises in the design, production and installation of bespoke machines under contract with individual customers, which are usually private medical companies. The draft financial statements recognise profit before tax of $950,000 and total assets of $7.5 million.

The audit senior has left the following note for your attention:

'One of Kowloon Co's major customers is the Bay Medical Centre (BMC), a private hospital. In June 2015 a contract was entered into, under the terms of which Kowloon Co would design a new radiotherapy machine for BMC. The machine is based on a new innovation, and is being developed for the specific requirements of BMC. It was estimated that the design and production of the machine would take 18 months with estimated installation in December 2016. As at 31 December 2015, Kowloon Co had invested heavily in the contract, and design costs totalling $350,000 have been recognised as work in progress in the draft statement of financial position. Deferred income of $200,000 is also recognised as a current liability, representing a payment made by BMC to finance part of the design costs. No other accounting entries have been made in respect of the contract with BMC.

As part of our subsequent events review, inspection of correspondence between Kowloon Co and BMC indicates that the contract has been cancelled by BMC as it is unable to pay for its completion. It appears that BMC lost a significant amount of funding towards the end of 2015, impacting significantly on the financial position of the company. The manager responsible for the BMC contract confirms that BMC contacted him about the company's financial difficulties in December 2015.

The matter has been discussed with Kowloon Co's finance director, who has stated that he is satisfied with the current accounting treatment and is not proposing to make any adjustments in light of the cancellation of the contract by BMC. The finance director has also advised that the loss of BMC as a customer will not be mentioned in the company's integrated report, as the finance director does not consider it significant enough to warrant discussion.

Kowloon Co is currently working on six contracts for customers other than BMC. Our audit evidence concludes that Kowloon Co does not face a threat to its going concern status due to the loss of BMC as a customer.'

Your review of the audit work performed on going concern supports this conclusion.

Required:

(i) Comment on the matters to be considered, and recommend the actions to be taken by the auditor; and (7 marks)

(ii) Explain the audit evidence you would expect to find in your review of the audit working papers. (5 marks)

(Total: 25 marks)

38 RETRIEVER *Walk in the footsteps of a top tutor*

Timed question with online tutor debrief

(a) Kennel & Co, a firm of Chartered Certified Accountants, is the external audit provider for the Retriever Group (the Group), a manufacturer of mobile phones and laptop computers. The Group obtained a stock exchange listing in July 2012. The audit of the consolidated financial statements for the year ended 28 February 2013 is nearing completion.

You are a manager in the audit department of Kennel & Co, responsible for conducting engagement quality control reviews on listed audit clients. You have discussed the Group audit with some of the junior members of the audit team, one of whom made the following comments about how it was planned and carried out:

'The audit has been quite time-pressured. The audit manager told the juniors not to perform some of the planned audit procedures on items such as directors' emoluments and share capital as they are considered to be low risk. He also instructed us not to use the firm's statistical sampling methods in selecting trade receivables balances for testing, as it would be quicker to pick the sample based on our own judgement.

'Two of the juniors were given the tasks of auditing trade payables and going concern. The audit manager asked us to review each other's work as it would be good training for us, and he didn't have time to review everything.

'I was discussing the Group's tax position with the financial controller, when she said that she was struggling to calculate the deferred tax asset that should be recognised. The deferred tax asset has arisen because several of the Group's subsidiaries have been loss making this year, creating unutilised tax losses. As I had just studied deferred tax at college I did the calculation of the Group's deferred tax position for her. The audit manager said this saved time as we now would not have to audit the deferred tax figure.

'The financial controller also asked for my advice as to how the tax losses could be utilised by the Group in the future. I provided her with some tax planning recommendations, for which she was very grateful.'

Required:

In relation to the audit of the Retriever Group, evaluate the quality control, ethical and other professional matters arising in respect of the planning and performance of the Group audit. (13 marks)

(b) The audit committee of the Group has contacted Kennel & Co to discuss an incident that took place on 1 June 2013. On that date, there was a burglary at the Group's warehouse where inventory is stored prior to despatch to customers. CCTV filmed the thieves loading a lorry belonging to the Group with boxes containing finished goods. The last inventory count took place on 30 April 2013.

The Group has insurance cover in place and Kennel & Co's forensic accounting department has been asked to provide a forensic accounting service to determine the amount to be claimed in respect of the burglary. The insurance covers the cost of assets lost as a result of thefts.

It is thought that the amount of the claim will be immaterial to the Group's financial statements, and there is no ethical threat in Kennel & Co's forensic accounting department providing the forensic accounting service.

Required:

In respect of the theft and the associated insurance claim:

(i) Identify and explain the matters to be considered, and the steps to be taken in planning the forensic accounting service; and

(ii) Recommend the procedures to be performed in determining the amount of the claim.

Note: The total marks will be split equally between each part. (12 marks)

(Total: 25 marks)

Calculate your allowed time, allocate the time to the separate parts..............

39 SPANIEL *Walk in the footsteps of a top tutor*

You are a manager in Groom & Co, a firm of Chartered Certified Accountants. You have just attended a monthly meeting of audit partners and managers at which client-related matters were discussed. Information in relation to two clients, which were discussed at the meeting, is given below:

(a) Spaniel Co

The auditor's report on the financial statements of Spaniel Co, a long-standing audit client, for the year ended 31 December 2012 was issued in April 2013, and was unmodified. In May 2013, Spaniel Co's audit committee contacted the audit engagement partner to discuss a fraud that had been discovered. The company's internal auditors estimate that $4.5 million has been stolen in a payroll fraud, which has been operating since May 2012.

The audit engagement partner commented that neither tests of controls nor substantive audit procedures were conducted on payroll in the audit of the latest financial statements as in previous years' audits there were no deficiencies found in controls over payroll. The total assets recognised in Spaniel Co's financial statements at 31 December 2012 were $80 million. Spaniel Co is considering suing Groom & Co for the total amount of cash stolen from the company, claiming that the audit firm was negligent in conducting the audit.

Required:

Explain the matters that should be considered in determining whether Groom & Co is liable to Spaniel Co in respect of the fraud. (12 marks)

(b) Bulldog Co

Bulldog Co is a clothing manufacturer, which has recently expanded its operations overseas. To manage exposure to cash flows denominated in foreign currencies, the company has set up a treasury management function, which is responsible for entering into hedge transactions such as forward exchange contracts. These transactions are likely to be material to the financial statements. The audit partner is about to commence planning the audit for the year ending 31 July 2013.

Required:

Discuss why the audit of financial instruments is particularly challenging, and explain the matters to be considered in planning the audit of Bulldog Co's forward exchange contracts. (8 marks)

(Total: 20 marks)

40 YORK CO *Walk in the footsteps of a top tutor*

(a) According to ISA 240 *The Auditor's Responsibilities Relating to Fraud in an Audit of Financial Statements*:

'When identifying and assessing the risks of material misstatement due to fraud, the auditor shall, based on a presumption that there are risks of fraud in revenue recognition, evaluate which types of revenue, revenue transactions or assertions give rise to such risks.'

Required:

Discuss why the auditor should presume that there are risks of fraud in revenue recognition and why ISA 240 requires specific auditor responses in relation to the risks identified. (7 marks)

(b) You are the manager responsible for the audit of York Co, a chain of health and leisure clubs owned and managed by entrepreneur Phil Smith. The audit for the year ended 30 November 2015 is nearing completion and the draft financial statements recognise total assets of $27 million and profit before tax of $2.2 million. The audit senior has left the following file notes for your consideration during your review of the audit working papers:

(i) Cash transfers

During a review of the cash book, a receipt of $350,000 was identified which was accompanied by the description 'BD'. Bank statements showed that the following day a nearly identical amount was transferred into a bank account held in a foreign country. When I asked the financial controller about this, she requested that I speak to Mr Smith, as he has sole responsibility for cash management. According to Mr Smith, an old friend of his, Brian Davies, has loaned the money to the company to fund further expansion and the money has been invested until it is needed. Documentary evidence concerning the transaction has been requested from Mr Smith but has not yet been received.

(7 marks)

(ii) Legal dispute

At the year end York Co reversed a provision relating to an ongoing legal dispute with an ex-employee who was claiming $150,000 for unfair dismissal. This amount was provided in full in the financial statements for the year ended 30 November 2014 but has now been reversed because Mr Smith believes it is now likely that York Co will successfully defend the legal case. Mr Smith has not been available to discuss this matter and no additional documentary evidence has been made available since the end of the previous year's audit. The auditor's report was unmodified in the previous year. **(6 marks)**

Required:

Evaluate the implications for the completion of the audit, recommending any further actions which should be taken by your audit firm.

Note: The split of the mark allocation is shown against each of the issues above.

(Total: 20 marks)

41 TONY GROUP *Walk in the footsteps of a top tutor*

(a) A high-quality audit features the exercise of professional judgement by the auditor, and importantly, a mind-set which includes professional skepticism throughout the planning and performance of the audit.

Required:

Explain the meaning of the term professional skepticism, and discuss its importance in planning and performing an audit. (5 marks)

You are an audit manager in Soprano & Co, working on the audit of the Tony Group (the Group), whose financial year ended on 31 March 2015. This is the first time you have worked on the Group audit. The draft consolidated financial statements recognise profit before tax of $6 million (2014 – $9 million) and total assets of $90 million (2014 – $82 million). The Group manufactures equipment used in the oil extraction industry.

Goodwill of $10 million is recognised in the Group statement of financial position, having arisen on several business combinations over the last few years. An impairment review was conducted in March 2015 by Silvio Dante, the Group finance director, and this year an impairment of $50,000 is to be recognised in respect of the goodwill.

Silvio has prepared a file of documentation to support the results of the impairment review, including notes on the assumptions used, his calculations, and conclusions. When he gave you this file, Silvio made the following comment:

'I don't think you should need any evidence other than that contained in my file. The assumptions used are straightforward, so you shouldn't need to look into them in detail. The assumptions are consistent with how we conducted impairment reviews in previous years and your firm has always agreed with the assumptions used, so you can check that back to last year's audit file. All of the calculations have been checked by the head of the Group's internal audit department.'

Silvio has also informed you that two members of the sales team are suspected of paying bribes in order to secure lucrative customer contracts. The internal audit team were alerted to this when they were auditing cash payments, and found significant payments to several new customers being made prior to contracts being signed. Silvio has asked if Soprano & Co would perform a forensic investigation into the alleged bribery payments.

Required:

(b) (i) Discuss how professional skepticism should be applied to the statement made by Silvio; and (6 marks)

(ii) Explain the principal audit procedures to be performed on the impairment of goodwill. (5 marks)

(c) Recommend the procedures to be used in performing a forensic investigation on the alleged bribery payments. (4 marks)

(Total: 20 marks)

42 HERON *Walk in the footsteps of a top tutor*

(a) You are a manager in Lark & Co, responsible for the audit of Heron Co, an owner-managed business which operates a chain of bars and restaurants. This is your firm's first year auditing the client and the audit for the year ended 31 March 2012 is underway. The audit senior sends a note for your attention:

'When I was auditing revenue I noticed something strange. Heron Co's revenue, which is almost entirely cash-based, is recognised at $5.5 million in the draft financial statements. However, the accounting system shows that till receipts for cash paid by customers amount to only $3.5 million. This seemed odd, so I questioned Ava Gull, the financial controller about this. She said that Jack Heron, the company's owner, deals with cash receipts and posts through journals dealing with cash and revenue. Ava asked Jack the reason for these journals but he refused to give an explanation.

'While auditing cash, I noticed a payment of $2 million made by electronic transfer from the company's bank account to an overseas financial institution. The bank statement showed that the transfer was authorised by Jack Heron, but no other documentation regarding the transfer was available.

'Alarmed by the size of this transaction, and the lack of evidence to support it, I questioned Jack Heron, asking him about the source of cash receipts and the reason for electronic transfer. He would not give any answers and became quite aggressive.'

Required:

(i) **Discuss the implications of the circumstances described in the audit senior's note; and (6 marks)**

(ii) **Explain the nature of any reporting that should take place by the audit senior. (3 marks)**

(b) You are also responsible for the audit of Coot Co, and you are currently reviewing the working papers of the audit for the year ended 28 February 2012. In the working papers dealing with payroll, the audit junior has commented as follows:

'Several new employees have been added to the company's payroll during the year, with combined payments of $125,000 being made to them. There does not appear to be any authorisation for these additions. When I questioned the payroll supervisor who made the amendments, she said that no authorisation was needed because the new employees are only working for the company on a temporary basis. However, when discussing staffing levels with management, it was stated that no new employees have been taken on this year. Other than the tests of controls planned, no other audit work has been performed.'

Required:

In relation to the audit of Coot Co's payroll:

Explain the meaning of the term 'professional scepticism', and recommend any further actions that should be taken by the auditor. (6 marks)

(Total: 15 marks)

REPORTING

43 RAVEN & CO *Walk in the footsteps of a top tutor*

You are an audit manager working for Raven & Co, a firm of Chartered Certified Accountants. You specialise in the audits of companies in the information technology industry. Issues have recently arisen in relation to two different clients which require your attention.

(a) Gull Co is a large, private company which is currently owned by the Brenner family, who own the majority of the company's shares. Following the completion of the audit this year, the finance director, Jim Brenner, contacted you and told you that the family is considering listing the company on the stock exchange. They would like to recruit one of your audit partners for a six-month period to help prepare for the listing. As the board is concerned that the necessary skills and personnel to support the listing are not currently present within the company, Jim Brenner has also requested that your firm assist them in identifying and recruiting new members to the board.

Currently, most of the executive director roles are performed by family members, except for the directors of operations and human resources, who are both long-serving employees. The board operates no audit committee and there is only one non-executive director, who works elsewhere as an IT consultant. Other than the recruitment of new board members, Gull Co is not planning on making any changes to its governance structure prior to or subsequent to listing.

Gull Co has a financial year ending 31 March 2017, and audit planning is scheduled to take place in January 2017.

Required:

In relation to the information provided for Gull Co, comment on:

(i) The ethical and professional matters in relation to the recruitment requests made by Gull Co

(ii) The implications the governance structure and proposed listing may have on the audit process.

Note: The total marks will be split equally between each part. (10 marks)

(b) The audit of Crow Co, a designer and manufacturer of mobile information technologies, for the year ended 30 June 2016 is nearly complete and the auditor's report is to be signed imminently. The following outstanding matters still require your consideration. The draft reported profit before tax and total assets for the year are $65 million (2015 – $111 million) and $650 million (2015 – $910 million) respectively. Crow Co is not a listed company.

Military research project

During the year $7 million of expenses relating to a new military research project were recorded in the statement of profit or loss. The audit team was given brief summaries of the costs incurred but when asked for further corroborating evidence, management stated that they had signed a confidentiality agreement with the military and were unable to provide any further details. The only additional information provided was that they anticipated the project to last for three years and that it may lead to a highly lucrative contract.

Fire

During the year a major catastrophe took place when a fire caused significant damage to the operations of the company, leading to production ceasing for several months. While operations have resumed, repairs are ongoing and it is anticipated that full production will not resume for at least another six months. Audit procedures revealed that the matter has been fully and satisfactorily reflected and disclosed in the financial statements and that it does not pose a significant risk to the going concern status of Crow Co.

Required:

In respect of each of the matters described above, discuss the implications for the auditor's report and recommend any further actions necessary.

Note: The total marks will be split equally between each matter. (10 marks)

(Total: 20 marks)

44 BOSTON *Walk in the footsteps of a top tutor*

You are the manager responsible for the audit of Boston Co, a producer of chocolate and confectionery. The audit of the financial statements for the year ended 31 December 2015 is nearly complete and you are reviewing the audit working papers. The financial statements recognise revenue of $76 million, profit before tax for the year of $6.4 million and total assets of $104 million.

The summary of uncorrected misstatements included in Boston Co's audit working papers, including notes, is shown below. The audit engagement partner is holding a meeting with the management team of Boston Co next week, at which the uncorrected misstatements will be discussed.

	Statement of profit or loss		**Statement of financial position**	
	Debit	**Credit**	**Debit**	**Credit**
Summary of uncorrected misstatements:	$	$	$	$
Impairment	400,000			400,000
Borrowing costs		75,000	75,000	
Irrecoverable debt	65,000			65,000
Investment		43,500	43,500	
	465,000	118,500	118,500	465,000

(i) During the year Boston Co impaired one of its factories. The carrying value of the assets attributable to the factory as a single, cash-generating unit totalled $3.6 million at the year end. The fair value less costs of disposal and the value in use were estimated to be $3 million and $3.5 million respectively and accordingly the asset was written down by $100,000 to reflect the impairment. Audit procedures revealed that management used growth rates attributable to the company as a whole to estimate value in use. Using growth rates attributable to the factory specifically, the audit team estimated the value in use to be $3.1 million.

(ii) Interest charges of $75,000 relating to a loan taken out during the year to finance the construction of a new manufacturing plant were included in finance charges recognised in profit for the year. The manufacturing plant is due for completion in November 2016.

(iii) One of Boston Co's largest customers, Cleveland Co, is experiencing financial difficulties. At the year end Cleveland Co owed Boston Co $100,000, against which Boston Co made a 5% specific allowance. Shortly after the year end Cleveland Co paid $30,000 of the outstanding amount due but has since experienced further problems, leading to their primary lender presenting a formal request that Cleveland Co be liquidated. If successful, only secured creditors are likely to receive any reimbursement.

(iv) During the year Boston Co purchased 150,000 shares in Nebraska Co for $4.00 per share. Boston Co classified the investment as a financial asset held at fair value through profit or loss. On 31 December 2015, the shares of Nebraska Co were trading for $4.29. At the year end the carrying value of the investment in Boston Co's financial statements was $600,000.

Required:

(a) Explain the matters which should be discussed with management in relation to each of the uncorrected misstatements, including an assessment of their individual impact on the financial statements; and

(b) Assuming that management does not adjust any of the misstatements, discuss the effect on the audit opinion and auditor's report.

The following mark allocation is provided as guidance for this question:

(a) 14 marks

(b) 6 marks

(Total: 20 marks)

45 HOPPER GROUP *Walk in the footsteps of a top tutor*

Timed question with online tutor debrief

You are an audit manager at Rockwell & Co, a firm of Chartered Certified Accountants. You are responsible for the audit of the Hopper Group, a listed audit client which supplies ingredients to the food and beverage industry worldwide.

The audit work for the year ended 30 June 2015 is nearly complete, and you are reviewing the draft auditor's report which has been prepared by the audit senior. During the year the Hopper Group purchased a new subsidiary company, Seurat Sweeteners Co, which has expertise in the research and design of sugar alternatives.

The draft financial statements of the Hopper Group for the year ended 30 June 2015 recognise profit before tax of $495 million (2014 – $462 million) and total assets of $4,617 million (2014: $4,751 million). An extract from the draft auditor's report is shown below:

Basis of modified opinion (extract)

In their calculation of goodwill on the acquisition of the new subsidiary, the directors have failed to recognise consideration which is contingent upon meeting certain development targets. The directors believe that it is unlikely that these targets will be met by the subsidiary company and, therefore, have not recorded the contingent consideration in the cost of the acquisition. They have disclosed this contingent liability fully in the notes to the financial statements. We do not feel that the directors' treatment of the contingent consideration is correct and, therefore, do not believe that the criteria of the relevant standard have been met. If this is the case, it would be appropriate to adjust the goodwill balance in the statement of financial position.

We believe that any required adjustment may materially affect the goodwill balance in the statement of financial position. Therefore, in our opinion, the financial statements do not give a true and fair view of the financial position of the Hopper Group and of the Hopper Group's financial performance and cash flows for the year then ended in accordance with International Financial Reporting Standards.

Emphasis of Matter Paragraph

We draw attention to the note to the financial statements which describes the uncertainty relating to the contingent consideration described above. The note provides further information necessary to understand the potential implications of the contingency.

Required:

(a) **Critically appraise the draft auditor's report of the Hopper Group for the year ended 30 June 2015, prepared by the audit senior.**

Note: You are NOT required to re-draft the extracts from the auditor's report. **(10 marks)**

(b) The audit of the new subsidiary, Seurat Sweeteners Co, was performed by a different firm of auditors, Fish Associates. During your review of the communication from Fish Associates, you note that they were unable to obtain sufficient appropriate evidence with regard to the breakdown of research expenses. The total of research costs expensed by Seurat Sweeteners Co during the year was $1·2 million. Fish Associates has issued a qualified audit opinion on the financial statements of Seurat Sweeteners Co due to this inability to obtain sufficient appropriate evidence.

Required:

Comment on the actions which Rockwell & Co should take as the auditor of the Hopper Group, and the implications for the auditor's report on the Hopper Group financial statements. **(6 marks)**

(c) **Discuss the quality control procedures which should be carried out by Rockwell & Co prior to the auditor's report on the Hopper Group being issued.** **(4 marks)**

(Total: 20 marks)

Calculate your allowed time, allocate the time to the separate parts..............

46 DARREN *Walk in the footsteps of a top tutor*

You are a manager in the audit department of Nidge & Co, a firm of Chartered Certified Accountants, responsible for the audit of Darren Co, a new audit client operating in the construction industry. Darren Co's financial year ended on 31 January 2015, and the draft financial statements recognise profit before tax of $22.5 million (2014 – $20 million) and total assets of $370 million, including cash of $3 million. The company typically works on three construction contracts at a time.

The audit is nearly complete and you are reviewing the audit working papers. The audit senior has brought several matters to your attention:

(a) Darren Co is working on a major contract relating to the construction of a bridge for Flyover Co. Work started in July 2014, and it is estimated that the contract will be completed in September 2015. The contract price is $20 million, and it is estimated that a profit of $5 million will be made on completion of the contract. The full amount of this profit has been included in the statement of profit or loss for the year ended 31 January 2015. Darren Co's management believes that this accounting treatment is appropriate given that the contract was signed during the financial year, and no problems have arisen in the work carried out so far. **(8 marks)**

(b) A significant contract was completed in September 2014 for Newbuild Co. This contract related to the construction of a 20-mile highway in a remote area. In November 2014, several large cracks appeared in the road surface after a period of unusually heavy rain, and the road had to be shut for ten weeks while repair work was carried out. Newbuild Co paid for these repairs, but has taken legal action against Darren Co to recover the costs incurred of $40 million. Disclosure on this matter has been made in the notes to the financial statements. Audit evidence, including a written statement from Darren Co's lawyers, concludes that there is a possibility, but not a probability, of Darren Co having to settle the amount claimed. **(6 marks)**

(c) For the first time this year, the financial statements are presented as part of an integrated report. Included in the integrated report are several key performance indicators, one of which states that Darren Co's profit before tax has increased by 20% from the previous year. **(6 marks)**

Required:

Discuss the implications of the matters described above on the completion of the audit and on the auditor's report, recommending any further actions which should be taken by the auditor. (Total: 20 marks)

47 BRADLEY *Walk in the footsteps of a top tutor*

The audit of Bradley Co's financial statements for the year ended 31 August 2014 is nearly complete, and the auditor's report is due to be issued next week. Bradley Co operates steel processing plants at 20 locations and sells its output to manufacturers and engineering companies. You are performing an engagement quality control review on the audit of Bradley Co, as it is a significant new client of your firm. The financial statements recognise revenue of $2.5 million, and total assets of $35 million.

(a) The audit senior who has been working on the audit of Bradley Co made the following comment when discussing the completion of the audit with you:

'We received the final version of the financial statements and the chairman's statement to be published with the financial statements yesterday. I have quickly looked at the financial statements but the audit manager said I need not perform a detailed review on the financial statements as the audit was relatively low risk. The manager also said that he had discussed the chairman's statement with the finance director so no further work on it is needed.'

Required:

Explain the quality control and other professional issues raised by the audit senior's comment in relation to the completion of the audit. (7 marks)

(b) The schedule of proposed adjustments to uncorrected misstatements included in Bradley Co's audit working papers is shown below, including notes to explain each matter included in the schedule. The audit partner is holding a meeting with management tomorrow, at which the uncorrected misstatements will be discussed.

		Statement of profit or loss		*Statement of financial position*	
Proposed adjustments to uncorrected misstatements:		*Debit* $	*Credit* $	*Debit* $	*Credit* $
1	Share-based payment scheme	300,000			300,000
2	Restructuring provision		50,000	50,000	
3	Estimate of additional provision required for slow-moving inventory	10,000			10,000
Totals		310,000	50,000	50,000	310,000

1 A share-based payment scheme was established in January 2014. Management has not recognised any amount in the financial statements in relation to the scheme, arguing that due to the decline in Bradley Co's share price, the share options granted are unlikely to be exercised. The audit conclusion is that an expense and related equity figure should be included in the financial statements.

2 A provision has been recognised in respect of a restructuring involving the closure of one of the steel processing plants. Management approved the closure at a board meeting in August 2014, but announced the closure to employees in September 2014. The audit conclusion is that the provision should not be recognised.

3 The estimate relates to slow-moving inventory in respect of a particular type of steel alloy for which demand has fallen. Management has already recognised a provision of $35,000, which is considered insufficient by the auditor.

Required:

(i) Explain the matters which should be discussed with management in relation to each of the uncorrected misstatements; and (9 marks)

(ii) Assuming that management does not adjust the misstatements, justify an appropriate audit opinion and explain the impact on the auditor's report. (4 marks)

(Total: 20 marks)

48 MARR *Walk in the footsteps of a top tutor*

(a) The IAASB has conducted a review of the structure and content of auditors' reports in which several suggestions were made with the aim of improving the disclosure of matters included in the auditor's report, including those relating to going concern status. As a result of the review, auditor's reports issued for periods ending on or after 15 December 2016 will contain a statement within the auditor's responsibilities section that they conclude on the appropriateness of management's use of the going concern basis of accounting.

Required:

Explain the suggestions made by the IAASB in respect of additional disclosures in the auditor's report regarding going concern status, and discuss the benefits of such disclosures. (8 marks)

(b) You are an audit manager in Taylor & Co, a firm of Chartered Certified Accountants, responsible for the audit of Marr Co, with a year ended 28 February 2014. The draft financial statements recognise profit for the year of $11 million. The audit for the year end is nearing completion, and several matters have been highlighted for your attention by the audit senior, Xi Smith. The matters have been discussed with management and will not be adjusted in the financial statements:

1 In January 2014 a major customer went into administration. There was a balance of $2.5 million owing to Marr Co from this customer at 28 February 2014, which is still included in trade receivables.

2 A court case began in December 2013 involving an ex-employee who is suing Marr Co for unfair dismissal. Lawyers estimate that damages of $50,000 are probable to be paid. The financial statements include a note describing the court case and quantifying the potential damages but no adjustment has been made to include it in the statement of financial position or the statement of profit or loss.

Xi Smith has produced a draft auditor's report for your review, an extract of which is shown below:

Extract 1

Basis for opinion and disclaimer of opinion

We have performed our audit based on a materiality level of $1.5 million. Our audit procedures have proven conclusively that trade receivables are materially misstated. The finance director of Marr Co, Rita Gilmour, has refused to make an adjustment to write off a significant trade receivables balance. Therefore in our opinion the financial statements of Marr Co are materially misstated and we therefore express a disclaimer of opinion because we do not think they are fairly presented.

Extract 2

Emphasis of Matter paragraph

Marr Co is facing a legal claim for an amount of $50,000 from an ex-employee. In our opinion this amount should be recognised as a provision but it is not included in the statement of financial position. We draw your attention to this breach of the relevant IFRS Standard.

Required:

Critically appraise the proposed auditor's report of Marr Co for the year ended 28 February 2014.

Note: You are NOT required to re-draft the extracts from the auditor's report.

(12 marks)

(Total: 20 marks)

49 POODLE GROUP *Walk in the footsteps of a top tutor*

You are the manager responsible for the audit of the Poodle Group (the Group) and you are completing the audit of the consolidated financial statements for the year ended 31 March 2013. The draft consolidated financial statements recognise revenue of $18 million (2012 – $17 million), profit before tax of $2 million (2012 – $3 million) and total assets of $58 million (2012 – $59 million). Your firm audits all of the components of the Group, apart from an overseas subsidiary, Toy Co, which is audited by a small local firm of accountants and auditors.

The audit senior has left a file note for your attention. You are aware that the Group's annual report and financial statements are due to be released next week, and the Group is very reluctant to make any adjustments in respect of the matters described.

(a) Toy Co

The component auditors of Toy Co, the overseas subsidiary, have been instructed to provide the Group audit team with details of a court case which is ongoing. An ex-employee is suing Toy Co for unfair dismissal and has claimed $500,000 damages against the company. To comply with local legislation, Toy Co's individual financial statements are prepared using a local financial reporting framework. Under that local financial reporting framework, a provision is only recognised if a cash outflow is virtually certain to arise. The component auditors obtained verbal confirmation from Toy Co's legal advisors that the damages are probable, but not virtually certain to be paid, and no provision has been recognised in either the individual or consolidated financial statements. No other audit evidence has been obtained by the component auditors. **(7 marks)**

(b) Trade receivable

On 1 June 2013, a notice was received from administrators dealing with the winding up of Terrier Co, following its insolvency. The notice stated that the company should be in a position to pay approximately 10% of the amounts owed to its trade payables. Poodle Co, the parent company of the Group, includes a balance of $1.6 million owed by Terrier Co in its trade receivables. **(7 marks)**

(c) Chairman's statement

The draft chairman's statement, to be included in the Group's annual report, was received yesterday. The chairman comments on the performance of the Group, stating that he is pleased that revenue has increased by 20% in the year. **(6 marks)**

Required:

In respect of each of the matters described:

(i) Assess the implications for the completion of the Group audit, explaining any adjustments that may be necessary to the consolidated financial statements, and recommending any further procedures necessary; and

(ii) Describe the impact on the Group auditor's report if these adjustments are not made.

(Total: 20 marks)

50 HENDRIX *Walk in the footsteps of a top tutor*

(a) You are the manager responsible for the audit of Dylan Co, a listed company, and you are reviewing the working papers of the audit file for the year ended 30 September 2012. The audit senior has left a note for your attention:

'Dylan Co outsources its entire payroll, invoicing and credit control functions to Hendrix Co. In August 2012, Hendrix Co suffered a computer virus attack on its operating system, resulting in the destruction of its accounting records, including those relating to Dylan Co. We have therefore been unable to perform the planned audit procedures on payroll, revenue and receivables, all of which are material to the financial statements. Hendrix Co has manually reconstructed the relevant figures as far as possible, and has supplied a written statement to confirm that they are as accurate as possible, given the loss of accounting records.'

Required:

(i) Comment on the actions that should be taken by the auditor, and the implications for the auditor's report; and (7 marks)

(ii) Discuss the quality control procedures that should be carried out by the audit firm prior to the auditor's report being issued. (3 marks)

(b) You are also responsible for the audit of Squire Co, a listed company, and you are completing the review of its interim financial statements for the six months ended 31 October 2012. Squire Co is a car manufacturer, and historically has offered a three-year warranty on cars sold. The financial statements for the year ended 30 April 2012 included a warranty provision of $1.5 million and recognised total assets of $27.5 million. You are aware that on 1 July 2012, due to cost cutting measures, Squire Co stopped offering warranties on cars sold. The interim financial statements for the six months ended 31 October 2012 do not recognise any warranty provision. Total assets are $30 million at 31 October 2012.

Required:

Assess the matters that should be considered in forming a conclusion on Squire Co's interim financial statements, and the implications for the review report.

(5 marks)

(Total: 15 marks)

51 SNIPE *Walk in the footsteps of a top tutor*

Timed question with online tutor debrief

You are the partner responsible for performing an engagement quality control review on the audit of Snipe Co. You are currently reviewing the audit working papers and draft auditor's report on the financial statements of Snipe Co for the year ended 31 January 2012. The draft financial statements recognise revenue of $8.5 million, profit before tax of $1 million, and total assets of $175 million.

(a) During the year Snipe Co's factory was extended by the self-construction of a new processing area, at a total cost of $5 million. Included in the costs capitalised are borrowing costs of $100,000, incurred during the six-month period of construction. A loan of $4 million carrying an interest rate of 5% was taken out in respect of the construction on 1 March 2011, when construction started. The new processing area was ready for use on 1 September 2011, and began to be used on 1 December 2011. Its estimated useful life is 15 years.

Required:

In respect of your file review of non-current assets:

Comment on the matters that should be considered, and the evidence you would expect to find regarding the new processing area. (8 marks)

(b) Snipe Co has in place a defined benefit pension plan for its employees. An actuarial valuation on 31 January 2012 indicated that the plan is in deficit by $10.5 million. The deficit is not recognised in the statement of financial position. An extract from the draft auditor's report is given below:

Explanation of adverse opinion in relation to pension

The financial statements do not include the company's pension plan. This deliberate omission contravenes accepted accounting practice and means that the accounts are not properly prepared.

Auditor's opinion

In our opinion, because of the significance of the matter discussed below, the financial statements do not give a true and fair view of the financial position of Snipe Co as at 31 January 2012, and of its financial performance and cash flows for the year then ended in accordance with International Financial Reporting Standards.

Required:

Critically appraise the extract from the proposed auditor's report of Snipe Co for the year ended 31 January 2012.

Note: you are NOT required to re-draft the extract of the auditor's report. (7 marks)

(Total: 15 marks)

Calculate your allowed time, allocate the time to the separate parts..............

UK SYLLABUS ONLY

52 KANDINSKY *Walk in the footsteps of a top tutor*

Malevich & Co is a firm of Chartered Certified Accountants offering audit and assurance services to a large portfolio of clients. You are a manager in the audit department responsible for the audit of two clients, Kandinsky Ltd and Viola Ltd.

(a) Kandinsky Ltd is a manufacturer of luxury food items including chocolate and other confectionery which are often sold as gift items individually or in hampers containing a selection of expensive items from the range of products. The company has a financial year ended 31 July 2015, much of the planned audit work has been completed, and you are reviewing issues which have been raised by the audit senior. Due to an economic recession sales of products have fallen sharply this year, and measures have been implemented to support the company's cash flow. You are aware that the company only has £150,000 in cash at the year end.

Extracts from the draft financial statements and other relevant information are given below.

	Note	*July 2015 (Draft)* £000	*July 2014 (Actual)* £000
Revenue		2,440	3,950
Operating expenses		(2,100)	(2,800)
Finance charge		(520)	(500)
(Loss)/profit before tax		(180)	650
Total assets		10,400	13,500
Long-term liabilities – bank loan	1	3,500	3,000
Short-term liabilities – trade payables	2	900	650
Disclosed in notes to financial statements:			
Undrawn borrowing facilities	3	500	1,000
Contingent liability	4	120	–

Notes:

1 The bank loan was extended in March 2015 by drawing on the borrowing facilities offered by the bank. The loan carries a fixed interest rate and is secured on the company's property including the head office and manufacturing site. The first repayment of loan capital is due on 30 June 2016 when £350,000 is due to be paid.

2 Kandinsky Ltd renegotiated its terms of trade with its main supplier of cocoa beans, and extended payment terms from 50 days to 80 days in order to improve working capital.

3 The borrowing facilities are due to be reviewed by the bank in April 2016 and contain covenants including that interest cover is maintained at 2, and the ratio of bank loan to operating profit does not exceed 4:1.

4 The contingent liability relates to a letter of support which Kandinsky Ltd has provided to its main supplier of cane sugar which is facing difficult trading conditions.

Required:

In respect of the audit of Kandinsky Ltd:

Identify and explain the matters which may cast significant doubt on the Kandinsky Ltd's ability to continue as a going concern; and recommend the audit procedures to be performed in relation to the going concern matters identified. (13 marks)

(b) You are also responsible for the audit of Viola Ltd, a small engineering company located in the Midlands with a financial year ended 31 March 2015. The auditor's report for the financial year then ended, which was issued in September 2015, contained an Emphasis of Matter paragraph outlining the going concern issues facing the company, but was otherwise unmodified.

The finance director of Viola Ltd phoned you yesterday to discuss some recent developments at the company. His comments are shown in the note below:

'I am getting in touch to update you on our situation and to ask for your firm's advice.

As you know, in the last financial year the company lost several contracts and we had to make a number of staff redundant. In recent months further contracts have been lost and Viola Ltd has faced severe working capital problems, resulting in the sale of some of our plant in order to meet liabilities as they fall due. We are restricted on the assets which can be sold as the company's bank loan is secured by a floating charge over non-current assets. In November 2015 the accounts recognised net liabilities of £500,000 and without securing further finance, the future of the company does not look good.

We are tendering for three new contracts to supply components to local car manufacturers. However, our bank is reluctant to extend our borrowing facilities until the contracts are secured, which may not be for another few months.

My fellow directors are becoming concerned about the possibility of our creditors applying for compulsory liquidation of the company, which we want to avoid if possible. We also wish to avoid a creditor's voluntary liquidation. Can you please advise me on the alternatives which are available given the company's precarious financial situation? I need you to explain the procedures involved with any alternatives which you can recommend, and describe the impact on the employees and directors of the company.'

Required:

Respond to the instructions in the note from the finance director. (12 marks)

(Total: 25 marks)

53 COXON *Walk in the footsteps of a top tutor*

Hunt & Co has provided non-audit services such as corporate finance and tax planning for Coxon Ltd in the past. Coxon Ltd ran a chain of high street stores selling books, CDs and computer games. Unfortunately, it could not compete with internet sites selling the same goods at a much cheaper price, and since 2012 the company had been loss making. The company was placed into compulsory liquidation last week due to being unable to pay its debts as they fall due.

The finance director, James Corgan, has contacted your firm, seeking advice on several issues to do with the liquidation; his comments are shown in the note below:

'We had thought for some time that the company was in financial difficulties, having lost market share to competitors, but we hoped to turn the company around. Things came to a head in January 2014 when the accounts showed a net liabilities position for the first time, and several loan covenants had been breached. However, we decided to continue to trade in order to maximise cash inflows, keep staff employed for a few months longer, and try to negotiate finance from new providers. During this period we continued to order goods from several suppliers.

However, the cash position deteriorated and in May 2014 creditors applied to the court for the compulsory winding up of the company. The court has appointed liquidators who are about to commence the winding up.

As you can imagine, myself and the other directors are very worried about the situation. Please provide me with explanations on the following matters. We have heard that we may be personally liable for some of the company's debts. Is this correct, and what are the potential consequences for us? Also, can you explain the impact of the compulsory liquidation process for our employees and for creditors?'

Required:

Respond to the instructions in the note from the finance director. **(13 marks)**

54 HAWK (A) *Walk in the footsteps of a top tutor*

(a) You are a manager in Lapwing & Co. One of your audit clients is Hawk Ltd which operates commercial real estate properties typically comprising several floors of retail units and leisure facilities such as cinemas and health clubs, which are rented out to provide rental income.

Your firm has just been approached to provide an additional engagement for Hawk Ltd, to review and provide a report on the company's business plan, including forecast financial statements for the 12-month period to 31 May 2013. Hawk Ltd is in the process of negotiating a new bank loan of £30 million and the report on the business plan is at the request of the bank. It is anticipated that the loan would be advanced in August 2012 and would carry an interest rate of 4%. The report would be provided by your firm's business advisory department and a second partner review will be conducted which will reduce any threat to objectivity to an acceptable level.

Extracts from the forecast financial statements included in the business plan are given below:

Statement of profit or loss (extract)

	Note	*FORECAST 12 months to 31 May 2013*	*UNAUDITED 12 months to 31 May 2012*
		£000	£000
Revenue		25,000	20,600
Operating expenses		(16,550)	(14,420)
Operating profit		8,450	6,180
Profit on disposal of Beak Retail	1	4,720	–
Finance costs		(2,650)	(1,690)
Profit before tax		10,520	4,490

Statement of financial position

	Note	*FORECAST 12 months to 31 May 2013*	*UNAUDITED 12 months to 31 May 2012*
Assets		£000	£000
Non-current assets			
Property, plant and equipment	2	330,150	293,000
Current assets			
Inventory		500	450
Receivables		3,600	3,300
Cash and cash equivalents		2,250	3,750
		6,350	7,500
Total assets		336,500	300,500
Equity and liabilities			
Equity			
Share capital		105,000	100,000
Retained earnings		93,400	92,600
Total equity		198,400	192,600
Non-current liabilities			
Long-term borrowings	2	82,500	52,500
Deferred tax		50,000	50,000
Current liabilities			
Trade payables		5,600	5,400
Total liabilities		138,100	107,900
Total equity and liabilities		336,500	300,500

Notes:

(1) Beak Retail is a retail park which is underperforming. Its sale is currently being negotiated, and is expected to take place in September 2012.

(2) Hawk Ltd is planning to invest the cash raised from the bank loan in a new retail and leisure park which is being developed jointly with another company, Kestrel Ltd.

Required:

In respect of the engagement to provide a report on Hawk Ltd's business plan:

(i) Identify and explain the matters that should be considered in agreeing the terms of the engagement; and Note: You are NOT required to consider ethical threats to objectivity. (6 marks)

(ii) Recommend the procedures that should be performed in order to examine and report on the forecast financial statements of Hawk Ltd for the year to 31 May 2013. (12 marks)

(b) You are also responsible for the audit of Jay Ltd, a company with a year ended 30 September 2011, in relation to which an unmodified auditor's report was issued in December 2011. Jay Ltd operates two separate divisions both of which manufacture food supplements – 'Jay Sport' manufactures food supplements targeted at athletes, and 'Jay Plus' is targeted at the general public. The audit engagement partner, Bill Kingfisher, sent you the following email this morning:

To: **Audit manager**

From: **Bill Kingfisher, audit engagement partner, Jay Ltd**

Regarding: **Jay Ltd – financial results**

Hello

I have just received some worrying news from the finance director of Jay Ltd. The company's latest results are not looking good – I have attached an extract from the latest management accounts for your information.

It seems that one of the key ingredients used in the 'Jay Sport' range has been found to have harmful side effects, so very few sales from that range have been made in the current financial year. The company is struggling to manage its working capital and meet interest payments on loans.

In light of all this, the directors are anxious about the future of the company, and I have been asked to attend a meeting with them tomorrow to discuss their concerns over the financial performance and position of Jay Ltd.

I am asking you to prepare briefing notes for my use in the meeting with the directors, in which you:

(i) Examine the financial position of Jay Ltd and determine whether the company is insolvent; and **(4 marks)**

(ii) Evaluate, reaching a recommendation, the options available to the directors in terms of the future of the company. **(9 marks)**

Thank you.

Attachment: Extract from Jay Ltd's management accounts at 31 May 2012 (unaudited)

Statement of financial position

	£000
Property, plant and equipment	12,800
Inventory	500
Trade receivables	400
Cash	0
Total assets	13,700
Share capital	100
Retained earnings	(1,050)
Long-term borrowings (secured with a fixed charge over property, plant and equipment)	12,000
Trade payables (including employees' wages of £300,000)	1,250
Bank overdraft	1,400
Total equity and liabilities	13,700

Statement of profit or loss (extract)

	£000	£000	£000
Revenue	50	1,450	1,500
Operating costs	(800)	(1,200)	(2,000)
Operating loss/profit	(750)	250	(500)
Finance costs			(800)
Loss before tax			(1,300)

Required:

Respond to the partner's email. **(13 marks)**

Note: the split of the mark allocation is shown within the partner's email.

Professional marks will be awarded in part (b) for the presentation and clarity of your answer. **(4 marks)**

(Total: 35 marks)

55 BUTLER (A) *Walk in the footsteps of a top tutor*

(a) Butler Ltd is a new audit client of your firm. You are the manager responsible for the audit of the financial statements for the year ended 31 May 2011. Butler Ltd designs and manufactures aircraft engines and spare parts, and is a subsidiary of a multi-national group. Extracts from the draft financial statements are shown below:

Statement of financial position	*31 May 2011*	*31 May 2010*
	Draft	*Actual*
Assets	£ million	£ million
Non-current assets		
Intangible assets (note 1)	200	180
Property, plant and equipment (note 2)	1,300	1,200
Deferred tax asset (note 3)	235	20
Financial assets	25	35
	1,760	1,435
Current assets		
Inventory	1,300	800
Trade receivables	2,100	1,860
	3,400	2,660
Total assets	5,160	4,095
Equity and liabilities		
Equity		
Share capital	300	300
Retained earnings	(525)	95
	(225)	395
Non-current liabilities		
Long-term borrowings (note 4)	1,900	1,350
Provisions (note 5)	185	150
	2,085	1,500
Current liabilities		
Short-term borrowings (note 6)	800	400
Trade payables	2,500	1,800
	3,300	2,200
Total equity and liabilities	5,160	4,095

Notes to the statement of financial position:

Note 1 Intangible assets comprise goodwill on the acquisition of subsidiaries (£80 million), and development costs capitalised on engine development projects (£120 million).

Note 2 Property, plant and equipment includes land and buildings valued at £25 million, over which a fixed charge exists.

Note 3 The deferred tax asset has arisen following several loss-making years suffered by the company. The asset represents the tax benefit of unutilised tax losses carried forward.

Note 4 Long-term borrowings include a debenture due for repayment in July 2012, and a loan from Butler Ltd's parent company due for repayment in December 2012.

Note 5 Provisions relate to warranties provided to customers.

Note 6 Short-term borrowings comprise an overdraft (£25 million), a short-term loan (£60 million) due for repayment in August 2011, and a bank loan (£715 million) repayable in September 2011.

You have received an email from the audit partner responsible for the audit of Butler Ltd:

To: **Audit manager**

From: **Audit partner**

Regarding: **Butler Ltd – going concern issues**

Hello

I understand that the audit work on Butler Ltd commences this week. I am concerned about the future of the company, as against a background of economic recession, sales have been declining, several significant customer contracts have been cancelled unexpectedly, and competition from overseas has damaged the market share previously enjoyed by Butler Ltd.

(i) Please identify and explain any matters arising from your review of the draft statement of financial position, and the cash flow forecast, which may cast significant doubt on the company's ability to continue as a going concern. The cash flow forecast has just been sent to me from the client, and is attached. It covers only the first three months of the next financial year, the client is currently preparing the forecasts for the whole 12 month period. Please be sceptical when reviewing the forecast, as the assumptions may be optimistic. **(10 marks)**

(ii) In addition, please recommend the principal audit procedures to be carried out on the cash flow forecast. **(8 marks)**

Thank you.

Attachment: Cash flow forecast for the three months to 31 August 2011

	June 2011	*July 2011*	*August 2011*
	£ million	£ million	£ million
Cash inflows			
Cash receipts from customers (note 1)	175	195	220
Loan receipt (note 2)		150	
Government subsidy (note 3)			50
Sales of financial assets	50		
Total cash inflows	225	345	270
Cash outflows			
Operating cash outflows	200	200	290
Interest payments	40	40	40
Loan repayment			60
Total cash outflows	240	240	390
Net cash flow for the month	(15)	105	(120)
Opening cash	(25)	(40)	65
Closing cash	(40)	65	(55)

Notes to the cash flow forecast:

This cash flow forecast has been prepared by the management of Butler Ltd, and is based on the following assumptions:

(1) Cash receipts from customers should accelerate given the anticipated improvement in economic conditions. In addition, the company has committed extra resources to the credit control function, in order to speed up collection of overdue debts.

(2) The loan expected to be received in July 2011 is currently being negotiated with our parent company, Rubery Ltd.

(3) The government subsidy will be received once our application has been approved. The subsidy is awarded to companies which operate in areas of high unemployment and it subsidises the wages and salaries paid to staff.

Required:

Respond to the email from the audit partner. **(18 marks)**

(b) The management of Butler Ltd is concerned that given the company's poor liquidity position, the company could be placed into compulsory liquidation.

Required:

(i) **Explain the procedures involved in placing a company into compulsory liquidation; and** **(4 marks)**

(ii) **Explain the consequences of a compulsory liquidation for Butler Ltd's payables (creditors), employees and shareholders.** **(3 marks)**

(Total: 25 marks)

56 ASPECTS OF INSOLVENCY *Walk in the footsteps of a top tutor*

(a) **Explain the differences between fraudulent and wrongful trading and the consequences for company directors.** **(6 marks)**

(b) **Explain how an auditor would determine whether a company is insolvent under the provisions of the UK Insolvency Act 1986.** **(2 marks)**

(c) **State the circumstances under which a company may be obliged to liquidate.** **(2 marks)**

(d) **Explain the consequences of compulsory liquidation and how it may affect company stakeholders.** **(5 marks)**

(e) **Explain the meaning of and describe procedures involved in a member's voluntary liquidation.** **(5 marks)**

(Total: 20 marks)

INT SYLLABUS ONLY

57 KANDINSKY *Walk in the footsteps of a top tutor*

Malevich & Co is a firm of Chartered Certified Accountants offering audit and assurance services to a large portfolio of clients. You are a manager in the audit department responsible for the audit of two clients, Kandinsky Co and the Rothko University, both of which have a financial year ended 31 July 2015. The audits of both clients are being completed and you are reviewing issues which have been raised by the audit seniors.

(a) Kandinsky Co is a manufacturer of luxury food items including chocolate and other confectionery which are often sold as gift items individually or in hampers containing a selection of expensive items from the range of products. Due to an economic recession sales of products have fallen sharply this year, and measures have been implemented to support the company's cash flow. You are aware that the company only has $150,000 in cash at the year end.

Extracts from the draft financial statements and other relevant information are given below.

	Note	*July 2015 (Draft)*	*July 2014 (Actual)*
		$000	$000
Revenue		2,440	3,950
Operating expenses		(2,100)	(2,800)
Finance charge		(520)	(500)
(Loss)/profit before tax		(180)	650
Total assets		10,400	13,500
Long-term liabilities – bank loan	1	3,500	3,000
Short-term liabilities – trade payables	2	900	650
Disclosed in notes to financial statements:			
Undrawn borrowing facilities	3	500	1,000
Contingent liability	4	120	–

Notes:

1 The bank loan was extended in March 2015 by drawing on the borrowing facilities offered by the bank. The loan carries a fixed interest rate and is secured on the company's property including the head office and manufacturing site. The first repayment of loan capital is due on 30 June 2016 when $350,000 is due to be paid.

2 Kandinsky Co renegotiated its terms of trade with its main supplier of cocoa beans, and extended payment terms from 50 days to 80 days in order to improve working capital.

3 The borrowing facilities are due to be reviewed by the bank in April 2016 and contain covenants including that interest cover is maintained at 2, and the ratio of bank loan to operating profit does not exceed 4:1.

4 The contingent liability relates to a letter of support which Kandinsky Co has provided to its main supplier of cane sugar which is facing difficult trading conditions.

Required:

In respect of the audit of Kandinsky Co:

(i) Identify and explain the matters which may cast significant doubt on the company's ability to continue as a going concern; and (9 marks)

(ii) Recommend the audit procedures to be performed in relation to the going concern matters identified. (6 marks)

(b) The Rothko University, a public sector entity, is a small university with approximately 2,000 students, which was established 10 years ago and specialises in vocational study programmes leading to the award of degrees in business, accountancy, finance, law and marketing. The highest performing students achieve a distinction on completing their degree programme, indicating excellence in the knowledge and understanding of their subject. Students pay tuition fees of $10,000 per year, and the degree programme is typically three years long.

The audit work in respect of the year ended 31 July 2015 is almost complete, but the audit senior has not yet completed the audit work in respect of performance information which is being published with the annual financial statements for the first time this year. It is a requirement in the jurisdiction in which the Rothko University is located that the performance information is audited as part of the external audit.

Details on the performance information are given below.

Performance area	*Performance measure*	*2015 result*
Graduation rate	% of students who complete their degree programme	85%
Academic performance	% of students achieving a distinction	20%
Employability	% of students who on graduation obtain graduate level employment	65%
Course satisfaction	% of students who rate their university experience as excellent or very good	70%

Required:

(i) Discuss the relevance and measurability of the reported performance information.

(ii) Recommend the examination procedures to be used in auditing the performance information.

Note: The total marks will be split equally between each part. (10 marks)

(Total: 25 marks)

58 PUBLIC SECTOR ORGANISATIONS *Walk in the footsteps of a top tutor*

(a) Define the terms 'performance audit' and 'performance information'. (2 marks)

(b) Suggest 4 performance targets which could be measured for each of the following public sector organisations:

(i) Local police department (2 marks)

(ii) Local hospital (2 marks)

(iii) Local council (2 marks)

(c) State 2 stakeholder groups that would rely on the performance information produced by the public sector organisations in part (b) and explain what they might use that information for. (6 marks)

(d) Explain the difficulties encountered by auditors when auditing performance information. (6 marks)

(Total: 20 marks)

Section 3

ANSWERS TO PRACTICE QUESTIONS – SECTION A

RISK ASSESSMENT

1 ZED COMMUNICATIONS GROUP *Walk in the footsteps of a top tutor*

Top tutor tips

Part (a) asks audit risks. This is the most frequently examined type of risk and students should be able to properly describe the risks as either risks of material misstatement or detection risks.

Part (b) requires matters to be considered before relying on the work of the client's internal audit department. This requires text book knowledge to be applied to the details of the scenario. Look out for information that indicates the internal audit department is experienced and qualified as this will indicate evidence of competence.

Part (c) asks for procedures in respect of the shareholding in the joint venture and the licence acquired during the year. Procedures are very regularly examined as a follow on from audit risks. Make sure the procedures are adequately described so that the person performing the procedure will know what to do.

Briefing notes

To: Vincent Vega, audit engagement partner

From: Audit engagement manager

Subject: Audit planning – ZCG

Introduction

These briefing notes have been prepared to assist in the audit planning of ZCG, and contain an evaluation of audit risk and a discussion of the matters to be considered in determining whether to place reliance on the Group's internal audit department. The notes also include the recommended audit procedures to be performed on the classification of the investment in WTC and on the measurement of a licence acquired on 1 January 2015.

(a) Evaluation of audit risks

Recognition of 50% equity shareholding in WTC

The 50% equity shareholding is likely to give rise to a joint venture under which control of WTC is shared between ZCG and Wolf Communications Co.

IFRS 11 *Joint Arrangements* requires that an investor which has joint control over a joint venture should recognise its investment using the equity method of accounting.

Audit risk arises in that despite owning 50% of the equity shares of WTC, ZCG may not actually share control with Wolf Communications, for example, if Wolf Communications retains a right to veto decisions or if ZCG cannot appoint an equal number of board members in order to make joint decisions with board members appointed by Wolf Communications. If ZCG does not have joint control, then WTC should not be treated as a joint venture.

Assuming that there is shared control, an audit risk arises in that ZCG may not have correctly applied equity accounting, thereby potentially over or understating ZCG's investment and resulting in incorrect presentation in the consolidated statement of financial position and statement of profit or loss. The cost of the investment in WTC represents 7.5% of ZCG's total assets at 31 August 2016, thus the investment is material to the Group.

Amortisation of licence to operate in Farland

The licence acquired on 1 January 2015 should be recognised as an intangible asset and amortised on a systematic basis over its useful life.

According to IAS®38 *Intangible Assets,* the amortisation method should reflect the pattern of benefits, or if the pattern cannot be determined reliably, the straight-line method of amortisation should be used.

Amortisation should begin when the asset is available for use, meaning when it is in the location and condition necessary for it to be capable of operating in the manner which management intends. ZCG therefore should begin to amortise the licence on 1 July 2016 and amortise over the remaining licence period of eight and a half years.

The audit risk is that amortisation did not commence at the right point in time or that it has been determined using an inappropriate useful life, leading to over or understatement of the amortisation charge to profit as well as the carrying value of the intangible asset.

Assuming that it is appropriate to use the straight-line method, amortisation for the year to 31 December 2016 should be $3.8 million (65/8.5 × 6/12). This represents 1.3% of extrapolated revenue for the year of $297 million (198 × 12/8) and is therefore material, and the amortisation will be more material next year when a full year's charge to profit is made.

Impairment of the Farland licence

IAS 38 does not require an annual impairment review to be conducted for all intangible assets. However, management should consider whether there are indicators of impairment and if necessary perform an impairment review on the licence.

The competitor's actions which appear to have reduced customer demand to a level below that anticipated is an indicator of potential impairment, so management must calculate the recoverable amount of the licence and compare to its carrying value in order to determine if the asset is impaired.

Therefore there is a risk that the licence is overstated in value, and operating profit also overstated if any necessary impairment has not been recognised.

Revenue recognition

Revenue recognition is complex and is a significant accounting issue with the risk of error increased by the fact that the Group is implementing the new requirements of IFRS 15 Revenue from Contracts with Customers for the first time this year.

With the adoption of any new financial reporting standard, there is an audit risk in that the new requirements are unfamiliar to the preparers of the financial statements. There may be errors in the understanding and application of the new rules, especially in areas of judgement, and controls may not have been sufficiently robust over any necessary systems changes.

Further, it is surprising that there are no comments in the latest internal audit report on the new controls which should have been implemented during the year in relation to the new requirements of IFRS 15. It is anticipated that internal audit should have been involved in testing the newly implemented controls for effectiveness. This may imply that the controls may not be fit for purpose and again increases control risk and therefore audit risk in this area.

We will need to ensure that we document the systems and controls in place and evaluate the significance of any control risk in order that we respond appropriately to any risks of material misstatement which are identified.

The audit team members themselves may be unfamiliar with the new requirements, creating a detection risk. Any necessary changes in accounting policy may not have been appropriately accounted for and disclosed in accordance with IAS 8 *Accounting Policies, Changes in Accounting Estimate and Errors*.

Given the significance of revenue recognition to the Group's financial statements, the potential misapplication of IFRS 15 and IAS 8 gives rise to a significant audit risk.

ZCG is supplying customers with a multiple-element contract and is providing access to a mobile phone network and a fixed landline and broadband service. The key audit risk arises in relation to whether ZCG accounts for the elements of the contract separately in accordance with IFRS 15 which requires the revenue to be derived from the contract to be allocated to each component.

ZCG should have robust systems in place to ensure that contracts can be 'unbundled', enabling the revenue from each part of the contract to be separately determined, otherwise there is a significant risk that the revenue element attributable to each component of the customer contracts will be over or understated.

There is also a risk that the timing of revenue recognition will not be in line with ZCG meeting its performance obligations, also a requirement of IFRS 15. Contracts vary in length, lasting two or three years, and there is an audit risk that the timing of revenue recognition is not appropriate.

The fact that total revenue, when extrapolated for the 12-month period, is expected to increase by 35% could indicate that revenue is being recognised too early. This could indicate a misapplication of IFRS 15, possibly changes to accounting policies which have been made on adoption of IFRS 15 are not appropriate.

IFRS 15 contains significant disclosure requirements and there is a risk that ZCG fails to provide sufficient disclosure on a range of matters relevant to its contracts with customers, including the significant judgements made in applying IFRS 15 to those contracts and sufficient disaggregation of the necessary disclosures.

Given the significant volume of individual customer contracts and the complexity of the accounting treatment, revenue recognition is a significant audit risk.

Right to use network capacity

The payment of $17.8 million to acquire access to network capacity represents 3% of total assets and 6% of extrapolated revenue for the year, thus the amount is material.

It seems that risk and reward does not pass to ZCG in respect of the assets being used and the seller retains control over the use of its network assets. Therefore the network capacity should not be recognised as an intangible asset of ZCG and the Group is currently adopting an inappropriate accounting treatment which has resulted in intangible assets being overstated.

The accounting treatment for these rights should be discussed with ZCG as soon as possible. The most appropriate accounting treatment would seem to be for ZCG to record the cost of the right to use the network capacity as a prepayment and recognise the cost in profit or loss on a straight-line basis over the term of the agreements and this accounting treatment should be reflected in the financial statements as soon as possible.

The audit team will need to be made aware of the risk that prepayments and operating expenses are over or understated if the cost has not been treated as a prepayment and/or is not released to profit or loss over an appropriate period.

A further risk is the payment to the network provider is for a specified amount of access to the network provider's network. There is a risk is that ZCG has exceeded the allocated allowance and that any necessary additional payment due for excess usage is not recognised in the financial statements.

Internal controls and fraud risk

The internal audit department has reported that internal controls are 'working well'. This statement will need to be substantiated but gives the impression that control risk is likely to be low. The work of the internal control department will be discussed in more detail in the next section of the briefing notes.

However, it is worth noting that two frauds have been found to be operating during the year, giving rise to audit risk. Although the total monetary amount attributable to the frauds is less than 1% of revenue, therefore immaterial, the fact that the frauds have occurred indicates that there are significant internal control deficiencies which could mean that other frauds are operating. We will need to carefully plan our audit approach to expenses and payroll in light of the increased fraud risk.

The lack of approval and authorisation of expenses discovered by internal audit is concerning as this appears to involve higher level management and may call into question management integrity.

We should review the work of internal audit to establish if this is an area where controls have been overridden or if there are current gaps within the control framework. We should review and update our systems notes to identify where reliance can potentially be placed on controls and where there are deficiencies.

The issue uncovered by internal audit in relation to payroll suggests that there is inadequate control over the Group's IT system. Access controls, which form part of the Group's general IT controls, are weak which means that other areas of the system may be vulnerable.

This significantly increases control risk and as a result presents a significant area of audit risk. We will need to ensure that we carefully plan our approach as this may mean that there are areas of the system where no reliance can be placed on internal controls and appropriate alternative procedures will need to be applied.

Segmental reporting

Being a listed entity, ZCG should provide segmental information in the notes to the financial statements in accordance with IFRS 8 *Operating Segments*.

The audit risk is that the segmental information provided is not sufficiently detailed and/or not based on the information reported internally to the Group's chief operating decision maker.

There are some unusual trends in the segmental revenue figures from the management accounts. For example, revenue from south east Asia appears to have increased significantly – if the 2016 revenue figure is extrapolated to a 12-month period, the projected revenue from that segment is $49.5 million, an increase of 65% compared to 2015.

There is a risk that revenues have been misallocated between segments and that the disclosure is inaccurate.

(b) Matters which should be considered in determining the amount of reliance, if any, which can be placed on the work of ZCG's internal audit department

According to ISA 610 *Using the Work of Internal Auditors*, the external auditor may decide to use the work of the audit client's internal audit function to modify the nature or timing, or reduce the extent, of audit procedures to be performed directly by the external auditor.

Note that in some jurisdictions the external auditor may be prohibited, or restricted to some extent, by law or regulation from using the work of the internal audit function. Therefore Tarantino & Co should consider whether it is prohibited by the law or regulations which it must adhere to from relying on the work of ZCG's internal audit department or using the internal auditors to provide direct assistance.

Tarantino & Co must evaluate the internal audit department to determine whether its work is suitable by evaluating:

- The extent to which the internal audit function's organisational status and relevant policies and procedures support the objectivity of the internal auditors
- The level of competence of the internal audit function, and
- Whether the internal audit function applies a systematic and disciplined approach, including quality control.

One of the key issues to be evaluated is objectivity – the internal audit department should be unbiased in their work and be able to report their findings without being subject to the influence of others. The fact that the latest internal audit report is addressed to ZCG's finance director could indicate that there is a conflict of interest, as the internal audit department should report directly to the audit committee or to those charged with governance in order to maintain their independence.

The internal audit team is managed by a qualified accountant who is presumably technically competent, though the nature and status of his qualification should be determined. Tarantino & Co should consider whether the rest of the internal audit department is staffed by professional accountants, whether ZCG has a training programme in place for the internal auditors, for example, to ensure that they are up to date with new IFRS requirements such as IFRS 15, and whether there are sufficient resources for the internal auditors to carry out their duties in a large multi-national organisation.

When assessing competency, consideration must also be given to the overall findings which were reported regarding the deficiencies in the current internal control system. The internal audit department has concluded that controls are working well despite there being two instances of fraud in the year which may have more serious ramifications than first suggested.

The scope of work carried out in this area and the resultant recommendations will need to be reviewed. This may further suggest that the internal audit department is not free to investigate or report their findings due to the current reporting chains.

If there are doubts over either the objectivity or the competence of the internal audit department, then Tarantino & Co should not rely on their work.

In order to determine whether the internal audit department works in a systematic and disciplined way, Tarantino & Co should consider matters including the nature of documentation which is produced by the department and whether effective quality control procedures are in place such as direction, supervision and review of work carried out.

If Tarantino & Co wants to use the internal audit function to provide direct assistance, then the firm should:

- obtain written agreement from an authorised representative of the entity that the internal auditors will be allowed to follow the external auditor's instructions, and that the entity will not intervene in the work the internal auditor performs for the external auditor, and
- obtain written agreement from the internal auditors that they will keep confidential specific matters as instructed by the external auditor and inform the external auditor of any threat to their objectivity.

If these confirmations cannot be obtained, then the internal auditors should not be used to provide direct assistance.

UK syllabus: In the UK, ISA 610 prohibits the use of internal auditors in providing direct assistance to the external auditor; direct assistance is the use of internal auditors to perform audit procedures under the direction, supervision and review of the external auditor. However, the internal auditors can be used to provide non-direct assistance, for example, we may review their reports on risk management as a way of obtaining business understanding and identifying business risks and risks of material misstatement.

(c) (i) Audit procedures on the classification of the 50% shareholding in WTC

- Obtain the legal documentation supporting the investment and agree the details of the investment including:
  - The date of the investment
  - Amount paid
  - Number of shares purchased
  - The voting rights attached to the shares
  - The nature of the profit sharing arrangement between ZCG and Wolf Communications
  - The nature of access to WTC's assets under the terms of the agreement
  - Confirmation that there is no restriction of ZCG's shared control of WTC
- Read board minutes to confirm the approval of the investment and to understand the business rationale for the investment.
- Read minutes of relevant meetings between ZCG and Wolf Communications to confirm that control is shared between the two companies and to understand the nature of the relationship and the decision-making process.
- Obtain documentation such as WTC's organisational structure to confirm that ZCG has successfully appointed members to the board of WTC and that those members have equal power to the members appointed by Wolf Communications.

(ii) Audit procedures on the measurement of the operating licence to operate in Farland

- Obtain the licence agreement and confirm the length of the licence period to be 10 years from the date it was granted.
- Confirm whether the licence can be renewed at the end of the 10-year period, as this may impact on the estimated useful life and amortisation.
- Re-perform management's calculation of the amortisation charged as an expense in 2016.
- Discuss with management the process for identifying an appropriate amortisation method and where relevant, how the pattern of future economic benefits associated with the licence have been determined.
- Confirm with management that the Farland network became operational on 1 July 2016.
- Review a sample of contracts with customers in Farland to verify that contracts commenced from the operational date of 1 July 2016.
- Enquire with management on the existence of any factors indicating that a shorter useful life is appropriate, for example, the stability of market demand in Farland or possible restrictions on the network capacity in Farland.

- Review management accounts and cash flow forecasts to confirm that Farland is generating an income stream and is predicted to continue to generate cash.
- Obtain a written representation from management confirming that there are no indications of impairment of the licence of which management is aware.

Conclusion

These briefing notes highlight that there are a number of audit risks to be addressed, in particular revenue recognition, and fraud risks appear to be significant issues requiring a robust response from the audit team. We will need to carefully consider whether it is appropriate to receive direct assistance from the internal audit department.

Examiner's comments

This question followed the pattern of previous examinations and was set at the planning stage of the audit/assurance cycle. The context of the question was a large company looking to expand its international presence through different means.

Part (a) was a standard audit risk requirement and should have been an area where candidates were able to score strong marks for identifying audit risks from the scenario and describing the effects on the financial statements and elements of audit risk. This part of the question was disappointingly answered by many candidates. There is a tendency for weaker candidates to produce long but irrelevant answers. There is no place in this requirement for describing the audit risk model or discussing ethical issues. If ethical issues were required in question 1 this would be flagged as a separate requirement. In this scenario the client was not a new client and had pre-existing international revenue streams, demonstrated by the prior year segmental revenue comparatives, therefore discussing detection risk due to a lack of auditor knowledge of the client or inability to audit international revenue was not relevant. The risks in this type of question are flagged up in the scenario and should be addressed using up to date knowledge of financial reporting standards to describe appropriate accounting treatment and highlighting the potential impact of errors on the financial statements. Generally, the direction of the error will be required to score well, simply stating that intangibles may be over or understated will not gain full credit as this does not demonstrate the level of knowledge which is required. As in previous audit risk questions, there is credit available for calculating and concluding on the materiality of a balance in the financial statements. A majority of candidates are able to correctly select the appropriate benchmark for materiality (e.g. assessing an asset or liability in the context of total assets rather than on revenue or profits) but frequently answers were presented with materiality based on prior year rather than current year figures. Audit risk continues to be an area that candidates find difficult and particularly it continues to be noted that many candidates fail to engage with the information provided in enough depth, specifically when provided with extracts from financial statements. Candidates are again reminded that in order to provide a full answer in relation to audit risk they should utilise and analyse all the information that is provided.

Candidates were also required to discuss the considerations to be taken into account when assessing whether and how to use internal audit to assist the external auditor. The majority of candidates were able to list the criteria as per ISA 610 *Using the Work of Internal Auditors*, to assess against and relate that back to the scenario, which was an improvement on the last time this standard was examined.

Finally candidates were required to provide the principal audit procedures to obtain audit evidence in relation to the classification of a joint venture and the measurement of an intangible asset. The majority of candidates performed satisfactorily in this requirement but again many had not read the requirement carefully enough and described tests covering other FS assertions than those required – for example assessing the cost of the joint venture which was not relevant to the classification risk, or failing to take into account that the intangible had been purchased in the prior year so the cost would have been audited at that point so audit procedures should have focused on confirming the brought forward figure and any adjustments for amortisation or impairment.

There were four professional marks available, and most candidates secured most of these marks by providing an introduction and using headings to create an appropriate structure for their answer. However, presentation was not always good and candidates are reminded to pay attention to determining an appropriate layout for their answer.

Marking scheme

		Marks
(a)	**Evaluation of audit risk** Generally up to 2 marks for each well explained audit risk. In addition, 1 mark for each correct materiality calculation to a maximum of 2 marks and 1 mark for each relevant calculation such as trends. – Recognition of 50% equity shareholding in WTC – Amortisation of licence to operate in Farland – Possible impairment of licence – Right to use network capacity – First-time adoption of IFRS 15 – Revenue recognition – max 5 marks if discuss a range of issues specific to IFRS 15 including multiple element contracts, timing of recognition, disclosure requirements, volume of transactions – Internal controls and fraud risk – up to 4 marks for a detailed discussion of fraud risk – Segmental reporting	
	Maximum	**14**
(b)	**Internal audit** Generally up to 2 marks for discussion of each relevant matter: – General introduction, comment on prohibition in some jurisdictions – Objectivity – Competence – Disciplined and systematic approach – Using the internal auditors to provide direct assistance	
	Maximum	**7**
(c)	**Audit procedures** Generally 1 mark for each well explained audit procedure: (i) **Investment in WTC** – Obtain the legal documentation supporting the investment and agree the details of the investment (max 2 marks for details of items to be verified) – Read board minutes for approval of the investment understanding of the business rationale for the investment – Read minutes of relevant meetings between ZCG and Wolf Communications to confirm shared control and shared decision-making process – Confirm that ZCG has successfully appointed members to the board of WTC and that board decisions are made equally	
	Maximum	**4**

(ii) **Amortisation of licence** – Obtain the licence agreement and confirm the length of the licence period – Confirm whether the licence can be renewed at the end of the 10-year period – Re-perform management's calculation of the amortisation charged as an expense in 2016 – Discuss with management the process for determining the method of amortisation – Review management accounts to confirm that the Farland network became operational on 1 July 2016 and that Farland is generating a revenue stream from that date – Review customer contracts to confirm network operational from 1 July 2016 – Enquire with management on the existence of factors indicating that a shorter useful life is appropriate – Review management accounts and cash flow forecasts to confirm that Farland is generating an income stream and is predicted to continue to generate cash – Obtain a management representation to confirm that there are no indications of impairment of the licence of which management is aware	
Maximum	**6**
Professional marks – generally 1 mark each for heading, introduction, structure and clarity of explanations	**4**
Total	**35**

2 VANCOUVER GROUP *Walk in the footsteps of a top tutor*

Top tutor tips

Part (a) asks why analytical procedures are performed as part of the risk assessment procedures. Some students may struggle with this so don't waste time thinking for too long on this requirement. There are plenty of other marks to be earned on other parts.

Part (b) asks for audit risks and analytical procedures. Students should be aware of the need to perform analytical procedures in the exam to help identify audit risks as this has been examined several times before. Calculators are an essential item for this exam and easy marks can be achieved for calculations.

Part (c) asks for discussion of two ethical issues. Ethical issues can appear more than once on the same exam and students should not be surprised if this happens. In order to score well, consider the significance of the issues in addition to explaining them and suggesting actions to address the issues.

Briefing notes

To: Albert Franks, audit engagement partner

From: Audit manager

Subject: Vancouver Group audit planning

Introduction

These briefing notes are prepared for use in the audit team briefing for the Vancouver Group (the Group). Following a meeting between the audit partner and the Group finance director and a member of the Group audit committee, and using information provided, audit risks have been identified and explained. Analytical procedures have been used to identify several audit risks, and the briefing notes also explain why analytical procedures are required as part of risk assessment. Finally, the briefing notes discuss the ethical implications of suggestions made by the Group audit committee.

(a) Analytical procedures and risk assessment

According to ISA 520 *Analytical Procedures*, analytical procedures are the evaluation of financial information through analysis of plausible relationships between both financial and non-financial data. Analytical procedures can involve comparisons of financial data including trend analysis and the calculation and comparison of ratios. Analytical procedures include comparisons of the Group's financial information with, for example:

- Comparable information for prior periods
- Anticipated results of the Group, such as budgets or forecasts
- Expectations of the auditor, or
- Comparable information from competitors.

Analytical procedures performed at the planning stage help the auditor to identify and respond appropriately to risk, and to assist the auditor in obtaining an understanding of the audited companies within the Group.

ISA 315 *Identifying and Assessing the Risks of Material Misstatement through Understanding the Entity and its Environment* requires the auditor to perform analytical procedures as part of risk assessment procedures at the planning stage of the audit to provide a basis for the identification and assessment of risks of material misstatement at the financial statement and assertion levels.

An example of how analytical procedures assist the auditor is that performing analytical procedures may alert the auditor to a transaction or event of which they were previously unaware, therefore prompting the auditor to investigate the matter, obtain understanding of the matter and plan appropriate audit procedures to obtain sufficient appropriate audit evidence. Therefore analytical procedures are an essential part of developing the audit strategy and audit plan.

Analytical procedures may also help the auditor to identify the existence of unusual transactions or events, such as significant one-off events. Unusual amounts, ratios, and trends might also indicate matters which indicate risk. Unusual or unexpected relationships which are identified by these procedures may assist the auditor in identifying risks of material misstatement, especially risks of material misstatement due to fraud.

Without performing analytical procedures, the auditor would be unable to identify risks of material misstatement and respond accordingly. This would increase detection risk, making it more likely that an inappropriate audit opinion could be issued.

(b) Audit risk evaluation including analytical procedures

Selected analytical procedures and associated audit risk evaluation

	2016	*2015*
Operating margin	27/375 × 100 = 7.2%	38/315 × 100 = 12.1%
Return on capital employed	27/66 + 181 = 10.9%	38/67 + 153 = 17.3%
Interest cover	27/4 = 6.8	38/3 = 12.7
Effective tax rate	10/33 × 100 = 30.3%	15/35 × 100 = 42.9%
Receivables days	62/375 × 365 = 60 days	45/315 × 365 = 52 days
Current ratio	97/120 = 0.8	83/95 = 0.9

Operating costs

Analytical procedures reveals that the Group's revenue has increased by 19%, but that operating expenses have disproportionately increased by 25.6%, resulting in the fall in operating margin from 12.1% in 2015 to 7.2% in 2016.

This is a significant change, and while the higher costs incurred could be due to valid business reasons, the trend could indicate operating costs are overstated or sales are understated.

There is a risk that some of the costs involved in modernising the Group's warehousing facilities have been incorrectly treated as revenue expenditure when this should have been capitalised.

The trend in operating margin is consistent with the change in return on capital employed which has also fallen. The treatment of the costs involved in the modernisation of the Group's warehouse facilities will need detailed investigation to ensure that costs have been classified appropriately.

Revenue

However, given the finance director's comment that operations have not changed significantly during the year, the increase in revenue of 19% seems surprising, given that this is a significant increase, and there is therefore also a risk that revenue could be overstated.

Detailed testing of the Group's revenue recognition policies will be required to verify that revenue is appropriately stated and recorded in the correct period.

Finance costs

The Group's interest cover has declined sharply, and finance costs have increased by 33%. This could indicate that finance costs are overstated, however, given that the Group has taken out additional debenture finance during the year, and also now has an overdraft, an increase in finance costs is to be expected and is more likely to simply reflect the significant drop which the Group has experienced in its operating profit levels.

The debenture may contain a covenant in relation to interest cover, and if so, there is a risk that the covenant may have been breached. While this is a business risk rather than an audit risk, the matter may require disclosure in the financial statements, leading to a risk of material misstatement if necessary disclosures are not made.

Tax expense

The comparison of effective tax rates shows that the effective tax rate is much lower in 2016. This could be due to the utilisation of Toronto Co's tax losses which seems to have taken place due to the reduction in the Group's deferred tax asset this year. However, this is a complex issue and there is a risk that the tax expense is understated in comparison with the previous year.

Given the ongoing tax investigation regarding potential underpayment of tax, this is a significant audit risk. Depending on the possible outcome of the tax investigation, there may be a need to provide for additional tax liabilities and any penalties which may be imposed by the tax authorities.

Details of the investigation and its findings so far will need to be considered and the probability of the tax authorities finding against the Group should be considered as part of our detailed audit testing to verify that liabilities are complete or that disclosures for contingent liabilities are complete.

Receivables

The receivables days figure has increased from 52 days in 2015 to 60 days in 2016. This could be due to poor credit control.

If this is a significant risk to the Group the issues involved may need to be disclosed according to IFRS 7 *Financial Instruments: Disclosure*, hence there is a risk of inadequate disclosure.

The increase in receivables days may also indicate an overstatement of receivables balances.

Provisions

The provisions balance has halved in value from $12 million in 2015 to $6 million in 2016. This could indicate that the provisions balance is understated and operating profit overstated, if there is not a valid reason for the reduction in value of the liability.

Possibly if the onerous lease contracts have now expired, then that could justify the change in value, but this will need to be confirmed.

In addition, provisions may be required in respect of dilapidation costs for leased properties, and there is a risk of understated liabilities if any such provisions have not been recognised.

The results of the analytical review should be reconsidered once any necessary adjustments are made to the financial statements in light of potential misstatements identified below.

Modernisation of warehousing facilities

Overall, property, plant and equipment has increased by $43 million or 23% which is a significant movement, representing 11.7% of total assets. A total amount of $25 million has been spent on modernising the warehousing facilities which is material, representing 6.8% of total assets.

The modernisation programme explains part of the increase in property, plant and equipment but given that depreciation would have been charged, the reasons for the large increase must be carefully considered. As part of our audit work we will need to ensure that we understand how all of this movement has occurred as there are several risks of material misstatement associated with the expenditure.

Treatment of expenditure

There is a risk that the amounts capitalised into non-current assets are not correct in that capital and revenue expenditure may not have been correctly identified and accounted for separately.

According to IAS 16 *Property, Plant and Equipment*, modernisation costs which give rise to enhanced future economic benefit should be capitalised where the costs are directly attributable, whereas costs which do not create future economic benefit should be expensed.

It would seem that costs such as replacing electrical systems should be capitalised, but other incidental costs which may have been incurred such as repairing items within the warehouses should be expensed.

Depreciation

In addition, there is a risk that the various components of each warehouse have not been treated as separate components and depreciated over a specific useful life. IAS 16 requires that each part of an item of property, plant and equipment with a cost which is significant in relation to the total cost of the item must be depreciated separately.

Items such as computer systems are likely to be significant components of the warehouses and as such should be accounted for as discrete assets in their own right.

Failure to correctly determine the significant components of the capital expenditure could lead to misstatement of the assets' carrying values and depreciation expenses.

Borrowing costs

There is also an issue with the finance costs in respect of the $5 million debenture taken out to finance the modernisation programme. If the criteria of IAS 23 *Borrowing Costs* are met, in particular if the modernisation of the warehouses meets the definition of a qualifying asset, then borrowing costs should be capitalised during the period of modernisation.

A qualifying asset is an asset which takes a substantial period of time to get ready for its intended use or sale, so depending on the length of time that the modernisation programme has taken, it may meet the definition so borrowing costs would need to be capitalised.

There is therefore a risk that borrowing costs have not been capitalised if the qualifying asset definition has been met, and equally a risk that borrowing costs may have been capitalised incorrectly if the definition has not been met. The borrowing costs, however, may not be material in isolation.

If any accounting errors have occurred in the amounts capitalised into property, plant and equipment, then non-current assets may be over or understated, as would be the depreciation charge calculated on the carrying value of those assets.

Disposal of shares in Calgary Co

A comparison of the statement of profit or loss for both years shows that the profit made on the disposal of shares in Calgary Co has been separately disclosed as part of profit in the year ending 31 July 2016. The profit recognised is material at 30.3% of profit before tax. Several errors seem to have been made in accounting for the disposal and in respect of its disclosure.

Profit on disposal

It is not correct that this profit on disposal is recognised in the statement of profit or loss. According to IFRS 10 *Consolidated Financial Statements*, changes in a parent's ownership interest in a subsidiary which does not result in the parent losing control of the subsidiary are treated as equity transactions. Any difference between the amount by which the non-controlling interests are adjusted and the fair value of the consideration paid or received is recognised directly in equity and attributed to the owners of the parent.

This appears to have been incorrectly accounted for as there should not be a profit on disposal within the statement of profit or loss. Therefore profit before tax is overstated by $10 million. The tax charge may be overstated if it has been calculated based on profit including the gain made on the share disposal.

Non-controlling interest

While the non-controlling interest has been recognised in equity, the Group's profit for the year has not been attributed and disclosed between the Group and the non-controlling interest.

There is also a risk that the disclosure requirements of IFRS 12 *Disclosure of Interests in Other Entities* are not followed, in particular in relation to the change in group structure which has taken place during the year, as IFRS 12 specifically requires disclosure relating to the consequences of changes in a group's ownership interest in a subsidiary which does not result in a loss of control.

Goodwill

IAS 38 *Intangible Assets* requires that goodwill is tested annually for impairment regardless of whether indicators of potential impairment exist.

The goodwill of $30 million recorded in the statement of financial position is unchanged from the prior year, indicating that no impairment has been recorded in the current financial year. It could be that management has performed an impairment review and concluded that no impairment is necessary.

There is a risk that management has not conducted a thorough review or not carried out a review and goodwill may be overstated. This will require investigation as part of our detailed audit procedures.

Management bias

The sale of shares to an institutional investor creates an inherent risk of management bias as management may feel under pressure to return favourable results.

This could explain the positive trends in revenue shown by the analytical review and could also explain the incorrect presentation of the profit on disposal which has incorrectly inflated profit by $10m.

Deferred tax asset

There is a risk that the deferred tax asset is overstated. According to IAS 12 *Income Taxes*, a deferred tax asset is recognised for an unused tax loss carry-forward or unused tax credit if, and only if, it is considered probable that there will be sufficient future taxable profit against which the loss or credit carry-forward can be utilised.

While it appears that some of the deferred tax asset has been utilised this year, there remains a risk that if it is no longer recoverable, then the amount would need to be written off. Audit work should be planned to confirm the recoverability of the amount recognised.

Audit committee – lack of financial reporting expert

Guidance on the composition of audit committees suggests that a financial reporting expert should be included in the committee. This is to ensure that the functions of the audit committee in relation to financial reporting are carried out effectively, for example, in ensuring that accounting policies are appropriate. The lack of an expert increases the risk that incorrect accounting treatments will occur, and is effectively a control risk.

(c) Ethical matters to be considered by our firm

Tax investigation

The ACCA's *Code of Ethics* states that an advocacy or self-review threat may be created when the firm represents an audit client in the resolution of a tax dispute, for example, before a tribunal or court.

The advocacy threat arises because the audit firm will take a position to promote the client's interests at the tribunal, leading to a threat to objectivity. The self-review threat arises where the matter which is the subject of the investigation and tribunal will have an impact on the financial statements on which the audit firm will express an opinion.

The existence and significance of any threat will depend on a number of factors including:

- Whether the firm has provided the advice which is the subject of the tax dispute
- The extent to which the outcome of the dispute will have a material effect on the financial statements on which the firm will express an opinion.

In this case the threat is lessened by the fact that it was another firm of accountants, Victoria & Co, which provided the tax planning advice to the Group, but the materiality of the matter will need to be carefully considered by Montreal & Co before they agree to take on the engagement to provide the necessary support to the Group.

The significance of any threat created shall be evaluated and safeguards applied when necessary to eliminate the threat or reduce it to an acceptable level. Examples of such safeguards include:

- Using professionals who are not members of the audit team to perform the service.
- Having a tax professional provide advice to the audit team on the Group's tax position, and review the financial statement treatment.

The *Code* states that where the taxation services involve acting as an advocate for an audit client before a public tribunal or court in the resolution of a tax matter and the amounts involved are material to the financial statements on which the firm will express an opinion, the advocacy threat created would be so significant that no safeguards could eliminate or reduce the threat to an acceptable level. Therefore, the firm shall not perform this type of service for an audit client.

What constitutes a 'public tribunal or court' shall be determined according to how tax proceedings are heard in the particular jurisdiction.

Appointment as a non-executive director and serve on audit committee

This would seem inappropriate as one of the functions of the audit committee is to oversee the external audit function, and it would not be possible for an audit partner of the firm to remain objective when evaluating matters such as determining the audit fee.

The Code specifically states that if a partner or employee of the firm serves as a director or officer of an audit client, the self-review and self-interest threats created would be so significant that no safeguards could reduce the threats to an acceptable level. Accordingly, no partner or employee shall serve as a director or officer of an audit client.

Hence, Montreal & Co must explain to the Vancouver Group that unfortunately it will not be possible for an audit partner to be appointed to serve as a non-executive director of the Group. The provision of the tax investigation service should also be discussed, and the audit committee's approval for Montreal & Co to provide the service should be obtained, depending on the materiality of the matter to the financial statements and the deployment of safeguards to reduce threats to an acceptable level.

Conclusion

These briefing notes have provided an assessment of the audit risks to be considered in planning the audit of the Vancouver Group, including analytical procedures and an explanation of the need for these procedures to be performed. There are several significant threats to our firm's objectivity which need to be discussed with the client prior to the audit fieldwork commencing.

Examiner's comments

The question followed the pattern of previous examinations and was set at the planning stage of the audit and candidates were presented with three requirements, which covered the use of analytical procedures at planning, identifying audit risks and ethics.

Candidates were asked to explain why analytical procedures are a fundamental part of audit planning and this requirement was generally well-answered by the majority of candidates. Good answers were tailored to the specifics of the situation and provided relevant examples.

Candidates were the required to identify audit risks, including through the use of analytical procedures. The best answers demonstrated that a methodical approach had been applied to the information in the scenario, and strong candidates had clearly worked through the information logically, calculating the key ratios and trends from the information provided, identifying the risk factors from the calculations and the remaining information, assessing materiality before going on to explain the risk fully and specifically in terms of how the risk could impact the financial statements. Candidates are reminded that when discussing risk relating to a specific accounting treatment, well explained answers will include an evaluation of the potential impact of the risk factor on the financial statements. A disappointing number of candidates failed to calculate any ratios or trends from the information supplied and thus provided weak answers and were unable to identify an appropriate number of audit risks for the marks available. Conversely some candidates calculated every trend or ratio possible, which was excessive and demonstrated poor time management; for example there was insufficient information in the question to calculate inventory or trade payable days so these ratios did not add to their answer.

Audit risk continues to be an area that candidates find difficult and particularly it continues to be noted that many candidates fail to engage with the information provided in enough depth, specifically when provided with extracts from financial statements. Candidates are again reminded that in order to provide a full answer in relation to audit risk they should utilise and analyse all the information that is provided.

Finally candidates were required to discuss the ethical issues relevant to the audit firm and to recommend any necessary actions. Performance in this area was mixed and it was clear that many candidates did not know the requirements of the Code of Ethics. For example a sizeable number of candidates advised that the audit engagement partner could simultaneously become a non-executive director on the audit committee of the entity under audit and failed to identify that the Code expressly prohibits this due to the extent of the self-review and self-interest threats which would be created. This demonstrates a lack of knowledge of the ethical requirements and a lack of professional judgment. Candidates are reminded that they must revise and be comfortable with the content of the code of ethics. Most candidates were however, able to highlight that there was a potential advocacy and self-review risk from representing the client in a tax enquiry but did not condition this on either grounds of materiality or that the firm had not been previously involved in the client's tax affairs.

There were four professional marks available and most candidates were able to earn the presentation marks by providing a clear introduction and conclusion and using headings to create an appropriate structure for their answer. Many candidates did not articulate their points in a clear or logical order and therefore many missed out on the logical flow and clarity marks.

ACCA Marking scheme		
		Marks
(a)	**Analytical procedures and risk assessment** Generally up to 1½ marks for each point explained: – Definition/examples of analytical procedure – Helps to identify risk of material misstatement – Helps to develop business understanding – Helps in developing the audit strategy and audit plan	
	Maximum	**5**
(b)	**Audit risk evaluation** Generally 1 mark for each ratio (including comparative) calculated, and ½ mark for relevant trends calculated, up to a maximum of 5 marks. In addition, up to 1 mark for discussion of audit risks in relation to the ratios calculated. Risks in relation to ratio analysis could include: – Overstatement of operating expenses – Overstatement of revenue due to finance director's comments – Interest cover and risk relating to disclosure – –Change in effective tax rates and risk tax expense incorrect – Ongoing investigation and risk of fines and penalties which need to be provided for – Liquidity issues and risk relating to disclosure – Increase in receivables days and overstatement of trade receivables – Onerous lease provision has halved in value, risk of understatement of liability	

	Other audit risks – up to 1½ marks for each risk identified and explained: – Allow 1 mark for each correct calculation and comment on materiality – Whether capital and revenue expenditure appropriately accounted for in respect of the modernisation programme – Whether assets have been accounted for using the concept of significant components – Treatment of borrowing costs and whether eligible for capitalisation – –The gain on disposal of shares in Calgary Co is incorrectly recognised in profit for the year – Non-controlling interest has not been disclosed in respect of profit for the year – Risk of inadequate disclosure regarding the rationale for, and consequences of, the share disposal – Risk of overstatement of goodwill as no evidence of impairment review – Management bias due to sale of shares to institutional investor – Deferred tax – risk of overstatement if the amount is not a recoverable asset – Lack of financial reporting expert on the Group audit committee increases the risk of incorrect accounting treatments	
	Maximum	**18**
(c)	**Ethical issues** Generally up to 1 mark for each relevant matter discussed: – Advocacy threat (1 mark where risk is explained) – Self-review threat (1 mark where risk is explained) – Extent of threat lessened because another firm provided the tax planning – Consider the materiality of the matter to the FS – If matter is immaterial, then the service can be provided as long as safeguards in place (1 mark for each safeguard suggested) – Where matter is material, the service should not be provided – Appointment of audit partner to audit committee creates objectivity threat – Code prohibits appointment of audit firm member as director of audit client – Matters to be discussed with client's audit committee and the audit firm's ethical partner	
	Maximum	**8**
	Professional marks Generally 1 mark for heading, 1 mark for introduction, 1 mark for use of headings within the briefing notes, 1 mark for clarity of comments made	
	Maximum	**4**
Total		**35**

3 DALI *Walk in the footsteps of a top tutor*

Top tutor tips

Part (a) asks for audit risks and additional information needed to help evaluate audit risk. Audit risk comprises the risk that the financial statements contain material misstatement and detection risk. Risk of material misstatement is usually due to non-compliance with an accounting standard. Think about the requirements of the relevant accounting standards and what the client might be doing incorrectly. Detection risks include auditing a client for the first time or where there is a tight reporting deadline.

Additional information is essentially the evidence you would gather in respect of the risks. For example, with the government grant you would want a copy of the grant terms and conditions to assess whether the grant conditions had been met. Where there is a subsequent requirement for audit procedures as in part (b), these are areas of audit risk that should be included in your answer to part (a).

Part (b) asks for procedures in respect of work in progress and the government grant. Procedures should be specific in terms of what the auditor needs to do to obtain the evidence they need.

Briefing notes

To: **Audit partner**

From: **Audit manager**

Subject: **Audit planning in respect of Dali Co**

Introduction

These briefing notes are prepared to assist in the audit planning meeting for Dali Co, our manufacturing client supplying machinery and equipment to the quarrying industry. The notes contain an evaluation of audit risk along with recommendations of the additional information which is relevant to audit risk evaluation. The notes also explain the principal audit procedures to be performed in respect of the valuation of work in progress, and the government grant received during the year.

(a) (i) Audit risk evaluation

Stock exchange listing and pressure on results

The listing obtained during the year can create inherent risk at the financial statement level because management may feel under pressure to achieve good results in this financial year.

The flotation raised equity capital, so there will be new shareholders who will want to see strong performance in the expectation of a dividend pay-out.

In addition, the introduction of the cash-settled share-based payment plan motivates management to produce financial statements which show a favourable performance and position which is likely to lead to an increase in the company's share price.

There is a risk that revenue and profits may be overstated. Revenue has increased by 2.2% and profit before tax by 6.5%, which may indicate overstatement.

Disclosure for listed companies

This is the first set of financial statements produced since Dali Co became listed.

There is a risk that the new finance director will not be familiar with the requirements specific to listed companies, for example, the company now falls under the scope of IAS 33 *Earnings per Share* and IFRS 8 *Operating Segments* for the first time. There is a risk of incomplete or inaccurate disclosures in respect of these standards and also in respect of any listing rules in the jurisdiction in which the company is listed.

Foreign exchange transactions

Dali Co purchases many components from foreign suppliers and is therefore likely to be transacting and making payments in foreign currencies.

According to IAS ® 21 *The Effects of Changes in Foreign Exchange Rates*, transactions should be initially recorded using the spot rate, and monetary items such as trade payables should be retranslated at the year-end using the closing rate. Exchange gains and losses should be recognised within profit for the year.

The risk is that the incorrect exchange rate is used for the translation and retranslation, or that the retranslation does not happen at the year end, in which case trade payables and profit could be over or understated, depending on the movement in the exchange rate. The company may have entered into hedging arrangements as a way to reduce exposure to foreign exchange fluctuations.

There is a risk that hedging arrangements are not identified and accounted for as derivatives according to IFRS ® 9 *Financial Instruments* which could mean incomplete recognition of derivative financial assets or liabilities and associated gains or losses.

Payment in advance and revenue recognition under contract with customers

For items where significant design work is needed, Dali Co receives a payment in advance. This gives rise to risk in terms of when that part of the revenue generated from a sale of goods is recognised.

According to IFRS 15 *Revenue from Contracts with Customers*, revenue should only be recognised as control is passed, either over time or at a point in time. The timing of revenue recognition will depend on the contractual terms with the customer, with factors which may indicate the point in time at which control passes including the transference of the physical asset, transference of legal title, and the customer accepting the significant risks and rewards related to the ownership of the asset.

It is likely that the payments in advance should be treated as deferred revenue at the point when the payment is received as the conditions for recognition of revenue are unlikely to have been met at this point in time.

There is a risk that revenue is recognised too early, especially given the risk of management bias and the incentive to overstate revenue and profit as discussed above.

There is additional audit risk created if a customer were to cancel a contract part way through its completion, the bespoke work in progress may be worthless and would need to be written off according to IAS 2 *Inventories*. There is therefore a risk of overstated work in progress.

New directors

During the year several new non-executive directors were appointed, as well as a new finance director.

While this may serve to strengthen the corporate governance structure including the control environment, equally the introduction of new personnel could mean inexperience and a control risk, particularly if the finance director is lacking in experience.

Some of the suggestions and accounting treatments made by the finance director indicate that their knowledge of the applicable financial reporting framework is weak, signalling that errors may occur in the preparation of the financial statements.

Cash-settled share-based payment scheme

This falls under the scope of IFRS 2 *Share-based Payment* which states that the liability in respect of the plan should be measured at fair value at the year end.

The increase in the share price from $2.90 at flotation to $3.50 (projected) at the year-end indicates that a liability should be recognised at 31 December 2015 based on the fair value of the liability which has accrued up to that date, with the expense recognised in the statement of profit or loss.

This accounting treatment has not been followed leading to understated liabilities and overstated profit, and the disclosure in respect of the plan may not be sufficient to meet the requirements of IFRS 2 which requires extensive disclosures including the effect of share-based payment transactions on the entity's profit or loss for the period and on its financial position.

Revaluation of property

The decision to revalue the company's manufacturing sites creates several risks. First, revaluation involves establishing a current market price or fair value for each property included in the revaluation, which can be a subjective exercise, leading to inherent risk that the valuations may not be appropriate.

A risk also arises in that IAS 16 *Property, Plant and Equipment* requires all assets in the same class to be revalued, so if any properties which are manufacturing sites have not been included in the revaluation exercise, the amounts recognised will not be correct.

There is also a risk that depreciation has not been recalculated on the new, higher value of the properties, leading to overstatement of non-current assets and understatement of operating expenses.

IAS 16 also requires a significant level of disclosure in relation to a policy of revaluation, so there is a risk that the necessary disclosures are incomplete.

The revaluation gain recognised in equity represents 3.9% of total assets and is therefore material to the financial statements.

Deferred tax recognition

IAS 12 *Income Taxes* requires deferred tax to be recognised in respect of taxable temporary differences which arise between the carrying amount and tax base of assets and liabilities, including the differences which arise on the revaluation of non-current assets, regardless of whether the assets are likely to be disposed of in the foreseeable future.

The finance director's suggestion that deferred tax should not be provided for is therefore incorrect, and at present liabilities are understated, representing an error in the statement of financial position.

There is no profit impact, however, as the deferred tax would be recognised in equity.

Depending on the rate of tax which would be used to determine the necessary provision, it may not be material to the financial statements.

Government grant recognition

The government grant represents 11.1% of total assets and is material to the financial statements.

A risk arises in relation to the recognition of the grant. IAS 20 *Accounting for Government Grants and Disclosure of Government Assistance* requires that a grant is recognised as income over the period necessary to match the grant received with the related costs for which they are intended to compensate.

Therefore, the $2 million relating to costs incurred this year should be recognised as income, but the remainder should be released to profit on a systematic basis; in this case it would seem appropriate to release on a straight line basis until July 2020.

The risk is that the grant has been recognised on an inappropriate basis leading to over or understated profit for the year. The part of the grant not recognised in profit should be recognised in the statement of financial position.

IAS 20 allows classification as deferred income, or alternatively the amount can be netted against the assets to which the grant relates. There is therefore also a risk that the amount is recognised elsewhere in the statement of financial position, leading to incorrect presentation and disclosure.

If the terms of the grant have been breached, the grant or an element of it may need to be repaid. There is therefore a risk that if there is any breach, the associated provision for repayment is not recognised, understating liabilities.

Inventory valuation

Work in progress is material at 13.3% of total assets and has increased by 26.3% in the current year.

The valuation of work in progress is likely to be complex as many different jobs for different customers are ongoing at the year end, and each will have a different stage of completion and cost base at the year end.

There are also issues more generally with the valuation of inventory, due to the customer returns of items which have recently occurred showing that there are problems with the quality of the goods supplied.

For items which have been returned, the net realisable value is likely to be less than the cost of the item indicating that a write-off may be necessary to reduce the value of the inventory according to IAS 2.

The increase in the inventory holding period, as demonstrated by the increase in inventory days, shows that inventory has become more slow-moving during the year also indicating that inventory may be overstated.

Provision in respect of returned goods

A provision should be recognised where a reliable estimate can be made in relation to a probable outflow of economic resources and an obligating event has taken place.

The fact that Dali Co replaces faulty products free of charge indicates that a provision should be recognised based on the best estimate of the future economic outflow.

The risk is that no provision or an insufficient provision in relation to the warranty has been recognised, leading to understated liabilities and operating expenses.

Working capital

The preliminary analytical review reveals that Dali Co is struggling to manage its working capital. The liquidity ratios provided show that the operating cycle has increased from 165 days in 2014 to 205 days in 2015.

The company may be finding it difficult to collect cash from customers, as the receivables period has increased by 20 days, and in turn the payment period to suppliers has increased by five days.

If there is doubt over the collectability of receivables, then certain balances may need to be written off, and there is a risk of overstatement of receivables and understatement of operating expenses if bad debts are not recognised.

Tutorial note

Credit will be awarded for other relevant audit risks.

(ii) Recommended additional information

- Details of the stock exchange listing during the year including the terms of the flotation, number of equity shares issued and amount of equity capital raised.
- Any information available in relation to the flotation, for example, investor prospectus, pre- and post-flotation press releases, communications with the stock exchange registrar.
- Information on the specific listing rules relevant to the stock exchange, for example, the corporate governance code and disclosures necessary in company annual reports and financial statements.
- Details on the planned foreign stock exchange listing in 2016 including the jurisdiction, the strategic rationale for seeking the listing and proposed timescales.

- Information on the background and experience of the new non-executive directors and the new finance director, for example, their professional qualifications and previous employment or directorships held.
- A full set of forecast financial statements including a statement of cash flows to assess the working capital issues faced by the company.
- Details on the valuation of properties including the date of the revaluation and information on the valuer such as their professional qualification and relationship with the company and a copy of the valuation report.
- Documentation on the cash-settled share-based payment scheme to gauge the number of members of the scheme and its potential materiality to the financial statements.

> ***Tutorial note***
>
> *Credit will be awarded for other relevant information which would be available at this stage of the audit to help in the evaluation of audit risk.*

(b) (i) Audit procedures in respect of the valuation of work in progress

- Obtain a schedule itemising the jobs included in work in progress at the year end, cast it and agree the total to the general ledger and draft financial statements.
- Agree a sample of items from the schedule to the inventory count records.
- For a sample of jobs included on the schedule:
  - Agree costs to supporting documentation such as supplier's invoice and payroll records;
  - For any overheads absorbed into the work in progress valuation, review the basis of the absorption and assess its reasonableness;
  - Assess how the degree of completion of the job has been determined at the year end and agree the stage of completion of the job to records taken at the inventory count;
  - Agree the details of the job specification to customer order; and
  - Confirm that net realisable value is greater than cost by agreeing the contract price and cash received from the customer post year end.
- To assess the completeness of work in progress, select a sample of customer orders and trace through to the list of jobs included in work in progress.

(ii) Audit procedures in respect of the recognition and measurement of the government grant

- Obtain the documentation relating to the grant to confirm the amount, the date the cash was received, and the terms on which the grant was awarded.
- Review the documentation for any conditions attached to the grant, for example, is there a requirement that a certain number of people are employed at the manufacturing plant?
- Discuss with management the method of recognition of the amount received, in particular how much of the grant has been recognised in profit and the treatment of the amount deferred in the statement of financial position.
- For the part of the grant relating to wages and salaries, confirm that the grant criteria have been complied with by examining payroll records and timesheets to verify that $2m has been spent on wages in the deprived area.
- For the part of the grant relating to continued operation of the manufacturing site, determine the basis on which this is being released into profit and recalculate to confirm accuracy of management's calculations.
- Review forecasts and budgets in relation to the manufacturing site to assess the likelihood of its continued operations until 2020.
- Using the draft financial statements, confirm the accounting treatment outlined by discussion with management has been applied and recalculate the amounts recognised.
- Confirm the cash received to bank statement and cash book.

Conclusion

These briefing notes indicate that there are many areas of potential audit risk to be considered when developing the audit strategy for Dali Co, and that additional information should be requested from the client to be obtained as soon as possible to facilitate a more in-depth evaluation of certain audit risks identified. The audit procedures recommended in respect of work in progress and the government grant received will provide assurance on these significant issues.

Examiner's comments

Candidates were required to provide an analysis of audit risks for a manufacturer of bespoke and generic machines. Performance on this requirement was good with the majority of candidates correctly describing audit risks rather than business risks. This is an area that most candidates are well prepared on, however stronger answers were able to develop and apply the relevant accounting treatment. Those able to identify specific areas of the financial statements which would be affected and to correctly identify whether the risk was over or understatement tended to score the strongest marks. A significant minority of candidates thought that the client was new to the firm as opposed to simply having a change in manager and spent time addressing opening balances and new client procedures which were not relevant to the question. Candidates are again reminded to read the question carefully and consider the context of the scenario both in terms of client history and timeframe before answering the question.

Candidates were further required to provide additional information needed to effectively plan the audit and candidates showed a marked improvement over previous sittings where this requirement has been examined. This type of question requires candidates to identify information that would be available in advance of the audit that would assist in the planning of the audit. Such information would generally help in the identification or evaluation of risks rather than the information available at the year-end for performing audit procedures. This is particularly relevant as the question was set almost a month prior to the year-end so financial statements and year-end balances would not yet be available.

Candidates were further required to provide audit procedures for the valuation of work in progress (WIP) and a government grant. With respect to the former, candidates often cited the need for an expert to value WIP rather than focusing on the components of cost and NRV in the machines. Similarly, there were a number of candidates who requested written representations from management on WIP despite the figure not being an issue where the knowledge was confined to management or one of management's intentions.

Candidates are once again reminded that a written representation is not a suitable substitute for sufficient appropriate evidence. The audit procedures relevant to the grant were generally well described.

There were four professional marks available, and most candidates secured most of these marks by providing an introduction and using headings to create an appropriate structure for their answer. However, presentation was not always good and candidates are reminded to pay attention to determining an appropriate layout for their answer.

ACCA marking scheme

			Marks
(a)	(i)	Evaluation of audit risks Up to 2 marks for each audit risk evaluated, and 1 mark for relevant calculations (e.g. materiality, trends): – Stock exchange listing and pressure on results – Disclosure for listed companies – Foreign exchange transactions and potential derivatives (up to 3 marks) – Payment in advance and revenue recognition – Potential for cancelled contracts and implication for valuation of work in progress – New directors – Cash-settled share-based payment scheme – Revaluation of property – Deferred tax recognition – Government grant recognition and potential for repayment if terms are breached – Inventory valuation – Provision in respect of returned goods – Working capital	
		Maximum	**18**
	(ii)	Additional information 1 mark for each relevant piece of relevant information recommended. The list below is indicative, and credit should be given for other relevant recommendations: – Details of the stock exchange listing during the year – Information on the specific listing rules relevant to the stock exchange – Details on the planned foreign stock exchange listing – Information on the background and experience of the new non-executive directors and the new finance director	

	– A full set of draft financial statements including a statement of cash flows – Details on the valuation of properties such as date of valuation and name of the valuer – Documentation on the cash-settled share-based payment scheme	
	Maximum	**5**

(b)	(i) Audit procedures on the valuation of work in progress
	1 mark for each well explained audit procedure:
	– Obtain a schedule itemising the jobs included in work in progress at the year end, cast it and agree the total to the general ledger and draft financial statements
	– Agree a sample of items from the schedule to the inventory count records
	– For a sample of jobs included on the schedule:
	  – Agree costs to supporting documentation such as supplier's invoice and payroll records
	  – For any overheads absorbed into the work in progress valuation, review the basis of the absorption and assess its reasonableness
	  – Assess how the degree of completion of the job has been determined at the year end and agree the stage of completion of the job to records taken at the inventory count
	  – Agree the details of the job specification to customer order
	  – Confirm that net realisable value is greater than cost by agreeing the contract price and cash received from the customer post year end
	– To assess the completeness of work in progress, select a sample of customer orders and trace through to the list of jobs included in work in progress	

	Maximum	**4**
	(ii) Audit procedures in respect of the government grant 1 mark for each well explained audit procedure: – Obtain the documentation relating to the grant to confirm the amount, the date the cash was received, and the terms on which the grant was awarded – Review the documentation for any conditions attached to the grant, for example, is there a requirement that a certain number of people are employed at the manufacturing plant? – Discuss with management the method of recognition of the amount received, in particular how much of the grant has been recognised in profit and the treatment of the amount deferred in the statement of financial position – For the part of the grant relating to continued operation of the manufacturing plant, determine the basis on which this is being released into profit, assess its reasonableness and recalculate to confirm accuracy of management's calculations – Review forecasts and budgets in relation to the manufacturing plant to assess the likelihood of its continued operations until 2020 – Using the draft financial statements, confirm the accounting treatment outlined by discussion with management has been applied and recalculate the amounts recognised – Confirm the cash received to bank statement and cash book	
	Maximum	**4**
	Professional marks for headings, introduction, conclusion and quality of explanations provided	4
Total		**35**

4 TED *Walk in the footsteps of a top tutor*

Top tutor tips

Part (a) asks for matters to consider when developing the audit strategy for a new audit client. Think of the elements included in an audit strategy and then tailor this to a new audit client.

Part (b) focuses on audit risk, i.e. the risk that the financial statements contain material misstatement or detection risk. Risk of material misstatement is usually due to non-compliance with an accounting standard. Think about the requirements of the relevant accounting standard and what the client might be doing incorrectly. Detection risks include auditing a client for the first time or where there is a tight reporting deadline.

Part (c) asks for procedures in respect of the portfolio of short term investments and EPS. Procedures should be specific in terms of what the auditor needs to do to obtain the evidence they need. Where there is a requirement asking for procedures, these are items of potential risk and should therefore have been included in your answer for audit risks.

Briefing notes

To: **Jack Hackett, audit partner**

From: **Audit manager**

Subject: **Audit planning of Ted Co**

Introduction

These briefing notes are prepared for the use of the audit team in planning the audit of Ted Co, our firm's new audit client which develops and publishes computer games. The briefing notes discuss the planning matters in respect of this being an initial audit engagement; evaluate the audit risks to be considered in planning the audit; and recommend audit procedures in respect of short-term investments and the earnings per share figure disclosed in the draft financial statements.

(a) In an initial audit engagement there are several factors which should be considered in addition to the planning procedures which are carried out for every audit. ISA 300 *Planning an Audit of Financial Statements* provides guidance in this area.

Review of predecessor auditor's working papers

Unless prohibited by laws or regulation, arrangements should be made with the predecessor auditor, for example, to review their working papers. Therefore communication should be made with Crilly & Co to request access to their working papers for the financial year ended 31 May 2014. The review of the previous year's working papers would help Craggy & Co in planning the audit, for example, it may highlight matters pertinent to the audit of opening balances or an assessment of the appropriateness of Ted Co's accounting policies.

It will also be important to consider whether any previous years' auditors' reports were modified, and if so, the reason for the modification.

Professional clearance

As part of the client acceptance process, professional clearance should have been sought from Crilly & Co. Any matters which were brought to our firm's attention when professional clearance was obtained should be considered for their potential impact on the audit strategy.

There should also be consideration of the matters which were discussed with Ted Co's management in connection with the appointment of Craggy & Co as auditors. For example, there may have been discussion of significant accounting policies which may impact on the planned audit strategy.

Opening balances

Particular care should be taken in planning the audit procedures necessary to obtain sufficient appropriate audit evidence regarding opening balances, and procedures should be planned in accordance with ISA 510 *Initial Audit Engagements – Opening Balances*.

For example, procedures should be performed to determine whether the opening balances reflect the application of appropriate accounting policies and determining whether the prior period's closing balances have been correctly brought forward into the current period.

Understanding of the business

With an initial audit engagement it is particularly important to develop an understanding of the business, including the legal and regulatory framework applicable to the company. This understanding must be fully documented and will help the audit team to perform effective analytical review procedures and to develop an appropriate audit strategy. Obtaining knowledge of the business will also help to identify whether it will be necessary to plan for the use of auditors' experts.

Independent review partner

Craggy & Co may have quality control procedures in place for use in the case of initial engagements, for example, the involvement of another partner or senior individual to review the overall audit strategy prior to commencing significant audit procedures. Compliance with any such procedures should be fully documented.

Audit team

Given that this is a new audit client, that it is newly listed, and because of other risk factors to be discussed in the next part of these briefing notes, when developing the audit strategy consideration should be given to using an experienced audit team in order to reduce detection risk.

(b) Management bias

The first audit risk identified relates to Ted Co becoming a listed entity during the year. This creates an inherent risk at the financial statement level and is caused by the potential for management bias. Management will want to show good results to the new shareholders of the company, in particular the institutional shareholders, and therefore there is an incentive for the overstatement of revenue and profit. The analytical review shows a significant increase in profit before tax of 48.1%, indicating potential overstatement.

There is a related risk of overstatement due to Dougal Doyle and his family members retaining a 30% equity interest in Ted Co, which is an incentive for inflated profit so that a high level of dividend can be paid.

It appears that governance structures are not strong, for example, there are too few non-executive directors, and therefore Dougal Doyle is in a position to be able to dominate the board and to influence the preparation of the financial statements. This increases the risk of material misstatement due to management bias.

There is also a risk that management lacks knowledge of the reporting requirements specific to listed entities, for example, in relation to the calculation and disclosure of earnings per share which is discussed later in these briefing notes.

E-commerce

With 25% of revenue generated through the company's website, this represents a significant revenue stream, and the income generated through e-commerce is material to the financial statements. E-commerce gives rise to a number of different audit risks, including but not limited to the following. For the auditor, e-commerce can give rise to detection risk, largely due to the paperless nature of the transactions and the fact there is likely to be a limited audit trail, making it difficult to obtain audit evidence.

For the same reason, control risk is increased, as it can be hard to maintain robust controls unless they are embedded into the software which records the transaction. The auditor may find it difficult to perform tests on the controls of the system unless audit software is used, as there will be few manual controls to evaluate.

A risk also arises in terms of the recognition of sales revenue, in particular cut-off can be a problem where sales are made online as it can be difficult to determine the exact point at which the revenue recognition criteria of IFRS 15 *Revenue from contracts with customers* have been met. Hence, over or understatement of revenue is a potential risk to be considered when planning the audit.

Ted Co also faces risks relating to the security of the system, for example, risks relating to unauthorised access to the system, and there is an increased risk of fraud. All of these risks mean that there is high audit risk in relation to the revenue generated from the company's website.

Licence income

The licence income which is deferred in the statement of financial position represents 13.4% of total assets and is therefore material.

There is a risk that the accounting treatment is not appropriate, and there are two separate risks which need to be considered. First, it may be the case that the revenue from the sale of a licence should not be deferred at all. The revenue recognition criteria of IFRS 15 need to be applied to the transaction, and if, for example, it were found that Ted Co has no continuing management involvement and that all risk and reward had been transferred to the buyer, then the revenue should be recognised immediately and not deferred. This would mean a significant understatement of revenue and profit.

Second, if it is appropriate that the revenue is deferred, for example, if Ted Co does retain managerial involvement and has retained the risk and reward in relation to the licence arrangement, then the period over which the revenue is recognised could be inappropriate, resulting in over or understated revenue in the accounting period.

Foreign exchange transactions

Ted Co's products sell in over 60 countries and the products are manufactured overseas, so the company is involved with foreign currency transactions which can be complex in nature. There is a risk that the requirements of IAS 21 *The Effects of Changes in Foreign Exchange Rates* have not been followed. For example, if transactions have not been retranslated to Ted Co's functional currency at the date of the transaction, then the amounts involved may be over or understated. There is also a risk that outstanding receivables and payables have not been retranslated at the year-end closing exchange rate, leading to over or understatement of assets and liabilities and unrecorded exchange gains or losses.

The treasury management function is involved with forward exchange contracts, meaning that derivatives exist and should be accounted for in accordance with IFRS 9 *Financial Instruments*. This is a complex accounting issue, and there are numerous audit risks arising. There is a risk that not all forward exchange contracts are identified, leading to incomplete recording of the balances involved. There is also a risk in determining the fair value of the derivative at the year end, as this can be judgmental and requires specialist knowledge. There is also a risk that hedge accounting rules have not been properly applied, or that inadequate disclosure of relevant risks is made in the notes to the financial statements.

Portfolio of equity shares

The cost of the portfolio of investments represents 6% of total assets and is material to the statement of financial position. The fall in value of the portfolio of $2 million represents 25% of profit before tax, and is therefore material to the statement of profit or loss.

The investment portfolio is recognised at cost, but this is not the correct measurement basis. The investments should be accounted for in accordance with IFRS 9 which requires financial assets to be classified and then measured subsequent to initial recognition at either amortised cost or at fair value through profit or loss. Speculative investments in equity shares should be measured at fair value through profit or loss because the assets are not being held to collect contractual cash flows. It seems that the current accounting treatment is incorrect in that assets are overstated, and it is significant that the draft profit for the year is overstated by $2 million.

Further, there is a new team dealing with these complex treasury management transactions involving financial instruments. There may be a lack of knowledge and experience which adds to the risks outlined above in relation to the foreign exchange transactions, derivatives and portfolio of equity shares.

Earnings per share

Ted Co must calculate and disclose its earnings per share figure (EPS) in accordance with IAS 33 *Earnings per Share*. It appears that the calculation has not been performed in accordance with the requirements of the standard and is incorrect. IAS 33 requires EPS to be calculated based on the profit or loss for the year attributable to ordinary shareholders as presented in the statement of profit or loss, but in the draft financial statements it has been calculated based on an adjusted profit figure. This is not in accordance with IAS 33, which only allows EPS based on an alternative profit figure to be disclosed in the notes to the financial statements as an additional figure, and should not be disclosed on the face of the financial statements. The earnings figure used as the basis of the calculation should also not be based on profit before tax but on the post-tax profit.

In addition, it appears that the denominator used in the EPS calculation is incorrect. It should be based on the weighted average number of shares which were in issue during the financial year, but the calculation shows that it is based on the number of shares in issue at the year end. Due to the share issue in December 2014, the weighted average will need to be determined and used in the calculation.

There is a risk relating to inadequate disclosure, for example, a diluted EPS needs to be presented, as does a comparative for the previous year. The incorrect calculation and disclosure of EPS is a significant issue, especially given the company becoming listed during the year, which will focus the attention of investors on the EPS this year.

Rapid growth

The analytical review which has been performed indicates rapid growth has occurred during the year. Revenue has increased by 46.3%, and profit before tax by 48.1%. The growth in the number of transactions could indicate a control risk, in that systems and personnel may struggle to keep pace with the volume of transactions which are being processed, leading to accounting errors being made. This is exacerbated by the lack of an internal audit department to provide assurance on systems and controls.

Profit margins

The trend in gross profit and operating profit margins could indicate a misstatement. The ratios are as follows:

	2015			*2014*		
Gross margin	65,000/98,000	=	66.3%	40,000/67,000	=	59.7%
Operating margin	12,000/98,000	=	12.2%	9,200/67,000	=	13.7%

The increase in the gross margin at the same time as the decrease in the operating margin could indicate that expenses such as depreciation and amortisation have been misclassified between cost of sales and other operating expenses. The disproportionate changes in the two margins could also indicate that cost of sales is understated, for example, due to incomplete recording of expenses.

Intangible assets – development costs

There has been a significant increase in the amount of development costs capitalised as an intangible asset. There is a risk that this amount is overstated. Development costs should only be recognised as an asset when the criteria for capitalisation from IAS 38 Intangible Assets have been met. For example, the ability of the development costs to generate economic benefit should be demonstrated, along with the existence of resources to complete the development.

As discussed earlier, there is an incentive for management to maximise profits, so it would be in management's interests to capitalise as much of the development costs as possible. The intangible asset currently recognised represents 43.3% of total assets, and is highly material to the financial statements.

Inventory

Any year-end inventory counts held at the overseas manufacturing locations will already have taken place, so the audit strategy should focus on alternative methods of obtaining evidence regarding the existence of inventories at the year end. Due to the overseas locations of inventory counts, a detection risk may be created from the fact that it may not be possible for the audit firm to attend any inventory counts which take place at a later date.

Opening balances

As this is an initial audit engagement, our firm should be alert to the fact that opening balances may be misstated. There is no evidence that the previous audit firm were lacking in competence, and the audit opinion for the prior year was unmodified, but there is the risk that inappropriate accounting policies have been used, and that opening balances may not be correct.

(c) (i) Audit procedures on the portfolio of short-term investments

- Agree the fair value of the shares held as investments to stock market share price listings at 31 May 2015.
- Confirm the original cost of the investment to cash book and bank statements.
- Discuss the accounting treatment with management and confirm that an adjustment will be made to recognise the shares at fair value.
- Review the notes to the financial statements to ensure that disclosure is sufficient to comply with the requirements of IFRS 9.
- Enquire with the treasury management function as to whether there have been any disposals of the original shares held and reinvestment of proceeds into the portfolio.
- Review board minutes to confirm the authorisation and approval of the amount invested.
- Review documentation relating to the scope and procedures of the new treasury management function, for example, to understand how the performance of investments is monitored.
- For any investments from which dividends have been received, confirm the number of shares held to supporting documentation such as dividend received certificates or vouchers.

(ii) Audit procedures on earnings per share

- Discuss with management the requirements of IAS 33 and request that management recalculates the EPS in accordance with those requirements.
- Review board minutes to confirm the authorisation of the issue of share capital, the number of shares and the price at which they were issued.
- Inspect any other supporting documentation for the share issue, such as a share issue prospectus or documentation submitted to the relevant regulatory body.
- Confirm that the share issue complies with the company's legal documentation (e.g. the memorandum and articles of association).
- Recalculate the weighted average number of shares for the year to 31 May 2015.
- Recalculate EPS using the profit as disclosed in the statement of profit or loss and the weighted average number of shares.

- Discuss with management the existence of any factors which may impact on the calculation and disclosure of a diluted EPS figure, for example, convertible bonds.
- Read the notes to the financial statements in respect of EPS to confirm that disclosure is complete and accurate and complies with IAS 33.

Tutorial note

Credit will be awarded for other, relevant audit procedures recommended.

Conclusion

These briefing notes have shown that the audit risk of this engagement is relatively high, largely due to the existence of potential management bias, rapid growth and a number of complex balances and transactions. As this is our firm's first audit of Ted Co, an audit strategy needs to be developed to focus on these areas, as well as dealing with the additional planning issues which arise on an initial audit engagement.

Examiner's comments

This question was set in the planning phase of the audit of a new audit client, Ted Co. The company was a computer games designer and publisher which had experienced significant growth in recent years, and had become listed in its home jurisdiction during the financial year. Information was provided on the company's financial background, its operations and corporate governance structure. Extracts from the financial statements were provided along with the Earnings per Share (EPS) figure calculated by the company's finance director.

The first requirement asked candidates to discuss the matters specific to an initial audit engagement which should be considered in developing the audit strategy. Given that Ted Co was a new audit client this was a very relevant requirement. The answers were very mixed in quality, with the best answers concentrating on practical matters such as reviewing the previous audit firm's working papers, planning procedures to obtain evidence on opening balances, and ensuring that the audit team developed a thorough understanding of the business.

Unfortunately the majority of candidates provided generic answers discussing whether or not the firm could take on the audit, engagement letters, fees, customer due diligence and checking to see if the previous auditors had been correctly removed from office. It was not relevant to discuss whether the audit firm should take on the client and associated acceptance issues as it was clearly expressed in the scenario that this decision had already been taken and consequently answers of this nature scored limited credit.

Other weaker answers discussed general audit planning matters such as the need to determine a materiality level. This was not tailored to the specifics of this scenario as this would be relevant for any audit. Candidates are reminded to answer the specific question that has been set, which in this case should have meant answers focusing on matters relevant to planning an initial audit engagement after the engagement has been accepted.

Some candidates wrote a lot for the marks available. Candidates are reminded that the marks for each requirement are a guide as to how long should be spent on answering the question. In some cases the answers to Q1 (a) ran to several pages, leading to time pressure on subsequent answers.

Requirement (b) asked candidates to evaluate the audit risks to be considered in planning the audit. There were some excellent answers to this requirement, with many responses covering a range of audit risks, all well explained, and all relevant to the scenario. The best answers demonstrated that a methodical approach had been applied to the information in the scenario, and the better candidates had clearly worked through the information logically, identifying the risk factors, then going on to explain them fully and specifically. The audit risks that were generally dealt with well included those relating to the foreign currency transactions and to the portfolio of short term investments. The risk relating to whether research and development costs could be capitalised was also identified by the majority of candidates, but the issue of amortisation was not often discussed.

To achieve a good mark for this type of requirement, candidates should look for a range of audit risks, some of which are risks of material misstatement and some are detection risks. Candidates however do not need to categorise the risks they are discussing or to spend time explaining the components of the audit risk model.

When discussing audit risks relating to a specific accounting treatment, well explained answers will include an evaluation of the potential impact of the risk factor on the financial statements, for example, in this scenario there was a risk that the short term investments were overstated in value and that profit also was overstated. Materiality should be calculated when possible, as this allows prioritisation of the risks identified. Strong candidates, as well as providing detailed analysis and explanation of the risks, also attempted to prioritise the various risks identified thus demonstrating appropriate judgment and an understanding that the audit partner would want to know about the most significant risks first. Candidates are reminded that it is those risks that could result in a material misstatement in the financial statements, which need to be identified and addressed.

Weak answers included answer points that were too vague to be awarded credit. Comments such as 'there is a risk this has not been accounted for properly', 'there is risk that this is not properly disclosed' and 'there is a risk that the accounting standard has not been followed' are unfortunately too common and will not earn marks due to the lack of specificity. It would be beneficial for candidates to review their answers and to consider whether what they have written would provide the audit engagement partner with the necessary knowledge to understand the risk profile of the client in question.

Other common weaknesses in answers include the following points:

- Discussing business risks instead of audit risks – in particular business risks relating to theft of inventory, security issues in relation to e-commerce and exposure to foreign currency fluctuations were often discussed, sometimes in a lot of detail, but usually the related audit risk was not developed.
- Incorrect comments on accounting treatments – for example discussing that the licenses granted by Ted Co should be treated as intangible assets.
- Lack of knowledge on some accounting issues – in particular many candidates clearly did not know how EPS should be calculated and therefore did not realise that the finance director's calculation was incorrect or how short term investments should be measured.
- Evaluation of the company's corporate governance structure, but not linking this to audit risk.
- Incorrect materiality calculations.

Requirement (c) asked candidates to recommend audit procedures to be performed on the portfolio of short term investments and on the EPS figure. Some candidates proved able to provide a good list of recommendations, but this was the minority. Answers tended to be better in relation to the investment portfolio, with many candidates appreciating that determining the short-term nature of the investments was an important issue and that the fair value of the shares at the year end could be agreed to stock market listings. However, most candidates could only provide vague suggestions such as 'discuss with the board' or 'agree to supporting documentation', and in relation to the fair value of the share many candidates could only suggest to 'rely on an expert' which was not necessary given that the investment relates to the shares of listed companies. Some candidates tried to make the recommended procedures much too complicated, not fully appreciating that traded equity shares can be easily valued and documented.

The procedures in relation to EPS were often very vague, with many candidates only able to suggest a recalculation of components of the calculation provided, or check the board had approved the calculation, neither of which were relevant given that the calculation was incorrect. Very few candidates picked up on the fact that the weighted average number of shares would need to be verified given that the company had a share issue during the year.

There were four professional marks available, and most candidates secured most of these marks by providing an introduction and using headings to create an appropriate structure for their answer. However, presentation was not always good and candidates are reminded to pay attention to determining an appropriate layout for their answer.

The adapted papers for the UK and Ireland (IRL) candidates contained an adapted version in which the requirements were not separated out and given specific mark allocations and some extra background information had been included in the question. The candidates attempting these adapted papers dealt well with the style of question requirements, and mostly devoted an appropriate amount of time to the discussion of each of the requirements.

ACCA Marking scheme		
		Marks
(a)	**Initial audit engagement**	
	Generally up to 1½ marks for each point discussed, including:	
	– Communicate with the previous auditor, review their working papers	
	– Consider whether any previous auditor reports were modified	
	– Consider any matters which were raised when professional clearance was obtained	
	– Consider matters discussed with management during our firm's appointment	
	– Need to develop thorough business understanding	
	– Risk of misstatement in opening balances/previously applied accounting policies	
	– Firm's quality control procedures for new audit clients	
	– Need to use experienced audit team to reduce detection risk	
	Maximum	6
(b)	**Evaluation of audit risk**	
	Generally up to 1½ marks for each point discussed, and 1 mark for each calculation of materiality.	
	– Management bias due to recent stock market listing – pressure on results	
	– Management bias due to owner's shareholding – incentive to overstate profit	
	– Management lacks knowledge and experience of the reporting requirements for listed entities	
	– Weak corporate governance, potential for Dougal to dominate the board	

- Revenue recognition – should the revenue be deferred
- Revenue recognition – whether deferred income recognised over an appropriate period
- E-commerce (allow up to 3 marks for discussion of several risks factors)
- Foreign exchange transactions – risk of using incorrect exchange rate
- Forward currency contracts – risk derivatives not recognised or measured incorrectly
- Portfolio of investments – risk fair value accounting not applied
- New team dealing with complex issues of treasury management
- EPS – incorrectly calculated (allow 3 marks for detailed discussion)
- EPS – risk of incomplete disclosure
- Rapid growth – control risk due to volume of transactions
- Profit margins – risk expenses misclassified (also allow 1 mark for each margin correctly calculated with comparative)
- Development costs – risk of over-capitalisation of development costs
- Inventory – year-end counts already taken place, difficulties in attending inventory counts
- Opening balances (give mark here if not given in (a) above)

Maximum **17**

(c) (i) **Procedures on portfolio of investments**

Generally 1 mark for each procedure explained:

- Agree the fair value of the shares held as investments to stock market share price listings
- Confirm the original cost of the investment to cash book and bank statements
- Discuss the accounting treatment with management and confirm that an adjustment will be made to recognise the shares at fair value
- Review the notes to the financial statements to ensure that disclosure is sufficient to comply with the requirements of IFRS 9
- Enquire with the treasury management function regarding disposals and reinvestment
- Review board minutes to confirm the authorisation and approval of the amount invested
- Confirm the number of shares held to supporting documentation such as dividend received vouchers
- Review documentation relating to the scope and procedures of the new treasury management function

(ii) **Procedures on EPS**

Generally 1 mark for each procedure explained:

- Discuss with management the requirements of IAS 33 ad request that management recalculates the EPS in accordance with those requirements
- Review board minutes to confirm the authorisation of the issue of share capital, the number of shares and the price at which they were issued
- Confirm the share issue complies with the company's legal documentation such as the memorandum and articles of association
- Inspect any other supporting documentation for the share issue, such as a share issue prospectus
- Recalculate the weighted average number of shares for the year to 31 May 2015
- Recalculate EPS using the profit as disclosed in the statement of profit or loss and the weighted average number of shares
- Discuss with management the existence of any factors which may impact on the calculation and disclosure of a diluted EPS figure, for example, convertible bonds

– Read the notes to the financial statements in respect of EPS to confirm that disclosure is complete and accurate and complies with IAS 33	
Maximum	**8**
Professional marks Overall presentation, structure and logical flow of the briefing notes and for the clarity of the evaluation and discussion provided.	
Maximum	**4**
Total	**35**

5 CONNOLLY *Walk in the footsteps of a top tutor*

Top tutor tips

The first requirement asks for business risks, i.e. the risk the company does not meet its strategic objectives. These are the issues that management are concerned about. Explain the impact of the issue to the company's profits or cash flows.

Part (b) focuses on risk of material misstatement, i.e. the risk that the financial statements contain material misstatement. This is usually due to non-compliance with an accounting standard. Think about the requirements of the relevant accounting standard and what the client might be doing incorrectly.

Part (c) asks for procedures in respect of the newly acquired brand name. Procedures should be specific in terms of what the auditor needs to do to obtain the evidence they need.

Part (d) requires discussion of ethical issues arising as a result of the loan guarantee and the request for advice. Make sure you include identification of the threats, explanation of those threats, discussion of whether the threats are significant and finally how to safeguard against them. There are seven marks available for this requirement. Simply stating 'this is a threat' will not earn marks.

Don't forget to present your answer in a briefing note format and include an introduction and a conclusion as well as subheadings to get the professional marks.

Briefing notes

To: **Audit partner**

From: **Audit manager**

Subject: **Audit planning for Connolly Co, year ending 31 December 2014**

Introduction

These briefing notes are prepared to assist in planning the audit of Connolly Co, our client operating in the pharmaceutical industry. Specifically, the briefing notes will evaluate the business risks facing our client, identify and explain four risks of material misstatement, recommend audit procedures in relation to a new brand acquired during the year, and finally explain ethical threats to our firm.

(a) Business risks

Licensing of products

A significant regulatory risk relates to the highly regulated nature of the industry in which the company operates. If any of Connolly Co's products fail to be licensed for development and sale, it would mean that costs already incurred are wasted. Research and development costs are significant. For example, in 2014 the cash outflow in relation to research and development amounted to 7.5% of revenue, and the failure to obtain the necessary licences is a major threat to the company's business objectives.

Patent infringements

In developing new products and improving existing products, Connolly Co must be careful not to breach any competitor's existing patent. In the event of this occurring, significant legal costs could be incurred in defending the company's legal position. Time and effort must be spent monitoring product developments to ensure legal compliance with existing patents. Similarly, while patents serve to protect Connolly Co's products, if a competitor were found to be in breach of one of the company's patents, costs of bringing legal action against that company could be substantial.

Advertising regulations

The company risks running inappropriate advertising campaigns, and failing to comply with local variations in regulatory requirements. For example, if television campaigns to promote products occurred in countries where this is not allowed, the company could face fines and reputational damage, with consequences for cash flow and revenue streams.

Skilled personnel

The nature of Connolly Co's operations demands a skilled workforce with the necessary scientific knowledge to be able to develop new drugs. Loss of personnel, especially to competitors in the industry, would be a drain on the remaining resources and in the worst case scenario it could delay the development and launch of new products. It may be difficult to attract and retain skilled staff given the pending court case and potential reputational damage to the company.

Diversification and rapid growth

During the year Connolly Co has acquired a new brand name and range of products, and has also diversified into a new market, that of animal health products. While diversification has commercial and strategic advantages, it can bring risks. Management may struggle to deal with the increased number of operations which they need to monitor and control, or they may focus so much on ensuring the success of the new business segments that existing activities are neglected. There may also be additional costs associated with the diversification which puts pressure on cash and on the margins of the enlarged business. This may be the reason for the fall in operating profit of 10.8% and for the decline in operating margin from 24% to 20%.

Cash flow and liquidity issues

Connolly Co seems to be struggling to maintain its cash position, as this year its cash flow is negative by $1.2 million. Contributing factors to this will include the costs of acquiring the 'Cold Comforts' brand name, expenditure to launch the new animal-related product line, and the cash outflow in relation to on-going research and development, which has increased by 7.1% in the year. The first two of these are one-off issues and may not create a cause for concern over long-term cash management issues, but the company must be careful to maintain a positive cash inflow from its operating activities to provide a sound foundation for future activities.

Companies operating in this industry must be careful to manage cash flows due to the nature of the product lifecycle, meaning that large amounts have to be expended long before any revenue is generated, in some cases the time lag may be many years before any cash inflow is derived from expenditure on research activities.

The fact that the company has approached its bank to make cash available in the event of damages of $3 million having to be paid out indicates that the company is not very liquid, and is relying to some degree on external finance. If the bank refuses to extend existing borrowing facilities, the company may have to find finance from other sources, for example, from an alternative external provider of funds or from an issue of equity shares, which may be difficult to achieve and expensive. The company has relatively high gearing, which may deter potential providers of finance or discourage potential equity investors.

If finance is refused, the company may not be able to pay liabilities as they fall due, and other operational problems may arise, for example, an inability to continue to fund in-progress research and development projects. Ultimately this would result in a going concern problem, though much more information is needed to assess if this is a risk at this year end.

Court case and bad publicity

The court case against the company will create reputational damage. Publicity over people suffering side effects while participating in clinical trials will undoubtedly lead to bad publicity, affecting market share especially if competitors take advantage of the situation. It is also likely that the bad publicity will lead to increased scrutiny of the company's activities making it more vulnerable should further problems arise.

Risk of overtrading

The fall in operating margin and earnings per share is a worrying sign for shareholders, though for the reasons explained above this may not be the start of a long-term trend as several events in this year have put one-off pressure on margins. However, there could be a risk of overtrading, as the company's revenue has increased by 5.2%.

(b) Risks of material misstatement

Inherent risk of management bias

Connolly Co's management is attempting to raise finance, and the bank will use its financial statements as part of their lending decision. There is therefore pressure on management to present a favourable position. This may lead to bias in how balances and transactions are measured and presented. For example, there is a risk that earnings management techniques are used to overstate revenue and understate expenses in order to maximise the profit recognised. Estimates included in the financial statements are also subject to higher risk. ISA 540 *Auditing Accounting Estimates, Including Fair Value Accounting Estimates, and Related Disclosures* states that auditors shall review the judgements and decisions made by management in the making of accounting estimates to identify whether there are indicators of management bias.

Research and development costs – recognition

There is a significant risk that the requirements of IAS 38 *Intangible Assets* have not been followed. Research costs must be expensed and strict criteria must be applied to development expenditure to determine whether it should be capitalised and recognised as an intangible asset. Development costs are capitalised only after technical and commercial feasibility of the asset for sale or use have been established, and Connolly Co must demonstrate an intention and ability to complete the development and that it will generate future economic benefits. The risk is that research costs have been inappropriately classified as development costs and then capitalised, overstating assets and understating expenses.

A specific risk relates to the drug which was being developed but in relation to which there have been side effects during the clinical trials. It is unlikely that the costs in relation to this product development continue to meet the criteria for capitalisation, so there is a risk that they have not been written off, overstating assets and profit.

Development costs – amortisation

When an intangible asset has a finite useful life, it should be amortised systematically over that life. For a development asset, the amortisation should correspond with the pattern of economic benefits generated from the sale of associated goods. The risk is that the amortisation period has not been appropriately assessed. For example, if a competitor introduces a successful rival product which reduces the period over which Connolly Co's product will generate economic benefit, this should be reflected in a reduction in the period over which that product is amortised, resulting in an increased amortisation charge. The risk if this does not happen is that assets are overstated and expenses are understated.

Patents – recognition and amortisation

The cost of acquiring patents for products should be capitalised and recognised as an intangible asset as the patent provides protection over the economic benefit to be derived. If patent costs have been expensed rather than capitalised, this would understate assets and overstate expenses. Once recognised, patents should be amortised over the period of their duration, and non-amortisation will overstate assets and understate expenses.

Court case – provisions and contingent liabilities

The court case which has been brought against Connolly Co may give rise to a present obligation as a result of a past event, and if there is a probable outflow of economic benefit which can be measured reliably, then a provision should be recognised. The clinical trial took place in 2013, so the obligating event has occurred. Depending on the assessment of probability of the case going against Connolly Co, it may be that instead of a provision, a contingent liability exists. This would be the case if there is a possible, rather than probable, outflow of economic benefit. The risk is that either a necessary provision is not recognised, understating liabilities and expenses, or that a contingent liability is not appropriately disclosed in the notes to the financial statements, in accordance with IAS 37 *Provisions, Contingent Liabilities and Contingent Assets*.

Legal fees relating to the court case should also be accrued if they have been incurred before the year end, and failure to do so will understate current liabilities and understate expenses.

Segmental reporting

The diversification into the new product area relating to animal health may warrant separate disclosure according to IFRS 8 *Operating Segments*. This requires listed companies to disclose in a note to the financial statements the performance of the company disaggregated over its operating or geographical segments, as the information is viewed by management. As the new product area has been successful and contributes 15% to revenue, it could be seen as a significant operating segment, and disclosure of its revenue, profit and other figures may be required. The risk is non-disclosure or incomplete disclosure of the necessary information.

Tutorial note

More than the required number of four risks of material misstatement have been included in this answer for illustrative purposes. Credit will be awarded for the identification and explanation of other relevant risks, e.g. in relation to the acquired brand name.

(c) Recommended audit procedures

- Review board minutes for evidence of discussion of the purchase of the acquired brand, and for its approval.
- Agree the cost of $5 million to the company's cash book and bank statement.
- Obtain the purchase agreement and confirm the rights of Connolly Co in respect of the brand.
- Discuss with management the estimated useful life of the brand of 15 years and obtain an understanding of how 15 years has been determined as appropriate.
- If the 15-year useful life is a period stipulated in the purchase document, confirm to the terms of the agreement.
- If the 15-year useful life is based on the life expectancy of the product, obtain an understanding of the basis for this, for example, by reviewing a cash flow forecast of sales of the product.

- Obtain any market research or customer satisfaction surveys to confirm the existence of a revenue stream.
- Consider whether there are any indicators of potential impairment at the year end by obtaining pre year-end sales information and reviewing terms of contracts to supply the products to pharmacies.
- Recalculate the amortisation expense for the year and agree the charge to the financial statements, and confirm adequacy of disclosure in the notes to the financial statements.

(d) Ethical threats

There are two ethical threats relevant to the audit firm.

Guarantee in respect of bank loan

The provision of such a guarantee represents a financial interest in an audit client, and creates a self-interest threat because the audit firm has an interest in the financial position of the client. The audit firm may be reluctant to request adjustments to the financial statements that would result in the firm having to honour the guarantee.

If an audit firm guarantees a loan to an audit client, the self-interest threat created would be so significant that no safeguards could reduce the threat to an acceptable level unless the loan or guarantee is immaterial to both the audit firm and the client.

In this case the loan would be material as it represents 5% of Connolly Co's total assets, and would also be considered material in nature because of the company's need for the additional finance.

UK syllabus: Ethical Standard section 2 states that audit firms, persons in a position to influence the conduct and outcome of the audit and immediate family members of such persons shall not make a loan to, or guarantee the borrowings of, an audited entity or its affiliates unless this represents a deposit made with a bank or similar deposit-taking institution in the ordinary course of business and on normal business terms. An intimidation as well as a self-interest threat arises when an audit firm makes a loan to, or guarantees a loan in respect of, an audited entity.

Advice on accounting and management information systems

If the advice was given, it would constitute the provision of a non-assurance service to an audit client. Services related to IT systems including the design or implementation of hardware or software systems may create a self-review threat. This is because when auditing the financial statements the auditor would assess the systems which they had recommended, and may be reluctant to criticise them if they are ineffective.

There is also a risk of assuming the responsibility of management, especially as Connolly Co has little experience in this area, so would rely on the auditor's suggestions and be less inclined to make their own decision.

In the case of an audit client which is a public interest entity, an audit firm shall not provide services involving the design or implementation of IT systems which form a significant part of the internal control over financial reporting or which generate information which is significant to the client's accounting records or financial statements on which the firm will express an opinion.

Therefore the audit firm should not provide a service to give advice on the accounting systems. With further clarification on the nature of the management information systems and the update required to them, it may be possible for the audit firm to provide a service to Connolly Co, as long as those systems are outside of the financial reporting system. However, it may be prudent for the audit firm to decline offering any advice on systems to the client.

These ethical issues should be discussed with those charged with governance of Connolly Co, with an explanation provided as to why the audit firm cannot guarantee the loan or provide the non-audit service to the company.

UK syllabus: Ethical Standard section 5 states that the audit firm shall not undertake an engagement to design, provide or implement information technology systems for an audited entity where the systems concerned would be important to any significant part of the accounting system or to the production of the financial statements and the auditor would place significant reliance upon them as part of the audit of the financial statements; or for the purposes of the information technology services, the audit firm would undertake part of the role of management.

Conclusion

Connolly Co faces a variety of business risks, some of which are generic to the industry in which it operates, while others are more entity-specific. A number of risks of material misstatement have been discussed, and the audit planning must ensure that appropriate responses are designed for each of them. The purchase of a new brand will necessitate detailed audit testing. Two ethical issues have been raised by requests from the client for our firm to provide a loan guarantee and to provide advice on systems, both of which create significant threats to independence and objectivity, and the matters must be discussed with the client before advising that we are unable to provide the guarantee or to provide the systems advice.

Examiner comments

This question centred on planning the audit of a listed company operating in the pharmaceutical industry. Candidates were provided with background information about the company's products and the environment in which the company, Connolly Co, operated. In addition, information was provided in the form of minutes from a meeting with Connolly's Finance Director, covering several issues relevant to the audit. These included details of requests made to the company's bank for further finance, a successful diversification into a new market, the acquisition of a new brand during the year, an on-going court case against the company following problems during a medical trial of its products, and an out of date management information system. Key financial information in the form of extracts from projected financial statements along with comparative information was also provided in the scenario.

The first requirement asked candidates to evaluate the business risks faced by Connolly Co. This requirement was generally well attempted, and in fact for many candidates this was the best attempted out of all of the question requirements. Most candidates proved able to identify and discuss many of the relevant business risks within their briefing notes and the risks surrounding non-compliance with stringent regulations, the risk of losing the licenses necessary to produce pharmaceutical products, the lack of cash to support on-going product development, the risks attached to diversifying into a new market, and reputational risks associated with the court case against the company were generally well discussed.

The best answers made full use of the information provided and performed analysis of the financial information, allowing for identification of the less obvious but often pertinent risks, such as that without the revenue derived from the new market entered into during the year the company's total revenue would have fallen by a significant amount. Furthermore strong candidates, as well as providing detailed analysis and explanation of the risks, also attempted to prioritise the various risks identified thus demonstrating appropriate judgment and an understanding that the audit partner would want to know about the most significant risks first.

The key weakness present in many answers continues to be the poor quality of explanations. Weaker answers tended to just repeat facts given in the scenario with little attempt to discuss or evaluate them. Some answers began with a lengthy discussion of the definition of business risk and its components which was not necessary and demonstrates a lack of judgment when the briefing notes are being requested by an audit partner. Further many answers were very repetitive and did not consider the number of distinct business risks that would be required for the marks available. Many candidates discussed at length risks over going concern that were tenuous or lacked appropriate explanation. Many candidates also confused business risk and audit risk and therefore provided responses that were not relevant to the question.

Requirement (b) asked candidates to identify and explain four risks of material misstatement to be considered in planning the audit and performance in this area was very mixed. There were some excellent answers to this requirement, with many candidates achieving close to full marks. Most candidates were able to identify the risks surrounding inappropriate accounting treatment which could lead to material misstatements, and were also able to quantify the materiality of the matters discussed. The risks that were most commonly discussed related to provisions, recognition of research and development costs, the valuation of potentially obsolete inventory, and the segmental reporting that would be likely required in relation to the new market entered into during the year.

The best answers were well structured in how they explained the potential misstatement and included in their evaluation of each risk an identification of the risk factor from the scenario (e.g. the court case ongoing against the company), a determination of materiality where possible given the information in the question, a clear comment on the appropriateness of the accounting treatment where relevant, and the impact on the financial statements (e.g. non-recognition of a provision in relation to the court case could lead to an understatement of liabilities and an overstatement of operating profit). Only the better candidates identified that requesting additional finance from the bank to cover the damages from the court case implied that the outcome was probable rather than possible and should be provided for.

Weaker answers failed to observe the number of risks of material misstatement that had been asked for, with a significant minority wasting valuable time and providing five or more risks even though credit could only be awarded for four risks. Many candidates discussed a risk of material misstatement relating to accounting for the loan that had been applied for, but given that this had not yet been received it would not give rise to a risk of this nature in this reporting period. Other candidates discussed at length the issue of going concern and that the company's financial statements should be prepared on a break-up basis but there was certainly not enough evidence in the scenario to justify this as a risk of material misstatement.

Other weaknesses in relation to this requirement included:

- Incorrect materiality calculations or stating that a balance was material with no justification;
- Lack of understanding of some accounting treatments, e.g. saying that intangible assets must be measured at fair value;
- Vague attempts to explain the risk of material misstatement along the lines of 'there is a risk it is not accounted for properly' or 'there is a risk the relevant accounting standard is not followed' – these points are too vague to score marks.

Requirement (c) asked candidates to recommend the principal audit procedures to be performed in respect of a brand name that had been acquired during the year. Answers to this requirement were very mixed, as is typical for requirements relating to audit procedures. The best answers provided well explained procedures that clearly set out how the test would be performed and where appropriate the documentation that would be used. Weaker answers contained vague or very brief lists that were not specific enough to constitute an audit procedure and therefore did not earn marks. Examples of weaker answer points include 'assess value of the brand' (this is not an audit procedure – how should the assessment take place?), 'discuss accounting treatment with management' (what specifically should be discussed?), 'look at the purchase contract' (what information should the auditor be looking for within the contract?). Candidates should ensure that procedures contain an actual instruction describing an action to be performed to satisfy a specific objective.

A minority of candidates thought that rather than acquiring a specific asset i.e. the brand, as stated in the question, a company had been purchased. This led to candidates providing irrelevant audit procedures and wrongly discussing the accounting treatment for goodwill. Candidates are reminded to read the question extremely carefully.

The final requirement asked candidates to discuss the ethical issues arising from the engagement and to recommend appropriate actions. There were two matters present in the scenario that were appropriate to discuss – the fact that Connolly Co's bank had asked the audit firm to guarantee the loan extension that had been requested, and that the audit firm had been asked to give advice on the new management information system planned to be introduced the following year.

This requirement was generally well attempted with the majority of candidates correctly identifying the two issues and providing some relevant discussion for each. Most candidates were able to explain the ethical threats associated with the issues and recognised that the significance of the threats would need to be determined. Many candidates appreciated that due to Connolly Co's listed status it qualified as a public interest entity, and therefore the threats to objectivity were heightened. Many candidates demonstrated sound judgment by concluding that the services should not be provided to the audit client as it would be unlikely that safeguards could reduce the threats to an acceptable level. However, credit was awarded where candidates mentioned the types of safeguards that could be considered.

Weaker answers for this requirement identified the wrong ethical threats or failed to identify the significance of the company's listed status, concluding that it would be acceptable to provide the services. Other answers digressed into discussions on the general ethical issues surrounding the testing of medicines on animals or humans, which was not relevant to the question requirement.

There were four professional marks available, and most candidates secured most of these marks by providing an introduction and using headings and well-structured paragraphs to create an appropriate structure for their answer.

The UK and Ireland (IRL) adapted papers had a slightly different style in that the question requirements were not separated out and some extra information had been included in the question. The candidates attempting these adapted papers dealt well with the style of question requirements, and on the whole devoted an appropriate amount of time to the discussion of each of the requirements. It was pleasing to see that candidates attempting these papers were often able to directly link business risks to risks of material misstatement, providing focused answers.

ACCA marking scheme		
		Marks
(a)	**Evaluation of business risks** Generally up to 1½ marks for each business risk evaluated. In addition, 1 mark for relevant trends calculated and used as part of the risk evaluation. – Regulatory risk – licensing of products – Regulatory risk – patent infringement – Regulatory risk – advertising – Skilled workforce – Risk of diversification – Cash flow issues – negative trend/cash management issues – Cash flow issues – reliance on further bank finance (allow up to 3 marks here if several points covered) – Cash flow issues – timing of cash flows – Court case – bad publicity and further scrutiny – Risk of overtrading	
	Maximum	**11**
(b)	**Risks of material misstatement** Up to 2 marks for each risk identified and explained – 4 risks only. Also allow up to 1 mark for appropriate and correct materiality calculations. – Management bias – Development costs – recognition – Development costs – amortisation – Patent costs – Court case – provision or contingent liability – Segmental reporting	
	Maximum	**8**
(c)	**Procedures in relation to purchased brand name** Generally 1 mark for each relevant, well described audit procedure: – Review board minutes for evidence of discussion of the purchase, and for its approval – Agree the cost of $5 million to the company's cash book and bank statement – Obtain the purchase agreement and confirm the rights of Connolly Co – Discuss with management the estimated useful life of the brand of 15 years and obtain an understanding of how 15 years has been determined as appropriate – If the 15-year useful life is a period stipulated in the purchase document, confirm to the terms of the agreement – If the 15-year useful life is based on the life expectancy of the product, review a cash flow forecast of sales of the product – Obtain any market research or customer satisfaction surveys – Consider whether there are any indicators of potential impairment – Recalculate the amortisation expense for the year and confirm adequacy of disclosure in notes to the financial statements	
	Maximum	**5**

(d)	**Ethical matters** Generally up to 1 mark for each point discussed: – Loan guarantee is a financial self-interest threat – The loan is material and guarantee should not be given – The advice on systems would be a non-audit service – Self-review threat created – Threat of assuming management responsibility – Service can only be provided if systems unrelated to financial reporting – In this case the advice relating to accounting systems must not be given – Advisable not to provide the advice on management information systems – Discuss both matters with management/those charged with governance	
	Maximum	**7**
	Professional marks Generally 1 mark for heading, 1 mark for introduction, 1 mark for use of headings within the briefing notes, 1 mark for clarity of comments made.	
	Maximum	**4**
Total		**35**

6 STOW GROUP *Walk in the footsteps of a top tutor*

Top tutor tips

Part (a) requires you to explain the risks of material misstatement, commenting on their materiality. A risk of material misstatement needs to relate to the financial statements in some way – figures, disclosures, or basis of preparation. Ultimately, the financial statements will be materially misstated if the client has not complied with the relevant accounting standard. Your answer should give reasons why the accounting treatment is wrong.

Materiality calculations are the easy marks to earn. If there is a figure mentioned in the scenario, calculate the percentage of profits or assets it represents and state whether this is material or not material. As a general rule of thumb use the lower materiality thresholds: 5% profit before tax, 1% assets, ½% revenue.

The question also asks for any further information that may be needed. This is a common requirement in more recent exams and you should try to identify other information that would help you with your risk assessment.

Part (b) asks for 'principal' audit procedures in respect of the disposal. Principal procedures are the procedures that should be performed to obtain the best quality evidence or the most important evidence.

Part (c) is a straightforward requirement considering whether reliance can be placed on the work of the internal audit department, including any ethical issues.

There are four professional marks available for the **structure, presentation of the briefing notes and the clarity of the explanations.** Your answer should be labelled 'Briefing Notes'.

You should identify who the briefing notes are intended for. For the introduction, use the words from the requirement. The body of the answer should have a clear structure including underlined headings for each risk. Don't forget to include a conclusion summarising the key points identified.

Briefing notes

To: **Audit Partner**

From: **Audit Manager**

Subject: **Planning issues for the Stow Group, year ending 31 December 2013**

Introduction

These briefing notes contain an explanation of the risks of material misstatement to be considered in planning the audit of the Stow Group. The risks which have been explained focus on a restructuring of the Group which has taken place during the year. Materiality has been considered where information permits, and further information which would be useful in planning the audit has also been identified. The briefing notes also contain recommended audit procedures to be performed in respect of the disposal of Broadway Co. In addition, the Group finance director's suggestion that our firm makes use of the new subsidiary's internal audit team when performing our audit has been discussed, along with the ethical implication of the suggestion.

(a) (i)

and (ii) Zennor Co

Materiality of Zennor Co

To evaluate the materiality of Zennor Co to the Group, its profit and assets need to be retranslated into \$. At the stated exchange rate of 4 Dingu = \$1, its projected profit for the year is \$22.5 million (90 million Dingu/4) and its projected total assets are \$200 million (800 million Dingu/4).

Zennor Co's profit represents 11.3% of Group projected profit for the year (22.5/200), and its assets represent 8% of Group total assets (200/2,500). Zennor Co is therefore material to the Group and may be considered to be a significant component of it. A significant component is one which is identified by the auditor as being of individual financial significance to the group.

Zenner Co is likely to be considered a significant component due to its risk profile and the change in group structure which has occurred in the year.

The goodwill arising on the acquisition of Zennor Co amounts to 2.4% (60/2,500) of Group assets and is material.

Because the balances above, including goodwill, are based on a foreign currency, they will need to be retranslated at the year end using the closing exchange rate to determine and conclude on materiality as at the year end.

Materiality needs to be assessed based on the new, enlarged group structure. Materiality for the group financial statements as a whole will be determined when establishing the overall group audit strategy. The addition of Zennor Co to the group during the year is likely to cause materiality to be different from previous years, possibly affecting audit strategy and the extent of testing in some areas.

Risks of material misstatement

Retranslation of Zennor Co's financial statements

According to IAS 21 *The Effects of Changes in Foreign Exchange Rates*, the assets and liabilities of Zennor Co should be retranslated using the closing exchange rate. Its income and expenses should be retranslated at the exchange rates at the dates of the transactions.

The risk is that incorrect exchange rates are used for the retranslations. This could result in over/understatement of the assets, liabilities, income and expenses that are consolidated, including goodwill. It would also mean that the exchange gains and losses arising on retranslation and to be included in Group other comprehensive income are incorrectly determined.

Measurement and recognition of exchange gains and losses

The calculation of exchange gains and losses can be complex, and there is a risk that it is not calculated correctly, or that some elements are omitted, for example, the exchange gain or loss on goodwill may be missed out of the calculation.

IAS 21 states that exchange gains and losses arising as a result of the retranslation of the subsidiary's balances are recognised in other comprehensive income. The risk is incorrect classification, for example, the gain or loss could be recognised incorrectly as part of profit for the year

Initial measurement of goodwill

In order for goodwill to be calculated, the assets and liabilities of Zennor Co must have been identified and measured at fair value at the date of acquisition. Risks of material misstatement arise because the various components of goodwill each have specific risks attached, for example:

- Not all assets and liabilities may have been identified, for example, contingent liabilities and contingent assets may be omitted
- Fair value is subjective and based on assumptions which may not be valid.

There is also a risk that the cost of investment is not stated correctly, for example, that any contingent consideration has not been included in the calculation.

Subsequent measurement of goodwill

According to IFRS 3 *Business Combinations*, goodwill should be subject to an impairment review on an annual basis. The risk is that a review has not taken place, and so goodwill is overstated and Group operating expenses understated if impairment losses have not been recognised.

Consolidation of income and expenses

Zennor Co was acquired on 1 February 2013 and its income and expenses should have been consolidated from that date. There is a risk that the full year's income and expenses have been consolidated, leading to a risk of overstated Group profit.

Disclosure

Extensive disclosures are required by IFRS 3 to be included in the notes to the Group financial statements, for example, to include the acquisition date, reason for the acquisition and a description of the factors which make up the goodwill acquired. The risk is that disclosures are incomplete or not understandable.

Intra-group transactions

There will be a significant volume of intra-group transactions as the Group is supplying Zennor Co with inventory. There is a risk that intra-group sales, purchases, payables and receivables are not eliminated, leading to overstated revenue, cost of sales, payables and receivables in the Group financial statements.

There is also a risk that intercompany transactions are not identified in either/both companies' accounting systems.

The intra-group transactions are by definition related party transactions according to IAS 24 *Related Party Disclosures*, because Zennor Co is under the control of the Group. No disclosure of the transactions is required in the Group financial statements in respect of intra-group transactions because they are eliminated on consolidation. However, both the individual financial statements of the Group company supplying Zennor Co and the financial statements of Zennor Co must contain notes disclosing details of the intra-group transactions. There is a risk that this disclosure is not provided.

In addition, the cars may be supplied including a profit margin or mark up, in which case a provision for unrealised profit should be recognised in the Group financial statements. If this is not accounted for, Group inventory will be overstated, and operating profit will be overstated.

Completeness of inventory

There is a risk that cars which are in transit to Zennor Co at the year end may be omitted from inventory. The cars spend a significant amount of time in transit and awaiting delivery to Zennor Co, and without a good system of controls in place, it is likely that items of inventory will be missing from the Group's current assets as they may have been recorded as despatched from the seller but not yet as received by Zennor Co.

The inventory in transit to Zennor Co represents 2.3% of Group total assets (58/2,500) and is therefore material to the consolidated financial statements.

Tutorial note

Credit will also be awarded where answers discuss the issue of whether the arrangement is a consignment inventory arrangement, and the relevant risks of material misstatement.

Further information in relation to Zennor Co:

- Prior years' financial statements and auditor's reports.
- Minutes of meetings where the acquisition was discussed.
- Business background, e.g. from the company's website or trade journals.

- Copies of systems documentation from the internal audit team.
- Confirmation from Zennor Co's previous auditors of any matters which they wish to bring to our attention.
- Projected financial statements for the year to 31 December 2013.
- A copy of the due diligence report.
- Copies of prior year tax computations.

> ***Tutorial note***
>
> *Credit will also be awarded for discussions of risks of material misstatement and relevant audit procedures relating to the initial audit of Zennor Co by Compton & Co, e.g. increased risk of misstatement of opening balances and comparatives.*

Broadway Co

Materiality

The profit made on the disposal of Broadway Co represents 12.5% of Group profit for the year (25/200) and the transaction is therefore material to the Group financial statements.

Given that the subsidiary was sold for $180 million and that a profit on disposal of $25 million was recognised, the Group's financial statements must have derecognised net assets of $155 million on the disposal. This amounts to 6.2% of the Group's assets and is material. This is assuming that the profit on disposal has been correctly calculated, which is a risk factor discussed below.

Risk of material misstatement

Derecognition of assets and liabilities

On the disposal of Broadway Co, all of its assets and liabilities which had been recognised in the Group financial statements should have been derecognised at their carrying value, including any goodwill in respect of the company.

There is therefore a risk that not all assets, liabilities and goodwill have been derecognised leading to overstatement of those balances and an incorrect profit on disposal being calculated and included in Group profit for the year.

Profit consolidated prior to disposal

There is a risk that Broadway Co's income for the year has been incorrectly consolidated. It should have been included in Group profit up to the date that control passed and any profit included after that point would mean overstatement of Group profit for the year.

Calculation of profit on disposal

There is a risk that the profit on disposal has not been accurately calculated, e.g. that the proceeds received have not been measured at fair value as required by IFRS 10 *Consolidated Financial Statements*, or that elements of the calculation are missing.

Classification and disclosure of profit on disposal

IAS 1 *Presentation of Financial Statements* requires separate disclosure on the face of the financial statements of material items to enhance the understanding of performance during the year. The profit of $25 million is material, so separate disclosure is necessary. The risk is that the profit is not separately disclosed, e.g. is netted from operating expenses, leading to material misstatement.

Extensive disclosure requirements exist in relation to subsidiaries disposed of, e.g. IAS 7 *Statement of Cash Flows* requires a note which analyses the assets and liabilities of the subsidiary at the date of disposal. There is a risk that not all necessary notes to the financial statements are provided.

Tutorial note

It is possible that Broadway Co represents a disposal group and a discontinued operation, and credit will be awarded for discussion of relevant risks of material misstatement and audit procedures in respect of these issues.

Treatment of the disposal in parent company individual financial statements

The parent company's financial statements should derecognise the original cost of investment and recognise a profit on disposal based on the difference between the proceeds of $180 million and the cost of investment. Risk arises if the investment has not been derecognised or the profit has been incorrectly calculated.

Tax on disposal

There should be an accrual in both the parent company and the Group financial statements for the tax due on the disposal. This should be calculated based on the profit recognised in the parent company. There is a risk that the tax is not accrued for, leading to overstated profit and understated liabilities. There is also a risk that the tax calculation is not accurate.

Tutorial note

As Compton & Co is no longer the auditor of Broadway Co, there is no need for any further information in relation to audit planning, other than that needed to perform the audit procedures listed below.

(b) Procedures to be performed on the disposal of Broadway Co

- Obtain the statement of financial position of Broadway Co as at 1 September 2013 to confirm the value of assets and liabilities which have been derecognised from the Group.
- Review prior year Group financial statements and audit working papers to confirm the amount of goodwill that exists in respect of Broadway Co and trace to confirm it is derecognised from the Group on disposal.

- Confirm that the Stow Group is no longer listed as a shareholder of the company.
- Obtain legal documentation in relation to the disposal to confirm the date of the disposal and confirm that Broadway Co's profit has been consolidated up to this date only.
- Agree or reconcile the profit recognised in the Group financial statements to Broadway Co's individual accounts as at 1 September 2013.
- Perform substantive analytical procedures to gain assurance that the amount of profit consolidated from 1 January to 1 September 2013 appears reasonable and in line with expectations based on prior year profit.
- Recalculate the profit on disposal in the Group financial statements to confirm arithmetical accuracy.
- Agree the proceeds received of $180 million to legal documentation, and to cash book/bank statements.
- Confirm that $180 million is the fair value of proceeds on disposal and that no deferred or contingent consideration is receivable in the future.
- Review the Group statement of profit or loss and other comprehensive income to confirm that the profit on disposal is correctly disclosed as part of profit for the year (not in other comprehensive income) on a separate line.
- Using a disclosure checklist, confirm that all necessary information has been provided in the notes to the Group financial statements.
- Obtain the parent company's statement of financial position to confirm that the cost of investment is derecognised.
- Using prior year financial statements and audit working papers, agree the cost of investment derecognised to prior year's figure.
- Recalculate the profit on disposal in the parent company's financial statements.
- Reconcile the profit on disposal recognised in the parent company's financial statements to the profit recognised in the Group financial statements.
- Obtain management's estimate of the tax due on disposal, recalculate the figure and confirm the amount is properly accrued at parent company and at Group level.
- Review any correspondence with tax authorities regarding the tax due.
- Possibly the tax will be paid in the subsequent events period, in which case the payment can be agreed to cash book and bank statement.

(c) Internal audit team and ethical issue

It is not improper for Marta to suggest that Compton & Co use the work of Zennor Co's internal audit team. ISA 610 *Using the Work of Internal Auditors* contains requirements relating to the evaluation of the internal audit function to determine in what areas, and to what extent, the work of internal audit can be used by the external audit firm.

It would be beneficial for Compton & Co to use the internal audit team as it may result in a more efficient audit strategy, for example, the internal audit team's monitoring of controls should have resulted in a strong control environment, so a less substantive approach can be used on the audit.

In addition, the internal audit team should be able to provide Compton & Co with systems documentation and information on control activities which have been implemented. This will help the audit firm to build its knowledge and understanding of the new audit client. The internal audit team will also be able to assist Compton & Co in gaining more general business understanding with respect to the new subsidiary.

Compton & Co may also decide to rely on audit work performed by the internal audit team, for example, they may be asked to attend inventory counts of cars held at the port and awaiting delivery to Zennor Co.

All of the benefits described above are particularly significant given Zennor Co's overseas location, as reliance on the internal audit team would reduce travel time and costs which would be incurred if the external auditor had to perform the work themselves. However, there will be a limit to the amount of work that can be delegated to the internal audit team.

Before deciding to what extent the work of internal audit can be used, ISA 610 requires the external auditor to evaluate various matters, including the extent to which the internal audit function's organisation status and policies and procedures support the objectivity of the function; the level of competence of the internal audit team; and whether the internal audit function applies a systematic and disciplined approach, including quality control.

To perform these evaluations the external auditor may wish, for example, to discuss the work of the team with Jo Evesham including a consideration of the level of supervision, review and documentation of work performed, and also review the qualifications held by members of the team.

The fact that the internal audit team does not report to an independent audit committee may reduce the reliance that can be placed on their work as it affects the objectivity of work performed.

If Compton & Co chooses to use the work of the internal audit team, this will be relevant to the audit of both Zennor Co's individual financial statements, and the Group financial statements and will affect the audit strategy of both.

Marta states that reliance on the internal audit team will reduce the external audit fee, and the Group audit committee has requested that the Group audit fee remains the same as last year. An audit firm being pressured to reduce inappropriately the extent of work performed in order to reduce fees is an example of an intimidation threat.

It should be brought to Marta's attention that the audit fee will not necessarily be reduced by reliance on internal audit, especially as this is the first year that Compton & Co have audited Zennor Co, so there will be a lot of work to be performed in developing knowledge and understanding of the client whether or not the firm chooses to rely on the work of the internal audit team.

Conclusion

The Stow Group's financial statements contain a high risk of material misstatement this year end, due to the restructuring which has taken place. The audit plan will contain numerous audit procedures to reduce the identified risks to an acceptable level. Compton & Co may choose to place reliance on Zennor Co's internal audit team, but only after careful consideration of their competence and objectivity, and communication between the external and internal audit teams must be carefully planned for.

Examiner's comments

This question involved the Stow Group, which had undergone some reorganisation during the year. A subsidiary had been disposed of, and a new foreign subsidiary had been acquired. Information was provided in the form of notes of a meeting that had been held with the Group's finance director. The notes described the acquisition of the foreign subsidiary Zennor Co and the goodwill arising on the acquisition, the disposal of Broadway Co, and gave information about some trading between group companies. In addition, some detail was provided on Zennor Co's internal audit team.

The requirements were based on planning the audit. The first requirement asked candidates to explain the risks of material misstatement to be considered in planning the Group audit, and to comment on materiality. This type of requirement is standard for P7, many candidates made a reasonable attempt at this requirement. Almost all candidates could at least identify several risks of material misstatement and determine their materiality, however the quality of explanation varied dramatically between scripts.

The best dealt with issues included the acquisition of the new subsidiary, with the majority of candidates correctly retranslating its figures into the Group's currency and discussing the risks relating to the re-translation process. Other matters generally well dealt with was the measurement of goodwill on acquisition and the risks associated with the elimination of balances arising on transactions between Group companies.

The main weakness seen in candidate's answers to this requirement was that of inadequately explained risks of material misstatements. While most candidates could identify a risk, only a small minority could adequately explain the risk. For example, having identified a risk, say in the recognition of goodwill, some candidates would simple suggest that 'this should be accounted for properly' or that 'the auditor must ensure that this is calculated properly', or simply 'this needs to be accounted for in accordance with accounting standards'.

Unfortunately this type of comment does not adequately answer the question requirement and where candidates supplied this type of explanation in their answers they would be unlikely to generate sufficient marks to pass this question requirement. Candidates are reminded that practicing past questions and carefully reviewing the model answers are the best way to prepare for this type of requirement, in order to understand exactly what is being asked for in the question requirement and to develop skill in explaining the risks identified.

Very few candidates picked up on some of the less obvious risks of material misstatement such as the tax implication of the disposal of Broadway.

Other common errors and weaknesses in answering this requirement included:

- Discussing business risks and failing to develop these into risks of material misstatement.
- Discussing detection risks, which are not part of the risk of material misstatement.
- Incorrectly calculating the amount of profit that should be consolidated for the subsidiaries during the year.
- Stating that Zennor Co's assets and liabilities should be recognised on a time-apportioned basis due to the subsidiary being acquired part way through the year.
- Stating that goodwill on acquisition should be cancelled out and not recognised in the group accounts because it is an inter-company transaction.
- Discussing that Broadway Co's assets and liabilities should be classified as held for sale at the year end, when in fact the subsidiary had been sold some months prior to the year end.
- Providing long discussions on the use of component auditors at the year end, which was not relevant to the scenario.
- Simply saying that a balance is material without demonstrating that this is the case.

Requirement (a) (ii) asked candidates, in the context of planning the Group audit, to identify further information that would be needed. Answers to this requirement were very mixed. Sound answers identified that information such as the due diligence report on the acquisition of Zennor Co and its previous years financial statements and auditors' reports would useful in planning the audit, as well as business background given that it is a first-year audit. Some answers gave audit procedures rather than information requirements, which was not asked for. Again candidates are encouraged to review similar past exam requirements and their model answers to gain an understanding of the type of information that would be useful in planning the audit.

The next requirement required candidates to recommend the principal audit procedures to be performed in respect of the disposal of Broadway Co. While there does seem to have been an improvement in the way that some candidates describe audit procedures, with many candidates scoring enough marks to pass this requirement, many answers were too vague to score well on this requirement. It was common to see procedures suggested such as 'agree to supporting documentation', or simply 'discuss with management' without any suggestion of what documentation should be looked at, and for what purpose, or the relevant matters that may be discussed with management. Procedures need to be specific to score well.

Requirement (c) focused on a suggestion by the Group's finance director that the external audit firm should use Zennor Co's internal audit team as much as possible in order to reduce the audit fee. Some information was provided about the internal audit team, the work they had performed, and the fact that it reports to the board of directors in the absence of an audit committee. The finance director had also requested that the audit fee should not be increased from the previous year. Candidates were asked to discuss how the finance director's suggestions impact on audit planning and to comment on relevant ethical issues.

This requirement was generally quite well answered. Most candidates knew the main requirements of the relevant ISA and could to some extent apply them to the scenario. Many candidates picked up on the fact that Zennor Co not having an audit committee would impact on the control environment of the company, and that the work of the internal audit team would need to be evaluated before any reliance could be placed on it. Most candidates could describe the impact that using the work of internal audit could have on the overall audit strategy, though this was often only very briefly mentioned, and few candidates suggested the type of work that the internal audit team could perform with relevance to the audit. On the whole though, this issue was quite well dealt with. The issue in relation to the audit fee was also generally well answered. Almost all candidates could identify the ethical threats raised, and attempted to evaluate them in the context of the scenario. However a significant minority of candidates thought that the finance director's suggestion was some kind of contingent fee arrangement, which was not correct, and there were the usual suggestions that the finance director should be 'disciplined' or 'sacked' due to her improper suggestions, which did not earn credit.

To summarise on this question, the answers on risk of material misstatement were unsatisfactory, especially given that this is a regularly examined area. Candidates need to improve on the quality of their explanations of the risks identified. Simply stating that a balance or transaction may be 'risky' without explaining why, and calculating its materiality is not enough to score well in this type of question. There were also relatively easy marks lost in many scripts where candidates had failed to provide any additional information requests, or due to audit procedures being inadequately described. For many candidates the requirement where they demonstrated the best level of understanding was in relation to internal audit and ethical matters.

ACCA marking scheme			
			Marks
(a)	(i)	Risks of material misstatement, materiality and further information requests Generally up to 1½ marks for each risk identified and explained (to a maximum of 4 marks for identification only): **Zennor Co** – Retranslation of Zennor Co's financial statements – Exchange gains and losses arising on retranslation – Goodwill not measured correctly at initial recognition – Goodwill not tested for impairment before the year end – Time apportionment of Zennor Co's income and expenses – Incomplete or inadequate disclosure – Cancellation of intercompany balances – Disclosure of related party transactions – Completeness of inventory **Broadway Co** – Derecognition of assets, liabilities and goodwill – Time apportionment of profit up to date of disposal – Calculation of profit on disposal – Classification and presentation regarding the disposal – Treatment in parent company financial statements – Accrual for tax payable Generally 1 mark for each of the following calculations/comments on materiality: – Appropriate retranslation of Zennor Co figures into \$ – Calculate materiality of Zennor Co to the Group – Determine if Zennor Co is a significant component – Calculate materiality of goodwill arising on acquisition – Calculate materiality of inventory in transit to the Group	
		Maximum	**12**

(ii)	1 mark for each piece of additional information identified: – Prior years' financial statements and auditor's reports – Minutes of meetings where the acquisition was discussed – Business background, e.g. from the company's website or trade journals – Copies of systems documentation from the internal audit team – Confirmation from Zennor Co's previous auditors of any matters that they wish to bring to our attention – Projected financial statements for the year to 31 December 2013 – A copy of the due diligence report – Copies of prior year tax computations	
	Maximum	**4**
(b)	**Audit procedures** Generally 1 mark for each well described audit procedure: – Confirm the value of assets and liabilities which have been derecognised from the Group – Confirm goodwill that exists is derecognised from the Group – Confirm that the Stow Group is no longer listed as a shareholder – Obtain legal documentation in relation to the disposal to confirm the date of the disposal and confirm that Broadway Co's profit has been consolidated up to this date only – Agree or reconcile the profit recognised in the Group FS to Broadway Co's individual accounts as at 1 September 2013 – Analytical procedures to gain assurance that the amount of profit consolidated from 1 January to 1 September 2013 appears reasonable – Recalculate the profit on disposal in the Group FS – Agree proceeds received to legal documentation/cash book/bank statements – Confirm that no deferred or contingent consideration is receivable – Review disclosure of profit on disposal – Review disclosure in the Group FS – Obtain the parent company's statement of financial position to confirm that the cost of investment is derecognised – Recalculate the profit on disposal in the individual FS – Reconcile the profit on disposal recognised in the parent company's FS to the profit recognised in the Group FS – Obtain management's estimate of the tax due on disposal, recalculate and confirm the amount is properly accrued – Review any correspondence with tax authorities – Agree post year-end payment to cash book and bank statement	
	Maximum	**8**
(c)	**Reliance on internal audit** Generally 1 mark for each discussion point: – Impact on audit strategy, e.g. reliance on controls – Impact on audit planning, e.g. systems documentation/business understanding – Specific work can be performed, e.g. inventory counts – Could lead to significant reduction in audit costs – Need to evaluate how much reliance can be placed (objectivity, competence, quality control, etc.) – up to 3 marks – Reliance will impact Group audit as well as individual audit – Pressure on fee is an intimidation threat – Fee unlikely to be maintained given the change in Group structure	
	Maximum	**7**
	Professional marks to be awarded for: – Use of headings – Introduction – Logical flow/presentation – Conclusion	
	Maximum	**4**
Total		**35**

7 GROHL *Walk in the footsteps of a top tutor*

Top tutor tips

Part (a) (i) and (ii) requires evaluation of both business risks and risks of material misstatement. This is a common requirement as it enables the examiner to ensure that students understand both types of risks. Business risks should be considered from the perspective of the client i.e. risks to profit, cash flow, reputation, survival of the company. Risks of material misstatement are the risks to the financial statements. For risks of material misstatement it is important to identify the balances or disclosures that could be wrong and to explain why this might be the case. Risks of material misstatement result from non-compliance with accounting standards so try to remember the relevant accounting standard and what the accounting treatment should be. Vague answers stating that there is a risk that the relevant accounting standard might not have been followed will not earn marks. State the requirements of the standards.

Part (a) (iii) asks for discussion of ethical issues. Whilst this requirement is often covered in Q4 of the exam, students should be prepared for any syllabus area being tested in any question of the exam.

There are four professional marks available for the **structure, presentation of the briefing notes and the clarity of the explanations.** Your answer should be labelled 'Briefing Notes'. You should identify who the briefing notes are intended for. For the introduction, use the words from the requirement. The body of the answer should have a clear structure including headings for each risk. Don't forget to include a conclusion summarising the key points identified.

Part (b) deals with matters and procedures in respect of an insurance claim. Matters questions require consideration of the materiality of the claim, discussion of the appropriate accounting treatment for the potential receivable and the risk to the financial statements if the matter is not accounted for correctly.

Procedures should be specific enough that another audit team member would know what to do if they were asked to perform the procedure. Be as specific as possible to ensure the marks are awarded.

(a) Briefing notes

To: **Audit Partner**

From: **Audit Manager**

Subject: **Audit planning and ethical issues in respect of Grohl Co**

Introduction

These briefing notes evaluate the business risks facing Grohl Co, and identify and explain four risks of material misstatement to be considered in planning the audit of the financial statements for the year ended 30 November 2012. In addition, two ethical issues are discussed and relevant actions recommended.

(i) Business risks

Imported goods – exchange rate fluctuations

Grohl Co relies on a key component of its production process being imported from overseas. This exposes the company to exchange rate volatility and consequentially cash flow fluctuations. The company chooses not to mitigate this risk by using forward exchange contracts, which may not be a wise strategy for a business so reliant on imports. Exchange gains and losses can also cause volatility in profits, and as the company already has a loss for the year, any adverse movements in exchange rates may quickly increase this loss.

Imported goods – transportation issues

Heavy reliance on imports means that transportation costs will be high, and with fuel costs continuing to increase this will put pressure on Grohl Co's margins. It is not just the cost that is an issue – reliance on imports is risky as supply could be disrupted due to aviation problems, such as the grounding of aircraft after volcanic eruptions or terrorist activities.

Reliance on imported goods increases the likelihood of a stock out. Unless Grohl Co keeps a reasonable level of copper wiring as inventory, production would have to be halted if supply were interrupted, creating idle time and inefficiencies, and causing loss of customer goodwill.

Reliance on single supplier

All of Grohl Co's copper wiring is supplied by one overseas supplier. This level of reliance is extremely risky, as any disruption to the supplier's operations, for example, due to financial difficulties or political interference, could result in the curtailment of supply, leading to similar problems of stock outs and halted production as discussed above.

Quality control issues

Since appointing the new supplier of copper wiring, Grohl Co has subsequently experienced quality control issues with circuit boards, which could result in losing customers (discussed further below). This may have been due to changing supplier as part of a cost-cutting exercise. Given that the new supplier is overseas, it may make resolving the quality control issues more difficult. Additional costs may have to be incurred to ensure the quality of goods received, for example, extra costs in relation to electrical testing of the copper wiring. The company's operating margins for 2012 are already low at only 4% (2011 – 7.2%), and additional costs will put further pressure on margins.

High-technology and competitive industry

Grohl Co sells into a high-technology industry, with computers and mobile phones being subject to rapid product development. It is likely that Grohl Co will need to adapt quickly to changing demands in the marketplace, but it may not have the resources to do this.

Grohl Co operates in a very competitive market. With many suppliers chasing the same customer base, there will be extreme pressure to cut prices in order to remain competitive. As discussed above, the company's operating margins are already low, so competition based on price would not seem to be an option.

Reliance on key customers

Grohl Co relies on only 20 key customers to generate its domestic revenue, which accounts for approximately half of its total revenue. In a competitive market, it may be difficult to retain customers without cutting prices, which will place further pressure on profit margins. In addition, the product quality issue in November could mean that some contracts are cancelled, despite Grohl Co's swift action to recall defective items, meaning a potentially significant loss of revenue.

Furthermore, Grohl Co will have to refund dissatisfied customers or supply alternative products to them, putting strain on cash flows and operating margins.

Regulatory issues

New regulations come into force within a few months of the year end. It would appear that the existing production facilities do not comply with these regulations, and work has only recently begun on the new and regulation-compliant production line, so it is very unlikely that the new regulations can be complied with in time. This creates a significant compliance risk for Grohl Co, which could lead to investigation by the regulatory authority, and non-compliance may result in forced cessation of production, fines, penalties and bad publicity. There may also be additional on-going costs involved in complying with the new regulations, for example, monitoring costs, as well as the costs of the necessary capital expenditure.

Additional finance taken out – liquidity/solvency issues

A loan representing 16.7% of total assets was taken out during the year. This is a significant amount, increasing the company's gearing, and creating an obligation to fund interest payments of $1.2 million per annum, as well as repayments of capital in the future. Grohl Co does not appear to be cash-rich, with only $130,000 cash available at the year end, and having built up an overdraft of $2.5 million in July, working capital management may be a long-term problem for the company. The current and quick ratios also indicate that Grohl Co would struggle to pay debts as they fall due.

Profitability

The draft statement of profit or loss indicates that revenue has fallen by 9.4%, and operating profit fallen by 50%. Overall, the company has made a loss for the year. In 2012 finance charges are not covered by operating profit, and it would seem that finance charges may not yet include the additional interest on the new loan, which would amount to $500,000 ($30m × 4% × 5/12). The inclusion of this additional cost would increase the loss for the year to $800,000. This may indicate going concern problems for the company.

Change in key management

The loss of several directors during the year is a business risk as it means that the company may lose important experience and skills. It will take time for the new directors to build up business knowledge and to develop and begin to implement successful business strategies.

(ii) Risks of material misstatement

Foreign currency transactions – initial recognition

The majority of Grohl Co's copper wiring is imported, leading to risk in the accounting treatment of foreign currency transactions. According to IAS 21 *The Effects of Changes in Foreign Exchange Rates,* foreign currency transactions should be initially recognised having been translated using the spot rate, or an average rate may be used if exchange rates do not fluctuate significantly. The risk on initial recognition is that an inappropriate exchange rate has been used in the translation of the amount, causing an inaccurate expense, current liability and inventory valuation to be recorded, which may be over or understated in value.

Foreign currency transactions – exchange gains and losses

Further risk arises in the accounting treatment of balances relating to foreign currency at the year end. Payables denominated in a foreign currency must be retranslated using the closing rate, with exchange gains or losses recognised in profit or loss for the year. The risk is that the year end retranslation does not take place, or that an inappropriate exchange rate is used for the retranslation, leading to over or understated current liabilities and operating expenses. Risk also exists relating to transactions that are settled within the year, if the correct exchange gain or loss has not been included in profit. Inventory should not be retranslated at the year end as it is a non-monetary item, so any retranslation of inventory would result in over or undervaluation of inventory and profit.

Product recall – obsolete inventory

There is a quantity of copper wiring which appears to have no realisable value as it has been corroded and cannot be used in the production of circuit boards. This inventory should be written off, as according to IAS 2 *Inventories,* measurement should be at the lower of cost and net realisable value. The risk is that inventory has not been reduced in value, leading to overstated current assets and overstated operating profit. The risk is heightened if Grohl Co has not adequately identified and separated the corroded copper wiring from the rest of its inventory. This is quite likely, given that the corrosion cannot be spotted visually and relies on the copper being tested.

Product recall – refunds to customers

Due to the faulty items being recalled, some customers may have demanded a refund instead of a replacement circuit board. If the customer had already paid for the goods, a provision should be recognised for the refund, as the original sale and subsequent product recall would create an obligation. If the customer had not already paid for the goods and did not want a replacement, then the balance on the customer's receivables account should be written off. Depending on whether the customer had paid before the year end, there is a risk of overstated profits and either understated provisions or overstated current assets if the necessary adjustment for any refunds is not made.

Additional finance – capitalisation of new production line

The new production process would appear to be a significant piece of capital expenditure, and it is crucial that directly attributable costs are appropriately capitalised according to IAS 16 Property, *Plant and Equipment* and IAS *23 Borrowing Costs.* Directly attributable finance costs must be capitalised during the period of construction of the processing line, and if they have not been capitalised, non-current assets will be understated and profit understated. There is also a risk that due to the company's low level of profit, there is pressure on management to understate expenses. This could be achieved by treating items of revenue expenditure as capital expenditure, which would overstate non-current assets and overstate profit.

New regulations – valuation of existing production facilities

There is a risk that the existing production facilities are impaired. This is due to the new regulations which come into force next year, and may make at least part of the existing facilities redundant when the new production line is ready for use. IAS 36 *Impairment of Assets* identifies adverse changes in the legal environment as an external indicator of potential impairment. If management does not perform an impairment review to identify the recoverable amount of the production facilities, then the carrying value may be overstated. Profit would also be overstated if the necessary impairment loss were not recognised.

Additional finance – measurement and disclosure of loan

The loan taken out is a financial liability and must be accounted for in accordance with IFRS *9 Financial Instruments,* which states that financial liabilities must be classified and measured at amortised cost using the effective interest method (unless an option is taken to measure at fair value). The risk is that amortised cost has not been applied, meaning that finance costs have not accrued on the loan. The fact that the finance cost in the draft statement of profit or loss has remained static indicates that this may have happened, resulting in understated finance costs and understated liabilities.

There is also a risk that necessary disclosures under IFRS *7 Financial Instruments: Disclosures* have not been made. The notes to the financial statements should contain narrative and numerical disclosures regarding risk exposures, and given the materiality of the loan, it is likely that disclosure would be necessary.

Tutorial note

More than the required number of four risks of material misstatement have been identified and explained in the answer above. Credit will be awarded for any four relevant risks, such as cut-off problems in relation to overseas transactions.

(iii) Ethical issues

An audit manager of Foo & Co is being interviewed for the position of financial controller at Grohl Co. Familiarity or intimidation threats may be created by employment with an audit client.

The familiarity threat is caused by the relationship that Bob Halen will have with the audit team, having worked at the firm. This may cause the audit team to fail to challenge him sufficiently and lose professional scepticism. The more junior members of the audit team may also feel intimidated by him as his previous position was as audit manager. He will also be aware of the firm's audit methodology and procedures, making it easier for him to circumvent procedures.

If a former member of the audit team or partner of the firm has joined the audit client in a position that can influence the preparation of the financial statements, and a significant connection remains between the firm and the individual, the threat would be so significant that no safeguards could reduce the threat to an acceptable level. Therefore it is crucial that Foo & Co ensures that no significant connection between the audit firm and Bob Halen remains, for example, by ensuring that he does not continue to participate or appear to participate in the firm's business or professional activities, and by making sure that he is not owed any material sum of money from the audit firm. If a significant connection were to remain, then the threat to objectivity would be unacceptably high, and Foo & Co would have to consider resigning as auditors of Grohl Co.

In the event of Bob Halen accepting the position and no significant connection between him and the firm remaining, the existence and significance of familiarity and intimidation threats would need to be considered and appropriate safeguards, such as modifying the audit plan and changing the composition of the audit team, put in place.

Any work that Bob Halen may have recently performed on Grohl Co should be subject to review, as there may have been a self-interest threat if Bob knew he was going to apply for the role at the same time as performing work for the client. However, as audit planning has yet to commence, this may not be an important issue.

Foo & Co should have in place policies and procedures which require members of an audit team to notify the audit firm when entering employment negotiations with the client. The firm's policies and procedures should be reviewed to ensure they are adequate and they may need to be communicated again to members of staff.

Tutorial note

It is not certain or even implied that Bob has deliberately tried to hide his intention to join Grohl Co – but credit will be awarded where candidates assume this to be the case. Equally, credit will be awarded for comments recognising that it is appropriate that Bob has been removed from the audit team.

As to the comment regarding whether the audit can be conducted on a contingent fee basis, this is not allowed according to ACCA's *Code of ethics*. Contingent fee arrangements in respect of audit engagements create self-interest threats to the auditor's objectivity and independence that are so significant that they cannot be eliminated or reduced to an acceptable level by the application of any safeguards.

The audit fee must not depend on contingencies such as whether the auditor's report on the financial statements is modified or unmodified. The basis for the calculation of the audit fee is agreed with the audited entity each year before significant audit work is undertaken.

Conclusion

The audit of Grohl Co should be approached as high risk, due to the number of business risks and risks of material misstatement explained in these briefing notes. An audit strategy must be developed to minimise the overall level of audit risk, and strong quality control procedures must be adhered to throughout the audit. In addition, the ethical issue relating to Bob Halen must be brought to the attention of our firm's Ethics Partner as soon as possible.

(b) Matters to consider

The amount of $5 million that has been claimed is material to the draft financial statements, representing 2.7% of total assets. It represents 40% of revenue for the year, and if adjusted would turn the loss currently recognised of $300,000 to a profit of $4.7 million.

The claim represents a contingent asset, which, according to IAS *37 Provisions, Contingent Liabilities and Contingent Assets* should not be recognised until such time as the inflow of economic benefits is virtually certain. If the inflow of benefits is probable rather than virtually certain, then the matter should only be disclosed in a note to the financial statements.

The issue here is whether the amount claimed can be considered as virtually certain or even probable to be received. The business insurance taken out by Grohl Co might only cover business interruption caused by certain circumstances or events, such as terrorist acts or natural disasters. And it may only apply if the whole business operation is curtailed, rather than just activities in one location.

The amount claimed appears unrealistic. Production was halted for one week at one location only, so to claim an amount equivalent to 40% of the company's total annual revenue seems extreme, making it very unlikely that the claim would be approved by the insurance provider.

For these reasons, an adjustment to the financial statements would seem inappropriate, certainly until confirmation has been received from the insurance provider. If the financial statements are adjusted to include a receivable of $5 million, the audit firm should consider this as a very high risk issue, because of the potential impact on the auditor's report of the potentially material and possibly pervasive misstatement.

Recommended procedures

- Obtain a copy of the insurance claim made and confirm that $5 million is the amount claimed.
- Enquire as to the basis of the $5 million claimed, and review any supporting documentation such as extracts of management accounts showing lost income for the period of halted production.
- Scrutinise the terms of Grohl Co's insurance policy, to determine whether production halted in Grohl Co's circumstances would be covered.
- Seek permission to contact the insurance provider to enquire as to the status of the claim, and attempt to receive written confirmation of the likelihood of any payment being made.
- Review correspondence between Grohl Co and the insurance provider, looking for confirmation of any amounts to be paid.
- Contact Grohl Co's lawyers to enquire if there have been any legal repercussions arising from the insurance claim, for example, the insurance company may have disputed the claim and the matter may now be in the hands of legal experts.

Examiner's comments

This question was split into four question requirements. The scenario and requirements involved the planning of the audit, and information was given on the business background and recent developments of the client company, as well as some financial information. There were also ethical issues embedded in the scenario.

It was clear that the majority of candidates were familiar with audit planning questions and seemed comfortable with the style of the question and with the amount of information that had been given in the scenario. There was little evidence of time pressure despite the length of the question.

Requirement (a) (i) asked candidates to evaluate the business risks faced by the company.

This was by far the best answered requirement of the exam, with most candidates identifying and explaining a range of relevant business risks, which on the whole were developed in enough detail. Most candidates tended to be able to discuss at least six different business risks, with foreign exchange issues, the loss of several executives, reliance on a single supplier and too few customers, and the problems of operating in a high technology industry being the most commonly risks discussed.

For candidates who achieved lower marks on this requirement, the problem was that they did not develop their discussion enough to achieve the maximum marks per point. Some of the answers just repeated the business issue as stated in the question without discussing any of the impact on the business at all. Most candidates discussed going concern, which was relevant, but instead of relating going concern to specific matters such as liquidity problems and the large loan, it was simply mentioned as a conclusion in relation to every business risk discussed, and therefore was not specific enough to earn credit.

Many answers could have been improved in relation to business risk evaluation by including some simple analysis of the financial information made available, for example through the calculation of profit margins and trends. This would have been an easy way to develop the point that financial performance was suffering, as well as liquidity being poor.

Requirement (a) (ii) was less well answered. Candidates were asked to identify and explain four risks of material misstatement to be considered in planning the audit. (Note the UK and IRL adapted papers had a slightly different requirement with no specific number of risks of material misstatement required. Answers were very mixed for this requirement. Some candidates clearly understood the meaning of a risk of material misstatement, and could apply their knowledge to the question requirement, resulting in sound explanations. However, despite this being a regularly examined topic and the cornerstone of audit planning under the Clarified ISAs, the majority of answers were unsatisfactory.

First, many candidates included a discussion about this being a first year audit which would result in a risk of material misstatement, but this was both incorrect and showed that the question had not been read carefully enough. Then, when attempting to explain a risk of material misstatement, many candidates could do little more than state a financial reporting rule, and then say the risk was that 'this would be incorrectly accounted for'. It was not clear if this type of vague statement was down to candidates being reluctant to come to a decision about whether a balance would be over or understated, or if they thought that their answer was specific enough. Very few answers were specific enough on the actual risk of misstatement to earn credit.

The matters that tended to be better explained were the risks of misstatement to do with inventory obsolescence, impairment of property plant and equipment, and the finance costs associated with the new loan.

On a general note, many candidates seemed confused between a business risk and a risk of material misstatement, and some answers mixed up the two. Candidates are reminded that it is an essential skill of an auditor to be able to identify both types of risk, and that they are related to each other, but they are not the same thing.

Requirement (a) (iii) focused on ethical issues. The requirement was to discuss the ethical issues raised in the scenario and to recommend actions to be taken by the audit firm. There were two ethical issues of relevance to planning the audit – the contingent fee that had been requested by the audit client, and the matter of the previous audit manager potentially gaining employment at the client. Answers here were mixed, and generally the answers in relation to the contingent fee were better than those in relation to employment at a client company. On the contingent fee most candidates seemed confident in their knowledge, and correctly identified that a contingent fee is not allowed for an audit engagement, and recommended sensible actions such as ensuring a discussion of the matter with those charged with governance. The majority of candidates had the correct knowledge here, and could apply appropriately to the question. As usual, candidates appear reasonably comfortable with the ethics part of the syllabus, but are reminded that to score well on ethical requirements in P7, they must do more than just identify a threat.

On the matter of the previous audit manager going to work at the audit client answers were unsatisfactory. Most could identify that it was an ethical threat, and could suggest which threat(s) arose, but were less competent at explaining why the threat arose in the first place. Most answers suggested at least one safeguard, usually involving reviews of work performed and ensuring that the manager has no further involvement with the audit, which were fine, but many also made inappropriate suggestions along the lines of 'forbidding' the manager to work at the client, 'prohibiting' the audit client from taking on the manager, and 'disciplining' the manager himself. Very few answers considered the key ethical issue of considering whether the audit manager retained any connection with the audit firm.

Some answers had incorrectly assumed that the manager was being loaned to the client on a temporary basis, rather than taking up a permanent position, and some thought that he would be involved in both the audit and the preparation of financial statements. It is important to read the scenario carefully and to take time to think through the information that has been given before starting to write an answer.

The requirements discussed so far attracted a maximum of four professional marks. Generally candidates presented their answer in a logical and appropriate manner, and a significant number of answers included both an introduction and an appropriate conclusion. Most answers used headings to separate their answer points and generally the presentation was improved from previous sittings.

Requirement (b) asked candidates to recommend the audit procedures that should be carried out in respect of an insurance claim that had been submitted by the client just before the year end. The wording of the requirement should have been familiar to candidates as it has been used in many previous exam questions. The scenario contained a brief description which should have made candidates sceptical of the claim being eligible to be recognised as a receivable – particularly the fact that the claim was highly material, and if recognised would have turned the company's loss into a profit, and also the fact that the amount being claimed seemed very unrealistic when compared to the annual revenue. Unfortunately very few candidates picked up on these matters, and did not question the amount of the claim or the timing of it, and very few answers specified the impact that it would have on the financial statements. Most answers included one materiality calculation but not the impact the adjustment would have on the reported loss for the year.

While some answers correctly discussed the accounting and disclosure requirements for a contingent asset, a number of answers incorrectly thought that the claim should result in some kind of provision or liability.

The audit procedures that were recommended were mixed in quality. Most candidates suggested a review of the terms and conditions of the insurance policy to see if the situation was covered, and most also recommended reviewing the actual claim and contacting the insurance provider. All of these are valid and appropriate procedures and generally were well described. Some answers tended to state that the matter should be 'discussed with management' with no further explanation, or that 'an expert should be consulted' but with no description of what evidence the expert should be asked to provide, or even who the expert should be. Too many candidates seemed to want to rely on representations and discussions about the possible outcome of the insurance claim when there were other stronger sources of audit evidence available.

ACCA marking scheme			
			Marks
(a)	(i)	**Business risks** Up to 2 marks for each business risk evaluated (up to a maximum of 3 marks in total if risks identified but not evaluated): – Exchange rate risk – Imports – transportation costs and potential for disrupted supply – Reliance on one supplier – Quality control issues – High-tech/competitive industry – Reliance on key customer contracts – Regulatory issues – Liquidity/solvency issues – Poor profitability – Change in key management	
		Maximum	**12**

(ii) **Risk of material misstatement**	
Up to 2 marks for each risk of material misstatement identified and explained to a maximum of four risks (up to a maximum of 2 marks in total for identification only):	
– Initial translation of foreign exchange transactions	
– Retranslation and exchange gains and losses	
– Obsolete inventory	
– Refunds to customers	
– Capitalisation of borrowing costs to new production line	
– Impairment of old production line	
– Loan classification, measurement and disclosure	
Maximum	**8**
(iii) **Ethical issues**	
Generally 1 mark per comment:	
– Explain why familiarity threat arises	
– Explain why intimidation threat arises	
– Significant connections should be evaluated	
– If significant connections remain, firm should resign	
– If continue with audit, consider modifying audit approach and change audit team	
– Review any work recently performed on Grohl Co audit by Bob Halen	
– Consider firms policies and procedures	
– Contingent fee not acceptable	
– The basis for calculation of the audit fee must be agreed with client	
Maximum	**6**
Professional marks:	
Generally 1 mark for heading, 1 mark for introduction, 1 mark for use of headings within the briefing notes, 1 mark for clarity of comments made	
Maximum	**4**
(b) **Insurance claim**	
Generally 1 mark per matter/procedure:	
Matters:	
– Accounting treatment for contingent asset	
– Claim may not be covered by insurance	
– Amount of the claim seems unreasonable	
– Materiality	
– Potential risk of material misstatement and impact on report	
Procedures:	
– Inspect claim and supporting documentation	
– Inspect insurance terms and conditions	
– Review correspondence	
– Communicate with insurance provider	
– Enquiry with lawyers	
Maximum	**5**
Total	**35**

8 JOVI GROUP *Walk in the footsteps of a top tutor*

Top tutor tips

Part (a) (i) requires an explanation of why materiality should be reassessed as the audit progresses. This is a mainly knowledge based requirement.

(a) (ii) asks for an assessment of the key audit findings for the completion of the audit. The key audit findings are clearly identifiable with a subheading and are also numbered. Work your way through the 9 notes in turn explaining why each is significant. The requirement specifies that you consider if there is a risk of material misstatement and the adequacy of the evidence obtained. Do not give additional procedures as you have been specifically told not to do this.

Part (b) requires advantages and disadvantages of joint audits. This is rote-learned knowledge and should therefore be quite straightforward.

(a) (i) Materiality

Materiality is a matter of judgement, and is commonly determined using a numerical approach based on percentages calculated on revenue, profit before tax and total assets. ISA 320 *Materiality in Planning and Performing an Audit* requires that the auditor shall revise materiality for the financial statements as a whole in the event of becoming aware of information during the audit that would have caused the auditor to determine a different level of materiality initially.

It may be that during the audit, the auditor becomes aware of a matter which impacts on the auditor's understanding of the client's business and which leads the auditor to believe that the initial assessment of materiality was inappropriate and must be revised. For example, the actual results of the audit client may turn out to be quite different to the forecast results on which the initial level of materiality was based.

Or, a change in the client's circumstances may occur during the audit, for example, a decision to dispose of a major part of the business. This again would cause the auditor to consider if the previously determined level of materiality were still appropriate.

If adjustments are made to the financial statements subsequent to the initial assessment of materiality, then the materiality level would need to be adjusted accordingly.

The initial calculation of materiality for the Jovi Group was based on the client's listed status, and therefore on an assumption of it being high risk. It is therefore important that any events, such as those explained above, are taken into account in assessing a new level of materiality for this client to ensure that sufficient appropriate evidence is obtained to support the audit opinion.

(ii) Audit implications

Property disposal

A material profit has been recognised on the disposal of a property, and the asset derecognised. This may not be the correct accounting treatment, as the sales agreement contains an option to repurchase, and the transaction may be a financing arrangement rather than a genuine sale. Further work needs to be carried out to determine the substance of the transaction. If it is in substance a loan secured on the value of the property, then the asset should be reinstated and a loan payable recognised on the statement of financial position, with finance charges accruing according to IFRS 9 *Financial Instruments.* Profit is overstated by a material amount if the disposal has been incorrectly accounted for.

Revaluation

The revaluation gain recognised of $800,000 is below the level of materiality set initially which was $900,000. However, the level of materiality has now been revised to $700,000, meaning that the gain now needs to be subject to audit procedures to ensure there is no material misstatement. Further audit work may be needed to ensure that this is the only property that should be revalued, given that all assets in the same class should be subject to revaluation.

Actuarial loss

The loss recognised is material to the financial statements, but only limited procedures have been conducted. Axle Co is a service organisation, and audit procedures should be carried out according to ISA 402 *Audit Considerations Relating to an Entity Using a Service Organisation.* Auditors are required to gain an understanding of the service organisation either from the user entity, which in this case is the Jovi Group (the Group), or by obtaining a report on the service organisation.

The procedures that have been conducted so far are not sufficient, as written confirmation and agreement to Axle Co's records do not provide evidence as to the basis of the valuation of the pension plan, which has a material impact on the Group financial statements. The audit team themselves should perform procedures to provide evidence as to the measurement of the plan and the actuarial loss, and not simply rely on the accounting records of the service organisation.

Goodwill impairment

Goodwill has remained at the same amount in the financial statements, but the goodwill may be overstated in value. One of the subsidiaries, Copeland Co, has suffered a 25% reduction in revenue. This is an indicator of impairment of goodwill, and a written representation and arithmetical check is not sufficient appropriate evidence for such a material and subjective matter. Further audit work should be conducted on management's assumptions used in the impairment review of goodwill relating to Copeland Co. As Sambora & Co performs the audit of Copeland Co, the firm should have sufficient business understanding to challenge management's assumptions on the impairment review of goodwill.

Goodwill classification

A trading division relating to one-third of a subsidiary's net assets is held for sale at the year end. Any goodwill relating to this trading division should be reclassified out of goodwill and into the disposal group of assets held for sale. It may be a subjective and complex process to determine how much of the subsidiary's goodwill should be allocated to the trading division which is held for sale. It may be that no goodwill is attached to this trading division, but this should be confirmed through further audit procedures.

The two matters explained above both indicate that the Group's goodwill figure could be materially overstated and that further audit procedures should be performed.

Associate

The statement of financial position recognises an associate at $4.23 million in both the current and prior periods. It is unusual to see no movement in this figure, especially given that the statement of profit or loss recognises a share of profit generated from the associate, which should normally result in an increase in the value of the associate recognised as an investment of the Group.

It is unacceptable not to obtain evidence in respect of the associate. The audit team should enquire as to the accounting entries that have been made in relation to the associate and confirm whether no movement in the investment is reasonable.

Assets held for sale

There seems to be incorrect and incomplete disclosure in relation to the disposal group of assets held for sale. As discussed above, it seems that no goodwill has been allocated to the disposal group, which needs further investigation. In addition, the disposal group of assets should not be disclosed under the non-current assets heading but should be disclosed in a separate category on the statement of financial position.

Also, any liabilities associated with the disposal group should be presented separately from other liabilities. It is not clear from the draft accounts whether the $7.8 million disclosed as assets held for sale is just non-current assets, or whether it is a net figure including both assets and liabilities. It is required by IFRS *5 Non-Current Assets Held for Sale and Discontinued Operations* that the assets and liabilities of disposal groups should not be offset and must be presented separately within total assets and total liabilities. Therefore, procedures should be performed to determine how the $7.8 million has been calculated, and to ensure appropriate disclosure of any liabilities of the disposal group.

The assets of a disposal group should also be re-measured if necessary to fair value less cost to sell, if this is lower than carrying value. The audit team needs to determine whether management has conducted a review of the value of assets held in the disposal group. The amounts recognised may be overstated.

Finally, the sale of the trading division would seem to meet the definition of a discontinued operation according to IFRS 5, as its assets were held for sale at the year end, and it is likely to constitute a separate major line of business. IFRS 5 requires that the face of the statement of profit or loss discloses a single figure in respect of discontinued operations, comprising the post-tax profit or loss of the discontinued operation and the post-tax gain or loss recognised on any measurement of its assets to fair value, less cost to sell. The Group's statement of profit or loss does not include any figure in relation to the trading division which is being sold. Audit procedures should be performed to determine whether this is necessary.

Regarding evidence obtained, the external confirmation from the buyer is a reliable source of evidence. However, it was obtained a number of months ago, since when circumstances may have changed. The buyer should be contacted again to reconfirm at a date closer to the signing of the auditor's report their intention to purchase the trading division.

Non-controlling interest

The statement of financial position correctly discloses the non-controlling interest as a component of equity, as required by IAS *1 Presentation of Financial Statements.* However, the statement of profit or loss does not disclose the profit for the year or total comprehensive income for the year attributable to the non-controlling interest. Therefore the audit team must enquire as to whether this disclosure will be made by management.

Finance cost

A loan of $8 million was taken out in October 2011, carrying a 2% interest charge. This would mean finance costs of $120,000 ($8 million × 2% × 9/12) should be accrued for. However, the Group's finance cost has increased by $40,000 only. Therefore the finance cost may not have been recognised in full, overstating profit and understating liabilities. Work should be performed to understand the components of the finance charge recognised, as other finance costs may have ceased during the year. The notes to the financial statements should also be reviewed to ensure there is adequate disclosure of the loan taken out.

(b) In a joint audit, two or more audit firms are responsible for conducting the audit and for issuing the audit opinion. The main advantage of a joint audit of May Co is that the local audit firm's understanding and experience of May Co will be retained, and that will be a valuable input to the audit. At the same time, Sambora & Co can provide additional skills and resources where necessary.

The country in which May Co is located may have different regulations to the rest of the Group, for example, there may be a different financial reporting framework. It makes sense for the local auditors, therefore, to retain some input to the audit as they will have detailed knowledge of such regulations.

The fact that May Co is located in a distant location means that from a practical point of view it may be difficult for Sambora & Co to provide staff for performing the bulk of the audit work. It will be more cost effective for this to be carried out by local auditors.

Two audit firms can also stand together against aggressive accounting treatments. In this way, a joint audit works to enhance the quality of the audit. The benchmarking that takes place between the two firms raises the level of service quality.

The main disadvantage is that for the Group, having a joint audit is likely to be more expensive than appointing just one audit firm. However, the costs are likely to be less than if Sambora & Co took sole responsibility, as having the current auditors retain an involvement will at least cut down on travel expenses. And the small local firm will probably offer a cheaper audit service than Sambora & Co.

For the audit firms, there may be problems in deciding on responsibilities, allocating work, and they will need to work very closely together to ensure that no duties go underperformed, and that the quality of the audit is maintained.

Examiner's comments

This question was split into three requirements. The scenario was based on the completion of a group audit, and candidates were given draft consolidated financial statements and a selection of key audit findings, based on the audit work that had already been performed.

Requirement (a) (i) asked for an explanation of why auditors need to reassess materiality as the audit progresses. This was linked to a part of the scenario where it was explained that the materiality level applied to the audit of the Group has been reduced. Answers were usually limited here to a definition of materiality and a suggestion of how an appropriate materiality figure is determined, and few answers actually answered the question requirement. Those that did tended to focus on risk assessment and the auditor uncovering new information about the client as the audit progresses. These points are both valid, but very few answers discussed them, or any other relevant points, in sufficient detail.

Requirement (a) (ii) asked candidates to assess the implications of the key audit findings provided on the completion of the audit. Guidance was given on this requirement, instructing candidates that they needed to consider risk of material misstatement and the adequacy of the audit evidence obtained.

Candidates were also specifically instructed not to recommend further audit procedures. The scenario provided nine key audit findings to be assessed.

This is a good example of a question requirement where candidates were expected to think on their feet and not rely on rote learnt facts. The candidates that did as the question instructed and took time to think about the information in the scenario scored well, and there were some sound answers. However the majority of candidates could not apply their knowledge to this scenario, leading to unfocused answers that did not actually answer the question requirement. Answers were on the whole unsatisfactory. Candidates tended to approach the key audit findings in a logical way, working through them in the order presented in the question. However, for each key audit finding most answers simply stated that audit evidence was not adequate without explaining why, and then gave a list of audit procedures, which was specifically not asked for. As in Q1(a) (ii), answers were inadequate at explaining risks of material misstatement, and in fact were worse in this question, maybe because audit completion is less frequently examined than audit planning. Candidates made mistakes in calculating materiality, using the wrong basis for most calculations, and generally did not understand the part of the information provided that dealt with other comprehensive income and its components.

Some key audit findings were better answered, mainly because marks could be awarded for financial reporting issues which candidates seemed comfortable discussing, namely the property disposal that could have been a financing arrangement, and the potential impairment of goodwill. However, all other key audit findings were inadequately dealt with, with some in some cases not even warranting an attempt at an answer, even though the issues, when thought through, were not difficult. For example, the key issue in relation to the actuarial loss that has been suffered was that a written representation is not sufficient evidence for such a material figure, and that no work had been done to consider the competence of the service organisation which had provided the figures. In relation to the associate, candidates did not seem sceptical of the fact that there was no movement on the statement of financial position, which in itself indicates a potential misstatement. A significant number of answers thought that the auditor need not obtain audit evidence for a material balance if it had not moved during the year.

Requirement (b) asked for a discussion of the advantages and disadvantages of a joint audit being performed on a newly acquired subsidiary. Most candidates could identify at least two advantages and two disadvantages, though often they were not discussed at all and the answer amounted to little more than a list of bullet points, which would not have attracted many marks. Some answers seemed to confuse a joint audit with an audit involving component auditors, and some used the fact that the foreign audit firm was a small firm to argue that it could not possibly be competent enough to perform an audit or have a good ethical standing.

Most answers identified the cost implications for the client, and the advantage of involving a local firm who would have knowledge of the local law and regulations.

ACCA marking scheme	
	Marks
(a) (i) **Materiality**	
Up to 1 mark for each comment:	
– Recognise materiality is subjective	
– Auditor's business understanding may change during the audit, making some balances and transactions material	
– Client's circumstances may change during the audit, making some balances and transactions more material	
– Adjustments to the accounts mean materiality has to be revised	
– Recognise the high-risk status of the client	
Maximum	4
(ii) **Audit completion issues**	
Up to 2 marks for each audit completion issue assessed:	
– Property disposal/sale and leaseback	
– Property revaluation	
– Actuarial loss	
– Goodwill impairment	
– Goodwill classification into assets held for sale	
– Associate	
– Presentation of assets held for sale (separate and not netted off)	
– Measurement of assets held for sale	
– Lack of disclosure of discontinued operation	
– Non-controlling interest	
– Finance cost and loan	
Maximum	15
(b) **Joint audit**	
Up to 1 mark for each advantage/disadvantage discussed:	
– Retain local auditors' knowledge of May Co	
– Retain local auditors' knowledge of local regulations	
– Sambora & Co can provide additional skills and resources	
– Cost effective – reduce travel expenses, local firm likely to be cheaper	
– Enhanced audit quality	
– But employing two audit firms could be more expensive	
– Problems in allocating work – could increase audit risk	
Maximum	6
Total	**25**

9 CS GROUP *Walk in the footsteps of a top tutor*

Top tutor tips

Part (a) (i) requires explanation of the implications of the acquisition of a subsidiary on the planning of the audit of CS Group. A good way to approach this requirement is to think about the planning aspects of a single company audit and apply them to the group situation e.g. risk assessment, materiality assessment, etc.

Part (a) (ii) asks for evaluation of the risks of material misstatement for both the individual financial statements of the parent and the consolidated financial statements. Risks of material misstatement are the risks to the financial statements. It is important to identify the balances or disclosures that could be wrong and to explain why this might be the case. Risks of material misstatement result from non-compliance with accounting standards so try to remember the relevant accounting standard and what the accounting treatment should be. Vague answers stating there is a risk the relevant accounting standards have not been followed will not earn marks. State the requirements of the standards.

Part (a) (iii) asks for principal audit procedures to be performed in respect of goodwill. Procedures should be specific enough that another audit team member would know what to do if they were asked to perform the procedure. Be as specific as possible to ensure the marks are awarded.

(a) (i) Implications of the acquisition of Canary Co for audit planning Individual financial statement audit

Our firm has been appointed auditor of the new subsidiary which was acquired on 1 February 2012. This means that we must plan the audit of its individual financial statements, and then consider its implications for the audit of the consolidated financial statements.

First, we must plan to develop an understanding of the company, including its environment and internal control, as required by ISA 315 *Identifying and* Assessing *the Risks of Material Misstatement through Understanding the Entity and Its Environment. We* must obtain an understanding of the relevant industry, regulatory and other external factors, the nature of the company's operations, ownership and governance structures, its selection and application of accounting policies, its objectives and strategies, and the measurement and review of its financial performance. Without this knowledge of the business we will be unable to properly perform risk assessment.

From our audit of the CS Group we will already have knowledge of the pottery industry, however, Canary Co's operations are different in that it specialises in figurines and makes some sales online.

The auditor should obtain an understanding of internal controls relevant to the audit. Therefore we must document our understanding of Canary Co's accounting systems and internal controls. This is important given that Canary Co has different IT systems to the rest of the group.

Canary Co makes sales online, and due to the likely complexity of the online sales system, consideration should be given as to whether the use of an expert is required, or whether computer-assisted audit techniques (CAATs) can be used to obtain sufficient evidence on revenue.

It will take time to gain this knowledge and to properly document it. Given that the company's year end is less than one month away, it is important that we plan to begin this work as soon as possible, to avoid any delay to the audit of either the individual or the consolidated financial statements. We need to arrange with the client for members of the audit team to have access to the necessary information, including the accounting system, and to hold the necessary discussions with management. Once we have gained a thorough understanding of Canary Co we will be in a position to develop an audit strategy and detailed audit plan.

We have been provided with the CS Group's forecast revenue and profit for the year, but need to perform a detailed preliminary analytical review on a full set of Canary Co's financial statements to fully understand the financial performance and position of the company, and to begin to form a view on materiality. This review will also highlight any significant transactions that have occurred this year.

As this is an initial audit engagement, we are required by ISA 300 *Planning an Audit of Financial Statements* to communicate with the predecessor auditor. If this has not yet occurred, we should contact the predecessor auditor and enquire regarding matters which may influence our audit strategy and plan. We may request access to their working papers, especially in respect of any matters which appear contentious or significant. We should also review the prior year audit opinion as this may include matters that impact on this year's audit.

As the opening balances were audited by another firm, we should plan to perform additional work on opening balances as required by ISA 510 *Initial Audit Engagements – Opening Balances.*

Consolidated financial statements audit

As Canary Co will form a component of the consolidated financial statements on which we are required to form an opinion, we must also consider the implications of its acquisition for the audit of the CS Group accounts. ISA 600 *Special Considerations – Audits of Group Financial Statements (Including the Work of Component Auditors)* requires that the group auditor must identify whether components of the group are significant components. Based on the forecast results Canary Co is a significant component, as it represents 11.9% of forecast consolidated revenue, and 23.5% of forecast consolidated profit before tax.

As our firm is auditing the individual financial statements of Canary Co, our risk assessment and planned response to risks identified at individual company level will also be relevant to the audit of the consolidated financial statements. However, we must also plan to obtain audit evidence in respect of balances and transactions which only become relevant on consolidation, such as any inter-company transactions that may occur.

A significant matter which must be addressed is that of the different financial year end of Canary Co. We will have audited Canary Co's figures to its year end of 30 June 2012, but an additional month will be consolidated to bring the accounts into line with the 31 July year end of the rest of the CS Group. Therefore, additional procedures will have to be planned to gain audit evidence on significant events and transactions of Canary Co which occur in July 2012. This may not entail much extra work, as we will be conducting a review of subsequent events anyway, as part of our audit of the individual financial statements.

It may be that Canary Co's year end will be changed to bring into line with the rest of the CS Group. If so, we need to obtain copies of the documentary evidence to demonstrate that this has been done.

When performing analytical procedures on the consolidated financial statements, we must be careful that when comparing this year's results with prior periods, we are making reasonable comparisons. This is because Canary Co's results are only included since the date of acquisition on 1 February 2012 and comparative figures are not restated. Calculations such as return on capital employed will also be distorted, as the consolidated statement of financial position at 31 July 2012 includes Canary Co's assets and liabilities in full, but the consolidated statement of profit or loss will only include six months' profit generated from those assets.

Materiality needs to be assessed based on the new, enlarged group structure. Materiality for the group financial statements as a whole shall be determined when establishing the overall group audit strategy. The addition of Canary Co to the group during the year is likely to cause materiality to be different from previous years, possibly affecting audit strategy and the extent of testing in some areas.

Finally, we must ensure that sufficient time and resource is allocated to the audit of the consolidated financial statements as there will be additional work to perform on auditing the acquisition itself, including the goodwill asset, the fair value of assets acquired, the cash outflows, the contingent consideration, and the notes to the financial statements. As this is a complex area we should consider allocating this work to a senior, experienced member of the audit team. Relevant risks of material misstatement and audit procedures in respect of goodwill are discussed later in these notes.

(ii) Risks of material misstatement

General matters

Changes to corporate structure such as large acquisitions, moving into new lines of business and the installation of significant new IT systems related to financial reporting may indicate risks of material misstatement. The CS Group has been involved in all three of these during the financial year, so the audit generally should be approached as high risk.

Goodwill

The client has determined goodwill arising on the acquisition of Canary Co to be $45 million, which is material to the consolidated financial statements, representing 8.2% of total assets. The various components of goodwill have specific risks attached. For the consideration, the contingent element of the consideration is inherently risky, as its measurement involves a judgement as to the probability of the amount being paid.

Currently, the full amount of contingent consideration is recognised, indicating that the amount is certain to be paid. IFRS 3 (Revised) *Business Combinations* requires that contingent consideration is recognised at fair value at the time of the business combination, meaning that the probability of payment should be used in measuring the amount of consideration that is recognised at acquisition. This part of the consideration could therefore be overstated, if the assessment of probability of payment is incorrect.

Another risk is that the contingent consideration does not appear to have been discounted to present value as required by IFRS 3, again indicating that it is overstated.

The same risk factors apply to the individual financial statements of Crow Co, in which the cost of investment is recognised as a non-current asset.

The other component of the goodwill calculation is the value of identifiable assets acquired, which IFRS 3 requires to be measured at fair value at the date of acquisition. This again is inherently risky, as estimating fair value can involve uncertainty. Possibly the risk is reduced somewhat as the fair values have been determined by an external firm.

Goodwill should be tested for impairment annually according to IAS 36 *Impairment of Assets,* and a test should be performed in the year of acquisition, regardless of whether indicators of impairment exist. There is therefore a risk that goodwill may be overstated if management has not conducted an impairment test at the year end. If the impairment review were to indicate that goodwill is overstated, there would be implications for the cost of investment recognised in Crow Co's financial statements, which may also be overstated.

Loan stock

Crow Co has issued loan stock for $100 million, representing 18.2% of total assets, therefore this is material to the consolidated financial statements. The loan will be repaid at a significant premium of $20 million, which should be recognised as finance cost over the period of the loan using the amortised cost measurement method according to IFRS *9 Financial Instruments.* A risk of misstatement arises if the premium relating to this financial year has not been included in finance costs.

In addition, finance costs could be understated if interest payable has not been accrued. The loan carries 5% interest per annum, and six months should be accrued by the 31 July year end, amounting to $2.5 million. Financial liabilities and finance costs will be understated if this has not been accrued.

There is also a risk of inadequate disclosure regarding the loan in the notes to the financial statements. IFRS *7 Financial Instruments: Disclosures* requires narrative and numerical disclosures relating to financial instruments that give rise to risk exposure. Given the materiality of the loan, it is likely that disclosure would be required.

The risks described above are relevant to Crow Co's individual financial statements as well as the consolidated financial statements.

Online sales

There is a risk that revenue is not recognised at the correct time, as it can be difficult to establish with online sales when the revenue recognition criteria of IFRS 15 *Revenue from contracts with customers* have been met. This could mean that revenue and profits are at risk of over or understatement. This is a significant issue as 30% of Canary Co's sales are made online, which approximates to sales of $4.8 million or 3.6% of this year's consolidated revenue, and will be a higher percentage of total sales next year when a full year of Canary Co's revenue is consolidated.

Prior to the acquisition of Canary Co, the CS Group had no experience of online sales, which means that there will not yet be a group accounting policy for online revenue recognition.

There may also be risks arising from the system not operating effectively or that controls are deficient leading to inaccurate recording of sales.

Canary Co management

As this is the first time that Canary Co's management will be involved with group financial reporting, they will be unfamiliar with the processes used and information required by the CS Group in preparing the consolidated financial statements. There is a risk that information provided may be inaccurate or incomplete, for example in relation to inter-company transactions.

Financial performance

Looking at the consolidated revenue and profit figures, it appears that the group's results are encouraging, with an increase in revenue of 8% and in profit before tax of 1.2%.

However, this comparison is distorted, as the 2012 results include six months' revenue and profit from Canary Co, whereas the 2011 results are purely Crow Co and Starling Co. A more meaningful comparison is made by removing Canary Co's results from the 2012 figures, enabling a comparison of the results of Crow Co and Starling Co alone:

	$ million *2012 forecast Crow Co*	$ million *2012 forecast Starling Co*	$ million *2012 forecast Crow Co and Starling Co*	$ million *2011 Actual Crow Co and Starling Co*	% change
Revenue	69	50	119	125	(4.8%)
Profit before tax	3.5	3	6.5	8.4	(22.6%)

The analysis reveals that Crow Co and Starling Co combined have a significantly reduced profit for the year, with revenue also slightly reduced. The apparent increase in costs may be caused by one-off costs to do with the acquisition of Canary Co, such as due diligence and legal costs. However there remains a risk of misstatement as costs could be overstated or revenue understated.

Possible manipulation of financial statements

A risk of misstatement arises in relation to Canary Co as its financial statements have been prone to manipulation. In particular, its management may have felt pressure to overstate revenue and profits in order to secure a good sale price for the company. The existence of contingent consideration relating to the Group's post acquisition revenue is also a contributing factor to possible manipulation, as the Group will want to avoid paying the additional consideration.

Grant received

Starling Co has received a grant of $35 million in respect of environmentally friendly capital expenditure, of which $25 million has already been spent. There is a risk in the recognition of the grant received. According to IAS 20 *Accounting for Government Grants and Disclosure of Government Assistance* government grants shall be recognised as income over the periods necessary to match them with the related costs which they are intended to compensate. This means that the $35 million should not be recognised as income on receipt, but the income deferred and released to profit over the estimated useful life of the assets to which it relates. There is a risk that an inappropriate amount has been credited to profit this year.

A further risk arises in respect of the $10 million grant which has not yet been spent. Depending on the conditions of the grant, some or all of it may become repayable if it is not spent on qualifying assets within a certain time, and a provision may need to be recognised. $10 million represents 1.8% of consolidated assets, likely to be material to the CS Group financial statements. It is likely to form a much greater percentage of Starling Co's individual assets and therefore be more material in its individual financial statements.

New IT system

A new system relevant to financial reporting was introduced to Crow Co and Starling Co which may indicate a risk of material misstatement. Errors may have occurred in transferring data from the old to the new system, and the controls over the new system may not be operating effectively.

Further, if Canary Co is not using the same IT system, there may be problems in performing its consolidation into the CS Group, for example, in reconciling inter-company balances.

Starling Co finance director

One of the subsidiaries currently lacks a finance director. This means that there may be a lack of personnel with appropriate financial reporting and accounting skills, increasing the likelihood of error in Starling Co's individual financial statements, and meaning that inputs to the consolidated financial statements are also at risk of error. In addition, the reason for the finance director leaving should be ascertained, as it could indicate a risk of material misstatement, for example, if there was a disagreement over accounting policies.

(iii) Audit procedures relating to goodwill

- Obtain the legal purchase agreement and confirm the date of the acquisition as being the date that control of Canary Co passed to Crow Co.
- From the legal purchase agreement, confirm the consideration paid, and the details of the contingent consideration, including its amount, date potentially payable, and the factors on which payment depends.
- Confirm that Canary Co is wholly owned by Crow Co through a review of its register of shareholders, and by agreement to legal documentation.
- Agree the cash payment of $125 million to cash book and bank statements.
- Review the board minutes for discussion regarding, and approval of, the purchase of Canary Co.

- Obtain the due diligence report prepared by the external provider and confirm the estimated fair value of net assets at acquisition.
- Discuss with management the reason for providing for the full amount of contingent consideration, and obtain written representation concerning the accounting treatment.
- Ask management to recalculate the contingent consideration on a discounted basis, and confirm goodwill is recognised on this basis in the consolidated financial statements.

Tutorial note

Procedures relating to impairment testing of the goodwill at the year end are not relevant to the requirement, which asks for procedures relating to the goodwill initially recognised on acquisition.

Examiner's comments

This question was based on the planning of a group audit when there had been a change in the group structure during the year. A wholly-owned subsidiary had been acquired, and candidates were given descriptions of some significant transactions and events, as well as limited financial information.

It was obvious that the majority of candidates were familiar with this part of the syllabus. Candidates also seem comfortable with the style of the question and with the amount of information that had been given in the scenario.

Requirement (a) (i) asked candidates to identify and explain the implications of the acquisition of the new subsidiary for the audit planning of the individual and consolidated financial statements. Most answers to this requirement identified the main planning implications, such as the determination of component and group materiality levels, the audit firm's need to obtain business understanding and assess the control environment in relation to the new subsidiary, and practical aspects such as the timings and resources needed for the group audit. Weaker answers to this requirement tended to just list out financial reporting matters, for example, that in the group financial statements related party transactions would have to be disclosed, and inter-company balances eliminated, but failed to link these points sufficiently well to audit planning implications.

The next part of the question dealt with risk assessment, requiring in (a) (ii) that candidates evaluate the risk of material misstatement to be considered in planning the individual and consolidated financial statements. The majority of answers focused on the correct type of risk (i.e. inherent and control risks), though some did discuss detection risks, which are irrelevant when evaluating the risk of material misstatement. Answers to (a) (ii) tended to cover a wide range of points but very often did not discuss the points in much depth.

For example, almost all candidates identified that accounting for goodwill can be complex, leading to risk of misstatement, but few candidates explained the specific issues that give rise to risk. Similarly, most identified that the grant that had been received by one of the subsidiaries posed risk to the auditor, but most answers just suggested (often incorrectly) an accounting treatment and said little or nothing about the specific risk of misstatement. Many answers also went into a lot of detail about how particular balances and transactions should be audited, recommending procedures to be performed by the auditor, which was not asked for. Weaker answers simply stated an issue, for example, that a grant had been received, and said the risk was that it would not be accounted for properly. Clearly this is not really an evaluation, as required, and will lead to minimal marks being awarded.

It was pleasing to see many candidates determining the materiality of the transactions and balances to the individual company concerned and to the group. However, candidates are reminded that materiality should be calculated in an appropriate manner. For example, the materiality of an asset or liability should usually be based on total assets and not on revenue.

Candidates' understanding of the relevant financial reporting issues varied greatly. Most understood the basics of accounting for grants received, the revenue recognition issues caused by online sales, and that contingent consideration should be discounted to present value. However, knowledge on accounting for loan stock that had been issued by the parent company was inadequate, and very few properly discussed how the probability of paying the contingent consideration would affect its measurement at the reporting date.

Candidates attempting the UK and IRL adapted papers are reminded that the syllabus is based on International Financial Reporting Standards. References to, and discussions of, accounting treatments under UK GAAP are not correct and cannot be given credit. For example, a significant minority of answers discussed the amortisation of goodwill, which is not permitted under IFRS Standards (though it is correct under UK GAAP) and so could not be given any marks for this discussion.

The issues that were dealt with well included:

- The due diligence on Canary Co that had been provided by an external valuer
- The measurement of contingent consideration at present value
- Online sales creating risks to do with revenue recognition
- The control risks arising as a result of a new IT system
- The non-coterminous year end of Canary Co.

The issues that generally were inadequately evaluated included:

- The recognition and measurement of loan stock issued by Crow Co
- The classification and measurement of the grant received by Starling Co

The financial information provided in relation to the group – very few answers performed any analytical review on the performance of the group and its components.

Requirement (a) (iii) asked candidates to recommend the principal audit procedures to be performed in respect of goodwill initially recognised on the acquisition of Canary Co. Generally candidates did well on this requirement, with many providing well described, relevant procedures. This represented a definite improvement from previous sittings. Most answers considered the need to look at source documentation regarding the acquisition, the importance of assessing the fair values attributed to Canary Co at acquisition, and the need to assess the probability of the contingent consideration being paid.

ACCA marking scheme	
	Marks
(a) (i) **Audit implications of Canary Co acquisition** Up to 1½ marks for each implication explained (3 marks maximum for identification): – Develop understanding of Canary Co business environment – Document Canary Co accounting systems and controls – Perform detailed analytical procedures on Canary Co – Communicate with previous auditor – Review prior year audit opinion for relevant matters – Plan additional work on opening balances – Determine that Canary Co is a significant component of the Group – Plan for audit of intra-company transactions – Issues on auditing the one month difference in financial year ends – Impact of acquisition on analytical procedures at Group level – Additional experienced staff may be needed, e.g. to audit complex goodwill	
Maximum	**8**
(ii) **Risk of material misstatement** Up to 1½ marks for each risk (unless a different maximum is indicated below): – General risks – diversification, change to group structure – Goodwill – contingent consideration – estimation uncertainty (probability of payment) – Goodwill – contingent consideration – measurement uncertainty (discounting) – Goodwill – fair value of net assets acquired – Goodwill – impairment – Identify that the issues in relation to cost of investment apply also in Crow Co's individual financial statements (1 mark) – Loan stock – premium on redemption – Loan stock – accrued interest – Loan stock – inadequate disclosure – Identify that the issues in relation to loan stock apply to cost of investment in Crow Co's individual financial statements (1 mark) – Online sales and risk relating to revenue recognition (additional 1 mark if calculation provided on online sales materiality to the Group) – No group accounting policy for online sales – Canary Co management have no experience regarding consolidation – Financial performance of Crow Co and Starling Co deteriorating (up to 3 marks with calculations) – Possible misstatement of Canary Co revenue and profit – Grant received – capital expenditure – Grant received – amount not yet spent – New IT system – Starling Co – no finance director in place at year end	
Maximum	**18**

(iii) **Goodwill**

Generally 1 mark per specific procedure (examples shown below):

- Confirm acquisition date to legal documentation
- Confirm consideration details to legal documentation
- Agree 100% ownership, e.g. using Companies House search/register of significant shareholdings
- Vouch consideration paid to bank statements/cash book
- Review board minutes for discussion/approval of acquisition
- Obtain due diligence report and agree net assets valuation
- Discuss probability of paying contingent consideration
- Obtain written representation regarding contingency
- Recalculate goodwill including contingency on a discounted basis

Maximum	5

Professional marks for the overall presentation, structure and logical flow of the briefing notes, and for the clarity of the evaluation and discussion provided.

Maximum	4
Total	**35**

10 JOLIE *Walk in the footsteps of a top tutor*

Top tutor tips

Part (a) requires you to evaluate business risk, i.e. events, conditions, circumstances, actions or inactions that could adversely affect Jolie Co's ability to achieve its objectives and execute its strategies. It is important that your answer is specific to the information in the scenario, and that you **evaluate** the risks identified. You should therefore introduce examples from the scenario into your answer and then explain the potential business consequence(s) of each example you have introduced.

There are professional marks available in part (a) **for the format of the answer and the clarity of the evaluation.** Your answer should be labelled 'briefing note'. It should identify the intended purpose of the briefing note by including a subject line. For the introduction use the words from the requirement. The briefing notes should have a clear structure including headings and a conclusion summarising the key points identified.

Part (b) requires you to identify and explain **five** risks, i.e. you should state what the risk is, and then explain the potential impact on the financial statements.

Part (c) requires audit procedures for the **valuation** of a **purchased** brand name. It is important that you address the specific requirements otherwise you are not answering the question set.

(a) **Briefing notes**

To: Toni Pacino

From: Audit manager

Subject: Business risks facing Jolie Co

Introduction

These briefing notes evaluate the business risks facing our firm's new audit client, Jolie Co, which operates in the retail industry, and has a year ended 30 November 2010.

Ability to produce fashion items

The company is reliant on staff with the skill to produce high fashion clothes ranges, and also with the ability to respond quickly to changes in fashion. If Jolie Co fails to attract and retain skilled designers then the clothing ranges may not be desirable enough to attract customers in the competitive retail market. The high staff turnover in the design team indicates that Jolie Co struggles to maintain consistency in the design team. This could result in deterioration of the brand name deterioration of the brand name and, ultimately, reduced sales.

There would be a high cost associated with frequently recruiting – this would have an impact on operating margins.

Inventory obsolescence and margins

There is a high operational risk that product lines will go out of fashion quickly, because new ranges are introduced so quickly to the stores (every eight weeks), leading to potentially large volumes of obsolete inventory. These product lines may be marked down to sell at a reduced margin.

The draft results show that operating margins have already reduced from 17.9% in 2009 to 16.8% in 2010. Any significant mark down of product lines will cause further reductions in margins.

Wide geographical spread of business operations

Jolie Co operates a large number of stores, many distribution centres, and has an outsourced function which is located overseas. This type of business model could be hard to control, increasing the likelihood of inefficiencies, system deficiencies, and theft of inventories or cash.

E-commerce – volume of sales

On-line sales now account for $255 million ($250 per order × 1,020,000 orders). In the previous year, on-line sales accounted for $158 million ($300 per order × 526,667 orders). This represents an increase of 61.4% (255 – 158/158 × 100%). One of the risks associated with the on-line sales is the scale of the increase in the volume of transactions, especially when combined with a new system introduced recently. There is a risk that the system will be unable to cope with the volume of transactions, leading possibly to unfilled orders and dissatisfied customers. This would harm the reputation of the company and the JLC brand.

The company has recently upgraded its computer system to integrate sales into the general ledger. A disaster plan should have been put into place, for use in the event of a system shutdown or failure. The risk is that no plan is in place and the business could lose a substantial amount of revenue in the event of the system failure.

E-commerce – security of systems

It is crucial that the on-line sales system is secure as customers are providing their credit card details to the site. Any breach of security could result in credit card details being stolen, and Jolie Co may be liable for losses suffered by customers if their credit card details were used fraudulently. There would clearly be severe reputational issues in this case. Additionally, the system must be secure from virus infiltration, which could cause system failure, interrupted sales, and loss of customer goodwill.

E-commerce – tax and regulatory issues

There are several compliance risks, which arise due to on-line sales. Overseas sales expose Jolie Co to potential sales tax complications, such as extra tax to be paid on the export of goods to abroad, and additional documentation on overseas sales that may be needed to comply with regulations. Another important regulatory issue is that of data protection. Jolie Co faces the risk of non-compliance with any data protection regulation relevant to customers providing personal details to the on-line sales system.

Jolie Co is now making sales overseas. If these sales are made in a different currency to Jolie Co's currency, the business will be exposed to exchange rate fluctuations which will have an impact on the company's profit margin.

Tutorial note

Credit will be awarded for other e-commerce related risks, such as the risk of obsolescence (leading to the need to continually update the website and system), and associated costs; and the risk of not having enough staff skilled in IT and e-commerce issues.

Outsourcing of phone ordering system

The fact that Jolie Co engaged the outsource provider offering the least cost could lead to business risks. Staff at the call centre may not be properly motivated, due to low wages being paid, and may fail to provide a quality service to Jolie Co's customers, leading to loss of customer goodwill. As the call centre is overseas, the staff may have a different first language to Jolie Co's customers, leading to customer frustration if they are not understood, and incorrect orders possibly being made. In addition, there may be staff shortages due to the low wage offered, leading to delay in answering calls and lost sales.

Overseas call centres are not always popular with customers, so Jolie Co may find that fewer customers use this method of purchase. However, the on-line system is there as an alternative for customers, and is proving popular, so this may not be a significant risk for the company.

The fact that Jolie Co opted for the lowest cost provider for the phone ordering system could pose a potential problem in that the provider may not be sustainable in the long term. If the provider fails to generate sufficient profit or cash, it may shut down, leaving Jolie Co without a crucial part of the sales generating system.

Ethical Trading Initiative

Jolie Co has aligned itself to an initiative supporting social and environmental well-being, presumably to promote its corporate social responsibility. The risk associated with this is that the claims that products have been produced in a responsible way can easily be undermined if the supply chain is not closely managed and monitored. Such claims are often closely scrutinised by the public and pressure groups, and any indication that Jolie Co's products have not been sourced responsibly will lead to loss of customer goodwill and waste of expenditure on the advertising campaign.

Distribution centres

There is a risk of non-compliance with the operating licence issued by the local government authority. The authority will monitor the operating hours of the distribution centres, and also the noise levels created by them. Breaches of the terms of the licence could lead to further revocations of licences, causing huge operational problems for Jolie Co if the centres are forced to close for any period of time. Fines and penalties may also be imposed due to the breach of the licence.

Financial performance

Total revenue has decreased by $80 million, or 5.2% (80/1,535 × 100). Operating profit has also fallen, by $30 million, or 10.9% (30/275 × 100). The information also shows that the average spend per order has fallen from $300 to $250. These facts may signify cause for concern, but operating expenses for 2010 are likely to include one-off items, such as the costs of the new on-line sales system, and the advertising of the 'fair-trade' initiative. The fall in spend per customer could be a symptom of general economic difficulties. The company has increased the volume of on-line transactions significantly; so on balance the overall reduction in profit and margins is unlikely to be a significant risk at this year-end, though if the trend were to continue it may become a more pressing issue.

Jolie Co's finance costs have increased by $3 million, contributing to a fall in profit before tax of 13%. The company has sufficient interest cover to mean that this is not an immediate concern, but the company should ensure that finance costs do not escalate.

Conclusion

Jolie Co faces a number of operational and compliance risks, the most significant of which relate to the need for constant updating of the product lines and the potential for obsolete inventory. The new on-line sales system also raises risks in terms of security, systems reliability and the sheer volume of transactions. Jolie Co must also carefully manage the risk of non-compliance with local government authority regulations. The trend in financial performance should be carefully monitored, as further reductions in revenue and margins could indicate that a change in business strategy is needed.

(b) Risks of material misstatement

Valuation of inventory

High fashion product lines are likely to become out-of-date and obsolete very quickly. Jolie Co aims to have new lines in store every eight weeks, so product lines have only a short shelf life. Per IAS 2 *Inventories*, inventory should be valued at the lower of cost and net realisable value, and could be easily overvalued at the year-end if there is not close monitoring of sales trends, and necessary mark downs to reflect any slow movement of product lines. The decline in revenue could indicate that the JLC brand is becoming less fashionable, leading to a higher risk of obsolete product lines.

Orders made over the phone or by the internet are prone to higher levels of returns than items purchased in a store, as the customer may find that the item is not the correct size, or they do not like the item when it arrives. The risk is insufficient provision has been made in the financial statements for pre year-end sales being returned post year-end.

Completeness/existence of inventory

Jolie Co has 210 stores and numerous distribution centres. It may be hard to ensure that inventory counting is accurate in this situation. There may be large quantities of inventory in-transit at the year-end, which may be missed from counting procedures, meaning that the inventory quantities are incomplete. Equally, it may be difficult for the auditor to verify the existence of inventory if it cannot be physically verified due to being in-transit at the year-end. Inventory could be the subject of fraudulent financial reporting, as it would be relatively easy for management to 'inflate' quantities of inventory to increase the amount recognised on the statement of financial position. The clothing items could also be at risk of theft, making inventory records inaccurate.

Unrecorded revenue

The on-line and phone sales systems could contribute to a risk of misstated revenue figures. Firstly, the on-line sales system is integrated with the general ledger, so sales made through the system should automatically be recorded in the accounting system.

However, the system is new, and it is possible that the integration is not functioning as expected. The scenario does not state whether the phone sales system is integrated, but it is unlikely given that the function is outsourced, so a similar risk of unrecorded transactions may arise here.

Sales made in store will include a proportion of cash sales. The risk is that the cash could be misappropriated, and the revenue unrecorded.

Over-capitalisation of IT/website costs

The on-line sales system has been upgraded at significant cost. There is a risk that costs have been incorrectly capitalised.

Only costs relating to the development phase of the project should be capitalised, but costs of planning, and all costs when the website is operational should be expensed. Software development costs follow similar accounting principles. Hence there is a risk of overvalued assets and unrecognised expenses.

Overvaluation of the brand name

The JLC brand name is recognised as an intangible asset, which is the correct accounting treatment for a purchased brand.

The risk is that the asset is overvalued, for two reasons. Firstly, if no amortisation is being charged on the asset, management are assuming that there is no end to the period in which the brand will generate an economic benefit. This may be optimistic, and there is a risk that the brand is overvalued, and operating expenses incomplete if there is no annual write-off. An intangible asset which is not being amortised should be subject to an annual impairment review according to IAS 38 *Intangible Assets*.

If no such review has been conducted, the asset could be overvalued. The falling revenue figures could indicate that the asset is overvalued.

Secondly, a significant amount has been spent on promoting the brand name during the year. This amount should be expensed, and if any has been capitalised, the brand is overvalued, and operating expenses incomplete.

Overvaluation of properties

There are two indications from the scenario that properties may need to be tested for impairment, and so could be overvalued.

The first is the potential for distribution centres' operating licences to be revoked. If this were to occur, the asset would cease to provide economic benefit, triggering the need for an impairment review. Secondly, the average revenue per store has fallen.

IAS 36 *Impairment of Assets* suggests that worse economic performance than expected is an indicator that an asset could be impaired. For these reasons, both stores and distribution centres have the potential to be overvalued.

Unrecognised provision/undisclosed contingency

The revocation of an operating licence could lead to a fine or penalty being paid to the local authority. Two licences have been revoked during the year. The risk is that Jolie Co has not either provided for any amount payable, or disclosed the existence of a contingent liability in accordance with IAS 37 *Provisions, Contingent Liabilities and Contingent Assets*.

Opening balances and comparative figures

As this is our first year auditing Jolie Co, extra care should be taken with opening balances and comparative figures, as they were not audited by our firm. Additional audit procedures will need to be planned.

Tutorial note

More than the required number of risks of material misstatement have been described in the answer above. Credit may be awarded for the discussion of other, relevant risks to a maximum of five risks of material misstatement.

(c) Principal audit procedures in respect of the JLC brand

- Agree the cost of the brand to supporting documentation provided by management. A purchase invoice may not be available depending on the length of time since the acquisition of the brand name.
- Agree the cost of the brand to prior year audited financial statements.
- Review the monthly income streams generated by the JLC brand, for indication of any decline in sales.
- Review the results of impairment reviews performed by management, establishing the validity of any assumptions used in the review, such as the discount rate used to discount future cash flows, and any growth rates used to predict the cash inflows from revenue.
- Perform an independent impairment review on the brand, and compare to management's impairment review.
- Review the level of planned expenditure on marketing and advertising to support the brand name, and consider its adequacy to maintain the image of the brand.
- Inquire as to the results of any customer satisfaction or marketing surveys, to gain an understanding as to the public perception of the JLC brand as a high fashion brand.
- Consider whether non-amortisation of brand names is a generally accepted accounting practice in the fashion retail industry by reviewing the published financial statements of competitors.
- Discuss with management the reasons why they feel that non-amortisation is a justifiable accounting treatment.

Tutorial note

As this is a first year audit, no marks will be awarded for procedures relating to prior year working papers of the audit firm.

Examiner's comments

Requirement (a) asked for an evaluation of business risks. The audit client operated in the retail industry and had recently initiated several strategies aimed at expansion, including e-commerce.

It was clear that most candidates were prepared for this type of requirement, and on the whole performed well. Answers tended to display reasonable application skills, with some candidates prioritising the risks identified, and reaching an overall conclusion. There was much less evidence here of 'knowledge-dumping' than in answers to other requirements. Some answers worked through the scenario, and for each risk identified explained the potential impact on the business. Some answers also made connections between different aspects of the client's business, for example, that joining the Fair Trade Initiative would have cost repercussions at a time when profit margins were reducing.

However, answers still left a lot of room for improvement. Common weaknesses in answers to the requirement included:

- Repeating large chunks of text from the scenario with no explanation provided
- Not actually explaining or evaluating a risk identified – just saying 'this is a risk'
- Providing detailed definitions of business risk, which was not asked for
- Providing audit procedures for risks, again not asked for
- Providing recommendations for mitigating the risk, not asked for

There was far too much emphasis on going concern risk, often raised indiscriminately for every risk area identified. In addition, it is worth noting that very few candidates used the figures provided in the scenario to identify risk exposure. The client's revenue and profit had fallen from the previous year, and some simple financial analysis could have revealed falling profit margins and worsening interest cover. This type of analysis is not difficult or time consuming, and is something that demonstrates mark-generating application skills.

Finally, some candidates simply failed to answer the question requirement. A minority of candidates took the opportunity to provide many pages of answer which just described how you would plan an audit in general, including descriptions of contacting the previous auditor, determining materiality levels, and meeting the client to discuss the engagement. All of this was totally irrelevant, and failed to generate any marks. Candidates are reminded that they must answer the specific question requirement, and not the requirement they would like to have been asked.

There were professional marks available in connection with requirement (a). Most candidates attempted the briefing notes format by including an appropriate heading and introduction. It seemed that by the end of their answer however, candidates had forgotten about the professional marks, as it was rare to see a conclusion provided on the business risk evaluation. Candidates are reminded that resources are available on ACCA's website providing guidance on the importance of professional marks.

Requirement (b) asked candidates to identify and explain risks of material misstatement from the scenario. The quality of answers to this requirement was unsatisfactory. The minority of candidates who scored well on this requirement provided a succinct explanation of the risk of material misstatement, clearly stating the potential impact of the risk identified on the financial statements. Some answers, which were by far the majority, tended to just outline an accounting treatment with no mention of the actual risk itself. Another common weakness was to discuss the detection risk which may arise with a new audit client, which is not a risk of material misstatement.

Given that risks of material misstatement have featured in several previous examinations it was somewhat surprising that the majority of candidates could not provide a satisfactory answer, especially when requirement (a) had asked for a business risk evaluation, which should then lead into the identification of risks of material misstatement as part of audit methodology.

Some candidates used the financial information provided to identify risks of material misstatement, rarely with any success. Common statements of this type were along the lines of 'revenue is reduced, so there is a risk of understatement'.

Finally, there was a tendency for candidates to provide more than the required number of risks of material misstatement, which is clearly a waste of time.

Requirement (c) asked candidates to recommend principal audit procedures in relation to the valuation of a purchased brand name, which was recognised at cost in the financial statements. Some candidates scored well here, providing well written procedures specific to the valuation of an intangible asset. Some answers recognised that procedures should focus on determining whether or not the brand was impaired and whether the non-amortisation policy was appropriate. The most common errors here included:

Mis-reading the scenario and thinking the brand was internally generated (the scenario clearly stated that the brand had been purchased several years ago).

Mis-reading the scenario and thinking the brand was amortised (the scenario clearly states it is not amortised).

Providing detailed explanations of the requirements of IAS 38 *Intangible Assets* (not asked for).

ACCA marking scheme		
		Marks
(a)	Briefing note evaluating business risks ½ mark for each risk identified (to max 4 marks) and up to 1½ further marks for explanation: – High fashion items/high staff turnover in design team – Obsolete inventory and pressure on margins – Widespread geographical business model hard to control – Volume of e-commerce sales – ability of systems to cope – Security of e-commerce operations – Tax and regulatory issues on e-commerce – Foreign exchange risk on new overseas transactions – Outsourcing of phone operations – quality issues – Outsourcing of phone operations – unpopular with customers – Long-term sustainability of outsourced function – Ethical Trading Initiative – supply chain issues – Potential restrictions on operation of distribution centres – Financial performance – general comments on revenue/ profitability/margins Up to 2 marks for calculation of margins, trends, etc.	
	Maximum	**15**
	Professional marks	**4**
	Maximum	**19**
(b)	**Risks of material misstatement** ½ mark for identification, up to 1½ further marks for explanation, FIVE matters only – Inventory valuation – Inventory existence – Unrecorded revenue – Capitalisation of IT/website costs – Valuation of brand name – Valuation of properties – Recognition of provision/contingent liability – Opening balances and comparatives (1 mark only)	
	Maximum	**10**

(c) **Audit procedures: brand name**	
1 mark per specific procedure	
– Agree cost to supporting documentation/prior year accounts	
– Review assumptions used in management impairment review	
– Perform independent impairment review	
– Review planned level of expenditure to support the brand	
– Review results of any marketing/customer satisfaction surveys	
– Consider if non-amortisation is GAAP for this industry	
– Discuss reasons for non-amortisation with management	
Maximum	6
Total	35

OTHER ASSIGNMENTS

11 ROPE *Walk in the footsteps of a top tutor*

Top tutor tips

The wording of this question is more unusual than previous prospective financial information questions. In this question, some of the assumptions used to prepare the forecast have been provided and the requirement is to evaluate the appropriateness of the forecast. Think about whether the assumptions are reasonable, for example, whether the cash receipts from customers are reduced to reflect the usual level of irrecoverable debts experienced by the company. The requirement also asks for procedures which should be performed which is more typical in relation to forecast questions.

(a) The cash flow forecast of Rope Co

When a company has prepared a cash flow forecast as part of their assessment of going concern, in accordance with ISA 570 *Going Concern* the auditor needs to evaluate the reliability of the underlying data used to prepare the forecast and to determine whether there is adequate support for the assumptions underlying the forecast. There are a number of issues relating to the forecast which raise concerns about the assessment of Rope's going concern status and therefore warrant further investigation.

Receipts from customers

There was little growth in cash receipts in the second half of the year ended 30 September 2016 (0.8%), yet in each consequent six-month period management predicts a significant rise in receipts of between 1.7% and 3.0%.

This could be based on overly optimistic forecasts in relation to sales growth for the same period. If sales forecasts are too optimistic, this could eliminate the forecast small positive cash flows, which could leave the company in a net overdraft position for the entire two-year period.

The movement in relation to customer receipts is a key assumption underpinning the return to a positive cash position and needs to be scrutinised further.

Salaries and other payments

While annual receipts from customers and payments to suppliers are forecast to rise during the forecast period by 8.5% and 9.4%, respectively, the amounts attributable to salaries and other operating payments are only forecast to rise by 4.1%.

This is based on management's simple assumption of a general 2% annual inflation in these costs. This seems to be overly simplistic and will require further investigation. Salary costs could be forecast using a more sophisticated methodology based on required employee numbers and average wages/salaries.

The significant forecast increase in sales suggests that operating activities will increase over the next two years and it might be expected that staff requirements may increase in line with this. For similar reasons, it is likely that a larger increase in other operating costs would be required to match the increased administrative burden of producing and selling more goods and/or services.

Sale of investments

Management is planning to sell some investments in listed shareholdings for $500,000 to repay a loan to the chief executive. At 30 September 2016, however, the fair value of the investments was only $350,000. As the fair value of these investments is revalued at the end of each year based upon the current share price, this is assumed to reflect the amount at which the shares were trading at the end of September. Management is therefore expecting the shares to increase in value by $150,000 in the space of two years, which represents a 43% rise. This is an extremely optimistic assumption in comparison to average rates of growth across most stock markets.

It therefore appears likely that there will be a shortfall in the amount raised to repay Mr Stewart. Rope Co will therefore have to supplement the amount received from selling investments with cash from other sources, which will lead to a reduction in the cash position in comparison to the forecasts.

Repayment of the bank loan

The bank loan is due for repayment 15 months after the year end. Management is assuming that they will be able to fund the repayment with a new loan facility from the same finance provider. Without any agreement in place from the provider, this represents a significant assumption.

Without a new facility Rope Co will have no means with which to repay their obligation, which could lead to the lender taking action to recover the loan amount. This could include seizing assets which were provided as security over the loan or commencing insolvency proceedings.

In either case, this could have a significant impact on Rope's ability to trade into the foreseeable future and, therefore, the loan repayment event represents a material uncertainty which may need to be fully disclosed in the financial statements of Rope Co in accordance with IAS 1 *Presentation of Financial Statements*.

Missing cash flows

There seems to be a lack of consideration of a number of non-operating cash flows which one might expect to see in a two-year forecast. For example, most companies maintain a practice of regular replacement of old, inefficient tangible non-current assets as opposed to making larger, less regular replacements which may create a significant drain on cash resources in one particular year. The forecast currently has no allocation for capital investment. In a similar fashion, there are no cash flows related to tax and dividend payments. It is possible that such transactions have been overlooked in the preparation of the forecast.

Further audit procedures

- Obtain a copy of the latest interim financial statements and compare the actual post year-end sales performance with the forecast sales upon which the cash flow forecast is based.
- Discuss with management the rationale for the expected increase in customer receipts and where possible confirm this to customer correspondence, orders or contracts.
- Inspect the documentation detailing the terms of the loan with Mr Stewart to confirm the amount outstanding and the agreed date of repayment.
- Inspect the terms of the bank loan to confirm the final amount due for repayment, the date of repayment and whether any assets have been accepted as security for the loan.
- Enquire of management whether they have entered into any negotiations with their bank, or any other financial institution, to provide a replacement loan in January 2018. If so, request corroborating evidence such as signed agreements, agreements in principle or correspondence with the financial institutions.
- Enquire of management whether they have any contingency plans in place to repay both loans on time should they not be able to raise the required amount through selling investments and obtaining new loan agreements.
- Perform an analytical review of actual monthly payroll costs incurred obtained from the payroll department. Include any available payment periods after 30 September 2016 to help ascertain whether management's assumptions regarding salaries are appropriate. Seek corroborating evidence for any fluctuations in cost such as HR records confirming pay awards and changes in staff.
- Perform an analytical review of actual other operational costs and consider the level of other costs as a percentage of sales. Compare this to the levels included in the forecast. Investigate any significant differences.
- Corroborate the lack of investment in new tangible non-current assets by performing an analytical review of the levels of additions and disposals over the last, say, five years to see if this supports the absence of any allocation for this in the short-term future and consider this in light of our understanding of the entity and its production process.
- Compare the cash flow forecasts to any capital expenditure forecasts prepared by Rope Co to ensure that the cash flow forecast is consistent with this. Ask management to explain any differences identified.

- Review the non-current asset register and identify any assets with a zero or negligible carrying value which could indicate that the assets have fulfilled their useful lives and are due for replacement.
- Inspect the cash book post year end to see if there are any significant cash transactions which do not appear to have been included in the forecasts, in particular cash transactions relating to purchases or disposals of assets and dividend payments.
- Review the outcome of previous forecasts prepared by management to assess how effective management has been in the past at preparing accurate forecasts.
- Obtain written representations from management confirming that they have no intention to either purchase or dispose of non-current assets or to pay dividends over the next two years.

(b) Matters relating to the loan from Mr J Stewart

Related party transaction

As a key member of staff at Rope Co, the loan from the chief executive represents a related party transaction. As such, the transaction and related outstanding balances must be fully disclosed in the financial statements in accordance with IAS 24 *Related Party Disclosures*.

This means that the nature of the related party relationship, the nature and the amount of the loan, the amounts outstanding at the year end and the terms and conditions of the loan, including a description of the fixed charge, must be disclosed in the notes to the financial statements.

Interest free loan measurement

The loan was received during the current year ended 30 September 2016. The loan liability should have been initially recorded at its fair value, which would normally be the transaction price of $500,000. IFRS 9 Financial Instruments, however, states that in the case of an interest free loan, the fair value should be measured as the present value of all future cash flows discounted using the prevailing market rates for similar instruments.

While it will be difficult to identify a similar instrument due to the nature of the relationship between the lender and the company, a similar instrument should be identified based upon the currency used, the loan term and any other similar factors, for example, a three-year, $ loan from a bank.

At the year end, the outstanding loan liability should have been measured using the amortised cost method and the effective interest calculated should be recognised as a finance charge in the statement of profit or loss.

Further audit procedures

- Inspect the loan agreement to confirm the amounts loaned to the company, and the other relevant terms including the rate of interest, the repayment date and the associated penalties for late payment.
- Inspect the related party disclosures in the financial statements to ensure that they provide sufficient information and accurately reflect the terms and amounts relating to the transaction.

- Additional procedures will need to be performed regarding the completeness of related party transactions as the loan with Mr Stewart was not identified through normal audit procedures.
- The market rate used in the calculation of the fair value of the loan should be compared to a range of suitable instruments, e.g. three-year bank loans, to ascertain its appropriateness. Following this, the calculation should be checked for arithmetical accuracy.
- The amount recorded for the initial loan value and the year-end value should be recalculated using the appropriate discount factor and market rate to confirm the arithmetical accuracy of management's calculations.
- Review the loan liability recognised in the financial statements to ensure that the appropriate, discounted figure has been used.
- Reconcile the effective interest rate for 2016 from the amortised cost calculation to the finance charges in the statement of profit or loss to confirm that this is appropriately included in profits.

Examiner's comments

Part (a) required candidates to appraise the forecast and suggest further procedures in assessing the use of the report as part of the going concern review during the audit. This was generally well answered by the majority of candidates attempting the question.

In part (b) candidates were required to discuss a loan from the chief executive to the company. This had been provided during the year being audited and the audit was still ongoing. Stronger candidates appropriately recognised this as a related party transaction and commented on the materiality and disclosure requirements before going on to describe procedures to perform. There were a significant number of candidates who had failed to take in to account the date the loan was provided and assumed it was missed in the prior year audit so instead focused their answers on a perceived lack of integrity of the directors, inappropriate levels of disclosure in prior year financial statements and audit qualifications.

Marking scheme

		Marks
	Generally up to 1½ marks for each well explained matter and 1 mark for each well explained procedure recommended:	
(a)	**Cash flow forecast**	
	Matters	
	– Potential overestimation of cash receipts from customers	
	– Lower than forecast sales may lead to net overdraft	
	– Potential underestimation of salary and other operating payments	
	– Simplistic assumption of cost inflation	
	– Investments do not match management's forecast disposal valuation	
	– Assumption of growth in value of investments is very optimistic	
	– Ability to repay loans dependent upon other assumptions	
	– Lack of specific consideration of non-operating cash flows	
	Procedures	
	– Review latest interim financial statements	
	– Discuss forecast sales and customer receipts with management	
	– Inspect J Stewart loan agreement	
	– Inspect terms of bank loan	
	– Enquire of management whether they have begun renegotiations regarding bank loan facility	

	– Enquire with management about contingency plans	
	– Perform analytical review of payroll costs	
	– Perform analytical review of other operating costs	
	– Inspect non-current asset registers	
	– Inspect post year-end cash book	
	– Review outcomes of previous management forecasts	
	– Obtain written representations from management (max ½ mark)	
	Maximum	**14**
(b)	**J Stewart loan**	
	Matters	
	– Provision of the loan represents a related party transaction	
	– Disclosure requirements of RPT	
	– Calculation of fair value for an interest free loan	
	– Determination of market rates for a similar instrument	
	– Valuation of loan at end of year using amortised cost method	
	Procedures	
	– Inspect terms of loan agreement	
	– Inspect related party disclosures in the financial statements	
	– Additional procedures in relation to potential other RPTs	
	– Compare market rate used to range of suitable instruments	
	– Recalculate initial and year-end loan amounts	
	– Reconcile effective interest rate from amortised cost calculation to statement of P&L	
	Maximum	**6**
Total		**20**

12 WATERS *Walk in the footsteps of a top tutor*

Top tutor tips

Matters to consider before accepting an engagement should be a straightforward as this question has been asked on many previous exam papers. Think about what might cause the accountancy firm to decline the work.

Examination procedures need to focus on assessing the reasonableness of the assumptions used in the forecast. Remember that these transactions have not happened as of yet so you will not be able to inspect invoices, etc. Instead, think about how the client determined the forecast figures and assess whether that is reasonable. Analytical procedures and inquiries will be the main procedures to use. There may be some documents you can inspect such as quotations for new equipment.

Part (bi) is quite tricky. You will either know this or not. If not, don't waste time trying to think of an answer. Move on to the next part which is more straightforward and has been asked before in previous exams. You can always come back to any difficult questions later on once you have answered everything you can on the rest of the paper.

(a) **(i)** Before accepting the engagement to examine Waters Co's prospective financial information, there are several matters to be considered.

Ethical matters

A significant matter is whether it is ethically acceptable to perform the engagement. The engagement would constitute a non-assurance service provided to an audited entity which may create self-interest, self-review and advocacy threats to independence.

In this case, the advocacy threat may be deemed particularly significant as Hunt & Co could be perceived as promoting the client's position to the bank. The engagement should only be provided if safeguards can be used to reduce the threat to an acceptable level, which may include:

- Having a professional accountant who was not involved with the non-assurance service review the non-assurance work performed or otherwise advise as necessary.
- Discussing ethical issues with those charged with governance of the client.
- Using separate teams to work on the audit and on the PFI engagement.

As well as ethical matters, ISAE 3400 *The Examination of Prospective Information* requires that certain matters are considered before the engagement is accepted.

Scope of the work

Hunt & Co must also consider the specific terms of the engagement. For example, the firm will need to clarify whether the bank has requested an assurance report to be issued, and what exact information will be included in the application to the bank. It is likely that more than just a forecast statement of profit or loss is required, for example, a forecast statement of cash flows and accompanying narrative, including key assumptions is likely to be required for a lending decision to be made.

Intended use of the information

ISAE 3400 also requires that consideration should be given to the intended use of the information, and whether it is for general or limited distribution. It seems in this case the assurance engagement and its report will be used solely in connection with raising bank finance, but this should be confirmed before accepting the engagement.

Period covered by the PFI

The period covered by the prospective financial information and the key assumptions used should also be considered. ISAE 3400 states that the auditor should not accept an engagement when the assumptions used are clearly unrealistic or when the auditor believes that the prospective financial information will be inappropriate for its intended use. For example, the assumption that the necessary capital expenditure can take place by September 2014 may be overly optimistic.

Resources and skills

The firm should also consider whether there are staff available with appropriate skills and experience to perform the PFI engagement, and the deadline by which the work needs to be completed. If the work on the cinemas is scheduled to be completed by September 2014, presumably the cash will have to be provided very soon, meaning a tight deadline for the engagement to be performed.

(ii) Examination procedures

- Agreement that the accounting policies used in preparing the forecast statement of profit or loss are consistent with those used in historical financial information and comply with IFRS Standards.
- The forecast should be cast to confirm accuracy.
- The time frame of the work to be carried out needs to be discussed with management, with enquiry being made to ascertain how the work can be carried out in such a short period of time, for example, will all cinemas be closed for the period of refurbishment? This will help to confirm the accuracy of the revenue and expenses recognised.
- Review of market research documents and review of prices charged by competitors showing new technology films to support the assumption regarding increase in price and consumer appetite for the films.
- Analytical review followed by discussion with management on the trend in revenue, which is forecast to increase by 22.9% and 7% in the years to 30 April 2015 and 2016 respectively.
- Consider the capacity of the cinemas and the number of screenings which can take place to assess the reasonableness of projected revenue.
- Analytical review of the composition of operating expenses to ensure that all expenses are included at a reasonable amount. In 2014, operating expenses are 80.7% of revenue, but this is forecast to reduce to 73.4% in 2015 and to 69.8% in 2016, indicating understatement of forecast expenses.
- Review the list of operating expenses to ensure that any loss to be recognised on the disposal of old equipment has been included, or that profit on disposal has been netted off.
- Quotations received from potential suppliers of the new technology should be reviewed to verify the amount of the capital expenditure and therefore that depreciation included in the forecast statement of profit or loss appears reasonable.
- Recalculation of depreciation expense and confirmation that depreciation on the new technology has been included and correctly calculated and agrees to the forecast statement of financial position.
- Recalculation of finance cost to ensure that interest payable on the new bank loan has been included, with confirmation of the rate of interest to bank documentation.
- Review of capital expenditure budgets, cash flow forecasts and any other information to accompany the forecast statement of profit or loss for consistency, and confirmation that the amount planned to be spent on the cinemas can be met with the amount of finance applied for as well Waters Co's own cash balance.

(b) (i) There are three stages typically involved in money laundering. The first is placement, which is when cash obtained through criminal activity is first placed into the financial system. Business owners who have illegally obtained funds can use a cash-intensive business to mix legitimate cash receipts from business activity with the funds they wish to launder. For Waters Co, the fact that most customers are likely to pay in cash indicates that it would be easy for genuine and illegal cash to be mixed up and banked, thereby placing the illegal cash into the financial system.

The second stage is layering. This is when cash is disguised by passing it through complex transactions involving many layers, making the transactions difficult to trace. This often involves moving the cash internationally, which adds a layer of complexity to the layering process. Waters Co transfers sums of cash to overseas bank accounts, indicating that layering may be taking place.

The final stage is integration, which is when the illegally gained funds are moved back into the legitimate economy. At this point the funds have become 'clean' and are invested in property or financial instruments or otherwise spent. Waters Co is planning to invest a large sum of cash, $8 million, in its cinema upgrade and refurbishment programme, which could be the integration stage of money laundering.

(ii) There are many elements which should be in place as part of an anti-money laundering programme, which are outlined in ACCA's Technical Factsheet 145 *Anti-Money Laundering Guidance for the Accountancy Sector.*

The audit firm must appoint a Money Laundering Reporting Officer (MLRO), who should have a suitable level of seniority and experience; usually this would be a senior partner in the audit firm. Suspicions of money laundering should be reported to the MLRO, who considers whether the matter should be referred to agencies such as the Serious Organised Crime Agency, and prepares and keeps the appropriate documentation.

There are also firm-wide elements of an anti-money laundering programme. A training programme is essential, to ensure that individuals are aware of the relevant legislation and regulations regarding money laundering. Individuals should also be trained in the firm's identification, record keeping and reporting policies. Individuals should also be trained in the money laundering risk factors, and be able to identify such risk factors and respond appropriately, and in matters such as tipping off offences.

An important part of anti-money laundering is customer due diligence, or know your client procedures. This means that audit firms must establish the identity of clients using documents such as certificates of incorporation and passports, and should obtain information about business activities in order to gain an understanding of matters such as sources of income, and the rationale for business transactions.

Finally, the audit firm must ensure that it maintains records of client identification procedures, and of all transactions relevant to audit clients, for example, the receipt of cash for services performed. This is important to ensure that the audit firm does not inadvertently become party to a transaction involving money laundering.

Tutorial note

Credit will be given for other relevant elements of an anti-money laundering programme to a maximum of four different matters.

Examiner's comments

This question focused on two issues – prospective financial information and money laundering. It was well attempted by many candidates, indicating that these syllabus areas had been studied and understood. There was however, a lack of application to the scenario, especially in relation to the first requirement.

The scenario centred on Waters Co, an audit client, that had approached your firm to provide a report on prospective financial information which would be used by the company's bank in making a significant lending decision. The amount advanced would be used to upgrade the cinemas operated by Waters Co and a forecast statement of profit or loss was provided in the scenario, along with some of the assumptions used in its preparation by management.

Requirement (a(i)) asked candidates to explain the matters to be considered by the audit firm before accepting the engagement to report on the prospective financial information. The quality of answers here was quite good, with almost all candidates making a reasonable attempt to discuss relevant matters including ethical issues, resource availability, the scope of the engagement and the nature of the assumptions used in the forecast. Where candidates scored less well on this requirement it was often due to lack of application to the scenario. A minority of answers amounted to little more than a bullet point list, often posed as questions (e.g. 'are there any ethical matters to consider', 'who is the report for', 'why is the report needed'), and while these are matters to consider the lack of any application to the scenario limits the amount of credit that can be awarded.

Requirement (aii) asked for examination procedures to be used in respect of the forecast statement of profit or loss, assuming the engagement is accepted. This was also quite well attempted by many candidates, who used the information provided to generate specific and relevant enquiries and other procedures. Weaker answers tended to write very vague comments which were not tailored to the scenario or explained, or were just incorrect, such as. 'obtain representations', 'agree forecast to audited financial statements', 'check whether assumptions are realistic', 'perform analytical procedures'.

The second part of the question focused on money laundering, and in contrast to previous sittings where this subject has been examined, the answers were generally of a reasonable standard. Requirement (bi) asked candidates to explain the stages used in money laundering and to comment on why Waters Co had been identified as high risk; and requirement (bii) asked for four recommendations in respect of an anti-money laundering programme that audit firms should have in place. Most answers were reasonably well attempted, and most candidates demonstrated knowledge of both the stages of money laundering, and the elements of an anti-money laundering programme. The weaker answers tended to simply be too short, limiting the marks that could be awarded. Some answers failed to comment on why Waters Co had been assessed as having a high risk of money laundering, even though the reasons were fairly obvious from the information provided.

ACCA marking scheme

			Marks
(a)	(i)	**Matters to consider before accepting the review engagement** Up to 1½ marks for each matter explained: – Independence – types of threats raised – Appropriate safeguards – Competence and time frame – Elements to be included in the application and intended use – Key assumptions and time period covered	
		Maximum	6
	(ii)	**Examination procedures** 1 mark for each described procedure. Also allow 1 mark for relevant analytical procedures used in the explanation of procedures. – Agreement that the accounting policies used in preparing the forecast information are consistent with those used in historical financial information – The forecast should be cast to confirm accuracy – Review of capital expenditure forecasts – Quotations received from potential suppliers of the new technology should be reviewed – The time frame of the work to be carried out needs to be discussed with management – Review of market research documents and review of prices charged by competitors – Analytical review followed by discussion with management on the trend in revenue – Revenue is forecast to increase by 22.9% and 7% in the years to 30 April 2015 and 2016 respectively – Analytical review of the composition of operating expenses – In 2014, operating expenses are 80.7% of revenue, but this is forecast to reduce to 73.4% in 2015 and to 69.8% in 2016 – Recalculation of depreciation expense and agreement to forecast statement of financial position – Recalculation of finance cost to ensure that interest payable with confirmation of the rate of interest to bank documentation	
		Maximum	8
(b)	(i)	**Stages of money laundering** Up to 2 marks for each stage explained with relevance to Waters Co: – Placement – cash based business and mixing of illegal and legitimate sources of cash – Layering – complex transactions to hamper tracing the cash such as transfer overseas – Integration – investing or spending cash to place it into the legitimate economy	
		Maximum	5
	(ii)	**Elements of an anti-money laundering programme** Up to 1½ marks for each element recommended: – MLRO – senior person, responsibilities – Firm-wide training programme – Know your client procedures – Record keeping	
		Maximum	6
Total			**25**

13 HAWK *Walk in the footsteps of a top tutor*

Top tutor tips

Part (a) (i) asks for matters to be considered in agreeing the terms of engagement for an examination of a forecast. This is the matters that need to be included in the engagement letter for this assignment. A good approach to take for this question is to identify matters that could lead to misunderstandings in future that the firm would want clarifying in writing. Knowledge of audit engagement letters can also be used and adapted to this type of engagement.

Part (a) (ii) requires the procedures to be performed on the forecast. It is important to remember that these events and transactions have not yet happened and therefore cannot be agreed to supporting documentation in the same way as historical figures. You need to generate procedures which will help you assess whether the assumptions used in the forecast are reasonable.

Part (bi) deals with a different client and asks for audit procedures to be performed in respect of the closure of the factory. As a provision has been set up for the closure costs, procedures should focus on whether the provision is an obligation at the year end.

Part (b) (ii) asks for discussion of difficulties measuring and reporting on social and environmental performance. This is again rote-learned knowledge from the text book which can be applied to the specific KPIs mentioned in the scenario to make it relevant.

(a) (i) Management's responsibilities

The terms of the engagement should set out management's responsibilities for the preparation of the business plan and forecast financial statements, including all assumptions used, and for providing the auditor with all relevant information and source data used in developing the assumptions. This is to clarify the roles of management and of Lapwing & Co, and reduce the scope for any misunderstanding.

The intended use of the business plan and report

It should be confirmed that the report will be provided to the bank and that it will not be distributed or made available to other parties. This will establish the potential liability of Lapwing & Co to third parties, and help to determine the need and extent of any liability disclaimer that may be considered necessary. Lapwing & Co should also establish that the bank will use the report only in helping to reach a decision in respect of the additional finance being sought by Hawk Co.

The elements of the business plan to be covered by the engagement

The extent of the engagement should be agreed. Lapwing & Co need to determine whether they are being asked to report just on the forecast financial statements, or on the whole business plan including any narrative descriptions or explanations of Hawk Co's intended future business activities. This will help to determine the scope of the work involved and its complexity.

The period covered by the forecasts

This should be confirmed when agreeing the terms of the engagement, as assumptions become more speculative as the length of the period covered increases, making it more difficult for Lapwing & Co to substantiate the acceptability of the figures, and increasing the risk of the engagement. It should also be confirmed that a 12-month forecast period is sufficient for the bank's purposes.

The nature of the assumptions used in the business plan

It is crucial that Lapwing & Co determine the nature of assumptions, especially whether the assumptions are based on best estimates or are hypothetical. This is important because ISAE 3400 *The Examination of Prospective Financial Information* states that the auditor should not accept, or should withdraw from, an engagement when the assumptions are clearly unrealistic or when the auditor believes that the prospective financial information will be inappropriate for its intended use.

The planned contents of the assurance report

The engagement letter should confirm the planned elements of the report to be issued, to avoid any misunderstanding with management. In particular, Lapwing & Co should clarify that their report will contain a statement of negative assurance as to whether the assumptions provide a reasonable basis for the prospective financial information, and a conclusion as to whether the prospective financial information is properly prepared on the basis of the assumptions and is presented in accordance with the relevant financial reporting framework. The bank may require the report to be in a particular format and include specific wordings in order to make their lending decision.

(ii) General procedures

- Recalculate the forecast financial statements to confirm the arithmetic accuracy.
- Agree the unaudited figures for the period to 31 May 2012 to management accounts, and agree the cash figure to bank statement or bank reconciliation.
- Confirm the consistency of the accounting policies used in the preparation of the forecast financial statements with those used in the last audited financial statements.
- Consider the accuracy of forecasts prepared in prior periods by comparison with actual results and discuss with management the reasons for any significant variances.
- Perform analytical procedures to assess the reasonableness of the forecast financial statements. For example, finance charges should increase in line with the additional finance being sought.
- Discuss the extent to which the joint venture with Kestrel Co has been included in the forecast financial statements.
- Review any agreement with Kestrel Co, or minutes of meetings at which the joint venture has been discussed to understand the nature, scale, and timeframe of the proposed joint business arrangement.
- Review any projected financial information for the joint venture, and agree any components relating to it into the forecast financial statements.

Forecast statement of profit or loss

- Consider the reasonableness of forecast trends in the light of auditor's knowledge of Hawk Co's business and the current and forecast economic situation and any other relevant external factors.
- Discuss the reason for the anticipated 21.4% increase in revenue with management, to understand if the increase is due to the inclusion of figures relating to the joint venture with Kestrel Co, or other factors.
- Discuss the trend in operating profit with management – the operating margin is forecast to improve from 30% to 33.8%. This improvement may be due to the sale of the underperforming Beak Retail Park.
- Obtain a breakdown of items included in forecast operating expenses and perform an analytical review to compare to those included in the 2012 figures, to check for any omissions.
- Using the cost breakdown, consider whether depreciation charges have increased in line with the planned capital expenditure.
- Request confirmation from the bank of the potential terms of the $30 million loan being negotiated, to confirm the interest rate at 4%. Consider whether the finance charge in the forecast statement of profit or loss appears reasonable. (If the loan is advanced in August, it should increase the company's finance charge by $1 million ($30 million × 4% × 10/12).)
- Discuss the potential sale of Beak Retail with management and review relevant board minutes, to obtain understanding of the likelihood of the sale, and the main terms of the sale negotiation.
- Recalculate the profit on the planned disposal, agreeing the potential proceeds to any written documentation relating to the sale, vendor's due diligence report, or draft legal documentation if available.
- Agree the potential proceeds on disposal to management's cash flow forecast, and confirm that operating cash flows relevant to Beak Retail are not included from the anticipated date of its sale.
- Discuss the reason for not including current tax in the profit forecast.

Forecast statement of financial position

- Agree the increase in property, plant and equipment to an authorised capital expenditure budget, and to any plans for the joint development with Kestrel Co.
- Obtain and review a reconciliation of the movement in property, plant and equipment. Agree that all assets relating to Beak Retail are derecognised on its disposal, and that any assets relating to the joint development with Kestrel Co are recognised in accordance with capital expenditure forecasts, and are properly recognised per IFRS 11 *Joint Arrangements*.
- Discuss the planned increase in equity with management to understand the reason for any planned share issue, its date and the nature of the share issue (rights issue or issue at full market price being the most likely).
- Perform analytical procedures on working capital and discuss trends with management, for example, receivables days is forecast to reduce from 58 to 53 days, and the reason for this should be obtained.

> ***Tutorial note***
>
> *Credit will be awarded for other examples of ratios calculated on the figures provided such as inventory turnover and average payables payment period.*

- Agree the increase in long-term borrowings to documentation relating to the new loan, and also to the forecast cash flow statement (where it should be included as a cash flow arising from financing activities).
- Discuss the deferred tax provision with management to understand why no movement on the balance is forecast, particularly given the planned capital expenditure.
- Obtain and review a forecast statement of changes in equity to ensure that movements in retained earnings appear reasonable. (Retained earnings are forecast to increase by $800,000, but the profit forecast for the period is $10.52 million – there must be other items taken through retained earnings such as a planned dividend.)
- Agree the movement in cash, and the forecast closing cash position to a cash flow forecast.

(b) Briefing notes

From: Audit manager

To: Audit partner

Subject: Osprey Co

Introduction

These briefing notes will firstly recommend the principal audit procedures to be performed in respect of the costs of closure of the factory involved in the environmental contamination. I will also discuss the difficulties in measuring and reporting on environmental and social performance.

(i) Recommended audit procedures

- Review board minutes for discussion of the closure and restructuring, noting the date the decision was made to restructure, which should be before the year end.
- Obtain any detailed and formal plan relating to the closure of the factory and relocation of its operations, noting the date the plan was approved, which should be before the year end.
- Discuss with management any indication that the company has started to implement the plan prior to the year end, e.g. the date of any public announcement, the date that plant began to be dismantled.
- Physically inspect the factory prior to the year end for evidence that dismantling has commenced.

Tutorial note

The procedures outlined above should establish whether a constructive obligation exists at the year end, in which case it is appropriate to recognise a provision according to IAS 37 Provisions, Contingent Liabilities and Contingent Assets. If there is no detailed formal plan in place, and no evidence that a valid expectation exists that the company will carry out the restructuring at the year end, then no provision should be recognised.

- Obtain a breakdown of the $1.25 million costs of closure and review to ensure that only relevant costs have been included, e.g. redundancy payments, lease cancellation fees. This is an important procedure for the potential overstatement of the provision.
- Cast the schedule for arithmetic accuracy.
- Agree a sample of relevant costs included in the provision to supporting documentation, e.g. redundancy payments to employees' contracts, lease cancellation fees (if any) to lease agreement.
- Enquire as to whether any gain is expected to be made on the sale of assets, and ensure that if so, the gain has not been taken into account when measuring the provision.

Tutorial note

IAS 37 prescribes that only costs necessarily entailed by the restructuring and not associated with the ongoing activities of the business may be included in the provision. In practice this means that very few costs can be included, and costs to do with relocation of employees, plant and equipment and inventories, retraining staff, investments in new infrastructure are not included as they are related to ongoing activities.

- Review the relevant disclosure note to the financial statements for accuracy and adequacy, where the provision should be treated as a separate numerical class and a description of it given.

Tutorial note

Credit will also be awarded for procedures relevant to ascertaining whether the factory closure constitutes a discontinued operation, and procedures relevant to any consequential disclosure requirements.

(ii) Measuring and reporting on social and environmental performance

Many companies attempt to measure social and environmental performance by setting targets or key performance indicators (KPIs), and then evaluating whether they have been met. The results are often published to enable a comparison to be made year on year or between companies. But it can be difficult to measure social and environmental performance for a number of reasons.

First, targets and KPIs are not always precisely defined. For example, Osprey Co may state a target of reducing environmental damage caused by its operations, but this is very vague. It is difficult to measure and compare performance unless a target or KPI is made more specific, for example, a target of reducing electricity consumption by 5% per annum.

Second, targets and KPIs may be difficult or impossible to quantify, with Osprey Co's planned KPI on employee satisfaction being a good example. This is a very subjective matter, and while there are methods that can be used to gauge the levels of employee satisfaction, whether this can result in a meaningful statistic is questionable.

Third, systems and controls are often not established well enough to allow accurate measurement, and the measurement of socio-environmental matters may not be based on reliable evidence. In Osprey Co's case, it may not be possible to quantify how much toxic chemical has been leaked from the factory.

Finally, it is hard to compare these targets and KPIs between companies, as they are not strictly defined, so each company will set its own target. It will also be difficult to make year on year comparisons for the same company, as targets may change in response to business activities. For example, if Osprey Co were to expand its operating, its energy and water use would increase, making its performance on environmental matters look worse. Users would need to understand the context in order to properly appraise why a target had not been met.

Conclusion

These briefing notes have shown that the environmental incident at Osprey Co will have an impact on our audit in that detailed audit procedures will need to be conducted to gain evidence regarding whether or not a provision for costs of closure should be recognised, and if so, its measurement. In addition, Osprey Co's intention to publish socio-environmental targets and KPIs is commendable, but it will be difficult for management to measure and report on these matters due to their often subjective nature.

Examiner's comments

This question was in two sections. Part (a) dealt with an engagement to report on prospective financial information. Part (b) covered the audit of a factory closure, and the difficulties in measuring environmental and social performance. Generally candidates performed better on part (a) than part (b).

The first part of the question related to an audit client, Hawk Co that had requested its auditor to provide a report on forecast financial statements included in a business plan, which would be used to help secure a loan. The scenario contained extracts from a forecast statement of profit or loss and a forecast statement of financial position.

Requirement (a) (i) asked candidates to identify and explain the matters that should be considered in agreeing the terms of engagement. Candidates were specifically told not to consider ethical threats to objectivity. Answers varied greatly in quality for this requirement. The best answers focused on matters that should be discussed with the client, such as management's responsibilities, the nature of the assumptions used in the forecasts and the planned contents of the review report and explained why those matters should form part of the terms of the engagement. Most answers discussed that negative assurance should be given, and explained the importance of determining the intended user of the report including issues to do with the use of a liability disclaimer. A significant number of candidates achieved high marks on this requirement. Weaker answers discussed only matters such as fee arrangements and deadlines, which, while relevant, are not enough to score well. Some answers discussed ethical issues, which specifically were not required, and others explained matters that would be more relevant to the initial acceptance of the engagement rather than agreeing terms with the client, such as whether the firm had the competence to perform the work.

The second requirement, (a) (ii) asked candidates to recommend the procedures that should be used to examine and report on the forecast financial statements to be included in the business plan. The best answers made good use of the forecast financial statements that had been provided, and gave procedures that were both well described and relevant to the specific content of the financial statements. Many candidates also performed analytical procedures to determine unusual trends and relationships in the figures and information provided, which helped to generate very exact procedures. Sound answers had a range of procedures, some general, some focused on income and expenses, some focused on assets, liabilities and equity. Weaker answers tended to state simple enquiries, for example 'ask management who prepared the forecasts', or 'ask why sales has increased' without any further development. Another problem arose in answers that seemed not to realise that the figures were forecasts, so source documentation would not be available in the same way that it is for an audit of historical information. For example, many answers suggested agreeing assets purchased to invoices from suppliers, or the forecast increase in share capital to share certificates, but these items would not yet exist as they relate to future transactions. The one area that was missing from almost all answers was the need to ensure internal consistency in all forecast figures, so for example cross-checking from the forecast financial statements to a capital expenditure budget and to cash flow forecasts.

Another problem with weaker answers was that they tended not to always provide procedures. For example, some answers contained a lengthy discussion as to whether a part of the business that was planned to be sold should be accounted for as a held-for-sale group of assets, which is not very relevant to the question requirement. These answers seemed to be drifting into an assessment of potential material misstatements, which was not asked for.

The second part of this question was generally not well answered. This part of the question dealt with a client which had suffered an environmental accident resulting in the closure of a factory. The audit engagement partner had asked for briefing notes to be prepared in which the principal audit procedures to be performed in respect of the cost of closure of the factory were recommended. Answers were often lacking in focus. Sound answers recommended a range of procedures specific to the types of cost that would normally be included in a cost of closure provision, such as redundancy costs. Very few candidates recognised that the date at which an obligation arose in relation to the closure of the factory was crucial, and many could recommend little more than asking for written representations. There was often discussion of the recognition criteria for provisions contained in IAS 37 *Provisions, Contingent Liabilities and Contingent Assets*, but little on the specific accounting requirements in relation to a restructuring, which could have prompted some specific procedures.

Requirement (b) (ii) was a discussion on the difficulties in measuring and reporting on environmental and social performance. Candidates often struggled to write more than a few bullet points here, and sometimes wrote from the point of view of the auditor trying to obtain evidence on key performance indicators. However, most answers did identify difficulties in defining performance measures on what can be quite intangible matters, and many also discussed the problems in quantifying socio-environmental issues.

Requirement (b) also contained 4 professional marks in relation to the briefing notes requested by the audit partner. Most candidates attempted a correct format and structure for the briefing notes, and the use of paragraphs, headings and an introduction meant that many candidates scored well here.

ACCA marking scheme			
			Marks
(a)	(i)	**Matters to be included in the terms of agreement** Up to 1½ marks for each matter identified and explained (2 marks maximum for identification): • Management's responsibilities • Intended use of the information and report • The contents of the business plan • The period covered by the forecasts • The nature of assumptions used in the forecasts • The format and planned content of the assurance report	
		Maximum	**6**
	(ii)	**Procedures on forecast financial information** Up to 1 mark for each procedure (brief examples below): • Re-calculate forecast • Consistency of accounting policies used • Discuss how joint venture has been included • General analytical procedures • Discuss trends – allow up to 3 marks for calculations performed and linked to procedures • Review and compare breakdown of costs • Recalculate profit on disposal, agreement of components to supporting documentation • Agree increase in property, plant and equipment to capital expenditure budget • Discuss working capital trends – allow 2 marks for calculations performed and linked to procedures • Agree movement in long-term borrowings to new loan documentation • Obtain and review forecast statement of changes in equity and confirm validity of reconciling items	
		Maximum	**15**
(b)	(i)	**Audit procedures on costs of closure** Generally 1 mark per specific procedure, examples given below: • Review board minutes for discussion and date of decision • Review detailed, formal plan and date of its approval – Review any public announcement and the date it was made • Physically inspect factory prior to year end for evidence of dismantling of assets • Consider whether costs included are relevant (redundancies and lease cancellation fees are the most common type of relevant costs included) • Agree relevant costs to supporting documentation • Review note to financial statements for accuracy and completeness	
		Maximum	**6**

(ii) **Problems in measuring and reporting on social and environmental performance** Up to 1½ marks per comment discussed • Difficulties in defining and measuring targets and KPIs • Problems in quantifying some measures, e.g. employee satisfaction • Inadequate systems and controls to accurately measure • Difficult to compare between companies or over time **Maximum**	4
Professional marks for the overall presentation of the notes, and the clarity of the explanation and assessment provided. **Maximum**	4
Total	**35**

14 APRICOT *Walk in the footsteps of a top tutor*

Top tutor tips

Part (a) Examination procedures need to focus on assessing the reasonableness of the assumptions used in the forecast. Remember that these transactions have not happened as of yet so you will not be able to inspect invoices, etc. Instead, think about how the client determined the forecast figures and assess whether that is reasonable. Analytical procedures and inquiries will be the main procedures to use. There may be some documents you can inspect such as quotations for new fixtures.

Part (b) is more general and simply asks what the contents of a typical PFI assurance report are. This requires little more than pre-learnt knowledge.

(a) Recommended procedures to be performed on the cash flow forecast include:

Accuracy checks:

- Agree the opening cash position to cash book and bank statement/bank reconciliation.
- Cast the forecast to confirm arithmetical accuracy.

Cash receipts:

- Assess whether the assumption regarding the split of revenue between cash and credit sales is accurate by considering whether it is in line with knowledge of the business.
- Agree the forecast cash receipts from cash sales to the forecast revenue figures in the profit forecast for January, February and March 2010.
- Verify the 10% discount has been accounted for in calculating the cash sales by recalculation.
- Agree the 10% discount to a small sample of invoices raised.
- Recalculate the pattern of receipts from credit customers by applying the stated average credit terms to actual sales in October, November and December 2009, and the forecast sales for January, February and March 2010.

- Review the latest aged receivables analysis available for confirmation of the pattern of payment from credit customers.

Purchases:

- Recalculate the pattern of cash flows relating to purchases by applying the stated credit terms to the forecast purchases figures in the profit forecast.
- Using the latest available information, calculate a supplier's payment ratio to compare with the stated usual credit terms applied to purchases of 30 days.
- Agree the 12% discount to invoices received, supplier statement reconciliations, or signed contracts with suppliers.

Other operating cash outflows:

- Discuss with the management of Apricot Co the relationship between sales and operating cash outflows. It appears that outflows could be understated, as salaries and expenses are static, whereas cash receipts from sales are increasing over the period.
- Agree the monthly salary cash outflow to latest available payroll records, and to the profit forecast.
- Obtain a breakdown of the contents of the overheads cash outflow category and review the schedule for any non-cash items which should not be included, e.g. depreciation and amortisation, bad debt expenses.
- Compare the components of the overhead cash outflow to a breakdown of operating expenses included in the profit forecast, looking for omissions.

Non-recurring cash flows:

- Agree the cost of the licence to supporting documentation, e.g. any correspondence already received from the issuing body, and compare the cost of $35,000 to the cost of the previous year's licence.
- Confirm that the 2009 licence expires in December and that the new licence will be required in January 2010 by reviewing the terms of the licence.
- Discuss the inspections required for the new licence to be granted, and ascertain if the inspections have yet taken place, and if so, the results of the inspection.
- Review the board minutes, and minutes of shareholder meetings for approval of the dividend payment in February 2010.

Cash flows associated with the new premises:

- For the new fixtures, agree the estimated cost to supplier price lists, or to any quotations received.
- Discuss the timing of the cash outflow in relation to fixtures with management. Presumably the fixtures can only be put into place once the premises have been acquired, which is planned for the end of March. It seems likely that the fixtures will not be purchased until April, in which case the cash payment is recognised too early in the forecast.
- For the premises, agree the potential purchase price to correspondence with the vendor and solicitors.

- Obtain a breakdown of the potential cost of $500,000 and review to ensure the cost is complete, i.e. have legal fees, stamp duty and other associated costs been included.
- Review board minutes for approval of the purchase, and approval that the finance will be raised from Pik Choi.

General enquiries:

Enquire with the preparer of the forecast regarding the following:

- Enquire as to the competence and experience of the preparer of the forecast.
- No finance costs or tax payments appear to have been included – have they been omitted or are there no finance or tax payments in the three-month period?
- Are there any other costs to be incurred in relation to the new premises in the three-month period? e.g. recruitment costs for new staff, any additional working capital requirements, installation of plant and fixtures to the new premises.
- Discuss the reason for the acquisition of the new premises.
- Enquire whether any payments in advance or deposits will need to be made; currently the full amount is forecasted to be paid on the date of acquisition.
- Enquire about any other potential sources of finance in case Pik Choi fails to provide the full amount required, or in case the new premises cost more than the estimated amount.

(b) Main contents of an assurance report

ISAE 3400 *The Examination of Prospective Financial Information* provides guidance on the content of an assurance report given when a professional accountant has examined forecasts or projections.

- Title and addressee.
- Identification of the prospective financial information (PFI); this should be by reference to a page number, or to the titles of the statements which have been evaluated. There should also be a reference to the period that the PFI covers.
- A reference to ISAE 3400 or relevant national standards applicable to the examination of PFI. This adds credibility to the report because it has been prepared according to a recognised regulatory statement.
- A statement that management is responsible for the PFI including the assumptions on which it is based. There should be a page reference for the assumptions, as these are a key component of the PFI.
- Where applicable, a reference to the purpose and/or restricted distribution of the prospective financial information. The report should caution readers that because the PFI is based on hypothetical assumptions, the events and figures contained in the PFI may not necessarily occur as expected. There should also be a caution as to the potential use of the PFI.
- A statement of negative assurance as to whether the assumptions provide a reasonable basis for the PFI. This would be stated as follows: 'nothing has come to our attention which causes us to believe that the assumptions do not provide a reasonable basis for the projection...'.

- A conclusion as to whether the PFI is properly prepared on the basis of the assumptions and is presented in accordance with the relevant financial reporting framework.
- Appropriate caveats concerning the achievability of the results indicated by the PFI.
- The date, name of the audit firm, and a signature.

The following points are not specifically referred to in ISAE 3400, but would commonly be included by firms providing assurance reports on PFI:

- A reference to the engagement letter and to the specific procedures that were requested, and have been carried out.
- A statement that the procedures carried out were those specified by the company and the third party to whom the report is issued.
- Details of any errors and exceptions found.

If the auditor believes that the presentation and disclosure of the PFI is not adequate, the auditor should express a qualified or adverse conclusion. If one or more significant assumptions do not provide a reasonable basis for the PFI, the auditor should express an adverse conclusion on the report. A modified conclusion due to lack of sufficient appropriate evidence should be expressed if conditions preclude application of one or more procedures considered necessary in the circumstances.

ACCA marking scheme		
		Marks
(a)	**Procedures on cash flow forecast**	
	Generally 1 mark per specific procedure from ideas list:	
	– Accuracy checks – recalculation	
	– Agree opening cash position	
	– Recalculate patterns of cash in and out for credit sales and purchases	
	– Agree patterns using aged receivables analysis/working capital ratios	
	– Agree discounts received and allowed to invoices/contracts/ correspondences	
	– Agree derivation of figures from profit forecast	
	– Agree monthly salary expense to payroll	
	– Review content of overheads – check non-cash expenses not included	
	– Review for missing outflows e.g. tax and finance charges	
	– Agree premises costs e.g. to legal documents	
	– Discuss timing of fixtures cash flow	
	– General enquiries with the preparer of the forecast	
	Maximum	**15**
(b)	**Content of an assurance report**	
	Up to 1 mark per point if explained:	
	– Title/addressee (½ mark)	
	– Identification of PFI	
	– Management responsibility	
	– Purpose of PFI	
	– Restricted use of PFI	
	– Negative assurance conclusion re assumptions	
	– Conclusion on presentation	
	– When may modifications be necessary/explanation of errors found	
	– Reference to engagement letter (½ mark)	
	– Statement/reference to procedures carried out (½ mark)	
	Maximum	**5**
Total		**20**

15 SANZIO *Walk in the footsteps of a top tutor*

Top tutor tips

Part (a) asks for the purpose of a due diligence assignment. This is the reason for performing a due diligence review i.e. what benefits can be generated for the client. The requirement also asks for a comparison of the scope of a due diligence assignment and an audit. Here you should identify not just the differences but the similarities as well.

Part (bi) asks for the information you would require to assist in your valuation of the Titian Tyres' intangible assets, primarily the customer database and the licence. The customer database is an internally generated asset therefore won't be included in the financial statements of Titian Tyres. Remember that the value of an asset is dependent on the expected future cash flows so identify information that would help assess the level of future cash flows that could be generated from the assets.

Part (bii) asks for enquiries to be made regarding the contingent liability included in the notes to the financial statements. Here you should be trying to assess the likelihood of payment and the potential amount of the payment.

(a) The purpose of due diligence

Information gathering

Due diligence is the process of fact finding to help reduce the risk involved in investment decisions. It is used when gathering information about a target company, for the purpose of ensuring that the acquirer has full knowledge of the operations, financial performance and position, legal and tax situation, as well as the general commercial background of the target. In particular, due diligence helps to uncover potential problems before a decision regarding the acquisition is made.

Verification of management representations

During a sale, the vendor may make representations to the potential acquirer which it is essential to verify. As an example, the vendor may state that the company has recently had a health and safety or fire safety investigation or that since their last year end they have replaced ageing property, plant and equipment. Due diligence can be used to substantiate such claims.

Identification of assets and liabilities

One of the key reasons for performing due diligence is to identify the assets and liabilities of the target company, which is vital when trying to value the target company. It is particularly important to attempt to identify and value the intangible assets of the target company, including their brands, customer databases and development costs. Internally generated intangibles will not be included on the statement of financial position and are particularly difficult to assess.

The valuation of liabilities is also critical because the acquirer will have to settle these in the future. This must be appropriately planned for and considered during the negotiation of the acquisition price. Contingent liabilities are particularly significant because, by their nature, the amount required to settle them and the likelihood of settlement are uncertain.

Operational issues

As well as the risk associated with the valuation of a business, the acquirer must also consider operational implications which could jeopardise a proposed acquisition, such as high staff turnover, the need to renegotiate supplier or customer contracts or contracts with lenders, and future changes in the product mix of the target company. Any of these could lead to operational problems in the future and could be considered potential 'deal breakers' or, at the very least, be used to negotiate the acquisition price.

Acquisition planning

Due diligence will also assess the potential commercial benefits and drawbacks of the acquisition. For example, it could be used to calculate the potential economies of scale from aligning the supply chains of the buyer and the target company. On the other hand, there are post-acquisition costs to consider, such as the costs of reorganisation and the potential staff turnover which may be experienced.

Scope of a due diligence assignment compared to an audit

With due diligence, the scope is focused primarily on fact finding, which means that the investigation will draw on a much wider range of sources than those connected with the current financial statements. These include:

- Several years' worth of historical financial statements
- Management accounts
- Profit and cash flow forecasts
- Recent business plans and internal strategies/objectives
- Employee contracts, particularly those of management
- All binding contracts, such as supply contracts, lease agreements and loan agreement
- Discussions with management, employees and third parties.

While many of these items may be reviewed during an audit of historical financial statements, it is likely that due diligence will require a much wider range of information.

The objective of an audit is to provide reasonable assurance that the financial statements are free from material misstatement. In contrast, the aim of due diligence is to provide the acquirer with a set of information which has been collated and, most likely, reviewed by the practitioner. Unless requested by the client, the practitioner will not express any conclusion with regard to the accuracy of the information provided. In this case, due diligence is performed as an 'agreed upon procedures' assignment.

If the practitioner is requested to provide assurance regarding the accuracy of the information provided, the due diligence service would be performed as a limited assurance review engagement. This is a lower level of assurance than that provided in an audit due to the reduced procedures performed during due diligence.

The type of work performed during due diligence is quite different to an audit, as a due diligence investigation uses, primarily, analytical procedures and enquiry as a means of gathering information. Very few, if any, substantive procedures are carried out, unless they are specifically requested by the client or there are specific issues which cause concern and therefore need more detailed investigation. This is in contrast to an audit, where a comprehensive range of tests of control and substantive tests are performed.

Due diligence is much more 'forward looking' than an audit. Much of the time during a due diligence investigation will be spent assessing forecasts and predictions. This is in contrast to an audit, where procedures only tend to consider future events if they are directly relevant to the year-end financial statements, for example, contingencies, or going concern problems.

In contrast to an audit, when it is essential to evaluate systems and controls, the due diligence investigation will not conduct detailed testing of the accounting and internal control systems, unless specifically requested to do so.

(b) (i) Intangible assets

Customer database

- A copy of the financial statements for the year ended 30 June 2015 to identify the current carrying value of any purchased intangibles relating to the database, such as computer software.
- A copy of the original purchase agreement for the software to identify the age of the software and when any product licences expire.
- A copy of the original purchase/ongoing maintenance contracts for the software to identify the continuing costs of maintaining the system at its current level of efficiency.
- Historic records of sales by customer to verify management's statement that repeat customers make up over 60% of annual sales.
- Copies of a sample of recent automated customer communications; these can be traced to customer bookings/sales records to confirm the current efficacy of the system.
- Sales forecasts for the foreseeable future to assess the potential future cash flows attributable to the customer database system to assess its value when determining the potential purchase price.
- Confirmation of the current price of similar database software to assess the market value/fair value of the asset.

Licence

- A copy of the original purchase agreement for the licence to confirm the $5 million cost and the exclusivity of the agreement.
- The original purchase agreement can also be used to identify whether any further incremental/contingent considerations or royalties are due in the future.

- A copy of the licence agreement to confirm whether the licence is for a fixed period of time or not and to confirm the exclusivity of the licence.
- A breakdown of the sales figures relating to the new tyres; these can be used to compare the performance of the new tyres to existing brands.
- Forecasts showing the expected future sales attributable to the new tyres to confirm the continued inflow of economic benefit from the asset.

(ii) Contingent liabilities

The following enquiries should be made of the management of Titian Tyres Co:

- Enquire of management and ascertain if any legal advice has been sought to determine who is liable to pay compensation in these cases, Titian Tyres Co or the supplier of the parts.
- Enquire whether management has sought any legal advice with regard to the likelihood of having to settle the claims or not.
- Enquire if management has records showing how many vehicles have been fitted with the faulty parts and whether these have been used in any estimates of the likely settlement costs.
- Discuss with management the level of claims which have been settled since the year end. Compare this with the original estimation to establish how effective management has been in making these estimates
- Enquire of management for how long the company used the faulty parts and for what portion of this time period the known claims relate to.
- Discuss with management the details of any new claims which have been made since the year end which were not included in any estimations of the cost of settlement included in the contingent liability disclosure in the financial statements.
- Discuss with management their assessment of any risk that further claims will be made which they are currently unaware of.
- Enquire of management if other quality problems have been experienced with other parts from the same supplier.

Examiner's comments

This question was the most popular choice of the optional questions, and was answered by a significant number of candidates.

Candidates were required to provide a description of the purpose of a due diligence assignment and to demonstrate an understanding of the purpose of due diligence by providing a comparison with a statutory audit of financial statements. The majority of candidates attempting this part of the question scored well demonstrating sound knowledge of this area of the syllabus.

The remainder of the question focused on the work that may be performed during a due diligence assignment and specifically around the valuation of specific assets and liabilities within a target company. The question here asked for further information that may be required and enquiries that would be made in order to provide assurance on such items.

Candidates produced the strongest answers with respect to the valuation of a purchased licence albeit often focusing on initial recording rather than current values/impairment. The valuation of an internally generated database proved harder as many candidates quoted the financial reporting rules and concluded it should not be presented within the financial statements. This was often despite having previously described the purpose of due diligence as a method of identifying assets and liabilities not included in the financial statements which nevertheless would form part of the fair values at acquisition. Candidates would benefit from reviewing the question as a whole in order to consider how the different sections and requirements fit together. More effective planning, prior to writing, would allow candidates to demonstrate a better understanding of these connections.

The final item related to a contingent liability that was presented in the target company's financial statements. Answers to this were of mixed quality but it was disappointing how many candidates again lost sight of the assignment being one of due diligence and made comments regarding the financial statements disclosure requirement. Again candidates are reminded that more effective use of reading and planning time would allow a clearer understanding of what is being asked for and that time should be spent ensuring that answers are tailored to the specifics of the question.

ACCA marking scheme	
	Marks
(a) Purpose and scope of due diligence	
Generally up to 1 mark for each description of the purpose of due diligence and up to 1 mark for each point of comparison with an audit.	
Purpose:	
– Gathering information to reduce risk of investment decisions	
– Verification on management representations	
– Identification and valuation of assets and liabilities	
– Identification of operational concerns and synergies	
– Assistance with acquisition planning	
Scope:	
– Range of sources used	
– Level of assurance/type of engagement	
– Types of procedure performed	
– Forward looking v mainly historical	
– No controls testing	
Maximum	**6**
(b) **(i) Additional Information**	
Up to 1 mark for each piece of information recommended and adequately explained.	
– Database:	
– 30 June 2015 financial statements (carrying value)	
– Original software purchase agreement	
– Software maintenance contract	
– Historic records of sales by customer	
– Sample customer communications	
– Sales forecasts	
Licence:	
– Original purchase agreement (cost)	
– Original purchase agreement (incremental/contingent consideration)	
– Licence terms and conditions	
– Sales figures for new brand	
– Forecast sales for new brand	

(ii) Enquiries Up to 1 mark for enquiry recommended and adequately explained. – Legal advice regarding who bears the liability – Legal advice regarding likelihood of settlement – Basis of estimation of liability – Settlement of claims since year end – How long faulty parts used for – New claims since year end – Risk of further claims – Quality problems with other parts	
Maximum	**14**
Total	**20**

16 BALTIMORE *Walk in the footsteps of a top tutor*

Top tutor tips

Part (a) requires discussion of the benefits of a due diligence review being performed prior to the acquisition of a company. There were indications in the scenario that the client did not have the skill to do this and you are expected to identify these points and use them in your answer.

Part (b) asked for matters to focus on during the due diligence review. A due diligence review is performed to find information relevant to the client's decision regarding the acquisition. Therefore you should identify the matters that might deter them from going ahead with the acquisition or might encourage them to go ahead with the acquisition.

Part (c) is a straightforward requirement asking for the type of conclusion, i.e. level of assurance, to be issued on the due diligence review and to compare this to an audit.

(a) Three benefits of due diligence to Baltimore Co

Identification of assets and liabilities

One of the objectives of a due diligence review is for the assets and liabilities of the target company to be identified and valued. Therefore a benefit of due diligence to Baltimore Co is to gain an understanding of the nature of assets and liabilities which are being acquired, as not all assets and liabilities of Mizzen Co are recognised in its financial statements. For example, Mizzen Co has built up several customer databases, which, being internally generated, will not be recognised as assets in its statement of financial position, but these could be valuable assets to Baltimore Co.

Identification of operational issues

The due diligence review should uncover more information about operational issues, which may then help Baltimore Co's management to decide whether to go ahead with the acquisition. For example, only one of Mizzen Co's revenue streams appears to be directly relevant to Baltimore Co's expansion plans, so more information is needed about the other operations of Mizzen Co to determine how they may be of benefit to Baltimore Co. The due diligence review should cover a wide range of issues, such as reviews of the company's legal and tax positions, which may uncover significant matters.

Expertise

An externally provided due diligence review, as opposed to a review conducted by management of Baltimore Co, is likely to provide information in a time-efficient, impartial manner. Baltimore Co's management has not previously dealt with an acquisition, whereas the audit firm has the financial and business understanding and expertise to provide a quality due diligence review. A review report issued by Goleen & Co will add credibility to the planned acquisition, which may help secure the bank loan which is needed to fund the acquisition.

Tutorial note

Credit will be awarded for other relevant benefits which are discussed.

(b) Matters to focus on in the due diligence review

Equity owners of Mizzen Co and involvement of BizGrow

The nature of the involvement of the venture capitalist company, BizGrow, is a crucial issue which must be the starting point of the due diligence review. Venture capitalists provide equity when a company is incorporated, and typically look for an exit route within three to seven years. Mizzen Co was incorporated four years ago, so it will be important to determine whether BizGrow retains its original equity holding in Mizzen Co, and if so, whether the acquisition of BizGrow's shares by Baltimore Co would be compatible with the planned exit route.

Key skills and expertise

It appears that the original founders of Mizzen Co, Vic Sandhu and Lou Lien, are crucial to the success of Mizzen Co and it would be in Baltimore Co's interests to keep them involved with the business. However, Vic and Lou may wish to focus on further work involving IT innovation rather than Baltimore Co's planned website and without Vic and Lou's expertise the acquisition may be much less worthwhile. However, there could be other employed personnel with the necessary skills and experience to meet Baltimore Co's needs, or much of the skill and expertise could be provided from freelancers, who will not be part of the acquisition.

Internally generated intangible assets

Mizzen Co is likely to have several important internally generated intangible assets, which will not be recognised in its individual accounts but must be identified and measured as part of the due diligence review. First, Vic and Lou have innovated and developed new website interfaces, and the review must determine the nature of this intellectual property (IP), and whether it belongs to Vic and Lou or to Mizzen Co. The measurement of this asset will be very difficult, and it is likely to form an important part of the acquisition deal if Baltimore Co want to acquire the IP to use in its new website.

There are also several customer databases which need to be measured and included in the list of assets acquired, which again may be difficult to measure in value. It is important for the due diligence review to confirm the relevance of the databases to Baltimore Co's operations, and that the databases contain up-to-date information.

Premises

Mizzen Co currently operates from premises owned by BizGrow and pays a nominal rent for this. Presumably if the acquisition were to go ahead, this arrangement would cease. The due diligence review should consider the need for new premises to be found for Mizzen Co and the associated costs. Possibly there is room for Mizzen Co to operate from Baltimore Co's premises as the operations do not appear to need a large space. The rental agreement may be fixed for a period of time and cancellation may incur a penalty.

Other tangible assets

Mizzen Co appears to own only items such as computer equipment and fixtures and fittings. It needs to be clarified whether these assets are owned or held under lease, and also whether any other tangible assets, such as vehicles, are used in the business. Any commitments for future purchases of tangible assets should be reviewed.

Accounting policy on revenue recognition

Mizzen Co has some fairly complex revenue streams, and the due diligence review should establish that the accounting policies in place are reasonable and in line with IFRS 15 *Revenue from contracts with customers*. The revenue generated from website development and maintenance should be split into two components, with the revenue for website development recognised once the website has been provided to the customer, but the revenue for maintenance spread over the contract period. There is a risk that revenue is recognised too early, inflating Mizzen Co's profit.

The revenue recognition policy for annual subscriptions should also be scrutinized, with revenue relating to future periods being deferred.

Sustainability and relevance of revenue streams

The financial statements indicate that revenue has increased each year, and that in the last year it has increased by 23.7%. This is an impressive growth rate and work must be done to analyse the likelihood of revenue streams being maintained and further growth being achieved. For example, the proportion of website development and two year maintenance contracts which are renewed should be investigated. Not all of Mizzen Co's revenue streams seem very relevant to Baltimore Co's operations, so how these may be managed post-acquisition should be considered.

Operating expenses

The financial extracts indicate a potentially unusual trend in relation to operating expenses. In 2011 and 2012, operating expenses represented 60% and 58.3% of revenue respectively. In 2013, this had reduced to 49.6%. This may be due to economies of scale being achieved as the company grows, or possibly expenses are understated or revenue overstated in 2013. As freelance web designers have been used in 2013, operating expenses may have been expected to have increased in proportion to revenue. The due diligence review should perform detailed analysis on the operating costs incurred by the company to gain assurance that expenses are complete and accurately recorded.

With the exception of 2010, the finance cost has remained static at $250,000 per annum. The due diligence review must uncover what this finance cost relates to, and whether it will continue post-acquisition. It may be a bank loan or it could be a payment made to BizGrow, as venture capitalist companies often impose a management charge on companies which they have invested in. Baltimore Co will need to understand the nature of any liability in relation to this finance charge.

Cash position and cash management

Mizzen Co's cash position should be confirmed. Given that the company appears to have limited need for capital expenditure and working capital, and given the level of profits which has been made in the last three years, it could be expected that the company would be cash-rich. The due diligence review should confirm how the cash generated by the company since incorporation has been used, for example, in dividend payments to BizGrow and to Vic and Lou.

Additional information required

- Contract or legal documentation describing the nature of the investment which BizGrow made when Mizzen Co was incorporated, and detailing the planned exit route.
- A register of shareholders showing all shareholders of Mizzen Co.
- An organisational structure, in order to identify the members of management and key personnel and their roles within Mizzen Co.
- A list of employees and their roles within the company, and their related obligations including salary, holiday entitlements, retirement plans, health insurance and other benefits provided by Mizzen Co, and details of compensation to be paid in the case of redundancy.
- A list of freelance web designers used by Mizzen Co, and a description of the work they perform.
- The key terms of contracts or agreements with freelance web designers.
- A list of all IT innovations which have been created and developed by Mizzen Co, and details of any patent or copyright agreements relating to them.
- Agreements with employees regarding assignment of intellectual property and confidentiality.
- Copies of the customer databases showing contact details of all people or companies included on the list.
- A list of companies which have contracts with Mizzen Co for website development and maintenance.
- A copy of all contracts with customers for review of the period for which maintenance is to be provided.
- A breakdown of the revenue which has been generated from making each database available to other companies, and the dates when they were made available.
- A summary of the controls which are in place to ensure that the database details are regularly updated.
- A copy of the rental agreement with BizGrow, to determine whether any penalty is payable on cancellation.

- Non-current asset register showing descriptions and values of all assets used in the business.
- Copies of any lease agreements, for example, leases of computer equipment, photocopiers, etc.
- Details of any capital expenditure budgets for previous accounting periods, and any planned capital expenditure in the future.
- Mizzen Co's stated accounting policy on revenue recognition.
- Systems and controls documentation over the processing of revenue receipts.
- An analysis of expenses included in operating expenses for each year and copies of documentation relating to ongoing expenses, such as salaries and other overheads.
- Copies of management accounts to agree expenses in the audited accounts are in line and to perform more detailed analytical review.
- The full set of financial statements and auditor's reports for each year since the company's incorporation, to:
  - Confirm the assets and liabilities recognised
  - Agree the level of dividends paid each year
  - Review all of the accounting policies used in preparing the financial statements
  - Find the details of any related party transactions that have occurred
  - Review the statement of cash flows for each year.
- Any agreements with banks or other external providers of finance, including finance advanced and relevant finance charges, or confirmation that no such finance has been provided to Mizzen Co.

> ***Tutorial note***
>
> *Credit will be awarded for other relevant information which would be required as part of the due diligence review.*

(c) Due diligence conclusion

Due diligence is a specific example of a direct reporting assurance engagement. The form of the report issued in this type of engagement is covered by ISAE 3000 *Assurance Engagements other than Audits or Reviews of Historical Financial Information*, and ISRE 2400 *Engagements to Review Historical Financial Statements* also contains relevant guidance.

The main difference between a review report and an auditor's report is the level of assurance that is given. In a review report a conclusion is expressed in a negative form. The conclusion would start with the wording 'based on our review, nothing has come to our attention...'

This type of conclusion is used because the nature of a due diligence review is that only limited assurance has been obtained over the subject matter. The procedures used in a review engagement are mainly enquiry and analytical review which can only provide limited assurance.

Tutorial note

Credit is equally awarded where answers discuss the due diligence assignment as being based on agreed upon procedures, in which case no assurance is provided.

In comparison, in an audit of historical information, the auditor will use a wide variety of procedures to obtain evidence to give reasonable assurance that the financial statements are free from material misstatement. This means that an opinion expressed in a positive form can be given.

Examiner's comments

This question focused on due diligence, a topic that has appeared in P7 examinations several times previous to this sitting. The scenario described a due diligence assignment to be performed on the target company Mizzen Co, at the request of Baltimore Co. The history and activities of the target company was described in some detail, and some financial information provided for the last four years. For Baltimore Co this would be their first acquisition, and was being considered as a means to diversify the company's operations.

Requirement (a) asked candidates to discuss three benefits to Baltimore Co of a due diligence review being performed on Mizzen Co. While some reasonable answers were given, possibly by candidates who had practiced the past exam question containing a similar requirement, on the whole answers were unsatisfactory. The following factors contributed to inadequate performance in relation to this requirement:

- Writing answers that were much too brief for the marks available – it was common to see three sentences given as an answer to this requirement, which cannot be enough for a 6 mark requirement.
- At the other extreme, some very lengthy answers were given that usually failed to answer the question requirement and instead either simply wrote in detail on how a due diligence assignment should be performed, or suggested in some detail the operational benefits to Baltimore Co of acquiring Mizzen Co.
- Many answers failed to limit to three benefits and instead provided a bullet point list of benefits that were not discussed at all.

Requirement (b) was the main part of the question, and asked candidates to identify and explain the matters that the due diligence review would focus on, and to recommend the additional information needed.

The answers provided to this requirement were extremely mixed in quality. There were some exceptionally sound answers, explaining relevant matters in sufficient depth, and using the financial information provided to come up with reasonable points. These answers also provided relevant requests for additional information.

However, the majority of answers were unsatisfactory. Most candidates picked up at least a few marks by identifying some of the matters that the review would focus on, but many candidates let themselves down by failing to explain the matters that they had identified in any real depth. It was common for answers to simply contain a list of bullet points with very little explanation at all, and only a limited amount of marks can be awarded to answers of this type.

Some points were better dealt with, including the following:

- Most answers picked up on the fact that Mizzen Co used premises owned by the venture capitalist company, and the fact that this arrangement would probably cease on the acquisition.
- Many candidates realised that the two founders of Mizzen Co were crucial to the company's success and that without them the acquisition would probably be pointless.
- Many candidates used the financial information to some extent, though sometimes only in a very limited way, but most picked up on the fact that Mizzen Co was paying finance charges, and so information would be needed to understand what those charges relate to.
- Many answers considered that revenue recognition would be a matter to focus on due to the relatively complex nature of the company's revenue streams.
- Some answers performed a little analytical review on the financial information to reveal that expenses were not increasing in line with revenue, and that this would need to be investigated.

The answers that were unsatisfactory, as well as containing inadequately explained points as mentioned above, also tended to focus too much on financial reporting matters, for example giving very lengthy discussions on the calculation of goodwill. While the accounting treatment of some items certainly was relevant to the answer, just focusing on these matters meant that candidates did not provide a broad enough range of comments to score well.

Another factor leading to poor marks for this requirement was that many candidates simply failed to recommend any additional information at all that would be needed in the review. Many candidates missed out on marks here, for example for recommending that a statement of financial position, management accounts and cash flow forecasts would be needed.

Some candidates supplied a lengthy discussion of matters relating to the acceptance of the due diligence assignment, such as agreeing fees and clarifying deadlines, which was not asked for.

Requirement (c) required candidates to describe the type of conclusion that would be issued for a due diligence report and to compare this to an auditor's report. This was well answered by most candidates, who compared the type of assurance that could be offered for a due diligence assignment with that given in an auditor's report, and linked this to the type of work that is carried out. Credit was awarded for different types of answers, as some discussed due diligence as being performed as agreed upon procedures rather than a review engagement, either of which is appropriate.

ACCA marking scheme	
	Marks
(a) **Benefit of due diligence** Up to 2 marks for each benefit discussed for a maximum of three benefits: – Identification of assets and liabilities – Valuation of assets and liabilities – Review of operational issues – Examination of financial position and performance – Added credibility and expertise – Added value for negotiation of purchase price – Other advice can be given, e.g. on obtaining finance	
Maximum	**6**

(b)	**Areas to focus on and additional information** Generally up to 1½ marks for each explanation of area to focus on: – Equity owners of Mizzen Co and involvement of BizGrow – Key skills and expertise – Internally generated intangible assets – Premises – Other intangible assets – Accounting policy on revenue recognition – Sustainability and relevance of revenue streams – Operating expenses – Finance charges – Cash management 1 mark for each specific additional information recommended: – Contract or legal documentation dealing with BizGrow's investment – A register of shareholders showing all shareholders of Mizzen Co – An organisational structure – A list of employees and their role within the company, obligations and compensation – A list of freelance web designers used by Mizzen Co, and a description of the work they perform – The key terms of contracts or agreements with freelance web designers – A list of all IT innovations which have been created and developed by Mizzen Co, and details of any patent or copyright agreements relating to them – Agreements with employees regarding IP and confidentiality – Copies of the customer databases – A list of companies which have contracts with Mizzen Co for website development and maintenance – A copy of all maintenance contracts with customers – A breakdown of the revenue that has been generated from making each database available to other companies, and the dates when they were made available – A summary of the controls which are in place to ensure that the database details are regularly updated – A copy of the premises rental agreement with BizGrow – Non-current asset register – Copies of any lease agreements – Details of any capital expenditure budgets for previous accounting periods, and any planned capital expenditure in the future – Mizzen Co's stated accounting policy on revenue recognition – Systems and controls documentation over the processing of revenue receipts – Analysis of expenses included in operating expenses for each year – Copies of management accounts – The full set of financial statements and auditor's reports – Any agreements with banks or other external providers of finance	
	Maximum	**16**
(c)	**Conclusion on due diligence** Generally 1 mark for each discussion point: – Due diligence report to express conclusion of negative assurance – Limited assurance due to nature of work performed – Audit opinion is a positive opinion of reasonable assurance	
	Maximum	**3**
Total		**25**

17 JACOB *Walk in the footsteps of a top tutor*

Top tutor tips

Part (a) asks for benefits of externally provided due diligence prior to the acquisition of a company. Try and think of reasons why the client might not be able to do the due diligence for themselves.

Part (b) requires the information you would require for your due diligence review. Think about the information that would help you identify whether there are any financial, operational, tax or legal issues with the company being acquired. Is there anything happening that would deter the client from purchasing the company? Is there anything that would impact the price that they would be prepared to pay for the company?

(a) There are many potential benefits to the potential purchaser of a company in having a due diligence review.

Identification of assets and liabilities

One benefit is that by conducting a due diligence review, the assets and liabilities of Locke Co can be identified and a potential value placed on them. Without a due diligence review it will be difficult for management to negotiate a fair price for Locke Co, as the price paid should include consideration of assets and liabilities not necessarily shown in the accounts, for example, any contingent liabilities which may exist in connection with warranties provided to customers of Locke Co.

Identification of operational issues

The due diligence review should uncover more information about operational issues, which may then help Jacob Co's directors in deciding whether to go ahead with the acquisition. For example, Locke Co may need to relocate its head office, as it is currently located on the owners' family estate. If this is the case, significant expense could be involved in building or purchasing new premises, or the head office function could be merged with that of Jacob Co. Either way, it is a practical operational issue that will need to be planned for, if the acquisition were to go ahead.

Expertise

A third benefit is that an externally provided due diligence review, as opposed to a review conducted by management of Jacob Co, is likely to provide information in a time-efficient, impartial manner. The audit firm has the financial and business understanding and expertise to provide a quality due diligence review. The management of Jacob Co can focus their attention on operational issues, for example, considering how best to merge the acquired business into existing operations, leaving the detailed due diligence review to be performed by independent experts.

Tutorial note

The answer above includes three benefits (as required). Credit will be awarded for explanation of any three benefits which are specific to the scenario. Other benefits could include an assessment of the significance of the court case against the company, and its potential impact on the valuation of the business; enhanced credibility provided by an external due diligence review; and a review of the terms and conditions of the significant bank loan, and its potential impact on the future liquidity profile of Locke Co.

(b) Further information to be requested could include:

Directors, and any other key management personnel's contracts of employment – these will be needed to see if there are any contractual settlement terms if the contract of employment is terminated after the acquisition. The family members who founded the company may be looking for an exit route and may not wish to be involved with the company after acquisition, so sizeable amounts could be payable to them on termination of their contracts.

An organisational structure should be obtained, in order to identify the members of management and key personnel and their roles within Locke Co. After acquisition, Jacob Co may wish to retain the services of some members of key management, while others may be made redundant as activities with Jacob Co are streamlined.

Details of any legal arrangement, such as a lease, covering the use of the family owned property by the company. Jacob Co's management may wish to relocate and/or merge Locke Co's head office function. If there is a formal lease arrangement currently in place, there could be early termination penalties to be paid on early termination of the lease.

Purchase documentation regarding the land obtained for the purpose of building a new head office. This will provide information on the location and size of the land. Jacob Co may wish to consider an alternative use for this land, or its sale, or possibly not including the land in the acquisition deal, if it does not wish to go ahead with the construction of the new premises. A copy of planning permission, if any has been sought, regarding the planned construction of a new head office should also be obtained.

Prior-year audited financial statements, and management accounts for this financial year – this information can be used to verify the assertion that Locke Co has enjoyed rapid growth. The financial statements will also provide useful information regarding contingent liabilities, the liquidity position of the company, accounting policies, and the value of assets. Further information should be sought regarding the market value of assets if the financial statements have been prepared using the historical cost convention.

The most recent management accounts for the current year should be analysed. They will reveal any significant change in the company's position or performance since the last audited accounts, for example, if revenue has decreased significantly, or further finance taken out.

Forecasts and budgets for future periods will enable an analysis of the future prospects of the company. Attention should be paid to the cash flow forecast in particular, given that the company has seasonal cash inflows, and uses an overdraft for several months of the year. Expansion in the past should not lead to an assumption that expansion will continue, and the assumptions underpinning the forecasts and budgets should be carefully considered for validity.

The signed loan agreement should be reviewed. Jacob Co will need to know the exact amount and terms of the loan, including the interest rate, any other finance charges, whether the loan is secured on company assets, the repayment terms, and any covenants attached to the loan. The amount is described as significant, and Jacob Co should be wary of taking on this amount of debt without a clear understanding of its associated risk exposure.

Details should also be obtained regarding the overdraft facility, such as the maximum facility that is extended to the company, the interest rate, when the facility is due for renewal or review, and how many months on average the facility is used in a financial year. If the acquisition were to go ahead, Locke Co could prove to be a cash drain on the group. Jacob Co may plan to alleviate this by an inter-company loan of cash during the winter months, but the seasonality of the cash flows must be clearly understood before an acquisition decision is made.

Legal correspondence pertaining to the court case should be obtained. This should show the amount of damages claimed against the company, and the timescale as to when the case should go to court. The correspondence should also show the amount of legal fees incurred so far, and give an indication as to the future amount of fees likely to be paid. A review of the board minutes of Locke Co may indicate the likelihood of the court case going against the company. Jacob Co will need a detailed understanding of the financial consequences of this legal matter if they are to acquire the company.

Information should also be sought regarding the bad publicity caused by the court case. A copy of any press statements made by company representatives would be useful background information.

It is stated that Locke Co enjoys a 'good reputation'. Information to substantiate this claim should be sought, such as the results of customer satisfaction surveys, or data showing the level of repeat customers. Any exaggeration of the claim regarding the company's reputation could mean that Jacob Co can negotiate a lower purchase price, and will need to consider the impact of Locke Co's reputation on its own operations.

Details of warranties offered to customers should be obtained, including the length of period covered by the warranty, and any limits on the amount that can be claimed under warranty, to consider the level of contingent liability they may represent. If significant potential warranty claims exist, this should be reflected in the price offered to acquire Locke Co.

The contract between Locke Co and Austin Co should be obtained and scrutinised. It is essential to understand exactly what services are performed by the service organisation – which could include bookkeeping, payroll, preparation of management accounts and dealing with tax issues. The cost of the outsourcing should also be considered, as well as the reputation of Austin Co. These are important considerations, as Jacob Co may wish to bring the accounting function back in-house, most likely to streamline Locke Co's accounting systems with that of Jacob Co.

Examiner's comments

This was the second most popular of the optional questions, and focused on due diligence. The scenario described a potential acquisition being planned by an audit client of your firm.

Requirement (a) required an explanation of three benefits of an externally provided due diligence review to the audit client. This was reasonably well answered, though many answers were not made very specific to the scenario and tended to discuss the benefits of any due diligence review rather than an externally provided one. Also, a significant number of candidates provided more than three benefits, which was a waste of time.

Requirement (b) asked for additional information to be made available for the firm's due diligence review. Answers were satisfactory, and the majority of candidates did not struggle to apply their knowledge to the scenario, usually providing some very focused answers dealing well with the specifics of the question scenario.

Most answers seemed to use a logical approach – working through the information provided to generate answer points, and this meant that on the whole most of the key issues from the scenario were covered in the answer. A small proportion of answers also included irrelevant discussions of the type of report that would be provided to the client, or a discussion of ethical issues which were not asked for.

ACCA marking scheme

		Marks
(a)	**Benefits of due diligence**	
	Up to 2 marks for each benefit explained (only three benefits required):	
	– Identify and value assets and liabilities to be acquired	
	– Identify and allow planning for operational issues	
	– Provision by external experts – technically competent and time efficient	
	– Assessment of potential impact of court case	
	– Evaluation of the liquidity position of Locke Co	
	– Enhanced credibility provided by an independent review	
	Maximum	6
(b)	**Information required**	
	Generally ½ mark for identification and up to 1 further mark for explanation (maximum 3 marks for identification):	
	– Service contracts of directors	
	– Organisational structure	
	– Lease/arrangement regarding head office	
	– Details of land purchased	
	– Planning permission for new head office	
	– Prior year accounts and management accounts	
	– Forecasts and budgets	
	– Loan agreement	
	– Overdraft facility details	
	– Legal correspondence	
	– Customer satisfaction surveys	
	– Details of warranty agreements	
	– Outsourcing agreement	
	Maximum	14
Total		20

18 FASTER JETS *Walk in the footsteps of a top tutor*

Top tutor tips

For part (a) (i) you are asked for additional information to plan the audit of land. When planning, you are identifying risks and determining an appropriate response to those risks. Think about the risks specific to the land to help you identify what additional information could be helpful. For part (ii), draw on your knowledge on ISA 620 for matters to consider when assessing the work of an auditor's expert.

Part (b) focuses on difficulties in measuring and reporting on social and environmental performance. This is knowledge taken from the study materials and should not pose too many problems. For part (ii), you are asked for procedures to gain assurance on the performance information in the scenario. Identify ways of proving the claims made in order to generate procedures.

(a) **(i)** Additional information needed to plan the audit of land includes the following:

- Details of the reason for the purchase, to understand the business rationale, e.g. is the land held for capital appreciation?
- Does management have any specific plans for how Faster Jets Co may make use of the land in the future, e.g. are there plans to construct buildings and if so what will be their purpose?
- The date of purchase to ascertain how long it has taken for the land to increase in value by $2 million and whether this seems reasonable.
- Whether the land was purchased for cash or if finance was taken out to raise the $12.5 million paid.
- Who is renting the land? This could establish whether the arrangement is with a related party, and the type of rental arrangement.
- What is the land being used for? As the legal owner, Faster Jets Co should be aware of its use and any associated risks, e.g. activities close to airports may convey security risks, e.g. terrorism.
- The location of the purchased land – this is necessary to plan the logistics of the audit.
- Does the company hold any other investment property, and if so, is that also held at fair value? The accounting treatment should be consistent for all investment property.
- What is management's rationale for the accounting policy choice to measure the land at fair value? It will result in profit for the year including the $2 million fair value increase.
- Establish who holds the title deeds to the land as this may need to be inspected.

(ii) Matters to consider before placing reliance on the work of the auditor's expert

ISA 620 *Using the Work of an Auditor's Expert* contains requirements relating to the objectivity and capabilities of the auditor's expert, the scope and objectives of their work, and assessing their work.

Objectivity

The auditor shall evaluate whether the auditor's expert has the necessary objectivity and that this should include inquiry regarding interests and relationships which may create a threat to the expert's objectivity. The audit firm will need to ensure that the expert has no connection to Faster Jets Co, for example, that they are not a related party of the company or any person in a position of influence over the financial statements. If the expert's objectivity is threatened, less reliance can be placed on their work.

Competence

The competence of the expert should also be considered; this should include considering the expert's membership of appropriate professional bodies. Any doubts over the competence of the expert will reduce the reliability of audit evidence obtained. The expert should in this case have experience in valuing land, and be familiar with the framework for measuring fair value in accordance with IAS 40 *Investment Property* and IFRS 13 *Fair Value Measurement*.

Scope of work

The auditor should agree the scope of work with the expert. This may include agreement of the objectives of the work, how the expert's work will be used by the auditor and the methodology and key assumptions to be used. In assessing the work performed by the expert, the auditor should confirm that the scope of the work is as agreed at the start of the engagement. If the expert has deviated from the agreed scope of work, it is likely to be less relevant and reliable.

Relevance of conclusions

The relevance and adequacy of the expert's findings or conclusions should be evaluated. This will involve consideration of the source data which was used, the appropriateness of assumptions and the reasons for any changes in methodology or assumptions. The conclusion should be consistent with other relevant audit findings and with the auditor's general understanding of the business. Any inconsistencies should be investigated as they may indicate evidence which is not reliable.

(b) (i) The difficulties in measuring and reporting on social and environmental performance

It is common for companies to produce a report on corporate social responsibility (CSR), and in some countries this is a requirement. CSR reports contain a wide variety of key performance indicators (KPIs) relating to the social and environmental targets which the company is aiming to achieve. It can be difficult to measure and report on social and environmental KPIs for a number of reasons.

Measurements of social and environmental performance are not always easy to define. For example, Faster Jets Co aims to develop an education programme, which is vague in terms of measurement. The measurement only becomes precisely defined when a KPI which is capable of being quantified is attached to it, for example, the number of free education days provided in a year. It can also be difficult to identify key stakeholders and the KPIs which each stakeholder group is interested in.

Also, targets and KPIs may be difficult to quantify in monetary terms. For example, Faster Jets Co's provision of free flights to charitable organisations can be quantified in terms of the number of flights donated, but the actual value of the flights is more questionable as this could be measured at cost price or market value. The monetary value may not even be very relevant to users of the CSR report.

In addition, systems and controls are often not established well enough to allow accurate measurement, and the measurement of social and environmental matters may not be based on reliable evidence. However, this is not always the case, for example, the accounting system should be able to determine accurately the amount of cash donated to charity and the amount spent on vehicle fuel.

Finally, it is hard to compare these targets and KPIs between companies, as they are not strictly defined, so each company will set its own target. It will also be difficult to make year on year comparisons for the same company, as targets may change in response to business activities.

(ii) Procedures to gain assurance on the validity of the performance measures

- Obtain a summary of all amounts donated to charitable causes and agree a sample to the cash book.
- For large donations above a certain limit (say $10,000) confirm that authorisation for the payment has been made, e.g. by agreeing to minutes of management meetings.
- Review correspondence with charities for confirmation of the amounts paid.
- Review relevant press releases and publicity campaigns, e.g. the free flight scheme and the local education schemes are likely to have been publicised.
- For the $750,000 spent on the local education scheme, obtain a breakdown of the amounts spent and scrutinise to ensure all relate to the scheme, e.g. payments to educators.
- Obtain a sample of classroom registers to confirm attendance of children on certain days.
- For the free flights donated to charity, perform analytical review to confirm that the average value of a flight seems reasonable – the average being $700 ($560,000/800).
- For a sample of the 800 free flights, obtain confirmation that the passenger was a guest of Faster Jets Co, e.g. through correspondence with the passenger and relevant charity.
- Agree a sample of business miles travelled in vehicles to a mileage log, and fuel costs to employee expenses claims forms and the general ledger.

Examiner's comments

This question featured Faster Jets Co, an airline company, and focused on two separate areas; planning the audit of land and verifying social and environmental performance information.

The first part of the question focused on planning the audit work relating to several large plots of land that had been purchased by the company during the year and were being accounted for as investment property in the company's financial statements. The first requirement asked candidates to explain the additional information that would be required to plan the audit of the land. This type of requirement is often seen in audit planning questions and again, as in previous sittings, disappointingly candidates tended to provide specific audit procedures rather than considering information that would be helpful in determining the type of procedures that would be relevant. Candidates for future examinations should bear in mind that answer points for this type of requirement can be phrased as questions, e.g. 'what is management's future plans for the land?', as this helps to determine its classification as investment property. Many candidates may find this type of requirement difficult if they have limited practical audit experience, in which case it is especially important to use past questions to practise how to answer these questions.

The second requirement asked candidates to explain the matters to be considered in assessing the reliance to be placed on the work of an auditor's expert being used in the audit of the land. This was much better answered than the first requirement, with almost all answers identifying that the auditor's expert must be independent and competent. However most answers went little further than explaining those two matters, indicating little knowledge of the requirements of ISA 620 *Using the Work of an Auditor's Expert* in relation to agreeing the scope of the expert's work, and evaluating the relevance of their conclusions. The answers to this requirement were also often very brief, amounting to little more than a few sentences or bullet points. Candidates are reminded that the number of marks available should be used as a guide for the number of points and depth required. A couple of bullet points or brief sentences are unlikely to be sufficient to score the marks that were available here.

The second part of the question focused on measuring and reporting on social and environmental information. The audit firm in the scenario had been asked to perform an assurance engagement on Faster Jets Co's corporate social responsibility (CSR) report, and a number of CSR objectives and targets were provided along with the performance indicators for 2014 to be included in the CSR report. The first requirement asked for a discussion of the difficulties in measuring and reporting on social and environmental performance. This short requirement was well attempted by many candidates, with most identifying that it can be difficult to define and quantify CSR measures, that systems are often not in place to capture the relevant information and that comparisons are difficult due to the lack of a regulatory framework. This again indicates that many candidates had practised past exam questions, as this type of requirement has featured in paper P7 paper on several previous occasions.

Candidates found the final requirement of this question more difficult, as they were asked for recommendations of procedures that could be used to gain assurance on the validity of the performance information included in the CSR report. The main weakness in responses was that candidates simply repeated the same procedures for each of the performance measures given, even if they weren't appropriate. For example, one of the performance measures related to free flights that had been donated to charities, and many candidates recommended that this should be agreed to bank statements or cash book even though it is not a cash transaction. Candidates are encouraged to think about whether the procedures they are recommending are sensible in the context of the scenario. As is often the case when presented with a requirement to detail procedures, many candidates provided procedures that were not well explained, and in many cases weren't procedures at all, e.g. 'review the free flights', 'inspect the education days', 'confirm the vehicle fuel'. This type of comment cannot be given credit as it is too vague and does not answer the question requirement.

ACCA marking scheme

			Marks
(a)	(i)	**Further information requirements** 1 mark for each further information point explained: – The reason for the purchase - rationale – Any specific plans for how Faster Jets Co may make use of the land in the future – The date of purchase – How the land was purchased - cash or finance – Who is leasing the land? Possible related party – What is the land being used for? – The location of the purchased land – this is necessary to plan the logistics of the audit – Does the company hold any other investment property? – What is management's rationale for the accounting policy choice to measure the land at fair value?	
	(ii)	**Matters to consider regarding the use of the auditor's expert** Up to 1½ marks for each of the following explained: – Objectivity – Competence – Scope of work – Relevance and reasonableness of conclusions	
		Maximum	**10**
(b)	(i)	**Difficulties in measuring and reporting on social and environmental performance** Up to 1½ marks for each point discussed: – Measures are difficult to define – Measures are difficult to quantify – Systems not set up to capture data – Hard to make comparisons	
		Maximum	**4**
	(ii)	**Procedures on Faster Jets Co's performance measures** Generally 1 mark for a well explained procedure: – Obtain a summary of all amounts donated to charitable causes and agree to cash book – For large donation confirm that authorisation for the payment has been made – Review correspondence with charities – Review relevant press releases and publicity campaigns – For the $750,000 spent on the local education scheme, obtain a breakdown of the amounts spent and scrutinise to ensure all relate to the scheme, e.g. payments to educators – Obtain a sample of registers to confirm attendance of children on certain days – For the free flights donated to charity, perform analytical review to confirm that the average value of a flight seems reasonable – the average being $700 – For a sample of the 800 free flights, obtain confirmation that the passenger was a guest of Faster Jets Co – Agree a sample of business miles travelled in vehicles and fuel costs to employee expenses claims forms	
		Maximum	**6**
Total			**20**

19 NEWMAN & CO *Walk in the footsteps of a top tutor*

Top tutor tips

Parts (a) and (b) of this question require knowledge of some core topics, i.e. professional and ethical matters and gathering evidence, and the ability to apply the knowledge to the specific, and slightly more unusual scenarios described.

You should take a methodical approach in applying your knowledge to the scenario in part (a), and work through the list of **professional and ethical** matters that apply to the consideration of accepting any assurance engagement.

In part (b), although these are not figures presented within the financial statements, in generating audit procedures to try to verify the figures you should treat them in the same way, i.e. think about the documentation Newman & Co might have which could be used to verify the information; think about all of the different types of evidence available to an auditor; and generate procedures that are relevant for the organisation described and the KPIs being verified.

Part (c) of the question tested an aspect of audit reporting, specifically ISA 720 *The Auditor's Responsibilities in Relation to Other Information in Documents Containing Audited Financial Statements.* This question highlights the importance of breadth of knowledge across the syllabus.

(a) Matters that should be considered in making acceptance decision

Objectivity

The proposed assurance engagement represents a non-audit service. ACCA's *Code of Ethics* does not prohibit the provision of additional assurance services to an audit client, however, the audit firm must carefully consider whether the provision of the additional service creates a threat to objectivity and independence of the firm or members of the audit team.

For example, when the total fees generated by a client represent a large proportion of a firm's total fees, the perceived dependence on the client for fee income creates a self-interest threat. Due to the nature of the proposed engagement, self-review and advocacy threats may also be created, as the Sustainability Report is published with the audited financial statements, and the audit firm could be perceived to be promoting the interests of its client by providing an assurance report on the key performance indicators (KPIs).

Newman & Co should only accept the invitation to provide the assurance engagement after careful consideration of objectivity, and a review as to whether safeguards can reduce any threat to objectivity to an acceptable level. As Eastwood Co is a 'major client', the fee level from providing both the audit and the assurance services could breach the permitted level of recurring fees allowed from one client. The fact that the company is listed means that the assessment of objectivity is particularly important and a second partner review of the objectivity of the situation may be considered necessary.

[**UK syllabus**: Ethical Standard section 5 suggests that the audit engagement partner should assess the significance of any threat to objectivity created by the potential provision of the non-audit service and should consider whether there are safeguards that could be applied and which would be effective to eliminate the threat or reduce it to an acceptable level. If such safeguards can be identified and are applied, the non-audit service may be provided. However, where no such safeguards are applied, the only course is for the audit firm either not to undertake the engagement to provide the non-audit service in question or not to accept (or to withdraw from) the audit engagement.]

The fact that a separate team, with no involvement with the audit, will be working on the KPIs strengthens the objectivity of the assignment.

Eastwood Co's requirements

Assurance engagements can vary in terms of the level of work that is expected, and the level of assurance that is required. This will clearly impact on the scale of the assignment. For example, Eastwood Co may require specific procedures to be performed on certain KPIs to provide a high level of assurance, whereas a lower level of assurance may be acceptable for other KPIs.

Newman & Co should also clarify the expected form and content and expected wording of the assurance report itself, and whether any specific third party will be using the Sustainability Report for a particular purpose, as this may create risk exposure for the firm.

Competence

The audit firm's sustainability reporting assurance team has only been recently established, and the firm may not have sufficient experienced staff to perform the assurance engagement. The fundamental principle of professional competence and due care requires that members of an engagement team should possess sufficient skill and knowledge to be able to perform the assignment, and be able to apply their skill and knowledge appropriately in the circumstances of the engagement.

Some of Eastwood Co's KPIs appear quite specialised – verification of CO_2 emissions for example, may require specialist knowledge and expertise. Newman & Co could bring in experts to perform this work, if necessary, but this would have cost implications and would reduce the recoverability of the assignment.

Scale of the engagement

The Sustainability Report contains 75 KPIs, and presumably a lot of written content in addition. All of these KPIs will need to be verified, and the written content of the report reviewed for accuracy and consistency, meaning that this is a relatively large engagement. Newman & Co should consider whether the newly established sustainability reporting assurance team has enough resources to perform the engagement within the required time scale, bearing in mind the time pressure which is further discussed below.

Time pressure

Given that the financial statements are scheduled to be published in four weeks, it is doubtful whether the assurance assignment could be completed, and a report issued, in time for it to be included in the annual report, particularly given the global nature of the assignment. Newman & Co may wish to clarify with Eastwood Co's management whether they intend to publish the assurance report within the annual report, as they have done previously, or whether a separate report will be issued at a later point in time, which would allow more time for the assurance engagement to be conducted.

Fee level and profitability

Such a potentially large scale assignment should attract a large fee. Costs will have to be carefully managed to ensure the profitability of the engagement, especially considering that overseas travel will be involved, as presumably much of the field work will be performed at Eastwood Co's Sustainability Department in Fartown. The fee level would need to be negotiated bearing in mind the specialist nature of the work, and the urgency of the assignment, both of which mean that a high fee could be commanded.

Global engagement

The firm's sustainability reporting team is situated in a different country to Eastwood Co's Sustainability Department. Although this does not on its own mean that the assignment should not be taken on, it makes the assignment logistically difficult.

Members of the assurance department must be willing to travel overseas to conduct at least some of their work, as it would be difficult to perform the engagement without visiting the department responsible for providing the KPIs. Other locations may also need to be visited. There are also cost implications of the travel, which will need to be built into the proposed fee for the engagement. Language may also present a barrier to accepting the engagement, depending on the language used in Fartown's location.

Risk

Eastwood Co is a large company with a global presence. It is listed on several stock exchanges, and so it appears to have a high public profile. In addition, pressure groups are keen to see the added credibility of an assurance report issued in relation to the KPIs disclosed. For all of these reasons, there will be scrutiny of the Sustainability Report and the assurance report.

Newman & Co should bear in mind that this creates a risk exposure for the firm. If the assignment were taken, the firm would have to carefully manage this risk exposure through thorough planning of the engagement and applying strong quality control measures. The firm would also need to ensure that the fee is commensurate with the level of risk exposure. Given the inconsistency that has come to light regarding one of the draft KPIs, which appears to overstate charitable donations made by the company, we may need to consider that management are trying to show the company's KPIs in a favourable way, which adds to the risk of the engagement.

Commercial consideration

If Newman & Co does not accept the assurance engagement, the firm risks losing the audit client in future years to another firm that would be willing to provide both services. As Eastwood Co is a prestigious client, this commercial consideration will be important, but should not override any ethical considerations.

(b) (i) Procedures to verify the number of serious accidents in the workplace

- Review records held by human resources, which summarise the number and type of accidents reported in the workplace.
- Review the accident log book from a sample of locations.
- Discuss the definition of a 'serious' accident (as opposed to a 'minor' accident) and establish the nature of criteria applied to an accident to determine whether it is serious.

- Review correspondence with legal advisors which may indicate legal action being taken against Eastwood Co in respect of serious accidents in the workplace.
- Review minutes of board meetings for discussions of any serious accidents and associated repercussions for the company.
- Ascertain through discussion with management and/or legal advisors, if Eastwood Co has any convictions for health and safety offences during the year (which could indicate that serious accidents have occurred).
- Enquire as to whether the company has received any health and safety visits (the regulatory authority would usually perform one if an employee has a serious accident). Review documentation from any health and safety visits for evidence of any serious accidents.
- Consider talking to employees to identify if any accidents have not been recorded in the accident book.

(ii) Procedures to verify the annual training spend per employee

- Review Eastwood Co's approved training budget in comparison to previous years to ascertain the overall level of planned spending on training.
- Obtain a breakdown of the total training spend and review for any items mis-classified as training costs.
- Agree significant components of the total training spend to supporting documentation such as contracts with training providers and to invoices received from those providers.
- Agree the total amount spent on significant training programmes to cash book and/or bank statements.
- Using data on total number of employees provided by the payroll department, recalculate the annual training spend per employee.

(c) (i) Auditor's responsibility

Other information is defined as financial and non-financial information included in a document containing audited financial statements and the auditor's report. Examples include a Chairman's Statement, Directors' Report, and in Eastwood Co's case a Sustainability Report.

The auditor must read the other information in order to identify any information contained within any of the financial or non-financial information in the annual report that is apparently materially incorrect based on, or materially inconsistent with, the knowledge acquired by the auditor in the course of performing the audit.

A material inconsistency arises where the other information contradicts information in the audited financial statements, and may possibly raise doubt about the audit opinion. Effectively, a material inconsistency undermines the credibility of the audit opinion.

In the event of a material inconsistency being discovered, the auditor shall determine whether the financial statements or other information needs to be revised, so that the inconsistency is removed.

If the inconsistency is not resolved, the auditor's responsibilities depend on whether it is the other information, or the financial statements that have not been corrected.

If the financial statements have not been revised, and therefore contain an item which the auditor believes to be materially misstated, then the auditor's opinion should be modified.

If management refuse to remove the inconsistency, the auditor should communicate this to those charged with governance.

In extreme situations, where a material inconsistency remains uncorrected by management, it may be necessary for the audit firm to withdraw from the audit. In such cases legal advice should be sought, to protect the interests of the audit firm.

Guidance is found in ISA 720 (Revised) *The Auditor's Responsibilities Relating to Other Information in Documents Containing Audited Financial Statements*.

If the other information is received before the date of the auditor's report, a separate section should be included in the auditor's report under the heading 'Other Information'. In this section the auditor should:

- Identify the other information obtained prior to the date of the auditor's report.
- State that the auditor has not audited the other information and accordingly does not express an opinion or conclusion on that information.
- Include a description of the auditor's responsibilities with respect to other information.
- State either that the auditor has nothing to report, or a description of the material misstatement.

Therefore, if management refuses to change the other information, the auditor should provide a description of the inconsistency in the 'Other Information' section of the auditor's report.

Alternatively the auditor may withhold the auditor's report or withdraw from the engagement.

Further actions are also available to auditors in the UK who have the right to speak at general meetings of company members, and could therefore highlight the inconsistency to shareholders in this way, if it remains unresolved.

(ii) Action to be taken

Eastwood Co's Sustainability Report contains a material inconsistency, as the figure disclosed for charitable donations of $10.5 million is different from that disclosed in a note to the financial statements of $9 million.

Audit procedures indicate that the figure in the note is correctly stated at $9 million. The audit work performed on this figure should be reviewed to ensure that sufficient and appropriate evidence has been gained to support the conclusion that $9 million is correct.

The matter should be discussed with management, who should be asked to amend the disclosure in the Sustainability Report and the Chairman's Statement to the correct figure of $9 million. Management should be presented with the results of our audit work, to justify if necessary that the figure of $9 million is correct. The inclusion of the wrong figure in the draft information could be a genuine mistake, in which case management should be happy to make the change.

If management refuse to change the other information, the audit team may wish to consider why this is the case, as it hints that management may lack integrity. Areas of the audit where evidence was dependent on management representations may need to be reviewed.

The matter should be communicated to those charged with governance.

As Eastwood Co is listed on several stock exchanges, the auditor should consider whether any additional responsibilities exist in relation to the other information issued in the annual report, as required by Listing Requirements. For example, some jurisdictions may require the auditor to apply specific procedures, or in the case of a misstatement, refer to the matter in the auditor's report.

If management refuse to change the disclosure in the other information, then the auditor's report should provide a description of the inconsistency in the 'Other Information' section of the report.

UK Syllabus: The audit firm should carefully review the content of the director's report for reference to the charitable donations (required under the Companies Act 2006). The director's report should be consistent with the figure disclosed in the note to the financial statements. The auditor must state in the auditor's report whether the information given in the directors' report is consistent with the information in the financial statements. Any inconsistency would therefore be highlighted in the auditor's report.

Examiner's comments

Requirement (a) asked candidates to identify and explain the matters that should be considered in evaluating whether the audit firm should perform an assurance engagement on the client's Sustainability Report.

It was clear that most candidates knew the matters that should be considered (ethical constraints, resources, knowledge, timescale, fees etc.), and most candidates took the right approach to the question, by working through the various 'matters' and applying them to the question. The fact that this was not an audit engagement did not seem to faze candidates, and there were many sound answers to this requirement.

Some answers evaluated the many ethical problems with taking on the assurance engagement as well as providing the audit for 'a major client', and appreciated that with only four weeks to complete the work, it would probably be impossible to ensure quality work could be performed on a global scale to such a tight deadline by an inexperienced team.

Some answers also picked up on the fact that the client's listed status would probably prevent the audit firm from conducting the assurance engagement, and certainly the situation would need to be discussed with, and approved by the audit committee.

However, some answers were much too brief for the marks available, amounting to little more than a bullet point list of matters to be considered but with no application to the scenario. Without application it was not possible to pass this requirement. Other common mistakes included:

- Ignoring the fact that the client was already an existing audit client, so discussing the need to contact its auditors for information.
- Not reading the question and thinking that you had been approached to perform the audit.
- Only discussing the potential problems and not identifying the benefits of providing the service (e.g. it would provide experience for the newly established assurance team).
- Ignoring information given in the question (e.g. saying that the firm would need to ask about the use of the assurance report – when the question clearly states that it would be published in the annual report with the financial statements).

Requirement (b) asked for procedures that could be used to verify two Key Performance Indicators (KPIs) – the number of serious accidents in the workplace, and the average annual spend on training per employee. A fair proportion of answers were sound, with precise procedures recommended.

But, many recommended procedures relied too much on observation and enquiry, and ignored the fact that the client was a global company with 300,000 employees which led to some bizarre and meaningless procedures being given, such as 'observe a serious accident', 'inspect the location of a serious accident', 'ask how much is spent on training', and 'look at the training room to see how many chairs are there'. None of these could verify the KPIs and are pointless.

Requirement (c) focused on other information published with financial statements. In the scenario an inconsistency had been discovered between a figure relating to charitable donations which had been stated at $9 million in a note to the financial statements, and $10.5 million in the Chairman's Statement and Sustainability Report. The requirement was to explain the auditor's responsibility, and to recommend actions to be taken. This requirement was inadequately attempted overall. Answers were usually extremely brief, and it was clear that most candidates did not know the requirements of ISA 720 *The Auditor's Responsibilities in Relation to Other Information in Documents Containing Audited Financial Statements.* Most answers took a guess that the matter would need to be discussed with management, and that if unresolved there would be some kind of impact on the auditor's report (an 'except for' opinion was the usual recommendation). But few could say more than this about the issue. Some candidates assumed that some kind of money laundering was taking place, leading to irrelevant discussions of reporting the situation to outside authorities.

ACCA marking scheme			
(a)		**Identify and explain acceptance matters**	*Marks*
		½ mark for each matter identified (to max 4 marks) and up to 1½ further marks for explanation – Objectivity (up to 3 marks allowed) – Client's specific requirements – Competence – Large scale engagement – Fee level and profitability – Time pressure – Global engagement – Risk – Commercial consideration	
		Maximum	**12**
(b)	(i)	**Procedures on number of serious accidents**	
		1 mark per specific procedure – HR records review – Accident book review – Determine criteria for serious accident – Review legal correspondence – Review board minutes – Review documentation of health and safety inspections – Ascertain any convictions for breach of health and safety rules	
	(ii)	**Procedures on average training spend**	
		1 mark per specific procedure – Review approved training budget – Review components of total spend for mis-classified items – Agree sample of invoices/contracts with training providers – Agree sample to cash book/bank statement (½ only) – Recalculate average	
		Maximum	**5**
(c)	(i)	**Auditor's responsibilities regarding other information**	
		1 mark per comment – Definition/examples of other information – Auditor reads to look for material inconsistency – Implication if inconsistency in financial statements not resolved (qualification) – Communicate with TCWG if not resolved with management – Consider withdrawal or legal advice – Other Information section of the auditor's report – UK: Speak at general meeting	
	(ii)	**Action by Newman & Co**	
		1 mark per comment – Review audit work on charitable donations – Discuss inconsistency with management/those charged with governance – If refuse to change the figure, reconsider reliance on representations from management – Consider any additional responsibilities – Implication for auditor's report	
		Maximum	**8**
Total			**25**

20 CHESTNUT *Walk in the footsteps of a top tutor*

Top tutor tips

Part (a) covers the syllabus area of forensic accounting and asks for ethical and professional issues if your firm investigates the fraudulent activity. Think about the threats that could arise and how they could be safeguarded. Remember to explain and evaluate the significance of the threats.

Part (b) requires the matters to be considered when planning the fraud investigation. Forensic accounting was the subject of a technical article in 2008 and this provides guidance on how to plan and perform such engagements.

Part (c) is a current issues question asking for arguments for and against the prohibition of auditors providing non-audit services to audit clients. Remember to deal with both sides of the argument and set these answers out under two subheadings to make it clear you are dealing with both aspects.

(a) An investigation into the alleged fraudulent activity is a forensic investigation. If Cedar & Co were to conduct the forensic investigation, this would be a non-audit service performed for an audit client. Specifically, this investigation would be deemed a litigation support service.

Tutorial note

Litigation support services may include activities such as acting as an expert witness, calculating estimated damages or other amounts that might become receivable or payable as the result of litigation or other legal dispute, and assistance with document management and retrieval.

Before a firm accepts an engagement to provide a non-audit service to an audit client, a determination should be made as to whether providing such a service would create a threat to independence. Self-review, self-interest and advocacy threats to independence may arise.

Self-review threat

The self-review threat exists because the forensic investigation will determine the monetary amount of the fraud, and the amount which Chestnut Co will attempt to recover from the fraudsters. Given the potential scale of the fraud, it could be that the amounts involved are material to the financial statements and therefore the audit team would be reviewing figures determined by members of the audit firm.

In addition, the forensic investigation team will, as part of their work, review systems and controls over expenses claimed by Chestnut Co's employees. This means that the forensic investigation team are also exposed to a self-review threat, as they will be reviewing systems and controls which have been considered during the audit of Chestnut Co's financial statements.

Advocacy threat

The advocacy threat arises because going to court and speaking as an expert witness in relation to the fraud would be seen as the audit firm promoting the interests of its client and supporting a position taken by management in an adversarial context.

Self interest threat

A self-interest threat could also arise, as the forensic investigation may be a lucrative source of income for Cedar & Co. This could create the perception that Cedar & Co is reliant on Chestnut Co for income and impairs the objectivity of the firm.

The firm should evaluate the significance of these threats. In particular, the firm should consider the potential materiality of the amounts involved in the fraud, and the degree of subjectivity that may be involved in determining the amounts involved. If the matter is material, and would involve significant judgements, then no safeguards would reduce the threat to an acceptable level and the forensic investigation should not be conducted by the audit firm.

It is likely, however, that the investigation would not involve a significant degree of judgement and the investigation could be performed as long as safeguards were used, such as:

- Having a senior member of the audit firm, who was not involved in the forensic investigation, review the results of the investigation and the impact on the financial statements
- Performing a second partner review on the audit of Chestnut Co; and
- Ensuring that the forensic investigation is not performed by anyone involved in the audit engagement. Possibly the investigation could be performed by a different office of the firm.

The ethical situation must be discussed with those charged with governance of Chestnut Co. Depending on any relevant regulation in Chestnut Co's jurisdiction, it may not be possible for the audit firm to carry out this non-audit assignment, or it may be permitted with the approval of those charged with governance (or an audit committee, if one exists).

Furthermore, the fundamental ethical principles apply to all professional assignments, including a forensic investigation.

Professional competence and due care

Forensic investigations are specialist assignments and may require very specific skills, which will not be possessed by individuals unless they have undergone specific training. Cedar & Co must consider whether there are any members of the firm who possess the necessary skills before accepting the assignment.

It is likely that relatively senior staff will need to be assigned to the investigation, which will bring necessary authority and experience to the investigation team. It should be considered whether Cedar & Co is able to divert senior staff from other assignments at short notice. Resourcing the team could be a problem.

Confidentiality

In addition, confidentiality is a crucial issue in such investigations as members of the investigation team will have access to sensitive information which will be used as evidence in court. Any breach of confidentiality could jeopardise the integrity of the legal proceedings against the fraudsters. Anyone involved with the investigation must be made aware of these issues and confidentiality agreements should be signed.

(b) Discuss the purpose, nature and scope of the investigation. In particular, confirm whether evidence gathered will be used in criminal proceedings and in support of an insurance claim.

Confirm that Chestnut Co's objectives are to identify those involved with the fraud, and to quantify the amount of the fraud. This will help to clarify the terms of the engagement, which will be detailed in an engagement letter.

Determine the time-scale involved, whether Jack Privet needs the investigation to commence as soon as possible and the deadline for completing the investigation. This is necessary to determine the resources needed to perform the investigation, and whether resources need to be diverted from other assignments.

Enquire as to how many sales representatives have been suspended (i.e. are suspected of involvement in the fraud). This will help the firm to determine the potential scale of the investigation.

Gain an understanding as to how the fraud came to light (e.g. was it uncovered by internal audit or a member of the sales department) and who reported their suspicions to Jack Privet. This information will indicate how the investigation should commence (e.g. by interviewing the whistle-blower).

Determine whether Chestnut Co will provide resources to help with the investigation, e.g. members of the internal audit team could provide assistance in obtaining evidence.

Ask for Jack Privet's opinion as to why the fraud had not been prevented or detected by the company's internal controls. In particular, enquire if there has been a breakdown in controls over authorisation of expenses.

Determine whether recommendations to improve controls are required as an output of the investigative work.

Discuss the investigative techniques which may be used (e.g. interviewing the alleged fraudsters, detailed review of all expense claims made by sales representatives, analytical review of expenses) and ensure that investigators will have unrestricted access to individuals and documentation.

Enquire as to whether the police have been informed, and if so, the name and contact details of the person informed. It is likely that a criminal investigation by the police will take place as well as Cedar & Co's own investigation.

Confirm that Chestnut Co grants permission to Cedar & Co's investigation team to communicate with third parties such as the police and the company's lawyers regarding the investigation.

(c) The issue of auditors providing non-audit services to audit clients has been topical for many years, and there are many arguments for and against their outright prohibition.

In favour of prohibition

Those arguing in favour of outright prohibition suggest that this would be a **simple way to eliminate the threats to objectivity**, which the provision of non-audit services to audit clients creates. Typically, management, self-interest and self-review threats arise, which result in the perception that the auditor cannot be objective when performing the audit service.

In particular, non-audit services can be very lucrative, leading potentially to a self-interest threat. The greater the volume and financial significance of the non-audit services provided, the greater the risk that the auditor will have relationship and economic reasons not to challenge management's views and positions with the necessary degree of professional scepticism.

It has also been argued that outright prohibition would **benefit the market, allowing smaller audit firms to provide the services** which larger firms would no longer be able to offer to their audit clients.

Tutorial note

Credit will be awarded for appropriate examples of regimes in which there is tight regulation on the provision of non-audit services, such as the US Sarbanes-Oxley legislation.

Against prohibition

However, there are also many arguments against outright prohibition. By having the same firm provide the audit and the non-audit service, the client benefits in two ways. The audit firm will already possess a good knowledge and understanding of the client and its operating environment, resulting in deeper insight and a better quality service being provided. This will then lead to **cost benefits**, as the non-audit service will be provided in a more efficient way.

Audit firms would also argue that participation in services such as due diligence reviews and forensic investigations, **allows the audit firm to understand their clients' business** and risks better and to obtain insights into management's objectives and capabilities which are useful in an audit context.

Finally, **non-audit services can be safely provided as long as steps are taken to assess potential threats to objectivity**, and to adequately address those risks, for example, by the use of separate teams to provide audit and non-audit services.

The UK Corporate Governance Code requires the audit committee to review and monitor the external auditor's independence and objectivity. This includes the audit committee evaluating approving the provision of non-audit services by the audit firm.

To conclude, a principles-based approach to the provision of non-audit services, in which such services can be provided as long as risks are assessed and managed, appears to benefit both audit firms and their clients.

Examiner's comments

This was the most popular of the optional questions, and focused on a forensic investigation into a fraud that had been uncovered at an audit client. One of the requirements focused on ethical issues, probably explaining the popularity of this question.

Requirement (a) required an assessment of the ethical and professional issues raised by the request from the audit client to investigate the fraudulent activity. Most answers were satisfactory, identifying the main ethical threats (advocacy, self-review etc.) raised by the scenario and explaining them to an extent. Some answers also discussed whether the audit firm would have the necessary skills and resources to perform such a specialist piece of work. Some answers however tended to focus on why the audit firm had not discovered the fraud during the previous audit, and the possibility of the audit firm being sued for negligence or the need to 'discipline' the audit manager. Some answers also contained irrelevant discussions of the responsibilities of management and auditors in relation to fraud, and other answers used the fundamental principles as a framework for their answer, probably as this had been set on a previous exam paper, but with a completely different question requirement.

Requirement (b) asked candidates to explain the matters that should be discussed in a meeting with the client, in terms of planning the forensic investigation. Some answers were very satisfactory, covering a wide range of matters including the timeframe, the required output of the investigation, and access to the client's accounting systems amongst others. Some answers however tended to simply list out the procedures that would be performed in conducting the investigation, or explain to the client's management the controls that should have been in place to stop the fraud in the first place.

Requirement (c) focused more theoretically on the debate over whether audit firms should be prohibited from providing non-audit services to their audit client. Although most candidates seemed prepared for a question of this type, most approached the question by discussing the pros and cons of audit firms offering non-audit services to their clients, rather than discussing whether prohibition would be desirable. There is some overlap between the two approaches, but the way that candidates tackled this requirement indicated that a rote-learnt answer had been provided, rather than evidence of candidates thinking on their feet and coming up with their own opinion on the matter. A lot of answers simply explained several ethical threats and concluded that because threats may exist auditors should not provide non-audit services to their clients. This is not a broad enough response to the question requirement.

ACCA marking scheme		
		Marks
(a)	**Ethical and professional issues** Generally 1 mark per issue assessed: – Non-audit service creates self-review threat – Non-audit service creates advocacy threat – Significance of threat to be evaluated – Significance depends on materiality and subjectivity – Examples of safeguards (1 mark each) – Competence to provide service – Resources to provide service – Confidentiality agreements	
	Maximum	**7**
(b)	**Matters to be discussed** Generally 1 mark for each matter explained: – Purpose, nature and scope of investigation – Confirm objectives of investigation – Time-scale and deadline – Potential scale of the fraud – How fraud reported to finance director – Possible reasons for fraud not being detected by internal controls – Resources to be made available to investigation team – Whether matter reported to police	
	Maximum	**7**
(c)	**Provision of non-audit services** Generally 1 mark per comment discussed and 1 mark for conclusion: – Simple way to eliminate threats to objectivity – Examples of threats e.g. lucrative nature of non-audit services – Benefit to audit market of outright prohibition – Benefits to client of auditor providing non-audit services – Benefits to audit firm of providing non-audit services – Safeguards should be used to reduce threats arising – Principles-based approach versus prescriptive approach	
	Maximum	**6**
Total		**20**

EVALUATION AND REVIEW

21 THURMAN *Walk in the footsteps of a top tutor*

Top tutor tips

This question examines the review stage of the audit but in a different way to the usual 'matters and evidence' questions seen in past exams. The question asks for comment on whether the evidence obtained is sufficient and appropriate. Has enough work been done? Has the most reliable form of evidence been obtained? Enquiries and written representations are the least reliable forms of evidence so ideally there will be better evidence than this on file. Think about what evidence you would expect to be on file. Compare this with the evidence that has been obtained. Any difference between what you would do and what has been done indicates that sufficient appropriate evidence has not been obtained. This should then form your answer to the next part of the requirement which asks for further procedures.

(a) Assets held for sale

(i) Audit evidence obtained

The evidence does not appear to be sufficient to draw a conclusion on the appropriateness of classifying the property and any other related assets and liabilities as held for sale. A discussion with management regarding the accounting treatment is relevant, as the audit team will need to understand management's rationale. However, management's explanation should not be accepted at face value and should be corroborated through further audit procedures. It is not sufficient to simply put management's justification for the accounting treatment on the audit file and conclude that it is correct. For example, the factory can only be classified as held for sale if it is available for immediate sale in its current condition, which may not be the case.

In terms of the manual journal, checking that it is arithmetically correct, while relevant, is not sufficient evidence. Further evidence should be obtained in order to conclude that the basis of the calculation is in accordance with IFRS 5 Non-current Assets Held for Sale and Discontinued Operations and there should be consideration as to whether other requirements of the standard other than those related to the reclassification and measurement of the asset have been complied with. For example, the results specific to the factory may need to be disclosed as a discontinued operation in the statement of profit or loss and the statement of cash flows. No audit evidence appears to have been obtained in respect of these issues.

(ii) Further audit procedures

- Review board minutes to confirm that the sale of the factory has been approved and to agree the date of the approval to the board minutes and relevant staff announcements.

- Obtain correspondence with estate agents to confirm that the factory is being actively marketed.
- Obtain confirmation, for example, by a review of production schedules, inventory movement records and payroll records, that production at the factory has stopped and thus it is available for immediate sale.
- Use an auditor's expert to confirm the fair value of the property and agree that this figure has been used in the impairment calculation.
- Using management accounts, determine whether the factory is a separate major line of business in which case its results should be disclosed as a discontinued operation.

(iii) Report to those charged with governance

ISA 265 *Communicating Deficiencies in Internal Controls to Those Charged with Governance and Management* requires the auditor to communicate significant deficiencies in internal control to those charged with governance and management. In deciding whether a control deficiency is significant, one of the matters which should be considered is the importance of the control to the financial reporting process. Controls over the period-end financial reporting process such as controls over non-recurring journal entries can be important as they often deal with one-off material matters which are being accounted for outside the normal accounting system.

Therefore the journal posted by the finance director should be subject to some form of internal control, for example, approval by the board or the audit committee. The report to those charged with governance should recommend that controls are established over period-end journals posted to ensure their accuracy and validity.

In addition, the finance director should not be asking the audit team to check his figures. This could be perceived as a self-review threat to independence. This should potentially be flagged to the audit committee.

The fact that there is, according to the finance director, no one else at the company with relevant knowledge is concerning. The audit committee should be made aware of this and appropriate steps taken to ensure that sufficiently knowledgeable personnel are hired or appropriate training is provided to existing staff.

(b) Capital expenditure

(i) Audit work performed

The audit work has revealed that internal controls have not been operating and this should have led to more extensive testing of capital expenditure, rather than the audit programme being completed as planned. Generally, the audit team should extend audit testing on capital expenditure, for example, by extending sample testing and reducing the level of materiality applied in audit tests.

The audit team should also investigate why the controls are not operating, considering whether they are being deliberately ignored or overridden, whether time pressure or lack of resources is making the controls difficult to operate, or if there is a suspicion of collusion and possible fraud.

The procedures on the purchase of the vehicles do not appear to cover all relevant assertions, for example, there is nothing to confirm that Thurman Co has correctly depreciated the vehicles or that they are actually owned and being used by the company, or even that they exist.

(ii) Further audit procedures

- Obtain the insurance documents to confirm that Thurman Co is paying the relevant insurance for the vehicles.
- Physically verify the vehicles and confirm that they are being used by employees on company business.
- Obtain the log book/vehicle registration document and other relevant ownership documents such as those issued by the vehicle licensing body, to confirm the right of Thurman Co to recognise the vehicles.
- Trace the vehicles to the company's non-current asset register.
- Recalculate the depreciation which should have been charged on the vehicles and agree to the statement of profit or loss for the year.

(iii) Report to those charged with governance

The auditor should report to those charged with governance that there appears to be a deficiency in internal controls. While the audit team's findings do not indicate that a fraud is taking place, the lack of segregation of duties and the failure to obtain appropriate authorisation makes it easy for assets to be misappropriated and creates a significant fraud risk.

The audit firm should explain the implications of the control deficiencies to management and recommend improvements. For example, authorisation should be a pre-requisite for any order over a certain monetary amount. Thurman Co should also be encouraged to improve the control environment, for example, by training staff on the importance of controls and setting an appropriate tone at the top so that there is no tolerance of controls being ignored or deliberately circumvented.

(c) Payroll

(i) Audit work

The audit work in respect of the payroll needs to be much more thorough. Simply agreeing the amounts to the reports issued by Jackson Co provides no evidence on the completeness, accuracy or validity of the payroll figures recognised in the financial statements. The audit team seems to have relied on Jackson's year-end reports as being accurate and the requirements of ISA 402 *Audit Considerations Relating to an Entity Using a Service Organisation* do not appear to have been followed.

The audit team needs to obtain assurance on the controls which Jackson Co has implemented in order to assess the risk of material misstatement in the payroll figures and to respond to the risk with appropriate audit procedures. The controls which Thurman Co uses to verify the information received from Jackson Co also need to be understood. With the permission of Thurman Co, the audit team should contact Jackson Co with the objective of obtaining more information which can be used to assess how the payroll has been processed, and the controls which are in place. The controls in place at Thurman Co should be documented and tested.

It is recommended that further substantive procedures should be carried out to provide a wider range of evidence on the payroll expense recognised in the financial statements.

In relation to the casual employees, the fact that the amount involved is immaterial means that the audit team does not need to perform any further detailed audit procedures as there is no risk of material misstatement. However, as there is a risk over the completeness of these costs, the controls in place to ensure this process is effectively managed should be discussed with management and documented.

(ii) Further audit procedures

- Review the service agreement between Thurman Co and Jackson Co to understand the exact work which is conducted by Jackson Co as a service organisation.
- Read all reports made by Jackson Co during the year to identify any risks of misstatement in the payroll figure.
- Discuss and document relevant controls in place at Thurman Co over the information received from Jackson Co and the management of casual employees, and perform tests of controls on a sample basis.
- The amount of unpaid taxes in respect of the casual workers should be quantified by recalculations of the amounts due.
- Read any user manuals or systems overviews to assess the efficacy of controls in place over the processing of payroll.
- If necessary, obtain a type 1 or type 2 report from Jackson Co to obtain further assurance on the controls which the service organisation has in place.
- Perform a substantive analytical review on payroll, preparing an auditor's expectation of the payroll figures and comparing it to that recognised in the financial statements and discussing any variance with management.
- Perform test of detail by selecting a sample from the payroll records and agreeing the amounts to payslips and HR records.

(iii) Report to those charged with governance

The fact that casual employees are being paid from petty cash without being put onto the company's payroll indicates that Thurman Co may not be complying with relevant regulations, for example, that appropriate payroll taxes are not being paid. Despite the amounts involved being immaterial, the potential non-compliance should be reported to those charged with governance, along with a recommendation that all employees, whether casual or not, should be processed through the company's payroll system. There may be implications for the financial statements if fines or penalties are imposed by the tax authorities in respect of the non-compliance.

Examiner's comments

This question was set in the completion stage of the audit and as is generally the case with completion questions, it was focused on the accounting treatment and audit evidence obtained on three issues. In this case, candidates were also required to discuss the impact of the issues found on the report to those charged with governance. Candidates generally demonstrated a good knowledge of the financial reporting implications of the areas and were often able to identify that the evidence obtained was insufficient and suggest further procedures. For many candidates the control weaknesses in the company and the implication of a deficiency in controls on further audit strategy and testing was not always identified. Candidates' responses to the matters to include in the report were variable with some candidates discussing auditor's report qualifications (despite no errors being flagged) or giving general answers to the contents of the report with no reference to the scenario in the exam.

Marking scheme

		Marks
	Generally 1 mark for each relevant point of discussion and well explained audit procedure:	
(a)	**Asset held for sale**	
	(i) **Audit evidence**	
	• Discussion is relevant but management's assertions must be corroborated	
	• Discussion alone is not sufficient to reach an audit conclusion	
	• Evidence not obtained on whether IFRS 5 classification criteria have been met	
	• Evidence not obtained on whether disclosure of discontinued operations is necessary	
	(ii) **Further procedures**	
	• Review board minutes to confirm the sale approval and date	
	• Correspondence with estate agents to confirm that the factory is being actively marketed	
	• Confirmation, for example, by a review of production schedules, inventory movement records and payroll records that production at the factory has stopped	
	• Auditor's expert to confirm the fair value of the property	
	• Determine whether the factory is a separate major line of business and should be disclosed as a discontinued operation	
	(iii) **Report to those charged with governance**	
	• Should be controls in place over year-end journals (2 marks for detailed discussion)	
	• Finance director should not have to ask the audit team to check his work	
	Maximum	9
(b)	**Capital expenditure**	
	(i) **Audit evidence**	
	• Testing should have been extended after the control deficiency was identified	
	• Reason for the controls not operating effectively should be investigated	
	• Increases the fraud risk in relation to capital expenditure	
	• Not all assertions have been covered by audit testing in respect of the vehicles purchased	

(ii) **Further audit procedures** • Obtain the insurance documents to confirm that Thurman Co is paying the relevant insurance for the vehicles • Physically verify the vehicles and confirm that they are being used by employees on company business • Obtain the log book and other relevant ownership documents to confirm the right of Thurman Co to recognise the vehicles • Trace the vehicles to the company's fixed asset register • Recalculate the depreciation which should have been charged on the vehicles		
(iii) **Report to those charged with governance** • Explain the deficiencies and the implications, i.e. increased fraud risk • Recommend improvements to specific controls and to the general control environment		
	Maximum	7
(c) **Payroll**		
(i) **Audit work** • Agreeing payroll to the service organisation's report does not provide sufficient evidence on completeness, accuracy or validity of the amounts • The controls at the service organisation must be assessed for their adequacy • No further work needed on the petty cash payments to casual workers as the amount is not material		
(ii) **Further audit procedures** • Review the service agreement between Thurman Co and Jackson Co to understand the exact work which is conducted by Jackson Co as a service organisation • Read all reports made by Jackson Co during the year to identify any risks of misstatement in the payroll figure • Discuss and document relevant controls in place at Thurman Co over the information received from Jackson Co and the management of casual employees, and perform tests of controls on a sample basis • Recalculate the amount of any unpaid tax which may be due to the tax authorities • Read any user manuals or systems overviews to assess the efficacy of controls in place over the processing of payroll • If necessary, obtain a type 1 or type 2 report from Jackson Co to obtain further assurance on the controls which the service organisation has in place • Perform a substantive analytical review on payroll, preparing an auditor's expectation of the payroll figures and comparing it to that recognised in the financial statements and discussing any variance with management • Perform test of detail by selecting a sample from the payroll records and agreeing the amounts to payslips and HR records		
(iii) **Report to those charged with governance** • There is not a significant control deficiency as the amounts involved are immaterial • Potential non-compliance with regulations, e.g. tax regulation should be reported • Recommend that all workers are put through payroll to ensure compliance		
	Maximum	9
Total		**25**

22 ADDER GROUP *Walk in the footsteps of a top tutor*

Top tutor tips

For 'Matters and evidence' questions, use the 'MARE' approach to make it easier to score the required number of marks.

First, consider the materiality of the issue. Next discuss the appropriate accounting treatment and give the risks of material misstatement that would arise if the appropriate treatment is not followed. Finally, the evidence is what you would expect to be recorded on the audit file when you come to review it. Be specific about the evidence, don't say 'supporting documentation', suggest what that documentation would be and what it would show.

Assume that half of the marks will be for matters and half of the marks will be for evidence.

(a) **(i)** The sale and leaseback transaction is material to the Group statement of financial position. The proceeds received on the sale of the property, equivalent to the fair value of the assets, represents 23.3% of Group assets, and the carrying value of the assets disposed of were $27 million ($35 million – $8 million), representing 18% of Group assets. In addition, the profit recognised on the disposal represents 40% of the Group's profit for the year, so it is highly material to the statement of profit or loss.

The accounting treatment does not appear to be in accordance with IFRS 16 *Leases*. IFRS 16 says the accounting treatment of a sale and leaseback depends on whether a performance obligation, as defined in IFRS 15 *Revenue from Contracts with Customers,* has been satisfied. Adder Group will be obtaining substantially all of the asset's remaining benefits, suggesting that control has not passed to the buyer.

Therefore, the transfer of the asset does not represent a 'sale'. As such, the asset should remain recognised in the statement of financial position, and the proceeds received from the sale should be recognised as a financial liability.

Therefore the Group's profit is materially overstated, and the total assets and liabilities are materially understated.

The following adjustments should be recommended to management:

DR	Property, plant and equipment	$27 million
DR	Profit or loss	$8 million
CR	Financial liability	$35 million

The complex should be depreciated over the final four months of the year, giving rise to depreciation of $0.5 million ($27 million/ 20 years × 4/12). The adjustment required is:

DR	Profit or loss	$0.5 million
CR	Property, plant and equipment	$0.5 million

The finance charge on the financial liability which has accrued since the transfer of the asset should be quantified, its materiality determined, and the appropriate adjustment communicated to management.

If the adjustments are not made, the Group financial statements will contain a material misstatement, with implications for the auditor's opinion, which would be modified due to a material misstatement following the misapplication of IFRS 16 to the sale and leaseback transaction.

Evidence:

- A copy of the lease, signed by the buyer-lessor, and a review of its major clauses to confirm that control of the asset remains with the Group.
- Review of forecasts and budgets to confirm that economic benefit is expected to be generated through the continued use of the property complex.
- Agreement of the $35 million cash proceeds to the bank statement and cash book.
- Physical inspection of the property complex to confirm that it is being used by the Group.
- Confirmation of the fair value of the property complex, possibly using an auditor's expert, in which case the expert's report should be included in the audit working papers.
- Where fair value has been established using an auditor's or management expert, evaluation of the expert's work including confirmation that the fair value is determined according to the applicable financial reporting framework, and that all assumptions are reasonable.
- Minutes of a discussion with management regarding the accounting treatment and including an auditor's request to amend the financial statements.
- A copy of insurance documents stating that the Group is responsible for insuring the property complex.
- Recalculation of finance charge and depreciation expense in relation to the leased asset.

(ii) The Group's interest in Baldrick Co is material, as the company's assets are equivalent to 12% of total Group assets, and its loss is equivalent to 25% of the Group's profit.

It is questionable whether Baldrick Co should have been accounted for as an associate. An associate arises where there is significant influence over an investee, according to IAS 28 *Investments in Associates and Joint Ventures*. Significant influence is typified by an equity shareholding of 20–50%, so the Group's shareholding of 52% would seem to indicate that the Group exercises control, rather than significant influence.

However, it may be that even with a 52% shareholding, the Group cannot exercise control, for example, if it is prevented from doing so due to agreements between other shareholders, or because it cannot appoint members to the board of Baldrick Co. This would be unusual though, so audit evidence must be sought on the nature of the shareholding in Baldrick Co and whether the Group actually exercises control or significant influence over the company. Baldrick Co not having been integrated into the Group's activities is not a valid reason for its non-consolidation as a subsidiary.

If the Group does have a controlling interest, and Baldrick Co remains recognised as an associate, the Group financial statements will be materially misstated, with implications for the auditor's opinion, which would be modified due to the application of an inappropriate accounting treatment.

If Baldrick Co should be treated as a subsidiary rather than an associate, then the company's loss for the year should be consolidated from the date of acquisition which was 1 January 2015. Therefore, a loss of $1.25 million ($5 million × 3/12) should be consolidated into Group profit. The loss which has already been recognised, assuming that equity accounting has been correctly applied, would be $650,000 ($5 million × 3/12 × 52%), therefore an additional loss of $600,000 needs to be recognised.

In addition, there are presentation issues to consider. Equity accounting requires the investment in the associate to be recognised on one line in the statement of financial position, and the income from the associate to be disclosed on one line of the statement of profit or loss.

Treating Baldrick Co as a subsidiary will require a line-by-line consolidation, which will have a significant impact on numerous balances within the financial statements.

The combination of adjustments in relation to the sale and leaseback transaction and the consolidation of Baldrick Co as a subsidiary may be considered pervasive to the Group financial statements, and if so, and the necessary adjustments are not made, then the audit opinion could be adverse.

Evidence:

- Agreement of the cash paid to acquire Baldrick Co to cash book and bank statements.
- Review of board minutes for discussion of the change in Group structure and for authorisation of the acquisition.
- Review of legal documentation pertaining to the acquisition of Baldrick Co, to confirm the number of equity shares acquired, and the rights attached to the shareholding, e.g. the ability to appoint board members.
- Inspection of other supporting documentation relating to the acquisition such as due diligence reports.
- Notes of discussion with management regarding the exercise of control over Baldrick Co, e.g. the planned level of participation in its operating and financial decisions.
- Review of forecasts and budgets to assess the plans for integrating Baldrick Co into the Group.
- Ensure that correct time apportionment has been applied in calculating the amount of losses recognised in the consolidation of Baldrick Co.
- Evaluation and recalculation of amounts recognised in Group equity in respect of Baldrick Co, in particular the determination of pre- and post-acquisition results.

(b) The storage of the potentially hazardous chemicals raises concerns that the Group may not be complying with regulations such as health and safety legislation. The auditor needs to consider the requirements of ISA 250 *Consideration of Laws and Regulations in an Audit of Financial Statements*, which states that while it is management's responsibility to ensure that the entity's operations are conducted in accordance with the provisions of laws and regulation, the auditor does have some responsibility in relation to compliance with laws and regulations, especially where a non-compliance has an impact on the financial statements.

The auditor is required by ISA 315 *Identifying and Assessing the Risks of Material Misstatement Through Understanding the Entity and its Environment* to gain an understanding of the legal and regulatory framework in which the audited entity operates. This will help the auditor to identify non-compliance and to assess the implications of non-compliance. Therefore the auditor should ensure a full knowledge and understanding of the laws and regulations relevant to the storage of items in the Group's warehouses is obtained, focusing on health and safety issues and the implications of non-compliance.

ISA 250 requires that when non-compliance is identified or suspected, the auditor shall obtain an understanding of the nature of the act and the circumstances in which it has occurred, and further information to evaluate the possible effect on the financial statements.

Therefore procedures should be performed to obtain evidence about the suspected non-compliance, for example, to identify any further instances of non-compliance in the Group's other warehouses.

Management may not be aware that the warehouse manager is allowing the storage of these potentially hazardous items. ISA 250 requires the matter to be discussed with management and where appropriate with those charged with governance. The auditor must therefore ignore the warehouse manager's threats and communicate the suspected non-compliance as required by ISA 250. Given the potential severity of the situation, and that the chemicals may not be safe, there is the risk of injury to the Group's employees or the general public, and the matter should be communicated as soon as possible.

The auditor needs to consider the potential implications for the financial statements. The non-compliance could lead to regulatory authorities imposing fines or penalties on the Group, which may need to be provided for in the financial statements. Audit procedures should be performed to determine the amount, materiality and probability of payment of any such fine or penalty imposed.

In terms of reporting non-compliance to the relevant regulatory authorities, ISA 250 requires the auditor to determine whether they have a responsibility to report the identified or suspected non-compliance to parties outside the entity. In the event that management or those charged with governance of the Group fail to make the necessary disclosures to the regulatory authorities, the auditor should consider whether they should make the disclosure. This will depend on matters including whether there is a legal duty to disclose or whether it is considered to be in the public interest to do so. Confidentiality is also an issue, and if disclosure were to be made by the auditor, it would be advisable to seek legal advice on the matter. This is very much a worst case scenario, however, as the Group's management is likely to make the necessary disclosures, and should be encouraged by the auditor to do so.

There is also an ethical issue arising from the warehouse manager's aggressive attitude and threatening behaviour. It would seem that the manager has something to hide, and that he was the only person who knew about the storage of the chemicals. He may have been bribed to allow the storage of the dangerous chemicals. His behaviour amounts to intimidation of the auditor, which is not acceptable behaviour, and those charged with governance should be alerted to the situation which arose. ISA 260 *Communication with Those Charged with Governance* requires the auditor to communicate significant difficulties encountered during the audit, which may include examples of lack of co-operation with the auditor, and imposed limitations on auditors performing their work.

The final issue is that the Group should review its policy of requiring limited documentation for contracts less than $10,000. This would seem to be inappropriate because it may lead to other instances of unknown items being stored in the Group's warehouses. This would seem to be a significant control deficiency, and should be reported to those charged with governance in accordance with both ISA 260 and ISA 265 *Communicating Deficiencies in Internal Control with Those Charged with Governance and Management*. The auditor could recommend improvements to the controls over the storage of items which should prevent any further non-compliance with laws and regulations from occurring.

Examiner comments

This question was split into two requirements. The first, requirement (a), asked candidates to comment on the matters to be considered and explain the audit evidence they would expect to find in a review of the working papers relating to the audit of the Adder Group. Candidates who have practised past exam papers will be familiar with requirements of this type, and with scenarios set in the completion stage of the audit.

The first issue related to a sale and leaseback arrangement. The Adder Group had derecognised the asset and recognised a profit on disposal. Candidates had to discuss whether the accounting treatment appeared appropriate. Answers on the whole were good. Most candidates proved able to confidently discuss whether the lease had been appropriately classified and accounted for. In addition almost all candidates correctly determined the materiality of the balances and could provide some specific and well explained points on audit evidence.

The second issue related to the acquisition of a 52% shareholding in Baldrick Co, which had been accounted for as an associate in the consolidated financial statements. Again, candidates were able to identify that the accounting treatment seemed incorrect, and could explain their reasoning. Fewer candidates appreciated that the loss-making status of Baldrick Co was the possible explanation for the Group's reluctance to consolidate it as a subsidiary and therefore that the Group's profits were overstated. Most candidates could provide some evidence points, with the most commonly cited being the board approval of the acquisition and agreeing the cash paid to bank statements. Fewer candidates could suggest how the audit firm should obtain evidence on the exercise of control by the parent company or on the mechanics of the consolidation that should have taken place.

Requirement (b) focused on laws and regulations, continuing to use the Adder Group as the scenario. Information was provided about suspicious activity in the Group's storage facility warehouses, where it was implied that internal controls were deficient and that hazardous materials were being kept, possibly against relevant laws and regulations. An employee had threatened the audit senior when questioned about the situation. Candidates were asked to discuss the implications of this situation for the completion of the Group audit.

Most candidates identified the obvious issues, namely that this was likely to be a breach of laws and regulations, internal controls were poor, and that an intimidation threat existed. Beyond this, the quality of answers varied dramatically. The best answers used a methodical approach to explain the auditor's responsibilities in relation to a suspected breach of laws and regulations; including the need to obtain more evidence, the auditor's reporting responsibilities, and the need to consider client confidentiality as well as possibly reporting the matter in the public interest. It was pleasing to see many candidates deal well with these issues, as well as the ethical threat raised by the employee's behaviour.

Weaker answers focused solely on the potential money laundering implications, which while not irrelevant should not have been the only matter discussed. In addition, weaker answers simply stated facts without much attempt to apply the requirements of the relevant auditing standard to the scenario. Some candidates suggested that the audit firm was responsible for ensuring that the Group was complying with relevant laws and regulations, saying that the audit firm should 'ensure compliance', and there were occasionally suggestions that the audit senior should be 'disciplined' for not taking further action when threatened by the employee of the Group. These comments, especially the latter, demonstrate a lack of judgment or real understanding of the role of the auditor in this regard.

This question was for many candidates the best attempted question on the exam. For requirement (a) it was encouraging that so many scripts discussed financial reporting matters with confidence, and crucially, were able to link those matters to relevant audit evidence points; for requirement (b) it was pleasing to see candidates indicate knowledge of the relevant ISA and demonstrate some application skills.

ACCA Marking scheme

			Marks
		Generally up to 1½ marks for each matter discussed, and 1 mark for each well explained procedure:	
(a)	(i)	**Sale and leaseback**	
		Matters:	
		– Correct determination of materiality	
		– IFRS 16 treatment	
		– Assets and liabilities understated, profit overstated	
		– Adjustment recommended	
		– Depreciation should be re-measured	
		– Finance charge accrual	
		– Implications for auditor's report if not adjusted	
		Evidence:	
		– A copy of the lease	
		– Forecasts and budgets	
		– Physical inspection of the property complex	
		– Confirmation of the fair value of the property	
		– Evaluation of the expert's work	
		– Bank statement and cash book	
		– Minutes of a discussion with management	
		– A copy of insurance documents	
		– Recalculation of finance charge and depreciation	
	(ii)	**Baldrick Co**	
		Matters:	
		– Correct determination of materiality of Baldrick Co	
		– If Group exercises control, Baldrick Co is a subsidiary not an associate	
		– Need to determine nature of the Group's interest in Baldrick Co	
		– Impact on audit opinion is at least qualification due to material misstatement	
		– Discussion of impact on Group profit if Baldrick Co is treated as a subsidiary	
		– Presentation issues	
		– Impact could be pervasive in combination with the sale and leaseback	

Evidence:

- Cash book and bank statements
- Board minutes for authorisation of the acquisition and disposal
- Legal documentation pertaining to the acquisition of Baldrick Co
- Other supporting documentation such as due diligence reports
- Notes of discussion with management regarding control
- Plans for integrating Baldrick Co into the Group
- Ensure that losses from the date of acquisition only are consolidated
- Evaluation and recalculation of amounts recognised in Group equity in respect of Baldrick Co

Maximum 16

(b) Completion issues and laws and regulations

Generally up to 1½ marks for each point discussed:

- Storage of hazardous chemicals likely to be a breach of laws and regulations
- Auditor needs to understand laws and regulations applicable to the Group
- Further evidence should be obtained about the storage of chemicals
- Implications for the financial statements to be considered, e.g. provisions for fines and penalties
- Matter to be reported as soon as possible to those charged with governance
- Auditor may have a legal duty to disclose, or consider disclosing in the public interest
- Intimidation and threatening behaviour should be reported to those charged with governance
- Control deficiency and recommendation to be communicated to those charged with governance
- The audit firm may wish to seek legal advice regarding the situation

Maximum 9

Total 25

23 FRANCIS GROUP *Walk in the footsteps of a top tutor*

Top tutor tips

This question is a typical 'matters and evidence' question. Use the 'MARE' approach. First, consider the materiality of the issue. Next discuss the appropriate accounting treatment and give the risks of material misstatement that would arise if the appropriate treatment is not followed. Finally, the evidence is what you would expect to be recorded on the audit file when you come to review it. Be specific about the evidence, don't say 'supporting documentation', and suggest what that documentation would be and what it would show.

There are three issues to deal with and each has its own mark allocation therefore deal with both matters and evidence for the acquisition of Teapot, then the property complex, and finally the intercompany balances. Don't deal with matters for all three then evidence for all three as the structure of the requirements and the mark allocations indicates that this is not appropriate presentation.

(a) Measurement of goodwill on acquisition

The goodwill arising on the acquisition of Teapot Co is material to the Group financial statements, representing 6% of total assets.

The goodwill should be recognised as an intangible asset and measured according to IAS 38 *Intangible Assets* and IFRS 3 *Business Combinations*. The purchase consideration should reflect the fair value of total consideration paid and payable, and there is a risk that the amount shown in the calculation is not complete, for example, if any deferred or contingent consideration has not been included.

The non-controlling interest has been measured at fair value. This is permitted by IFRS 3, and the decision to measure at fair value can be made on an investment by investment basis. The important issue is the basis for measurement of fair value. If Teapot Co is a listed company, then the market value of its shares at the date of acquisition can be used and this is a reliable measurement. If Teapot Co is not listed, then management should have used estimation techniques according to the fair value hierarchy of inputs contained in IFRS 13 *Fair Value Measurement*. This would introduce subjectivity into the measurement of non-controlling interest and goodwill and the method of determining fair value must be clearly understood by the auditor.

The net assets acquired should be all identifiable assets and liabilities at the date of acquisition. For such a significant acquisition some form of due diligence investigation should have been performed, and one of the objectives of this would be to determine the existence of assets and liabilities, even those not recognised in Teapot Co's individual financial statements. There is a risk that not all acquired assets and liabilities have been identified, or that they have not been appropriately measured at fair value, which would lead to over or understatement of goodwill and incomplete recording of assets and liabilities in the consolidated financial statements.

The fair value adjustment of $300,000 made in relation to Teapot Co's property is not material to the Group accounts, representing less than 1% of total assets. However, the auditor should confirm that additional depreciation is being charged at Group level in respect of the fair value uplift.

Though the value of the depreciation would not be material to the consolidated financial statements, for completeness and accuracy the adjustment should be made.

The auditor should also consider if any further adjustments need to be made to Teapot Co's net assets to ensure that Group accounting policies have been applied. IFRS 3 requires consistency in accounting policies across Group members, so if the necessary adjustments have not been made, the assets and liabilities will be over or understated on consolidation.

Evidence:

- Agreement of the purchase consideration to the legal documentation pertaining to the acquisition, and a review of the documents to ensure that the figures included in the goodwill calculation are complete.
- Agreement of the $75 million to the bank statement and cash book of the acquiring company (presumably the parent company of the Group).
- Review of board minutes for discussions relating to the acquisition, and for the relevant minute of board approval.
- A review of the purchase documentation and a register of significant shareholders of Teapot Co to confirm the 20% non-controlling interest.

- If Teapot Co's shares are not listed, a discussion with management as to how the fair value of the non-controlling interest has been determined and evaluation of the appropriateness of the method used.
- If Teapot Co's shares are listed, confirmation that the fair value of the non-controlling interest has been calculated based on an externally available share price at the date of acquisition.
- A copy of any due diligence report relevant to the acquisition, reviewed for confirmation of acquired assets and liabilities and their fair values.
- An evaluation of the methods used to determine the fair value of acquired assets, including the property, and liabilities to confirm compliance with IFRS 3 and IFRS 13.
- Review of depreciation calculations, and recalculation, to confirm that additional depreciation is being charged on the fair value uplift.
- A review of the calculation of net assets acquired to confirm that Group accounting policies have been applied.

Impairment

IAS 38 requires that goodwill is tested annually for impairment regardless of whether indicators of potential impairment exist. The goodwill in relation to Teapot Co is recognised at the same amount at the year end as it was at acquisition, indicating that no impairment has been recognised. It could be that management has performed an impairment review and has concluded that there is no impairment, or that no impairment review has been performed at all.

However, Group profit has declined by 30.3% over the year, which in itself is an indicator of potential impairment of the Group's assets, so it is unlikely that no impairment exists unless the fall in revenue relates to parts of the Group's activities which are unrelated to Teapot Co. There is a risk that Group assets are overstated and profit overstated if any necessary impairment has not been recognised.

Evidence:

- Discussion with management regarding the potential impairment of Group assets and confirmation as to whether an impairment review has been performed.
- A copy of any impairment review performed by management, with scrutiny of the assumptions used, and re-performance of calculations.
- The auditor's impairment evaluation and calculation compared with that of management.

Loan

The loan is material, representing 13.3% of the Group's total assets.

The loan taken out to finance the acquisition should be accounted for under IFRS 9 *Financial Instruments*. It should be initially measured at fair value, and classified according to whether it is subsequently measured at amortised cost or at fair value. As the loan is not held for trading, it should be measured at amortised cost unless Group management decides to use the fair value option.

Assuming subsequent measurement is based on amortised cost, an effective interest rate should be calculated to allocate the premium to be paid on maturity over the 20-year life of the loan, meaning that the annual finance charge will be more than just the actual interest paid. There is a risk that the finance charge does not include an element relating to the premium, in which case both the finance charge and the liability are understated.

Tutorial note

It is not necessary for candidates to calculate the effective interest on the loan or the correct value of the finance charge for the year.

IFRS 7 *Financial Instruments: Disclosure* contains extensive disclosure requirements, for example, information on the significance of financial instruments and on the nature and extent of associated risks. There is a risk of incomplete disclosure in relation to the loan taken out.

Evidence:

- Recalculate the finance charge in relation to the loan, to ensure that the loan premium has been correctly accrued.
- Agreement of the loan receipt and interest payment to bank statement and cash book.
- Review of board minutes for approval of the loan to be taken out.
- A copy of the loan agreement, reviewed to confirm terms including the maturity date, premium to be paid on maturity and annual interest payments.
- A copy of the note to the financial statements which discusses the loan to ensure all requirements of IFRS 7 and IFRS 13 have been met.

(b) Property complex

The carrying value of the property complex is material to the Group financial statements, representing 3.6% of total assets.

The natural disaster is a subsequent event, and its accounting treatment should be in accordance with IAS 10 *Events after the Reporting Period.* IAS 10 distinguishes between adjusting and non-adjusting events, the classification being dependent on whether the event provides additional information about conditions already existing at the year end. The natural disaster is a non-adjusting event as it indicates a condition which arose after the year end.

Disclosure is necessary in a note to the financial statements to describe the impact of the natural disaster, and quantify the effect which it will have on next year's financial statements.

The demolition of the property complex should be explained in the note to the financial statements and reference made to the monetary amounts involved. Consideration should be made of any other costs which will be incurred, e.g. if there is inventory to be written off, and the costs of the demolition itself.

The contingent asset of $18 million should not have been recognised. Even if the amount were virtually certain to be received, the fact that it relates to the non-adjusting event after the reporting period means that it cannot be recognised as an asset and deferred income at the year end.

The financial statements should be adjusted to remove the contingent asset and the deferred income. The amount is material at 4% of total assets. There would be no profit impact of this adjustment as the $18 million has not been recognised in the statement of profit or loss.

Evidence:

- A copy of any press release made by the Group after the natural disaster, and relevant media reports of the natural disaster, in particular focusing on its impact on the property complex.
- Photographic evidence of the site after the natural disaster, and of the demolished site.
- A copy of the note to the financial statements describing the event, reviewed for completeness and accuracy.
- A schedule of the costs of the demolition, with a sample agreed to supporting documentation, e.g. invoices for work performed and confirmation that this is included in the costs described in the note to the financial statements.
- A schedule showing the value of inventories and items such as fixtures and fittings at the time of the disaster, and confirmation that this is included in the costs described in the note to the financial statements.
- A copy of the insurance claim and correspondence with the Group's insurers to confirm that the property is insured.
- Confirmation that an adjustment has been made to reverse out the contingent asset and deferred income which has been recognised.

(c) Intercompany trading

The intercompany receivables and payables represent 4.4% of Group assets and are material to the consolidated statement of financial position. The inventory is also material, at 11% of Group assets.

On consolidation, the intercompany receivables and payables balances should be eliminated, leaving only balances between the Group and external parties recognised at Group level. There is a risk that during the consolidation process the elimination has not happened, overstating Group assets and liabilities by the same amount.

If the intercompany transaction included a profit element, then the inventory needs to be reduced in value by an adjustment for unrealised profit. This means that the profit made by Marks Co on the sale of any inventory still remaining in the Group at the year end is eliminated. If the adjustment has not been made, then inventory and Group profit will be overstated.

Evidence:

- Review of consolidation working papers to confirm that the intercompany balances have been eliminated.
- A copy of the terms of sale between Marks Co and Roberts Co, scrutinised to find out if a profit margin or mark-up is part of the sales price.

- A reconciliation of the intercompany balances between Roberts Co and Marks Co to confirm that there are no other reconciling items to be adjusted, e.g. cash in transit or goods in transit.
- Copies of inventory movement reports for the goods sold from Marks Co to Roberts Co, to determine the quantity of goods transferred.
- Details of the inventory count held at Roberts Co at the year end, reviewed to confirm that no other intercompany goods are held at the year end.

Examiner's comments

This question contained information relevant to the audit completion of the Francis Group. Specifically, three issues had been highlighted by the audit senior, and candidates were asked in respect of each issue to comment on the matters to be considered and explain the audit evidence they should expect to find during a review of the audit working papers. This type of requirement is common in paper P7, and it was encouraging to see that many candidates had obviously practised past exam questions containing similar requirements. Most candidates approached each of the issues in a sensible manner by firstly determining the materiality of the matters involved, considering the appropriate financial reporting treatment and risk of misstatement, and then providing some examples of appropriate audit evidence relevant to the matters discussed. However, the question was not well attempted by all, and it was usually a lack of knowledge of financial reporting requirements, and / or an inability to explain the relevant audit evidence that let some candidates down.

Requirement (a) related to an acquisition of a subsidiary that had taken place during the year. A goodwill calculation had been provided, along with information regarding a fair value adjustment relevant to the net assets of the subsidiary at acquisition. In addition, a loan had been taken out to finance the acquisition and information relating to the interest rate and loan premium was given in the scenario. Candidates were able to achieve a good mark here if they tackled each component of the information provided in turn and used that approach to deliver a structured answer.

In relation to the goodwill calculation, many candidates identified that no impairment had been recognised, and therefore that the goodwill balance may be overvalued. Only the strongest candidates mentioned that a significant drop in the Group's profit for the year meant that it would be very likely that an impairment loss should be recognised. It was worrying to see how many candidates referred to the need for goodwill to be amortised over a useful life – a practice that has not been allowed under IFRS 3 *Business Combinations* for many years. Fewer candidates touched on the measurement issues in relation to the non-controlling interest component of goodwill, which was usually ignored in answers. Looking at the fair value adjustment to net assets, most candidates recognised that this would be a subjective issue and that ideally an independent valuer's report or due diligence report would be required as audit evidence to justify the adjustment. Weaker candidates thought that the accounting treatment of goodwill was incorrect and set about correcting the perceived errors.

The loan element tended to be well dealt with – most candidates seemed to be aware of the principles of IFRS 9 *Financial Instruments* in discussing the financial reporting implications of the loan taken out to finance the acquisition, and the need to measure the loan at amortised cost including the premium was frequently identified. It was encouraging to see many candidates also refer to the extensive disclosure requirements that would be necessary in relation to the acquisition itself, as well as the loan, and that a significant risk would be insufficient disclosure in the notes to the financial statements.

Some incorrect accounting treatments frequently discussed included:

- Goodwill should be amortised over an estimated useful life (discussed above)
- Goodwill only needs to be tested for impairment when indicators of impairment exist
- Non-controlling interest should not be part of the goodwill calculation
- Borrowing costs should be capitalised into the cost of investment / goodwill figures
- Fair value adjustments are not required and are an indication of fraudulent financial reporting.

The evidence points provided by candidates for this requirement tended to revolve around recalculations of the various balances, and confirming figures to supporting documentation such as the loan agreement, purchase documentation and due diligence reports. These were all valid evidence points but it would benefit candidates to consider a wider range of evidence that may be available especially in relation to the more subjective and therefore higher risk elements, for example a discussion with management regarding the need for an impairment review of goodwill or a review and assessment of the methods used to determine the fair value of the non- controlling interest.

Requirement (b) related to a natural disaster that had taken place two months after the year end, resulting in the demolition of the Group's head office and main manufacturing site. The Group had claimed under its insurance an amount in excess of the value of the demolished property, and the whole amount of the claim was recognised in the statement of financial position as a current asset and deferred income. This requirement was generally well answered, with almost all candidates correctly determining the materiality of the property complex and the contingent asset. Most candidates also appreciated that the auditor should consider the event to be a non-adjusting event after the reporting date, requiring disclosure in the notes to the financial statements, in line with the requirements of IAS 10 *Events after the Reporting Period*. The audit evidence suggested was usually relevant and sensible, tending to focus on the insurance claim, discussing the need for demolition with management, and evidence from documents such as health and safety reports on the necessity for the demolition. Many answers identified that a key part of the audit evidence would be in the form of a review of the sufficiency of the required notes to the financial statements describing and quantifying the financial implications of the non-adjusting event. In a minority of scripts candidates suggested that the event was actually an adjusting event and that impairment of the property complex should be recognised in this financial year. Weaker answers to this requirement suggested that the event should be recognised by impairing the property complex and recognising the contingent asset. However, encouragingly even where candidates had discussed the incorrect accounting treatment, the evidence points provided were generally appropriate to the scenario.

Requirement (c) briefly described the details of intercompany trading that had taken place between components of the Group resulting in intercompany receivables and payables in the individual financial statements of the components, and inventory within the recipient company including a profit element. Most candidates correctly determined that at Group level the intercompany transactions should be eliminated and that a provision for unrealised profit would be necessary to remove the profit element of the transaction. Most candidates also correctly calculated the relevant materiality figures and could provide a couple of evidence points. The main concern with responses to this requirement was that they were often brief, with the audit evidence described usually amounting to little more than recalculations and 'check the elimination has happened'.

In summary the question was well attempted by many candidates, with the matters to consider element of the requirements usually better attempted than the audit evidence points. It was clear that many candidates had practised past questions of this type and were well prepared for the style of question requirement.

The UK and IRL adapted papers were slightly different in that the requirements were not broken down and therefore marks were not allocated to each separate issue. This did not seem to affect how candidates approached the question, and again it was generally well attempted. It was however much more common to see references to incorrect financial reporting requirements, specifically that goodwill must be amortised over an estimated useful life.

Candidates are reminded that if they choose to attempt the UK or IRL adapted paper, the financial reporting requirements are still based on IFRS Standards, as in the INT paper, and therefore discussing financial reporting requirements of UK and Irish GAAP will not score credit.

ACCA marking scheme	
	Marks
Generally 1 mark for each matter considered/evidence point explained: (a) **Teapot Co** **Matters:** – Materiality of the goodwill – Purchase price/consideration to be at fair value – Risk of understatement if components of consideration not included – Non-controlling interest at fair value – determination of fair value if Teapot Co is listed – Non-controlling interest at fair value – determination of fair value if Teapot Co is not listed – Use of fair value hierarchy to determine fair value – Risk that not all acquired assets and liabilities have been separately identified – Risk in the measurement of acquired assets and liabilities – judgmental – Additional depreciation to be charged on fair value uplift – Group accounting policies to be applied to net assets acquired on consolidation – Impairment indicator exists – fall in revenue – Impairment review required regardless for goodwill – Risk goodwill and Group profit overstated if necessary impairment not recognised – Loan – initial measurement at fair value – Loan – subsequent measurement at amortised cost – Risk effective interest not properly applied – understated finance cost and liability – Risk of inadequate disclosure in relation to financial liability **Evidence:** – Agreement of the purchase consideration – Agreement of the $75 million to the bank statement and cash book – Review of board minutes for discussions relating to the acquisition – A review of the purchase documentation and a register of significant shareholders of Teapot Co to confirm the 20% NCI – If Teapot Co's shares are not listed, a discussion with management as to how the fair value of the non-controlling interest has been determined – If Teapot Co's shares are listed, confirmation that the fair value of the non-controlling interest has been calculated based on an externally available share price at the date of acquisition – A copy of any due diligence report relevant to the acquisition	

	– An evaluation of the methods used to determine the fair value of acquired assets – Review of depreciation calculations, and recalculation – A review of the calculation of net assets acquired – Discussion with management regarding the potential impairment of Group assets – A copy of any impairment review performed by management – Recalculate the finance charge in relation to the loan, to ensure that effective interest has been correctly applied – Agreement of the loan receipt and interest payment – Review of board minutes for approval of the loan to be taken out – A copy of the loan agreement, reviewed to confirm terms – A copy of the note to the financial statements to ensure disclosure requirements have been met	
	Maximum	**12**
(b)	**Subsequent event** **Matters:** – Materiality of the asset (calculation) and significance to profit – Identify event as non-adjusting – Describe content of note to financial statements – Consider other costs, e.g. inventories to be written off – Contingent asset/deferred income should not be recognised **Evidence:** – A copy of any press release/media reports – Photographic evidence of the site after the natural disaster and of the demolished site – A copy of the note to the financial statements describing the event – A schedule of the costs of the demolition, with a sample agreed to supporting documentation – A schedule showing the value of inventories and items such as fixtures and fittings – A copy of the insurance claim – Confirmation of the removal of the contingent asset from the financial statements	
	Maximum	**7**
(c)	**Intercompany trading** **Matters:** – Materiality of the intercompany balance and the inventory – At Group level the intercompany balances must be eliminated – If they are not eliminated, Group current assets and liabilities will be overstated – A provision for unrealised profit may need to be recognised in respect of the inventory **Evidence:** – Review of consolidation working papers to confirm that the intercompany balances have been eliminated – A copy of the terms of sale scrutinised to find out if a profit margin or mark-up is part of the sales price – A reconciliation of the intercompany balances between Roberts Co and Marks Co to confirm that there are no other reconciling items to be adjusted, e.g. cash in transit or goods in transit – Copies of inventory movement reports for the goods sold from Marks Co to Roberts Co to determine the quantity of goods transferred – Details of the inventory count held at Roberts Co at the year end, reviewed to confirm that no other intercompany goods are held at the year end	
	Maximum	**6**
Total		**25**

24 COOPER *Walk in the footsteps of a top tutor*

Top tutor tips

Part (a) is a typical 'matters and evidence' question. Use the 'MARE' approach. First, consider the materiality of the issue. Next discuss the appropriate accounting treatment and give the risks of material misstatement that would arise if the appropriate treatment is not followed. Finally, the evidence is what you would expect to be recorded on the audit file when you come to review it. Be specific about the evidence, don't say 'supporting documentation', suggest what that documentation would be and what it would show.

Part (b) deals with a professional issue where a section of the prior year financial statements have not been audited. What will it mean for this year's audit? What should the auditor do to rectify the issue?

(a) (i) Matters to consider:

The factories are a class of assets which is material to the statement of financial position, representing 25% of total assets. The factories manufacturing the chemical which is to be phased out are half of the total class of assets, representing 12.5% of total assets and therefore material.

The new government regulation indicates that the products made in these factories will be phased out by 2017. According to IAS 36 *Impairment of Assets*, this is an indicator of potential impairment of the assets. IAS 36 gives examples of indicators that an asset may be impaired in value, one of which is significant adverse changes which have taken place or are expected to take place in the technological, market, economic or legal environment in which the entity operates.

Management should have conducted an impairment review to determine the recoverable amount of the factories, which would be the greater of the fair value less cost to sell and the value in use of the assets.

The new government regulation is potentially going to detrimentally affect the revenue generating ability of the factories, and hence their value in use to Cooper Co. This means that the recoverable amount of the factories may be less than their carrying value of $30 million, and that an impairment loss should be recognised. If any necessary impairment loss is not recognised, then property, plant and equipment, and operating profit will be overstated.

However, sales are still buoyant and may continue to be so until the product is discontinued, so an impairment test may reveal that there is no impairment to be recognised. This is likely to be the case if the factories can be used to produce an alternative product, possibly the new product which is being researched.

The $1 million which has been spent on the feasibility study into a new product must be treated as an operating expense.

There is a risk that management has capitalised the expenditure as an intangible asset, which is not appropriate. Under IAS 38 *Intangible Assets*, research costs must not be capitalised.

In the longer term, if a replacement chemical cannot be developed to replace the one being discontinued, there may be going concern issues for Cooper Co. However, this does not impact the financial statements for this year.

Evidence:

- A copy of the government regulation stating that the product made by the factories is to be phased out in 2017.
- Agreement of the carrying value of the factories making this product to the non-current asset register and general ledger at an amount of $30 million.
- A review of forecast financial statements and management accounts to confirm the amount of revenue still being generated by the factories.
- A copy of management's impairment test, including an assessment of the validity of any assumptions used and confirmation that they are in line with auditor's understanding of the business.
- A discussion with management regarding the potential future use of the factories, and whether the potential new product can be produced by them.
- Confirmation that the research costs are included in operating expenses, and have not been capitalised.

(ii) Hannah Osbourne is a related party of Cooper Co. This is according to IAS 24 *Related Party Disclosures*, which states that a member of key management personnel is a related party of the reporting entity. ISA 550 *Related Parties* requires that the auditor evaluates whether identified related party relationships and transactions have been appropriately accounted for and disclosed in accordance with the applicable financial reporting framework. In addition, ISA 550 requires that where a significant related party transaction outside of the entity's normal course of business is identified, the auditor shall:

Inspect the underlying contracts or agreements, if any, and evaluate whether:

- The business rationale (or lack thereof) of the transactions suggests that they may have been entered into to engage in fraudulent financial reporting or to conceal misappropriation of assets;
- The terms of the transactions are consistent with management's explanations; and
- The transactions have been appropriately accounted for and disclosed in accordance with the applicable financial reporting framework.

The auditor shall also obtain audit evidence that the transactions have been appropriately authorised and approved.

IAS 24 states that a related party transaction should be disclosed if it is material. Based on monetary value the amount of the transaction is not material, based on either the book value or the market value of the car, as it represents less than 1% of total assets and of profit using either measure of value.

However, the materiality should also be judged based on the significance of the transaction to the person involved. The car's market value of $75,000 could be deemed significant to Hannah, especially if she is not going to settle the amount, meaning effectively that she has been given the car for free by the company.

And, because the transaction is with a member of key management personnel, it is effectively material by nature, regardless of monetary amount. Therefore disclosure of the transaction in the notes to the financial statements will be necessary to avoid a material misstatement.

In relation to a material related party transaction, IAS 24 requires disclosure of the nature of the related party relationship along with information about the transaction itself, such as the amount of the transaction, any relevant terms and conditions, and any balances outstanding.

If the related party transaction has not been disclosed, the auditor should consider the implications for the auditor's report, which may need to be modified on the grounds of material misstatement.

Finally the auditor should consider the recoverability of the $50,000 outstanding, given that the invoice was raised several months before the year end and the amount has not yet been paid. If the amount is not recoverable and needs to be written off, this will not be material in monetary terms for Cooper Co but an adjustment would be advisable to avoid overstatement of receivables and operating profit.

Evidence:

- A review of the notes to the financial statements to confirm that sufficient disclosure has been made to comply with the requirements of IAS 24.
- A copy of the invoice raised, and agreement to the receivables ledger to confirm the amount of $50,000 which is outstanding.
- A copy of any contract or other document pertaining to the sale of the car to Hannah, and a review of its terms and conditions, e.g. specification of when the amount is due for payment.
- A post year-end review of the bank statement and cash books to confirm if the amount has been received in the subsequent events period.
- Confirmation that the carrying value of $50,000 has been removed from the non-current asset register and general ledger.
- Confirmation that any profit or loss recognised on the disposal has been recognised in profit for the year.
- A review of board minutes to confirm the transaction was appropriately authorised.
- A written representation from management stating that management has disclosed to the auditor the identity of the entity's related parties and all the related party relationships and transactions of which they are aware, and that management has appropriately accounted for and disclosed such relationships and transactions in accordance with the requirements of IAS 24.

(b) A material misstatement exists in the prior year financial statements. Expenditure relating to the development of an internally generated brand name must be treated as an expense and is prohibited from recognition as an internally generated brand name under IAS 38 *Intangible Assets*. While being immaterial to prior year total assets, at 0.5% of total assets at 31 January 2013, the costs of developing the brand name amounts to 6% of the prior year's profit. If the costs had been correctly accounted for, prior year profit would be $18.8 million.

The amount is still recognised at this year end. According to IAS 8 *Accounting Policies, Changes in Accounting Estimates and Errors*, due to its materiality, the error must be adjusted for retrospectively by amending comparatives and restating retained earnings at the beginning of the earliest period presented.

If an adjustment is not made, the financial statements will contain a material misstatement, intangible assets and retained earnings will both be overstated, with implications for the auditor's report.

Rose & Co should inform Cooper Co's management of the situation and request that adjustment is made to the financial statements. The audit firm may be reluctant to do this, as it will amount to an admission of negligence while performing the prior year's audit, which may lead to legal action being taken against the firm. However, disclosure to the client must be made in the interests of professionalism and integrity.

The audit should include procedures to ensure that the prior year adjustment has been properly made, and that relevant disclosures have been given in the notes to the financial statements.

The situation raises doubts about the quality control procedures which were applied to last year's audit. Rose & Co should consider a detailed review of last year's audit to understand how a material balance could have been left unaudited. For example, were the costs of developing the brand name subject to a last-minute adjustment by the client after the final review of the financial statements had taken place?

It seems likely that proper review procedures did not take place and that the audit was not properly directed and supervised. Consideration should be made as to whether any other balances or transactions in the prior year financial statements should be reviewed. The audit firm's quality control procedures as a whole should be reviewed to ensure they are adequate and comply with ISQC 1 *Quality Controls for Firms that Perform Audits and Reviews of Financial Statements, and Other Assurance and Related Services Engagements* and ISA 220 *Quality Control for an Audit of Financial Statements*. There may be implications for other audits which have been conducted.

Examiner comments

This question scenario was set at the completion stage of the audit of Cooper Co and candidates were well prepared for this type of question, as it was well attempted by many of the candidates that chose to answer it.

The first requirement presented information on two separate issues uncovered during the audit that have been brought to your attention by the audit senior – factories that are producing a chemical that would be phased out in three years' time and a vehicle that was sold to the company's finance director. The wording of this requirement would have been familiar to candidates who had practised past exam papers, and specifically candidates were required to comment on the matters to be considered in relation to each of the issues, and the audit evidence that should be found during a review of the audit working papers. There were some excellent answers here, with many candidates achieving close to the maximum marks. Most candidates correctly identified that possible impairment was the main matter to consider in relation to the factories, and discussed the issue well.

However, there were two common problems visible in answers. Firstly, there was an over emphasis on going concern issues, even though the scenario explicitly stated that sales of output from the factories was still buoyant. While it was correct to identify that without a replacement for the product there would be an impact on the company's revenue in the future, this was not a pressing issue for this year's audit. Secondly, in relation to the feasibility study into a replacement chemical, many candidates spent time detailing the capitalisation criteria for development costs, even when they had already stated in their answer that the amounts would have to be expensed as a research cost. This wasted valuable time as the capitalisation criteria were not relevant to their answer. Worryingly, a significant minority of answers commented on the need for a provision to be made for the loss of revenue that would happen in future years, which displays a lack of understanding over some fairly basic accounting principles.

The second issue was often well dealt with, with many answers correctly identifying the related party transaction and explaining the associated issues, including the necessary disclosure of the transaction in the financial statements. However there were often errors in the calculation of materiality, with candidates thinking that the vehicle had been sold for $50 million to the finance director, indicating that they had failed to read the question carefully. Weaker answers often stated that the sale was 'illegal' or 'unethical', or that the accounting treatment was wrong, and that assets should always be revalued to fair value immediately prior to sale.

For both issues, while the comments on the matters to consider were often good, the evidence points were usually weaker. Candidates lost marks by not providing an explanation of why the evidence would be necessary, which was a specific requirement of the question. For example while most candidates suggested a review of management's impairment calculations, this was rarely expanded upon. Similarly it was often recommended that a copy of the government regulation should be on file and reviewed, but the purpose of this review was seldom explained. In relation to the related party transaction, few procedures other than checking the invoice and obtaining written representations were usually given, and while these are relevant again the purpose of the evidence was not usually explained.

Requirement (b) briefly described an issue that had arisen regarding the same audit client but in relation to a section of the previous year's audit file that had not been completed. The section related to the development of an internally generated brand name which had been capitalised as an intangible asset and was still recognised in the financial statements. Candidates were asked to explain the implications for the completion of this year's audit, explain any other professional issues arising and to make recommendations as to an appropriate course of action. This requirement was not well answered. Many candidates did not know the correct accounting treatment for internally generated brand names, and discussed the capitalisation criteria which were not relevant, or impairment or amortisation of the brand name, which were also not relevant. Most could correctly determine the materiality of the brand, but far fewer identified the key issue, which was that a prior period adjustment would be necessary to correct the material misstatement that existed in the prior year's financial statements. Few candidates discussed the quality control issues that this raised in any detail, with the most common comment being that the audit partner should be 'disciplined'.

ACCA marking scheme	
	Marks
(a) (i) **Factories** Generally up to 1½ marks for each matter and up to 1 mark for each evidence point explained: **Matters:** – Materiality of factories to statement of financial position – Government regulation is an indicator of impairment – Management need to conduct an impairment review – Implication for financial statements if factories are overstated – Impairment review may reveal that factories are not overstated – Research costs may not be capitalised – No going concern issues this year but could be a longer term problem **Evidence:** – A copy of the government regulation – Agreement of the carrying value of the factories making this product to the non-current asset register and general ledger – A review of forecast financial statements and management accounts to confirm the amount of revenue still being generated by the factories – A copy of and assessment of management's impairment test – A discussion with management regarding the potential future use of the factories, and whether the potential new product can be produced by them – Confirmation that the research costs are included in operating expenses, and have not been capitalised	
Maximum	8

	(ii) **Related party transaction** Generally up to 1½ marks for each matter and up to 1 mark for each evidence point explained: **Matters:** – Hannah is a member of key management personnel and therefore a related party – Auditor required to review documents and to consider whether transaction authorised – Materiality should not be based solely on monetary calculations – it is material by nature – The amount is outstanding and may need to be written off – Disclosure needed in notes to financial statements – Implications for auditor's report if appropriate disclosure not made **Evidence:** – A review of the notes to the financial statements to confirm that sufficient disclosure has been made – A copy of the invoice raised, and agreement to the receivables ledger – A copy of any contract or other document pertaining to the sale of the car to Hannah, and a review of its terms and conditions – A post year-end review of the bank statement and cash books to confirm if the amount has been received subsequent to the year end – Confirmation that the carrying value of $50,000 has been removed from the non-current asset register and general ledger – Confirmation that profit or loss on disposal has been included in profit or loss – A review of board minutes to confirm the transaction was appropriately authorised – A written representation from management **Maximum**	7
(b)	**Prior year material misstatement** Generally 1 mark per point explained: – The prior year error is material at 6% of profit for 2013 – A prior year adjustment is required – If no adjustment is made the audit opinion for 2014 will be modified – The client must be informed of the error – Potential for legal action against the audit firm – Audit of 2014 financial statements to include procedures on the prior year adjustment – Quality control on prior year audit was lacking and should be investigated – May be implications for firm-wide quality control procedures **Maximum**	5
Total		**20**

25 DASSET *Walk in the footsteps of a top tutor*

Top tutor tips

This question is a typical 'matters and evidence' question. First, consider the materiality of the issue. Next discuss the appropriate accounting treatment and give the risks of material misstatement that would arise if the appropriate treatment is not followed. Finally, the evidence is what you would expect to be recorded on the audit file when you come to review it. Be specific about the evidence, don't say 'supporting documentation', suggest what that documentation would be and what it would show.

Part (b) tests your knowledge of the auditor responsibilities in respect of laws and regulations.

(a) (i) Matters which should be considered

Impairment of assets

The mine is recognised at $10 million, representing 5.7% of Dasset Co's total assets, and therefore material to the statement of financial position.

The accident has caused part of the mine to be unusable, which indicates that it has become impaired. IAS 36 *Impairment of Assets* requires that an impairment review should be conducted when there is an indicator of potential impairment, and therefore management should have performed a review to determine the recoverable amount of the mine.

If an impairment review has not been performed, and no adjustment made to the carrying value of the mine, then assets will be overstated and profit overstated. One-third of the mine has become unusable, so presumably no future economic benefit can be derived. Therefore one-third of the mine's carrying value may need to be written off.

This amounts to $3.33 million, which represents 18.5% of profit for the year. The impairment write off is therefore potentially material to Dasset Co's profit.

A worst case scenario is that more than one-third of the mine is unusable. It could be that all of the mine is unsafe and should be shut down, or possibly the National Coal Mining Authority may withdraw its licence to operate the Ledge Hill mine completely. In either case, the impairment loss would then be extended to the full value of the mine, increasing the materiality of the matter in the financial statements.

Another consideration is there is likely to be some equipment which is contained in the tunnels which can no longer be used. It is possible that some of the equipment may be recovered, but it is likely that a large proportion of it will have to be abandoned and written off, increasing the impairment loss to be recognised.

IAS 1 *Presentation of Financial Statements* requires that an individual item of income or expense which is material should be disclosed separately, and gives impairment of assets as an example of a circumstance which may warrant separate disclosure.

The costs which have been incurred and are yet to be incurred to ensure the safety of the mine in the future should be treated as capital expenditure at the time when the costs are incurred. There may also be costs to be incurred in making the unusable tunnels safe, for example, entrances may need to be blocked up. These costs should be expensed as they do not relate to future economic benefit and so do not meet the definition of an asset. There is a risk that capital and revenue expenses have not been appropriately classified.

Provisions and liabilities

There has also been damage caused to some properties situated above the mine. Dasset Co may need to recognise a provision in relation to any costs it will suffer in relation to repairing or demolishing the properties. According to IAS 37 *Provisions, Contingent Liabilities and Contingent Assets*, a provision should be recognised if there is a present obligation as a result of a past event, a probable outflow of economic benefits, and a reliable estimate can be made.

It seems that the criteria have been met, as the accident happened before the year end and gives rise to an obligating event. Dasset Co is meeting all expenses of the residents who have been relocated, so the company appears to be acknowledging responsibility for the accident and its impact on the residential properties. The damage to the properties will result in a cash outflow for the company whether they have to be demolished or repaired, and the expert should be able to provide a reliable estimate of the amount. Therefore a provision should be recognised.

The company may suffer further cash outflows as a result of the accident, and consideration needs to be made as to whether a provision or a contingent liability should be recognised in respect of them. The residents may claim further damages against the company, for example, for stress caused by the accident, and compensation for expenses such as damaged fixtures in the properties.

There may also be a clause in the National Coal Mining Authority's operating licence that imposes a fine on Dasset Co in the event of any non-compliance with health and safety regulations. Any such fines may need to be recognised as provisions or contingent liabilities.

There is a risk that provisions have not been appropriately recognised, leading to overstated profit and understated liabilities, or that contingent liabilities have not been disclosed accurately and completely.

Going concern

Finally, there may be going concern implications as a result of the accident. Given the relatively small size of the Ledge Hill mine in relation to the company's total operations, it is unlikely that the closure of part, or even all, of the mine alone would create a risk to going concern. However, bad publicity may create difficult trading conditions, and a claim for high compensation from the group of local residents could place the company's cash flow under strain. If these factors cast significant doubt on going concern, then disclosures should be made in the note to the financial statements.

The very worst case scenario is that the National Coal Mining Authority could withdraw the company's operating licence completely, which would cause it to cease operational existence. This may be very unlikely; however, it would mean that the financial statements should be prepared on the break up basis.

(ii) Evidence

- A copy of the operating license, reviewed for conditions relating to health and safety and for potential fines and penalties which may be imposed in the event of non-compliance.
- A written representation from management on their intention (or not) to bring the non-compliance to the attention of the National Coal Mining Authority.
- A copy of board minutes where the accident has been discussed to identify the rationale behind the non-disclosure.
- A copy of reports issued by engineers or other mining specialists confirming the extent of the damage caused to the mine by the accident.
- Any quotes obtained for work to be performed to make the mine safe and for blocking off entrances to abandoned tunnels.
- Confirmation that the undamaged portion of the mine is operational, e.g. from reviewing a specialist's report.
- A copy of the surveyor's report on the residential properties, reviewed for the expert's opinion as to whether they should be demolished.
- A review of correspondence entered into with the local residents who have been relocated, to confirm the obligation the company has committed to in respect of their relocation.
- Copies of legal correspondence, reviewed for any further claims made by local residents.
- A review of the Ledge Hill Mine accident book, for confirmation that no one was injured in the accident.
- A copy of management's impairment review, if any, evaluated to ensure that assumptions are reasonable and in line with auditor's understanding of the situation.
- Confirmation that impairment losses have been recognised as an operating expense.
- A review of draft disclosure notes to the financial statements where provisions and contingent liabilities have been discussed.
- A review of cash flow and profit forecasts, forming a view on the overall going concern status of the company.

(b) Responsibilities to report the accident to the National Coal Mining Authority

Dasset operates in a highly regulated industry, and Burton & Co must consider the requirements of ISA 250 *Consideration of Laws and Regulations in an Audit of Financial Statements*. ISA 250 states that it is management's responsibility to ensure that operations are conducted in accordance with relevant law and regulations. The auditor is expected to obtain a general understanding of the applicable legal and regulatory framework and how the entity is complying with that framework.

In this case, there is a suspected non-compliance with the National Coal Mining Authority's health and safety requirements. The accident may have been caused by using unsafe equipment or mining methods which failed to meet the authority's strict requirements. Management has not informed the authority, which may be for a genuine belief that there is no need to make a report concerning the accident, or it could be because management has something to hide and does not wish to come under the scrutiny of the authority.

ISA 250 states that if the auditor becomes aware of information concerning an instance of non-compliance or suspected non-compliance with laws and regulations, the auditor shall obtain an understanding of the nature of the act and the circumstances in which it has occurred; and further information to evaluate the possible effect on the financial statements. Further audit procedures will therefore be necessary.

The matter should be discussed with those charged with governance, as required by ISA 250. Management should be asked to confirm the reason why the authority has not been notified of the accident, and a written representation should be obtained. Burton & Co may wish to encourage management to disclose the accident to the authority.

ISA 250 also requires that the auditor shall determine whether the auditor has a responsibility to report the identified or suspected non-compliance to parties outside the entity. Burton & Co needs to carefully evaluate their legal responsibility to report suspected non-compliance to the National Coal Mining Authority, and legal advice should be obtained to determine the appropriate course of action.

Confidentiality is an issue, as usually auditors cannot disclose information obtained during the audit to external parties without the prior consent of the client. However, this may be overridden in some cases by legislation or court order. In certain cases, disclosure in the public interest may warrant disclosure without client consent. Again, legal advice would be helpful here, to determine whether confidentiality can or should be breached and a report made to the National Coal Mining Authority if management fails to do so.

Examiner's comments

This question was in the style of a typical paper P7 question, set in the completion stage of an audit, and asking candidates to comment on the matters to be considered, and he audit evidence that should be expected to be found during the review of the audit files by the audit manager. Candidates were well prepared for this type of question, and it was quite well attempted by many of the candidates that chose to attempt it.

The scenario involved a coal mining company operating in a highly regulated environment. An accident had caused significant damage to one of the coal mines, and to residential properties located in its vicinity.

Management had agreed to meet some expenses relating to the relocation of the residents of these properties, which may need to be demolished in the future. Management had not reported the accident to the relevant regulatory body.

Requirement (a) contained standard wording for a P7 requirement, asking candidates to comment on the matters to consider and the evidence that should be found in undertaking a review of the audit file and financial statements of the company. There were some sound answers, and most candidates correctly identified impairment, provisions or contingent liabilities and going concern as the main financial reporting issues that would need to be considered, and in many cases a range of appropriate evidence was described. The impairment issue tended to be the best dealt with, and as usual in this type of question, many candidates demonstrated a sound understanding of the financial reporting matter and linked this to its audit implication.

Where candidates performed less well on this requirement, it tended to be due to focusing on just one issue, and dealing only very briefly with other matters. For example, in some scripts almost all of the answer discussed the impairment issue, and only touched on provisions in a couple of sentences at the end. In other scripts the answer focused on going concern, almost to the exclusion of any other matters. Some answers displayed a lack of basic financial accounting knowledge, suggesting that lost revenue should be provided for. Audit evidence points were often not well described, sometimes too vague to be awarded any credit, for example 'discuss with management' or 'check properly disclosed' – these comments are pretty meaningless as they have no context.

Requirement (b) focused on management's decision not to report the accident to the regulatory authority, asking candidates to discuss the auditor's responsibilities and recommend the actions to be taken by the auditor in respect of this. Most candidates had some basic knowledge of the auditor's responsibilities in relation to law and regulations, but not many could capitalise on this knowledge through proper application to the scenario. Many answers focused on the lack of integrity of management, suggesting that the audit firm should 'discipline' the company's directors. Other answers were too vague and brief, simply suggesting without any real explanation that the auditor should report to the regulatory authority, and failing to justify this as an appropriate course of action. The best answers applied the requirements of the relevant ISA to the scenario and recommended an appropriate course of action.

ACCA marking scheme

			Marks
(a)	(i)	**Matters to consider** Generally 1 mark for each point made: – Materiality of the mine to total assets – Impairment review should have been performed – Materiality of the potential write off to profit – No impairment write off means overstated assets and profit – Potentially all of the mine may be closed down and therefore impaired – Equipment which cannot be recovered also needs to be written off – Improvements to health and safety should be capitalised – Costs of abandoning/sealing up collapsed tunnels should be expensed – Separate presentation of material impairment costs in financial statements – Provision to be recognised for damaged properties/relocation costs of local residents – Further claims may be made leading to provisions or contingent liabilities – The authority may impose fine/penalty – provision or contingent liability – Going concern disclosure if accident creates significant doubt – Break up basis if authority withdraw company's operating licence	

(ii) **Evidence** – Operating licence, reviewed for conditions relating to health and safety and for potential fines and penalties – A written representation from management on their intention (or not) to bring the non-compliance to the attention of the National Coal Mining Authority – A copy of board minutes where the accident has been discussed to identify the rationale behind the non-disclosure – A copy of reports issued by engineers or other mining specialists confirming the extent of the damage caused to the mine by the accident – Any quotes obtained for work to be performed to make the mine safe and for blocking off entrances to abandoned tunnel – Confirmation, possibly by physical inspection, that the undamaged portion of the mine is operational – A copy of the surveyor's report on the residential properties, reviewed for the expert's opinion as to whether they should be demolished – A review of correspondence entered into with the local residents who have been relocated, to confirm the obligation the company has committed to in respect of their relocation – Copies of legal correspondence, reviewed for any further claims made by local residents – A review of the Ledge Hill Mine accident book, for confirmation that no one was injured in the accident – A copy of management's impairment review, if any, evaluated to ensure that assumptions are reasonable and in line with auditor's understanding of the situation – Confirmation that impairment losses have been recognised as an operating expense – A review of draft disclosure notes to the financial statements where provisions and contingent liabilities have been discussed – A review of cash flow and profit forecasts, forming a view on the overall going concern status of the company **Maximum**	**14**
(b) **Responsibilities, actions and reporting** Generally 1 mark for each point discussed: – Management responsible for compliance with laws and regulations – Auditor responsible for understanding applicable laws and regulations – There is suspected non-compliance with laws and regulations and further procedures are necessary – Matter should be discussed with those charged with governance – Need to understand reason for non-disclosure/encourage management to disclose – The need for external reporting should be evaluated – Legal advice may be sought – Confidentiality may be overridden in some circumstances **Maximum**	**6**
Total	**20**

26 SETTER STORES *Walk in the footsteps of a top tutor*

Top tutor tips

This question is a typical 'matters and evidence' question. First, consider the materiality of the issue. Next discuss the appropriate accounting treatment and give the risks of material misstatement that would arise if the appropriate treatment is not followed. Finally, the evidence is what you would expect to be recorded on the audit file when you come to review it. Be specific about the evidence, don't say 'supporting documentation', suggest what that documentation would be and what it would show.

There are three issues to deal with and each has its own mark allocation therefore deal with both matters and evidence for the assets held for sale, then the sale and leaseback, and finally the licence. Don't deal with matters for all three then evidence for all three as the structure of the requirements and the mark allocations indicates that this is not appropriate presentation.

(a) Matters

The properties classified as assets held for sale are material to the financial statements as the year-end carrying value of $24 million represent 8% of total assets. The amount written off the assets' value at the date of classification as held for sale of $2 million represents less than 1% of revenue and 4.2% of profit before tax, which on both measures is immaterial to the statement of profit or loss and other comprehensive income.

Assets can only be classified as held for sale if the conditions referred to in IFRS 5 *Non-current Assets Held for Sale and Discontinued Operations* are met. The conditions include the following:

- Management is committed to a plan to sell
- The assets are available for immediate sale
- An active programme to locate a buyer is initiated
- The sale is highly probable, within 12 months of classification as held for sale (subject to limited exceptions)
- The asset is being actively marketed for sale at a sales price reasonable in relation to its fair value
- Actions required to complete the plan indicate that it is unlikely that the plan will be significantly changed or withdrawn.

There is a risk that the assets have been inappropriately classified if the above conditions have not been met.

IFRS 5 requires that at classification as held for sale, assets are measured at the lower of carrying value and fair value less costs to sell. This appears to have been correctly accounted for when classification occurred in October 2012. Though not specifically required by IFRS 5, an impairment review should take place at 31 January 2013, to ensure that there is no further impairment of the properties to be recognised at the year end. If an impairment review has not taken place, the assets may be misstated in value.

The assets should not be depreciated after being classified as held for sale, therefore audit procedures should confirm that depreciation has ceased from October 2012.

Disclosure is needed in the notes to the financial statements to include a description of the non-current assets classified as held for sale, a description of the facts and circumstances of the sale and its expected timing, and a quantification of the impairment loss and where in the statement of profit or loss and other comprehensive income it is recognised.

Evidence

- A copy of the board minute at which the disposal of the properties was agreed by management.
- Details of the active programme in place to locate a buyer, for example, instructions given to real estate agency, marketing literature.
- A copy of any minutes of meetings held with prospective purchasers of any of the properties, or copies of correspondence with them.
- Written representation from management on the opinion that the assets will be sold before October 2013.
- Subsequent events review, including a review of post year-end board minutes and a review of significant cash transactions, to confirm if any properties are sold in the period after the year end.
- Details of any impairment review conducted by management on the properties at 31 January 2013.
- A copy of the client's depreciation calculations, to confirm that depreciation was charged up to October 2012 but not subsequent to the reclassification of the assets as held for sale.

(b) Matters

The sale and leaseback arrangement relates to an asset with a carrying value of $27 million, which represents 9% of total assets and is material to the statement of financial position. The fair value of the asset (cash proceeds) is also material at 12.3% of total assets.

The accounting treatment for a sale and leaseback transaction should follow the requirements of IFRS 16 *Leases*. The transfer of the property would appear to be a sale, because the buyer will obtain the substantial remaining benefits of the asset. Therefore, Setter Stores should derecognise the property complex and instead recognise a right-of-use asset. The right-of-use asset will be measured as the proportion of the previous carrying amount that relates to the rights retained. This amounts to $11.7 million ($16m/$37m × $27m). The right-of use asset would be presented as an item of property, plant and equipment.

A lease liability will be recognised at $16 million, which is the present value of the annual payments.

A profit on disposal of $5.7 million will be recognised in profit or loss based on the rights transferred to the buyer (see journal below).

The following entry should have been posted:

DR Cash	$37 million
DR Right-of-use asset	$11.7 million
CR Property, plant and equipment	$27 million
CR Lease liability	$16 million
CR Profit or loss (bal. fig.)	$5.7 million.

Therefore property, plant and equipment is overstated by $15.3 million ($27m – $11.7m). $15.3 million represents 5.1% of total assets and is material.

An adjustment should be made and, if not, the audit firm should consider the implication for the auditor's opinion, which may be modified on the grounds of material misstatement.

In forthcoming accounting periods, depreciation should be calculated based on the $11.7 million carrying amount of the asset allocated over the remaining lease term of 8 years. Each year, interest arising on the lease liability will be recorded in profit or loss.

Evidence

- A copy of the lease, signed by the lessor, to confirm the major clauses.
- Physical inspection of the property complex to confirm it is being used by Setter Stores Co.
- Confirmation of the fair value of the property complex, possibly using an auditor's expert.
- Recalculation of the present value of the lease payments.
- Agreement of the $37 million cash proceeds to the bank statement and cash book.
- A schedule showing the adjustment required in the financial statements.
- Minutes of a discussion with management regarding the accounting treatment and including an auditor's request to amend the financial statements.

(c) Matters

The amount capitalised as an intangible asset is material to the statement of financial position, representing 5% of total assets.

According to IAS 38 *Intangible Assets*, an intangible asset is recognised in the financial statements if it meets the definition of an intangible asset, if it is probable that future economic benefits will flow to the reporting entity, and if its cost can be reliably measured. It would seem appropriate that the licence is recognised as an intangible asset as it has been purchased as a separable asset without physical substance and has a reliable cost. Management should be able to demonstrate the economic benefit that has been, or is expected to be, derived from the licence.

As the licence has a fixed term of five years, it should be amortised over that period. However, it appears that amortisation has not been charged, as the amount recognised at the year end is the original cost of the licence. Amortisation of $1.25 million (15 million/5 years × 5/12) should have been charged from 1 September to the year end. This amount represents less than 1% of revenue and only 2.6% of profit before tax, and is not considered material to profit.

Evidence

- A copy of the distribution licence, confirming the five-year period of the licence, and the cost of $15 million.
- Agreement of the cash paid to the bank statement and the cash book.
- Minutes of a discussion with management regarding the apparent non-amortisation of the licence, including any reasons given for the non-amortisation.
- Sales records in relation to the soft drink and also forecast sales, to determine the future economic benefit to be derived from the licence.

Examiner's comments

This question was in the style of a typical paper P7 question, set in the completion stage of an audit, and asking candidates to comment on the matters to be considered, and the audit evidence that should be expected to be found during the review of the audit files by the audit manager. Candidates were well prepared for this type of question, and as one of the optional questions, it was attempted by the majority of candidates.

Requirement (a) described a number of properties that had been classified as held for sale. Information was given on the carrying value and fair value less cost to sell of the properties. Most answers were satisfactory, largely because candidates were confident in explaining the relevant financial reporting requirements and applying them to the brief scenario. The audit evidence points were sometimes a little vague, for example 'discuss with management', 'get management representation', 'review board minutes', and only a limited amount of credit could be awarded for such comments. However generally there has been an improvement in how well audit evidence is described and in many cases the answer points were sufficiently precise and detailed.

Requirement (b) described how a sale and leaseback arrangement had been accounted for. Answers to this requirement varied greatly in quality. Some were excellent, covering all of the financial reporting issues and if not corrected could have implications for the auditor's opinion. In these cases, evidence points also tended to be adequate, focusing on the classification of the lease, and on the adjustment necessary in the financial statements. Inadequate answers discussed the points in a vague manner, seeming uncertain as to whether the accounting treatment was correct or not, resulting in the suggestion of a few unclear audit evidence points.

Requirement (c) concerned a distribution licence that had been purchased and capitalised as an intangible asset and held at cost. Candidates seemed more comfortable with this requirement than the preceding one, and many discussed all of the relevant financial reporting concerns, particularly in relation to amortisation and/or impairment of the asset. Audit evidence points were usually provided and reasonably well explained.

Overall this was a well attempted question by many. However candidates need to think carefully when calculating and commenting on materiality. Most candidates calculated the materiality of every figure given in the question in relation to each of revenue, profit before tax and assets. By this stage in their studies candidates should appreciate that often this is not necessary, for example there is little relevance in calculating an item of expense in relation to assets. Performing all of these calculations must take some time, and the irrelevant calculations will not generate marks.

ACCA marking scheme	
	Marks
(a) **Assets held for sale**	
Generally 1 mark for each matter considered/evidence point explained:	
Matters:	
– Assets held for sale are material (calculation)	
– Amount written off is not material (calculation)	
– Conditions required to classify assets as held for sale (up to 2 marks)	
– Re-measurement at classification appears correct	
– Further impairment review may be needed at year end	
– Depreciation should not be charged after reclassification	
– Disclosure in notes to financial statements	
Evidence:	
– Board minute at which the disposal of the properties was agreed	
– Details of the active programme in place to locate a buyer	
– A copy of any minutes of meetings held with prospective purchasers of any of the properties	
– Written representation from management that the assets will be sold before October 2013	
– Subsequent events review	
– Confirm depreciation ceased on reclassification	
– Details of any impairment review conducted by management	
Maximum	8
(b) **Sale and leaseback**	
Generally 1 mark for each matter considered/evidence point explained:	
Matters:	
– Asset is material (calculation)	
– IFRS 16 treatment	
– Recognise right-of-use asset	
– Accounting entries required – 2 marks	
– Materiality of adjustment	
– Implication for auditor's opinion	
– Future implications for depreciation and interest	
Evidence:	
– A copy of the lease	
– Physical inspection of the property complex	
– Confirmation of the fair value of the property complex	
– Recalculation of the PV of lease payments	
– Agreement of the $37 million to bank statement and cash book	
– A schedule showing the adjustment required in the FS	
– Minutes of a discussion with management	
Maximum	7
(c) **Distribution licence**	
Generally 1 mark for each matter considered/evidence point explained:	
Matters:	
– Materiality of the asset (calculation)	
– Identify event as intangible asset that should be capitalised	
– Identify that no amortisation has been charged	
– The non-amortisation is not material	
Evidence:	
– A copy of the licence	
– Agreement of cost to bank statement and cash book	
– Discussion with management regarding the non-amortisation	
– Sales records of the soft drink since 1 September 2012	
Maximum	5
Total	**20**

27 ROBSTER CO *Walk in the footsteps of a top tutor*

Top tutor tips

This is a relatively straightforward matters/evidence question, albeit concerning two complex, technical accounting areas. Matters to consider at the review stage include: whether potential areas of contention are material; what the relevant accounting guidance states, and the risk of material misstatement.

(a) (i) Leases

Matters to consider

Materiality

The amounts recognised in the statement of financial position in relation to the leases are material to the financial statements. The amount recognised in non-current assets amounts to 8% of total assets, and the total lease payable recognised amounts to 7.1% of total assets.

Accounting treatment

IFRS 16 *Leases* contains detailed guidance on the classification and recognition of leased assets.

A lessee must recognise a right to use an asset and a corresponding lease liability for all leases of more than 12 months (unless the asset is of low value).

Interest on the lease liability will be recorded as a finance charge in the statement of profit or loss.

Leased assets should be depreciated over the shorter of the lease term and the economic useful life of the asset.

Presentation and disclosure

The lease liability of $3.2 million should be split between current and non-current liabilities in the statement of financial position.

Extensive disclosure relating to leases should be made in the notes to the financial statements, including an analysis showing the amounts outstanding under the lease, and the timing of the cash outflows.

Audit evidence

- A review of the lease contract (using a copy of the lease obtained from the lessor) including consideration of the major clauses of the lease and length of the lease.
- A recalculation of the finance charge expensed during the accounting period, and agreement of the interest rate used in the lease contract.
- Agreement to the cash book of amounts paid to the lessor i.e. deposit and instalments paid before the year end.

- A recalculation of the depreciation charged, and agreement that the period used in the calculation is the shorter of the lease term and the useful life of the assets.
- A recalculation and confirmation of the split of the total lease liability between current and non-current liabilities.
- A confirmation of the adequacy of the disclosure made in the notes to the financial statements, and agreement of the future payments disclosed to the lease contract.

(ii) Financial assets

Matters to consider

Materiality

The financial assets are material to the statement of financial position as the amount recognised in non-current assets amounts to 2.8% of total assets. The gain recognised is material to the statement of profit or loss, representing 10.9% of profit before tax, and 3.3% of revenue.

Accounting treatment

Robster Co has classified financial assets as 'financial assets at fair value through profit or loss' as they are considered to be 'held for trading' investments.

IFRS 9 *Financial Instruments* states that financial assets are initially measured at fair value. Fair value is normally the price paid. Any transaction costs (such as legal or broker fees) are added to the initial carrying amount, unless the asset is classified to be measured at 'fair value through profit or loss.

Equity instruments are subsequently measured at either fair value through profit or loss, or fair value through other comprehensive income.

If an equity instrument is not held for trading, an irrecoverable election can be made to designate the equity instrument as fair value through other comprehensive income. This election would not be appropriate as Robster Co considers the assets to be 'held for trading' investments.

It would appear that Robster Co has correctly classified the financial assets.

Investments classified in this way must be measured at fair value each year end, with gains and losses taken into the statement of profit or loss as part of net profit for the year.

Disclosure

IFRS 7 *Financial Instruments: Disclosures* contains extensive disclosure requirements in relation to financial assets, including for example, a narrative description of how the risks in relation to the investments are managed and monitored, and quantitative disclosures including sensitivity analysis relating to the market risk associated with the valuation of investments.

Audit evidence

- A schedule showing all the investments held in the category, their purchase price and their year-end valuation.
- Agreement of the purchase prices of investments to supporting documentation, e.g. stockbrokers' statements.

- Agreement of the year end valuation for each investment to external sources of information, e.g. stock exchange website, financial press.
- Recalculation, and confirmation of the gain recognised in the statement of profit or loss.
- A review of the internal function which has been set up to manage the investments, to confirm that investments are generally short-term in nature, that the investments are managed as a portfolio, and that there is evidence of frequent transactions.
- Confirmation that the other information published with the financial statements, e.g. the operating and financial review, describes Robster Co's investment activities in line with the classification of investments as held for trading, and refers to the valuation and gain made during the year.
- A review of the proposed note to the financial statements confirming adherence to the disclosure requirements of IFRS 7, and recalculations of numerical disclosures.

(b) Guidance on reviews of interim financial statements is provided in ISRE 2410 *Review of Interim Financial Information Performed by the Independent Auditor of the Entity.* The standard states that the auditor should plan their work to gather evidence using analytical procedures and enquiry.

The auditor should perform analytical procedures in order to discover unusual trends and relationships, or individual figures in the interim financial information, which may indicate a material misstatement. Procedures should include the following:

- Comparing the interim financial information with anticipated results, budgets and targets as set by the management of the company.
- Comparing the interim financial information with:
  - comparable information for the immediately preceding interim period,
  - the corresponding interim period in the previous year, and
  - the most recent audited financial statements.
- Comparing ratios and indicators for the current interim period with those of entities in the same industry.
- Considering relationships among financial and non-financial information. The auditor also may wish to consider information developed and used by the entity, for example, information in monthly financial reports provided to the senior management or press releases issued by the company relevant to the interim financial information.
- Comparing recorded amounts or ratios developed from recorded amounts, to expectations developed by the auditor. The auditor develops such expectations by identifying and using plausible relationships that are reasonably expected to exist based on the accountant's understanding of the entity and the industry in which the entity operates.
- Comparing disaggregated data, for example, comparing revenue reported by month and by product line or operating segment during the current interim period with that of comparable prior periods.

As with analytical procedures performed in an audit, any unusual relationships, trends or individual amounts discovered which may indicate a material misstatement should be discussed with management. However, unlike an audit, further corroboration using substantive procedures is not necessary in a review engagement.

Examiner's comments

The first part of this question was a standard audit evidence question of the type seen in numerous previous examinations. Nearly all candidates correctly calculated and concluded on the materiality of both items, and considered the financial reporting implications of the information provided.

In terms of the leases, most candidates identified the correct financial reporting standard, and discussed the classification of the lease. The evidence points tended to be quite brief for this requirement, usually limited to 'check the lease document', 'check lease approved by management' and the inevitable 'get written representation'. Such comments are much too vague, and better answers provided more specific pieces of evidence that should be sought.

Requirement (a) (ii) was generally unsatisfactorily answered, and the information given in the question was often misinterpreted. Candidates tended to know the number of the relevant financial reporting standard for financial assets, but not the technical content of that standard. Despite the question clearly stating that the assets are all investments in listed companies, a significant proportion of candidates chose to base their answer around investment properties, and others seemed to think the assets were some kind of inventory, to be valued at the lower of cost and net realisable value. Even those candidates who appreciated that the assets were investments were confused by terminology, frequently stating that 'fair value through profit and loss' and 'held for trading' are contradictory, which is not the case. Most candidates thought that the revaluation gain should not be recognised in profit for the year, which again is not the case.

The evidence points were also inadequate for this requirement. Even a candidate lacking knowledge of the financial reporting issues for investments in listed companies should be able to suggest confirming the year end share price to an external source of information on share prices, such as the Financial Times, but unfortunately few candidates could even provide this as a piece of evidence.

Requirement (b) was unsatisfactorily answered by almost all candidates. This asked for the principal analytical procedures that should be used to gather evidence in a review of interim financial information. Candidates are repeatedly reminded that non-audit engagements are part of the syllabus, and likely to feature regularly in the examination. However, few candidates seemed to know the purpose of a review of interim financial information, which meant that their answers lacked clarity. Most answers could only suggest a comparison with the prior period, and hardly any answers mentioned the disaggregation of data, or comparison with budget. Only a handful of candidates seemed aware of the existence of ISRE 2410, *Review of Interim Financial Information Performed by the Independent Auditor of the entity,* on which the requirement is based.

Some candidates confused a 'review of interim financial information' with an 'interim audit', despite the short scenario describing a review of interim financial information for the avoidance of any such confusion.

ACCA marking scheme

			Marks
(a)	(i)	**Leases** Generally 1 mark per matter/evidence point: Matters: – Correct calculation and assessment of materiality – IFRS 16 treatment – Finance charge – Depreciation – Disclosure **Evidence** – Lease agreement – Recalculate depreciation and finance charge – Cash book for payments – Review of disclosures – Split current/non-current payable	
		Maximum	**9**
	(ii)	**Financial Assets** Generally 1 mark per matter/evidence point: **Matters:** – Correct calculation and assessment of materiality – Classification as held for trading – Assets shown at fair value – could be subjective – Disclosure **Evidence** – Agree purchase price – Agree fair value – Recalculate gain – Review of disclosures in notes – Review of disclosures in OFR/other information published with financial statements	
		Maximum	**5**
(b)		**Interim Financial Information** Generally 1 mark per procedure: – Comparison to corresponding interim last year – Comparison to last audited accounts – Comparisons to anticipated results – Comparisons to non-financial data/ratios – Comparisons to similar entities – Disaggregation of data	
		Maximum	**6**
Total			**20**

Section 4

ANSWERS TO PRACTICE QUESTIONS – SECTION B

PROFESSIONAL AND ETHICAL CONSIDERATIONS

28 THORNHILL & CO *Walk in the footsteps of a top tutor*

Top tutor tips

Part (a) asks for a discussion of how professional scepticism can be applied to the scenario. Professional scepticism requires an open and questioning mind. In this case, your firm is hvaing difficulty obtaining sufficient appropriate evidence from the client and from the component auditor. You need to consider the impact that this issue will have on your audit of the group.

In part (b) you are asked to discuss the ethical and professional issues arising as a result of the refusal to provide evidence and the request not to modify the auditor's report. This carries on from requirement (a) and goes further into the actions that your firm should take such as considering whether to resign and whether or not you should modify your auditor's report.

(a) Application of professional scepticism

Potential for material misstatement

Without support from the parent, it is unlikely that Northwest Co would be considered a going concern. There is therefore a risk in relation to the going concern status of Northwest Co and a risk of material misstatement in the financial statements if an incorrect basis of preparing the accounts is selected. Professional scepticism requires the auditor to remain alert for any circumstances which may cause the financial statements to be materially misstated especially in relation to going concern matters.

Internally generated evidence

In order to reach a satisfactory conclusion in this matter, it would be essential to receive formal confirmation of support from Valerian Co. The auditor must be sceptical of this form of evidence because it is prepared by management and this sort of internally generated evidence is, generally, not as reliable as other forms of externally generated evidence.

Use of judgment

The ability to provide support to Northwest Co is also a matter of judgment. The management of Valerian Co would need to forecast their own cash flows and make a judgment as to whether they will have sufficient capacity to meet Northwest Co's obligations in the event that the subsidiary cannot. Clearly, such forecasts are prone to uncertainty and management bias.

In this case Valerian Co is itself facing a material uncertainty regarding the outcome of the legal case. It is plausible that this could affect their ability to provide full support. The failure to supply a formal letter of support adds weight to this concern. The auditor must therefore remain sceptical when considering management's pledge of support to Northwest Co.

Suspicious behaviour

The group engagement partner's request not to modify the audit opinion should also promote scepticism. This is an unusual request and appears to be based on pressure by the directors of Valerian Co. This reinforces the suspicion that both the group auditor and the directors of Valerian Co may be trying to conceal some sort of problem. It is possible that the outcome of the legal case is less favourable than is currently suggested and this may require some form of modification to the group accounts. This may, in turn, trigger further repercussions which Valerian Co is seeking to avoid.

Heightened scepticism

Based upon these concerns, the auditor needs to remain sceptical and alert for other factors which raise concerns in relation to the going concern status of Northwest Co. They should also be sceptical of all judgements made by management, particularly in relation to the forecasts prepared to assist with the assessment of going concern. It is possible that they are being overoptimistic in their estimates in order to make forecasts appear better than is reasonable to expect.

(b) (i) **Offer of support by Valerian Co**

Insufficient evidence

Without the financial support of its parent company, Northwest Co would not be considered a going concern. A verbal pledge of support from Valerian Co would not be considered sufficient, reliable evidence in regard to this matter.

Ability to provide parental support

In addition to a letter of support, the auditor of Northwest Co would need to obtain sufficient appropriate evidence that Valerian Co can provide the support which they promise.

The statement by the group auditor that they have received adequate representations from the directors and legal advisers of the company does not constitute sufficient appropriate evidence. At the very least, the auditor of Northwest Co would need copies of those representations. While the representations from management would suffer from the same lack of reliability, representations from the legal advisers would represent third party evidence and, as such, be more reliable.

Uncertainty surrounding legal case

Given the uncertainty surrounding the court case and the gravity of preparing the financial statements on an incorrect basis, Thornhill & Co may seek further documentary evidence before concluding on the going concern status of the company. This could include correspondence between Valerian Co and their legal advisers, minutes of board meetings, copies of Valerian's assessments of going concern and their current statement of financial position.

Conduct of client and group auditor

The suspicious behaviour of both the directors and auditors of Valerian Co suggests that they are not being entirely honest with Thornhill & Co. If their statements regarding the likely outcome of the legal case are appropriate and there are no other concerns, then there is no reason why they would not be able to provide copies of the representations and a written letter of support to the auditor of Northwest Co.

This increases the need for professional due care during the audit process, particularly in relation to the re-appraisal of fraud risk and the potential for material misstatement in relation to the going concern status of the company and associated disclosures in the financial statements.

Further procedures

The auditor should communicate with those charged with governance of Northwest Co and explain the requirements to obtain sufficient appropriate evidence in this matter. The auditor should also explain the consequences of not receiving this information in terms of the impact this will have on the going concern status of the company and the adjustments they would be required to make to the financial statements.

Finally, the auditor should explain that if the additional evidence is not received and the recommended adjustments are not made, then this will lead to a modification of the auditor's report. The fact that necessary audit evidence is being withheld would constitute a limitation in the scope of the audit, which may result in a qualified opinion or a disclaimer of opinion being issued.

(ii) The request not to modify the auditor's report

Intimidation

By trying to influence the decisions in relation to the audit of Northwest Co, the group auditor is creating an intimidation threat to objectivity. IESBA's Code of Ethics for Professional Accountants defines this as the threat that a professional accountant will be deterred from acting objectively because of actual or perceived pressures.

Responsibility for the opinion

As the auditor of Northwest Co, the responsibility for determining the final audit opinion and wording of the auditor's report remains with Thornhill & Co. If, based upon the evidence obtained, the engagement partner believes that a modification to the auditor's report is necessary, then they should follow this through, regardless of the opinion of the group auditor and the board of the parent company. The group partner's 'oversight' of the whole audit is irrelevant to the audit of Northwest Co. As a company in its own right, it must be audited in accordance with International Standards on Auditing.

Transferring the debt to the parent

The suggestion to transfer the debts into the parent company would not resolve the problem. If the debt obligations were 'transferred' to the parent using an appropriate journal, they would be replaced by a matching liability to the parent company in the financial statements of Northwest Co, and the same problem would exist and while this would be eliminated in the consolidated accounts, this does not allow the auditor of Northwest Co to gather sufficient appropriate evidence in relation to the going concern status of the company.

Possible manipulation of the financial statements

It is possible that the group engagement partner is recommending some form of inappropriate accounting treatment to transfer the debt into the parent company without any matching liability in Northwest's accounts, for example, by transferring the debts and then consequently cancelling any obligations from Northwest Co due to Valerian Co. This form of accounting manipulation could be used to disguise the true financial position of the group and may constitute fraud. Any suggestion to pursue this line of action should be firmly refused.

Integrity of the group auditor

The overall integrity of the group engagement partner must be questioned. His aggressive attitude towards the audit of Northwest Co and his reluctance to cooperate by providing evidence in relation to the lawsuit indicate some form of inappropriate conduct in the audit of the parent company and group accounts. This matter should be discussed with the audit engagement partner and possibly with other senior partners, possibly including the firm's designated ethics partner. Further, the suggestion that 'he' would transfer the debt from Northwest Co to the parent company suggests that the auditor is becoming involved in the accounting transactions included in the financial statements and may suggest that the firm's independence is compromised.

Position as auditor of Northwest Co

Given the intimidation threat and the potential concerns relating to the audit of the parent and the group, Thornhill & Co may consider resignation from the audit of Northwest Co, if permitted, or may not seek re-election as auditor for the following year.

Examiner's comments

This question examined the concept of scepticism in the context of a group audit where the parent company was reluctant to provide more than verbal assurances that they would support the loss making subsidiary. The parent company was facing a law suit that they may lose and hence good candidates could explain and apply to concept of professional scepticism by questioning why the parent company would not put the support in writing and whether this might reflect uncertainty of the parent company's going concern status given the law suit.

Part b required the implications for the audit of the subsidiary in terms of evidence, reporting and pressure from the parent company auditor to refrain from modifying the audit opinion despite insufficient evidence being available.

The structure of the requirements led candidates to conclude the parent company might not be able to provide support, that a lack of evidence had been obtained in this regard, there was an ethical threat of intimidation and then discuss the auditor's report and the modification required. Disappointingly candidates often stated correctly that there was inability to collect sufficient appropriate evidence but the incorrectly proposed an adverse opinion.

Marking scheme	
	Marks
(a) **Professional scepticism**	
Generally 1 mark for each well discussed point made:	
• Risk of misstatement in relation to a material matter	
• Reliability of confirmation of internally generated evidence	
• Judgement required in relation ability to provide support	
• Material uncertainty facing parent company	
• Unusual behaviour of group engagement partner	
• Need to remain alert for other factors affecting going concern	
• Need to remain sceptical of all other matters requiring management judgment	
Maximum	**6**
(b) **Ethical and professional matters**	
Generally 1 mark for each well explained point and recommendation made:	
(i) **Support offered by Valerian Co**	
• Northwest Co would not be a going concern without support of parent	
• Verbal confirmation not sufficient evidence	
• Additional evidence that Valerian Co is capable of providing support	
• Examples of further evidence required (½ mark each, maximum of 2 marks)	
• Suspicious conduct of parent and group auditor	
• Need for professional due care and potential re-appraisal of fraud risk	
• Communication with those charged with governance	
• Possible modification of auditor's report if additional evidence not received	
(ii) **Request not to modify report**	
• Intimidation threat	
• Responsibility for audit opinion remains with Thornhill & Co	
• Transfer of debt to Valerian Co would not resolve the problem	
• Possible suggestion of inappropriate accounting treatment	
• Potential lack of integrity of group audit partner and potential fraud	
• Matter should be discussed with senior audit staff	
• Possible resignation as auditor	
Maximum	**14**
Total	**20**

29 CHENNAI & CO *Walk in the footsteps of a top tutor*

Top tutor tips

Part (a) deals with the differences between an audit and an assurance engagement as well as advantages and disadvantages of having an audit. This is quite straightforward knowledge from paper F8 and should not cause any problems for students.

Part (b) dealt with the request to perform a review of the internal controls of a listed client. Again, this should have been straightforward for most students. The key to scoring a good mark on ethical issues such as this is to discuss the significance of the threat as well as explaining the threat and suggesting safeguards. In this case, it was particularly important to identify that the client was listed as this makes the threat more significant and the safeguards need to focus on those applicable to listed entities.

(a) (i) Difference between an audit and a limited assurance review

An audit is a mandatory requirement in most countries, although some small companies below a certain threshold may be exempted. Limited assurance reviews are not usually required by law.

The scope of and procedures performed during an audit are determined by the audit firm in accordance with the auditing standards adopted by the professional regulatory body. The scope of a limited review is agreed by the firm providing the services and the client, although this must be in accordance with any relevant standards on assurance and related services adopted by professional regulators.

In particular, an audit involves a wide range of procedures used to obtain evidence, including both tests of controls and substantive procedures. The latter include inspection of documents, recalculation, observation, enquiry and analytical procedures, amongst others. Limited reviews use a narrower range of procedures, focusing primarily on enquiry and analytical procedures.

Overall, the level of assurance provided by an audit is much higher than that provided by a limited review. In an audit the practitioner expresses reasonable levels of assurance, whereas in a review engagement the practitioner expresses moderate levels of assurance.

This has a significant impact on the wording of the respective reports. In an auditor's report the practitioner expresses an opinion as to the fair presentation of the financial statements. An example of this would be:

'In our opinion the financial statements present fairly, in all material respects, the financial position of the company, its financial performance and its cash flows for the year ended in accordance with International Financial Reporting Standards.'

A review engagement report does not express any opinion on the fair presentation of the financial statements reviewed, instead the report expresses a conclusion based only upon the work performed. For example:

'Based on the review performed, nothing has come to our attention which causes us to believe that the accompanying financial statements are not fairly presented in all material respects in accordance with International Financial Reporting Standards.'

The review engagement report is often referred to as a negative form of opinion, whereas the auditor's report is referred to as a positive statement regarding the fair presentation of the financial statements.

(ii) Advantages and disadvantages to Delhi Co of having an audit

Advantages

One of the key differences between an audit and a review engagement is that an audit provides a reasonable level of assurance, whereas a review only provides limited assurance. This means that an audit provides stronger assurances to users of the financial statements regarding their accuracy and credibility.

This would be significant for Delhi Co for a number of reasons. The first is that the company now has an external shareholder, Robert Hyland, who is not part of the executive management team. With this separation of ownership and control comes an increased need to hold the management of the company accountable to the external shareholders and having a full audit will provide a much stronger form of accountability.

Second, Delhi Co has a bank loan facility which is due to expire in 2017. Given the ambitious expansion plans of Delhi Co, it is likely that the company will want to renew this facility and they may even seek to obtain more loan finance. If this is the case, it is very likely that the bank will seek a reasonable level of assurance over the financial statements.

By electing to have an annual audit now, it may avoid delays in 2017 when the company comes to renegotiate terms with the bank.

Finally, the internal management team needs good quality information on which to base their operational and strategic decisions. As the business grows and the significance of those decisions increases, it becomes more important that the management team has information that they can rely on. Having fully audited financial statements, as opposed to a limited review, will increase the confidence of management in the accuracy of the information used.

Another benefit of having a full audit now is that, whilst the business is currently under the audit exemption threshold, it is rapidly expanding and may soon exceed the threshold and be subject to mandatory audit. One of the key problems of auditing a business for the first time is that there is no existing assurance over the opening balances and comparative figures. In this case the first audit is much more time consuming, and therefore expensive, as the audit team has to invest more time investigating prior year figures. The requirement to review the prior year would be much less onerous if the company began to have their financial statements audited now while they were still relatively small and this would lead to a more efficient audit in the future.

Delhi Co also plans to expand its customer base. Trading internationally usually adds extra complications due to the added complexity in the supply chain, foreign exchange and simple lack of familiarity with the company. Customers may want assurances that any company they sign a trading agreement with has the resources to satisfy their contractual obligations. For this reason, having fully audited accounts, as opposed to accounts which have had a limited review, may give potential customers increased confidence in the financial position of Delhi Co and may improve their chances of forming new trade partnerships.

There has also been a recent change in the accounting department of Delhi Co. This is normal in a rapidly expanding business but it creates new challenges. Often the accounting systems of small companies are unsophisticated but as the company grows the systems soon become outdated and less effective. An audit incorporates a review of effectiveness of the internal control systems relevant to the production of the financial statements and any deficiencies identified by the auditor would be reported to management. Given the changes Delhi Co has experienced, a full audit may help them assess the effectiveness of their internal systems and make changes where necessary. The systems would not be assessed with a limited review.

The change in staff in the accounts department also increases the risk of misstatement of the financial statements due to their lack of familiarity with the company and the accounting systems. The fact that the new recruits are both part qualified further increases the risk of misstatement of the financial statements because the trainees may not be fully able to process all of the transactions and events relevant to the business. An audit is a more thorough investigation of the financial statements than a review and would be much more likely to identify misstatements, providing management with more reliable figures upon which to base their decisions.

Disadvantages

While an audit is a more thorough investigation, it is also more expensive than a review. For a small company an audit may be prohibitively expensive, whereas a review may be more affordable.

As the company is currently exempt, an audit may also be an unnecessary cost. Delhi Co already managed to raise a loan without the need for audited accounts. The external shareholder is also an ex-business partner of Mr Dattani and it is likely that they have a good working relationship. If Mr Hyland needs assurances, it is possible that Mr Dattani could satisfy this on an informal basis without the need to incur the costs of an audit. Mr Hyland also decided to invest knowing that the company was not subject to audit, so it may not be a concern of his.

An audit is also more invasive than a limited review and would require the staff of Delhi Co to provide more information to the auditor and give up more of their time than would be the case with a limited review. Given the relative inexperience of the accounts team, Mr Dattani may prefer to choose the less invasive limited review now and perform a full audit in the future when the team is more knowledgeable of the business.

(b) Mumbai Co

Review of internal controls

Reviewing the internal controls of an audit client which are relevant to the financial reporting system would create a self-review threat as the auditor would consequently assess the effectiveness of the control system during the external audit.

The design, implementation and maintenance of internal controls are also management responsibilities. If the auditor were to assist in this process, it may be considered that they were assuming these management responsibilities. This creates potential self-review, self-interest and familiarity threat. The latter arises because the audit firm could be considered to be aligning their views and interests to those of management.

The Code states that the threats caused by adopting management responsibilities are so significant that there are no safeguards which could reduce the threats to an acceptable level.

The only effective measures which could be adopted would be those which ensured the audit firm did not adopt a management responsibility, such as ensuring that the client has assigned competent personnel to be responsible at all times for reviewing internal control review reports and for determining which of the recommendations from the report are to be implemented.

Furthermore, if the client is listed and also an audit client, then the audit firm should not provide internal audit services which relate to a significant part of the internal controls relevant to financial reporting. Given that this is the main expertise of the audit firm, it is likely that they will be required to perform some work in this area and this service would therefore not be appropriate.

If Mumbai Co would like the firm to perform a review of internal controls not related to the financial reporting system, Chennai Co would need to consider whether they have the professional competencies to complete the engagement to the necessary standard of quality.

Concerns regarding deterioration in controls

One of the responsibilities of the auditor is to evaluate the design and implementation of the client's controls relevant to the audit in order to assist with the identification of risks of material misstatement. This includes the specific requirement to consider the risk of material misstatement due to fraud.

If deficiencies in internal controls are identified, the auditor has to assess the potential impact on the financial statements and design a suitable response in order to reduce audit risk to an acceptable level. The auditor is also responsible for communicating significant deficiencies in internal control to those charged with governance on a timely basis.

The audit committee has suggested that a number of internal control deficiencies have recently been identified which they were not previously aware of. This suggests that these were not issues identified or reported to those charged with governance by the auditor.

If these internal control deficiencies relate to systems relevant to the audit, it may suggest that the audit firm's consideration of the internal control system failed to detect these potential problems, which may indicate ineffective audit planning. If so, this increases the risk that the audit procedures designed were inappropriate and that there is a heightened risk that the audit team failed to detect material misstatements during the audit. In the worst case scenario this could mean that Chennai & Co issued an inappropriate audit opinion.

The circumstances are not clear though; the audit committee of Mumbai Co has not specified which controls appear to have deteriorated and whether these are related to the audit or not. There is also no indication of the potential scale of any fraud or inefficient commercial practice. It is possible that the risks resulting from the deficiencies are so small that they did not lead to a risk of material misstatement. In these circumstances, the audit team may have identified the deficiencies as not being significant and reported them to an appropriate level of operating management.

In order to assess this further, the manager should examine the audit file and review the documentation in relation to the evaluation of the internal controls of Mumbai Co and assess any subsequent communications to management and those charged with governance. The concerns raised by the audit committee should be noted as points to take forward into next year's audit, when they should be reviewed and evaluated as part of planning the audit for the 2017 year end.

Additionally, Chennai & Co should contact the audit committee of Mumbai Co to seek further clarification on the nature and extent of the deficiencies identified and whether this has resulted in any actual or suspected acts of fraud.

Examiner's comments

This question required candidates to provide advice to two clients around the difference between an audit and a limited assurance review and providing non-audit services. In relation to the differences between audit and limited review, most candidates demonstrated a sound understanding of both and were able to succinctly explain the differences between them including the different audiences for each. Strong answers were tailored based on the specifics of the scenario and therefore provided relevant advice to the client in question. For example strong answers highlighted that a full audit would be beneficial to the fast-growing client as it would give more credibility to the company, especially as it may be seeking bank finance. Candidates are reminded that at this level answers need to be responsive to the question requirements and should not simply be an exercise in reproducing everything that they know about a topic.

Candidates were also asked to advise a listed audit client, asking for a review of their control systems due to concerns about weaknesses in controls shortly after your firm had signed off the most recent auditor's report. Few candidates recognised the potential implications on the accuracy of the auditor's report which had been recently issued and that these potential weaknesses could undermine that opinion. Clearly further details were needed to establish if the deficiencies in control would have had any significant impact on those financial statements. Many candidates simply provided a discussion of the advantages to the client of having a review of the internal control system but failed to appreciate that undertaking such a review for a listed client would be prohibited by the Code, and this again demonstrated that many candidates did not have a good enough understanding of the requirement of the ethical guidelines. In such circumstances opting for a separate team is not an effective safeguard and the review should not be done.

ACCA Marking scheme

		Marks
(a)	Generally 1 mark available for each well explained point:	
(i)	**Audit v limited review**	
	– Regulatory requirements	
	– Determination of scope	
	– Nature of procedures	
	– Reasonable v moderate levels of assurance	
	– Audit opinion	
	'The financial statements are true and fair'	
	Review engagement conclusion	
	'Based on our review nothing has coming to our attention'	
	Negative v positive wording	
	Maximum	**4**
(ii)	**Advantages and disadvantages of audit**	
	– Accountability to external shareholder	
	– Renegotiation of loan facility	
	– Reliability of information for internal decisions	
	– Potential mandatory audit if company grows	
	– Overseas trading relationships	
	– Review of internal controls	
	– Risk of misstatement due to changes in accounting staff	
	– Cost of full audit	
	– Potentially no need for high level of assurance	
	– More invasive nature of audit	
	Maximum	**8**
(b)	**Mumbai Co**	
	Generally 1 mark for each well explained ethical and professional threat;	
	½ mark available for each recommended safeguard:	
	– Self-review threat	
	– Management responsibility: self-interest and familiarity threat	
	– No safeguards which can reduce management threat	
	– Possible safeguards to avoid management threat	
	– Restriction on internal audit services for listed clients	
	– Competence if review is not related to financial controls	
	– Responsibilities of auditor in relation to internal controls	
	– Possible deficiency in external audit procedures	
	– Nature/severity of deficiencies not clear	
	Maximum	**8**
Total		**20**

30 MONET & CO *Walk in the footsteps of a top tutor*

Top tutor tips

This question covers advertising, a potential intimidation threat from a client and a conflict of interest. Each requirement has its own mark allocation. Try and make as many points as there are marks available. Take care not just to identify and explain the issues in parts (b) and (c). Include in your answer the safeguards the firm should put in place to address the issues to provide a complete evaluation.

(a) Advertisement

Accountants are permitted to advertise subject to the requirements in the ACCA Code of Ethics and Conduct that the advert should 'not reflect adversely on the professional accountant, ACCA or the accounting profession'. The advert does not appear to be in keeping with this principle; it suggests that other firms of accountants charge inappropriately high fees and that the quality of their services is questionable. This discredits the services offered by other professional accountants as well as implying that the services offered by Monet & Co are far superior.

The advert states that the firm offers 'the most comprehensive range of finance and accountancy services in the country'. This is misleading; with 12 offices and only 30 partners Monet & Co is unlikely to be one of the largest accountancy firms in the country and is therefore unlikely to offer the most comprehensive range of services. If it is misleading, this statement must be withdrawn from the advertisement.

The advert also implies that they have the country's leading tax team; it is not possible to substantiate this claim as it is not possible to measure the effectiveness of tax teams and even if it were, no such measure currently exists. This is, therefore, also potentially misleading and should be withdrawn from the advert.

The suggestion that the tax experts are waiting to save the client money is inappropriate; no such guarantees can be made because tax professionals must apply relevant tax legislation in an objective manner. This may lead to a reduction in a client's current tax expense or it may not. Any failure to apply these regulations appropriately could raise questions about the professional behaviour of the practitioner.

Guaranteeing to be cheaper than other service providers is often referred to as 'lowballing'. This could create a potential self-interest threat to objectivity and it could also threaten professional competence and due care if the practitioner is unable to apply the appropriate professional standards for that level of fee.

[**UK syllabus:** Ethical Standard section 4 states that the audit engagement partner shall be satisfied and able to demonstrate that the audit engagement has assigned to it sufficient partners and staff with appropriate time and skill to perform the audit in accordance with all applicable auditing and ethical standards, irrespective of the audit fee to be charged.]

Offering business advice to audit clients creates a potential self-review threat to objectivity. It depends on the sort of advice offered but it is possible that the auditor in consequent years may have to audit aspects of the business affected by the advice given. This would be particularly relevant if the practitioner provided advice with regard to systems design. It would be possible to offer both services if Monet & Co can use different teams to provide each service. Given that they have 12 offices, it may be possible to keep these services completely separate and they may be able to offer both.

[**UK syllabus**: According to Ethical Standard section 5, offering a non-audit service such as business advice to audit clients potentially creates self-interest, self-review, management and advocacy threats to objectivity.]

Offering services for free as part of a promotion is not prohibited but, similar to lowballing, this increases the threat to competence and due care if sufficient time and resources are not allocated to the task. This may also devalue the services offered by Monet & Co as they may be perceived as being a promotional tool as opposed to a professional service.

Firms of accountants are permitted to offer free consultations, so this does not create any specific threats. The phrase 'drop in and see us' may cause a problem with potential clients though as it may not always be possible to expect to see senior staff members without an appointment. To avoid damaging the professional profile of the firm, Monet & Co would need to make sure they had a dedicated member of staff available to meet potential customers who is available without prior notice.

Finally, Monet & Co is not permitted to use the term 'Chartered Certified Accountants' because less than 50% of the partners of the firm are ACCA members. This reference should be removed.

(b) Renoir Co

Mr Cassatt's threat that he will seek an alternative auditor unless the audit is cheaper and less intrusive than the prior year constitutes an intimidation threat to objectivity. This has arisen because Mr Cassatt is trying to unduly influence the conduct of the audit of Renoir Co.

The audit manager or partner should arrange a meeting with the senior management of Renoir Co and the audit committee, if one exists, and they should explain how the audit has to be performed and how the fee is calculated. They should take care to explain the professional standards which they have to comply with and the terms of the engagement which the client agreed to, specifically that management should provide all necessary documents and explanations deemed necessary by the auditor to collect sufficient appropriate evidence. It should be explained that due to the need to comply with these standards, they cannot guarantee to reduce either the volume of procedures or the audit fee.

Monet & Co should also consider the integrity of Mr Cassatt. If the audit firm considers any threat created too significant, then they may wish to resign from the engagement. If not, it may be necessary to use more senior, experienced staff on the assignment who are less likely to be intimidated by Mr Cassatt while performing audit fieldwork.

If the audit proceeds, it should be ensured that the planning is performed by an appropriately experienced member of the audit team. This should be reviewed thoroughly by the audit manager and the partner to ensure that the procedures recommended are appropriate to the risk assessment performed. In this way Monet & Co can ensure that any unnecessary, and potential time wasting, procedures are avoided.

The audit manager should then make sure that Mr Cassatt is given adequate notice of the timing of the audit and provide him with a list of documentation which will be required during the course of the audit so that Renoir Co may prepare for the visit by the audit team. The manager could also recommend that Mr Cassatt and his team make specific time available to meet with the audit team and then request that the audit team use that time to ask all the necessary enquiries of the client. This should minimise any disruption experienced by the client during fieldwork.

The overdue fees create a self-interest threat. A self-interest threat may be created if fees due from an audit client remain unpaid for a long time, especially if not paid before the issue of the auditor's report for the following year.

The audit firm should determine the amount of fee which is unpaid, and whether it could be perceived to be a loan made to the client. It may be a relatively insignificant amount, and it may not be long overdue, in which case the threat to objectivity is not significant.

[**UK syllabus**: Ethical Standard section 4 states that ordinarily, any outstanding fees for the previous audit period are paid before the audit firm commences any new audit work. Where they are not, it is important for the audit engagement partner to understand the nature of any disagreement or other issue.]

If the self-interest threat is significant, then no audit work should be performed until the fees are paid. This decision, and the reason for it, should be communicated to the management of Renoir Co or their audit committee, if possible.

(c) Homer Winslow Co

The acquisition of the accountancy firm by Monet & Co creates a potential conflict of interest because Monet & Co will become the auditor of both Homer Winslow Co and their competitor Pissarro Co.

There is nothing ethically inappropriate having clients in the same industry; this is actually normal practice and allows firms of accountants to develop industry specialisms which allow them to offer high quality, expert services. It is therefore likely that firms will have clients which compete in the same industry.

Acting for two competing companies may give rise to ethical threats though. It may be perceived that the auditor cannot offer objective services and advice to a company where it also audits a competitor. The clients may also be concerned that commercially sensitive information may be inadvertently, or intentionally, passed on to the competitor via the auditor.

The main safeguard available is to disclose the potential conflict to all parties involved. If both Homer Winslow Co and Pissarro Co accept the situation, it is appropriate for Monet & Co to continue in its capacity as auditor to both as long as appropriate safeguards are put in place. These include:

- The use of separate engagement teams
- Issuing clear guidelines to the teams on issues of security and confidentiality
- The use of confidentiality agreements by audit team members
- Regular review of the safeguards by an independent partner.

Monet & Co must also evaluate whether there are sufficient resources available to conduct the audits of both companies using separate teams. If not, the audit firm will not be able to accept the additional work into the department.

If either Pissarro Co or Homer Winslow Co do not give their consent, then Monet & Co must resign as the auditor of one of the companies.

If this is the case, a number of ethical and commercial considerations should be made before deciding which client should be rejected. Monet & Co will need to consider the risk profile of both clients and should conduct appropriate acceptance/ continuance procedures for both clients prior to making any final decision. From a commercial perspective, Monet & Co may also consider which of the two clients provides the highest audit revenue. Homer Winslow Co appears to be the larger company currently but Pissarro Co is a rapidly expanding business which could be a more lucrative audit client in the future. In this case Monet & Co should also consider if they will be able to offer the range of services required by the rapidly expanding Pissarro Co without creating any self-interest or self-review threats to independence.

Monet & Co should also consider if any non-audit services are currently offered to the clients and whether additional services could be offered to either of them in the future. As a rapidly expanding business, it is possible that Pissarro Co will require more services than the established Homer Winslow Co.

Examiner's comments

This was the most popular of the optional questions and was answered by a significant number of candidates. Performance on this question was generally strong and most candidates were able to identify and discuss the relevant issues. The question focused on ethics and practice management, and candidates were required to critique the appropriateness of advertising being utilised by the firm. The majority of students were well prepared to answer this question with a format that has been used before, and were able to confidently identify and evaluate the ethical issues associated with the proposed advertisement

The second part of this question combined overdue fees with an intimidation threat and again was well answered. The final part dealt with a conflict of interest between two competing clients arising after an acquisition of another firm and candidates attempting this question tended to score well.

ACCA marking scheme			
			Marks
	Up to 1½ marks for each point of evaluation and up to 1 mark for each response recommended.		
(a)	**Advertisement**		
	–	Advert reflects adversely on other professional accountants	
	–	Misleading with regards to size of firm	
	–	Misleading comments regarding expertise of tax team	
	–	Threat to professional behaviour by guaranteeing to save tax	
	–	Lowballing – self-interest threat and threat to professional competence and due care	
	–	Potential self-review threat from business advice	
	–	Free consultations permitted	
	–	Remove misleading claims from advert	
	–	Separate teams for audit and other services advertised	
		Maximum	**7**
(b)	**Renoir Co**		
	–	Intimidation threat to objectivity	
	–	Meet senior management and explain the terms of the audit	
	–	Consider integrity of Jim Cassatt and implications for audit	
	–	Thorough performance and review of planning	
	–	Early notice of audit requirements and logistics	
	–	Self-interest threat created by overdue fees	
	–	Delay audit until fees paid (1 max)	
		Maximum	**7**
(c)	**Homer Winslow Co**		
	–	Conflict of interest	
	–	Normal to audit firms in the same industry	
	–	Threat to objectivity	
	–	Confidentiality threat	
	–	Full disclosure to both clients	
	–	Possible safeguards (½ each, 1 max)	
	–	Consideration of resources available	
	–	Possible resignation from one audit	
		Maximum	**6**
Total			**20**

31 BUNK & CO *Walk in the footsteps of a top tutor*

Top tutor tips

This question covers a range of professional issues that an accountancy firm could encounter. These issues don't just focus on ethical issues but other practice management and quality control issues as well. Each requirement has its own mark allocation therefore make sure you make enough points for each. Your answer to part (c) should contain almost twice as many points as your answer for part (b).

(a) When the audit client imposes fee pressure on the audit firm, an intimidation threat to objectivity arises. An intimidation threat is the threat that a professional accountant will be deterred from acting objectively because of actual or perceived pressures, and gives an example of an intimidation threat where the audit firm is being pressured to reduce inappropriately the extent of work performed in order to match the fee they can obtain to the work performed.

The matter should have been discussed with Wire Co's audit committee, with the audit firm stressing that the new locations would lead to an increased scope of the audit, and therefore the fee should increase rather than remain the same. It should also be brought to the attention of Bunk & Co's partner responsible for ethics.

The fee pressure has resulted in the materiality level being increased. This leads to a risk that insufficient audit evidence may have been obtained to support the audit opinion, with the risk heightened by the fact that some review procedures were not carried out. This in itself indicates that appropriate quality control procedures have not been applied to the audit. ISA 220 *Quality Control for an Audit of Financial Statements* requires the audit engagement partner to review the audit documentation to be satisfied that audit work is complete and that sufficient appropriate audit evidence has been obtained to support the conclusions reached and for the auditor's report to be issued.

There are also quality control issues with the selection of samples to be used in tests of detail. First, the use of judgmental sampling may result in sample sizes which are smaller than would have been selected using statistical sampling methods, or in the selection of items which are not representative of the whole population.

ISA 530 *Audit Sampling* requires the auditor to determine a sample size sufficient to reduce sampling risk to an acceptably low level, and to select items for the sample in such a way that each sampling unit in the population has a chance of selection. The risk is that the use of judgement has led to inappropriate audit conclusions being made.

Second, it seems that some items in the populations were completely excluded from the sample. There is a high risk that these items have not been subject to sufficient audit procedures and that the relevant assertions have not been covered by audit testing. For example, if the non-current assets have not been physically verified, and no other procedures relevant to their existence have been performed, then assets recognised in the financial statements may be overstated.

Given the pressure on fees which seems to be affecting the quality of audit work performed, Bunk & Co may wish to consider whether it is appropriate to continue with the audit engagement. The audit firm's concerns should be communicated to those charged with governance of Wire Co, and the audit committee should be made aware of the implications of the fee pressure on the audit.

(b) The off-shoring of audit work has become increasingly common in the audit profession in the last few years, with global audit firms using low-cost overseas audit offices or service centres to perform some audit procedures. There is no regulation to prohibit this practice, but quality control implications have been brought into question.

If the overseas office is performing only low-risk and non-judgmental work, the risk to audit quality is relatively low. However, it seems in the case of Wire Co's audit other more subjective tasks were included in the off-shoring arrangement, such as the review of board minutes. In order to properly assess the contents of the board minutes for audit implications, the work should be performed by an auditor with sufficient knowledge and understanding of the audit client to be able to identify matters which are significant in the context of that audit. It is unlikely that an auditor in an overseas office with no direct understanding or experience of Wire Co would be able to identify relevant matters for the attention of the rest of the audit team.

If Bunk & Co wishes to continue the off-shoring of audit procedures, then controls must be put in place to ensure that only appropriate tasks are included in the arrangement, and that monitoring and review procedures are performed to give comfort on the quality of the work performed. The audit firm must ensure that its firm-wide policies adhere to the requirements of ISQC 1 *Quality Control for Firms that Perform Audits and Reviews of Financial Statements, and Other Assurance and Related Services Engagements*, and that commercial considerations do not take priority over the performance of high quality audits.

Tutorial note

Credit will be awarded for other relevant comments on the issue of off-shoring audit work.

(c) Russell Bell moving from Wire Co to Bunk & Co to take up the position of audit partner creates potential self-interest, self-review or familiarity threats to objectivity if a member of the audit team has recently served as a director, officer, or employee of the audit client. Though the threats may be mitigated somewhat by him not being a formal member of the audit team of Wire Co, the fact that Russell helped the audit team by providing information about the audited entity means that the threats described above apply in this situation, and there is a perception of a lack of independence of the audit team.

The Code of Ethics requires that if, during the period covered by the auditor's report, a member of the audit team served as a director or officer of the audit client, or was an employee in a position to exert significant influence over the preparation of the client's accounting records or the financial statements on which the firm will express an opinion, that person may not be included in the audit team. Clearly Russell's former position as finance director of Wire Co means that this requirement should have been applied to him.

[**UK syllabus**: Ethical Standard section 2 contains similar guidance and a more specific requirement, stating that where a former director or a former employee of an audited entity, who was in a position to exert significant influence over the preparation of the financial statements, joins the audit firm, that individual shall not be assigned to a position in which he or she is able to influence the conduct and outcome of the audit for that entity or its affiliates for a period of two years following the date of leaving the audited entity.]

The matter should be discussed with Bunk & Co's partner responsible for ethics, and it should also be discussed with Wire Co's audit committee, who are responsible for oversight of auditor independence.

The second issue is that Russell retained a shareholding in Wire Co for six months after his appointment as an audit partner in Bunk & Co. This gives rise to a self-interest threat to objectivity, as it would have been in Russell's interests to act in such a way as to maximise his financial interest in Wire Co until the point when he sold his shares. There is a general prohibition on auditors holding a financial interest in an audit client, and when a financial interest arises, it should be disposed of immediately in the case of an audit team member, or as soon as possible in the case of an individual who is not a member of the audit team. Given Russell's seniority, and the fact that he seems to have closely advised the audit team on matters relating to Wire Co, he should have made the disposal immediately.

Concerns may arise over Bunk & Co's procedures in relation to staff and partner disclosure of financial interests in audited entities. Six months is a long period for the shares to have been held, and the firm should have procedures in place to ensure that such matters are monitored and quickly resolved. A review of the firm's procedures should take place, and Russell should be asked why he did not dispose of the shares more quickly.

Finally, the audit firm's policy on cross-selling non-audit services raises ethical issues. A self-interest threat is created when a member of the audit team is evaluated on or compensated for selling non-assurance services to that audit client. This is because the audit team member clearly has a financial interest in successful cross-selling, which may result in the selling of services which are inappropriate to the client, or which give rise to other ethical threats which exist when non-audit services are provided to audited entities.

The significance of the self-interest threat depends on:

- The proportion of the individual's compensation or performance evaluation which is based on the sale of such services
- The role of the individual on the audit team
- Whether promotion decisions are influenced by the sale of such services.

The Code of Ethics states that a key audit partner shall not be evaluated on or compensated based on that partner's success in selling non-assurance services to the partner's audit client. Therefore if Bunk & Co is to continue with this policy, care must be taken that partners' performance are not evaluated based on their success in cross-selling to their audit clients.

It is not prohibited for other audit team members to cross-sell, but safeguards must be in place to reduce the potential threat to an acceptable level, such as a review of audit work performed.

It may be prudent, however, for the audit firm to consider other ways to increase revenue and to evaluate staff performance which do not raise threats to objectivity.

[**UK syllabus**: Ethical Standard section 4 contains more restrictive requirements. It is not permissible for the performance evaluation of engagement team members to include elements relating to the cross-selling of goods and services to audited entities, and remuneration should not include elements based on such activity.]

Examiner comments

This question was broadly themed around audit quality and ethical issues and featured the audit of Wire Co, for which the auditor's report on the most recent financial statements had just been issued. The question was split into three short scenarios, with the requirement to comment on the quality control, ethical and professional issues contained in each with respect to the audit of Wire Co and the firm-wide policies of the audit firm. Candidates were also required to recommend any actions to be taken by the audit firm.

Part (a) described how the audit committee of Wire Co had refused to agree to an increase in audit fees despite an increase in the company's operations. Consequently the audit firm increased the materiality level used during the audit, reduced sample sizes used when obtaining audit evidence and cut out some review procedures. Many candidates attempted this part of the question well. Effective answers explained the intimidation threat to objectivity caused by fee pressure and went on to discuss the impact of each of the issues raised in the scenario on the quality of the audit that had been performed. It was pleasing to see many candidates discuss matters such as sampling risk and the need for review procedures to assure the quality of audit work and to reduce the audit firm's detection risk. Weaker answers tended to be repetitive, and for each of the issues simply say that "not enough evidence could be obtained" resulting in material misstatements and an inappropriate audit opinion.

Part (b) focused on the issue of off-shoring audit work, which had been discussed in an article. The scenario described how some of the audit work in relation to Wire Co had been performed by an overseas office. The work performed by the overseas office included numerical checks on calculations and reading the board minutes of Wire Co. Answers ranged in quality, with some good attempts which identified that while off-shoring can bring efficiencies to an audit, care must be taken in deciding the type of work that is performed by the overseas office. From this scenario it should have been identified that off-shoring procedures such as the reading of board minutes to identify audit issues was not appropriate, but relatively few answers mentioned this point. Weaker answers tended to suggest that overseas offices would be incompetent and unable to perform even the simplest of audit procedures. Some candidates misinterpreted the information provided and assumed that the scenario was about using component auditors in a group situation, which was not the case.

Part (c) centred on the fact that the former finance director of Wire Co had joined the audit firm as an audit partner, and while he was not involved with the audit, he had discussed Wire Co with the audit engagement partner. Most candidates realised that the former finance director could have influenced the partner and had motivation to do so given that he held shares in Wire Co for a period of time after joining the audit firm. Stronger candidates were able to clearly explain the specific ethical threats that arose from the scenario, provided sensible recommendations, and also commented on the audit firm needing stronger firm-wide policies in the event of recruiting new audit partners from audit clients. The scenario also stated that audit team members were being encouraged to cross-sell non-audit services to audit clients and that they would be appraised on this. The answers here tended not to focus on the problems caused by appraising staff on their success in selling services to audit clients but instead discussed generally the ethical problems of providing non-audit services to audit clients. While not irrelevant, these discussions tended to be very general and not applied to the information in the scenario, resulting in answers that lacked focus.

Generally, when candidates are discussing ethical threats they must take care to explain why a threat has arisen. Many answers simply stated that a threat existed, for example by saying "holding shares in a client is a self- interest threat" but did not develop the point further. This limits the amount of marks which can be awarded.

It was also clear that many candidates were not guided by the mark allocation for the various parts of the question, and a significant number of answers to part (c) were the same length as the answer to part (a). As mentioned earlier, candidates should bear the mark allocation in mind, and use it to determine how long to spend in answering each part of the question.

	ACCA Marking scheme	
		Marks
	Up to 1½ marks for each relevant point explained, to include 1 mark for each action recommended and ½ mark for identification of ethical threats.	
(a)	**Fee pressure and sampling risk**	
	– Intimidation threat identified and explained	
	– Fee should not remain the same when the scope of audit is increased	
	– Discuss with audit committee and communicate with those charged with governance	
	– Increased materiality level reduces audit work and increases DR	
	– Audit work to be reviewed for completeness and sufficiency (1 mark)	
	– Use of judgment increases sampling risk	
	– Sample cannot be representative of population as items excluded	
	Maximum	6
(b)	**Off-shoring audit work**	
	– No regulation to prohibit off-shoring arrangements	
	Increasingly common way to improve audit efficiency	
	– Lack knowledge and experience of the client	
	– Off-shoring should focus on low-risk and low-judgment areas	
	– Strong controls and monitoring should be in place	
	Maximum	5
(c)	**Recent service with audit client, financial self-interest and cross-selling services**	
	– Recent service with client creates self-interest, self-review and familiarity threats	
	– Persons joining audit firm from a client should not be part of that client's audit team	
	– Russell seems to have acted as if he were a member of the audit team	
	– A quality control review should be performed	
	– Russell's shareholding creates a self-interest threat	
	– The shareholding should have been disposed of immediately	
	– Consider why this did not happen – firm's policies should be reviewed	
	– Cross-selling creates a self-interest threat	
	– Key audit partners should not be evaluated based on cross-selling	
	– Other audit team members can cross-sell if appropriate safeguards are in place	
	Maximum	9
Total		20

32 RYDER & CO *Walk in the footsteps of a top tutor*

Top tutor tips

This question is split into four separate requirements covering a range of ethical and professional issues.

Take note of the mark allocation for each requirement and tailor the length of your answers accordingly. Part (a) is only worth 4 marks whereas part (d) is worth 7 marks. Therefore you need to allow more time for part (d) and consequently include more points.

(a) Business risk is defined in ISA 315 *Identifying and Assessing the Risks of Material Misstatement Through Understanding the Entity and its Environment*. The definition states that business risk is a risk resulting from significant conditions, events, circumstances, actions or inactions which could adversely affect an entity's ability to achieve its objectives and execute its strategies, or from the setting of inappropriate objectives and strategies.

Risk of material misstatement is defined in ISA 200 *Overall Objectives of the Independent Auditor and the Conduct of an Audit in Accordance with ISAs* as the risk that the financial statements are materially misstated prior to audit. Risk of material misstatement comprises inherent risk and control risk.

ISA 315 states that the auditor shall perform risk assessment procedures to provide a basis for the identification and assessment of risks of material misstatement at the financial statement and assertion levels. Business risks can be broken down into operational risk, financial risk and compliance risk. Each of these components can have a direct impact on the financial statements, and therefore understanding the components of business risk can help the auditor to identify risks of misstatement, and to design a response to that risk.

Some business risks impact the inherent risk component of risk of material misstatement. For example, the auditor may have identified that an audited entity has significant levels of debt with covenants attached. The business risk is that the covenants are breached and the debt recalled. An associated inherent risk at the financial statement level is that the financial statements could be manipulated to avoid breaching the debt covenant.

Other business risks impact on the control risk component of risk of material misstatement. For example, the auditor may have identified that an audited entity has a business risk due to having lost key members of personnel in the accounting department. This has a clear impact on control risk, as it means the accounting department is short of competent staff and errors are likely to go undetected and uncorrected.

Therefore the ISAs' approach to planning an audit is underpinned by the concept that it is essential for an auditor to understand the business risks of an audited entity in order to effectively identify and respond to risks of material misstatement.

(b) Outsourcing is when certain functions within a business are contracted out to third parties known as service organisations. It is common for companies to outsource one or more of it functions, with payroll, IT and human resources being examples of functions which are typically outsourced.

Outsourcing does have an impact on audit planning. ISA 402 *Audit Considerations Relating to an Entity Using a Service Organisation* requires the auditor to obtain an understanding of how the audited entity (also known as the user entity) uses the services of a service organisation in the user entity's operations, including the following matters:

- The nature of the services provided by the service organisation and the significance of those services to the audited entity, including the effect on internal control
- The nature and materiality of the transactions processed or accounts or financial reporting processes affected by the service organisation
- The degree of interaction between the activities of the service organisation and those of the audited entity
- The nature of the relationship between the audited entity and the service organisation, including the relevant contractual terms.

The reasons for the auditor being required to understand these matters is so that any risk of material misstatement created by the use of the service organisation can be identified and an appropriate response planned.

The auditor is also required under ISA 402 to evaluate the design and implementation of relevant controls at the audited entity which relate to the services provided by the service organisation, including those which are applied to the transactions processed by the service organisation. This is to obtain understanding of the control risk associated with the outsourced function, for example, whether the transactions and information provided by the service organisation is monitored and whether checks are performed prior to inclusion in the financial statements.

Information should be available from the audited entity to enable the understanding outlined above to be obtained, for example, through reports received from the service organisation, technical manuals and the contract between the audited entity and the service organisation.

The auditor may decide that further work is necessary in order to evaluate the risk of material misstatement associated with the outsourcing arrangement's impact on the financial statements. It is common for a report on the description and design of controls at a service organisation to be obtained.

A type 1 report focuses on the description and design of controls, whereas a type 2 report also covers the operating effectiveness of the controls. This type of report can provide some assurance over the controls which should have operated at the service organisation.

Alternatively, the auditor may decide to contact the service organisation to request specific information, to visit the service organisation and perform procedures, probably tests on controls, or to use another auditor to perform such procedures. All of these methods of evaluating the service organisation's controls require permission from the client and can be time consuming to perform.

The purpose of obtaining the understanding above is to help the auditor to determine the level of competence of the service organisation, and whether it is independent of the audited entity. This will then impact on the risk of material misstatement assessed for the outsourced function.

(c) A potential conflict between the interest of two audit clients arises from Ryder & Co offering advice to Crow Co on the tender being presented to Hatfield Co. A conflict of interest may create potential threats to objectivity, confidentiality or other threats to compliance with the fundamental ethical principles.

In this scenario, Ryder & Co faces the problem of potentially giving advice to one audit client in relation to another audit client, which threatens objectivity. There may also be problems to do with confidentiality of information, as either party could benefit from information obtained from the audit firm about the other party.

In dealing with conflicts of interest, the significance of any threats should be evaluated, and safeguards must be applied when necessary to eliminate the threats or reduce them to an acceptable level. The most important safeguard is disclosure by Ryder & Co. The audit firm should notify both Crow Co and Hatfield Co of the potential conflict of interest and obtain their consent to act.

Other possible safeguards could include:

- The use of separate engagement teams
- Procedures to prevent access to information (for example, strict physical separation of such teams, confidential and secure data filing)
- Clear guidelines for members of the engagement team on issues of security and confidentiality
- The use of confidentiality agreements signed by employees and partners of the firm; and
- Regular review of the application of safeguards by a senior individual not involved with relevant client engagements.

Ryder & Co may decide, having evaluated the threats and available safeguards, that the threats cannot be reduced to an acceptable level, in which case the firm should decline from giving advice to Crow Co regarding the tender.

(d) If Ryder & Co were to be involved with the events organised by Campbell Co, this could be perceived as a close business relationship. Such relationships can arise when an audit firm has a commercial relationship or common financial interest with an audit client. Examples in which a close business relationship can arise include:

- Having a financial interest in a joint venture with the client or a controlling owner, director or officer or other individual who performs senior managerial activities for that client.
- Arrangements to combine one or more services or products of the firm with one or more services or products of the client and to market the package with reference to both parties.
- Distribution or marketing arrangements under which the firm distributes or markets the client's products or services, or the client distributes or markets the firm's products or services.

[**UK syllabus**: Ethical Standard section 2 contains similar examples].

The proposal for Ryder & Co to invest some cash in the business opportunity would give a financial interest to the audit firm in the success of Campbell Co, especially because the profits from the events would be shared between the audit firm and its client. The fact that the audit client and firm are acting together in a joint business arrangement is further apparent from the joint marketing of the events, and that Ryder & Co would supply the speakers at the events.

A self-interest threat to objectivity arises, because Ryder & Co will benefit financially if the events are successful. An intimidation threat could also arise, as Campbell Co could threaten the audit firm with removal from office unless it supports the business opportunity and markets it to its other audit clients.

Ryder & Co must evaluate the significance of these threats, and whether there are safeguards available to reduce the threats to an acceptable level. Unless any financial interest is immaterial and the business relationship is insignificant to the firm and the client or its management, the threat created would be so significant that no safeguards could reduce the threat to an acceptable level. Therefore, unless the financial interest is immaterial and the business relationship is insignificant, the business relationship with Campbell & Co should not be entered into. The fact that the events are nationwide implies that it is a reasonably large operation and could therefore be assessed as significant.

[**UK syllabus**: Ethical standard section 2 contains similar guidance, stating that audit firms shall not enter into business relationships with an audited entity except where they are clearly inconsequential to either party].

There may also be more practical and commercial issues which Ryder & Co should consider, if the threats are considered insignificant enough for the business relationship to continue. The audit firm would need to consider if it has staff with the appropriate skills and expertise to present on technical matters. Also, assuming that it would be more senior staff who presented at the events, this may interfere with client work and leave the audit firm short of staff if the events coincided with busy periods of the year.

In addition, Ryder & Co would need to consider whether it has any surplus cash to invest in the business opportunity, the return which it could expect to receive, and whether it represents a good enough return on investment. An advantage of being involved in the events is that the firm could derive benefits from the marketing and brand awareness which it would be involved in, and possibly generate some new clients. However, these considerations are secondary to the assessment of threats and safeguards discussed above.

Examiner comments

This question contained four different issues with a common requirement to explain the ethical and professional matters relevant to each. This was the most popular of the Section B questions but performance varied tremendously.

Issue (a) focused on business risk and risk of material misstatement, asking candidates to explain each and to explain how identifying business risk relates to risk of material misstatement. Most candidates could attempt the definitions, but some went into far too much detail for the marks available. The relationship between the two types of risk was usually explained by way of example, which was acceptable, and many of the examples were appropriate. The most common mistake seen in answers here was to explain audit risk rather than risk of material misstatement.

Issue (b) focused on outsourcing, and asked candidates to consider, in the context of a manufacturing company that outsourced payroll, how the outsourcing would affect audit planning. There were some good attempts, with most answers identifying issues in relation to access to information, assessment of the internal controls at the service organisation, and the competence of the service organisation. Disappointingly, few answers mentioned type 1 and type 2 reports that are typically obtained in this situation, and many tried to focus on ethical matters such as independence, and therefore didn't specifically address the requirement.

Issue (c) was about a potential conflict of interest between two audit clients and confidentiality of information. The audit firm had been asked to provide advice on a tender for an important contract that one audit client was preparing in relation to a different audit client. Many candidates did correctly determine that a conflict of interest would arise and could recommend appropriate safeguards. However, many answers failed to identify the potential issues surrounding the confidentiality of client information. Some candidates tried to include a comment on every one of the ethical principles – many of which were irrelevant. It is a better exam technique to focus on the most relevant of the ethical threats, and not to try to cover all of them.

Issue (d) explained that the audit firm had been approached to invest in a business opportunity with an audit client, which proposed the audit firm invest some cash and supply personnel to work in a joint business venture, with profit being shared between the audit firm and the audit client. Most answers picked up on the potential for a close business relationship to be created with an audit client, and many could discuss that the severity of the ethical threats resulting from such an investment are unlikely to be acceptable. Some answers also considered the commercial angle, and many also reached an appropriate conclusion. Weaker answers listed out all of the possible threats to objectivity without any real application to the scenario.

In summary, the answers showed that many candidates have a good understanding of ethical issues and can apply that knowledge to deal with specific scenarios. There has been some improvement in the way that candidates discuss ethical matters, with threats usually being explained, their significance evaluated, and relevant safeguards suggested. Where candidates performed less well on this question it tended to be due to them not appropriately assessing the mark allocation. It was common to see most written in the answer to (a) and less for issues (c) and (d), when the mark allocation would suggest otherwise.

ACCA marking scheme		
		Marks
	Up to 1½ marks for each comment/explanation/definition:	
(a)	**Risk assessment**	
	– Definition of business risk (1 mark)	
	– Definition of risk of material misstatement (1 mark)	
	– Business risks impact on the financial statements and therefore risk of material misstatement	
	– Business risk impacts inherent risk	
	– Business risk impacts control risk	
	Maximum	4
(b)	**Outsourcing**	
	– Need to assess significance of outsourced function on financial statements	
	– Need to understand relationship and interaction between audited entity and service organisation	
	– Obtain understanding of the service organisation including internal controls	
	– Means of obtaining understanding – type 1 and type 2 reports	
	– Other means of obtaining understanding – requesting information, performing tests on controls at the service organisation	
	Maximum	4
(c)	**Conflict of interest**	
	– Identify/explain the conflict of interest	
	– Threats to objectivity and confidentiality created	
	– Safeguard of disclosure to both parties	
	– Other safeguards (½ mark each), e.g. separate teams confidentiality agreements review of situation by independent partner	
	– If threats too significant the advice should not be given	
	Maximum	5

(d)	**Business opportunity** – Close business relationship/financial interest in a client – Threats created – self-interest and intimidation – Can only be accepted if the interest is insignificant – Unlikely to be insignificant due to nationwide programme – Consider commercial angle – return on investment/cash availability – Skills and competence to provide speakers – Resource availability	
	Maximum	**7**
Total		**20**

33 CHESTER & CO *Walk in the footsteps of a top tutor*

Top tutor tips

This was a straightforward ethical and professional issues question and should not pose too many problems. There are three clients to deal with and the mark allocation for each is clearly shown. Make enough points for the marks available and remember to consider the significance of the issues as well as identifying them and explaining them. Safeguards should also be included in your answer.

(a) Tetbury Co

Chester & Co needs to conduct customer due diligence (know your client) procedures to ensure that anti-money laundering requirements are adhered to. This is especially important given the highly regulated nature of Tetbury Co's business. Background checks will need to be made on Juan Stanton and other members of management, and the nature of the business including the sources of income must be fully understood before deciding on accepting the audit appointment.

The competence of the audit firm in relation to the audit of a financial services firm should be evaluated, as it is a relatively specialised area. A self-interest threat to professional competence and due care is created if the engagement team does not possess, or cannot acquire, the competencies necessary to properly carry out the engagement.

Chester & Co should consider whether it is appropriate to be appointed as auditor to Tetbury Co from an ethical point of view. The Code states that before accepting a new client relationship, a professional accountant in public practice shall determine whether acceptance would create any threats to compliance with the fundamental principles. Threats to integrity may arise from questionable activities by management of the company or from inappropriate financial reporting.

It appears that Tetbury Co's management may lack integrity due to its past investigation by the financial services authority. Chester & Co should find out more about this matter, for example, reading press reports or contacting the financial services authority for more information.

In addition, the resignation of the previous auditors over a disagreement indicates a possible problem with management's integrity. There may also be ethical issues, for example, management may have intimidated the previous auditors over the financial reporting issue which prompted their resignation.

Chester & Co should request permission to contact the previous audit firm to obtain further information on the reasons behind the resignation, and if there are any other matters which should be considered in deciding whether to take on the audit appointment. It is important that all relevant facts are known before an acceptance decision is made. A threat to professional competence and due care arises where the appointment is accepted without full knowledge of relevant information.

Juan's comment about deficient controls is also a cause for concern, as it indicates that the audit would be high risk. While this alone does not mean that the audit should not be taken on, Chester & Co should consider whether the audit risk can be reduced to an acceptable level, for example, by using an experienced audit team and a substantive audit approach. As part of its client acceptance decision, Chester & Co should consider whether the fee for the audit outweighs the risk involved.

The audit firm could apply a safeguard such as securing Juan's commitment to improve the company's control environment before accepting the client.

Tetbury Co is owner-managed. This means that management comes to rely on the auditor for advice and recommendations and the audit firm could be perceived to be taking on the responsibilities of management. This is especially relevant to Juan's suggestion that the audit firm can provide business advice.

According to the Code, this situation gives rise to potential self-review and self-interest threats to objectivity. If the audit firm were to assume management responsibilities, then no safeguards can reduce the threat to an acceptable level. However, providing advice and recommendations to assist management in discharging its responsibilities is not assuming a management responsibility.

If the audit appointment is accepted, Chester & Co may wish to obtain written confirmation from management that it acknowledges responsibility for business decisions taken.

(b) Stratford Co

The request to attend a meeting with the company's bank can give rise to an advocacy threat to objectivity. The Code defines an advocacy threat as the threat that a professional accountant will promote a client's or employer's position to the point that the professional accountant's objectivity is compromised. In this case, the managing director may want the audit engagement partner to support a view that Stratford Co will be able to continue as a going concern and that the loan ultimately will be repaid. This means that the audit partner is promoting the client which leads to the creation of an advocacy threat.

In addition, from a legal perspective, the audit firm must be careful not to create the impression that they are in any way guaranteeing the future existence of the company or providing assurance on the draft financial statements. In legal terms, attending the meeting and promoting the interests of the client could create legal 'proximity', which increases the risk of legal action against the auditor in the event of Stratford Co defaulting on any loan provided by the bank.

It may be possible for a partner other than the audit engagement partner to attend the meeting with the bank, which would be a form of safeguard against the ethical threat. Chester & Co's partner responsible for ethics should consider the severity of the threat and whether this, or another safeguard, could reduce the threat to an acceptable level.

There is also an intimidation threat to objectivity caused by the managing director's hint at putting the audit out to tender. An audit firm being threatened with dismissal from a client engagement represents an intimidation threat. The managing director's actions should also lead to questions over his integrity, and the audit firm may wish to consider resigning from the audit if the threat becomes too severe.

A self-interest threat may be created if fees due from an audit client remain unpaid for a long time, especially if a significant part is not paid before the issue of the auditor's report for the following year. The audit firm should determine the amount of fee that is unpaid, and whether it could be perceived to be a loan made to the client. It may be a relatively insignificant amount, and it may not be long overdue as it relates to work performed less than four months ago, in which case the threat to objectivity is not significant.

(c) Banbury Co

Providing an actuarial valuation service is an example of providing a non-assurance service. The provision of such services can create threats to objectivity of self-review and self-interest. The self-review threat arises because the defined benefit pension plan on which Chester & Co has been asked to provide a valuation service is included in the statement of financial position, and the audit firm would need to audit the figure which has been generated by a member of the firm. The self-interest threat arises from the fee which would be paid to the firm.

Chester & Co needs to evaluate the significance of the threats and whether safeguards could be used to reduce the threats to an acceptable level. In assessing the self-review threat the following factors should be considered:

- Whether the valuation will have a material effect on the financial statements.
- The extent of the client's involvement in determining and approving the valuation methodology and other significant matters of judgement.
- The availability of established methodologies and professional guidelines.
- For valuations involving standard or established methodologies, the degree of subjectivity inherent in the item.
- The reliability and extent of the underlying data.
- The degree of dependence on future events of a nature that could create significant volatility inherent in the amounts involved.
- The extent and clarity of the disclosures in the financial statements.

A key matter to be considered is the materiality of the pension plan to Banbury Co's financial statements. Banbury Co is a listed company, and therefore a public interest entity. The Code states that an audit firm shall not provide valuation services to an audit client which is a public interest entity if the valuations would have a material effect, separately or in the aggregate, on the financial statements on which the firm will express an opinion.

Based on the 2012 financial statements, the pension liability at the year end represented only 0.3% of total assets and was immaterial. Chester & Co should consider whether there are any indications that the pension deficit may have become more significant during the year, which may have caused the balance to become material. In which case the audit firm should not provide the valuation service to Banbury Co.

An actuarial valuation involves significant subjectivity, for example, in determining the appropriate discount rate, and in estimating key variables to be used in the calculations. It is also unlikely that Banbury Co's management will possess sufficient knowledge and experience to have much involvement, if any, in the valuation. However, it may be possible to use safeguards to reduce the threats to an acceptable level.

Examples of such safeguards include:

- Having a professional who was not involved in providing the valuation service review the audit or valuation work performed; or
- Making arrangements so that personnel providing such services do not participate in the audit engagement.

Examiner's comments

This was the most popular of the Section B questions, and was generally well attempted. Three short scenarios were provided, describing a range of situations giving rise to ethical threats and other issues, with the requirement to identify and discuss the ethical and other professional issues raised, and to recommend any actions to be taken by the audit firm for each of the scenarios given. This is a fairly standard type of question for P7, and many candidates performed well, obviously having practiced some past exam questions.

Requirement (a) described a potential new audit client, a small owner-managed company providing financial services. There were several issues that candidates should have spotted in the scenario including a potential lack of integrity of the company's managing director, potential self-interest and self-review threats arising from the provision of non-audit services, threats arising from non-compliance with the regulatory body, and a potential for audit pre-conditions not to be met. The majority of candidates picked up on most of these issues and explained the ethical threats well. There has been a definite improvement in the way that candidates tackle this type of question, and in many cases close to the maximum marks were awarded.

Requirement (b) outlined the situation of an existing client facing going concern problems. The audit engagement partner had been asked to accompany the managing director to a meeting with the bank where additional finance would be sought, and there were intimidation threats in that the client had threatened to put the audit out for tender, and there were also outstanding fees. Again, candidates generally did well on this requirement, identifying and explaining the correct ethical threats, and on the whole recommending appropriate courses of action. The only problem in some scripts was a focus on the lack of integrity of the managing director, rather than discussing specific ethical threats raised.

Requirement (c) described the situation in which a listed client company had asked the audit firm to perform an actuarial valuation of its pension plan. The audit firm had an appropriately qualified person to perform the work, and as with the other requirements of this question, on the whole this was well attempted. Some answers failed to correctly calculate the materiality of the pension plan to the financial statements, and in some answers the fact that the client was a listed entity was not considered. However most candidates suggested an appropriate course of action in response to the ethical matters identified.

ACCA marking scheme

		Marks
	Generally 1 mark for each point identified and discussed:	
(a)	**Tetbury Co**	
	– Customer due diligence/know your client procedures	
	– Audit firm's competence to audit a financial services client	
	– Acceptance decision should also consider ethical threats	
	– Management integrity - investigation by financial services authority	
	– Management integrity - inappropriate financial reporting	
	– Management may have intimidated the previous auditors	
	– Contact previous auditors for further information	
	– Controls appear weak leading to high audit risk	
	– Responses to high risk should be considered, e.g. use of experienced audit team	
	– Confirm client's intention to improve controls	
	– Assuming management responsibility giving business advice	
	– Self-review and self-interest threats created	
	– Safeguard e.g. management acknowledge responsibility for business decisions	
	Maximum	8
(b)	**Stratford Co**	
	– Advocacy threat created by attending meeting	
	– Legal proximity may be created by attending meeting	
	– Intimidation threat from threat of removal from office	
	– Consider appropriate safeguards	
	– Integrity of the managing director questionable	
	– Overdue fees may represent self-interest threat	
	– But amount may be insignificant and not long overdue	
	Maximum	6
(c)	**Banbury Co**	
	– Valuation service creates self-review and self-interest threats	
	– Service cannot be provided if the pension deficit is material	
	– Calculate and comment on materiality in 2013 financial statements	
	– Other matters to consider including level of subjectivity, lack of informed management (1 mark each)	
	– Safeguards may be used to reduce threat to acceptable level (1 mark each)	
	Maximum	6
Total		**20**

34 WESTON & CO *Walk in the footsteps of a top tutor*

Top tutor tips

This question is split into two parts, with ethical and professional issues being part (b) and part (a) dealing with tendering.

For the tender document you need to identify ways in which you can sell your firm to the client. Try and match the firm with the prospective client from the information in the scenario. Don't just give rote learnt knowledge without applying it to the scenario.

The ethical requirement focuses on long association of senior personnel with an audit client. Identify the name of the threat and explain why long association creates an ethical issue. The requirement also asks for discussion of whether the engagement partner can become quality control reviewer of the same client in the future. Don't forget to include this in your answer.

(a) (i) Matters to be included in the audit proposal

Outline of Weston & Co

A brief outline of the audit firm, including a description of different services offered, and an outline of the firm's international locations. This will be important to Jones Co given that it wishes to expand into overseas markets and will be looking for an audit firm with experience in different countries. The document should also outline the range of services which Weston & Co can provide, and any specialism which the firm has in auditing recruitment companies.

Identify the audit requirements of Jones Co

There should be an outline of the statutory audit requirement in the country in which Jones Co is incorporated, to confirm that the company is now at the size which necessitates a full audit of the financial statements. As this is the first time an audit is required, it will be important to outline the regulatory framework and the duties of auditors and of management in relation to the audit requirement.

Audit approach

A description of the proposed audit approach, outlining the stages of the audit process and the audit methodology used by the firm should be given. The description should state that the audit will be conducted in accordance with ISA requirements. Weston & Co should emphasise the need for thorough testing of opening balances and comparatives given that this is the first year that the financial statements will be audited. The risk-based nature of the audit methodology should be explained, and that it will involve an assessment of accounting systems and internal controls. Controls may not be good given the limited resources of the accounting function, so the audit approach is likely to be substantive in nature.

The audit firm may at this stage wish to explain that while the audit should not be 'disruptive', the audit team will require some input from Jones Co's employees, especially the accountant, and other personnel including Bentley may need to make themselves available to respond to the audit firm's requests for information and to discuss matters relating to the audit.

The proposal should outline the various communications which will be made with those charged with governance during the audit process, and highlight the value added from such communications, for example, recommendations on any control deficiencies.

Deadlines

The audit firm should clarify the timescale to be used for the audit. Bentley has requested that the audit is completed within four months of the year end. This seems to be reasonable; it should be possible for the audit of a relatively small company with simple transactions and a full-time accountant to be completed within that timeframe.

Quality control and ethics

Weston & Co should clarify its adherence to the ACCA *Code of Ethics*, and to International Standards on Quality Control. This should provide assurance that the audit firm will provide an unbiased and credible auditor's report. This may be important for the venture capitalists who will wish to gain assurance on the financial information which they are provided with in relation to their investment.

Additional non-audit and assurance services

The audit proposal should describe the various non-audit and assurance related services which Weston & Co would be able to offer Jones Co. These may include, for example, business consultancy and corporate finance advice on overseas expansion and obtaining any necessary additional funding to help the planned overseas expansion. This discussion should clearly state and emphasise that the provision of such services is subject to meeting ethical requirements and will be completely separate from the audit service.

Tutorial note

Credit will be awarded for discussion of other matters which may be included in the audit proposal, where the matters are relevant to the audit of Jones Co.

(ii) Matters to be considered in determining the audit fee

Weston & Co needs to consider a number of matters in determining the audit fee. The commercial need for the firm to make a profit from providing the audit service needs to be considered alongside the client's expectations about the fee level and how it has been arrived at.

First, the audit firm should consider the costs of providing the audit service. This will include primarily the costs of the audit team, so the firm will need to assess the number and seniority of audit team members who will be involved, and the amount of time that they will spend on the audit. There may be the need for auditor's experts to be engaged, and the costs of this should be included if necessary.

Weston & Co will have standard charge out rates which are used when determining an audit fee and these should be used to estimate the total fee. Other costs such as travel costs should also be considered.

Bentley Jones has made some comments in relation to the audit fee which have ethical and other implications. First, he wants the audit fee to be low, and says that he is willing to pay more for other services. One of the problems of a low audit fee is that it can affect audit quality, as the audit firm could be tempted to cut corners and save time in order to minimise the costs of the audit.

Offering an unrealistically low audit fee which is below market rate in order to win or retain an audit client is known as lowballing, and while this practice is not prohibited, the client must not be misled about the amount of work which will be performed and the outputs of the audit. The issue for the client is that an unrealistically low audit fee is unlikely to be sustainable in the long run, leading to unwelcome fee increases in subsequent years.

[**UK syllabus**: Ethical Standard section 4 states that the audit engagement partner must be satisfied and able to demonstrate that the audit engagement has assigned to it sufficient partners and staff with appropriate time and skill to perform the audit in accordance with all applicable auditing and ethical standards, irrespective of the audit fee to be charged. This means that the audit fee should be high enough to allow the use of appropriate resources and that a low fee cannot be tolerated if it would impact on audit quality].

The second issue is that Bentley Jones has suggested that the audit fee should be linked to the success of the company in expanding overseas, on which he wants the audit firm to provide advice. This would mean that the audit fee is being determined on a contingent fee basis. Contingent fees are fees calculated on a predetermined basis relating to the outcome of a transaction or the result of the services performed by the firm.

A contingent fee charged by a firm in respect of an audit engagement creates a self-interest threat which is so significant that no safeguards could reduce the threat to an acceptable level. Accordingly, a firm shall not enter into any such fee arrangement.

[**UK syllabus**: Ethical Standard section 4 states that an audit shall not be conducted on a contingent fee basis].

Weston & Co should explain to Bentley Jones that the audit fee will be determined by the level of audit work which needs to be performed, and cannot be in any way linked to the success of Jones Co or advice which may be given to the firm by its auditors. The fee will be determined by the grade of staff that make up the audit team and the time spent by each of them on the audit.

Tutorial note

Credit will be awarded for discussion of other relevant current issues in relation to the setting of audit fees.

(b) Ethical threats created by long association of senior audit personnel and relevant safeguards

When a senior auditor acts for an audit client for a long period, several ethical problems can arise. First, the professional scepticism of the auditor can be diminished. This happens because the auditor becomes too accepting of the client's methods and explanations, so stops approaching the audit with a questioning mind.

Familiarity and self-interest threats are created by using the same senior personnel on an audit engagement over a long period of time. The familiarity threat is linked to the issues relating to the loss of professional scepticism discussed above, and is due to the senior auditor forming a close relationship with the client's personnel over a long period of time.

[**UK syllabus**: Ethical Standard section 3 describes similar ethical problems arising from long association of senior audit personnel with an audit client, stating that self-interest, self-review and familiarity threats to the auditor's objectivity may arise].

As with any ethical threat, the significance of the threat should be evaluated and safeguards which reduce the threat to an acceptable level put in place. Matters which should be considered in evaluating the significance of the ethical threat could include the seniority of the auditor involved, the length of time they have acted for the client, the nature, frequency and extent of the individual's interactions with the client's management or those charged with governance and whether the client's management team has changed.

Examples of safeguards which can be used include:

- Rotating the senior personnel off the audit team
- Having a professional accountant who was not a member of the audit team review the work of the senior personnel; or
- Regular independent internal or external quality control reviews of the engagement.

[**UK syllabus**: ES section 3 states that in the case of listed entities no one shall act as audit engagement partner for more than five years and that anyone who has acted as the audit engagement partner for a particular audited entity for a period of five years shall not subsequently participate in the audit engagement until a further period of five years has elapsed. Therefore it is appropriate that Bobby is removed from the position of audit partner at this time as he has acted in that capacity for five years. In addition, Bobby may not have any involvement with the audit of Ordway plc for the next five years. Performing quality control work forms part of participating in the audit engagement. Therefore Bobby cannot act as engagement quality control reviewer for the audit of Ordway plc, having stepped down as audit engagement partner].

In the case of a public interest company such as Ordway Co, the Code contains a specific requirement that an individual shall not be a key audit partner for more than seven years. After seven years the individual shall not be a member of the engagement team or be a key audit partner for the client for two years. This is known as the cooling off period, and during that period, the auditor shall not participate in the audit of the entity, provide quality control for the engagement, consult with the engagement team or the client regarding technical or industry-specific issues, transactions or events or otherwise directly influence the outcome of the engagement.

Because Ordway Co is a listed company, the audit firm must apply the requirements of the Code, remove Bobby from the audit team and not allow further contact with the client or the audit process. Therefore Bobby cannot act as engagement quality control reviewer for the audit of Ordway Co, having stepped down as audit engagement partner.

Examiner's comments

This question was by far the most popular of the Section B questions and in the most part was well attempted. The first part of the question focused on practice management and client acceptance issues. The scenario described a potential new audit client, Jones Co, a small but rapidly growing company with ambitions to expand internationally. The audit firm had been approached to tender for the audit of Jones Co, and this would be the first year that the company required an audit. The company had previously had limited assurance reviews performed on its financial statements, and had one accountant using an off-the shelf accounting package.

Requirement (ai) asked candidates to explain the specific matters to be included in the audit proposal document, other than those relating to the audit fee. This was quite well attempted by many, with almost all candidates understanding the main components of an audit proposal document such as a background of the audit firm, discussion of audit methodology, an outline of the firm's resources and timings and deadlines. Where candidates did not score well on this requirement was where the answer provided was very generic and was not made specific to the requirements of Jones Co. For example, some candidates ignored the fact that Jones Co had never previously been audited which would mean that management may have little appreciation of the audit process and as such the audit proposal should explain in some detail the responsibilities of management and the audit firm, and provide a detailed explanation of the audit process including key outputs.

Requirement (aii) went on to ask candidates to discuss the issues relating to determining the audit fee to be considered by the audit firm, assuming its appointment as auditor of Jones Co. Unfortunately many answers to this requirement did not identify the relevant matters in the question scenario, including the issue of contingent fees, intimidation on fees and lowballing that were implied by the comments made by the owner- manager of Jones Co. Better candidates were able to make the very valid point that the potential client needed a better understanding of the purpose of an audit and why it needs to be seen to be independent and tied this back to the content of the proposal document.

Where these matters were not discussed, answers tended to be generic, and simply focused on the fact that audit fees should be determined by time, resources and charge-out rates. Many of the weaker answers did not focus on the specific nature of the question requirement, and instead discussed matters that had little to do with the audit fee, such as self-review threats and other irrelevant acceptance procedures such as customer due diligence.

The final requirement moved to focus on a different audit client – Ordway Co, a listed company. The scenario briefly described that the current audit partner, having acted in that capacity for seven years was to be replaced by another partner, but wanted to stay in contact with the client and act as engagement quality control reviewer. Candidates were asked to explain the ethical threats raised by the long association of senior audit personnel with an audit client and the relevant safeguards to be applied. Candidates were also asked to determine whether the partner could in fact act as engagement quality control reviewer. This section was well attempted and most candidates correctly identified the familiarity threat and loss of professional scepticism that arises on a long association with an audit client, especially when dealing with senior audit personnel. Most candidates could also explain the relevant safeguards and demonstrated knowledge of the relevant requirements for listed entities. It was pleasing to see this syllabus area well understood by most candidates given its topical nature.

The issue of whether the audit partner could remain in contact with the client by acting as engagement quality control reviewer was less well understood. While many candidates correctly suggested that this could not happen for ethical reasons, many others thought that it would be appropriate as long as further quality control reviews took place. Other candidates misinterpreted the question and thought that the partner was leaving the audit firm to work at the client.

The information in the question was amended slightly for the UK and IRL adapted papers to make them relevant to the Financial Reporting Council's Ethical Codes, which the majority of candidates referred to in their answers.

ACCA marking scheme

					Marks
(a)	(i)	**Matters to be included in the audit proposal**			
		Generally up to 1½ marks for each matter explained:			
		–	Outline of the audit firm		
		–	Audit requirement of Jones Co		
		–	Audit approach (allow up to 3 marks for well explained points made relevant to scenario)		
		–	Deadlines		
		–	Quality control and ethics		
		–	Additional non-audit and assurance services		
				Maximum	**8**
	(ii)	**Matters to be considered in determining audit fee**			
		Generally up to 2 marks for each point discussed:			
		–	Fee to be based on staffing levels and chargeable hours		
		–	Low fees can result in poor quality audit work and increase audit risk		
		–	Lowballing and client expectation issues		
		–	Contingent fees not allowed for audit services		
				Maximum	**6**
(b)	**Long association of senior audit personnel**				
	Generally up to 1½ marks for each point discussed:				
	–	Loss of professional scepticism			
	–	Familiarity and self-interest threats to objectivity			
	–	Assessing the significance of the threat			
	–	Appropriate safeguards (1 mark each where well explained to max of 3 marks)			
	–	Specific rule applicable to public interest entities			
	–	Conclusion on whether partner can perform EQCR role			
				Maximum	**6**
Total					**20**

35 WELLER & CO *Walk in the footsteps of a top tutor*

Top tutor tips

This question is split into two parts, with ethical and professional issues being part (b) and part (a) dealing with tendering.

For the tender document you need to identify ways in which you can sell your firm to the client. Try and match the firm with the prospective client from the information in the scenario. Don't just give rote learnt knowledge without applying it to the scenario.

The ethical requirement is split into two parts so take each in turn explaining the issues that would be created by the suggestions and evaluating the significance of them, as well as suggesting any safeguards that could be applied.

(a) Matters to be included in tender document

Outline of Weller & Co

A brief outline of the audit firm, including a description of different services offered, and the firm's membership of an international network of audit firms. This should provide comfort to the Plant Group's audit committee that Weller & Co has the capability to audit its overseas subsidiary, and that the audit firm has sufficient resources to conduct the Plant Group audit now and in the future, given the Plant Group's rapid expansion.

Specialisms of Weller & Co

A description of areas of particular audit expertise, focusing on those areas of relevance to the Plant Group, namely the audit firm's telecoms audit department. The tender document should emphasise the audit firm's specialism in auditing this industry sector, which highlights that an experienced audit team can be assembled to provide a high quality audit.

Identify the audit requirements of the Plant Group

An outline of the requirements of the client, including confirmation that Weller & Co would be providing the audit service to each subsidiary, as well as to the parent company, and to the Plant Group. Weller & Co may also wish to include a clarification of the purpose and legal requirements of an audit in the jurisdictions of the components of the Plant Group, as requirements may differ according to geographical location.

Identify any audit-related services that may be required

Due to the Plant Group's listed status, there may be additional work to be performed. For example, depending on the regulatory requirements of the stock exchange on which the Plant Group is listed, there may be additional reporting requirements relevant to corporate governance and internal controls. This should be clarified and included in the tender document to ensure that the audit committee understands any such requirements, and that Weller & Co can provide an all-encompassing service.

Audit approach

A description of the proposed audit approach, outlining the stages of the audit process and the audit methodology used by the firm. Weller & Co may wish to emphasise any aspects of the proposed audit methodology which would be likely to meet the audit committee's requirement of a cost effective audit. The proposed audit approach could involve reliance to some extent on the Plant Group's controls, which are suggested to be good, and the tender document should explain that the audit firm will have to gauge the strength of controls before deciding whether to place any reliance on them.

Deadlines

The audit firm should clarify the timescale to be used for the audit. This is very important, given the audit committee's hope for a quick audit. It would be time pressured for the audit of all components of the Plant Group and of the consolidated financial statements to be completed in two months, especially given the geographical spread of the Plant Group. The audit firm may wish to propose a later deadline, emphasising that it may be impossible to conduct a quality audit in such a short timeframe.

Quality control and ethics

Weller & Co should clarify its adherence to the Code of Ethics and to International Standards on Quality Control. This should provide assurance that the audit firm will provide an unbiased and credible auditor's report. This may be particularly important, given the recent listing obtained by the Plant Group, and consequential scrutiny of the financial statements and auditor's report by investors and potential investors.

Fees

The proposed audit fee should be stated, with a breakdown of the main components of the fee. The audit firm may wish to explain that the audit fee is likely to be higher in the first year of auditing the Plant Group, as the firm will need to spend time obtaining business understanding and ensuring there is appropriate documentation of systems and controls. The tender document could explain that the audit is likely to become more cost effective in subsequent years, when the audit firm has gone through a learning curve.

Tutorial note

Credit will also be awarded for alternative comments regarding fees, for example, candidates may suggest that the audit fee will be relatively constant year on year (the reason being that initial costs are not passed on to the client in the first year of providing the audit service).

Additional non-audit services

The audit firm should describe any non-audit services that it may be able to provide, such as tax services or restructuring services, which may be relevant given the rapid expansion of the Plant Group. The provision of such services would have to be considered carefully by the audit firm due to the threat to objectivity that may be created, so the tender document should outline any safeguards that may be used to reduce risks to an acceptable level. This is particularly important, given the listed status of the Plant Group. This part of the tender document may remind the audit committee members that corporate governance requirements may prohibit the audit firm from offering certain non-audit services.

Tutorial note

Credit will be awarded for discussion of other matters that may be included in the tender document, if made relevant to the Plant Group.

(b) Ethical issues

Weller & Co must ensure that any efforts to increase the firm's revenue do not create any threats to objectivity and independence.

The suggestion to remunerate partners with a bonus on successful sale of a non-audit service to an audit client creates a potential self-interest threat to objectivity. A self-interest threat is created when a member of the audit team is evaluated on or compensated (remunerated) for selling non-assurance services to that audit client.

The significance of the threat depends on factors such as:

- The proportion of the individual's compensation or performance evaluation that is based on the sale of such services
- The role of the individual on the audit team; and
- Whether promotion decisions are influenced by the sale of such services.

In this case, the fact that the remuneration will be paid to the partner creates a significant threat to objectivity due to their influential position in the audit team. A key audit partner shall not be evaluated on or compensated (remunerated) based on that partner's success in selling non-assurance services to the partner's audit client. Therefore the bonus scheme should not be offered to partners as it creates an unacceptable threat to objectivity.

The Code of Ethics does not specifically state that managers should not be evaluated or remunerated for selling services to audit clients. It may be possible in the case of an audit manager having been remunerated for such a sale for safeguards to be put in place to reduce the threat to objectivity to an acceptable level, for example by having a review of the work of the manager in relation to the client. However, it would be more prudent for Weller & Co not to offer the remuneration scheme at all.

The second suggestion, regarding offering an 'extended audit' service to clients, also creates ethical problems. The issue is that providing an internal audit service to an audit client creates a self-review threat to independence, if the firm uses the internal audit work in the course of a subsequent external audit. The self-review threat arises because of the possibility that the audit team will use the results of the internal audit service, without appropriately evaluating those results or exercising the same level of professional scepticism as would be exercised when the internal audit work is performed by individuals who are not members of the firm. An acceptable safeguard would be for the internal audit engagement to be performed by a separate team.

The Code also states that performing a significant part of the client's internal audit activities increases the possibility that firm personnel providing internal audit services will assume a management responsibility. This threat cannot be reduced to an acceptable level, and the Code requires that audit personnel shall not assume a management responsibility when providing internal audit services to an audit client. Management responsibility may include, for example, performing procedures that are part of the internal control and taking responsibility for designing, implementing and maintaining internal control.

Accordingly, an audit firm may only provide internal audit services to an audit client where:

- The client designates an appropriate and competent resource, preferably within senior management, to be responsible at all times for internal audit activities and to acknowledge responsibility for designing, implementing, and maintaining internal control
- The client's management or those charged with governance reviews, assesses and approves the scope, risk and frequency of the internal audit services
- The client's management evaluates the adequacy of the internal audit services and the findings resulting from their performance
- The client's management evaluates and determines which recommendations resulting from internal audit services to implement and manages the implementation process; and
- The client's management reports to those charged with governance detail the significant findings and recommendations resulting from the internal audit services.

In the case of an audit client that is a public interest entity, an audit firm shall not provide internal audit services that relate to:

- A significant part of the internal controls over financial reporting.
- Financial accounting systems that generate information that is, separately or in the aggregate, significant to the client's accounting records or financial statements on which the firm will express an opinion.
- Amounts or disclosures that are, separately or in the aggregate, material to the financial statements on which the firm will express an opinion.

Where internal audit services are supplied to an audit client, they should be the subject of a separate engagement letter and billing arrangement, and should also be pre-approved by those charged with governance of the audited entity.

Examiner's comments

This question was marginally the most popular of the optional questions. Requirement (a) focused on tendering, and provided information in relation to a potential new audit client – a multinational, newly listed group requiring a cost effective audit to a tight deadline. The requirement, for eight marks, was to identify and explain the matters to be included in the tender document.

This was generally well attempted, with a significant minority of answers achieving close to full marks. The best answers went through each of the typical contents of a tender document and related them specifically to the Group in the question, resulting in focused and well explained answer points. Interestingly these answers were often relatively brief, but still managed to attract a high mark through application of knowledge to the question scenario. The more common areas discussed were the international network, audit specialism, fees and deadline, and the introduction of key members of the potential audit team.

Some answers tended to either be much too brief - sometimes little more than a list of bullet points, or did not answer the question requirement, and instead of explaining matters to be included in a tender document, discussed the matters that may impact client acceptance, such as whether the audit firm has sufficient resources, and whether a fee dependency would be created. Candidates are advised to read question requirements carefully and not to make assumptions about what is being asked for.

Requirement (b) focused on ethics. Two suggestions had been made to help an audit firm increase its revenue – one was to give managers and partners a financial reward for selling non-audit services to clients, and the other to provide an external audit service to clients. The requirement was to comment on the ethical and professional issues raised by the two suggestions. Answers tended to discuss one of the suggestions reasonably well, but then repeat almost identical points in relation to the second suggestion. There was some overlap given that both involved the provision of a non-audit service to an audit client, but there were enough separate points that could be made to avoid repetition. In relation to the financial incentives for partners and manager selling services to audit clients, hardly any candidates discussed the issue of the significance of the ethical threat depending on seniority and that partners couldn't have the arrangement. Many also discussed the self-interest threat in relation to the audit firm rather than its personnel.

In relation to the extended audit, most answers explained the self-review threat and suggested appropriate safeguards, usually that of separate teams. Fewer discussed the need for extended review procedures or for separate engagement letters and billing arrangements were the internal audit service provided to an audit client. Fewer still knew the position of the ethical codes in relation to this matter, and there was very little in the way of discussion of the topic as a current issue.

ACCA marking scheme	
	Marks
(a) **Matters to be included in tender document**	
Up to 1½ marks for each matter identified and explained with relevance to the maximum of 2 marks in total for matters identified only):	
– Outline of the audit firm including international network	
– Audit firm specialism in telecoms	
– Client audit requirements	
– Outline of audit firm's audit methodology	
– Deadlines	
– Discuss provision of audit-related services	
– Quality control and ethics	
– Fees	
– Discuss provision of non-audit services	
Maximum	**7**
(b) **Ethical matters**	
Up to 1 mark for each relevant comment:	
– Explain self-interest threat arising on bonus suggestion	
– Significance depends on seniority of person, materiality of compensation	
– Partners may not have this arrangement	
– Safeguard could be put in place for other audit team members	
– Explain self-review threat arising on internal audit service	
– Identify impact on professional scepticism	
– Explain management threat arising in internal audit service	
– Safeguards (1 mark each), e.g. separate team	
– Not allowed for public interest clients	
– Separate engagement letter/billing arrangements	
– Approval of those charged with governance	
Maximum	**8**
Total	**15**

36 DRAGON GROUP *Walk in the footsteps of a top tutor*

Top tutor tips

Part (a) requires little more than common sense regarding why auditors may not wish to continue auditing a particular client.

Part (b) requires a basic knowledge of the contents of a tender document. You then need to flesh this out by applying this knowledge to the specific information given.

Part (c) asks you to consider what professional issues you need to consider before accepting a new client. This could include any aspect of audit quality control, ethics or general practice management/administration.

Part (d) required some basic knowledge and then some common sense suggestions about the difficulty of cross-border audit.

(a) Reasons why a firm of auditors may decide not to seek re-election – any FOUR of the following:

Disagreement with the client

The audit firm may have disagreed with the client for a number of reasons, for example, over accounting treatments used in the financial statements. A disagreement over a significant matter is likely to cause a breakdown in the professional relationship between auditor and client, meaning that the audit firm could lose faith in the competence of management. The auditor would be reluctant to seek re-election if the disagreement were not resolved.

Lack of integrity of client

The audit firm may feel that management is not acting with integrity, for example, the financial statements may be subject to creative accounting, or dubious business ethics decisions could be made by management, such as the exploitation of child labour. The auditor would be likely not to seek re-election (or to resign) in this case to avoid being associated with the client's poor decisions.

Fee level

The audit firm could be unable to demand a high enough audit fee from the client to cover the costs of the audit. In this situation the audit firm may choose not to offer itself for re-election, to avoid continuing with a loss making audit engagement, and consequently to use resources in a more commercially advantageous way.

Fee payments

The audit firm could have outstanding fees which may not be fully recovered due to a client's poor cash flow position. Or, the client could be slow paying, causing the audit firm to chase for payment and possibly affecting the relationship between the two businesses. In such cases the audit firm may make the commercial decision not to act for the client any longer.

Resources

The audit firm may find that it lacks the resources to continue to provide the audit service to a client. This could happen if the client company grows rapidly, financially or operationally, meaning that a larger audit team is necessary. The audit firm may simply lack the necessary skilled staff to expand the audit team.

Competence

The audit firm could feel that it is no longer competent to perform an audit service. This could happen for example if a client company diversified into a new and specialised business operation of which the audit firm had little or no experience. The audit firm would not be able to provide a high quality audit without building up or buying in the necessary knowledge and skills, and so may decide not to be considered for re-election.

Overseas expansion

A client could acquire one or several material overseas subsidiaries. If the audit firm does not have an associate office in the overseas location, the firm may feel that the risk and resources involved in relying on the work of other auditors is too great, and so decide not to act for the client any longer.

Independence

There are many ethical guidelines in relation to independence which must be adhered to by auditors, and in the event of a potential breach of the guidelines, the audit firm may decide not to seek re-election. For example, an audit firm may need to increase the audit fee if a client company grows in size. This could have the effect of increasing the fee received from the client above the allowed thresholds. As there would be no ethical safeguard strong enough to preserve the perception of independence, in this case the audit firm would not be able to continue to provide the audit service.

> ***Tutorial note***
>
> *Other examples may be used to explain why the issue of independence could cause an audit firm not to seek re-election, e.g. audit firm takes on a financial interest in the client, close personal relationships develop between the firm and the client.*

Conflicts of interest

An audit firm may become involved in a situation where a conflict of interest arises between an existing audit client and another client of the firm. For example, an audit firm could take on a new audit client which is a competitor of an existing audit client. Although with the use of appropriate safeguards this situation could be successfully managed, the audit firm may decide that stepping down as auditor of the existing firm is the best course of action.

(b) Matters to be included in tender document

Brief outline of Unicorn & Co

This should include a short history of the firm, a description of its organisational structure, the different services offered by the firm (such as audit, tax, corporate finance, etc.), and the locations in which the firm operates. The document should also state whether it is a member of any international audit firm network. The geographical locations in which Unicorn operates will be important given the multi-national structure of the Dragon Group.

Specialisms of the firm

Unicorn & Co should describe the areas in which the firm has particular experience of relevance to the Dragon Group. It would be advantageous to stress that the firm has an audit department dedicated to the audit of clients in the retail industry, as this emphasises the experience that the firm has relevant to the specific operations of the group.

Identification of the needs of the Dragon Group

The tender document should outline the requirements of the client, in this case, that each subsidiary is required to have an individual audit on its financial statements, and that the consolidated financial statements also need to be audited. Unicorn & Co may choose to include here a brief clarification of the purpose and legal requirements of an audit. The potential provision of non-audit services should be discussed, either here, or in a separate section of the tender document (see below).

Outline of the proposed audit approach

This is likely to be the most detailed part of the tender document. Here the firm will describe how the audit would be conducted, ensuring that the needs of the Dragon Group (as discussed above) have been met. Typically contained in this section would be a description of the audit methodology used by the firm, and an outline of the audit cycle including the key deliverables at each phase of work. For example:

- How the firm would intend to gain business understanding at group and subsidiary level.
- Methods used to assess risk and to plan the audits.
- Procedures used to assess the control environment and accounting systems.
- Techniques used to gather evidence, e.g. the use of audit software.

How the firm would structure the audit of the consolidation of the group financial statements and how they would liaise with subsidiary audit teams.

The firm should clarify its adherence to International Standards on Auditing, ethical guidelines and any other relevant laws and regulations operating in the various jurisdictions relevant to the Dragon Group. The various financial reporting frameworks used within the group should be clarified.

Quality control

Unicorn & Co should emphasise the importance of quality control and therefore should explain the procedures that are used within the firm to monitor the quality of the audit services provided. This should include a description of firm-wide quality control policies, and the procedures applied to individual audits. The firm may wish to clarify its adherence to International Standards on Quality Control.

Communication with management

The firm should outline the various reports and other communication that will be made to management as part of the audit process. The purpose and main content of the reports, and the timing of them, should be outlined. Unicorn & Co may provide some 'added value' bi-products of the audit process. For example, the business risks identified as part of the audit planning may be fed back to management in a written report.

Timing

Unicorn & Co should outline the timeframe that would be used. For example, the audits of the subsidiaries' financial statements should be conducted before the audit of the consolidated financial statements. The firm may wish to include an approximate date by which the group audit opinion would be completed, which should fit in, if possible, with the requirements of the group. If Unicorn & Co feel that the deadline requested by the client is unrealistic, a more appropriate deadline should be suggested, with the reasons for this clearly explained.

Key staff and resources

The document should name the key members of staff to be assigned to the audit, in particular the proposed engagement partner. In addition, the firm should clarify the approximate number of staff to be used in the audit team and the relevant experience of the key members of the audit team. If the firm considers that external specialists could be needed, then this should be explained in this section of the document.

Fees

The proposed fee for the audit of the group should be stated, and the calculation of the fee should be explained, i.e. broken down by grade of staff and hourly/daily rates per grade. In addition, invoicing and payment terms should be described, e.g. if the audit fee is payable in instalments, the stages when each instalment will fall due.

Extra services

Unicorn & Co should ensure that any non-audit services that it may be able to offer to the Dragon Group are described. For example, subject to ethical safeguards, the firm may be able to offer corporate finance services in relation to the stock exchange listing that the group is seeking, although the provision of this non-audit service would need to be carefully considered in relation to independence issues.

(c) Evaluation of matters to be considered:

Size and location of the group companies

The Dragon Group is a large multi-national group of companies. It is extremely important that Unicorn & Co assesses the availability of resources that can be allocated to the audit team. The assignment would comprise the audit of the financial statements of all 20 current subsidiaries, the audit of the parent company's and the group's financial statements. This is a significant engagement which will demand a great deal of time.

The location of half of the group's subsidiaries in other countries means that the overseas offices of Unicorn & Co would be called upon to perform some or all of the audit of those subsidiaries. In this case the resource base of the relevant overseas offices should be considered to ensure there is enough staff with appropriate skills and experience available to perform the necessary audit work.

Unicorn & Co must consider if they have offices in all of the countries in which the Dragon Group has a subsidiary.

Depending on the materiality of the overseas subsidiaries to the group financial statements, it is likely that some overseas visits would be required to evaluate the work of the overseas audit teams. Unicorn & Co should consider who will conduct the visits (presumably a senior member of the audit team), and whether that person has the necessary skills and experience in evaluating the work of overseas audit teams.

Planned expansion of the group

In light of the comments above, Unicorn & Co should consider that the planned further significant expansion of the group will mean more audit staff will be needed in future years, and if any subsidiaries are acquired in other countries, the audit is likely to be performed by overseas offices. The firm should therefore consider not only its current resource base in the local and overseas offices, but whether additional staff will be available in the future if the group's expansion goes ahead as planned.

Relevant skills and experience

Unicorn & Co has an audit department specialising in the audit of retail companies, so it should not be a problem to find audit staff with relevant experience in this country.

On consolidation, the financial statements of the subsidiaries will be restated in line with group accounting policies and financial reporting framework, and will also be retranslated into local presentational currency. All of this work will be performed by the management of the Dragon Group. Unicorn & Co must evaluate the availability of staff experienced in the audit of a consolidation including foreign subsidiaries.

Timing

It is important to consider the timeframe when conducting a group audit. The audit of each subsidiary's financial statements should be carried out prior to the audit of the consolidated financial statements. Unicorn & Co should consider the expectation of the Dragon Group in relation to the reporting deadline, and ensure that enough time is allowed for the completion of all audits. The deadline proposed by management of 31 December is only three months after the year end, which may be unrealistic given the size of the group and the multi-national location of the subsidiaries. The first year auditing a new client is likely to take longer, as the audit team will need to familiarise themselves with the business, the accounting systems and controls, etc.

Mermaid Co – prior year modification

If Unicorn & Co accepts the engagement, the firm will take on the audit of Mermaid Co, whose financial statements in the prior year were in breach of financial reporting standards. This adds an element of risk to the engagement. Unicorn & Co should gather as much information as possible about the contingent liability, and the reason why the management of Mermaid Co did not amend the financial statements last year end. This could hint at a lack of integrity on the part of the management of the company.

The firm should also consider whether this matter could be significant to the consolidated financial statements, by assessing the materiality of the contingent liability at group level.

Further discussions should be held with the management of the Dragon Group in order to understand their thoughts on the contingency and whether it should be disclosed in the individual financial statements of Mermaid Co, and at group level. Contacting the incumbent auditors (after seeking relevant permission from the Dragon Group) would also be an important procedure to gather information about the modification.

Minotaur Co – different business activity

The acquisition of Minotaur Co represents a new business activity for the group. The retail business audit department may not currently have much, if any, experience of auditing a distribution company. This should be easily overcome, either by bringing in staff from a different department more experienced in clients with distribution operations, or by ensuring adequate training for staff in the retail business audit department.

Highly regulated/reliance on financial statements and auditor's report

The Group is listed on several stock exchanges, and is therefore subject to a high degree of regulation. This adds an element of risk to the engagement, as the management will be under pressure to publish favourable results. This risk is increased by the fact that a new listing is being sought, meaning that the financial statements and auditor's report of the group will be subject to close scrutiny by the stock exchange regulators.

There may be extra work required by the auditors due to the listings, for example, the group may have to prepare reconciliations of financial data, or additional narrative reports on which the auditors have to express an opinion under the rulings of the stock exchange. The firm must consider the availability of staff skilled in regulatory and reporting listing rules to perform such work.

Previous auditors of Dragon Group

Unicorn & Co should consider the reason why the previous audit firm is not seeking re-appointment, and whether the reason would impact on their acceptance decision. After seeking permission from the Dragon Group, contact should be made with the previous auditors to obtain confirmation of the reason for them vacating office (amongst other matters).

In conclusion, this is a large scale, multi-national group, which carries a fairly high level of risk. Unicorn & Co must be extremely careful to only commit to the group audit if it has the necessary resources, can manage the client's expectation in relation to the reporting deadline, is convinced of the integrity of management, and is confident to take on a potentially high profile client.

Tutorial note

Credit will be awarded in this requirement for discussion of ethical matters which would be considered prior to accepting the appointment as auditor of the Dragon Group. However, as the scenario does not contain any reference to specific ethical matters, marks will be limited to a maximum of 2 for a general discussion of ethical matters on acceptance.

(d) (i) **Definition:** A transnational audit means an audit of financial statements which are or may be relied upon outside the audited entity's home jurisdiction for the purpose of significant lending, investment or regulatory decisions.

Relevance: The Dragon Group is listed on the stock exchange of several countries, (and is planning to raise more finance by a further listing). This means that the group is subject to the regulations of all stock exchanges on which it is listed, and so is bound by listing rules outside of its home jurisdiction. The group also contains many foreign subsidiaries, meaning that it operates in a global business and financial environment.

(ii) **Transnational audit and audit risk** – any TWO of the following:

Application of auditing standards

Although many countries of the world have adopted International Standards on Auditing (ISAs), not all have done so, choosing instead to use locally developed auditing regulations. In addition, some countries use modified versions of ISAs. This means that in a transnational audit, some components of the group financial statements will have been audited using a different auditing framework, resulting in inconsistent audit processes within the group, potentially reducing the quality of the audit.

Regulation and oversight of auditors

Similar to the previous comments on the use of ISAs, across the world there are many different ways in which the activities of auditors are regulated and monitored. In some countries the audit profession is self-regulatory, whereas in other countries a more legislative approach is used. This also can impact on the quality of audit work in a transnational situation.

Financial reporting framework

Some countries use International Financial Reporting Standards, whereas some use locally developed accounting standards. Within a transnational group it is likely that adjustments, reconciliations or restatements may be required in order to comply with the requirements of the jurisdictions relevant to the group financial statements (i.e. the jurisdiction of the parent company in most cases). Such reconciliations can be complex and require a high level of technical expertise of the preparer and the auditor.

Corporate governance requirements and consequent control risk

In some countries there are very prescriptive corporate governance requirements, which the auditor must consider as part of the audit process. In this case the auditor may need to carry out extra work over and above local requirements in order to ensure group wide compliance with the requirements of the jurisdictions relevant to the financial statements. However, in some countries there is very little corporate governance regulation at all and controls are likely to be weaker than in other components of the group. Control risk is therefore likely to differ between the various subsidiaries making up the group.

Examiner's comments

Requirement (a) was a short factual requirement, not related to the detail of the question scenario, which asked candidates to explain four reasons why a firm of auditors may decide not to seek re-election as auditor. There were two main problems with answers to this requirement. Firstly, too few candidates actually provided an explanation of the reasons they gave. For example, an answer stated that the auditor had a disagreement with the client over something in the financial statements. While this is indeed a reason why the auditor may chose not to seek re-election, it is not an explanation, which would entail going on to say that the disagreement had caused a breakdown in the working relationship between the auditor and client, and that the auditor had lost faith in the competence and/or integrity of management.

Secondly, the requirement asked for **FOUR** reasons. It is a waste of time and effort to provide more than the required number of reasons.

The second requirement focused on the audit tendering process, and asked for matters to be included in a tender document to be presented to the Dragon Group. This requirement seemed to polarise candidates. Those candidates who tailored their answer to the question scenario tended to do well, with a significant proportion achieving close to the maximum marks available. However, candidates who provided a list of points to be included in ANY tender, regardless of the information provided about the prospective client, and about your audit firm, scored inadequately. In other words, it is important to apply knowledge to score well, as is true for any scenario-based question.

Sound answers to (b) appreciated that the point of the tender document is to sell your audit firm's services to the client, and recommended points to include such as the global positioning of both audit firm and prospective client, the specialism of the audit firm in retail, and the firm's ability to potentially provide services relating to the expansion plans of the group, such as due diligence.

Weak answers simply stated vague comments: 'we should discuss fees', 'we should set a deadline,' etc. Some answers confused a tender document with an engagement letter, and included points more suited to that document, such as a statement of responsibilities or a legal disclaimer.

Inadequate answers to (b) were those that seemed to confuse the requirements with those of (c). Candidates are reminded that it is important to read ALL of the requirements of a question before beginning their answer, to avoid such confusion. Examples of statements commonly seen in answers to (b) which are more relevant to (c) are:

- 'are we competent to audit the group'
- 'can we audit the goodwill and foreign exchange transactions which are complex'
- 'will any of our audit staff want to go abroad to work'
- 'do any of our partners hold shares in Dragon Group'.

These comments definitely do not belong in a tender document, which should highlight the audit firm's capabilities to service the prospective client, rather than question the firm's competence or ability to take on the assignment. Such comments indicate a failure to read and understand the question requirement, as well as a lack of commercial awareness.

Requirement (c) asked candidates to evaluate the matters that should be considered before accepting the audit engagement. Answers here were weak, despite this being a regularly examined syllabus area. Most answers were not tailored to the question, and just provided a list of questions or actions, such as 'get permission to contact previous auditor', or 'check the integrity of management', and 'do we have the skill to audit foreign currencies'.

Providing a list of such comments will not generate enough marks to pass the question requirement. Better answers discussed, amongst other points:

- the risk posed by the numerous stock exchange listings of the potential client, and whether the audit fee would be enough to compensate for that risk
- the practical difficulties entailed in co-ordinating an audit of more than 20 companies across many different countries
- the tight deadline imposed by the potential client, especially in light of this being a first year audit, and the learning curve that the audit firm would need to go through.

Some candidates appeared to think that the audit would be too much trouble – a sizeable number of scripts contained comments such as 'auditing a company far from our main office would be tedious and inconvenient'. I would suggest that most audit firms, on being successful in a tender for an audit as significant as this, would consider the inconvenience worthwhile.

Requirement (d) was the worst answered on the paper. Clearly, very few candidates had studied the issue of transnational audits, and answers displayed a lack of knowledge. (di) asked for a definition of transnational audit, and an explanation as to why the term was applicable to the Dragon Group audit. Only a small minority of candidates could provide the correct definition, the rest guessing from the scenario that it was 'an audit covering many countries', or 'an audit performed by several audit firms from different countries', neither of which is true. (d) (ii) asked for two features of a transnational audit that contribute to a high level of audit risk. Answers again appeared to be based mainly on guesswork, with common suggestions being 'language difficulties' and 'communication barriers'. However, some candidates could identify variations in auditing standards and financial reporting frameworks as issues contributing to high risk, but these points were rarely developed to their full potential.

ACCA marking scheme			
			Marks
(a)	**Identify and explain using examples why an audit firm may not seek re-election**		
	Generally 1 for explanation/example, any FOUR:		
	– Disagreement		
	– Lack of integrity		
	– Fee level		
	– Late payment of fees		
	– Resources		
	– Overseas expansion		
	– Competence		
	– Independence		
	– Conflict of interest		
		Maximum	**4**
(b)	**Contents of tender document**		
	Up to 1½ marks per matter described:		
	– Outline of firm		
	– Specialisms		
	– Audit requirement of Dragon Group		
	– Outline audit approach (max 3 marks if detailed)		
	– QC		
	– Communication with management		
	– Timing		
	– Key staff/resources		
	– Fees		
	– Extra services		
		Maximum	**8**
(c)	**Matters to consider re. acceptance**		
	Generally ½ mark for identification, 1 further mark for explanation, from ideas list:		
	– Large and expanding group – availability of staff now and in the future		
	– Use of overseas offices		
	– Visits to overseas audit teams		
	– Skills/experience in retail/foreign subsidiaries consolidation		
	– Timing – tight deadline		
	– Mermaid Co – implication of prior year modification		
	– Minotaur Co – implication of different business activity		
	– Highly regulated – risk/additional reporting requirements		
	– Reason for previous auditors leaving office		
		Maximum	**6**
(d)	(i) **Define transnational audit and relevance to Dragon Group**		
	1 mark for definition		
	2 marks for relevance to Dragon Group		
		Maximum	**3**
	(ii) **Audit risk factors in a transnational audit**		
	2 marks per point explained		
	– Auditing standards		
	– Regulation of auditors		
	– Financial reporting standards		
	– Corporate governance/control risk		
		Maximum	**4**
Total			**25**

37 MACAU & CO *Walk in the footsteps of a top tutor*

Top tutor tips

Part (a) requires evaluation of quality control, ethical and other professional matters arising. This is a regularly examined topic. Typical issues to look out for in such a question are: whether the work has been assigned to the appropriate level of staff, whether sufficient time has been allocated for the audit, whether sufficient appropriate evidence has been obtained (e.g. have the ISAs been followed), whether any ethical threats have been addressed appropriately and whether adequate quality control procedures have been performed in respect of the engagement such as adequate levels of supervision and review.

Part (b) is a typical completion requirement asking for 'matters and evidence'. This is examined very frequently and the 'MARE' approach can help to provide structure to answers. MARE stands for:

Materiality – calculate whether the issue is material.

Accounting treatment – state the required treatment and why the client's treatment is wrong.

Risk - to the financial statements and the impact on the audit opinion if not corrected.

Evidence – the evidence that would have been documented on the audit file by the person who audited the section being reviewed.

(a) Quality control, ethical and professional matters

The audit of Stanley Co does not seem to have been performed with a high regard for the quality of the audit and there appear to be several ways in which the ISA requirements have been breached.

Materiality

First, it is not appropriate that the materiality level was determined at the planning stage of the audit but has not been reviewed or adjusted since. ISA 320 *Materiality in Planning and Performing an Audit* requires the auditor to determine materiality for the financial statements as a whole at the planning stage of the audit, and to revise it as the audit progresses as necessary where new facts and information become available which impact on materiality. It may be the case that no revision to the materiality which was initially determined is necessary, but a review should have taken place and this should be clearly documented in the audit working papers.

Audit of property, plant and equipment

The audit of the packing machine has not been properly carried out, and there seems to be a lack of sufficient, appropriate audit evidence to support the audit conclusion. The cost of the asset is material, based on the initial materiality, therefore there is a risk of material misstatement if sufficient and appropriate evidence is not obtained. By the year end the asset's carrying value is less than materiality, presumably due to depreciation being charged, but this does not negate the need for obtaining robust audit evidence for the cost and subsequent measurement of the asset.

The packing machine should have been physically verified. Obtaining the order and invoice does not confirm the existence of the machine, or that it is in working order. In addition, without a physical verification, the audit team would be unaware of problems such as physical damage to the machine or obsolescence, which could indicate impairment of the asset.

Relying on the distribution company to provide evidence on the existence and use of the asset is not appropriate. ISA 500 *Audit Evidence* states that audit evidence obtained directly by the auditor is more reliable than audit evidence obtained indirectly or by inference. External confirmations can be used to provide audit evidence but in this case the external confirmation should corroborate evidence obtained directly by the auditor, rather than be the only source of evidence. The relationship between Stanley Co and Aberdeen Co should also be understood by the auditor, and evidence should be obtained to confirm whether or not the two companies are related parties, as this would impact on the extent to which the external confirmation can be relied upon as a source of evidence.

Inventory count

In respect of the inventory count attendance, the audit team should have discussed the discrepancies with management as they could indicate more widespread problems with the inventory count. Given the comment that the inventory count appeared unorganised, it is possible that count instructions were not being followed or that some items had not been included in the count.

One of the requirements of ISA 501 *Audit Evidence – Specific Considerations for Selected Items* is that while attending an inventory count, the auditor shall evaluate management's instructions and procedures for recording and controlling the results of the entity's physical inventory counting. It is not clear from the conclusion of the audit work whether the problems noted at the inventory count have been discussed with management. The auditor attending the inventory count should have raised the issues at the time and assessed whether a recount of all of the inventory was required.

Training may need to be provided to audit staff to ensure that they understand the auditor's role at an inventory count and can deal with problems which may arise in the appropriate manner.

The discrepancies noted at the inventory count should be subject to further audit work. The results of the test counts should be extrapolated over the population in order to evaluate the potential misstatement of inventory as a whole. The results should then be evaluated in accordance with ISA 450 *Evaluation of Misstatements Identified during the Audit* which requires that the auditor shall accumulate misstatements identified during the audit, other than those which are clearly trivial, and that misstatements should be discussed with management.

The issues raised by the way in which the inventory count was performed could represent a significant control deficiency and should be raised with those charged with governance in accordance with ISA 265 *Communicating Deficiencies in Internal Control to Those Charged with Governance and Management*.

Working paper review

The audit senior's comments in relation to the review by the manager and partner indicate that elements of ISA 220 *Quality Control for an Audit of Financial Statements* have been breached. ISA 220 requires that the engagement partner shall, through a review of the audit documentation and discussion with the engagement team, be satisfied that sufficient appropriate audit evidence has been obtained to support the conclusions reached and for the auditor's report to be issued. It appears that in this case the partner has not properly reviewed the working papers, instead relying on the audit senior's comment that there were no problems in the audit work. ISA 220 does state that the audit partner need not review all audit documentation, but only a 'quick look' at the working papers could indicate that areas of risk or critical judgement have not been reviewed in sufficient detail.

There is also an issue in that the manager and partner reviews took place at the same time and near the completion of the audit fieldwork. Reviews should happen on a timely basis throughout the audit to enable problems to be resolved at an appropriate time. Reviews should also be hierarchical and it appears that the audit partner has not reviewed the work of the audit manager.

Ethical considerations

Finally, there appears to be a potential threat to objectivity due to the audit engagement partner's brother providing a management consultancy service to the audit client. This amounts to a self-interest threat in that the partner's brother receives income from the audit client. The audit partner's objectivity is therefore threatened, and this is a significant risk due to his position of influence over the audit. He may even receive an introducer's commission from his brother.

The matter should be investigated further, and a senior member of the audit firm or the firm's partner responsible for ethics should discuss the comments made in Stanley Co's board minutes with Joe Lantau in order to evaluate the ethical threat and determine any necessary actions. The amount which is being paid to Mick Lantau should be made known, as well as whether the amount is a market rate, and whether other providers of management advice were considered by the company.

The partner's comments to the audit junior indicate a lack of integrity, and indicate that the partner may have something to hide, which increases the threat to objectivity. The audit partner may need to be removed from the audit and his work reviewed.

(b) (i) Matters to consider and actions to take

The work in progress represents 4.7% of total assets and is therefore material to the statement of financial position. The deferred income is also material at 2.7% of total assets.

Even though the correspondence with BMC is dated after the end of the reporting period, BMC was suffering from financial problems during the year ending 31 December 2015 which was notified to Kowloon Co before the year end. Therefore the cancellation of the contract appears to meet the definition of an adjusting event under IAS 10 *Events after the Reporting Period* because it confirms conditions which existed at the year end.

Management must consider whether it is still appropriate to recognise the work in progress as an asset. According to IFRS 15 *Revenue from Contracts with Customers*, costs incurred to fulfil a contract are recognised as an asset if and only if all of the following criteria are met:

- The costs relate directly to a contract (or a specific anticipated contract)
- The costs generate or enhance resources of the entity which will be used in satisfying performance obligations in the future; and
- The costs are expected to be recovered.

The cancellation of the contract indicates that the costs of the work in progress are not recoverable from BMC, in which case the balance should be written off. Management is not planning to amend the balances recognised at the year end, and the audit team should investigate the reasons for this. Possibly management is asserting that the machine design costs could be utilised for a different contract, despite the fact that the machine was developed specifically for BMC. Audit work should focus on the contractual arrangements between Kowloon Co and BMC, particularly in relation to the ownership of the rights to the design work which has taken place. If the design work has been based on an innovation by BMC, then it needs to be determined if this information can still be used.

If the design work which has been undertaken to date can be used by Kowloon and results in an ability to develop a new type of product for other customers, there is the possibility that the costs (excluding any research costs) could be capitalised in line with IAS 38 *Intangible Assets*. This should be discussed with the project manager and finance director to assess if this has been considered and if the capitalisation criteria of IAS 38 can be satisfied.

The accounting treatment of the deferred income also needs to be considered. Depending on the terms of the contract with BMC, the amount could be repayable, though this may not be the case given that it is BMC which has cancelled the contract. If part or all of the amount is repayable, it can remain recognised as a current liability. If it is not repayable, it should be released to the statement of profit or loss.

If the costs cannot be capitalised, then there is a loss which needs to be recognised. Assuming that the advance payment is non-refundable, the net position of the development cost and the deferred income balances result in a loss of $150,000. This represents 15.8% of profit for the year and is material. If any necessary adjustments are not made there will be implications for the auditor's report, which would contain a modified opinion due to material misstatement.

Due to the significance of the matter to the financial statements, the contract cancellation and loss of BMC as a customer should be discussed in the other information to be issued with the financial statements, in this case in the integrated report.

The audit firm must consider its responsibilities in respect of ISA 720 *The Auditor's Responsibilities Relating to Other Information in Documents Containing Audited Financial Statements*. ISA 720 requires the auditor to read the other information to identify material inconsistencies, if any, with the audited financial statements.

Depending on the wording used in the integrated report when referring to the company's activities during the year and its financial performance, omitting to mention the cancellation of the contract could constitute a material misstatement of fact or a material inconsistency.

The matter should be discussed with management, who should be encouraged not only to amend the financial statements but also to discuss the cancellation of the contract in the integrated report. If management refuses to make the necessary amendments and disclosures, the matter should be discussed with those charged with governance and/or the company's legal counsel.

(ii) Evidence

- A copy of the contract between Kowloon Co and BMC reviewed for terms, in particular on whether the cancellation of the contract triggers a repayment of the payment in advance and in relation to ownership of the rights to the development which has so far taken place.
- Copies of correspondence between Kowloon Co and BMC reviewed for implications of the cancellation of the contract.
- Written confirmation from BMC that the contract has been cancelled and the date of the cancellation.
- Written representation from the project manager confirming that BMC contacted him regarding their financial difficulties in December 2015.
- Notes of a discussion with the project manager to confirm if the work in progress could be used for a different contract or the feasibility of the design work leading to a new type of product which could be produced by Kowloon Co.
- Correspondence with legal counsel regarding the ownership of the machine and whether there are any legal implications following the contract cancellation and potential proposal to sell the machine to a different customer.
- Review of post year-end orders/board minutes to assess if any conclusion regarding completion of the machine has been made and if it can be sold to an alternative customer, whether any potential customer has been identified.
- Extracts from the financial statements and journals to confirm that the necessary adjustments have been made.
- A copy of the integrated report, reviewed to confirm whether the cancellation of the contract and loss of BMC as a customer has been discussed.

Examiner's comments

This question combined two familiar formats by asking candidates to comment on the quality of the audit work performed and discuss the quality control, ethical and professional issues raised in part (a) and to comment on the matters arising and evidence expected to be found in relation to a number of financial reporting issues in part (b).

In part (a), there was tendency to re-write statements of fact from the question which scored no marks but stronger candidates discussed the issues and explained why the firm's actions were clearly inappropriate. Very few candidates were able to discuss the need for materiality to be constantly reviewed throughout the audit in light of changing circumstances. However, most candidates picked up that a significant addition to property, plant and equipment sited at a supplier's premises needed to be physically verified and that reliance on third party evidence for existence was inappropriate in the circumstances. The inventory count had been poorly performed but few candidates developed this to consider where the real audit risks may lie and the need to inform management of the weakness in internal controls and for the auditors to investigate the discrepancies and extend their testing. Improper manager/partner review was highlighted by the majority of candidates but the implications of the partner's cursory review were not always followed through to a logical conclusion.

In relation to the matters to consider, candidates were faced with a situation where the client had encountered a cancelled manufacturing contract. Most candidates scored the materiality marks for both the value of WIP and deferred income. A significant number of candidates discussed how WIP should have been calculated and its composition without realising that this was irrelevant as it needed to be recognised at nil unless a further use for it could be validly identified. Stronger candidates identified that the client may be able to levy a compensation claim for breach of contract. A worrying number of candidates also believed that writing off a deferred income creditor was a cost rather than a credit to the statement of profit or loss which shows a more fundamental lack of accounting knowledge. Likewise, many candidates confused WIP with R&D contracts and raised irrelevancies such as depreciation. The question stated that going concern was not an issue yet many candidates discussed this in depth as part of their answer. Candidates must realise that if the question makes a statement of this nature then marks will not be awarded for discussion, regardless of the quality of their answer and are again reminded to read the question scenario carefully. Audit evidence required was generally well-answered and there were some straightforward marks achieved by a majority of candidates, specifically the needs to obtain the relevant contract, board minutes, the cancellation letter and evidence of funds received. Some candidates were over reliant on written representations from management which are never as compelling as third-party evidence.

ACCA Marking scheme

			Marks
(a)	**Quality control, ethical and other professional issues**		
	Generally up to 1 mark for each point explained:		
	–	Materiality should be reviewed as the audit progresses	
	–	Insufficient audit evidence obtained in relation to packing machine: 1 mark for comment on materiality 1 mark for comment on physical verification 1 mark for comment on external confirmation 1 mark for comment on whether the distribution company is a related party 1 mark for comment on assertions/inappropriate audit conclusion	
	–	Lack of organisation at inventory count should have been discussed with management	
	–	Test count discrepancies should be extrapolated over the population	
	–	Audit staff may need training on inventory count attendance	
	–	Misstatements should be accumulated and discussed with management	
	–	The inaccuracy of the client's test counts should be reported to management as a control deficiency	

		– Insufficient review performed by audit manager – Review left too late and should be ongoing during the audit – Potential self-interest threat regarding audit engagement partner's brother – Matter should be investigated and notified to audit firm's ethical partner – The audit partner lacks integrity, maybe has something to hide – The partner may need to be removed from the audit and his work reviewed	
		Maximum	**13**
(b)	**(i)**	**Matters and actions to take** Generally 1 mark per comment/recommended action explained: – Calculation and determination of materiality (1 mark for each of the work in progress and the deferred income) – Contract cancellation is an adjusting event after the reporting period – The work in progress should be written off and charged to profit unless it can be used on a different contract – The deferred income may be repayable, if not it should be released to profit – Reporting implications if necessary adjustments not made – Integrated report may be inconsistent with financial statements or contain a misstatement of fact – Auditor's responsibility to read the integrated report to identify inconsistencies/misstatements – Matters to be discussed with management/those charged with governance	
		Maximum	**7**
	(ii)	**Evidence** Generally 1 mark for a well explained audit evidence point: – A copy of the contract between Kowloon Co and BMC reviewed for terms, in particular on whether the cancellation of the contract triggers a repayment of the payment in advance and in relation to ownership of the rights to the development which has so far taken place – Copies of correspondence between Kowloon Co and BMC reviewed for implications of the cancellation of the contract – Written confirmation from BMC that the contract has been cancelled and the date of the cancellation – Written representation from the project manager confirming that BMC contacted him regarding their financial difficulties in December 2015 – Notes of a discussion with the project manager to confirm if the work in progress could be used for a different contract or the feasibility of the design work leading to a new type of product which could be produced by Kowloon Co – Correspondence with legal counsel regarding legal implications of selling to alternative customer – Review of orders/board minutes to identify if course of action has been determined and alternative customer identified – Extracts from the financial statements and journals to confirm that the necessary adjustments have been made – A copy of the integrated report, reviewed to confirm whether the cancellation of the contract has been discussed	
		Maximum	**5**
Total			**25**

38 RETRIEVER *Walk in the footsteps of a top tutor*

Top tutor tips

Part (a) requires evaluation of quality control, ethical and other professional matters arising. Whilst this requirement is often covered in Q4 of the exam, students should be prepared for any syllabus area being tested in any question of the exam.

Typical issues to look out for in such a question are: whether the work has been assigned to the appropriate level of staff, whether sufficient time has been allocated for the audit, whether sufficient appropriate evidence has been obtained (e.g. have the ISAs been followed), whether any ethical threats are apparent (e.g. threats to objectivity or competence).

Part (b) deals with a forensic accounting service for a client who has been burgled and requested assistance determining the amount of the insurance claim. The question is split into two sections: matters to be considered when planning and procedures to be performed. Forensic accounting was the subject of a technical article in 2008 and this provides guidance on how to plan and perform such engagements. For the procedures, a common sense approach can be taken to quantify the extent of the loss.

(a) There are many concerns raised regarding quality control. Audits should be conducted with adherence to ISA 220 *Quality Control for an Audit of Financial Statements* and it seems that this has not happened in relation to the audit of the Retriever Group, which is especially concerning, given the Group obtaining a listing during the year. It would seem that the level of staffing on this assignment is insufficient, and that tasks have been delegated inappropriately to junior members of staff.

Time pressure

The junior's first comment is that the audit was time pressured. All audits should be planned to ensure that adequate time can be spent to obtain sufficient appropriate audit evidence to support the audit opinion. It seems that the audit is being rushed and the juniors instructed not to perform work properly, and that review procedures are not being conducted appropriately. All of this increases the detection risk of the audit and, ultimately, could lead to an inappropriate opinion being given.

The juniors have been told not to carry out some planned procedures on allegedly low risk areas of the audit because of time pressure. It is not acceptable to cut corners by leaving out audit procedures. Even if the balances are considered to be low risk, they could still contain misstatements. Directors' emoluments are related party transactions and are material by their nature and so should not be ignored. Any modifications to the planned audit procedures should be discussed with, and approved by, senior members of the audit team and should only occur for genuine reasons.

Method of selecting sample

ISA 530 *Audit Sampling* requires that the auditor shall select items for the sample in such a way that each sampling unit in the population has a chance of selection. The audit manager favours non-statistical sampling as a quick way to select a sample, instead of the firm's usual statistical sampling method. There is a risk that changing the way that items are selected for testing will not provide sufficient, reliable audit evidence as the sample selected may no longer be representative of the population as a whole. Or that an insufficient number of items may be selected for testing.

The juniors may not understand how to pick a sample without the use of the audit firm's statistical selection method, and there is a risk that the sample may be biased towards items that appear 'easy to audit'. Again, this instruction from the audit manager is a departure from planned audit procedures, made worse by deviating from the audit firm's standard auditing methods, and likely to increase detection risk.

Audit of going concern

Going concern can be a difficult area to audit, and given the Group's listed status and the fact that losses appear to have been made this year, it seems unwise to delegate such an important area of the audit to an audit junior. The audit of going concern involves many subjective areas, such as evaluating assumptions made by management, analysing profit and cash flow forecasts and forming an overall opinion on the viability of the business.

The going concern audit programme should be performed by a more senior and more experienced member of the audit team. This issue shows that the audit has not been well planned as appropriate delegation of work is a key part of direction and supervision, essential elements of good quality control.

Review of work

The juniors have been asked to review each other's work which is unacceptable. ISA 220 requires that the engagement partner shall take responsibility for reviews being performed in accordance with the firm's review policies and procedures. Ideally, work should be reviewed by a person more senior and/or experienced than the person who conducted the work.

Audit juniors reviewing each other's work are unlikely to spot mistakes, errors of judgement and inappropriate conclusions on work performed. The audit manager should be reviewing all of the work of the juniors, with the audit partner taking overall responsibility that all work has been appropriately reviewed.

Deferred tax

It is concerning that the client's financial controller is not able to calculate the deferred tax figure. This could indicate a lack of competence in the preparation of the financial statements, and the audit firm should consider if this impacts the overall assessment of audit risk.

The main issue is that the junior prepared the calculation for the client. Providing an audit client with accounting and bookkeeping services, such as preparing accounting records or financial statements, creates a self-review threat when the firm subsequently audits the financial statements. The significance of the threat depends on the materiality of the balance and its level of subjectivity.

Clients often request technical assistance from the external auditor, and such services do not, generally, create threats to independence provided the firm does not assume a management responsibility for the client. However, the audit junior has gone beyond providing assistance and has calculated a figure to be included in the financial statements.

The Group is listed and generally the provision of bookkeeping services is not allowed to listed clients. The Code states that in the case of an audit client that is a public interest entity, a firm shall not prepare tax calculations of current and deferred tax liabilities (or assets) for the purpose of preparing accounting entries that are material to the financial statements on which the firm will express an opinion.

The calculation of a deferred tax asset is not mechanical and involves judgements and assumptions in measuring the balance and evaluating its recoverability. The audit junior may be able to perform a calculation, but is unlikely to have sufficient detailed knowledge of the business and its projected future trading profits to be able to competently assess the deferred tax position. The calculation has not been reviewed and poses a high audit risk, as well as creating an ethical issue for the audit firm.

The deferred tax balance calculated by the junior should be assessed for materiality, carefully reviewed or re-performed, and discussed with management. It is unclear why the junior was discussing the Group's tax position with the financial controller, as this is not the type of task that should normally be given to an audit junior.

Tax planning

The audit junior should not be advising the client on tax planning matters. This is an example of a non-audit service, which can create self-review and advocacy threats to independence. As discussed above, the audit junior does not have the appropriate level of skill and knowledge to perform such work.

The junior's work on tax indicates that the audit has not been properly supervised, and that the junior does not seem to understand the ethical implications created. As part of a good quality control system, all members of the audit team should understand the objectives of the work they have been allocated and the limit to their responsibilities.

(b) **(i)** **Planning a forensic investigation**

Planning the investigation will involve consideration of similar matters to those involved in planning an audit.

The planning should commence with a meeting with the client at which the investigation is discussed. In particular, the investigation team should develop an understanding of the events surrounding the theft and the actions taken by the client since it occurred. Matters that should be clarified with the client include:

- The objective of the investigation – to quantify the amount to be claimed under the insurance cover
- Whether the client has informed the police and the actions taken by the police so far
- Whether the thieves have been captured and any stolen goods recovered
- Whether the thieves are suspected to be employees of the Group

- Any planned deadline by which time the insurance claim needs to be submitted
- Whether the client has contacted the insurance company and discussed the events leading to the potential claim.

The insurance policy should be scrutinised to clarify the exact terms of the insurance, to ensure that both the finished goods and stolen lorry will be included in the claim. The period of the insurance cover should be checked, to ensure that the date of the theft is covered, and the client should confirm that payments to the insurance company are up to date, to ensure the cover has not lapsed.

The audit firm should also consider the resources that will be needed to conduct the work. Kennel & Co has a forensic accounting department, so will have staff with relevant skills, but the firm should consider if staff with specific experience of insurance claims work are available.

The client should confirm that the investigation team will have full access to information required, and are able to discuss the matter with the police and the insurance company without fear of breaching confidentiality.

The output of the investigation should be confirmed, which is likely to be a report addressed to the insurance company. It should be clarified that the report is not to be distributed to any other parties. Kennel & Co should also confirm whether they would be required to act as expert witness in the event of the thieves being caught and prosecuted.

Tutorial note

Credit will also be awarded for explanations of acceptance issues such as the need for a separate engagement letter drawn up to cover the forensic investigation, outlining the responsibilities of the investigation team and of the client. Fees should also be discussed and agreed.

(ii) Procedures

- Watch the CCTV to form an impression of the quantity of goods stolen, for example, how many boxes were loaded onto the lorry.
- If possible, from the CCTV, determine if the boxes contain either mobile phones or laptop computers.
- Inspect the boxes of goods remaining in the warehouse to determine how many items of finished goods are in each box.
- Agree the cost of an individual mobile phone and laptop computer to accounting records, such as cost cards.
- Perform an inventory count on the boxes of goods remaining in the warehouse and reconcile to the latest inventory movement records.
- Discuss the case with the police to establish if any of the goods have been recovered and if, in the opinion of the police, this is likely to happen.
- Obtain details of the stolen lorry, for example the licence plate, and agree the lorry back to the non-current asset register where its carrying value should be shown.

Examiner's comments

This question contained two separate requirements in relation to the same client, the Retriever Group. The first requirement was largely based around quality control and ethics, the second to do with a forensic investigation. The scenario provided was not long, and candidates did not appear to be time pressured when attempting this question.

Requirement (a) described various matters that had arisen during the performance of the audit as described one of the audit juniors, including time pressure, deviations from the audit plan, and the type of work that had been performed by the audit juniors, some of which was inappropriate. The requirement asked candidates to evaluate the quality control, ethical and other professional issues arising in the planning and performance of the audit. Answers on the whole were satisfactory, and candidates seemed comfortable with applying their knowledge of quality control requirements and ethical threats to the scenario.

Most answers were well structured, working through each piece of information and discussing the matters in a relevant way. There were a number of scripts where the maximum marks were awarded for this requirement.

The common strengths seen in many answers included:

- Identifying that the audit had not been planned well, as it was time pressured and the allocation of tasks to audit juniors was not commensurate with their knowledge and experience.
- Discussing the problems in the direction and supervision of the audit, including the significant issue of the audit manager instructing the juniors not to follow planned audit procedures.
- Appreciating that review procedures were not being performed in accordance with ISA requirements, and that audit juniors did not know the limit of their responsibilities.
- Explaining the ethical threats caused by the audit junior's inappropriate work on deferred tax and tax planning.
- Describing the lack of competence and integrity of the audit manager in allowing the audit to be performed to such poor quality.
- Recommending that the audit team members receive training on quality control and ethical issues, and that the audit files should be subject to a detailed quality control review with a view to some areas of the audit possibly being re-performed.

It was especially encouraging to see that most candidates were not just able to identify the problems but could also explain and evaluate them to some extent.

Requirement (b) contained a short scenario describing a burglary that had occurred at the Retriever Group. The Group's audit committee had asked the audit firm's forensic accounting department to provide a forensic accounting service to determine the amount to be claimed on the Group's insurance policy.

The requirement asked candidates to identify and explain the matters to be considered and steps to be taken in planning the forensic investigation, and for the procedures to be performed. Unfortunately answers to this requirement were overall unsatisfactory indicating that this is not a well understood part of the syllabus.

Some answers tended to include one or more of the following in relation to the first part of the requirement:

- A lengthy discussion of what a forensic investigation is, including long definitions, with no application to the scenario – this was not asked for. This tended to be based on rote learning and earned few, if any marks.
- An assumption that management had already quantified the amount to be claimed, and that the forensic investigation would 'audit' that amount – leading to mostly irrelevant answer points.
- A discussion about fraud and the lack of integrity of management for 'allowing' the fraud to take place – this was often accompanied by lengthy speculation about the control deficiencies that failed to prevent the burglary from happening.
- A focus on whether adequate safeguards could be put in place to allow the audit firm's forensic accounting department to perform the investigation – this is a valid consideration to an extent, but the question did clearly state that there was no ethical threat.
- A discussion on the accounting treatment necessary for the stolen goods – again, not asked for.

In relation to the second part of the requirement, while some answers gave well described and relevant procedures to quantify the loss, many focused exclusively on determining the volume of goods stolen and said nothing about the value of them. Many suggested discussing the amount to be claimed with the insurance provider and comparing our figure with theirs, clearly not understanding the point of the forensic investigation being to provide the amount to be claimed in the first place. On the plus side, most answers included suggestions that reconciliation should be performed between the latest inventory count records and the amount of goods currently in the warehouse, though these were not often presented as procedures.

On the whole it was clear that many candidates were unprepared for a question requirement of this type, and that again it is apparent that a significant number of candidates rely on rote learnt knowledge and have difficulty to develop relevant answer points for a given scenario. Some candidates barely attempted this requirement, which for scripts achieving a mark that is a marginal fail is obviously a significant issue.

ACCA marking scheme		
		Marks
(a)	**Quality control, ethical and other professional matters** Up to 2 marks for each matter evaluated (up to a maximum 3 marks for identification only) – Time pressure – Planned procedures ignored on potentially material item – Sampling method changed – increases sampling risk – Inappropriate review by juniors – Inappropriate delegation of tasks – Deferred tax – management not competent – Deferred tax – self-review/management responsibility threat – Tax planning – non-audit service with advocacy threat – Junior lacks experience for this work regardless of ethical issues – Junior not supervised/directed appropriately – Overall conclusion	
	Maximum	**13**

(b) (i) **Planning the forensic investigation**

Up to 1½ marks for each planning matter identified and explained (up to a maximum 2 marks for identification only)

- Develop understanding of the events surrounding the theft
- Meeting with client to discuss the investigation
- Confirm insurance policy details (period and level of cover)
- Agree output of investigation
- Confirm access to necessary information
- Discuss confidentiality and ability to discuss with police/insurance company
- Consider resources for the investigation team
- Deadlines/fees

(ii) **Procedures to be performed**

1 mark for each specific procedure recommended:

- Watch the CCTV
- If possible, from the CCTV, determine the type of goods stolen
- Determine how many items of finished goods are in each box
- Agree the cost of an individual item to accounting records
- Perform an inventory count and reconcile to the latest inventory movement records
- Discuss the case with the police to establish if any of the goods have been recovered
- Obtain details of the stolen lorry and agree to the non-current asset register

Maximum	**12**
Total	**25**

39 SPANIEL *Walk in the footsteps of a top tutor*

Top tutor tips

Part (a) addresses the issue of auditor liability and whether the audit firm has been negligent due to failure to detect a fraud. Knowledge of the conditions for a negligence claim to succeed and discussion of each of these conditions in turn should help to score the marks available.

Part (b) is a discussion question regarding the difficulties auditing financial instruments and the matters to be considered when planning the audit of forward exchange contracts. For the first part, think about the risks associated with financial instruments. For the planning aspects, think about what the auditor does at the planning stage of an audit and why, and apply it to the specific area of financial instruments.

(a) It is not the auditor's primary responsibility to detect fraud. According to ISA 240 *The Auditor's Responsibilities Relating to Fraud in an Audit of Financial Statements*, management is primarily responsible for preventing and detecting fraud. The auditor is required to obtain reasonable assurance that the financial statements are free from material misstatement whether caused by fraud or error.

The total amount estimated to have been stolen in the payroll fraud represents 5.6% of Spaniel's assets. If the amount has been stolen consistently over a 12-month period, then $3 million (8/12 × 4.5 million) had been stolen prior to the year end of 31 December 2012. $3 million is material, representing 3.8% of total assets at the year end. Therefore the fraud was material and it could be reasonably expected that it should have been discovered.

However, material misstatements arising due to fraud can be difficult for the auditor to detect. This is because fraud is deliberately hidden by the perpetrators using sophisticated accounting techniques established to conceal the fraudulent activity. False statements may be made to the auditors and documents may have been forged. This means that material frauds could go undetected, even if appropriate procedures have been carried out.

ISA 240 requires that an audit is performed with an attitude of professional scepticism. This may not have been the case. Spaniel Co is a long-standing client, and the audit team may have lost their sceptical attitude. Necessary tests of control on payroll were not carried out because in previous years it had been possible to rely on the client's controls.

It seems that ISAs may not have been adhered to during the audit of Spaniel Co. ISA 330 *The Auditor's Responses to Assessed Risks* requires that the auditor shall design and perform tests of controls to obtain sufficient appropriate audit evidence as to the operating effectiveness of relevant controls if the auditor's assessment of risks of material misstatement at the assertion level includes an expectation that the controls are operating effectively. It can be acceptable for the auditor to use audit evidence from a previous audit about the operating effectiveness of specific controls but only if the auditor confirms that no changes have taken place. The audit partner should explain whether this was the case.

Substantive procedures have not been performed on payroll either. This effectively means that payroll has not been audited.

This leads to a conclusion that the audit firm may have been negligent in conducting the audit. Negligence is a common law concept in which an injured party must prove three things in order to prove that negligence has occurred:

- That the auditor owes a duty of care
- That the duty of care has been breached
- That financial loss has been caused by the negligence.

Looking at these points in turn, Groom & Co owes a duty of care to Spaniel Co, because a contract exists between the two parties. The company represents all the shareholders as a body, and there is an automatic duty of care owed to the shareholders as a body by the auditor.

A breach of duty of care must be proved for a negligence claim against the audit firm to be successful. Duty of care generally means that the audit firm must perform the audit work to a good standard and that relevant legal and professional requirements and principles have been followed. For an audit firm, it is important to be able to demonstrate that ISAs have been adhered to. Unfortunately, it seems that ISAs have been breached and so the audit firm is likely to have been negligent in the audit of payroll.

Tutorial note

Credit will be awarded for references to legal cases as examples of situations where audit firms have been found to have been negligent in performing an audit, such as Re Kingston Cotton Mill.

Finally, a financial loss has been suffered by the audit client, being the amount stolen while the fraud was operating.

In conclusion, Spaniel Co is likely to be able to successfully prove that the audit firm has been negligent in the audit of payroll, and that Groom & Co is liable for some or all of the financial loss suffered.

(b) The audit of financial instruments

There are many reasons why financial instruments are challenging to audit. The instruments themselves, the transactions to which they relate, and the associated risk exposures can be difficult for both management and auditors to understand. If the auditor does not fully understand the financial instrument and its impact on the financial statements, it will be difficult to assess the risk of material misstatement and to detect errors in the accounting treatment and associated disclosures. Even relatively simple financial instruments can be complex to account for.

The specialist nature of many financial instruments means that the auditor may need to rely on an auditor's expert as a source of evidence. In using an expert, the auditor must ensure the objectivity and competence of that expert, and then must evaluate the adequacy of the expert's work, which can be very difficult to do where the focus of the work is so specialist and difficult to understand.

The auditor may also find that there is a lack of evidence in relation to financial instruments, or that evidence tends to come from management. For example, many of the financial reporting requirements in relation to the valuation of financial instruments are based on fair values. Fair values are often based on models which depend on management judgement. Valuations are therefore often subjective and derived from management assumptions which increase the risk of material misstatement.

It is imperative that the auditor retains professional scepticism in the audit of financial instruments, but this may be difficult to do when faced with a complex and subjective transaction or balance for which there is little evidence other than management's judgement.

There may also be control issues relating to financial instruments. Often financial instruments are dealt with by a specialist department and it may be a few individuals who exert significant influence over the financial instruments that are entered into. This specialist department may not be fully integrated into the finance function, leading to the accounting treatment being dealt with outside the normal accounting system. Internal controls may be deficient and there may not be the opportunity for much segregation of duty. However, some companies will have established strong internal controls around financial instruments, leading to a lower risk of material misstatement.

In planning the audit of Bulldog's financial instruments, the auditor must first gain an understanding of the relevant accounting and disclosure requirements. For example, the applicable financial reporting standards should be clarified, which are likely to be IFRS 9 *Financial Instruments* and IFRS 7 *Financial Instruments: Disclosures*. These standards can be complex to apply, and the auditor should develop a thorough understanding of how they relate to Bulldog's financial instruments.

The auditor must also obtain an understanding of the instruments in which Bulldog Co has invested or to which it is exposed, including the characteristics of the instruments, and gain an understanding of Bulldog's reasons for entering into the financial instruments and its policy towards them.

It is important that the resources needed to audit the financial instruments are carefully considered. The competence of members of the audit firm to audit these transactions should be assessed, and it may be that an auditor's expert needs to be engaged. If so, this should be explained to the client. Instructions will have to be drawn up and given to the expert to ensure that the work performed is in line with audit objectives and follows the relevant financial reporting requirements, for example, in relation to valuing the financial instruments.

The audit planning should include obtaining an understanding of the internal control relevant to Bulldog's financial instruments, including the involvement, if any, of internal audit. An understanding of how financial instruments are monitored and controlled assists the auditor in determining the nature, timing and extent of audit procedures, for example, whether to perform tests on controls.

Specific consideration should be given to understanding management's method for valuing financial instruments for recognition in the year-end financial statements. The valuation is likely to involve some form of estimate, and ISA 540 *Auditing Accounting Estimates, Including Fair Value Accounting Estimates and Related Disclosures* requires the auditor to obtain an understanding of how management makes accounting estimates and the data on which accounting estimates are based.

Finally, the materiality of the financial instruments should be determined and the significance of the risk exposure associated with them should be assessed.

Examiner's comments

This was the least popular of the section B questions, though for UK and IRL candidates this was less the case.

Requirement (a) provided a scenario which described that an audit firm had given an unmodified audit opinion on Spaniel's financial statements, and that subsequent to the auditor's report being issued a fraud had been discovered that had been operating during the period covered by the auditor's report. The scenario also pointed out that the audit firm had not performed audit procedures in relation to the area in which the fraud was occurring, namely payroll. The requirement asked candidates to explain the matters to be considered in determining the audit firm's liability to Spaniel Co in respect of the fraud.

There were some excellent answers to this requirement. The best ones clearly outlined the factors that have to be proven to determine negligence, and applied them methodically to the scenario. The materiality of the fraud was considered, the duty of care owed to the audit client, and the fact that the auditor may not have been exercising professional scepticism during the audit due to the long-standing nature of the audit appointment. It was also appropriate to discuss the responsibilities of management and auditors in relation to fraud, and whether it is appropriate for auditors to rely on the conclusions reached in previous year's audit.

Some answers tended to only provide a rote-learnt description of responsibilities in relation to fraud, and usually failed to reach an appropriate conclusion. With little application to the scenario there is limited scope for marks to be awarded.

Requirement (b) described a different audit client, Bulldog Co, which had expanded overseas and set up a treasury management function dealing with forward exchange contracts. The requirement was to discuss why the audit of financial statements is challenging and explain the matters to be considered in planning the audit of the forward exchange contracts. Answers here were extremely mixed in quality. Satisfactory answers focused on why financial instruments generally are difficult to audit, discussing their complex nature, the changing landscape of financial reporting requirements, the potential for both client and auditor to lack appropriate knowledge and skills, and the frequent need to rely on an expert. In terms of planning the audit, adequate answers focused on simple matters such as managing resources, obtaining an understanding of the nature of the contracts and the controls in relation to them, and assessing how management value the financial instruments.

Inadequate answers did not include much reference to audit at all, and simply listed out financial reporting rules, with no consideration of audit implications other than saying that financial instruments are complex and subjective.

There were very few references to relevant ISA requirements, and little evidence that the audit of complex matters such as financial instruments had been studied at all, even though it is a topical current issue.

ACCA marking scheme

		Marks
(a)	**Fraud and auditor's liability**	
	Generally up to 2 marks for each point explained:	
	– Auditor's responsibility in relation to fraud	
	– Materiality calculation of the fraud	
	– Reasons why fraud is hard to detect	
	– Audit firm may not have been sufficiently sceptical	
	– Non-adherence to ISAs on controls assessment and evidence obtained	
	– Discuss whether duty of care owed to client	
	– Discuss breach of duty of care	
	– Identify financial loss suffered and firm likely to have been negligent	
	Maximum	12
(b)	**Audit of financial instruments**	
	Generally up to 1½ marks for each point explained:	
	Why is audit of financial instruments challenging?	
	– Financial reporting requirements complex	
	– Transactions themselves difficult to understand	
	– Lack of evidence and need to rely on management judgement	
	– Auditor may need to rely on expert	
	– May be hard to maintain attitude of scepticism	
	– Internal controls may be deficient	
	Planning implications	
	– Obtain understanding of accounting and disclosure requirements	
	– Obtain understanding of client's financial instruments	
	– Determine resources, i.e. skills needed and need for an auditor's expert	
	– Consider internal controls including internal audit	
	– Determine materiality of financial instruments	
	– Understand management's method for valuing financial instruments	
	Maximum	8
Total		20

40 YORK CO *Walk in the footsteps of a top tutor*

Top tutor tips

Part (a) requires a discussion of the risks of fraud in revenue recognition. In this situation, fraud involves manipulating the revenue figure in the financial statements to show a different picture. Therefore your answer should consider the ways that management can achieve this.

Part (b) requires you to consider two issues and how the auditor should address them. Your answer should follow a logical process. Discuss the issue in the scenario and what it means for the audit or auditor. State any further evidence that is needed and the actions the auditor should take to form a conclusion on the issue. Finally, consider any reporting requirements.

(a) There are a number of reasons why there should be a presumption that there are risks of fraud in revenue recognition. One reason is that managers of companies are often under pressure, particularly in listed companies, to achieve certain performance targets. The achievement of those targets often impacts their job security and their compensation. These performance targets often include measures of revenue growth, providing an incentive for management to use earnings management techniques.

In other companies there may be incentives to understate revenues, for example, to reduce reported profits and, therefore, company taxation charges. This may be more relevant to private limited companies where management may not be under such pressure to achieve revenue based targets.

There is also usually a high volume of revenue transactions during a financial period. As the volume of transactions increases, the risk of failing to detect fraud and error using traditional, sample based auditing techniques also increases. This means that it is potentially easier for management to successfully manipulate these balances than other balances which are subject to a lower volume of transactions. Material misstatement through the manipulation of revenue recognition can be readily achieved by recording revenue in an earlier or later accounting period than is proper or by creating fictitious revenues.

Revenue recognition can also be a judgmental area. Examples include the recognition of revenues on long-term contracts, such as the construction of buildings, and from the provision of services. These require the estimation of the percentage of completion at the period end, increasing the scope for management to manipulate reported results.

As well as requiring judgement, revenue recognition can also be a complex issue. For example, some sales have multiple elements, such as the sale of goods and the separate sale of related maintenance contracts and warranties. This added complexity increases the risk of manipulation.

In some companies, for example, those in the retail industry, a high proportion of revenue may be earned through cash sales. This increases the risk of the theft of cash and the consequent manipulation of recorded revenues to conceal this crime.

Methods of revenue manipulation have also featured prominently in cases of accounting fraud, such as Enron and Worldcom. The prevalence of these methods in modern accounting frauds and the failure of auditors to detect this in these cases suggests that it is one of the more common methods of earnings management and one which auditors should rightly consider as high risk.

While revenue recognition in general may be considered a high risk area, it is not always the case; companies with simple revenue streams or a low volume of transactions may be considered at low risk of fraud through revenue manipulations. Accordingly ISA 240 *The Auditor's Responsibility Relating to Fraud in an Audit of Financial Statements* permits the rebuttable of the fraud risk presumption for revenue recognition. One example of simple revenue streams would be where a company leases properties for fixed annual amounts over a fixed period of time. If this is the case, the reasons for not treating revenue as a high fraud risk area must be fully documented by the auditor.

(b) (i) Cash transfers

This unusual, unexplained cash transfer into a foreign bank account may indicate that Phil Smith is using York Co to carry out money laundering. Money laundering is defined as the process by which criminals attempt to conceal the origin and ownership of the proceeds of their criminal activity, allowing them to maintain control over the proceeds and, ultimately, providing a legitimate cover for the sources of their income.

It is possible that the proceeds of criminal activity have been placed into York's bank account to enable them to transfer the funds into a foreign account, thus providing them with the appearance of legitimacy and creating a trail which is difficult to trace to the original source. This process is known as 'layering'. According to ACCA's Technical Factsheet 145 *Anti-money laundering guidance for the accountancy sector*, money laundering can result from a single transaction such as the cash placed into York Co's bank account.

The fact that Mr Smith retains sole control over cash management and that the financial controller has no oversight or involvement in this indicates weak controls over cash, for example, there appears to be no segregation of duty which may be the intention of Mr Smith to facilitate illegal activity. That he has failed to provide any documentary evidence, despite the request to do so by the audit team, only arouses suspicion further. It is also possible that the company is being used as a vehicle for money laundering without Mr Smith's knowledge. It is possible that the money has been accepted in good faith without the source of the funding being adequately verified.

The amount which has been transferred represents 1.3% of total assets, which is material to the financial statements. The engagement, and particularly matters relating to cash transactions, should now be considered as high risk and approached with a high degree of professional scepticism. The audit files should now be subject to an independent second partner review. The firm may also wish to seek legal advice given the potential legal implications of dealing with a client involved in money laundering.

To properly assess the impact of the transaction on the financial statements, the audit firm needs to understand the accounting entries which have been made. The debit side of the entry would be to cash, and the audit team should enquire as to where the credit side of the entry has been recognised. Possibly the credit has been recognised as revenue or possibly it has been contra'd against the cash payment which was made the next day.

The situation should be reported as soon as possible to the firm's Money Laundering Reporting Officer (MLRO). The MLRO is responsible for receiving and evaluating reports of suspected money laundering from colleagues within the firm. They will make a decision as to whether further enquiries are required and, if necessary, will make reports to the appropriate authorities.

Finally, care must now be taken during the remaining audit that no-one 'tips off' the client that their activity is being treated as suspicious and that a report will be made to the MLRO. 'Tipping off' the client could prejudice any consequent investigation and may itself be considered a criminal offence, depending on relevant legislation. According to Technical Factsheet 145, a tipping off disclosure may be made in writing or verbally, and either directly or indirectly so the audit team must ensure that when discussing the matter with Mr Smith, he is not alerted to the suspicions of money laundering.

(ii) Legal dispute

The creation of provisions and their reversal in consequent years is a commonly used creative accounting technique. As such, this is a potentially high risk area of the audit. The reversal of the provision in the current year increases the reported profit before tax by $150,000, which represents 6.8% of profit. This is therefore material and should be treated with appropriate professional scepticism.

In accordance with IAS 37 *Provisions, Contingent Liabilities and Contingent Assets*, the provision should only have been recorded originally if: York Co had an obligation as a result of a past event; if it was considered probable that an outflow of cash would occur; and if a reliable estimate of the amount was available. Given that this is a material amount, there should be audit evidence on the prior year file concerning the appropriateness of the original amount recorded.

It would be prudent to review the evidence held on the prior year audit file to assess the quality of evidence which was obtained relating to the assumptions made regarding the probability of payment. With legal disputes one would expect to see some documentary evidence from legal experts, such as the company's lawyers. It is unlikely that management assumptions and a written representation would have been considered appropriate as evidence in a matter where legal expertise is required.

For the same reason it is unlikely that the opinions of Mr Smith are likely to be considered as sufficient justification for reversing the provision in the current year. The lack of additional documentary evidence and Mr Smith's lack of availability to discuss the matter with the audit team further arouses suspicions of the validity of the decision to reverse the provision.

The audit manager should contact the client and request confirmation of Mr Smith's opinions from the company lawyers, along with any relevant documentation of legal proceedings or agreements reached with the ex-employee.

If the client is unable to provide any further documentation, then the provision should be reinstated in full. This should be noted on the summary of proposed adjustments to the financial statements and sent to the client along with a request that they amend all the adjustments identified.

Examiner's comments

The first part required candidates to discuss why auditors should presume that there is a risk of fraud in revenue recognition and this requirement was poorly answered with most candidates setting out lengthy explanations of the respective duties of the auditor and management for the identification and prevention of fraud and thereby not answering the question. Strong answers considered management bias and targets, judgments in complex business and cut-off errors.

The second part explored two unusual issues which had occurred in an entrepreneurial audit client. Many candidates were able to identify the potential money laundering transaction and identified the placement and layering stages which were involved. Most candidates answered this part of the question well and were able to identify; the need for proper evidence, the poor controls over payments, notification to the MLRO and avoiding tipping-off the client. Candidates were also asked to consider the release of a provision relating to a legal claim for which evidential documentation was not available. Most candidates discussed the implications of the reversal quite well but failed to identify the creative accounting and profit smoothing which was the purpose behind the provision reversal.

In both parts numerous candidates demonstrated poor exam technique and diverted into highlighting what would be included in the auditor's report which was not required.

ACCA Marking scheme

		Marks
(a)	**Fraud and revenue recognition**	
	Generally 1 mark for each point of discussion:	
	– Management targets/incentives	
	– High volume of transactions	
	– Use of judgement	
	– Complexity of accounting	
	– Cash sales	
	– Common in recent accounting frauds	
	– Not always complex/rebuttable permitted	
	Maximum	**7**
(b)	**Implications for completion of audit**	
	Generally 1 mark for each well explained implication for the audit or recommendation for further action:	
	(i) Cash transfers	
	– Indication of money laundering	
	– Layering	
	– Weakness in controls over cash	
	– Need to understand the accounting entries	
	– Failure to provide evidence	
	– Increased risk/need for scepticism	
	– Need for independent review	
	– Report to MLRO	
	– Care in avoiding 'tipping off'	
	Maximum	**7**

(ii) Legal dispute	
– Potential creative accounting	
– Material impact on profit for the year	
– Review evidence on previous file	
– Criteria for recognition (½ each to max of 1)	
– Insufficiency of current evidence	
– Request for further evidence (1 mark for each well described procedure to obtain further evidence)	
– Possible need to reinstate provision to be discussed with management	
Maximum	**6**
Total	**20**

41 TONY GROUP *Walk in the footsteps of a top tutor*

Top tutor tips

Part (a) deals with professional scepticism and a technical article was published prior to the exam on this topic. Students are reminded to pay attention to technical articles published by the examining team in the run up to the exam.

Part (b) then looks at how to apply professional scepticism to a situation. Think about whether there is any incentive for management to mislead the auditor and whether they are trying to withhold information or appear to be trying to influencing your audit procedures.

Part (c) is a straightforward requirement dealing with forensic procedures.

(a) Professional scepticism is defined in ISA 200 *Overall Objectives of the Independent Auditor and the Conduct of an Audit in Accordance with International Standards on Auditing* as an attitude that includes a questioning mind, being alert to conditions which may indicate possible misstatement due to error or fraud and a critical assessment of audit evidence.

ISA 200 requires the auditor to plan and perform an audit with professional scepticism, recognising that circumstances may exist which cause the financial statements to be materially misstated. It is important to use professional scepticism at all stages of the audit. Professional scepticism can reduce the risk of material misstatements caused by fraud going undetected.

Professional scepticism includes being alert to the existence of contradictory audit evidence and being able to assess assumptions and judgements critically and without bias, and being ready to challenge management where necessary. It is also important that the auditor considers the reliability of information provided by management during the audit.

Recently, regulatory bodies such as the IAASB have stressed the importance of the auditor's use of professional scepticism. The increased use of principles-based financial reporting frameworks such as IFRS Standards, and the prevalence of fair value accounting which introduces subjectivity and judgement into financial reporting are examples of the reasons why the use of professional scepticism by auditors is increasingly important. It is imperative that professional scepticism is applied to areas of financial reporting which are complex or highly judgmental.

Going concern assessments and related party transactions are also examples of areas where management must exercise judgement in determining the appropriate accounting treatment, and where the potential for management bias is high. Therefore these areas need to be approached with professional scepticism.

The application of professional scepticism is closely aligned with maintaining objectivity, and it is difficult to remain sufficiently sceptical when certain threats to objectivity are present. Ultimately, the exercise of professional scepticism should work to reduce audit risk by ensuring that the auditor has sufficient and appropriate evidence to support the audit opinion, and that all evidence obtained, especially in relation to areas of high risk of material misstatement, has been critically evaluated and is based on reliable information.

(b) **(i)** The finance director seems to be dictating the audit work to be performed. The audit manager should decide the extent of audit procedures in response to the risk of material misstatement identified. The manager should consider why the finance director seems so insistent that his file is used as the main source of audit evidence; he may be hiding something relevant to the impairment which would be revealed if the auditor looked at other sources of evidence.

The Group's profit before tax has fallen by 33.3%, indicating that a significant impairment loss amounting to more than the $50,000 calculated by the finance director may need to be recognised. There is a risk of material misstatement in that the impairment loss is understated, and there is a risk that management bias has resulted in an inappropriate determination of the loss. The auditor therefore needs to be sceptical and alert for factors indicating that the loss is greater than that calculated by the finance director. Impairment testing is a complex and subjective area, and could be easily manipulated by management wishing to reduce the size of the loss recognised.

The audit manager should obtain corroborative evidence regarding the assumptions used and not just confirm that the assumptions are in line with management's risk assessment or the prior year audit file. The reliability of this source of evidence is not strong as it is prepared by management. An important part of professional scepticism is challenging management's assumptions, especially in an area of high judgement such as impairment testing.

The internal auditor checking the figures is also not a reliable source of evidence, as it is client-generated. The internal auditor may have been pressured to confirm the finance director's calculations.

Professional scepticism should also be applied to the comment that the assumptions are the same as in previous years. New factors impacting on impairment may have arisen during this year, affecting the determination of the impairment loss and up-to-date evidence on the assumptions used in this year's calculation should be sought.

The audit team should also remain alert when auditing balances and transactions other than goodwill in case there are other areas where Silvio does not appear to be providing all evidence required or where he is suggesting the audit approach to be taken.

While his comment does not seem to be intimidating in nature, the audit team should recognise that if Silvio does have something to hide in relation to the goodwill impairment, he may become more aggressive, in which case the matter should be brought to the attention of the firm's ethics partner and discussed with those charged with governance of the Group.

(ii) Audit procedures – impairment of goodwill

The auditor should perform the following procedures:

- The assumptions used in the impairment test should be confirmed as agreeing with the auditor's understanding of the business based on the current year's risk assessment procedures, e.g. assess the reasonableness of assumptions on cash flow projections.
- Confirm that the impairment review includes the goodwill relating to all business combinations.
- Consider the impact of the auditor's assessment of going concern on the impairment review, e.g. the impact on the assumption relating to growth rates which have been used as part of the impairment calculations.
- Obtain an understanding of the controls over the management's process of performing the impairment test including tests of the operating effectiveness of any controls in place, for example, over the review and approval of assumptions or inputs by appropriate levels of management and, where appropriate, those charged with governance.
- Confirm whether management has performed the impairment test or has used an expert.
- The methodology applied to the impairment review should be checked by the auditor, with inputs to calculations, e.g. discount rates, agreed to auditor-obtained information.
- Develop an independent estimate of the impairment loss and compare it to that prepared by management.
- Confirm that the impairment calculations exclude cash flows relating to tax and finance items.
- Perform sensitivity analysis to consider whether, and if so how, management has considered alternative assumptions and the impact of any alternative assumptions on the impairment calculations.
- Check the arithmetic accuracy of the calculations used in the impairment calculations.

> ***Tutorial note***
>
> *Credit will be awarded for other relevant audit procedures recommended.*

(c) Forensic investigation

- Interview the two suspects and question them regarding the nature of the cash payments made to the customers prior to the signing of the contracts.
- Use computer-assisted audit techniques to identify all new customers in the year and any payments made to these customers, and total the amounts.
- Review the terms of the contracts with customers for any details of payments included in the contract, and understand the business rationale for any such payments.

Tutorial note

It would be unusual for the Group to be making any payments to customers, so these terms would need to be viewed with professional scepticism.

- Review the email and other correspondence entered into by the two suspects for any further information about the cash payments, e.g. specifically who the payments were discussed with.
- Perform tests of control on the authorisation of cash payments to find out if these payments were known to anyone operating in a supervisory capacity.

Examiner's comments

This question focused on professional scepticism, the audit of goodwill impairment, and a forensic investigation into alleged bribery payments made by several of the audit client's employees.

Requirement (a) was a discussion, asking candidates to explain the meaning of the term professional scepticism and to discuss its importance in planning and performing an audit. It was clear that many candidates had read and understood the contents of a recent article on the topic of professional scepticism. Most answers provided an appropriate definition of professional scepticism and went on to discuss how it links to audit quality. Stronger candidates also discussed how the auditor should apply professional scepticism when considering the risk of material misstatement associated with fraud and areas of the financial statements that rely on the application of judgment. Few candidates however, discussed the recent activities of the regulatory bodies in respect of professional scepticism.

The second part of the question, requirement (b), involved a scenario which described how the finance director of the Tony Group was insisting that the audit firm should rely on a file prepared by him in their audit of goodwill impairment. The file contained workings and assumptions and had been checked by the Group's head of internal audit. The requirement asked candidates to discuss how professional scepticism should be applied to the scenario, and to explain the principal audit procedures to be performed on the impairment of goodwill.

Many candidates were able to explain that the Group finance director was intimidating the audit firm, that his workings were not sufficient as a source of evidence, and that he may have something to hide. It was disappointing that few candidates appreciated that the Group's profit before tax had fallen significantly, and therefore the small impairment to goodwill suggested by the finance director was unlikely to be sufficient in the circumstances, and probably influenced by management bias. Most candidates did however realise that the audit firm should perform their own workings and not place complete reliance on the procedures that had been performed by the head of internal audit.

The requirement relating to procedures on goodwill impairment was poorly attempted. The evidence points provided by candidates for this requirement tended to revolve around recalculation or a discussion with management. Very few suggested specific procedures that would allow the auditor to develop their own expectation in terms of the impairment necessary, which could then be compared with the finance director's workings. This was disappointing, as impairment has featured in several P7 exams as an audit issue and is a topic that candidates should be better prepared to tackle. Many candidates did not answer the question, and simply described the accounting treatment for goodwill, or suggested procedures that were relevant to the calculation of goodwill at acquisition but not relevant to a review of its impairment.

Requirement (c) asked candidates to recommend the procedures to be used in performing a forensic investigation. This was in relation to alleged bribery, whereby members of the Group's sales team were suspected of making payments to customers in order to secure contracts. Answers to this requirement were weak. Many candidates gave no procedures at all, therefore not answering the question set, and instead described agreeing the scope of the work or whether the investigation could be performed for ethical reasons. Other candidates gave broad statements instead of procedures, such as "quantify the loss" without explaining how this could be done, or "interview the suspects" without saying what the purpose of this interview would be.

It was quite clear that many candidates had chosen to attempt this option question because they had read the relevant article on professional scepticism, but that they had very limited knowledge on either impairment audit issues or on forensic investigation procedures. To improve exam technique, candidates should ensure that they can have a good attempt at all requirements of a question before selecting that question in the exam.

ACCA Marking scheme

		Marks
(a)	**Professional scepticism discussion**	
	Generally up to 1½ marks for each point discussed, including:	
	– Definition of professional scepticism (1 mark for definition)	
	– Explaining professional scepticism	
	– Link between professional scepticism and ethics/objectivity	
	– Importance in relation to complex and subjective areas of the audit	
	– Importance in relation to the audit of going concern	
	– Discussion of regulatory bodies actions in relation to professional scepticism	
	Maximum	**5**
(b)	**(i) Applying professional scepticism**	
	Generally up to 1½ marks for each point discussed, and 1 mark for calculation of materiality.	
	Risk that impairment loss understated due to Group's fall in profit	
	The determination of the impairment loss is judgmental and subject to management bias	
	Auditor should question the reasons for finance director's insistence that no other audit work is needed	
	Evidence provided by the finance director is not reliable (client-generated)	
	Assumptions are unlikely to have stayed the same since last year	
	Audit team should remain alert for other instances where professional scepticism is needed	
	Possible threat of intimidation by the finance director	
	Maximum	**6**
	(ii) Procedures on impairment	
	Generally 1 mark for each procedure explained:	
	– Review all assumptions used in preparing projected cash flows	
	– Confirm that the impairment review includes the goodwill relating to all business combinations	
	– Consider impact of auditor's assessment of the Group's going concern status	
	– Consider operating effectiveness of any controls in place	
	– Confirm whether management has performed the impairment test or used an expert	
	– Recalculate amounts based on auditor-generated inputs	
	– Develop an independent estimate of the impairment loss and compare to that prepared by management	
	– Confirm that the impairment calculations exclude cash flows relating to tax and finance items	
	– Perform sensitivity analysis	
	– Check the arithmetic accuracy of the calculations	
	Maximum	**5**

(c)	**Procedures on alleged bribery payments** Generally 1 mark for each procedure explained: – Interview the two suspects – Identify all new customers in the year and any payments made to these customers – Review the terms of contracts with customers – Review the email and other correspondence entered into by the two suspects – Perform tests of control on the authorisation of cash payments	
	Maximum	**4**
Total		**20**

42 HERON *Walk in the footsteps of a top tutor*

Top tutor tips

Part (a) requires knowledge of the auditor's responsibilities when suspicious transactions are identified. Money laundering is a topic regularly examined and this requirement should be quite straightforward.

Part (b) covers professional scepticism and how to apply it. In this scenario the auditor has been given contradictory evidence from the client and the requirement asks for the further actions that should be taken by the auditor. You should think of ways in which to obtain further evidence to reach a conclusion as to which evidence can be relied on.

(a) (i) The circumstances described by the audit senior indicate that Jack Heron may be using his company to carry out money laundering. Money laundering is defined as the process by which criminals attempt to conceal the origin and ownership of the proceeds of their criminal activity, allowing them to maintain control over the proceeds and, ultimately, providing a legitimate cover for the sources of their income. Money laundering activity may range from a single act, such as being in possession of the proceeds of one's own crime, to complex and sophisticated schemes involving multiple parties, and multiple methods of handling and transferring criminal property as well as concealing it and entering into arrangements to assist others to do so.

Heron's business is cash-based, making it an ideal environment for cash acquired through illegal activities to be legitimised by adding it to the cash paid genuinely by customers and posting it through the accounts. It appears that $2 million additional cash has been added to the genuine cash receipts from customers. This introduction of cash acquired through illegal activities into the business is known as 'placement'.

The fact that the owner himself posts transactions relating to revenue and cash is strange and therefore raises suspicions as to the legitimacy of the transactions he is posting through the accounts. Suspicions are heightened due to Jack Heron's refusal to explain the nature and reason for the journal entries he is making in the accounts.

The $2 million paid by electronic transfer is the same amount as the additional cash posted through the accounts. This indicates that the cash is being laundered and the transfer is known as the 'layering' stage, which is done to disguise the source and ownership of the funds by creating complex layers of transactions. Money launderers often move cash overseas as quickly as possible in order to distance the cash from its original source, and to make tracing the transaction more difficult. The 'integration' stage of money laundering occurs when upon successful completion of the layering process, the laundered cash is reintroduced into the financial system, for example, as payment for services rendered.

The secrecy over the reason for the cash transfer and lack of any supporting documentation is another indicator that this is a suspicious transaction.

Jack Heron's reaction to being questioned over the source of the cash and the electronic transfer point to the fact that he has something to hide. His behaviour is certainly lacking in integrity, and even if there is a genuine reason for the journals and electronic transfer his unhelpful and aggressive attitude may cast doubts as to whether the audit firm wishes to continue to retain Heron Co as a client.

The audit senior was correct to be alarmed by the situation. However, by questioning Jack Heron about it, the senior may have alerted him to the fact that the audit team is suspicious that money laundering is taking place. There is a potential risk that the senior has tipped off the client, which may prejudice any investigation into the situation.

Tipping off is itself an offence, though this can be defended against if the person did not know or suspect that the disclosure was likely to prejudice any investigation that followed.

The amount involved is clearly highly material to the financial statements and will therefore have an implication for the audit. The whole engagement should be approached as high risk and with a high degree of professional scepticism.

The firm may wish to consider whether it is appropriate to withdraw from the engagement (if this is possible under applicable law and regulation). However, this could result in a tipping off offence being committed, as on withdrawal the reasons should be discussed with those charged with governance.

If Lark & Co continue to act as auditor, the audit opinion must be considered very carefully and the whole audit subject to second partner review, as the firm faces increased liability exposure. Legal advice should be sought.

(ii) The audit senior should report the situation in an internal report to Lark & Co's Money Laundering Reporting Officer (MLRO). The MLRO is a nominated officer who is responsible for receiving and evaluating reports of suspected money laundering from colleagues within the firm, and making a decision as to whether further enquiries are required and if necessary making reports to the appropriate external body.

Lark & Co will probably have a standard form that should be used to report suspicions of money laundering to the MLRO.

Tutorial note

According to ACCA's Technical Factsheet 145 Anti-Money Laundering Guidance for the Accountancy Sector, there are no external requirements for the format of an internal report and the report can be made verbally or in writing.

The typical content of an internal report on suspected money laundering may include the name of the suspect, the amounts potentially involved, and the reasons for the suspicions with supporting evidence if possible, and the whereabouts of the laundered cash.

The report must be done as soon as possible, as failure to report suspicions of money laundering to the MLRO as soon as practicable can itself be an offence under the money laundering regulations.

The audit senior may wish to discuss their concerns with the audit manager in more detail before making the report, especially if the senior is relatively inexperienced and wants to hear a more senior auditor's view on the matter. However, the senior is responsible for reporting the suspicious circumstances at Heron Co to the MLRO.

Tutorial note

ACCA's Technical Factsheet 145 states that: 'An individual may discuss his suspicion with managers or other colleagues to assure himself of the reasonableness of his conclusions but, other than in group reporting circumstances, the responsibility for reporting to the MLRO remains with him. It cannot be transferred to anyone else, however junior or senior they are.'

(b) The term professional scepticism is defined in ISA 200 *Overall Objectives of the Independent Auditor and the Conduct of an Audit in Accordance with ISAs* as follows: 'An attitude that includes a questioning mind, being alert to conditions which may indicate possible misstatement due to error or fraud, and a critical assessment of audit evidence'.

Professional scepticism means for example, being alert to contradictory or unreliable audit evidence, and conditions that may indicate the existence of fraud. If professional scepticism is not maintained, the auditor may overlook unusual circumstances, use unsuitable audit procedures, or reach inappropriate conclusions when evaluating the results of audit work. In summary, maintaining an attitude of professional scepticism is important in reducing audit risk.

The Code of Ethics also refers to professional scepticism when discussing the importance of the auditor's independence of mind. It can therefore be seen as an ethical as well as a professional issue.

In the case of the audit of Coot Co, the audit junior has not exercised a sufficient degree of professional scepticism when obtaining audit evidence. Firstly, the reliability of the payroll supervisor's response to the junior's enquiry should be questioned. Additional and corroborating evidence should be sought for the assertion that the new employees are indeed temporary.

The absence of authorisation should also be further investigated. Authorisation is a control that should be in place for any additions to payroll, so it seems unusual that the control would not be in place even for temporary members of staff.

If it is proved correct that no authorisation is required for temporary employees the audit junior should have identified this as a control deficiency to be included in the report to those charged with governance.

The contradictory evidence from comments made by management also should be explored further. ISA 500 *Audit Evidence* states that 'if audit evidence obtained from one source is inconsistent with that obtained from another... the auditor shall determine what modifications or additions to audit procedures are necessary to resolve the matter'.

Additional procedures should therefore be carried out to determine which source of evidence is reliable. Further discussions should be held with management to clarify whether any additional employees have been recruited during the year.

The amendment of payroll could indicate that a fraud ('ghost employee') is being carried out by the payroll supervisor. Additional procedures should be conducted to determine whether the supervisor has made any other amendments to payroll to determine the possible scope of any fraud. Verification should be sought as to the existence of the new employees. The bank accounts into which their salaries are being paid should also be examined, to see if the payments are being made into the same account.

Finally, the audit junior should be made aware that it is not acceptable to just put a note on the file when matters such as the lack of authorisation come to light during the course of the audit. The audit junior should have discussed their findings with the audit senior or manager to seek guidance and proper supervision on whether further testing should be carried out.

Examiner's comments

This question focused on money laundering and fraud. Two short scenarios relating to two audit clients were presented.

Part (a)'s scenario described a cash-based business whose owner manager was acting suspiciously in relation to the accounting for cash sales. A large sum of cash had been transferred to an overseas bank account and the transaction had no supporting evidence. The first requirement, (a) (i) was to discuss the implications of these circumstances. This open requirement allowed for discussion of many different implications for the audit firm, included suspected fraud and/or money laundering, a poor control environment, the ethical implications of the owners intimidating behaviour, and problems for the audit firm in obtaining evidence. Most candidates covered a range of points and the majority correctly discussed fraud and/or money laundering.

Weaker answers tended to focus on the materiality of the cash transferred to overseas, and seemed not to notice the client's suspicious behaviour. Candidates are reminded that they will often be expected to identify a key issue in a question scenario and that in a question of this type it is important to stop and think about what is happening in the scenario before rushing to start to write an answer. This question is a good example of one where a relatively short answer could generate a lot of marks – if the scenario has been properly thought through before writing the answer.

Requirement (a) (ii) asked for an explanation of any reporting that should take place by the audit senior. Candidates who had identified money laundering as an issue in (a) (i) usually scored well here, describing the need to report to the audit firm's Money Laundering Reporting Officer, and what should be reported to them. Weaker answers discussed the auditor's report or that the fraud/money laundering should be reported to the client's management - this is not good advice given that the owner- manager was the person acting suspiciously and would have resulted in him being tipped off.

Part (b) described a client where unauthorised additions had been made to payroll, and contradictory audit evidence had been obtained. Candidates were asked to explain the term 'professional scepticism' and to recommend further actions to be taken by the auditor. Answers here were reasonably good, with most candidates able to attempt an explanation of the term, and most identifying poor controls leading to a possible fraud involving the payroll supervisor. Some very specific further procedures were often recommended, and candidates often scored better on part (b) than part (a) for this question.

ACCA marking scheme	
	Marks
(a) (i) **Implications of the audit senior's note**	
1 mark for each matter discussed relevant to money laundering:	
– Definition of money laundering	
– Placement – cash-based business	
– Owner posting transactions	
– Layering – electronic transfer to overseas	
– Secrecy and aggressive attitude	
– Audit to be considered very high risk	
– Senior may have tipped off the client	
– Firm may consider withdrawal from audit	
– But this may have tipping off consequences	
Maximum	**6**
(ii) **Reporting that should take place**	
Generally 1 mark for each comment:	
– Report suspicions immediately to MLRO	
– Failure to report is itself an offence	
– Examples of matters to be reported	
– Audit senior may discuss matters with audit manager but senior responsible for the report	
Maximum	**3**
(b) **Professional scepticism**	
Generally 1 mark for each comment:	
– Definition of professional scepticism	
– Explain – alert to contradictory evidence/unusual events/fraud indicator (up to 2 marks)	
– Part of ethical codes	
– Coot Co – evidence is unreliable and contradictory	
– Absence of authorisation is fraud indicator	
– Additional substantive procedures needed	
– Management's comments should be corroborated	
– Control deficiency to be reported to management/those charged with governance	
– Audit junior needs better supervision/training on how to deal with deficiencies identified	
Maximum	**6**
Total	**15**

REPORTING

43 RAVEN & CO *Walk in the footsteps of a top tutor*

Top tutor tips

Part (a) focuses on the governance and ethics areas of the syllabus. Be prepared for more than one topic area being examined in the same question like this. When dealing with ethical threats, identify and explain the threat. Take the discussion further by considering the significance of the threat. In this case, the situation involves the audit partner which makes the threat more significant. Finish off the discussion by stating any safeguards or actions the firm should implement.

Part (b) is a typical audit reporting question. There are two matters which need to be discussed individually first of all in terms of whether the issues are material to the financial statements and what impact the issue has on the audit or the financial statements. Finally, state the impact to the auditor's opinion and report.

(a) (i) Ethical and professional matters

Temporary recruitment of audit partner

Seconding a member of staff to an audit client may create a self-review threat. This would arise if the member of staff returns to the audit firm and considers matters or documentation which is the result of work which they performed while on assignment to the client.

In this situation, it is likely that the individual would be involved in preparing the financial systems of Gull Co for the flotation. If this is the case, it would create a significant threat to objectivity. This would be reduced if the role was focused on non-financial matters.

Additionally, the member of staff would work alongside employees of the client on a daily basis. This would overstep the normal professional boundary between auditor and client and may compromise the objectivity of the member of staff due to their familiarity with employees of the client.

In order to reduce this threat, the member of staff seconded to Gull Co should not be a current or future member of the audit team.

An additional risk would be if the seconded member of staff assumed managerial responsibilities of the client. This is not permitted. Given that Gull Co has specifically requested a partner, it appears as though they require someone senior, indicating that they may need someone to either make or significantly influence decision making.

In order to reduce this risk, the use of a less senior member of staff with relevant experience of the flotation process could be proposed and make it clear in the contract that they are not able to make decisions for Gull Co and that decision making will always remain their responsibility.

Alternatively, it could be recommended that Gull Co recruit the assistance of either the management or transaction advisory services team to assist them with the flotation as a separate engagement, thus circumventing the ethical threats identified.

UK syllabus: Ethical Standard section 2 *Financial, business, employment and personal relationships,* states that an audit firm shall not enter into an agreement with an audited entity to provide a partner or employee to work for a temporary period as if that individual were an employee of the audited entity (a 'loan staff assignment') unless:

- the agreement is for a short period of time and does not involve staff or partners performing non-audit services which would not be permitted under Ethical Standard section 5 *Non-audit / Additional services,* and
- the audited entity agrees that the individual concerned will not hold a management position, and acknowledges its responsibility for directing and supervising the work to be performed, which will not include such matters as making management decisions or exercising discretionary authority to commit the audited entity to a particular position or accounting treatment.

Recruitment services

In relation to the request for Raven & Co to provide assistance in recruiting new members of the board, this could give rise to self-interest, familiarity or intimidation threats as the firm would essentially be advising on the recruitment of staff who will ultimately be in senior management positions and responsible for the running of and oversight of a listed company. These new members of staff may also go on to be included in any audit committee which the company sets up and will be responsible for assessing the independence of the external auditors. Being involved in any decision on who should be appointed to such a senior position is also likely to involve the firm taking on a management responsibility which is not appropriate. Given that Gull Co is potentially going to be a listed company, Raven & Co should not be involved in any activity which involves searching for suitable candidates or undertaking any reference checks of prospective candidates. This request should be turned down by Raven & Co due to the potential management responsibility involved.

Tutorial note

Credit will be awarded for relevant comments relating to the professional benefits of accepting the assignment.

(ii) Implications of governance and board structure on audit process

Structure of the board

As a private company with the majority of shares held by the Brenner family, the auditor's report addressed to the shareholders as a body would have been aimed predominantly at the Brenner family. However, the predominance of the Brenner family may undermine the independence of the board. The board may be accustomed to operating in the interests of the family as the majority shareholders. However, once the company is listed, the board will be required to consider the interests of the new shareholders as a group. The executive members of the board are either Brenner family members or long-term employees of the company and potentially loyal to the existing ownership.

With only one non-executive director, the board currently lacks independent oversight and the opinions and decisions of the executive board may not be subject to appropriate levels of challenge and scrutiny.

In addition, non-executive board members are specifically required to scrutinise the performance of management, consider the integrity of the financial statements, determine director remuneration and participate in the appointment and removal of directors. With limited experience outside IT consultancy and limited time, the current non-executive is unlikely to be able to fulfil these roles effectively on their own.

There is no indication that management lacks integrity but Raven & Co must remain sceptical of the motivations of the family, particularly leading up to a listing. There will be an incentive to overstate performance and position to inflate the value of the company. With little effective oversight of the executive board, Raven & Co must remain alert for this possibility, particularly when auditing matters involving management judgement in subsequent financial periods.

UK syllabus: As a company listed on the UK stock exchange, the company will be expected to comply with the UK Corporate Governance Code (the Code) or explain any departure from the Code in the annual report. The Code states that the board should include an appropriate combination of executive and non-executive directors (and, in particular, independent non-executive directors) such that no individual or small group of individuals can dominate the board's decision taking. The auditor, in line with Bulletin 2009/4 *Developments in corporate governance affecting the responsibilities of auditors in UK companies*, will be required to review the corporate governance statement produced by Gull plc for any inconsistencies and to report in line with the Bulletin.

Audit committee

The lack of any form of audit committee is a significant departure from corporate governance best practice. The audit committee fulfils a number of significant roles, including monitoring the integrity of the financial statements, reviewing internal financial controls, monitoring the independence of the external auditor and communicating with the external auditor on matters relating to the external audit. The audit committee should have a member with relevant financial expertise and this will become of even more importance once the company is listed.

In the absence of an audit committee, Raven & Co will have to communicate directly with the board including the requirement to communicate how the auditor has maintained their independence in line with ISA 260 *Communication with Those Charged with Governance*. This may affect the independence of Raven & Co, or at least the perception of their independence. It may also reduce the effectiveness of communications between the auditor and the company. The audit committee is responsible for communicating relevant matters, such as deficiencies in internal control, up to the executive board for their consideration. Without an audit committee, matters of significance to the audit may not be given sufficient prominence by the board. Further, the audit committee is responsible for reviewing the integrity of the financial statements and internal controls and currently there is no-one at Gull Co capable of carrying out this role. Overall this may make it harder for Raven & Co to discuss and communicate key findings from the audit including the auditor's qualitative assessment of the company's accounting practices. Also with the lack of an objective audit committee, it may be harder for Raven & Co fulfil their responsibilities to communicate any significant difficulties which are encountered during the audit.

Listed status

Further as a listed company, Gull Co will be subject to increased scrutiny and pressure to achieve performance levels, which may motivate the board to manipulate the financial statements to present an improved picture of performance. For Raven & Co, this increases the level of audit risk and is likely to have a significant impact on the firm's assessment of the risk of fraud and management override.

This is likely to have a significant impact on the firm's approach to auditing areas of the financial statements subject to judgement, such as management estimates and revenue recognition.

As a listed company, Gull Co may be required to produce more detailed financial statements probably in a shorter time frame and as mentioned above, the lack of financial expertise and lack of objective scrutiny by an audit committee may result in errors or omissions. This again increases the level of audit risk faced by Raven & Co and a lot more detailed testing may need to be performed to ensure compliance with appropriate accounting standards and listing rules.

Further, once listed, the auditor's report issued for Gull Co will be available to a much wider audience and will require additional disclosures in line with ISA 701 *Communicating Key Audit Matters in the Independent Auditor's Report*. This will add another level of work and complexity to the audit of Gull Co.

(b) Military research project

The research expenses represent 10.8% of profit for the year so they are material to the financial statements.

Raven & Co is unable to obtain sufficient appropriate evidence relating to the research expenses. Given the limitation imposed by management, the auditor will be unable to form a conclusion about the occurrence, completeness, accuracy or classification of the associated expenses.

ISA 705 (Revised) *Modifications to the Opinion in the Independent Auditor's Report* requires that when management imposes a limitation on the scope of the audit, the auditor should request that they remove the limitation. If management refuses, the auditor should communicate the matter to those charged with governance, explaining the implications of the matter and the impact on this year's audit opinion. In addition, as this is a matter which is likely to arise again in future audits, the auditor should stress that the compound effect of this and the likelihood that there may be development cost implications to consider in the future may give rise to both a material and pervasive matter, which would give rise to a disclaimer of opinion.

As well as the implications on the auditor's report, those charged with governance should be informed that in accordance with ISA 210 *Agreeing the Terms of Audit Engagements,* the auditor may not be able to accept the audit engagement in the future if management continues to impose the limitation on the scope of the auditor's work and the auditor believes that it may result in them disclaiming their opinion.

In the current year under these circumstances, it will be necessary to issue a modified opinion. Given the claimed value of the expenses, it is likely that the matter will be considered material but not pervasive to the financial statements and a qualified opinion will be issued.

A 'Basis for Qualified Opinion' paragraph should be included immediately after the audit opinion describing the matter giving rise to the modification.

Fire

Audit procedures have confirmed that the matter has been satisfactorily reflected in the financial statements. There are therefore no misstatements relevant to this matter and no modification to the audit opinion is necessary.

However, the accident caused the temporary suspension of operations for a number of months, with a significant impact on the results for the year. Overall, the associated reduction in sales and the expenses relating to the repairs have contributed to a $46 million reduction in profits. This may make interpretation of the current year's results difficult. Crow Co is still unable to operate at full capacity, so the matter will continue to affect performance in the following year.

This represents a major catastrophe which has had and continues to have a significant effect on the company's financial position. The disclosures provided by management in relation to this constitute a matter of fundamental importance to users, and should be referred to in an emphasis of matter paragraph by Raven & Co, as described in ISA 706 (Revised) *Emphasis of Matter Paragraphs and Other Matter Paragraphs in the Independent Auditor's Report*.

The auditor should include the paragraph in a separate section of the auditor's report with an appropriate heading that includes the term 'emphasis of matter'. It may be appropriate for the paragraph to be entitled 'Emphasis of matter – effects of a fire.' The placement of the paragraph depends on the auditor's judgement in terms of the significance and the nature of the matter being described. It is likely that in these circumstances it should be placed directly after the basis for qualified opinion paragraph.

The paragraph should clearly reference the matter being emphasised including a reference to where the full description of the matter may be found in the financial statements. The paragraph should make it clear that the audit opinion is not modified in respect of this matter.

Examiner's comments

This question was the most popular of the option questions and was centered on audit reporting and ethics with a corporate governance slant.

The first part of the question had two elements, an ethics part regarding other services which were generally well answered and a second element which required the implications the governance structure and a potential listing may have on the audit process. Many candidates appeared to interpret this as a requirement to comment on how the governance structure of the client fell below best practice and how to improve that structure and did not address the audit implications at all. This is particularly disappointing given the recent examiners article on the topic and again candidates are reminded to make sure that they read the requirements carefully. The second part of the question described two issues and candidates were required to discuss the implications for the auditor's report. Unfortunately many candidates deviated from the requirement and spent time discussing the accounting treatment and audit procedures for an area where there was a limitation on the scope the audit. Candidates also lost time discussing audit procedures on going concern, which was flagged as already satisfactorily covered. The understanding of auditor's reports and their usage continues to be a weak area for many candidates despite it being a core part of the syllabus.

Marking scheme

	Marks
(a) (i) **Ethical and professional matters**	
In general up to 1 mark for each well explained point:	
Temporary recruitment of audit partner	
• Potential self-review threat	
• Potential familiarity threat	
• Potential management decision making threat	
• Recommendations to reduce the potential threats described (1 mark each to a maximum of 2)	
Recruitment services	
• Potential self-interest, intimidation and familiarity threat	
• Management responsibility in appointing senior management	
• As listed entity, service cannot be provided	
• Decline engagement	
(ii) **Implications for audit process**	
In general up to 1 mark for each well explained point:	
• Lack of independence and oversight of board	
• Ineffective non-executive board	
• Need for increased auditor scepticism particularly in light of potential listing	
• Increased fraud/manipulation risk which will need to be reflected in audit approach	
• No effective audit committee	
• Communication in line with ISA 260 harder with no objective audit committee	
• Listed company with increased audit risk	
• Extended auditor's report requirements	
Maximum	**10**
(b) **Implications for the auditor's report and further actions**	
In general up to 1 mark for each well explained point and action point recommended:	
Military research	
• Expenses are material (must include relevant calculation)	
• Management imposed limitation on scope	
• Auditor should request that management removes the limitation	

- Communication of potential impact to those charged with governance
- Impact on continuation of audit engagement
- If limitation is not removed, audit opinion will be modified
- Matter is material but not pervasive - qualified opinion
- Basis for qualified opinion paragraph

Fire

- No modification of the audit opinion necessary
- The major catastrophe will have a significant impact on results and make their interpretation difficult
- Disclosures by management are of fundamental importance to users
- Emphasis of matter paragraph required
- EOM paragraph should describe the matter and where disclosures can be found in the financial statements and that opinion not modified in respect of this matter

Maximum	**10**
Total	**20**

44 BOSTON *Walk in the footsteps of a top tutor*

Top tutor tips

Part (a) asks for matters to be discussed with management in relation to four uncorrected misstatements. You can take the same approach as a 'matters' question i.e. state whether the issue is material, the accounting treatment required and the risk to the financial statements. For part (b) you need to state the impact to the auditor's report if the client does not amend the financial statements. Consider the aggregate effect of the misstatements to assess whether there is a material misstatement. State the impact to both the report and opinion as a result of the issues. Don't waste time stating the reporting implications if the issues are corrected as this is not part of the requirement.

(a) Matters to discuss at meeting

During the completion stage of the audit, the effect of uncorrected misstatements must be evaluated by the auditor, as required by ISA 450 *Evaluation of Misstatements Identified during the Audit*. This requires that the auditor obtains an understanding of management's reasons for not making recommended adjustments to the financial statements and that they take this into account when evaluating whether the financial statements as a whole are free from material misstatement.

In order to maintain accurate accounting records, management should be encouraged to record all misstatements to ensure that the risk of material misstatements in future periods is reduced due to the cumulative effect of immaterial uncorrected misstatements.

ISA 450 also requires that the auditor communicates with those charged with governance about uncorrected misstatements and the effect that they, individually or in aggregate, may have on the opinion in the auditor's report. Each of the matters included in the summary of uncorrected misstatements will be discussed below and the impact on the auditor's report considered individually and in aggregate.

(i) Impairment

When performing an impairment test, in accordance with IAS 36 *Impairment of Assets*, the carrying value of the asset (or cash generating unit) in question is compared to the recoverable amount of the asset. If the recoverable amount is lower than the carrying value an impairment loss should be recognised, reducing the asset down from its carrying value to the recoverable amount.

The recoverable amount is calculated as the higher of the fair value less costs to sell and value in use. In relation to the cash generating unit, Boston Co estimated that the greater of these two figures was the value in use at $3.5 million. This was compared to the carrying value of $3.6 million and the asset has been impaired by $100,000 accordingly.

The findings of audit procedures carried out suggest that an inappropriate estimate was used in the calculation of value in use. Boston Co applied the company's annual growth rates when estimating the cash flows attributable to the cash generating unit. A more relevant estimate for the growth rates, specific to the cash generating unit, was available and should have been used.

This would have generated a value in use of $3.1 million which is still higher than fair value less cost to sell of $3 million, and should be used as the recoverable amount. As management already impaired the asset to $3.5 million, a further impairment of $400,000 is required to value it appropriately at $3.1 million.

At the meeting management should be asked why they used the company's forecast growth rates, rather than the factory's growth rates and whether any matters have arisen since the audit to suggest that the growth rates used by the audit team are now inappropriate.

The adjustment represents 6.25% of profit and 0.4% of total assets. While not material to the statement of financial position, it is material to profit.

If management does not adjust for this or provide justifications as to why their valuation is more appropriate, then this will lead to a material misstatement of the financial statements.

(ii) Borrowing costs

Interest charges are borrowing costs. The borrowing costs relating to the construction of qualifying assets, such as property and plant, should be capitalised during the construction period, in accordance with IAS 23 *Borrowing Costs*.

As the manufacturing plant is not due for completion until November 2016, it is still a qualifying asset and the interest should have been capitalised. Boston Co has incorrectly expensed the interest as part of the finance charges for the year.

The correcting adjustment is therefore to reduce finance charges and to add the interest to the cost of the asset on the statement of financial position.

The charges of $75,000 represent 1.2% of profit and 0.07% of assets so are not material to either profit or the statement of financial position.

(iii) Cleveland Co

At the year end Boston Co would have recognised a net receivable of $95,000 as being due from their customer Cleveland Co. Although $30,000 has been received after the year end, the request to have the company liquidated indicates that any further payment is unlikely to be received.

In accordance with IAS 10 *Events After the Reporting Period*, this is an adjusting event indicating that management's assessment of the recoverability of the balance is inaccurate and that the remainder of the outstanding balance should be written off as an irrecoverable debt.

As Boston Co has previously provided for $5,000 management should provide for the remaining $65,000 in the financial statements for the year ended 31 December 2015. This will reduce trade receivables in the statement of financial position and profit before tax by $65,000.

At the meeting enquiries should be made as to whether any further correspondence has been received from either the management of Cleveland Co or the liquidators offering any form of reimbursement to Boston Co. If not, then the proposed adjustment should be encouraged.

The adjustment represents 1.0% of profit and 0.06% of total assets so is not material individually to either profit or the statement of financial position.

(iv) Investment in Nebraska

The investment in Nebraska has been designated as fair value through profit or loss. As such, the value at the year end must be adjusted to reflect the fair value of the investment and any gain or loss recognised in the statement of profit or loss.

The fair value of the investment at the year end is $643,500 (150,000 shares × $4.29). This represents an increase in the fair value of $43,500, which should be taken to the statement of profit or loss as a gain. The carrying value of the investment should also be increased by this amount.

$43,500 represents 0.7% of profit and 0.04% of total assets. It is therefore not material individually to either profit or the statement of financial position.

(b) Impact on the audit opinion and auditor's report

When considering their opinion, the auditor must conclude whether the financial statements as a whole are free from material misstatement. In order to do this, they must consider whether any remaining uncorrected misstatements are material, either on an individual basis or in aggregate.

The aggregate effect of the misstatements would be to overstate Boston Co's profit by $346,500 ($465,000 – $118,500). Total assets on the statement of financial position would also be overstated by this amount.

This represents 5.4% of profit and 0.3% of total assets. The overstatement would therefore be material to the statement of profit or loss on an aggregate basis but not to the statement of financial position.

However, as the necessary adjustment regarding the impairment of the factory building is individually material, management should be informed that if the valuation calculated by the audit team is more appropriate then failure to incorporate this adjustment will result in the auditor concluding that the financial statements are materially misstated. Based upon this, a modification to the audit opinion in accordance with ISA 705 *Modifications to the Opinion in the Independent Auditor's Report* will be required.

The type of modification depends on the significance of the material misstatement. In this case, the misstatement regarding the impairment is material to the financial statements, but is unlikely to be considered pervasive. This is supported by the fact that the adjustment is not material to the statement of financial position and it is therefore unlikely that the auditor will conclude that the financial statements as a whole are misleading.

Therefore a qualified opinion should be expressed, with the auditor stating in the opinion that the financial statements show a true and fair view 'except for' the effects of the matters described in the basis for qualified opinion paragraph.

The basis for qualified opinion paragraph should include a description of the matter giving rise to the qualification, including quantification of the financial effects of the misstatement.

The remaining uncorrected misstatements are, individually and in aggregate, immaterial to the financial statements and it will be at the discretion of management to amend and will have no impact on the auditor's report.

Although as previously mentioned because of the impact on future periods, management should be encouraged to amend for all misstatements. If management intends to leave these as uncorrected misstatements, written confirmation of their immaterial nature should be obtained via a written representation.

Examiner's comments

The question set out four potential audit adjustments and candidates were required to discuss each, considering the individual and aggregate impact on the auditor's report. The values of each potential adjustment were given in the question so there were materiality marks available and many candidates scored these but performed less well in discussing the associated issues. Most of the adjustments were relatively straightforward such as the capitalisation of loan interest, allowance for a bad debt and revaluation of investments and the issues around these were reasonably answered. The issue of impairment was less well answered. There was significant inconsistency in answers where candidates concluded that an issue was not material but concluded that the auditor's report required modification. Furthermore candidates need to ensure that they understand what Emphasis of Matter and Other Matters paragraphs are. They are not a substitute for a modified opinion and should only be used where there are significant issues that the auditor wants to bring to the attention of the users of the accounts.

ACCA Marking scheme

		Marks
(a)	**Summary of uncorrected misstatements**	
	In general up to 1 mark for each point of explanation and up to ½ mark for each appropriate calculation:	
	– Obtaining an understanding of management's reasons	
	– Encourage management to amend all misstatements	
	– Communicate effect of misstatements to those charged with governance	
(i)	**Impairment**	
	– Explanation of original calculation	
	– Inappropriate estimates used	
	– Revised impairments	
	– Justification of the proposed adjustment	
	– Request further clarification at meeting	
	– Matter is material individually	
(ii)	**Borrowing costs**	
	– Capitalisation rules	
	– Qualifying asset	
	– Identification of incorrect treatment of interest costs	
	– Explanation of adjustment	
	– Not material individually	
(iii)	**Cleveland**	
	– Liquidation is indication of further impairment	
	– Adjusting event after the reporting period	
	– Need to write off remainder of outstanding balance	
	– Request evidence of any further correspondence	
	– Not material individually	
(iv)	**Nebraska**	
	– Need to revalue investment to fair value at year end	
	– Calculation of fair value (½ max) and adjustment (½ max)	
	– Gain taken to statement of profit and loss	
	– Not material individually	
	Maximum	**14**
(b)	**Auditor's report**	
	– Aggregate impact on financial statements	
	– Material to profit	
	– Impairment individually material	
	– Modification of opinion due to a material misstatement	
	– Discussion of whether it is pervasive	
	– Qualified opinion	
	– Basis for qualified opinion paragraph	
	Maximum	**6**
Total		**20**

45 HOPPER GROUP *Walk in the footsteps of a top tutor*

Top tutor tips

Part (a) asks for a critical appraisal of the draft report extracts. Don't just focus on whether the opinion is appropriate. You should also think about the titles of the paragraphs included and whether the names are correct, the order they appear in, whether the required information that should be included has been included and whether the wording used is professional and appropriate.

In part (b) you need to discuss the reporting implications for the Group auditor's report as a result of the auditor's inability to obtain sufficient appropriate evidence for the subsidiary. This requires consideration of whether the issue is material to the Group financial statements.

Part (c) asks for quality control procedures to be carried out before issuing the auditor's report, i.e. what procedures are performed in a 'hot review'.

(a) Critical appraisal of the draft report

Type of opinion

When an auditor issues an opinion expressing that the financial statements 'do not give a true and fair view', this represents an adverse opinion. The paragraph explaining the modification should, therefore, be titled 'Basis for Adverse Opinion' rather than simply 'Basis of Modified Opinion'.

An adverse opinion means that the auditor considers the misstatement to be material and pervasive to the financial statements of the Hopper Group. Pervasive matters are those which affect a substantial proportion of the financial statements or fundamentally affect the users' understanding of the financial statements.

It is unlikely that the failure to recognise contingent consideration is pervasive; the main effect would be to understate goodwill and liabilities. This would not be considered a substantial proportion of the financial statements, neither would it be fundamental to understanding the Hopper Group's performance and position.

However, there is also some uncertainty as to whether the matter is even material. If the matter is determined to be material but not pervasive, then a qualified opinion would be appropriate on the basis of a material misstatement. If the matter is not material, then no modification would be necessary to the audit opinion.

Wording of opinion/report

The auditor's reference to 'the acquisition of the new subsidiary' is too vague; the Hopper Group may have purchased a number of subsidiaries to which this phrase could relate. It is important that the auditor provides adequate description of the event and in these circumstances it would be appropriate to name the subsidiary referred to.

The auditor has not quantified the amount of the contingent element of the consideration. For the users to understand the potential implications of any necessary adjustments, they need to know how much the contingent consideration will be if it becomes payable. The auditor should quantify the financial effects of any misstatements, unless it is impracticable to do so.

In addition to the above point, the auditor should provide more description of the financial effects of the misstatement, including full quantification of the effect of the required adjustment to the assets, liabilities, incomes, revenues and equity of the Hopper Group.

The auditor should identify the note to the financial statements relevant to the contingent liability disclosure rather than just stating 'in the note'. This will improve the understandability and usefulness of the contents of the auditor's report.

The use of the term 'we do not feel that the treatment is correct' is too vague and not professional. While there may be some interpretation necessary when trying to apply financial reporting standards to unique circumstances, the expression used is ambiguous and may be interpreted as some form of disclaimer by the auditor with regard to the correct accounting treatment. The auditor should clearly explain how the treatment applied in the financial statements has departed from the requirements of the relevant standard.

Tutorial note

As an illustration to the above point, an appropriate wording would be: 'Management has not recognised the acquisition-date fair value of contingent consideration as part of the consideration transferred in exchange for the acquiree, which constitutes a departure from International Financial Reporting Standards.'

The ambiguity is compounded by the use of the phrase 'if this is the case, it would be appropriate to adjust the goodwill'. This once again suggests that the correct treatment is uncertain and perhaps open to interpretation.

If the auditor wishes to refer to a specific accounting standard they should refer to its full title. Therefore instead of referring to 'the relevant standard' they should refer to IFRS 3 *Business Combinations*.

The opinion paragraph requires an appropriate heading. In this case the auditors have issued an adverse opinion and the paragraph should be headed 'Adverse Opinion'.

As with the basis paragraph, the opinion paragraph lacks authority; suggesting that the required adjustments 'may' materially affect the financial statements implies that there is a degree of uncertainty. This is not the case; the amount of the contingent consideration will be disclosed in the relevant purchase agreement, so the auditor should be able to determine whether or not the required adjustments are material.

Regardless, the sentence discussing whether or not the balance is material is not required in the auditor's report as to warrant inclusion in the report the matter must be considered material. The disclosure of the nature and financial effect of the misstatement in the basis paragraph is sufficient.

Finally, the emphasis of matter paragraph should not be included in the auditor's report. An emphasis of matter paragraph is only used to draw attention to an uncertainty/matter of fundamental importance which is correctly accounted for and disclosed in the financial statements. An emphasis of matter is not required in this case for the following reasons:

- Emphasis of matter is only required to highlight matters which the auditor believes are fundamental to the users' understanding of the business. An example may include an uncertainty relating to the future outcome of exceptional litigation. That is not the case with the Hopper Group and the contingent liability does not appear to be fundamental.
- Emphasis of matter is only used for matters where the auditor has obtained sufficient appropriate evidence that the matter is not materially misstated in the financial statements. If the financial statements are materially misstated, in this regard the matter would be fully disclosed by the auditor in the basis for qualified/adverse opinion paragraph and no emphasis of matter is necessary.

(b) Communication from the component auditor

The qualified opinion due to insufficient evidence may be a significant matter for the Hopper Group audit. While the possible adjustments relating to the current year may not be material to the Hopper Group, the inability to obtain sufficient appropriate evidence with regard to a material matter in Seurat Sweeteners Co's financial statements may indicate a control deficiency which the auditor was not aware of at the planning stage and it could indicate potential problems with regard to the integrity of management, which could also indicate a potential fraud.

It could also indicate an unwillingness of management to provide information, which could create problems for future audits, particularly if research and development costs increase in future years. If the group auditor suspects that any of these possibilities are true, they may need to reconsider their risk assessment and whether the audit procedures performed are still appropriate.

If the detail provided in the communication from the component auditor is insufficient, the group auditor should first discuss the matter with the component auditor to see whether any further information can be provided. The group auditor can request further working papers from the component auditor if this is necessary. However, if Seurat Sweeteners has not been able to provide sufficient appropriate evidence, it is unlikely that this will be effective.

If the discussions with the component auditor do not provide satisfactory responses to evaluate the potential impact on the Hopper Group, the group auditor may need to communicate with either the management of Seurat Sweeteners or the Hopper Group to obtain necessary clarification with regard to the matter.

Following these procedures, the group auditor needs to determine whether they have sufficient appropriate evidence to draw reasonable conclusions on the Hopper Group's financial statements. If they believe the lack of information presents a risk of material misstatement in the group financial statements, they can request that further audit procedures be performed, either by the component auditor or by themselves.

Ultimately the group engagement partner has to evaluate the effect of the inability to obtain sufficient appropriate evidence on the audit opinion of the Hopper Group. The matter relates to research expenses totalling $1.2 million, which represents 0.2% of the profit for the year and 0.03% of the total assets of the Hopper Group. It is therefore not material to the Hopper Group's financial statements. For this reason no modification to the auditor's report of the Hopper Group would be required as this does not represent a lack of sufficient appropriate evidence with regard to a matter which is material to the Group financial statements.

Although this may not have an impact on the Hopper Group audit opinion, this may be something the group auditor wishes to bring to the attention of those charged with governance. This would be particularly likely if the group auditor believed that this could indicate some form of fraud in Seurat Sweeteners Co, a serious deficiency in financial reporting controls or if this could create problems for accepting future audits due to management's unwillingness to provide access to accounting records.

(c) Quality control procedures prior to issuing the auditor's report

ISA 220 *Quality Control for an Audit of Financial Statements* and ISQC 1 *Quality Control for Firms that Perform Audits and Reviews of Historical Financial Information, and Other Assurance and Related Services Agreements* require that an engagement quality control reviewer shall be appointed for audits of financial statements of listed entities. The audit engagement partner then discusses significant matters arising during the audit engagement with the engagement quality control reviewer.

The engagement quality control reviewer and the engagement partner should discuss the failure to recognise the contingent consideration and its impact on the auditor's report. The engagement quality control reviewer must review the financial statements and the proposed auditor's report, in particular focusing on the conclusions reached in formulating the auditor's report and consideration of whether the proposed auditor's opinion is appropriate.

The audit documentation relating to the acquisition of Seurat Sweeteners Co will be carefully reviewed, and the reviewer is likely to consider whether procedures performed in relation to these balances were appropriate.

Given the listed status of the Hopper Group, any modification to the auditor's report will be scrutinised, and the firm must be sure of any decision to modify the report, and the type of modification made. Once the engagement quality control reviewer has considered the necessity of a modification, they should consider whether a qualified or an adverse opinion is appropriate in the circumstances.

This is an important issue, given that it requires judgement as to whether the matters would be material or pervasive to the financial statements.

The engagement quality control reviewer should ensure that there is adequate documentation regarding the judgements used in forming the final audit opinion, and that all necessary matters have been brought to the attention of those charged with governance.

The auditor's report must not be signed and dated until the completion of the engagement quality control review.

Tutorial note

In the case of the Hopper Group's audit, the lack of evidence in respect of research costs is unlikely to be discussed unless the audit engagement partner believes that the matter could be significant, for example, if they suspected the lack of evidence is being used to cover up a financial statements fraud.

Examiner's comments

This question examined reporting, group audits and quality reviews. Candidates were required to critically appraise a draft auditor's report. This approach to a reporting question has been seen many times in the past and answers were generally good in this area. A minority of candidates however incorrectly spent time discussing the accounting treatment for contingent liabilities rather than contingent consideration in an acquisition context. This often led to the conclusion that there was no requirement to modify the auditor's report therefore the shortcomings of the report were overlooked.

The second part of this question examined the impact of a qualification in a subsidiary auditor's report on the group auditor's report. In this case, stronger candidates identified that the limitation in scope as described in the question was immaterial and was unlikely to have an impact on the group auditor's report in isolation. Weaker candidates spent time considering the assessment of extent of reliance on component auditors or suggested that the error be corrected in the group financial statements reflecting inattention to the scenario which was clear that lack of evidence was the issue rather than an error to be adjusted. A significant proportion of candidates still propose adding other matter or emphasis of matter paragraphs into the auditor's report to draw attention to immaterial items that need not be disclosed.

Finally candidates were asked to describe quality control procedures which would be required for this listed client prior to the auditor's report being issued. This was particularly poorly answered with many candidates listing either general characteristics of quality control across the audit cycle or describing the general completion process tasks such as analytical review and disclosure check lists. The requirement to focus on the quality control review required for listed clients and in particular this client, with a modified auditor's report was often missed or only mentioned briefly as perform a 'hot' review. Some candidates suggested a cold review which would be performed after, not prior to, the issuance of the auditor's report.

ACCA marking scheme

		Marks
(a)	**Critical appraisal of auditor's report**	
	Generally up to 1½ mark for each relevant point of appraisal.	
	– Heading of 'basis paragraph' (1 max)	
	– Vagueness of description of subsidiary	
	– Quantification of contingent consideration	
	– Identification of note in financial statements	
	– Vagueness in relation to correct accounting treatment	
	– Quantification of the effects on the financial statements	
	– Vague reference to 'relevant accounting standard' (1 max)	
	– Opinion paragraph heading (1 max)	
	– Reference to materiality	
	– Pervasiveness of the matter	
	– Appropriate opinion qualified or unmodified	
	– Use of emphasis of matter paragraph	
	Maximum	**10**

(b)	**Audit of component** Generally up to 1 mark for each action and implication explained. – Consideration of significance to group – Discuss matter with component auditor – Discuss matter with management of Seurat Sweeteners Co or the Hopper Group – Sufficiency of audit evidence – Calculation of materiality – Materiality to the Hopper Group – No modification to the Hopper Group auditor's report – Potential communication to those charged with governance	
	Maximum	6
(c)	**Quality control procedures** Up to 1 mark for each procedure explained. – Appointment of reviewer for listed entities – Discuss lack of evidence in subsidiary – Discuss contingent consideration & review working papers – Review draft report wording – Review of working papers to support judgements in opinion – Signing of report after review complete	
	Maximum	4
Total		**20**

46 DARREN *Walk in the footsteps of a top tutor*

Top tutor tips

Requirements (a) and (b) requires discussion of the relevant accounting treatment in the same way as you would approach a 'Matters and evidence' question. To finish off, you need to explain the impact on the auditor's report if the issues are not resolved.

In part (c) you need to discuss how the auditor should address inconsistencies between the unaudited information in the integrated report and the audited financial statements including the reporting implications.

(a) The total estimated profit of $5 million which has been recognised in the statement of profit or loss represents 22.2% of profit for the year and is therefore material.

The construction contract should be accounted for in accordance with IFRS 15 *Revenue from Contracts with Customers* which states that when the outcome of a construction contract can be estimated reliably, contract revenue and contract costs associated with the construction contract shall be recognised as revenue and expenses respectively by reference to the stage of completion of the contract activity at the end of the reporting period.

Darren Co has recognised 100% of the contract profit even though the contract is not yet complete. The contract activity period is 15 months, and by the year end the contract activity has been ongoing for seven months only. Therefore the profit which has been recognised appears to be overstated, and it seems to have been recognised too early.

The audit firm should clarify Darren's accounting policy on construction contracts and confirm the method which is used to determine the stage of completion of contracts at the reporting date. IFRS 15 allows for a variety of methods to be used, for example, based on the proportion that contract costs incurred for work performed to date bear to the estimated total contract costs, or on surveys of work performed.

Further evidence should be obtained to determine the stage of completion of this contract at the reporting date, to enable the appropriate amount of revenue, costs and profit which should be recognised to be determined. Further procedures should be performed, including:

- The contract terms should be scrutinised for any terms relating to the completion of stages of the contract which may trigger the recognition of contract revenue.
- Surveys of work performed by 31 January 2015 should be reviewed to estimate the stage of completion at the reporting date.
- Correspondence with the customer should be read to confirm that the contract is progressing in a satisfactory way.

Further audit evidence is required, but based on the time period in months as a rough guide, it appears that the contract is 7/15 complete, and therefore profit in the region of \$2.3 million (\$5 million × 7/15) can be recognised, and that profit is overstated by \$2.7 million. The overstatement is material at 12% of profit before tax.

If any necessary adjustment is not made, then profit is overstated by a material amount. This gives rise to a material misstatement, and the audit opinion should be modified. A qualified 'except for' opinion should be given, and the Basis for Qualified Opinion paragraph should explain the reason for the qualification, including a quantification of the misstatement.

This is only one contract, and Darren Co typically works on three contracts at a time. Therefore further audit work may be needed in respect of any other contracts which are currently being carried out. If the same accounting treatment has been applied to other contracts, the misstatement may be even greater, and could potentially result in an adverse opinion if the accumulated misstatements were considered by the auditor to be both material and pervasive to the financial statements.

In addition, Darren Co may have been using an inappropriate accounting treatment in previous years, and therefore there may be misstatements in the opening balances. This should be discussed with management to determine how contracts have been accounted for historically. Any errors which may be discovered should be corrected retrospectively, leading to further adjustments to the financial statements.

(b) The amount claimed by Newbuild Co is material to the financial statements, representing 10.8% of total assets and 178% of profit before tax. It is also likely to be considered material by nature, as the possible payment is much larger than the amount of cash recognised in the financial statements at the year end.

The implications for the going concern status of Darren Co should be considered. The matter should be discussed with management to obtain an understanding of how Darren Co could meet any necessary cash payment. Due to the potential for such a sizeable cash payment, management should confirm that should the amount become payable, the company has adequate resources to fund the cash outflow, for example, through the existence of lending facilities.

The correct accounting treatment seems to have been applied. According to IAS 37 *Provisions, Contingent Liabilities and Contingent Assets*, if an amount is possible, rather than probable to be paid, then it is treated as a contingent liability, and a note to the accounts should be provided to describe the nature of the situation, an estimate of the possible financial effect and an indication of any uncertainties.

To ensure that IAS 37 has been complied with, the auditor should review the contents of the note for completeness and accuracy. Events after the reporting date should also be considered, for example, legal correspondence should be reviewed, to confirm that the probability of payment has not changed by the time of the auditor's report being signed.

Due to the size of the potential cash outflow, the auditor should consider including a Material Uncertainty Related to Going Concern section in the auditor's report.

The going concern section should include a clear reference to the note to the financial statements where the matter is disclosed. The paragraph should also make it clear that the audit opinion is not modified in respect of this matter.

(c) The key performance indicators (KPIs) included in an integrated report are by definition 'other information' according to ISA 720 (Revised) *The Auditor's Responsibilities Relating to Other Information in Documents Containing Audited Financial Statements*.

Other information is defined as financial and non-financial information included in a document containing audited financial statements and the auditor's report.

The requirement of ISA 720 is that the auditor shall read the other information, in order to identify any information contained within any of the financial or non-financial information in the annual report that is apparently materially incorrect based on, or materially inconsistent with, the knowledge acquired by the auditor in the course of performing the audit.

There appears to be an inconsistency because the KPI states that profit before tax has increased by 20%, but the increase shown in the financial statements is 12.5%. The auditor must use professional judgement to determine if this is a material inconsistency.

Assuming that this is deemed to be a material inconsistency, the auditor should consider whether the financial statements or the other information should be amended.

The audit completion procedures, including final analytical review and review of all working papers will determine whether the profit before tax figures as stated in the financial statements need to be amended. From the discussion above, it is likely that some adjustment to profit before tax will be needed regardless of the inconsistent KPI.

It is most likely that the KPI included in the integrated report should be changed in agreement with the movement in profit shown in the adjusted financial statements, and management should be asked to make the necessary change to the KPI.

The auditor may seek legal advice if management refuses to amend the KPI to remove the material inconsistency. All of the matters affecting the auditor's report should be discussed with those charged with governance.

If management refuse to change the other information, then the auditor's report should provide a description of the inconsistency in the 'Other Information' section of the report.

Alternatively the auditor may withhold the auditor's report or withdraw from the engagement.

Further actions are also available to auditors in the UK who have the right to speak at general meetings of company members, and could therefore highlight the inconsistency to shareholders in this way, if it remains unresolved.

These actions are very much a last resort, however, and management is likely to resolve the inconsistency rather than facing these consequences.

Examiner's comments

This question was based on the audit of Darren Co, a company operating in the construction industry and a new client of Nidge & Co. Information was provided in respect of three issues at the completion stage of the audit, and for each issue candidates were required to discuss the implication for the completion of the audit and for the auditor's report, and to recommend further actions to be taken. Generally the question was well attempted by many candidates who seemed well prepared for a question of this type.

Part (a) described how Darren's financial statements recognised all of the profit relating to a long-term construction contract even though it was only part completed at the year end. Candidates performed well on this requirement, providing answers which confidently discussed both the inappropriate accounting treatment and the implications for the audit opinion if the material misstatements identified were not corrected by management. Some candidates missed out on marks by not recommending any further actions or by only discussing the impact for the audit opinion itself and not the overall impact on the auditor's report, failing to mention the need for a Basis for Opinion paragraph within the auditor's report. Only the strongest candidates realised that this incorrect accounting treatment may have been applied to other contracts and that opening balances may be incorrect given that this was a new audit client.

Part (b) provided information on a completed contract in respect of which Darren Co was facing legal action due to problems that had arisen following completion. The scenario stated that disclosure on the matter had been made in the notes to the financial statements and that the audit evidence on file concluded there to be a possibility of Darren Co having to pay the damages claimed. Candidates again seemed confident of the accounting rules, yet many suggested that a provision should be made for the damages; this may be because candidates assumed that there "should" be some implication for the auditor's opinion given the facts of the scenario, but this was not the case. The other significant issue was that Darren Co could not afford to pay the damages given its small cash balance, and this could raise a threat to the going concern status of the company. Only the strongest candidates made this connection and were able to explain clearly the implications for the auditor's report. In this scenario the issue was that a disclosure would be sufficient, as long as there was only a possibility that the claim would need to be paid, but the crucial aspect was that audit firm would need to audit the disclosure carefully to obtain evidence as to its sufficiency especially given the potential impact on going concern. As in part (a), the further actions were generally not given, other than a generic suggestion to "discuss with management".

Part (c) briefly outlined that Darren Co had included as a key performance indicator in its integrated report the percentage increase in profit before tax. Candidates were provided with the information to calculate that the indicator was incorrect. It was unfortunate that a significant minority of candidates were unable to work out a simple percentage increase despite the information being clearly presented in the question scenario. Despite this, almost all answers identified that the stated key performance indicator was incorrect. The best answers explained that management should be asked to amend the figure in the integrated report, and the impact on the auditor's report. Weaker answers suggested that the opinion should be modified due to material misstatement which is incorrect. Again, there were few suggestions of further action to be taken other than "discuss with management".

The main weakness in answers to this question was a lack of specificity in the actions that had been recommended, and in many answers no actions were provided at all, severely limiting the marks that could be awarded.

ACCA Marking scheme		
		Marks
	Generally up to 1½ marks for each relevant point explained, with 1 mark for correct determination of materiality.	
(a)	**Bridge contract**	
	– Profit recognised is material	
	– Profit should be recognised by reference to stage of completion	
	– Profit appears to be overstated/recognised too early	
	– Further actions (1 mark each):	
	– Review company's stated accounting policy	
	– Review contract terms for revenue recognition trigger points	
	– Verify stage of completion using surveyor's reports	
	– Correspondence with customer to confirm contract progress	
	– Material misstatement leading to qualification of audit opinion	
	– Basis for Qualified Opinion paragraph	
	– Other contracts need to be reviewed	
	– Opening balances could also be materially misstated	
	Maximum	**8**
(b)	**Legal action**	
	– Possible cash payment material by monetary amount and by nature	
	– Going concern implication due to size of possible cash outflow	
	– Treatment as a contingent liability appears correct	
	– Further actions (1 mark each):	
	– Review post year-end legal correspondence	
	– Confirm financing in place if amount becomes payable	
	– Read note to accounts to ensure complete and accurate	
	– Material uncertainty related to going concern paragraph to highlight the significant uncertainty	
	– Content of the Material uncertainty related to going concern paragraph	
	Maximum	**6**
(c)	**KPI**	
	– KPIs included in integrated report are other information	
	– Read other information to identify material inconsistencies	
	– The profit increase KPI is not the same as reported in the financial statements giving rise to material inconsistency	
	– Further actions (1 mark each):	
	– Consider whether the FS or KPI should be amended	
	– Request amendment of the KPI once audit finalised	
	– Reporting implications	
	– Auditor should seek legal advice (1 mark)	
	– All matters should be discussed with those charged with governance (1 mark)	
	Maximum	**6**
Total		**20**

47 BRADLEY *Walk in the footsteps of a top tutor*

Top tutor tips

Part (a) asks for quality control and other professional issues raised in relation to the completion of the audit. Quality control issues are increasingly common in the P7 exam. Consider whether the audit has been performed in accordance with professional standards and whether the auditor has conducted the work with due professional care.

Part (b) (i) asks for matters to be discussed with management in relation to three uncorrected misstatements. You can take the same approach as a 'matters' question i.e. state whether the issue is material, the accounting treatment required and the risk to the financial statements.

For part (b) (ii) you need to state the impact to the auditor's report if the client does not amend the financial statements. Consider the aggregate effect of the misstatements to assess whether there is a material misstatement. State the impact to both the report and opinion as a result of the issues. Don't waste time stating the reporting implications if the issues are corrected as this is not part of the requirement.

(a) Quality control, ethical and other issues raised

It is a requirement of ISA 520 *Analytical Procedures* that analytical procedures are performed at the overall review stage of the audit. An objective of ISA 520 is that the auditor should design and perform analytical procedures near the end of the audit which assist the auditor when forming their opinion as to whether the financial statements are consistent with the auditor's understanding of the entity.

It is unlikely that the audit senior's 'quick look' at Bradley's financial statements is adequate to meet the requirements of ISA 520 and audit documentation would seem to be inadequate. Therefore if the audit senior, or another auditor, does not perform a detailed analytical review on Bradley's financial statements as part of the completion of the audit, there is a breach of ISA 520. Failing to perform the final analytical review could mean that further errors are not found.

The auditor will not be able to check that the presentation of the financial statements conforms to the requirements of the applicable financial reporting framework. It is also doubtful whether a full check on the presentation and disclosure in the financial statements has been made. The firm should evidence this through the use of a disclosure checklist.

The lack of final analytical review increases audit risk. Because Bradley Co is a new audit client, it is particularly important that the analytical review is performed as detection risk is higher than for longer-standing audit engagements where the auditor has developed a cumulative knowledge of the audit client.

The fact that the audit manager suggested that a detailed review was not necessary shows a lack of knowledge and understanding of ISA requirements. An audit client being assessed as low risk does not negate the need for analytical review to be performed, which the audit manager should know. Alternatively, the audit manager may have known that analytical review should have been performed, but regardless of this still instructed the audit senior not to perform the review, maybe due to time pressure. The audit manager should be asked about the reason for his instruction and given further training if necessary.

The manager is not providing proper direction and supervision of the audit senior, which goes against the principles of ISA 220 *Quality Control for an Audit of Financial Statements*, and ISQC1 *Quality Control for Firms that Perform Audits and Reviews of Financial Statements and other Assurance and Related Services Engagements*. Both of these discuss the importance of the audit team having proper direction and supervision as part of ensuring a good quality of audit engagement performance.

The second issue relates to the chairman's statement. ISA 720 (Revised) *The Auditor's Responsibilities Relating to Other Information in Documents Containing Audited Financial Statements* which requires the auditor to read the other information to identify material inconsistencies, if any, with the audited financial statements and the auditor's knowledge obtained during the audit.

The audit manager has discussed the chairman's statement but this does not necessarily mean that the manager had read it for the purpose of identifying potential misstatements, and it might not have been read at all.

Even if the manager has read the chairman's statement, there may not be any audit documentation to show that this has been done or the conclusion of the work. The manager needs to be asked exactly what work has been done, and what documentation exists. As the work performed does not comply with the ISA 720 requirements, then the necessary procedures must be performed before the auditor's report is issued.

Again, the situation could indicate the audit manager's lack of knowledge of ISA requirements, or that a short-cut is being taken. In either case the quality of the audit is in jeopardy.

(b) **(i)** **Evaluation of uncorrected misstatements**

During the completion stage of the audit, the effect of uncorrected misstatements must be evaluated by the auditor, as required by ISA 450 *Evaluation of Misstatements Identified during the Audit*. In the event that management refuses to correct some or all of the misstatements communicated by the auditor, ISA 450 requires that the auditor shall obtain an understanding of management's reasons for not making the corrections and shall take that understanding into account when evaluating whether the financial statements as a whole are free from material misstatement. Therefore a discussion with management is essential in helping the auditor to form an audit opinion.

ISA 450 also requires that the auditor shall communicate with those charged with governance about uncorrected misstatements and the effect that they, individually or in aggregate, may have on the opinion in the auditor's report.

Each of the matters included in the schedule of uncorrected misstatements will be discussed below and the impact on the auditor's report considered individually and in aggregate.

Share-based payment scheme

The adjustment in relation to the share-based payment scheme is material individually to profit, representing 12% of revenue. It represents less than 1% of total assets and is not material to the statement of financial position.

IFRS 2 *Share-based Payment* requires an expense and a corresponding entry to equity to be recognised over the vesting period of a share-based payment scheme, with the amount recognised based on the fair value of equity instruments granted. Management's argument that no expense should be recognised because the options are unlikely to be exercised is not correct.

IFRS 2 would classify the fall in Bradley's share price as a market condition, and these are not relevant to determining whether an expense is recognised or the amount of it.

Therefore management should be requested to make the necessary adjustment to recognise the expense and entry to equity of $300,000. If this is not recognised, the financial statements will contain a material misstatement, with consequences for the auditor's opinion.

Restructuring provision

The adjustment in relation to the provision is material to profit, representing 2% of revenue. It represents less than 1% of total assets so is not material to the statement of financial position.

The provision appears to have been recognised too early. IAS 37 *Provisions, Contingent Liabilities and Contingent Assets* requires that for a restructuring provision to be recognised, there must be a present obligation as a result of a past event, and that is only when a detailed formal plan is in place and the entity has started to implement the plan, or announced its main features to those affected.

A board decision is insufficient to create a present obligation as a result of a past event. The provision should be recognised in September 2014 when the announcement to employees was made.

Management should be asked to explain why they have included the provision in the financial statements, for example, there may have been an earlier announcement before 31 August 2014 of which the auditor is unaware.

In the absence of any such further information, management should be informed that the accounting treatment of the provision is a material misstatement, which if it remains unadjusted will have implications for the auditor's opinion.

Inventory provision

The additional slow-moving inventory allowance which the auditor considers necessary is not material on an individual basis to either profit or to the statement of profit or loss or the statement of financial position, as it represents only 0.4% of revenue and less than 1 % of total assets.

Despite the amount being immaterial, it should not be disregarded, as the auditor should consider the aggregate effect of misstatements on the financial statements. ISA 450 does state that the auditor need not accumulate balances which are 'clearly trivial', by which it means that the accumulation of such amounts clearly would not have a material effect on the financial statements. However, at 0.4% of revenue the additional provision is not trivial, so should be discussed with management.

This misstatement is a judgmental misstatement as it arises from the judgements of management concerning an accounting estimate over which the auditor has reached a different conclusion. This is not a breach of financial reporting standards, but a difference in how management and the auditor have estimated an uncertain amount.

Management should be asked to confirm the basis on which their estimate was made, and whether they have any reason why the provision should not be increased by the amount recommended by the auditor.

If this amount remains unadjusted by management, it will not on an individual basis impact the auditor's report.

(ii) Impact on auditor's report

Aggregate materiality position

In aggregate, the misstatements have a net effect of $260,000 ($310,000 – $50,000), meaning that if left unadjusted, profit will be overstated by $260,000 and the statement of financial position overstated by the same amount. This is material to profit, at 10.4% of revenue, but is not material to the statement of financial position at less than 1% of total assets.

Impact on auditor's report

The statement of profit or loss is materially misstated if the adjustments are not made by management. The auditor should modify the opinion in the auditor's report when the auditor concludes that, based on the audit evidence obtained, the financial statements as a whole are not free from material misstatement.

The type of modification depends on the significance of the material misstatement. In this case, the misstatements in aggregate are material to the financial statements, but are unlikely to be considered pervasive even though they relate to a number of balances in the financial statements as they do not represent a substantial proportion of the financial statements, and do not make them misleading when viewed as a whole.

Therefore a qualified opinion should be expressed, with the auditor stating in the opinion that except for the effects of the matters described in the basis for qualified opinion paragraph, the financial statements show a true and fair view.

The basis for qualified opinion paragraph should contain a description of the matters giving rise to the qualification. This should include a description and quantification of the financial effects of the misstatement.

Examiner's comments

This question scenario was set at the completion stage of the audit of Bradley Co, a significant new audit client, with the auditor's report due to be issued in the next week.

Requirement (a) provided some information in the form of a comment made by the audit senior, who indicated that there may have been some problems with the performance of the audit. The concerns raised included the lack of a detailed review of the final version of the financial statements and the chairman's statement had been discussed with the finance director but no further work had been conducted. The justification for not carrying out these tasks was the conclusion by the audit manager that the audit was relatively low risk. The requirement asked candidates to explain the quality control and other professional issues raised by the audit senior's comments.

Candidates did not perform well on this requirement, which was somewhat surprising as in the past questions on quality control issues have been well attempted. Only a minority of candidates were able to identify that the audit of a significant new client could not be classified as low risk, and that a final review would be needed on the financial statements at the completion stage of the audit. Very few candidates however mentioned that final analytical review is a requirement of ISA 520 *Analytical Procedures* and even fewer could explain why the final review is so important prior to the issuance of the auditor's report. In respect of the work performed on the chairman's statement, few candidates identified that there was a lack of documentation of the work performed, but most at least understood the auditor's responsibilities in relation to the chairman's statement.

Generally the answers to this requirement were not made relevant to the information given in the scenario and instead mentioned general features of quality control such as the need for supervision and review. This will earn minimal credit, as marks are severely limited when answer points are not related to the scenario. Many answers discussed at length the reporting implications of uncorrected inconsistencies in the chairman's statement, but discussing this in a lot of detail was not answering the question requirement.

Requirements (bi) and (bii) dealt with the evaluation of misstatements and their potential implications for the auditor's opinion and report. The information was presented as a schedule of proposed adjustments to uncorrected misstatements in relation to three issues – a share-based payment scheme, a restructuring provision, and slow-moving inventory. In each case the auditor's proposed correcting journal was presented, along with an explanation of the audit findings and audit conclusion on the matter.

Requirement (bi) asked for an explanation of the matters to be discussed with management in relation to each of the uncorrected misstatements, for nine marks, and requirement (bii) for four marks, asked candidates to justify an appropriate audit opinion assuming that management does not make the proposed adjustments.

Both requirement (bi) and (bii) were not well attempted. Answers were much too brief for the marks available and unfortunately many candidates could not competently demonstrate that they understand the topic of auditors' reports. Firstly in relation to the share-based payment, the required financial reporting requirements were not well understood, with most candidates suggesting that a provision should be created rather than an adjustment made to equity, which was disappointing as this detail was actually given in the question. In relation to the restructuring provision, many candidates did not consider the specific requirements of IAS 37 *Provisions, Contingent Liabilities and Contingent Assets* in relation to restructuring provisions, and instead applied the general recognition criteria for provisions to the scenario. The slow-moving inventory was better dealt with, as most candidates could explain that inventory should be measured at lower of cost and net realisable value. On the whole, the only marks that many candidates were awarded in this requirement were for materiality calculations. There seems to be very little knowledge or understanding of ISA 450 *Evaluation of Misstatements Identified during the Audit* with almost no candidates differentiating between judgmental misstatements and misstatements caused by a breach of IFRS Standards requirements.

The answers in relation to the impact on the auditor's report were also disappointing. Only the very best candidates considered the aggregate effect of the misstatements in discussing the audit opinion. Many attempted to aggregate the misstatements themselves, coming to the wrong total, even though this had been given in the question. Weaker candidates simply stated that each of the material misstatements would result in a qualified 'except for' opinion. Some candidates suggested that the inventory adjustment should be discussed in an Emphasis of Matter or Other Matter paragraph because it was immaterial, clearly demonstrating a complete misunderstanding of when it is appropriate to use these paragraphs. Candidates must learn when an Emphasis of Matter paragraph should be used; it is not a substitute to be used when the candidate cannot decide between a modified and an unmodified audit opinion.

Candidates must appreciate that the process of justifying an audit opinion and explaining the implication for the auditor's report is a core area of the syllabus. It is regularly examined and it should not come as a surprise to see this topic in the exam. The presentation of information in this question was in a new style, but this should not have made the question more difficult, in fact having information presented in the form of journals with totals given should make understanding the question easier. Further the structure of the requirement into two distinct sections should have helped candidates understand that they were being asked to consider the issues first and then to aggregate the effect of the misstatements before assessing the impact on the auditor's report.

ACCA marking scheme

			Marks
(a)		**Explanation of quality control and other professional issues**	
		Generally up to 1 mark for each point explained:	
		– Analytical review mandatory at the final review stage	
		– Objective to ensure that financial statements consistent with auditor's understanding	
		– A quick look unlikely to be sufficient	
		– The fact that it is deemed low-risk does not negate the need for analytical review	
		– Lack of analytical review increases audit risk	
		– Other information must be read with objective of identifying material inconsistencies	
		– Manager to be questioned to see what work has been done and what documentation exists	
		– Likely that chairman's statement needs to be properly read and audit conclusion documented	
		– Audit manager lacks understanding of ISA requirements	
		– Audit manager may need further training	
		Maximum	**7**
(b)	(i)	**Explain matters to be considered in forming audit opinion**	
		Generally 1 mark for each point explained:	
		– ISAs require auditor to understand management's reason for not adjusting misstatements	
		– ISAs require auditor to communicate impact of unadjusted misstatement on opinion	
		Share-based payment:	
		– Materiality assessment including appropriate calculation	
		– Fall in share price not valid reason for not recognising expense and credit to equity	
		– Material misstatement due to breach of financial reporting standards, encourage management to make necessary adjustment	
		Provision:	
		– Materiality assessment including appropriate calculation	
		– Provision recognised too early	
		– Material misstatement	
		– Consider if any additional information to explain recognition of provision	
		– Encourage management to make necessary adjustment	

Inventory allowance:	
– Materiality assessment including appropriate calculation	
– Discussion of difference between clearly trivial, immaterial and material items	
– Misstatement is a matter of judgment	
– Management should still be encouraged to make adjustment but no impact on audit opinion if not done	
Maximum	**9**
(ii) **Impact on auditor's report:**	
Generally up to 1 mark per point explained:	
– Determination of aggregate impact of adjustments and combined materiality	
– Material misstatement and modified opinion necessary	
– Discussion and conclusion as to whether opinion should be qualified or adverse	
– Basis for qualified opinion paragraph to include a description and quantification of the financial effects of the misstatement	
Maximum	**4**
Total	**20**

48 MARR *Walk in the footsteps of a top tutor*

Top tutor tips

Part (a) requires students to have read a recently issued technical article regarding improvements to the auditor's report. Students that had not read this would have struggled with this requirement. It is important to not just rely on study texts when preparing for this exam as current issues are also examinable which requires knowledge of what is happening in the real world.

Part (b) is a typical reporting question seen several times in previous exams and should not cause problems for students who are familiar with the format of an auditor's report and who have practised this style of question before. Work your way through the auditor's report and think about whether the wording is appropriate, the order of the paragraphs is correct, the names of the paragraphs are correct and ultimately, whether you agree with the opinion suggested.

(a) A quality audit should be accompanied by an informative auditor's report which delivers value to the entity's stakeholders and that the auditor's report should better explain key matters.

In respect of going concern, the auditor's report should include an auditor's conclusion on the appropriateness of management's use of the going concern assumption, and an explicit statement as to whether material uncertainties in relation to going concern have been identified. A description of management's responsibilities with respect to going concern will also be required.

It is clear that the financial crisis of recent years sparked a new debate into the appropriateness of the use of the going concern assumption by management, and into whether the auditor's report contains sufficient information about going concern matters.

Many users of financial statements have argued that going concern is such a critical issue that it should be discussed in more detail, and in an understandable way in the auditor's report. The previous auditor's report was criticised for containing insufficient information regarding going concern and added to the perceived expectation gap. The IAASB suggestion to include specific statements regarding going concern will add clarity on this matter.

The issue of auditors making an affirmative statement regarding going concern is likely to add more credibility to the financial statements, which will provide a level of comfort for all users of financial statements. Specifically for users such as providers of finance, they may be more willing to make lending decisions based on financial statements on which an affirmative statement in respect of going concern has been given by the auditor.

The disclosures include a statement regarding material uncertainties which relate to going concern. This can be seen to be informative and should help users to understand the subjective nature of the going concern assumption.

Overall, the suggestions should go some way to bridge the expectation gap but users of financial statements will need to treat statements made in relation to going concern with some caution, due to its highly subjective nature. The danger is that the auditor's affirmations may be seen as a guarantee of a company's future sustainability, which is clearly not their purpose.

It can be argued that the requirements of ISA 570 (Revised) *Going Concern* are sufficiently robust, and that including going concern as a specific matter in the auditor's report only when it is an issue provides the best clarity for users of the financial statements.

Tutorial note

Answers which refer to more recent IAASB documents on the proposed changes to auditor's reports will be given credit.

(b) In terms of structure, the basis for opinion and opinion paragraphs should not be combined together. When the auditor modifies the opinion on the financial statements, the auditor shall include a paragraph in the auditor's report which provides a description of the matter giving rise to the modification. Therefore the auditor's report needs to be amended to include two separate paragraphs.

The auditor should use the heading 'Basis for Qualified Opinion', 'Basis for Adverse Opinion', or 'Basis for Disclaimer of Opinion', as appropriate.

The paragraph states that audit procedures have 'proven conclusively' in respect of trade receivables. This term is misleading, implying that every transaction has been tested. Audit procedures provide a reasonable, but not absolute, level of assurance on the financial statements, and conclusive proof is not an appropriate term to be used in the auditor's report.

The amount of the potential adjustment to trade receivables and its financial impact should be included in the paragraph. If there is a material misstatement of the financial statements which relates to specific amounts in the financial statements (including quantitative disclosures), the auditor shall include in the basis for modification paragraph a description and quantification of the financial effects of the misstatement, unless impracticable. The relevant financial reporting standard should also be referred to.

The paragraph uses unprofessional wording by naming the finance director. The auditor's report should refer to management collectively and not single out one person as being responsible for the financial statements. In addition, it should not state that she 'refused' to make an adjustment.

The incorrect type of modified audit opinion seems to have been given. The trade receivables balance is material at $2.5 million, which is in excess of the materiality threshold of $1.5 million used in the audit and so a qualification due to material misstatement seems necessary. The auditor's report uses a disclaimer of opinion, which is used when the auditor cannot form an opinion, usually due to lack of audit evidence, which does not appear to be the case here.

In addition, the level of modification seems incorrect. The matter is material but is unlikely to be pervasive to the financial statements based on the level of profit of $11 million. Therefore a qualified 'except for' opinion is sufficient.

The use of an Emphasis of Matter paragraph in respect of the court case is not appropriate. An Emphasis of Matter paragraph is used to refer to a matter appropriately presented or disclosed in the financial statements which, in the auditor's judgement, is of such importance that it is fundamental to users' understanding of the financial statements.

The court case and its potential legal consequences are not material, being well below the materiality threshold of $1.5 million. The matter is certainly not fundamental to users' understanding of the financial statements. Due to the immaterial nature of the matter it need not be referred to in the auditor's report at all.

The auditor has reached the conclusion that the court case has not been accounted for correctly. The Emphasis of Matter paragraph should only be used to highlight matters which have been appropriately accounted for and disclosed within the financial statements, and its use to describe non-compliance with the relevant financial reporting standard is not appropriate.

Examiner comments

This question concentrated on auditors' reports, and also included a requirement in relation to a current issue.

Requirement (a) asked candidates to explain the suggestions made by the IAASB in respect of additional disclosures in the auditor's report regarding going concern status, and to discuss the benefits of such disclosures. This requirement was based on the IAASB's Invitation to Comment on Improving the Auditor's Report, an examinable document, and about which there had been a relevant article published for the benefit of candidates on ACCA's website. It was clear that many candidates who attempted this question had read the article and understood the main proposals, and marks were awarded for this knowledge. However, very few candidates made any attempt to discuss the proposals, as requested, which limited the marks that could be awarded. Some candidates had little awareness of the IAASB's Invitation to Comment, and instead gave an answer that simply outlined the existing requirements in relation to the auditor's responsibility in respect of going concern.

The UK and IRL adapted papers contained a slightly different requirement. The requirement was more general, asking for a discussion of whether including specific disclosures on going concern would improve the quality and usefulness of the auditor's report. Answers here tended to be good, with a real attempt made to properly discuss the issues and to reach an opinion and justified conclusion on the topic.

Requirement (b) asked for a critical appraisal of a proposed auditor's report. The report contained many errors of fact and of judgment, and well prepared candidates scored highly here. There were some quite obvious matters that most candidates discussed, for example that the structure of the report was not correct, the wording was not professional, the basis for opinion paragraph lacked sufficient detail, and the nature of the modification was wrong in the circumstances described in the scenario. Most candidates also commented on the incorrect use of the Emphasis of Matter paragraph and correctly determined the materiality of the two issues described in the scenario. Overall however, answers to this requirement were often too short for the marks available, and while most issues had been identified, they were not always well explained.

ACCA marking scheme

		Marks
(a)	**Discussion regarding the auditor's report**	
	In general **up to 1½ marks** for each relevant discussion point:	
	– Relevant introduction	
	– 1 mark for each correct suggestion:	
	– Suggestion of auditor's affirmation regarding use of going concern assumption	
	– Suggestion of description of material uncertainties regarding going concern	
	– Description of management responsibility regarding going concern	
	– Previous auditor's report had insufficient information	
	– Additional disclosures could add clarity and transparency	
	– Credibility of financial statements is enhanced	
	– May help to highlight the subjective nature of going concern assessment	
	– Drawbacks include the affirmation being perceived as a guarantee of financial health	
	Maximum	**8**
(b)	**Evaluation of draft auditor's report**	
	In general **up to 1½ marks** for each relevant point of evaluation:	
	– Incorrect presentation and combining of Opinion and Basis for Opinion paragraphs	
	– Wording regarding 'proven conclusively' is inappropriate	
	– Description of material misstatement should include quantification and impact on financial statements	
	– The relevant financial reporting standard should be referred to	
	– Unprofessional wording regarding the finance director	
	– Inappropriate opinion given – should be modified due to material misstatement not due to disclaimer of opinion	
	– Level of modification incorrect – it is material but not pervasive	
	– Court case not fundamental so not appropriate to include in Emphasis of Matter paragraph	
	– Emphasis of Matter should only be used for matters appropriately accounted for which is not the case	
	Maximum	**12**
Total		**20**

49 POODLE GROUP *Walk in the footsteps of a top tutor*

Top tutor tips

This question focuses on reporting implications in a group context but also required explanation of any adjustments and further audit procedures necessary.

There are three issues which need to be discussed, first of all in isolation i.e. one issue at a time. However, remember that the aggregate effects of misstatements should also be considered so finish off your answer by doing this.

When considering the implications for the auditor's report, remember to consider not just the opinion but any other paragraphs that may need to be added.

To earn the marks you will need to justify your answer, e.g. say whether the issue is material; justify why it is material but not pervasive.

(a) Toy Co

The amount claimed against Toy Co is material to consolidated profit, representing 25% of consolidated profit before tax. The amount is not material to consolidated total assets, representing less than 1% of that amount.

The same accounting policies should be applied across the Group in the consolidated financial statements. Therefore in accordance with IAS 37 *Provisions, Contingent Liabilities and Contingent Assets*, a provision should be recognised in the consolidated financial statements if the amount is probable to be paid. The adjustment needed is:

DR Operating expenses	\$500,000
CR Current liabilities – provisions	\$500,000

The audit evidence obtained by the component auditors is insufficient. Verbal evidence is not a reliable source of evidence. Further audit procedures should be performed, including:

- Obtain written evidence from Toy's legal advisors including a statement that in their opinion the damages are probable to be paid, and the basis of that opinion.
- Review the claim itself to confirm that \$500,000 is the amount claimed by the ex-employee.
- Inspect the board minutes of Toy Co for evidence of discussion of the claim, to obtain an understanding as to the reason for the claim and whether it has been disputed by Toy Co.

These further audit procedures may be performed by the component auditor, or by the Group audit team.

If, having obtained evidence to confirm that the damages are probable to be paid, the consolidated financial statements are not adjusted to include the provision, the consolidated statement of profit or loss will be materially misstated. This would result in a qualified 'except for' opinion due to the material, but not pervasive, nature of the material misstatement.

The report should contain a paragraph entitled 'Basis for Qualified Opinion' describing the matter giving rise to the qualification. A quantification of the financial effect of the misstatement should also be given.

The auditor should discuss the need for the adjustment with the client (including those charged with governance), and explain that a modified opinion will result from the material misstatement.

(b) Trade receivable

The trade receivable is material to the consolidated financial statements, representing 2.8% of total assets and 80% of profit before tax. The amount that is potentially irrecoverable is 90% of the total balance outstanding, i.e. $1.44 million. This amount is also material, representing 2.5% of total assets and 72% of profit before tax.

IFRS 9 *Financial Instruments* requires that impaired trade receivables are recognised at fair value, which is the present value of estimated cash inflows. According to the information provided by Terrier's administrators, it is likely that 10% of the amount outstanding will be paid and the remaining 90% should be written off. The adjustment needed is:

DR Operating expenses (irrecoverable debts expense) $1,440,000

CR Trade receivables $1,440,000

The amount should be adjusted in the financial statements for the year ended 31 March 2013, even though notice was not received until May 2013. This is because according to IAS 10 *Events After the Reporting Period*, an adjusting event is one that provides additional information about conditions existing at the year end.

If the financial statements are not adjusted for the impaired receivable, current assets will be overstated and profits overstated by $1.44 million. This is a very significant matter as the adjustment to profit is highly material.

Tutorial note

Credit will be awarded for comments relating to whether separate disclosure on the face of the statement of profit or loss is appropriate, due to the material and unusual nature of the item.

The auditor should perform additional procedures as follows:

- Obtain the notice from Terrier's administrators confirming that the company is insolvent and that only 10% of amount outstanding is likely to be paid.
- Obtain a written confirmation from the administrators stating the expected timing of the payment.
- Check post year-end cash receipts to see if any of the outstanding balance has been received from Terrier Co.
- Recalculate the impairment losses and trace the posting of the impairment into the general ledger and the financial statements.

If the consolidated financial statements are not adjusted for the irrecoverable amount, both the statement of financial position and the statement of profit or loss will be materially misstated. This would result in a qualified 'except for' opinion due to the material, but not pervasive, nature of the material misstatement.

Aggregate impact on the financial statements

The materiality and overall significance of the two matters discussed above should be considered in aggregate. When combined, the adjustment needed to net assets and to operating expenses is $1.94 million. This adjustment would reduce the draft consolidated profit before tax to only $60,000.

The auditor should discuss the need for the adjustment with the client (including those charged with governance), and explain that a qualified or adverse opinion will result from the material misstatements.

The combined misstatement could be considered both material and pervasive to the financial statements as the profit figure is so impacted by the adjustments necessary. In this case, the auditor should express an adverse opinion, stating that the financial statements do not show a true and fair view.

A paragraph should be included entitled 'Basis for Adverse Opinion', which describes the reason for the adverse opinion and provides quantification. This would be positioned after the opinion.

(c) Chairman's statement

Guidance is found in:

ISA 720 (revised) *The Auditor's Responsibilities Relating to Other Information in Documents Containing Audited Financial Statements*.

The requirement of ISA 720 is that the auditor shall read the other information, in order to identify any information contained within any of the financial or non-financial information in the annual report that is apparently materially incorrect based on, or materially inconsistent with, the knowledge acquired by the auditor in the course of performing the audit.

A material inconsistency arises where the other information contradicts information in the audited financial statements, and may possibly raise doubt about the audit opinion. Effectively, a material inconsistency undermines the credibility of the audit opinion.

In the event of a material inconsistency being discovered, the auditor shall determine whether the financial statements or other information needs to be revised, so that the inconsistency is removed.

If the inconsistency is not resolved, the auditor's responsibilities depend on whether it is the other information, or the financial statements that have not been corrected.

If the financial statements have not been revised, and therefore contain an item which the auditor believes to be materially misstated, then the audit opinion should be modified.

If management refuse to remove the inconsistency, the auditor should communicate this to those charged with governance.

In extreme situations, where a material inconsistency remains uncorrected by management, it may be necessary for the audit firm to withdraw from the audit. In such cases legal advice should be sought, to protect the interests of the audit firm.

In the Group's case, the chairman's statement contains an inconsistency, as according to the consolidated financial statements, revenue has increased by 5.9%, but the chairman states that revenue has increased by 20%.

The audit work performed on revenue should be reviewed to ensure that sufficient and appropriate evidence has been gained to support the figures in the financial statements.

The matter should be discussed with management, who should be asked to amend the disclosure in the chairman's statement. Management should be presented with the results of the audit work, to justify, if necessary, that the amendment needs to be made. The inclusion of the incorrect figure in the draft chairman's statement could be a genuine mistake, in which case management should be happy to make the change.

If the other information is received before the date of the auditor's report, a separate section should be included in the auditor's report under the heading 'Other Information'. In this section the auditor should:

- Identify the other information obtained prior to the date of the auditor's report.
- State that the auditor has not audited the other information and accordingly does not express an opinion or conclusion on that information.
- Include a description of the auditor's responsibilities with respect to other information.
- State either that the auditor has nothing to report, or a description of the material misstatement.

Therefore, if management refuses to change the other information, the auditor should provide a description of the inconsistency in the 'Other Information' section of the auditor's report.

Alternatively the auditor may withhold the auditor's report or withdraw from the engagement.

Further actions are also available to auditors in the UK who have the right to speak at general meetings of company members, and could therefore highlight the inconsistency to shareholders in this way, if it remains unresolved.

Examiner's comments

Many candidates chose to attempt this question, which focused on audit completion and auditors' reports, despite clearly having very little knowledge and understanding of this topic. Performance tended to be weak on this question overall.

The question was based in a Group audit scenario, in which three matters pertaining to the completion of the audit were described. The scenario made it clear that management was reluctant to adjust the consolidated financial statements in respect of the matters described.

Requirement (a) described the situation in relation to Toy Co, an overseas subsidiary of the Group that was audited by local auditors and reported under the local financial reporting framework, not IFRS Standards.

The main issue was that under the local financial reporting rules a claim against the company would not result in the recognition of a provision, but under IFRS Standards the provision should be recognised. The amount was correctly identified by almost all as material to the Group financial statements, and answers were generally satisfactory, despite the slightly complex scenario. Most candidates explained how an adjustment should be made at Group level and that if not made, the audit opinion should be qualified due to material misstatement. Some answers insisted, incorrectly, that the adjustment should be made in the subsidiary's individual financial statements. The fact that the audit evidence so far obtained was insufficient was not always identified, and only a minority of answers suggested the further audit procedures that should be conducted. Some answers were confused about the impact on the opinion and suggested various options including adverse, disclaimer or in some cases, both.

Requirement (b) provided a short description relating to a receivables balance outstanding in the parent company's financial statements for which payment was unlikely to be received due to the insolvency of the company owing the amount. Many candidates correctly identified this as an adjusting event after the reporting period, and determined that the amount was highly material.

Some answers tended to focus on the going concern status of both companies, or suggested that the matter should be disclosed in both sets of financial statements but not adjusted for. Comments on the audit opinion were also mixed here, with many incorrectly stating that the issue should be highlighted in an emphasis of matter paragraph if not adjusted by Group management.

Before moving on to look at requirement (c) there are two other comments to make in relation to how candidates dealt with the reporting implications of requirements (a) and (b). The first point is that very few candidates considered the issues of (a) and (b) in aggregate. This was important because in aggregate the potential adjustments had a significant impact on Group results, and a discussion of whether this would result in an adverse opinion was relevant. Candidates are encouraged to always look at the bigger picture and even though the scenarios are described separately, they should at some point in the answer be considered collectively.

The second issue is that very few answers went beyond discussing the impact on the audit opinion. However the question asked for impact on the auditor's report, so marks were available for describing the structure and content of the basis for opinion paragraph as well as the opinion itself.

Requirement (c) briefly described how the chairman's statement to be published in the Group's annual report, contained a statement that the Group's revenue had increased by 20%.

The vast majority of answers correctly determined that this was incorrect, revenue had actually increased by 5.9%. While there were some sound answers here from candidates who clearly understood the implications, unfortunately in many answers there was little else to be said, indicating a lack of knowledge of the auditor's responsibilities in relation to other information published with the financial statements, or the impact of such a misstatement on the auditor's report. Many answers suggested the use, incorrectly, of an emphasis of matter paragraph, but more suggested that there would be no impact at all on the auditor's report, and that the chairman's statement was nothing to do with the auditor's responsibilities.

	ACCA marking scheme	
		Marks
	Audit completion, adjustments necessary, additional audit procedures, implications for auditor's report	
	Generally up to 1 mark for each point assessed/procedure recommended:	
(a)	**Toy Co**	
	– Potential provision is material to Group accounts (calculation)	
	– Group accounting policy should be applied	
	– Adjustment needed to operating profit and current liabilities	
	– Recommend additional procedures (1 mark each)	
	– Material misstatement if not adjusted and qualified opinion	
	– Describe 'Basis for Qualified Opinion' paragraph	
	Maximum	**7**
(b)	**Trade receivable**	
	– Potential impairment of receivables is material to Group accounts (calculation)	
	– Account for as an adjusting event	
	– Adjustment needed to operating profit and current assets	
	– Recommend additional procedures (1 mark each)	
	– Material misstatement if not adjusted and qualified opinion	
	Potential adjustments in aggregate (marks can be awarded either in answer to (a) or (b))	
	– In aggregate, the two matters almost wipe out profit before tax	
	– Could be considered to be pervasive to financial statements leading to adverse opinion	
	– Must be discussed with those charged with governance	
	Maximum	**7**
(c)	**Chairman's statement**	
	– Auditor required to read other information which includes the draft chairman's statement	
	– Other information should be consistent with financial statements	
	– Inconsistencies undermine the audit opinion	
	– Draft chairman's statement contains a misstatement regarding revenue	
	– Review audit work performed on revenue	
	– Request draft chairman's statement to be amended	
	– Reporting implications	
	– Consider speaking at meeting of shareholders regarding the inconsistency	
	Maximum	**6**
Total		**20**

50 HENDRIX *Walk in the footsteps of a top tutor*

Top tutor tips

Part (a) (i) asks for actions to be taken by the auditor and the implications for the auditor's report. Here, you need to consider if there is anything further that can be done to obtain the evidence required. Implications for the auditor's report should consider not just the opinion but any other modifications that may be necessary.

Part (a) (ii) requires quality control procedures to be undertaken before issuing the report. Draw on your knowledge from the quality control chapter and specifically the pre-issuance quality control requirements for listed clients.

Part (b) requires matters to be considered in forming a conclusion on the interim financial statements. Even though this is not an audit engagement, the same approach can be taken as for other 'matters' questions. Refer to the materiality of the warranty provision made in the previous year, discuss the appropriate accounting treatment and what should be done. In terms of the opinion, remember that limited assurance will be given so the wording needs to reflect this.

(a) **(i)** There is a clear lack of audit evidence in respect of payroll, receivables and revenue. The written statement from Hendrix Co is not sufficient appropriate evidence on which to reach a conclusion regarding these balances and transactions which are material to the financial statements of Dylan Co.

The auditor should consider whether audit procedures alternative to those planned could be used to gather sufficient appropriate evidence. For example, procedures could be performed on the manual reconstruction of accounting records which has been performed by Hendrix Co, and receivables could still be contacted to confirm the balances outstanding at the year end. This would rely on the cooperation of Hendrix Co, who would have to allow the audit firm access to its accounting records and the reconstruction that has taken place.

The audit firm could request an extension to the agreed deadline for the completion of the audit to perform such additional work. This may be seen as a favourable option to the client, who presumably would want to avoid a modified audit opinion in the event that insufficient audit evidence was obtained.

Given that the accounting systems were affected in August, only one month before the financial year end, it may be possible to obtain sufficient appropriate evidence for the majority of transactions that occurred during the year, and that it is only a small proportion of transactions that cannot be confirmed, which may be immaterial to the financial statements. In this case, an unmodified opinion would be issued.

If further evidence cannot be obtained, the auditor should consider a modification to the auditor's opinion.

If the auditor is unable to obtain sufficient appropriate audit evidence on which to base the opinion, but the auditor concludes that the possible effects on the financial statements of undetected misstatements, if any, could be material but not pervasive, then a qualified opinion should be given. In this opinion, the auditor states that except for the possible effects of the potential misstatements of payroll, receivables and revenue, the financial statements give a true and fair view.

The auditor may conclude that the possible effects on the financial statements of undetected misstatements, if any, could be both material and pervasive, in which case the auditor should disclaim an opinion.

In this case, the auditor states that sufficient appropriate evidence has not been obtained to provide a basis for an audit opinion, and accordingly the auditor does not express an opinion on the financial statements.

It is required that potential modifications are communicated to those charged with governance. The reasons for the modification should be explained, and those charged with governance may be able to provide the auditor with further information and explanations. Given that Dylan Co is listed, the communication is likely to be with its audit committee.

A paragraph should be included entitled 'Basis for Qualified Opinion', or 'Basis for Disclaimer of Opinion' which describes the reason for the modified opinion and provides quantification of the issue.

As Dylan Co is listed, the auditor may refer to the matter in the Key Audit Matters section of the auditor's report if the opinion is not modified as the issue would have been discussed with the audit committee and may be something the auditor considers should be communicated to the users of the financial statements.

(ii) **Quality control**

ISA *220 Quality Control for an Audit of Financial Statements* requires that for audits of financial statements of listed entities, an engagement quality control reviewer shall be appointed. The audit engagement partner shall then discuss significant matters arising during the audit engagement with the engagement quality control reviewer.

In the case of Dylan's audit, clearly the lack of evidence in respect of significant financial statement balances and transactions, and its impact on the auditor's report should be discussed. The engagement quality control reviewer must review the financial statements and the proposed auditor's report, in particular focusing on the conclusions reached in formulating the auditor's report and consideration of whether the proposed auditor's opinion is appropriate. The audit documentation relating to payroll, receivables and revenue will be carefully reviewed, and the reviewer is likely to consider whether there are any alternative means of confirming the balances and transactions.

Given the listed status of Dylan Co, any modification to the auditor's report will be scrutinised, and the firm must be sure of any decision to modify the report, and the type of modification made. Once the engagement quality control reviewer has considered the necessity of a modification, they should consider whether a qualified or disclaimer of opinion is appropriate. This is an important issue, given that it is a matter of judgement whether the matters would be material or pervasive to the financial statements.

The engagement quality control reviewer should ensure that there is adequate documentation regarding the judgements used in forming the audit opinion, and that all necessary matters have been brought to the attention of those charged with governance.

The auditor's report may not be signed and dated until the completion of the engagement quality control review.

(b) Review of interim financial statements

Reviews of interim financial statements are governed by ISRE 2410 *Review of Interim Financial Information Performed by the Independent Auditor of the Entity.* Reviews are based on enquiries and analytical procedures, and having determined that Squire Co has changed its accounting treatment regarding the warranty provision, management must be asked to explain the reason for the change.

Interim financial statements should be prepared under the same financial reporting framework as annual financial statements. Therefore IAS *37 Provisions, Contingent Liabilities and Contingent Assets* should be applied.

It would appear correct that a warranty provision is not recognised for cars sold since 1 July 2012, as Squire Co has no obligation relating to those sales. However, cars sold previous to that date are subject to a three-year warranty, so a warranty provision should continue to be recognised for the obligation arising in respect of those sales. Therefore Squire's interim financial statements understate liabilities and overstate profits.

The warranty provision as at 30 April represented 5·5% of total assets, therefore material to the financial statements. If the same warranty provision still needs to be recognised at 31 October, it would represent 5% of total assets, therefore material to the interim financial statements.

ISRE 2410 requires that when a matter comes to the auditor's attention that leads the auditor to question whether a material adjustment should be made to the interim financial information, additional inquiries should be made, or other procedures performed. In this case, the auditor may wish to inspect sales documentation to ensure that warranties are no longer offered on sales after 1 July. The auditor should also review customer correspondence to ensure that warranties on sales prior to 1 July are still in place.

If as a result of performing the necessary procedures, the auditor believes that a material adjustment is needed in the interim financial information, the matter must be communicated to the appropriate level of management, and if management fail to respond appropriately within a reasonable period of time, to those charged with governance. In order to avoid a modification of the report, it is likely that adjustment would be made by management to the interim financial statements.

If the amount remains unadjusted, meaning that in the auditor's opinion the interim financial statements contain a material departure from the applicable financial reporting framework, the report on the review of interim financial information should contain a qualified or adverse conclusion. This is a modification of the conclusion, and the auditor must describe the reason for the modification, which is provided in a paragraph entitled 'Basis for Qualified Conclusion'.

The qualified conclusion would be worded as follows: 'Based on our review, with the exception of the matter described in the preceding paragraph, nothing has come to our attention that causes us to believe that the accompanying interim financial information does not give a true and fair view...'

Finally, the audit firm should consider whether it is possible to withdraw from the review engagement and resigning from the audit appointment.

Examiner's comments

This question, as is typical for question five in paper P7, focused on reporting. The scenario for requirement (a) described the loss of accounting records that had occurred one month before the year end of a listed audit client.

The records had been held by a service organisation, which had provided reconstructed records in respect of those that had been lost. Requirement (a) (i) asked candidates to comment on the actions that should be taken by the auditor, and the implication for the auditor's report. Most candidates correctly discussed that fact that the auditor was unable to obtain sufficient, appropriate audit evidence based on the reconstructed records, leading them to explain that the audit opinion should be disclaimed. Fewer candidates suggested that alternative procedures could be used to obtain evidence, and fewer still recognised that as the accounting records were available for eleven months of the year, the auditor's report may not necessarily be subject to a disclaimer of opinion, or even qualified at all if alternative procedures could take place. A small minority of answers discussed the fact that due to the client being a listed entity, it would most likely have back up records of its own and not be totally reliant on the service organisation in any case.

Some answers demonstrated a lack of knowledge on auditors' reports, stating incorrectly that an adverse opinion would be most appropriate, and few answers described the need for discussing the potential modification with those charged with governance, instead opting for resignation in the face of such 'incompetent' management.

Requirement (a) (ii) asked for a discussion of quality control procedures that should be carried out by the audit firm prior to the auditor's report being issued. Sound answers appreciated that because the client in the scenario was listed, an Engagement Quality Control review would be required, and the answers that described what such a review would entail achieved the maximum marks.

Most answers were too general however, simply describing the quality control procedures that would be relevant to any audit. Many answers were extremely brief, with little more than a sentence or two provided.

Requirement (b) was based on a scenario which described a review engagement that was taking place on the interim financial statements of another listed company. An accounting policy in relation to warranty provisions had been changed in the interim financial statements, and based on the information provided, candidates should have appreciated that the accounting treatment was incorrect. Figures were provided to enable materiality to be calculated. The requirement was to assess the matters that should be considered in forming an opinion on the interim financial statements, and the implications for the review report. Most answers were good at discussing the accounting treatment for the warranty provision, that the non-recognition was not appropriate, and the majority correctly assessed the materiality of the issue. Answers were inadequate in discussing the impact of this on the review report, being mostly unable to say much more than the auditor would need to mention it in the review report. There seemed to be a lack of knowledge on anything other than the standard wording for a review report, with many answers stating that the wording should be 'nothing has come to our attention' followed by a discussion that there actually was something to bring to shareholders' attention but with no recommendation as to how this should be done.

ACCA marking scheme

			Marks
(a)	(i)	Actions and implications in respect of the auditor's report	
		Up to 1½ marks for each action/implication	
		– Insufficient appropriate audit evidence so far obtained	
		– Extend audit procedures/perform other procedures	
		– Majority of transactions during the year likely to have sufficient evidence	
		– If no further evidence available, consider modification to opinion	
		– Discuss whether material or pervasive	
		– Description of report contents if opinion modified	
		– Communicate with those charged with governance	
		Maximum	7
	(ii)	Quality control procedures	
		Up to 1 mark for each comment:	
		– EQCR required as Dylan Co is listed	
		– EQCR to review sufficiency and appropriateness of evidence	
		– EQCR to consider judgement used in forming audit opinion	
		– EQCR to ensure matters communicated to TCWG	
		Maximum	3

(b)	Interim financial statement review Up to 1½ marks for each matter to be considered in forming conclusion/implication for report: – Interim financial information should use applicable financial reporting framework – Identify and explain unrecognised provision – Correct calculation of materiality (1 mark) – Communicate adjustment to management / TCWG – If amount unadjusted, the conclusion will be qualified – Reason for qualified conclusion to be explained in the report – Consider withdrawing from engagement/resign from audit	
	Maximum	**5**
Total		**15**

51 SNIPE *Walk in the footsteps of a top tutor*

Top tutor tips

Part (a) is a typical 'matters and evidence' question. First, consider the materiality of the issue. Next discuss the appropriate accounting treatment and give the risks of material misstatement that would arise if the appropriate treatment is not followed. Finally, the evidence is what you would expect to be recorded on the audit file when you come to review it. Be specific about the evidence, don't say 'supporting documentation', suggest what that documentation would be and what it would show.

Part (b) asks for a critical appraisal of the draft report extracts. Don't just focus on whether the opinion is appropriate. You should also think about the titles of the paragraphs included and whether the names are correct, the order they appear in, whether the required information that should be included has been included and whether the wording used is professional and appropriate.

(a) Matters to consider

The total cost of the new processing area of $5 million represents 2.9% of total assets and is material to the statement of financial position. The borrowing costs are not material to the statement of financial position, representing less than 1% of total assets; however, the costs are material to profit representing 10% of profit before tax.

The directly attributable costs, including borrowing costs, relating to the new processing area should be capitalised as property, plant and equipment. According to IAS 23 *Borrowing Costs,* borrowing costs that are directly attributable to the acquisition, construction or production of a qualifying asset should be capitalised as part of the cost of that asset. The borrowing costs should be capitalised only during the period of construction, with capitalisation ceasing when substantially all the activities necessary to prepare the qualifying asset for its intended use or sale are complete.

In this case, the new processing area was ready for use on 1 September, so capitalisation of borrowing costs should have ceased at that point. It seems that the borrowing costs have been appropriately capitalised at $100,000, which represents six months' interest on the loan ($4m × 5% × 6/12).

The new processing area should be depreciated from 1 September, as according to IAS 16 *Property, Plant and Equipment,* depreciation of an asset begins when it is in the location and condition necessary for it to be capable of operating in the manner intended by management.

There should therefore be five months' depreciation included in profit for the year ended 31 January 2012, amounting to $138,889 ($5m/15 years × 5/12).

Evidence

- A breakdown of the components of the $4.9 million capitalised costs (excluding $100,000 borrowing costs) reviewed to ensure all items are eligible for capitalisation.
- Agreement of a sample of the capitalised costs to supporting documentation (e.g. invoices for tangible items such as cement, payroll records for internal labour costs).
- A copy of the approved budget or capital expenditure plan for the extension.
- An original copy of the loan agreement, confirming the amount borrowed, the date of the cash receipt, the interest rate and whether the loan is secured on any assets.
- Documentation to verify that the extension was complete and ready for use on 1 September, such as a building completion certificate.
- Recalculation of the borrowing cost, depreciation charge and carrying value of the extension at the year end, and agreement of all figures to the draft financial statements.
- Confirmation that the additions to property, plant and equipment are disclosed in the required note to the financial statements.

(b) The **description and explanation** provided for the adverse opinion is not sufficient, for a number of reasons. Firstly, the matter is not quantified. The paragraph should clearly state the amount of $10.5 million, and state that this is material to the financial statements.

The paragraph does not say whether the pension plan is in surplus or deficit, i.e. whether it is an asset or a liability which is omitted from the financial statements.

There is **no description of the impact of this omission** on the financial statements. Wording such as 'if the deficit had been recognised, total liabilities would increase by $10.5 million, and shareholders' equity would reduce by the same amount' should be included.

It is **not clear whether any accounting for the pension plan has taken place** at all. As well as recognising the plan surplus or deficit in the statement of financial position, accounting entries are also required to deal with other items such as the current service cost of the plan, and any actuarial gains or losses which have arisen during the year. Whether these have been omitted as well, and their potential impact on profit or equity is not mentioned.

No reference is made to the relevant accounting standard IAS 19 *Employee Benefits.* Reference should be made in order to help users' understanding of the breach of accounting standards that has been made.

The **use of the word 'deliberate'** when describing the omission of the pension plan is not professional, sounds accusatory and may not be correct. The plan may have been omitted in error and an adjustment to the financial statements may have been suggested by the audit firm and is being considered by management.

It is **unlikely that this issue alone would be sufficient to give rise to an adverse opinion**. An adverse opinion should be given when misstatements are both material and pervasive to the financial statements. The amount of the deficit, and therefore the liability that should be recognised, is $10.5 million, which represents 6% of total assets. The amount is definitely material, but would not be considered pervasive to the financial statements.

The **titles and positioning of the two paragraphs** included in the extract are not appropriate. In this case, the titles are incorrect, and the paragraphs should be switched round, so that the basis for modification is provided **after** the opinion.

The opinion paragraph should be entitled 'Adverse Opinion'.

When the auditor modifies the opinion, the 'Basis for Adverse Opinion', should describe the matter giving rise to the modification.

Tutorial note

Where a misstatement is confined to specific elements of the financial statements, it would only be considered pervasive if it represents a substantial proportion of the financial statements.

Examiner's comments

This question was in two parts. Part (a) described the self-construction of new property, plant and equipment at a client. A loan had been taken out to help finance the construction, and financial information was provided in relation to the asset and the loan. Candidates were asked to comment on the matters that should be considered, and the evidence that should be found when conducting a file review of non-current assets.

Candidates should have been familiar with this type of question requirement, as it commonly features in P7. Sound answers contained a calculation and explanation of the materiality of the asset and of the borrowing costs that had been capitalised, followed by a discussion of the appropriate accounting treatment, including whether the borrowing cost should be capitalised, and when depreciation in relation to the asset should commence. There were some sound answers here, with candidates demonstrating sound knowledge of the relevant financial reporting standard requirements, and going on to provide some very well described and relevant audit procedures.

Weaker answers said that it was not possible to capitalise borrowing costs, or incorrectly thought that the construction should be accounted for as some kind of long-term construction contract. Procedures in the weaker answers tended to rely on representations from management and recalculations of every figure provided in the question.

Part (b) involved the critique of an extract from an auditor's report. The report contained an adverse opinion, which most candidates spotted, in relation to the non-recognition of a defined benefit pension deficit on the company's statement of financial position. There were some sound answers here, and candidates' performance in questions of this type has shown a definite improvement. Some answers not only identified but also provided an explanation of the problems with the auditor's report. The majority of answers suggested that an 'except for' qualification may be more suitable than an adverse opinion, and correctly calculated the materiality of the pension plan deficit to support their discussion.

A significant proportion of answers picked up on the order of the paragraphs in the report and on the incorrect wording used in the headings, and on the lack of explanation that had been provided in the report regarding the material misstatement. Fewer answers discussed the inappropriate use of the phrase 'deliberate omission'.

The weaker answers tended to just list out bullet points with no explanation, limiting the amount of marks that could be awarded. Other weaker answers attempted to discuss the appropriate accounting treatment for the pension, often incorrectly.

ACCA marking scheme			
			Marks
(a)	**New processing area**		
	Generally 1 mark for each matter/specific audit procedure:		
	Matters:		
	–	Materiality calculation	
	–	Borrowing costs are directly attributable to the asset	
	–	Borrowing costs should be capitalised during period of construction	
	–	Amounts are correctly capitalised	
	–	Depreciate from September 2011	
	–	Additions to non-current assets should be disclosed in note	
	Evidence:		
	–	Review of costs capitalised for eligibility	
	–	Agreement of sample of costs to supporting documentation	
	–	Copy of approved capital expenditure budget/discuss significant variances	
	–	Agreement of loan details to loan documentation	
	–	Recalculation of borrowing costs, depreciation, asset carrying value	
	–	Confirmation of completeness of disclosure in notes to FS	
		Maximum	**8**
(b)	**Auditor's report**		
	Generally 1 mark per comment:		
	–	Amounts not quantified	
	–	Impact on financial statements not described	
	–	Unclear from report if any accounting taken place	
	–	No reference made to relevant accounting standard	
	–	Use of word 'deliberate' not professional	
	–	Materiality calculation	
	–	Discuss whether adverse opinion appropriate (up to 2 marks)	
	–	Inappropriate headings	
	–	Paragraph order	
		Maximum	**7**
Total			**15**

UK SYLLABUS ONLY

52 KANDINSKY *Walk in the footsteps of a top tutor*

Top tutor tips

Part (a) is a straightforward going concern question asking for indicators of problems and audit procedures to be performed.

Part (b) asks for alternatives to a creditor's voluntary liquidation and the implications of these. Make sure you address all parts of the requirement.

(a) Going concern matters

Revenue and profitability

The extract financial statements show that revenue has fallen by 38.2%. Based on the information provided, operating profit was £1,150,000 in 2014 but is only £340,000 in 2015. Operating margins have fallen from 29.1% to 13.9% during the year and the fall in revenue and margin has caused the company to become loss-making this year.

These changes are highly significant and most likely due to the economic recession which will impact particularly on the sale of luxury, non-essential products such as those sold by Kandinsky Ltd. The loss-making position does not in itself mean that the company is not a going concern, however, the trend is extremely worrying and if the company does not return to profit in the 2016 financial year, then this would be a major concern. Few companies can sustain many consecutive loss-making periods.

Bank loan

The bank loan is significant, amounting to 33.7% of total assets this year end, and it has increased by £500,000 during the year. The company appears to be supporting operations using long-term finance, which may be strategically unsound. The loan is secured on the company's properties, so if the company defaults on the payment due in June 2016, the bank has the right to seize the assets in order to recoup their funds. If this were to happen, Kandinsky Ltd would be left without operational facilities and it is difficult to see how the company could survive. There is also a risk that there is insufficient cash to meet interest payments due on the loan.

Trade payables

The trade payables balance has increased by 38.5%, probably due in part to the change in terms of trade with its major supplier of raw materials. An extension to the payable payment period indicates that the company is struggling to manage its operating cycle, with the cash being generated from sales being insufficient to meet working capital requirements. Relations with suppliers could be damaged if Kandinsky Ltd cannot make payments to them within agreed credit terms, with the result that suppliers could stop supplying the company or withdraw credit which would severely damage the company's operations. There is also a risk that suppliers could bring legal action against the company in an attempt to recover the amounts owed.

Borrowing facility

Kandinsky Ltd has £500,000 available in an undrawn borrowing facility, which does provide a buffer as there is a source of cash which is available, somewhat easing the going concern pressures which the company is facing. However, the availability of the borrowing facility depends on certain covenants being maintained. The calculations below show that the covenants have now been breached, so the bank is within its right to withdraw the facility, leaving Kandinsky Ltd exposed to cash shortages and possibly unable to make payments as they fall due.

	Covenant	*2015*	*2014*
Interest cover	2	340/520 = 0.65	1,150/500 = 2.3
Borrowings to operating profit	4:1	3,500/340 = 10.3:1	3,000/1,150 = 2.6:1

Contingent liability

The letter of support offered to a supplier of raw materials exposes Kandinsky Ltd to a possible cash outflow of £120,000, the timing of which cannot be predicted. Given the company's precarious trading position and lack of cash, satisfying the terms of the letter would result in the company utilising 80% of their current cash reserve – providing such support seems unwise, though it may have been done for a strategic reason, i.e. to secure the supply of a particular ingredient. If the financial support is called upon, it is not certain that Kandinsky Ltd would have the means to make the cash available to its supplier, which may create going concern issues for that company and would affect the supply of cane sugar to Kandinsky Ltd. There may also be legal implications for Kandinsky Ltd if the cash could not be made available if or when requested by the supplier.

Audit procedures in relation to going concern matters identified

- Obtain and review management accounts for the period after the reporting date and any interim financial accounts which have been prepared. Perform analytical review to ascertain the trends in profitability and cash flows since the year end.
- Read the minutes of the meetings of shareholders, those charged with governance and relevant committees for reference to trading and financing difficulties.
- Discuss with management the strategy which is being developed to halt the trend in declining sales and evaluate the reasonableness of the strategy in light of the economic recession and auditor's knowledge of the business.
- Review the company's current order book and assess the level of future turnover required to break-even/make a profit.
- Analyse and discuss the cash flow, profit and other relevant forecasts with management and review assumptions to ensure they are in line with management's strategy and auditor's knowledge of the business.
- Perform sensitivity analysis on the forecast financial information to evaluate the impact of changes in key variables such as interest rates, predictions of sales patterns and the timing of cash receipts from customers.
- Calculate the average payment period for trade payables and consider whether any increase is due to lack of cash or changes in the terms of trade.

- Obtain the contract in relation to the borrowing facility to confirm the covenant measures and to see if any further covenants are included in the agreement.
- Review correspondence with the bank in relation to the loan and the borrowing facility to gauge the bank's level of support for Kandinsky Ltd and for evidence of deteriorating relationships between the bank and the company's management.
- Obtain the bank loan agreement to confirm the amount of the loan, the interest rate and repayment dates and whether the charge over assets is specific or general in nature.
- Review the bank loan agreement for any clauses or covenants to determine whether there are any breaches.
- Obtain the letter of support in relation to the supplier to confirm the conditions under which Kandinsky Ltd would become liable for payment of the £120,000.
- Discuss with management the reason for the letter of support being given to the supplier to understand the business rationale and its implications, including why the supplier approached Kandinsky Ltd for the letter of support.
- Inspect minutes of management meetings where those charged with governance discussed the letter of support and authorised its issuance.
- Obtain any further documentation available in relation to the letter of support, for example, legal documentation and correspondence with the supplier, to confirm the extent of Kandinsky Ltd's involvement with the supplier and that no further amounts could become payable.

(b) The net liabilities position indicates that Viola Ltd is insolvent, meaning that if the company were to dispose of all of its assets, there would not be sufficient funds to pay off the company's liabilities. In a situation of insolvency coupled with operational difficulties like those being faced by Viola Ltd, if the company wishes to avoid liquidation the best option would be to place the company in administration.

The aim of administration is to save the company if possible. The directors seek the assistance of experts and the company continues to operate. An insolvency practitioner is appointed to act as administrator, and will effectively take control of the company in an attempt to rescue it as a going concern. Administration protects the company from the actions of creditors while a restructuring plan is prepared. This is important for Viola Ltd, which is struggling to manage its working capital, meaning that some creditor's balances may be long overdue and the creditors may already be considering actions to recover the amounts owed.

Administration can commence without a court order. The directors themselves may be able to appoint an administrator, though this depends on the company's articles of association. Alternatively, the company (a majority of shareholders) or qualifying floating charge holders can apply for administration without going through the court. Given that Viola Ltd's bank loan is secured by a floating charge over the company's assets, the bank could have the right to appoint an administrator, depending on the terms of the floating charge. If the directors or the company commence appointing an administrator, notice must be given to any qualifying floating charge holders who are entitled to appoint an administrator.

Alternatively, administration proceedings can involve a court order. The company (a majority of shareholders), the directors, one or more creditors or in rare cases the Justice and Chief Executive of the Magistrates' Court can apply to court for an administration order. The court will consider the application and will grant the administration order if it appears that the company is unable to pay its debts.

Whichever method of appointment of an administrator is employed, the advantage for the company is that a moratorium over the company's debts commences. This means that no creditor can enforce their debt against the company during the period of administration and no security over the company's assets can be enforced. For Viola Ltd this would allow much needed breathing space and time to resolve the working capital problems and lack of cash.

The impact on the directors is that they will lose control of the company and all operational decisions will be made by the administrator. The administrator has the power to remove or appoint directors.

The administrator is likely to request that the directors prepare a statement of affairs detailing all of the company's assets and liabilities, information on the company's creditors and any security over assets.

Using the statement of affairs and other information, the administrator will prepare a proposal regarding the future of the company, in which the administrator recommends either a rescue plan to save the company, or states that the company cannot be saved. The proposal must be sent to all shareholders and creditors, and a creditors' meeting will be held at which the proposal will be accepted or rejected.

For Viola Ltd, the proposal is likely to focus on the probability of obtaining the new contracts which have been tendered for, and the availability of bank finance which depends on the contracts being secured. If the contracts are secured, then it may be possible to save the company. However, in the event that the contracts are not secured and there is limited demand from other customers, the administrator may well recommend liquidation of the company.

The employees will remain employed unless the administrator decides that redundancies are an appropriate measure, and this could be a feature of any proposal to save the company. It must be noted that if the administrator recommends the winding up of Viola Ltd, then the loss of jobs will be inevitable.

Administration can last for up to 12 months, but the administration period will end sooner if the administration has been successful, or where there is application to court by one or more creditors or by the administrator.

An alternative to administration is a voluntary liquidation, which can be initiated by creditors or by members. Liquidation means that the company will be wound up – the assets will be sold, proceeds used to pay the company's debts in a prescribed order, and any remaining funds would be distributed to the shareholders.

For a member's voluntary liquidation to take place, the shareholders must pass a resolution, which can be an ordinary or a special resolution depending on the articles of association. However, a member's voluntary liquidation can only take place if the directors make a declaration of solvency. This is a statutory declaration that the directors have made full enquiry into the affairs of the company, and their opinion is that it will be able to pay its debts. The declaration must also include a statement of the company's assets and liabilities. According to the information supplied, Viola Ltd is in a position of net liabilities and therefore it does not seem likely that the directors will be able to make this statement. Therefore a member's voluntary liquidation does not appear feasible.

The recommendation therefore is for the company to be placed into administration, as this will protect the company from the actions of creditors and allow the administrator to consider all relevant facts before making a proposal on the future of the company.

Examiner's comments

This question presented information relating to two different clients. Initially candidates were required to identify indicators in the scenario which gave rise to going concern issues and then to state procedures to audit the going concern status of the company. In general, this was well attempted and candidates scored high marks, however those using a columnar approach tended to lack depth in their explanation of the factors identified in the question and overlooked some of the more encompassing audit procedures that did not arise from a specific scenario point.

In the UK and IRL exam the second part of the question was set around alternatives to insolvency for a company in financial distress. Answers to this requirement were mixed. Many candidates provided good answers, showing that they understood this syllabus area and could apply their knowledge to the scenario. Weaker answers were too vague, and some clearly did know this syllabus area well enough to provide any reasonable advice.

ACCA marking scheme

		Marks
(a)	**Identify and explain going concern matters** Up to 2½ marks for matter identified and explained, to include 1 mark for relevant calculations: • Revenue, operating margins and profitability • Bank loan • Trade payables • Borrowing facility • Contingent liability **Audit procedures in respect of going concern matters** Up to 1 mark for each well explained procedure: • Obtain and review management accounts, perform analytical review to ascertain the trends in profitability and cash flows since the year end • Read the minutes of the meetings for reference to trading and financing difficulties • Discuss with management the strategy which is being developed to halt the trend in declining sales and evaluate the reasonableness of the strategies in light of the economic recession and auditor's knowledge of the business • Review the company's current order book and assess the level of future turnover to level required to breakeven/make a profit • Analyse and discuss the cash flow, profit and other relevant forecasts with management and review assumptions are in line with management strategy and auditor's knowledge of the business • Obtain the bank loan agreement to confirm the amount of the loan, the interest rate and repayment dates and whether the charge over assets is specific or general in nature • Review the bank loan agreement for any clauses or covenants to determine whether there are any breaches • Calculate the average payment period for trade payables and consider whether any increase is due to lack of cash or changes in the terms of trade	

- Obtain the contract in relation to the borrowing facility to confirm the covenant measures and to see if any further covenants are included in the agreement
- Discuss correspondence with the bank in relation to the loan and the borrowing facility to gauge the bank's level of support for Kandinsky Co and for evidence of deteriorating relationships between the bank and the company's management. Inspect minutes of management meetings where those charged with governance discussed the letter of support and authorised its issuance
- Obtain any further documentation available in relation to the letter of support, for example, legal documentation and correspondence with the supplier, to confirm the extent of Kandinsky Co's involvement with the supplier and that no further amounts could become payable

Maximum	**13**

(b) **Response to finance director's instructions**

Generally 1½ marks for each point explained

- Identify Viola Ltd as insolvent
- Purpose of administration
- Procedure – commencing administration without court order
- Procedure – commencing administration with a court order
- Moratorium over debts – advantage to the company
- Statement of affairs to be produced
- Administrator proposes rescue plan or liquidation
- Proposals agreed by members and creditors
- Impact on directors – loss control of the company
- Impact on directors – lose control of the company
- Impact on employees – depends on recommendation of administrator
- Period of administration and cessation of administration
- Members' voluntary liquidation is a possibility but depends on declaration of solvency being made

Maximum	**12**
Total	**25**

53 COXON *Walk in the footsteps of a top tutor*

Top tutor tips

This question requires knowledge of the difference between fraudulent and wrongful trading. You then need to apply that knowledge to the scenario to assess whether the directors are guilty of either offence.

The question also asks you to describe the impact of the compulsory liquidation for the employees and creditors. Make sure you identify all aspects of the requirement when the requirement is embedded within the scenario like this to avoid missing out on vital marks.

Personal liability of company directors

Normally, the directors of a company which is placed in liquidation do not have a personal liability for the debts of the company. However, the liquidator who is appointed to wind up the company will investigate the reasons for the insolvency, which includes an assessment of whether fraudulent or wrongful trading has taken place, in which case the directors may become liable to repay all or some of the company's debts.

Wrongful trading is defined under s.214 Insolvency Act 1986, and is the less serious of the two offences. Wrongful trading applies when:

- the company has gone into insolvent liquidation
- at some time before the commencement of the winding up of the company, the directors knew, or ought to have known, that there was no reasonable prospect that the company would avoid going into insolvent liquidation
- the directors did not take sufficient steps to minimise the potential loss to creditors.

In deciding whether or not a director of a company ought to have known or ascertained the company was insolvent, the liquidator will consider the general knowledge, skill and experience which may reasonably be expected of a reasonable diligent person carrying out the same functions as are carried out by that director. If a director has greater than usual skill, they would be judged by reference to their own capacity.

The liquidator needs to apply to the court to proceed with an action against a director for wrongful trading. If found guilty, the director faces a civil liability and can be ordered to make a contribution to the company's assets. A director is not likely to be found guilty if they can demonstrate that they took every step with a view to minimising the potential loss to the company's creditors which they ought to have taken.

Fraudulent trading is the more serious offence. Here, a director faces a criminal charge as well as a civil charge under the Insolvency Act. The definition of fraudulent trading is if in the course of the winding up of a company, it appears that any business of the company has been carried on with intent to defraud creditors of the company, or for any fraudulent purpose. Carrying on a business can include a single transaction.

It is harder to prove fraudulent trading than wrongful trading. Only those directors who took the decision to carry on the business, or played an active role are liable. If found guilty, directors may have to make personal contributions to the company's assets and the court can also impose fines or imprisonment on guilty directors.

In the case of Coxon Ltd's directors, it seems that there was a decision to continue to trade even when there were clear signs of the company's financial distress. The company continued to purchase goods even though the directors were aware of severe cash shortages and difficult trading conditions. Therefore the liquidator is likely to conclude that there is evidence of at least wrongful trading, especially on the part of the finance director, who should have known that the company was insolvent, and did not take all steps necessary to protect creditors.

Impact of compulsory liquidation for employees and creditors

In a compulsory liquidation the employees are automatically dismissed. The liquidator effectively takes over control of the company, assuming management responsibility. The liquidator can require directors and other staff to assist with matters such as preparing and submitting the statement of affairs.

With regard to creditors, they have no involvement with the actual liquidation process, other than having the right to hold a meeting at which they appoint their choice of insolvency practitioner to act as liquidator.

The main impact of liquidation for both employees and creditors is the allocation of company assets at the end of the winding up. There is a prescribed order of priority for allocating company assets. Employees' salaries in arrears (subject to a maximum amount), pension contributions and holiday pay are all preferential creditors. This means that these amounts will be paid after liquidator's costs and fixed charge holders but before all other creditors.

Unsecured creditors and floating charge holders are paid next, followed by preference shareholders and finally members (equity shareholders). Trade creditors are likely to be unsecured creditors, so rank after employees for payment. They are protected to an extent by the 'prescribed part' which is a proportion of assets which is set aside for unsecured creditors. This means that they may not receive the full amount owed to them, but should receive a percentage of what is owed.

ACCA marking scheme	
	Marks
Wrongful and fraudulent trading	
Up to 1.5 marks for each matter explained:	
• Liquidator assesses reason for insolvency including director's actions	
• Definition of wrongful trading	
• Elements which must be proven for wrongful trading (up to 2 marks)	
• Matters looked at by court to determine liability – skill and experience	
• Implication of being found guilty of wrongful trading	
• Definition of fraudulent trading	
• Comment on or application of the above to Coxon Ltd's situation	
• Employees automatically dismissed but may assist liquidator if required	
• Creditors have limited role in liquidation other than ability to appoint liquidator	
• Employees rank as preferential creditors	
• Creditors can be secured, or unsecured and paid from prescribed part	
• Details of any impairment review conducted by management	
Total	**13**

54 HAWK (A) *Walk in the footsteps of a top tutor*

Top tutor tips

Part (a) (i) asks for matters to be considered in agreeing the terms of engagement for an examination of a forecast. These are the matters that need to be included in the engagement letter for this assignment. A good approach to take for this question is to identify matters that could lead to misunderstandings in future that the firm would want clarifying in writing. Knowledge of audit engagement letters can also be used and tailored to this type of engagement.

Part (a) (ii) requires the procedures to be performed on the forecast. It is important to remember that these events and transactions have not yet happened and therefore cannot be agreed to supporting documentation in the same way as historical figures. You need to generate procedures which will help you assess whether the assumptions used in the forecast are reasonable.

Part (bi) asks you to examine the information to determine whether the company is insolvent i.e. does it have more liabilities than assets. This should be relatively straightforward.

Part (b) (ii) asks you to set out the options available to the directors for the future of the company. This requires rote learned knowledge from the text book about the key aspects of liquidation and administration. The requirement specifically asks you to provide a recommendation so you must reach a conclusion as to the best way forward for the company.

(a) **(i)** The terms of the engagement to review and report on Hawk Ltd's business plan and forecast financial statements should be agreed in an engagement letter, separate from the audit engagement letter. The following matters should be included in the terms of agreement:

Management's responsibilities

The terms of the engagement should set out management's responsibilities for the preparation of the business plan and forecast financial statements, including all assumptions used, and for providing the auditor with all relevant information and source data used in developing the assumptions. This is to clarify the roles of management and of Lapwing & Co, and reduce the scope for any misunderstanding.

The intended use of the business plan and report

It should be confirmed that the report will be provided to the bank and that it will not be distributed or made available to other parties. This will establish the potential liability of Lapwing & Co to third parties, and help to determine the need and extent of any liability disclaimer that may be considered necessary. Lapwing & Co should also establish that the bank will use the report only in helping to reach a decision in respect of the additional finance being sought by Hawk Ltd.

The elements of the business plan to be included in the review and report

The extent of the review should be agreed. Lapwing & Co need to determine whether they are being asked to report just on the forecast financial statements, or on the whole business plan including any narrative descriptions or explanations of Hawk Ltd's intended future business activities. This will help to determine the scope of the work involved and its complexity.

The period covered by the forecasts

This should be confirmed when agreeing the terms of the engagement, as assumptions become more speculative as the length of the period covered increases, making it more difficult for Lapwing & Co to substantiate the acceptability of the figures, and increasing the risk of the engagement. It should also be confirmed that a 12-month forecast period is sufficient for the bank's purposes.

The nature of the assumptions used in the business plan

It is crucial that Lapwing & Co determine the nature of assumptions, especially whether the assumptions are based on best estimates or are hypothetical. This is important because the auditor should not accept, or should withdraw from, an engagement when the assumptions are clearly unrealistic or when the auditor believes that the prospective financial information will be inappropriate for its intended use.

The planned contents of the assurance report

The engagement letter should confirm the planned elements of the report to be issued, to avoid any misunderstanding with management. In particular, Lapwing & Co should clarify that their report will contain a statement of negative assurance as to whether the assumptions provide a reasonable basis for the prospective financial information, and an opinion as to whether the prospective financial information is properly prepared on the basis of the assumptions and is presented in accordance with the relevant financial reporting framework. The bank may require the report to be in a particular format and include specific wordings in order to make their lending decision.

(ii) General procedures

- Recalculate the forecast financial statements to confirm arithmetic accuracy.
- Agree the unaudited figures for the period to 31 May 2012 to management accounts, and agree the cash figure to bank statement or bank reconciliation.
- Confirm the consistency of the accounting policies used in the preparation of the forecast financial statements with those used in the last audited financial statements.
- Consider the accuracy of forecasts prepared in prior periods by comparison with actual results and discuss with management the reasons for any significant variances.
- Perform analytical procedures to assess the reasonableness of the forecast financial statements. For example, finance charges should increase in line with the additional finance being sought.
- Discuss the extent to which the joint venture with Kestrel Ltd has been included in the forecast financial statements.

- Review any agreement with Kestrel Ltd, or minutes of meetings at which the joint venture has been discussed to understand the nature, scale, and timeframe of the proposed joint business arrangement.
- Review any projected financial information for the joint venture, and agree any components relating to it into the forecast financial statements.

Forecast statement of profit of loss

- Consider the reasonableness of forecast trends in the light of auditor's knowledge of Hawk Ltd's business and the current and forecast economic situation and any other relevant external factors.
- Discuss the reason for the anticipated 21.4% increase in revenue with management, to understand if the increase is due to the inclusion of figures relating to the joint venture with Kestrel Ltd, or other factors.
- Discuss the trend in operating profit with management – the operating margin is forecast to improve from 30% to 33.8%. This improvement may be due to the sale of the underperforming Beak Retail Park.
- Obtain a breakdown of items included in forecast operating expenses and perform an analytical review to compare to those included in the 2012 figures, to check for any omissions.
- Using the cost breakdown, consider whether depreciation charges have increased in line with the planned capital expenditure.
- Request confirmation from the bank of the potential terms of the £30 million loan being negotiated, to confirm the interest rate at 4%. Consider whether the finance charge in the forecast appears reasonable. (If the loan is advanced in August, it should increase the company's finance charge by £1 million (£30 million × 4% × 10/12).)
- Discuss the potential sale of Beak Retail with management and review relevant board minutes, to obtain understanding of the likelihood of the sale, and the main terms of the sale negotiation.
- Recalculate the profit on the planned disposal, agreeing the potential proceeds to any written documentation relating to the sale, vendor's due diligence report, or draft legal documentation if available.
- Agree the potential proceeds on disposal to management's cash flow forecast, and confirm that operating cash flows relevant to Beak Retail are not included from the anticipated date of its sale.
- Discuss the reason for not including current tax in the profit forecast.

Forecast statement of financial position

- Agree the increase in property, plant and equipment to an authorised capital expenditure budget, and to any plans for the joint development with Kestrel Ltd.
- Obtain and review a reconciliation of the movement in property, plant and equipment. Agree that all assets relating to Beak Retail are derecognised on its disposal, and that any assets relating to the joint development with Kestrel Ltd are recognised in accordance with capital expenditure forecasts, and are properly recognised per IFRS 11 *Joint Arrangements.*

- Discuss the planned increase in equity with management to understand the reason for any planned share issue, its date and the nature of the share issue (rights issue or issue at full market price being the most likely).
- Perform analytical procedures on working capital and discuss trends with management, for example, receivables days is forecast to reduce from 58 to 53 days, and the reason for this should be obtained.

> ***Tutorial note***
>
> *Credit will be awarded for other examples of ratios calculated on the figures provided such as inventory turnover and average payables payment period.*

- Agree the increase in long-term borrowings to documentation relating to the new loan, and also to the forecast cash flow statement (where it should be included as a cash flow arising from financing activities).
- Discuss the deferred tax provision with management to understand why no movement on the balance is forecast, particularly given the planned capital expenditure.
- Obtain and review a forecast statement of changes in equity to ensure that movements in retained earnings appear reasonable. (Retained earnings are forecast to increase by £800,000, but the profit forecast for the period is £10.52 million – there must be other items taken through retained earnings such as a planned dividend.)
- Agree the movement in cash, and the forecast closing cash position to a cash flow forecast.

(b) Briefing notes

To: **Audit partner**

From: **Audit manager**

Subject: **Jay Ltd – financial results and the future of the company**

Introduction

These briefing notes will examine the current financial position of Jay Ltd using the most recent available management accounts. The notes then go on to look at the future of the company, explaining the options available to the directors.

(i) Financial position of Jay Ltd

The company is clearly suffering from a shortage of cash and is reliant on a bank overdraft to manage its working capital. It is unlikely that this situation can be sustained in the long run. However, there is a difference between a company suffering from a cash shortage and a company which is insolvent. Insolvency exists when a company is unable to pay its payables even if it sold all of its assets, in other words the company is in a position of net liabilities.

In order to determine whether Jay Ltd is insolvent it is necessary to look at its net asset or net liability position, using figures from the latest management accounts:

	£000
Property, plant and equipment	12,800
Inventory	500
Trade receivables	400
Cash	0
Long-term borrowings	(12,000)
Trade payables	(1,250)
Bank overdraft	(1,400)
Net liabilities	(950)

Jay Ltd appears to be insolvent, as it is in a position of net liabilities at 31 May 2012.

Tutorial note

Credit will be awarded where candidates discuss further issues to do with the company being in a position of net liabilities, such as the directors needing to take care to avoid conducting wrongful trading, and the implications of it.

The management accounts show the very different results of 'Jay Sport' (JS) and 'Jay Plus' (JP). JS has clearly been badly affected by the revelation regarding one of its ingredients, with only a small amount of sales being made in the current financial year, and this business segment is loss-making overall. However, there seems to be continued demand for JP, which remains profitable. This indicates that the JP business segment may still be able to make a return for shareholders and creditors.

(ii) The future of the company – option 1: liquidation

It may be decided that liquidation or 'winding up' is the best course of action. In this case the company's assets will be sold and a distribution made to its creditors with the proceeds. There is an order of priority for allocating the proceeds raised. Using the information available for Jay Ltd, and ignoring liquidator's costs, the long-term borrowings are secured by a fixed charge over property and rank high in the order of priority and would be paid before the other payables. The employees' wages of £300,000 rank as a preferential creditor and are paid next. Any proceeds remaining would be paid to unsecured creditors, then any residual amount to the shareholders. It is unlikely that the shareholders would receive anything in this case.

The directors cannot themselves begin liquidation proceedings. If they decide that this would be the best course of action for Jay Ltd, they can recommend that a creditor's voluntary winding up should be instigated. In this case a liquidator is appointed by the company's creditors, and a liquidation committee comprising both shareholders and creditors is established, so that the creditors have input to the conduct of the liquidation. A member's voluntary liquidation is not an option, as this form of liquidation can only be used for a solvent company.

If the directors take no action, then a creditor may end up applying to the court for a compulsory winding up order. Any creditor who is owed more than £750 can apply for this action to take place. The directors may wish to avoid the company being placed into compulsory liquidation as this means that employees are automatically dismissed.

In any liquidation the directors will have to stand down to be replaced by the liquidator, unless the liquidator decides to retain them.

The future of the company – option 2: administration

Administration is a very different course of action. It aims to save the company, and an insolvency practitioner is appointed to take control of the company and to attempt to rescue it as a going concern. Administration protects the company from the actions of creditors while a restructuring plan is prepared.

Administration can commence without a court order. The directors themselves may be able to appoint an administrator where a company is unable to pay its debts, though this depends on the company's articles of association.

Alternatively, a majority of shareholders, the directors or one or more creditors can apply for administration through the court. It is likely to be more expensive and time consuming to apply to the court.

The administrator takes on the role of the directors, and within eight weeks of appointment must send a document to the company's shareholders and creditors in which they state their proposals for rescuing the company, or states that the company cannot be saved. In Jay Ltd's case, it is likely that the JS business segment would be discontinued, and further finance may need to be raised to support the JP segment.

Conclusions and recommendation

From the information available, it seems that the JP range is still profitable, and could represent a way for the company to remain a going concern. The damage to the JS range does not seem to have tarnished the JP products, and therefore a rescue plan for the company may be feasible.

However, further information is needed before a definite decision is made. In particular, there may be costs that the company would be committed to continue to pay in relation to JS even if that part of the business were to cease to operate, for example, non-cancellable leases. From the information provided, and assuming that no large commitments are included in the overheads of JS, I would recommend that the directors consider an administration order for the company, which will give some breathing space for an appropriate strategy to be devised.

Administration may also benefit Jay Ltd's shareholders, who will continue to own their shares in what may become more profitable and solvent business. It may also be preferential for the creditors for the company to continue to trade, as they may be more likely to receive the amounts owed to them through the continued operation of the company compared to a forced sale of its assets.

ACCA marking scheme	
	Marks
(a) (i) **Matters to be included in the terms of agreement** Up to 1½ marks for each matter identified and explained (2 marks maximum for identification): – Management's responsibilities – Intended use of the information and report – The contents of the business plan – The period covered by the forecasts – The nature of assumptions used in the forecasts – The format and planned content of the assurance report	
Maximum	6
(ii) **Procedures on forecast financial information** Up to 1 mark for each procedure (brief examples below): – General procedures examples: • Recalculate • Consistency of accounting policies used • Discuss how joint venture has been included • General analytical procedures – Procedures on statement of profit or loss: • Discuss trends – allow up to 3 marks for calculations performed and linked to procedures • Review and compare breakdown of costs • Recalculate profit on disposal, agreement of components to supporting documentation – Procedures on statement of financial position: • Agree increase in property, plant and equipment to capital expenditure budget • Discuss working capital trends – allow 2 marks for calculations performed and linked to procedures • Agree movement in long-term borrowings to new loan documentation • Obtain and review forecast statement of changes in equity and confirm validity of reconciling items	
Maximum	12
(b) (i) **Examine financial position and determine whether the company is insolvent** Generally 1 mark per comment: – Calculation of net liabilities position of Jay Ltd – Determination that Jay Ltd is insolvent – Explanation of meaning of insolvency – Discussion of different results of JS and JP business segments	
Maximum	4
(ii) **Evaluate the option available to the directors** Up to 1½ marks per comment: – Explanation of meaning of liquidation – Application of order of priority in allocating proceeds of liquidation – Discussion of means of appointing an administrator – Benefits of administration over liquidation – Identify that a definite decision depends on further information – Overall recommendation	
Maximum	9
Professional marks for the overall presentation of the notes, and the clarity of the explanation and assessment provided.	
Maximum	4
Total	35

55 BUTLER (A) *Walk in the footsteps of a top tutor*

Top tutor tips

Part (a) (i) requires analytical procedures to be performed to help identify going concern issues. Be careful not to spend too much time on the calculations to the detriment of talking about the risks.

Part (a) (ii) asks for audit procedures to be performed on the cash flow forecast. Procedures should focus on obtaining evidence to support the assumptions which provide the basis for the forecast. It is important to remember that these events and transactions have not yet happened and therefore cannot be agreed to supporting documentation in the same way as historical figures.

Part (b) requires the procedures involved with placing a company into compulsory liquidation and the consequences to the key stakeholder groups of doing this. This requires rote learned knowledge from the text book.

(a) (i) Assessment of draft statement of financial position.

The most obvious issue is that Butler Ltd currently does not have a positive cash balance. The statement of financial position includes an overdraft of £25 million. This lack of cash will make it difficult for the company to manage its operating cycle and make necessary interest payments, unless further cash becomes available.

Butler Ltd is in a position of net liabilities, as indicated by the negative shareholders' funds figure. The company's retained earnings figure is now negative. Net liabilities and significant losses are both examples of financial conditions listed in ISA (UK) 570 *Going concern,* which may cast doubt about the going concern assumption.

Note 3 indicates that Butler Ltd has been loss-making for several years. Recurring losses are a further indication of going concern problems. Few companies can sustain many consecutive loss-making periods.

There are several items recognised in the statement of financial position, which, if adjusted, would make the net liabilities position worse. For example, a deferred tax asset is recognised at £235 million. This asset should only be recognised if Butler Ltd can demonstrate that future profits will be sufficient to enable the recoverability of the asset. As Butler Ltd has been loss-making for several years, it is arguable that this asset should not be recognised at all. Additionally, an intangible asset relating to development costs of £120 million is recognised. One of the criteria for the capitalisation of such costs is that adequate resources exist for completion of the development. Given Butler Ltd's lack of cash, this criteria may no longer be applicable. If adjustments were made to write off these assets, the net liabilities would become £580 million.

Note 2 indicates that fixed charges exist over assets valued at £25 million. If Butler Ltd fails to make repayments to the creditor holding the charge over assets, the assets could be seized, disrupting the operations of Butler Ltd.

There are significant short-term borrowings due for repayment – notably a bank loan of £715 million due for repayment in September 2011. It is hard to see how Butler Ltd will be able to repay this loan given its current lack of cash. The cash flow forecast does not indicate that sufficient cash is likely to be generated post year end to enable this loan to be repaid.

Provisions have been classified as non-current liabilities. Given that the provisions relate to customer warranties, it is likely that some of the provisions balance should be classified as a current liability. This potential incorrect presentation impacts on assessment of liquidity, as incorrect classification will impact on the cash flow required to meet the warranties obligation.

Butler Ltd's poor financial position means it is unlikely to be able to raise finance from a third party.

Assessment of cash flow forecast

From an overall point of view, the cash flow forecast indicates that by the end of August, Butler Ltd will still be in a negative cash position. As discussed above, this is particularly concerning given that a loan of £715 million is due to be repaid in September.

The assumption relating to cash receipts from customers seems optimistic. It is too simplistic to assume that anticipated economic recovery will lead to a sudden improvement in cash collection from customers, even if additional resources are being used for credit control.

£200 million of the cash receipts for this three-month period relate to loans and subsidies which are currently being negotiated and applied for. These cash inflows are not guaranteed, and if not received, the overall cash position at the end of the period will be much worse than currently projected.

The cash inflow for June 2011 includes the proceeds of a sale of financial assets of £50 million. It is questionable whether this amount of cash will be generated, given the financial assets are recognised on the statement of financial position at £25 million. The assumed sales value of £50 million may be overly optimistic.

In conclusion, the cash flow forecast may not be reliable, in that assumptions are optimistic, and the additional funding is not guaranteed. This means that three months into the next financial year, the company's cash position is likely to have worsened, and loans and trade payables which are due for payment are likely to remain unpaid. This casts significant doubt as to the ability of Butler Ltd to continue operating as a going concern.

Tutorial note

Credit will be awarded for calculation and explanation of appropriate ratios relevant to Butler Ltd's going concern status.

(ii) Recommended audit procedures:

- Discuss with management the reasons for assuming that cash collection from customers will improve due to 'anticipated improvement in economic conditions'. Consider the validity of the reasons in light of business understanding.
- Enquire as to the nature of the additional resources to be devoted to the credit control function, e.g. details of extra staff recruited.
- For the loan receipt, inspect written documentation relating to the request for finance from Rubery Ltd. Request written confirmation from Rubery Ltd regarding the amount of finance and the date it will be received, as well as any terms and conditions.
- Obtain and review the financial statements of Rubery Ltd, to consider if it has sufficient resources to provide the amount of loan requested.
- For the subsidy, inspect the application made to the subsidy awarding body and confirm the amount of the subsidy.
- Read any correspondence between Butler Ltd and the subsidy awarding body, specifically looking for confirmation that the subsidy will be granted.
- Regarding operating expenses, verify using previous months' management accounts, that operating cash outflows are approximately £200 million per month.
- Enquire as to the reason for the increase in operating cash outflows in August 2011.
- Verify, using previous months' management accounts, that interest payments of £40 million per month appear reasonable.
- Confirm, using the loan agreement, the amount of the loan being repaid in August 2011.
- Enquire whether any tax payments are due in the three month period, such as VAT.
- Agree the opening cash position to cash book and bank statement/bank reconciliation, and cast the cash flow forecast.
- Ensure that a cash flow forecast for the full financial year is received as three months' forecast is inadequate for the purposes of the audit.
- Enquire if those charged with governance have assessed the going concern assumption for a period of 12 months from the date of approval of the financial statements.

Tutorial note

Marks would also be awarded for the more general procedures required under ISA 570 in relation to audit procedures on a cash flow forecast, such as evaluation of the reliability of underlying data, and requesting a written representation regarding the feasibility of plans for future action.

Conclusion

The review of the draft statement of financial position and cash flow forecast shows that there are many factors indicating that Butler Ltd is experiencing going concern problems. In particular, the lack of cash, and the significant amounts due to be paid within a few months of the year end cast significant doubt over the use of the going concern assumption in the financial statements. The company has requested finance from its parent company, but even if this is forthcoming, cash flow remains a significant problem.

(b) **(i)** A company is usually placed in compulsory liquidation by a payable (creditor), who uses compulsory liquidation as a means to recover monies owed by the company. The payable (creditor) must petition the court and the petition is advertised in the *London Gazette. There* are various grounds for a petition to be made for compulsory liquidation. The most common ground is that the company is unable to pay its debts. In this case the payable (creditor) must show that he or she is owed more than £750 by the company and has served on the company at its registered office a written demand for payment. This is called a statutory demand. If the company fails to pay the statutory demand in 21 days and does not dispute the debt, then the payable (creditor) may present a winding up petition at court.

The application for a winding up order will be granted at a court hearing where it can be proven to the court's satisfaction that the debt is undisputed, attempts to recover have been undertaken and the company has neglected to pay the amount owed.

On a compulsory winding up the court will appoint an Official Receiver, who is an officer of the court. Within a few days of the winding up order being granted by the court, the Official Receiver must inform the company directors of the situation. The court order is also advertised in the *London Gazette.*

The Official Receiver takes over the control of the company and usually begins to close it down. The company's directors are asked to prepare a statement of affairs. The Official Receiver must also investigate the causes of the failure of the company.

The liquidation is deemed to have started at the date of the presentation of the winding up petition.

At the end of the winding up of the company, a final meeting with payables (creditors) is held, and a final return is filed with the court and the Registrar. At this point the company is dissolved.

> ***Tutorial note***
>
> *Credit will be awarded to candidates who explain other, less common, means by which a company may face a compulsory liquidation:*
>
> *A shareholder may serve a petition for compulsory liquidation. The grounds for doing so would normally be based on the fact that that the shareholder is dissatisfied with the management of the company, and that it is therefore just and equitable to wind up the company. This action by the shareholder is only allowed if the company is solvent and if the shareholder has been a shareholder for at least six months prior to the petition.*
>
> *Very occasionally, if the Crown believes that a company is contravening legislation such as the Trading Standards legislation or is acting against the public or government interest, it is possible for the company to be liquidated compulsorily. This is very serious action to take and is not used very regularly.*

(ii) Payables (creditors) – The role of the Official Receiver (or Insolvency Practitioner, if appointed), is to realise the company's assets, and to distribute the proceeds in a prescribed order. Depending on the amount of cash available for distribution, and whether the debt is secured or unsecured, payables (creditors) may receive some, all, or none of the amount owed to them.

Employees – All employees of the company are automatically dismissed. A prescribed amount of unpaid employee's wages, accrued holiday pay, and contributions to an occupational pension fund rank as preferential debts, and will be paid before payables (creditors) of the company.

Shareholders – Any surplus that remains after the payment of all other amounts owed by the company is distributed to the shareholders. In most liquidations the shareholders receive nothing.

ACCA marking scheme			*Marks*
(a)	(i)	**Going concern matters** Up to 1½ marks per matter identified and explained (maximum 3 marks for identification): – Negative cash position – Net liabilities position – Recurring losses – Possible adjustment to deferred tax and development intangible asset exacerbate net liabilities position (allow 3 marks max) – Fixed charge over assets – Significant short term liabilities – Potential misclassified provisions – Forecast to remain in negative cash position – Assumptions re sales optimistic – Receipt of loan and subsidy not guaranteed – Assumption of sale value of financial assets could be optimistic	
		Maximum	**10**

	(ii)	**Procedures on cash flow forecast**	
		1 mark per specific procedure:	
		– Enquire regarding and consider validity of assumption re cash sales	
		– Inspect any supporting documentation re additional resources for credit control	
		– Seek written confirmation from Rubery Ltd re loan	
		– Review financial statements of Rubery Ltd re adequacy of resources	
		– Inspect subsidy application	
		– Seek third party confirmation that subsidy will be awarded	
		– Confirm cash outflows for operating expenses and interest appear reasonable	
		– Enquire about potentially missing cash outflows	
		– Agree date and amount of short term loan repayment to loan documentation	
		– Agree opening cash to cash book and bank statements	
		Maximum	**8**
(b)	(i)	**Procedures for compulsory liquidation**	
		1 mark each point explained:	
		– Creditors petition court for winding-up order	
		– Grounds for the petition must be demonstrated – usually an unpaid statutory demand	
		– Court appoints an Official Receiver	
		– Official Receiver informs company directors and takes control of company	
		– Shareholders can apply for compulsory liquidation (rare)	
		– The Crown can apply for compulsory liquidation (very rare)	
		Maximum	**4**
	(ii)	**Consequences for stakeholders**	
		1 mark each consequence explained:	
		– Payables (creditors)	
		– Employees	
		– Shareholders	
		Maximum	**3**
Total			**25**

56 ASPECTS OF INSOLVENCY *Walk in the footsteps of a top tutor*

Top tutor tips

This question is not taken from a previous exam, but has been added to the bank to give you the opportunity to practise requirements relating to the UK syllabus area of insolvency.

(a) Fraudulent trading

Fraudulent trading is where a company carries on a business with the intention of defrauding creditors or for any other fraudulent purposes.

This would include a situation where the director(s) of a company continue to trade whilst insolvent, and enter into debts knowing that the company will not be in a position to repay those debts.

The Insolvency Act 1986 governs situations where, in the course of a winding up, it appears that the business has been carried on with the intent to defraud creditors, or for any other fraudulent purpose.

Fraudulent trading is also a criminal offence under the Companies Act 2006.

A director who is found guilty of fraudulent trading can be made personally liable for the debts of the company (a civil liability under the Insolvency Act); be disqualified as a director for between two and fifteen years, and can be imprisoned for up to ten years.

Wrongful trading

Wrongful trading is when the director(s) of a company have continued to trade when they: 'knew, or ought to have concluded that there was no reasonable prospect of avoiding insolvent liquidation'.

A director can defend an action of wrongful trading if they can prove that they have taken sufficient steps to minimise the potential loss to creditors.

Wrongful trading is an action that can be taken only by a company's liquidator, once it has gone into insolvent liquidation (either voluntary or compulsory liquidation).

Unlike fraudulent trading, wrongful trading needs no finding of 'intent to defraud'. In addition, because wrongful trading is a civil offence (fraudulent trading is a criminal offence), it only needs to be proven 'on the balance of probabilities' (i.e. it is more likely than not that the director(s) are guilty of wrongful trading). Fraudulent trading needs to be proven 'beyond reasonable doubt' (i.e. it is almost certain that the director(s) are guilty of fraudulent trading).

For these reasons, wrongful trading is more common than fraudulent trading.

A director who is found guilty of wrongful trading can be made personally liable for the debts of the company; and be disqualified as a director for between two and fifteen years.

(b) An auditor would examine the financial position of a company in order to determine whether it is insolvent.

There are two tests for insolvency defined in the Insolvency Act 1986.

(i) if assets are exceeded by liabilities, or

(ii) if a company is failing to discharge its debts as and when they fall due.

If a company meets either criteria then it is technically insolvent.

(c) Compulsory liquidation

Companies may be obliged to liquidate if a winding up order is presented to a court, usually by a creditor or member. Such a petition may be made for a number of reasons, which include (Insolvency Act 1986):

- the company being unable to pay its debts; and
- it is just and equitable to wind up the company.

(d) Consequences of liquidation

If successful the court will appoint an official receiver (an officer of the courts) as liquidator. They may be replaced by a practitioner at a later date. The receiver investigates the company's affairs and the cause of its failure. The petition also has the following effects:

- all actions for the recovery of debt against the company are stopped.
- any floating charges crystallise.
- all legal proceedings against the company are halted and none may start unless the courts grant permission.
- the company must cease trading activity, unless it is necessary to complete the liquidation, e.g. completing work-in-progress.
- the directors relinquish power and authority to the liquidator, although they may remain in office; and
- employees are automatically made redundant. The liquidator may choose to re-employ them to help complete the liquidation process.

(e) Explanation of Member's Voluntary Liquidation

Liquidation is the process of terminating a company, thus ending its life. The assets of the company are physically liquidated, i.e. they are sold, so that cash can be used to pay off company creditors and equity holders.

Members' Voluntary Liquidation is used when a company is solvent.

In order to facilitate this the members must pass one of two resolutions:

- an ordinary resolution, where the articles provide for liquidation on the expiry of a fixed date or a specific event
- a special resolution, for any other reason.

Once this has been passed the directors must make a **declaration of solvency** stating that they are of the opinion that the company will be able to pay its debts within twelve months. A false declaration would constitute a criminal offence.

The company will then appoint a named insolvency practitioner to act as the liquidator. They will realise the company's assets and distribute the proceeds accordingly.

Once the liquidation process is complete the liquidator presents a report at the final meeting of the members, which is then submitted to the registrar of companies. The company will be dissolved three months later.

Marking scheme

		Marks
(a)	**Differences between fraudulent and wrongful trading**	
	Up to 1 mark per point	
	– Fraudulent: intention of defrauding	
	– Fraudulent: continuing to trade whilst insolvent	
	– Fraudulent: criminal offence	
	– Fraudulent: penalties	
	– Wrongful: should have known the company was insolvent	
	– Wrongful: action taken by liquidator	
	– Wrongful: civil offence	
	– Wrongful: penalties	
	Maximum	6
(b)	**Insolvency**	
	Up to 1 mark per point	
	• Liabilities exceed assets	
	• Failure to discharge liabilities when due	
	Maximum	2
(c)	**Circumstances when a company must liquidate**	
	Up to 1 mark per point	
	• Company is unable to pay its debts	
	• Just and equitable to wind up the company	
	Maximum	2
(d)	**Consequences of compulsory liquidation**	
	Up to 1 mark per consequence	
	Maximum	5
(e)	**Voluntary liquidation**	
	Up to 1 mark per point	
	• Terminating the company by liquidating assets	
	• Company is solvent	
	• Ordinary resolution or special resolution passed	
	• Make a declaration of solvency	
	• Appoint insolvency practitioner	
	• Liquidator presents final report to members	
	Maximum	5
Total		**20**

INT SYLLABUS ONLY

57 KANDINSKY *Walk in the footsteps of a top tutor*

Top tutor tips

Part (a) is a straightforward going concern question asking for indicators of problems and audit procedures to be performed.

Part (b) asks for a discussion of the relevance and measurability of the reported performance information. You need to think about whether the various stakeholder groups would be interested in such information or whether there is other information they would prefer to see (relevance). For measurability, think about whether the information would be readily available to report. Organisations may wish to report on performance matters but if that information is not reliably captured by the information systems the credibility of such information will be called into question.

(a) (i) Going concern matters

Revenue and profitability

The extract financial statements show that revenue has fallen by 38.2%. Based on the information provided, operating profit was $1,150,000 in 2014 but is only $340,000 in 2015. Operating margins have fallen from 29.1% to 13.9% during the year and the fall in revenue and margin has caused the company to become loss-making this year.

These changes are highly significant and most likely due to the economic recession which will impact particularly on the sale of luxury, non-essential products such as those sold by Kandinsky Co. The loss-making position does not in itself mean that the company is not a going concern, however, the trend is extremely worrying and if the company does not return to profit in the 2016 financial year, then this would be a major concern. Few companies can sustain many consecutive loss-making periods.

Bank loan

The bank loan is significant, amounting to 33.7% of total assets this year end, and it has increased by $500,000 during the year. The company appears to be supporting operations using long-term finance, which may be strategically unsound. The loan is secured on the company's properties, so if the company defaults on the payment due in June 2016, the bank has the right to seize the assets in order to recoup their funds. If this were to happen, Kandinsky Co would be left without operational facilities and it is difficult to see how the company could survive. There is also a risk that there is insufficient cash to meet interest payments due on the loan.

Trade payables

The trade payables balance has increased by 38.5%, probably due in part to the change in terms of trade with its major supplier of raw materials. An extension to the payable payment period indicates that the company is struggling to manage its operating cycle, with the cash being generated from sales being insufficient to meet working capital requirements. Relations with suppliers could be damaged if Kandinsky Co cannot make payments to them within agreed credit terms, with the result that suppliers could stop supplying the company or withdraw credit which would severely damage the company's operations. There is also a risk that suppliers could bring legal action against the company in an attempt to recover the amounts owed.

Borrowing facility

Kandinsky Co has $500,000 available in an undrawn borrowing facility, which does provide a buffer as there is a source of cash which is available, somewhat easing the going concern pressures which the company is facing. However, the availability of the borrowing facility depends on certain covenants being maintained. The calculations below show that the covenants have now been breached, so the bank is within its right to withdraw the facility, leaving Kandinsky Co exposed to cash shortages and possibly unable to make payments as they fall due.

	Covenant	*2015*	*2014*
Interest cover	2	340/520 = 0.65	1150/500 = 2.3
Borrowings to operating profit	4:1	3,500/340 = 10.3:1	3,000/1,150 = 2.6:1

Contingent liability

The letter of support offered to a supplier of raw materials exposes Kandinsky Co to a possible cash outflow of $120,000, the timing of which cannot be predicted. Given the company's precarious trading position and lack of cash, satisfying the terms of the letter would result in the company utilising 80% of their current cash reserve. Providing such support seems unwise, though it may have been done for a strategic reason, i.e. to secure the supply of a particular ingredient. If the financial support is called upon, it is not certain that Kandinsky Co would have the means to make the cash available to its supplier, which may create going concern issues for that company and would affect the supply of cane sugar to Kandinsky Co. There may also be legal implications for Kandinsky Co if the cash could not be made available if or when requested by the supplier.

(ii) Audit procedures in relation to going concern matters identified

- Obtain and review management accounts for the period after the reporting date and any interim financial accounts which have been prepared. Perform analytical review to ascertain the trends in profitability and cash flows since the year end.

- Read the minutes of the meetings of shareholders, those charged with governance and relevant committees for reference to trading and financing difficulties.

- Discuss with management the strategy which is being developed to halt the trend in declining sales and evaluate the reasonableness of the strategy in light of the economic recession and auditor's knowledge of the business.
- Review the company's current order book and assess the level of future turnover required to breakeven/make a profit.
- Analyse and discuss the cash flow, profit and other relevant forecasts with management and review assumptions to ensure they are in line with management's strategy and auditor's knowledge of the business.
- Perform sensitivity analysis on the forecast financial information to evaluate the impact of changes in key variables such as interest rates, predictions of sales patterns and the timing of cash receipts from customers.
- Calculate the average payment period for trade payables and consider whether any increase is due to lack of cash or changes in the terms of trade.
- Obtain the contract in relation to the borrowing facility to confirm the covenant measures and to see if any further covenants are included in the agreement.
- Review correspondence with the bank in relation to the loan and the borrowing facility to gauge the bank's level of support for Kandinsky Co and for evidence of deteriorating relationships between the bank and the company's management.
- Obtain the bank loan agreement to confirm the amount of the loan, the interest rate and repayment dates and whether the charge over assets is specific or general in nature.
- Review the bank loan agreement for any clauses or covenants to determine whether there are any breaches.
- Obtain the letter of support in relation to the supplier to confirm the conditions under which Kandinsky Co would become liable for payment of the $120,000.
- Discuss with management the reason for the letter of support being given to the supplier to understand the business rationale and its implications, including why the supplier approached Kandinsky Co for the letter of support.
- Inspect minutes of management meetings where those charged with governance discussed the letter of support and authorised its issuance.
- Obtain any further documentation available in relation to the letter of support, for example, legal documentation and correspondence with the supplier, to confirm the extent of Kandinsky Co's involvement with the supplier and that no further amounts could become payable.

(b) (i) The relevance and measurability of the reported performance information

Relevance

Performance information should be relevant to the users of that information. In the case of Rothko University, there is likely to be a wide range of interested parties including current and potential students who will be interested in the quality of the teaching provided and the likelihood of securing employment on completion of the university course. Other interested parties will include the government body which provides funding to the University, regulatory bodies which oversee higher education and any organisations which support the University's work, for example, graduate employers.

For current and potential students, performance measures such as the graduation rate and employability rate will be relevant as this will provide information on the success of students in completing their degree programmes and subsequently obtaining a job. This is important because students pay tuition fees to attend Rothko University and they will want to know if the investment in education is likely to result in employment. However, some students may be more interested in further study after graduation, so employability measures would be less relevant to them.

Students will be interested in the proportion of graduates who achieve a distinction as this may lead to better job prospects and a better return on the investment (of time and money) in their education. Finally, students will find the performance measure on course satisfaction relevant because it indicates that the majority of students rated the quality of the course as high, an important factor in deciding whether to enrol onto a degree programme. Stakeholders other than current and potential students may find other performance information more relevant to them, for example, potential graduate employers may be interested in the amount of work experience which is provided on the University's degree programme.

The performance measures are most relevant where they can be compared to the measures of other universities. Currently, the University has not provided comparative information and this is likely to make it difficult to assess the performance of the University over time and also makes the current year measures harder to gauge.

Measurability

In terms of measurability, as with many key performance indicators, it is sometimes difficult to precisely define or measure the performance information. Some of the measures are quite subjective, for example, the rating which a student gives to a course is down to personal opinion and it is difficult to substantiate, for example, the difference between a course rating of excellent and very good. Similarly, defining 'graduate level employment' could be subjective. Some measures will be easier to quantify, for example, the degree completion percentage, which will be based on fact rather than opinion.

There may also be problems in how the information is gathered, affecting the validity of the information. For example, only a sample of students may have completed a course evaluation, and possibly the most satisfied students were selected which will improve the measure.

(ii) Examination procedures

- Obtain a list detailing all of the University's performance objectives and the basis of measurement for each objective.
- Enquire of the University whether comparative information is available and if this information needs to be verified as part of the disclosure in the current year.
- For the graduation rate, obtain a list of students awarded degrees in 2015, and a list of all students who registered on the degree programme and use this information to recalculate the %.
- For academic performance, review minutes of meetings where degree results were discussed and approval given for the award of distinction to a number of students.
- For a sample of students awarded a distinction, confirm each student's exam results to supporting documentation, e.g. information in their student files, notices of exam results sent to the student and confirm that the grades achieved qualify for a distinction being awarded.
- Inspect any documentation issued at events such as degree award ceremonies to confirm the number of students being awarded a distinction.
- Obtain supporting documentation from the University for the employability rate and discuss with appropriate personnel, for example, the careers centre, the basis of the determination of the rate.
- For the employability rate, a confirmation could be sent to a sample of students asking for the details of their post-graduation employment.
- If the University supplies references for students seeking employment, inspect the references issued in 2015 and contact the relevant company to see if the student was offered employment.
- For course satisfaction, inspect the questionnaires or surveys completed by students from which the % was derived, and recalculate.
- Enquire if there is any other supporting documentation on course satisfaction, for example, minutes of student and lecturer meetings about the quality of courses.

Examiner's comments

This question presented information relating to two different clients. Initially candidates were required to identify indicators in the scenario which gave rise to going concern issues and then to state procedures to audit the going concern status of the company. In general, this was well attempted and candidates scored high marks, however those using a columnar approach tended to lack depth in their explanation of the factors identified in the question and overlooked some of the more encompassing audit procedures that did not arise from a specific scenario point.

The second part of the question differed between the International (INT) and Singapore (SGP) exams and the UK and Ireland (IRL) adapted exams. The INT and SGP exam focused on the audit of performance information, a relatively new topic in the relevant syllabus, and required candidates to discuss the relevance and measurability of key performance indicators (KPIs) in respect of a University and to describe how they might be audited. Well prepared candidates were able to discuss the issues surrounding measuring and determining relevant performance information and were able to draw on the information included in the recent examiners article on this topic to the scenario. Some candidates did not focus on the question requirement and attempted to describe the theory of public sector KPIs. Many candidates were unprepared and left this requirement out altogether.

ACCA marking scheme

			Marks
(a)	(i)	Identify and explain going concern matters Up to 2½ marks for matter identified and explained, to include 1 mark for relevant calculations: – Revenue, operating margins and profitability – Bank loan – Trade payables – Borrowing facility – Contingent liability	
		Maximum	**9**
	(ii)	Audit procedures in respect of going concern matters Up to 1 mark for each well explained procedure: – Obtain and review management accounts, perform analytical review to ascertain the trends in profitability and cash flows since the year end – Read the minutes of the meetings for reference to trading and financing difficulties – Discuss with management the strategy which is being developed to halt the trend in declining sales and evaluate the reasonableness of the strategies in light of the economic recession and auditor's knowledge of the business – Review the company's current order book and assess the level of future turnover to level required to breakeven/make a profit – Analyse and discuss the cash flow, profit and other relevant forecasts with management and review assumptions are in line with management strategy and auditor's knowledge of the business – Obtain the bank loan agreement to confirm the amount of the loan, the interest rate and repayment dates and whether the charge over assets is specific or general in nature – Review the bank loan agreement for any clauses or covenants to determine whether there are any breaches – Calculate the average payment period for trade payables and consider whether any increase is due to lack of cash or changes in the terms of trade – Obtain the contract in relation to the borrowing facility to confirm the covenant measures and to see if any further covenants are included in the agreement – Discuss correspondence with the bank in relation to the loan and the borrowing facility to gauge the bank's level of support for Kandinsky Co and for evidence of deteriorating relationships between the bank and the company's management. Inspect minutes of management meetings where those charged with governance discussed the letter of support and authorised its issuance – Obtain any further documentation available in relation to the letter of support, for example, legal documentation and correspondence with the supplier, to confirm the extent of Kandinsky's involvement with the supplier and that no further amounts could become payable	
		Maximum	**6**

(b) (i) The relevance and measurability of the reported performance information Generally up to 1 mark for each point explained: – 1 mark for explaining why each measure would be relevant to an existing or potential student (4 measures in total, so maximum 4 marks) – Problems in defining the measures – Problems in quantifying the measures – some are subjective – Issues in validity of the reported information – Lack of comparative information (ii) Examination procedures Up to 1 mark for well described procedures: – Obtain a list detailing all of the University's performance objectives and the basis of measurement for each objective – Discuss with University the availability of comparative information and requirement to include in current year report – For the graduation rate, obtain a list of students awarded degrees in 2015, and a list of all students who registered on the degree programme and use this information to recalculate the % – For academic performance, review minutes of meetings where degree results were discussed and approval given for the award of distinction to a number of students – Agree a sample of students' exam results to supporting documentation, e.g. information in their student files, notices of exam results sent to the students – Inspect any documentation issued at events such as degree award ceremonies to confirm the number of students being awarded a distinction – Obtain supporting documentation from the University for the employability rate and discuss with appropriate personnel, for example, the careers centre, the basis of the determination of the rate – For the employability rate, a confirmation could be sent to a sample of students asking for the details of their post-graduation employment – If the University supplies references for students seeking employment, inspect the references issued in 2015 and contact the relevant company to see if the student was offered employment – For course satisfaction, inspect the questionnaires or surveys completed by students from which the % was derived, and recalculate – Enquire if there is any other supporting documentation on course satisfaction, for example, minutes of student and lecturer meetings about the quality of courses	
Maximum	**10**
Total	**25**

58 PUBLIC SECTOR ORGANISATIONS *Walk in the footsteps of a top tutor*

Top tutor tips

This question is not taken from a previous exam, but has been added to the bank to give you the opportunity to practise requirements relating to the INT syllabus area of public sector performance information.

(a) **Performance audits** aim to provide management with assurance and advice regarding the effective functioning of its operational activities.

Performance information is information published by public sector bodies regarding their objectives and the achievement of those objectives.

(b) **Performance targets**

(i) **Local police department**

- Reduce the number of crimes by x%
- Reduce the number of offenders re-offending by x%
- Reduce the number of deaths caused by dangerous driving x%
- Increase public satisfaction to x%

(ii) **Local hospital**

- Reduce emergency department waiting times to a maximum of x hours
- Reduce the maximum waiting time for an operation to x weeks
- Reduce the number of infections contracted in the hospital by x%
- Reduce the number of re-admissions to hospital by x%

(iii) **Local council**

- Increase public satisfaction to x%
- To build x number of council houses in the next 5 years
- To spend $x on road maintenance and improvements each year
- To increase council tax by a maximum of the rate of inflation

Tutorial note

Credit will be awarded for any other relevant examples.

A target does not have to be SMART. Targets are typically more generalised than an objective.

(c) Stakeholder groups

(i) Police department

Stakeholder	**Use**
Government e.g. Home Office	To ensure that police departments are achieving the targets set by the government. To report to taxpayers on how government money in this area is being used to achieve the stated objectives.
Local residents	Residents may wish to know the level of crime in their area to assess the performance of their local police department.
Prospective residents	Prospective residents may use such information to decide whether to move to a particular town/city. If the crime rate is high they may decide not to move there.

(ii) **Local hospital**

Local residents	To assess the performance of their local hospital as this will be of importance if they were ever to be admitted to hospital.
Patients awaiting treatment	Patients awaiting treatment may have a choice of hospital from which to receive treatment. In this case, patients are likely to choose the option with the lowest infection rates, highest success rates for a particular operation/procedure, or the quickest treatment time.
Government e.g. Department for Health	To ensure that hospitals are achieving the targets set by the government. To report to taxpayers on how government money in this area is being used to achieve the stated objectives.

(iii) Local council

Local residents	To assess the performance of their local council and how their taxes are being used.
Suppliers/contractors	Suppliers/contractors will be interested to see the plans for the future to assess if there will be additional work being tendered. For example if the council has set a target to build an additional 1000 houses in the coming year, local building firms may be able to bid for the work.
Government e.g. Department for Communities and Local Government	To ensure that councils are achieving the targets set by the government. To report to taxpayers on how government money in this area is being used to achieve the stated objectives.

Tutorial note

Credit will be awarded for any other relevant examples e.g. employees to assess whether there is the possibility of redundancies if the target is to reduce costs significantly.

(d) Difficulties

All relevant information may not be reported (e.g. number of crimes or number of hospital infections) therefore it may appear as though there has been improvement when problems may not have been recorded completely.

Where information is completely recorded, accuracy of the information may be an issue. The public sector organisation needs to have good internal controls in place in respect of this information in the same way as internal controls would be expected to be in place in respect of financial information.

Definitions of certain targets and measures may be ambiguous resulting in matters going un-recorded due to public sector employees recording the information in a different way. Information may be classified differently by different members of staff unless thorough training is given.

Even so, information may not be comparable between different police departments/ hospitals/councils if each interpret the definitions in a different way.

There is also the risk that public sector departments will falsify the figures that have been reported if they are failing to meet the targets set by the government. This may be difficult for the auditor to detect as it is unlikely there will be alternative forms of corroborative evidence to highlight discrepancies.

Marking scheme

		Marks
(a)	**Definitions**	
	Up to 1 for each definition	
	– Performance audit	
	– Performance information	
	Maximum	**2**
(b)	**Performance targets**	
	½ mark per performance target. Max of 2 per public sector body.	
	Maximum	**6**
(c)	**Stakeholder groups**	
	½ mark per stakeholder group and ½ mark per reason for using the performance information. Max of 2 marks per public sector body	
	Maximum	**6**
(d)	**Difficulties**	
	Up to 1 ½ per point made.	
	– Completeness	
	– Accuracy	
	– Ambiguity of targets	
	– Comparability	
	– Risk of falsification	
	Maximum	**6**
Total		**20**

REFERENCES

The Board (2016) *IFRS 16 Leases*. London: IFRS Foundation.